THE PAPERS OF
BENJAMIN FRANKLIN

SPONSORED BY

The American Philosophical Society
and Yale University

Benjamin Franklin, Bronze Medal after Isaac Gosset

THE PAPERS OF

Benjamin Franklin

VOLUME 13 *January 1 through December 31, 1766*

LEONARD W. LABAREE, *Editor*

Helen C. Boatfield and James H. Hutson, Assistant Editors

New Haven and London YALE UNIVERSITY PRESS, 1969

Designed by Alvin Eisenman and Walter Howe,
and printed in the United States of America
at The Lakeside Press, R. R. Donnelley & Sons Company.

Library of Congress catalogue number: 59–12697
Standard book number: 1132–6

Editor's Note

James T. Babb, a member of the Administrative Board of this enterprise, died on June 21, 1968, when editorial preparation of the present volume was in progress. Roy F. Nichols, chairman of the Administrative Board, Richard H. Shryock, and Frederick B. Adams, Jr., also members, submitted their resignations in the spring of 1969, while this volume was in the printer's hands. All four gentlemen had served on the Board since its establishment in the winter of 1953–54. The editor records here, on behalf of his colleagues, past and present, as well as on his own account, our very great appreciation for the time and energy these men contributed to the undertaking and for the sympathetic and understanding support they gave us during these years.   L.W.L.

Contents

List of Illustrations

Scotia be ours, den New York and all de Continent beware." Farmers, armed only with rakes and pitchforks, are unable to protect the lion, but comment scornfully about the military gentry to the effect that "Whores and Cards, Hunting and Horse racing are more their concern than Commerce or Glory." At the extreme right gentlemen discuss calmly the lion's injury and at the extreme left Admiral Byng, who had lost Minorca, offers an inglorious explanation for his failure. In the lower right corner the French cock pecks at the fallen Union Jack, declaring: "I'll tear you to pieces for Clouts to Scare Crows." Reproduced by courtesy of Wilmarth S. Lewis.

Figure 3. Benjamin Franklin's Stamp Act Cartoon

The only known original example of Franklin's cartoon. It is printed on a piece of *Pro Patria* paper measuring $4^{15}\!/_{16}$ by $3\frac{1}{8}$ inches, with the verso blank. For the most part Franklin seems to have used copies printed on cards or on larger sheets of paper that bore the "Explanation" and "Moral" reprinted here on pp. 70–1. In Franklin's print (as compared to that of 1749, Figure 1) Britannia has lost all four limbs, instead of only her arms, but she is not suffering the further torture of disembowelment; by contrast, she seems here to be entirely deserted by friends and foes alike. Her shield and spear have again fallen, but the spear, having pierced one limb, is pointed menacingly at her breast. British ships, their commerce gone, are tied up in the distance, the brooms at their mastheads signaling that they are for sale. The cartoon is reproduced here by courtesy of the Library Company of Philadelphia.

Figure 4. Philadelphia Redrawing of the Stamp Act Cartoon

No evidence has been found to establish just when this copy of Franklin's Stamp Act Cartoon was made. Almost certainly the draftsman used as his model one of the several cards Franklin had sent to relatives and friends in Philadelphia during the early months of 1766. The year 1767, when indignation over the Townshend Duties flared up, seems a likely time for the production and distribution of this print, with the expanded "Explanation" that appeared, together with the "Moral," on the same sheet of paper. Examination of the two versions of the cartoon will reveal the variances in detail between them. Reproduced by courtesy of the American Philosophical Society.

Joseph Priestley's Electrified Chain

On the previously blank third page of Priestley's letter to Franklin of Sept. 21, 1766, he laid a looped metal chain, with the apex of the loop placed at the spot marked "a" in the upper right-hand corner of the page. He then sent an electrical charge through the chain from end to end. At that instant the chain "appeared like a bright flame" and the looped portion was "thrown back" about an inch and a half from "a" to "b." The scorch marks of the links show clearly on the paper. Priestley then wrote his explanatory account of the experiment (printed here as a postscript to the letter) all around the scorch marks, thereby providing Franklin on the same paper with both explanation and visual evidence of the experiment. Reproduced by courtesy of the American Philosophical Society.

This engraving faces the first page of Timothy Lane's letter to Franklin, Oct. 15, 1766, as printed in *Philosophical Transactions*, LVII, Part I, For the Year 1767 (London, 1768), p. 451. Lane's letter provides a key to the letters A–O of figure 1 and explains the lower-case letters in Figures 2 and 4. The Royal Society's regular engraver, James Mynde, doubtless prepared the engraving from sketches supplied by Lane to accompany his paper. Reproduced by courtesy of the Yale University Library.

Contributors to Volume 13

The ownership of each manuscript, or the location of the particular copy used by the editors of each rare contemporary pamphlet or similar printed work, is indicated where the document appears in the text. The sponsors and editors are deeply grateful to the following institutions and individuals for permission to print in the present volume manuscripts or other materials which they own.

INSTITUTIONS

American Antiquarian Society
American Philosophical Society
Assay Office, Birmingham, England
Boston Public Library
William L. Clements Library
Columbia University Library
Duke University Library
Fordham University Library
Harrowby Manuscript Trust, The Earl of Harrowby, Sandon Hall, Stafford
Harvard College Library
Haverford College Library
Historical Society of Pennsylvania
Landesbibliothek, Kassel
Library of Congress
Maryland Historical Society
Massachusetts Archives
Massachusetts Historical Society
New York Public Library
University of Pennsylvania Library
Philadelphia Contributionship, for the Insuring of Houses from Loss by Fire
Pierpont Morgan Library
Princeton University Library
Public Record Office, London
The Rosenbach Foundation
The Royal Society
The Royal Society of Arts
Salem County Historical Society, Salem, N.J.
Society for the Propagation of the Gospel in Foreign Parts
Yale University Library

INDIVIDUALS

William Logan Fox, Philadelphia
Boies Penrose, Devon, Pa.
William Pepper, Philadelphia
Dr. Myron Prinzmetal, Beverly Hills, Calif.
Dr. James W. Wister, Philadelphia

Method of Textual Reproduction

An extended statement of the principles of selection, arrangement, form of presentation, and method of textual reproduction observed in this edition appears in the Introduction to the first volume, pp. xxxiv-xlvii. A condensation and revision of the portion relating to the method of reproducing the texts follows here.

Printed Material:

In general Franklin's writings printed under his direction should be regarded as his ultimate intention and should therefore be reproduced without change, except as modern typography requires. In fact, however, newspapers and pamphlets were often set by two or more journeymen with different notions of spelling, capitalization, and punctuation. Although the resulting inconsistencies and errors did not represent Franklin's intentions, they are not eliminated by the editors. Again, in cases where Franklin's writings were printed by another, they were sometimes carelessly or willfully revised without his consent. He once complained, for example, that an English printer had so corrected and excised one of his papers "that it can neither scratch nor bite. It seems only to paw and mumble."[1] What was thus printed was obviously not what Franklin wrote, but, in the absence of his manuscript, the editors have no alternative but to reprint it as it stands. Still other Franklin letters are known only in nineteenth-century printings, vigorously edited by William Temple Franklin, Duane, or Sparks. Here, too, the editors follow the texts as printed, only noting obvious misreadings.

In reproducing printed materials, the following general rules are observed:

1. The place and date of composition of letters are set at the top, regardless of their location in the original printing.

2. Proper nouns, including personal names, which were often printed in italics, are set in roman, except when the original was italicized for emphasis.

1. BF to William Franklin, Jan. 9, 1768.

3. Prefaces and other long passages, though italicized in the original, are set in roman. Long italicized quotations are set in roman within quotation marks.

4. Words in full capitals are set in small capitals, with initial letters in full capitals if required by Franklin's normal usage.

5. All signatures are set in capitals and small capitals.

6. Obvious typographical errors are silently corrected. An omitted parenthesis or quotation mark, for example, is inserted when the other of the pair was printed.

7. Every sentence is closed with a period or other appropriate mark of punctuation (usually a question mark).

8. Longhand insertions in the blanks of printed forms are set in italics, with space before and after.

Manuscript Material:

a. *Letters* are presented in the following form:

1. The place and date of composition are set at the top, regardless of their location in the original.

2. The complimentary close is set continuously with the text.

3. Addresses, endorsements, and docketing are so labeled and printed at the end of the letter.

b. *Spelling* of the original is retained. When, however, it is so abnormal as to obscure meaning, the correct form is supplied in brackets or footnote, as: "yf[wife]."

c. *Capitalization* has been retained as written, except that every sentence is made to begin with a capital. When there is doubt whether a letter is a capital, it is printed as like letters are in the same manuscript, or, that guide failing, as modern usage directs.

d. Words underlined once in the manuscript are printed in *italics;* words underlined twice or written in large letters or full capitals are printed in SMALL CAPITALS.

e. *Punctuation* has been retained as in the original, except:

1. Every sentence ends with a period or other appropriate mark (usually a question mark), unless it is not clear where the sentence ends, when the original punctuation (or lack of it) is preserved.

2. Dashes used in place of commas, semicolons, colons, or periods are replaced by the appropriate marks; and when a sentence ends with both a dash and a period, the dash is omitted.

3. Commas scattered meaninglessly through a manuscript are eliminated.

4. When a mark of punctuation is not clear or can be read as one of two marks, modern usage is followed.[2]

5. Some documents, especially those of a legal character, lack all punctuation. This is supplied with restraint, and the fact indicated in a footnote. In some other, inadequately punctuated documents, it is silently added when needed for clarity, as in a long series of names.

f. *Contractions and abbreviations* in general are expanded except in proper names. The ampersand is rendered as "and," except in the names of business firms, in the form "&c.," and in a few other cases. Letters represented by the thorn or tilde are printed. The tailed "p" is spelled out as per, pre, or pro. Symbols of weights, measures, and monetary values follow modern usage, as: £34. Superscript letters are lowered. Abbreviations in current use are retained, as: Col., Dr., N.Y., i.e.

g. *Omitted or illegible words or letters* are treated as follows:

1. If not more than four letters are missing, they are silently supplied when there is no doubt what they should be.

2. The omission of more than four letters or one or more words is supplied conjecturally within brackets. The addition of a question mark within the brackets indicates uncertainty as to the conjecture.

3. Other omissions are shown as follows: [*illegible*], [*torn*], [*remainder missing*], or the like.

4. Missing or illegible digits are indicated by suspension points in brackets, the number of points corresponding to the estimated number of missing figures.

5. Blank spaces are left as blanks.

2. The typescripts from which these papers are printed have been made from photocopies of the manuscripts, and marks of punctuation are sometimes blurred or lost in photography. It has often been impossible to consult the originals in these cases.

h. *Author's additions and corrections.*

1. Interlineations and brief marginal notes are brought into the text without comment. Longer notes are brought into the text with the notation [*in the margin*].

2. Author's footnotes are printed at the bottom of the appropriate pages between the text and any editorial footnotes.

3. Canceled words and phrases are in general omitted without notice; if significant, they are printed in footnotes. The canceled passages of important documents, such as drafts of treaties, are brought into the text enclosed in angle brackets *before* the words substituted.

4. When alternative words and phrases have been inserted in a manuscript but the original remains uncanceled, the alternatives are given in brackets, preceded by explanatory words in italics, as: "it is [*written above:* may be] true."

5. Variant readings of several versions are noted if important.

Abbreviations and Short Titles

Acts Privy Coun., Col.	W. L. Grant and James Munro, eds., *Acts of the Privy Council of England, Colonial Series, 1613–1783* (6 vols., London, 1908–12).
ADS	Autograph document signed.[1]
ALS	Autograph letter signed.
Alvord and Carter, eds., *The Critical Period*	Clarence W. Alvord and Clarence E. Carter, eds., *The Critical Period 1763–1765* (*Collections,* Illinois State Hist. Lib., x; Springfield, Ill., 1915).
Alvord and Carter, eds., *The New Régime*	Clarence W. Alvord and Clarence E. Carter, eds., *The New Régime 1765–1767* (*Collections,* Illinois State Hist. Lib., xi; Springfield, Ill., 1916).
APS	American Philosophical Society.
Autobiog. (APS-Yale edit.)	Leonard W. Labaree, Ralph L. Ketcham, Helen C. Boatfield, Helene H. Fineman, eds., *The Autobiography of Benjamin Franklin* (New Haven, 1964).
BF	Benjamin Franklin
Bigelow, *Works*	John Bigelow, ed., *The Complete Works of Benjamin Franklin* . . . (10 vols., N.Y., 1887–88).
Board of Trade Journal	*Journal of the Commissioners for Trade and Plantations . . . April 1704 to . . . May 1782* (14 vols., London, 1920–38).
Cohen, *BF's Experiments*	I. Bernard Cohen, ed., *Benjamin Franklin's Experiments. A New Edition of Franklin's Experiments and Observations on Electricity* (Cambridge, Mass., 1941).
Colden Paps.	*The Letters and Papers of Cadwallader Colden.* New-York Historical Society *Collections* for 1917–23, 1934, 1935.

1. For definitions of this and other kinds of manuscripts, see above, i, xliv-xlvii.

DAB	*Dictionary of American Biography.*
Darlington, *Memorials*	William Darlington, *Memorials of John Bartram and Humphrey Marshall* (Phila., 1849).
Dexter, *Biog. Sketches*	Franklin B. Dexter, *Biographical Sketches of the Graduates of Yale College* . . . (6 vols., N.Y. and New Haven, 1885–1912).
DF	Deborah Franklin
DNB	*Dictionary of National Biography.*
DS	Document signed.
Duane, *Works*	William Duane, ed., *The Works of Dr. Benjamin Franklin* . . . (6 vols., Phila., 1808–18). Title varies in the several volumes.
Evans	Charles Evans, *American Bibliography* (14 vols., Chicago and Worcester, Mass., 1903–59). Surviving imprints are reproduced in full in microprint in Clifford K. Shipton, ed., *Early American Imprints, 1639–1800* (microprint, Worcester, Mass.).
Exper. and Obser.	*Experiments and Observations on Electricity, made at Philadelphia in America, by Mr. Benjamin Franklin,* . . . (London, 1751). Revised and enlarged editions were published in 1754, 1760, 1769, and 1774 with slightly varying titles. In each case the edition cited will be indicated, e.g., *Exper. and Obser.,* 1751 edit.
Gipson, *British Empire*	Lawrence H. Gipson, *The British Empire before the American Revolution* (14 vols., to date: Vols. 1–3, Caldwell, Idaho, 1936; Vols. 4–14, N.Y., 1939–69; Vols. 1–3, revised edit., N.Y., 1958–60).
Lib. Co. Phila.	Library Company of Philadelphia.
LS	Letter signed.
Montgomery, *Hist. Univ. Pa.*	Thomas H. Montgomery, *A History of the University of Pennsylvania from Its Foundation to A.D. 1770* (Phila., 1900).

Morgan, *Stamp Act Crisis*	Edmund S. and Helen M. Morgan, *The Stamp Act Crisis* (Chapel Hill, [1953]).
MS, MSS	Manuscript, manuscripts.
Namier and Brooke, *House of Commons*	Sir Lewis Namier and John Brooke, *The History of Parliament. The House of Commons 1754–1790* (3 vols., London and N.Y., 1964).
N.J. Arch.	William A. Whitehead and others, eds., *Archives of the State of New Jersey* (2 series, Newark and elsewhere, 1880–). Editors, subtitles, and places of publication vary.
N.Y. Col. Docs.	E. B. O'Callaghan, ed., *Documents relative to the Colonial History of the State of New York* (15 vols., Albany, 1853–87).
Pa. Arch.	Samuel Hazard and others, eds., *Pennsylvania Archives* (9 series, Phila. and Harrisburg, 1852–1935).
Pa. Col. Recs.	*Minutes of the Provincial Council of Pennsylvania* . . . (16 vols., Phila., 1838–53). Title changes with Volume 11 to *Supreme Executive Council.*
Pa. Gaz.	*The Pennsylvania Gazette.*
Pa. Jour.	*The Pennsylvania Journal.*
Phil. Trans.	The Royal Society, *Philosophical Transactions.*
PMHB	*Pennsylvania Magazine of History and Biography.*
Sibley's Harvard Graduates	John L. Sibley, *Biographical Sketches of Graduates of Harvard University* (Cambridge, Mass., 1873–). Continued from Volume 4 by Clifford K. Shipton.
Smyth, *Writings*	Albert H. Smyth, ed., *The Writings of Benjamin Franklin* . . . (10 vols., N.Y., 1905–07).
Sparks, *Works*	Jared Sparks, ed., *The Works of Benjamin Franklin* . . . (10 vols., Boston, 1836–40).
Statutes at Large, Pa.	*The Statutes at Large of Pennsylvania from 1682 to 1801, Compiled under the*

	Authority of the Act of May 19, 1887 ... (Vols. 2–16, [Harrisburg], 1896–1911). Volume 1 was never published.
Van Doren, *Franklin*	Carl Van Doren, *Benjamin Franklin* (N.Y., 1938).
Van Doren, *Franklin-Mecom*	Carl Van Doren, ed., *The Letters of Benjamin Franklin & Jane Mecom* (Memoirs of the American Philosophical Society, XXVII, Princeton, 1950).
Votes	*Votes and Proceedings of the House of Representatives of the Province of Pennsylvania, Met at Philadelphia ... 1750, and continued by Adjournments* (Phila., 1751–). Each annual collection of the journals of separate sittings is designated by the year for which that House was elected, e.g., *Votes, 1750–51.*
WF	William Franklin.
WTF, *Memoirs*	William Temple Franklin, ed., *Memoirs of the Life and Writings of Benjamin Franklin, LL.D., F.R.S., &c.* . . . (3 vols., 4to, London, 1817–18).

Genealogical references. An editorial reference to one of Benjamin Franklin's relatives may be accompanied by a citation of the symbol assigned to that person in the genealogical tables and charts in volume 1 of this work, pp. xlix-lxxvii, as, for example: Thomas Franklin (A.5.2.1), Benjamin Mecom (C.17.3), or Benjamin Franklin Bache (D.3.1). These symbols begin with the letter A, B, C, or D. Similarly, a reference to one of Deborah Franklin's relatives may be accompanied by a symbol beginning with the letter E or F, as, for example, John Tiler (E.1.1.2), or Mary Leacock Hall (F.2.2.3). Such persons may be further identified by reference to the charts of the White and Cash families printed in VIII, 139–42.

Chronology

January 1 through December 31, 1766

1766

January 2: BF publishes a letter in *The Public Advertiser*, over the signature "Pacificus Secundus," showing the folly of trying to reduce Americans to obedience to Parliament by force. During this and the following month, over a variety of signatures, he publishes several newspaper articles, defending the colonies and agitating for the repeal of the Stamp Act.

January 21: Partnership between BF and David Hall expires.

February 1: James Parker prepares a state of the account between BF and Hall; he concludes that BF owes Hall £993 11s. 6d.

February 13: BF examined before the Committee of the Whole of the House of Commons on the effects of the Stamp Act and on the advisability of continuing it. Several contemporaries credit his performance with contributing greatly to procuring its repeal.

February 22: The Committee of the Whole votes, 275 to 167, to repeal the Stamp Act.

February-March: About this time Joseph Priestley, with the encouragement and aid of BF and other London electricians, begins writing his *History of Electricity*, published in 1767.

March 18: Bill repealing the Stamp Act receives the royal assent, as does the Declaratory Act.

March 31-April 5: BF drafts a bill, at the request of a member of Parliament, for the repeal of the Currency Act of 1764 and for the emission of legal-tender paper money in the colonies; it receives no positive action.

April 12–15: BF composes a humorous petition to the House of Commons against the transportation of felons from Scotland to America.

June 15-August 16: BF and Sir John Pringle travel to the German resort, Bad Pyrmont; after spending about a fortnight, they visit Hanover and then Göttingen, where both are admitted to the Royal Academy of Sciences; from there they travel through Kassel, Frank-

fort, and Mainz, and then down the Rhine to Holland and thence
home to London.

September-October: BF has several conferences with Lord Shelburne,
secretary of state for the Southern Department. Among other matters
they discuss the establishment of a colony in the Illinois country, a
project conceived by his son and his Pennsylvania associates.

November 27–29: BF's essay, "On the Price of Corn, and Management
of the Poor," is published in *The London Chronicle.*

THE PAPERS OF
BENJAMIN FRANKLIN

VOLUME 13
January 1 through December 31, 1766

From Thomas Hutchinson

Letterbook copy: Massachusetts Archives, Office of the Secretary of State

Dear Sir   Boston Jan. 1. 1766

Upon a review of my last letter from you[1] I find that you asked my opinion upon an application to Parliament for repres[entation] from the colonies and that I omitted taking notice of your desire in my answer.

When the scheme of a stamp duty was first known in the colonies the general voice was that it would deprive them of the liberties of eng[lish] men unless they should have repres[entation] in Parliament, as soon as a suspicion arose that possibly representation might be admitted it was as generally agreed that a representation would be of no service. I find the committees of the colonies were all of that mind at New York.[2] Our great incendiary who when it was first talked of became an advocate for it and has often hinted it in his inflammatory Pieces is now silent because he finds the voice of the People against it.[3]

We shall never be easy again until the relation between the parent state and its colonies is ascertained. Some few imprudent writers have represented this relation to be such as to make no great distinction between english and french colonists whilst the general run of writers have encouraged an independence or at best an imperium in imperio[4] and these latter, such is our state, it is not safe to contradict.

We have a calm at present, the colonies in general having determined that business shall go on as if the act of Parl[iament] had

1. Perhaps BF's of Aug. 15, 1765 (not found), mentioned in Hutchinson's letter to him of Nov. 18, 1765; see above, XII, 379.

2. That is, at the Stamp Act Congress, held at New York, Oct. 7–24, 1765.

3. The "great incendiary," James Otis (1725–1783), had advocated colonial representation in Parliament in his *The Rights of the British Colonies Asserted and Proved* (Boston, 1764), *A Vindication of the British Colonies* (Boston, 1765), and *Considerations on Behalf of the Colonists in a Letter to a Noble Lord* (Boston, 1765). After attending the Stamp Act Congress Otis ceased pamphleteering.

4. Otis disapproved of this concept as much as Hutchinson did, declaring that "*imperium in imperio* [is] the greatest of all political solecisms." Bernard Bailyn, ed., *Pamphlets of the American Revolution 1750–1776*, I (Cambridge, Mass., 1965), 122.

not Passed. I held out in the Probate court until I was assured further violence was just at hand. I could not comply and thought it a favour that I was allowed to quit my Post without being obliged at the same time to quit the continent.[5] The governor by the act was restrained from appointing a successor for a longer term than 12 months but it is very doubtful whether ever I shall be able to reassume it and if the Place of Chief Justice had any emoluments in proportion to the importance of it, and to the time and labour which it requires I should not desire it. I am told business goes on in the courts of admiralty as well as the common law courts and I suppose I am the only instance of non compliance. What will be the next advance is uncertain but it seems impossible we should long remain quiet &c.

Doctor Franklin.

"Pacificus Secundus": Reply to "Pacificus"

Reprinted in *The Pennsylvania Chronicle, And Universal Advertiser*, February 16–23, 1767, from *The Public Advertiser*, January 2, 1766.

Franklin's contributions to the newspaper debate in England that followed the passage of the Stamp Act and the emergence of colonial opposition in 1765 continued into the early weeks of 1766. The problem of identifying his contributions and the grounds for attributing particular writings to him have been described in the last volume of this edition, pp. 243–4, and that explanation need not be repeated here, except to acknowledge once more the debt the present editors owe to the earlier studies of the subject made by Verner W. Crane. In reprinting in this volume the newspaper contributions of 1766 that can be certainly or probably attributed to Franklin, only the specific evidence for each particular piece will be cited in its annotation.

As the first paragraph of this one of two initial contributions of the new year makes clear, the *Public Advertiser* of Dec. 27, 1765, had published a letter signed "Pacificus" that advocated the use of military force to reduce the colonists to obedience. This satirical reply, signed "Paci-

5. Hutchinson resigned his office as probate judge of Suffolk County on Dec. 21, 1765, because he would not do business without stamped documents, although the ostensible reason for his resignation was his proposed trip to England to seek compensation for the destruction of his house by the mob in August 1765. See above, XII, 418 n.

ficus Secundus," printed in the *Public Advertiser*, Jan. 2, 1766, was reprinted in Goddard's *Pennsylvania Chronicle, and Universal Advertiser*, Feb. 16–23, 1767, as the first of two pieces in the latter issue specifically attributed to Franklin. An undated memorandum attributing to him authorship of twenty-one pieces reprinted in the *Chronicle*, 1767–69, appears to be in the hand of William Franklin, not in that of his father as stated above, XII, 406. With regard to many of these pieces the authorship is beyond question; as to the others it seems probable that William based his listings on some similar memorandum drawn up by his father or on some other direct information from him. This letter and the one from the *Gazetteer* signed "Homespun," which immediately followed this piece in the *Chronicle* as it does here, both fall into the second category.

Sir, [January 2, 1766]

PACIFICUS in your Paper of Friday last, tells us, that the inhabitants of New-England "are descended from the Stiff-Rumps in Oliver's Time;" and he accounts for their being "so tenacious of what they call their Rights and Liberties;" from the independent Principles handed down to them by their Forefathers, and that Spirit of Contradiction, which, he says, "is the distinguishing Characteristic of Fanaticism." But it seems the Inhabitants of Virginia and Maryland, who are descended from the Royalists of the Church of England, driven hence by those very Oliverian Stiff-Rumps, and never tinctured with Fanaticism, are, in the present Case, as stiff-rump'd as the others, and even led the Way in asserting what "they call their Rights."[6] So that this Hypothesis of Fanaticism appears insufficient to account for the Opposition universally given to the Stamp-Act in America; and I fancy the Gentleman thought so himself, as he mends it a little after, by lumping all the Americans under the general Character of "House-breakers and Felons."[7]

Supposing them such, his Proposal of "vacating all their Char-

6. The first strongly worded formal protest against the Stamp Act was the series of resolves of the Virginia House of Burgesses, May 30, 1765. See above, XII, 212–14.

7. In spite of objections from the colonists, the British government followed a policy of transporting many convicted felons to America rather than subject them to execution according to the harsh penal laws of the times. For three attacks on this policy by BF, see above, IV, 130–3; VIII, 351; and below, pp. 240–2. The transported felons, though often troublesome, constituted of course only a small fraction of the entire American population, though some British critics of the colonists chose to ignore that fact, professing to regard all of them as criminals or the descendants of criminals.

ters, taking away the Power of their Assemblies, and sending an armed Force among them, to reduce them all to a military Government, in which the Order of the commanding Officer is to be their Law," will certainly be a very *justifiable* Measure. I have only some Doubts as to the Expediency of it, and the Facility of carrying it into Execution. For I apprehend 'tis not unlikely they may set their Rumps more stiffly against this Method of Government, than ever they did against that by Act of Parliament:[8] But, on second Thoughts, I conceive it may possibly do very well: For though there should be, as 'tis said there are, at least 250,000 fighting Men among them, many of whom have lately seen Service; yet, as one Englishman is to be sure as good as five Americans, I suppose it will not require Armies of above 50,000 Men in the whole, sent over to the different Parts of that extensive Continent, for reducing them; and that a three or four Year's Civil War, at perhaps a less Expence than ten or twelve Millions a Year, Transports and Carriages included, will be sufficient to compleat *Pacificus*'s Pacification, notwithstanding any Disturbance our restless Enemies in Europe might think fit to give us while engaged in this necessary Work. I mention three or four Years only; for I can never believe the Americans will be able to spin it out to seventy, as the Hollanders did the War for their Liberties against Spain, how much soever it may be found the Interest of our own numerous Commissaries, Contractors, and Officers afraid of Half Pay, to continue and protract it.

It may be objected, that by ruining the Colonies, killing one half the People, and driving the rest over the Mountains, we may deprive ourselves of their Custom for our Manufactures: But a Moment's Consideration will satisfy us, that since we have lost so much of our European Trade, it can only be the Demand in America that keeps up, and has of late so greatly enhanced the Price of those Manufactures, and therefore a Stop put to that Demand will be an Advantage to us all, as we may thereafter buy our own Goods cheaper for our own Use at home. I can think of but one Objection more, which is, that Multitudes of our Poor may starve for Want of Employment. But our wise Laws have provided a Remedy for that. The Rich are to maintain them. I am, Sir, Your humble Servant, PACIFICUS SECUNDUS.

8. The Stamp Act.

"Homespun": Second Reply to "Vindex Patriae"

Printed in *The Gazetteer and New Daily Advertiser*, January 2, 1766

This is the second of two letters that Goddard reprinted in the *Pennsylvania Chronicle*, Feb. 16–23, 1767, the authorship of which is attributed to him there and in William Franklin's memorandum. It is his second response to a letter by "Vindex Patriae" printed in the *Gazetteer*, Dec. 23, 1765, refusing to admit the economic importance to Britain of colonial trade and denying the colonists' right to direct representation in Parliament before that body might properly tax them. Over the signature "N.N." Franklin had replied on the general question in the *Gazetteer* of December 28 (above, XII, 413–16), and now, writing in a lighter vein as "Homespun," he answered his opponent's aspersions on the American diet and easy dismissal of the effects a colonial boycott might have on trade.

[January 2, 1766]

VINDEX PATRIAE, a writer in your paper, comforts himself, and the India Company, with the fancy, that the Americans, should they resolve to drink no more tea, can by no means keep that resolution, their Indian corn not affording "an agreeable, or easy digestible breakfast." Pray let me, an American, inform the gentleman, who seems quite ignorant of the matter, that Indian corn, take it for *all in all,* is one of the most agreeable and wholesome grains in the world; that its green ears roasted are a delicacy beyond expression; that *samp, hominy, succatash,* and *nokehock,* made of it, are so many pleasing varieties; and that a *johny* or *hoecake,* hot from the fire, is better than a Yorkshire muffin.[9] But if Indian corn were as *disagreeable* and *indigestible* as the Stamp Act, does he imagine we can get nothing else for breakfast? Did he never hear that we have oatmeal in plenty, for water gruel or burgoo;[1] as good wheat, rye, and barley as the world affords, to make fru-

---

9. Samp: coarsely broken Indian corn, boiled and eaten with milk and sugar. Hominy: grains of Indian corn with the hulls removed, broken into a meal, either fine or coarse, and boiled. Succotash: beans and kernels of corn cooked together. Nokehock, or nocake: corn meal, which may be cooked in various ways such as johnny cake or hoecake. By "Yorkshire muffin" BF may have meant what is today usually called "Yorkshire pudding." For his more extended defense of Indian corn, see below, pp. 44–9.

1. A thick gruel or porridge.

menty;[2] or toast and ale; that there is every where plenty of milk, butter, and cheese; that rice is one of our staple commodities; that for tea, we have sage and bawm in our gardens, the young leaves of the sweet white hickery or walnut, and, above all, the buds of our pine, infinitely preferable to any tea from the Indies;[3] while the islands yield us plenty of coffee and chocolate? Let the gentleman do us the honour of a visit in America, and I will engage to breakfast him every day in the month with a fresh variety, without offering him either tea or Indian corn. As to the Americans using no more of the former, I am not sure they will take such a resolution; but if they do, I fancy they will not lightly break it. I question whether the army proposed to be sent among them, would oblige them to swallow a drop more of tea than they chuse to swallow; for, as the proverb says, though one man may *lead* a horse to the water, ten can't *make him drink*. Their resolutions have hitherto been pretty steadily kept. They resolved to wear no more mourning; and it is now totally out of fashion with near two millions of people;[4] and yet nobody sighs for Norwich crapes, or any other of the expensive, flimsey, rotten, black stuffs and cloths you used to send us for that purpose, with the frippery gauses, loves, ribbands, gloves, &c. thereunto belonging. They resolved last spring to eat no more lamb; and not a joint of lamb has since been seen on any of their tables, throughout a country of 1500 miles extent, but the sweet little creatures are all alive to this day, with the prettiest fleeces on their backs imaginable. Mr. VINDEX's very civil letter will, I dare say, be printed in all our provincial news papers, from Nova Scotia to Georgia; and together with the other *kind, polite,* and *humane* epistles of your correspondents PACIFICUS, TOM HINT, &c. &c. contribute not a little to strengthen us in every resolution that may be of advantage, to *our* country at least, if not to *yours*.   HOMESPUN.

2. Hulled wheat boiled in milk, with sugar, raisins, and other ingredients added.
3. The use of various forms of local vegetation, including the ones mentioned here, for the making of tea is often cited in the writings of this period. On William Allen's fondness for pine-bud tea, especially as a specific for the gout, see Lewis B. Walker, ed., *The Burd Papers. Extracts from Chief Justice William Allen's Letter Book* ([Pottsville, Pa.,] 1897), pp. 58–62.
4. For one of the earliest funerals in Philadelphia at which the customary marks of mourning were omitted, see above, XII, 240 n.

8

"F.B.": On the Paving of Chancery Lane

Printed in *The Gazetteer and New Daily Advertiser*, January 4, 1766

While there is no certainty that Franklin wrote this squib, the editors agree with Verner W. Crane (*Letters to the Press*, pp. 44–5) that "the probability . . . is strong enough to justify its inclusion" among his writings. The style and lightness of touch are characteristic; his interest in street paving appears several times in his other writings; and the signature "F.B.," reversing his own initials, is found also in four of his acknowledged pieces of this period; above, XII, 406–7, 411–13; and below, pp. 38–9, 182–4.

Chancery Lane, familiar haunt today of students of English and Anglo-American history as the site of the Public Record Office, runs from Fleet Street to Holborn. Originally called New Street, its name was changed to Chancery Lane after Edward III assigned the earlier House of Converts as the seat of the master of the rolls. This official, formerly only a custodian of records, gradually assumed a jurisdiction in the Court of Chancery next to that of the lord chancellor himself and heard cases in equity in Rolls Chapel or the court in Rolls Yard. For generations the street was notorious for its miry and malodorous condition, having no sewer arrangements until well into the seventeenth century. The Paving Act of 1765 (5 Geo. III, cap. 50) authorized the inhabitants of any square, street, or place to meet and agree to raise funds for its paving. The difficulties and delays attending procedure in the Court of Chancery, as notorious as the condition of the street in earlier times, continued until long after Franklin's time; in 1853 Charles Dickens brought them vividly to the attention of readers on both sides of the Atlantic through his novel *Bleak House*.

To the Printer.   [January 4, 1766]
By an advertisement in your paper of Wednesday last, I find, "the inhabitants of Chancery-lane are desired to meet at the Crown and Rolls, to consider about new paving the said street." I hope and pray they may not agree to it. *Chancery lane* is in every respect so like a *Chancery suit;* it is so very *long* a lane, so subject to *obstructions* and *delays,* one is so *unwilling* to enter into it, so *uneasy* and *unsafe* all the while one is going through it, and so *glad* to get out of it, that the very reflection on this similarity has often, to my great advantage, deterred me from law, and inclined me rather to end a dispute by arbitration. I therefore wish to see the lane continued in its present state (even after all the rest of the city shall be

9

new paved) as a standing *memento* that may be beneficial to my
fellow citizens.   F.B.

From James Parker   ALS: American Philosophical Society

Honoured Sir   Burlington, Jan. 4. 1766.
  About eight Days after mine per December Packet, yours of
Sept. 26 1765 per Capt. Robinson came to Hand:[5] The Chief Matter in yours, which my last will not serve for an Answer to, is that
part relating to Mr. Balfour:[6] Tho' I have the highest Sense of
your Kindness in what Answer you return'd him, yet I have now
wrote to them, and inclose it to you, first because I would not
put them to greater Charge than I can't help, and next that you
may see what I have wrote, which is Strictly true:[7] Indeed, I meet
with a good deal of hard Fortune; I am really £50 Sterl. out of

  5. For Parker's letter to BF of Dec. 20, 1765, see above, XII, 407–10; BF's
letter to Parker of Sept. 26, 1765, has not been found. The *Prince George,*
Capt. J. Robinson, arrived at Philadelphia during the last week of December.
Pa. Gaz., Jan. 2, 1766.
  6. John Balfour, Edinburgh bookseller, had written BF, Sept. 2, 1765, asking
for the recommendation of an "honest Attorney" in New York to bring suit
against Parker for a debt owed him and his brother-in-law and partner, Gavin
Hamilton, on account of a shipment of books they had sent Parker at BF's request; above, XII, 251–2. BF had apparently included an extract of Balfour's
letter in his to Parker of September 26.
  7. Parker's long letter of Jan. 3, 1766, to Messrs. Hamilton and Balfour is
among the Franklin Papers, APS. In it he explained that the first parcel of
these unwanted books had reached New York after he had given up business
there and had moved to Woodbridge, N.J. He had turned the books over to a
nephew (Samuel Parker, with the same name as James's own son), who was
just starting up in business in the city. The senior Parker had sent a first remittance out of his own pocket, though he had "not received 10s. in all for
your Books myself." His nephew, Parker thought, had sold about a third of
the books, "then broke and suddenly absconded," owing his uncle personally
about £300 in addition to the money received for the Hamilton and Balfour
books he had sold. The older man had then secured the shop and its contents
and turned them over to John Holt. Parker understood that Holt had sent the
Scottish booksellers "some Money," but soon James Rivington had arrived in
New York with such a large stock that other booksellers were nearly driven
out of competition. Parker promised to do what he could to straighten the
matter out when he got to New York in the following summer.

Pocket by their sending me those Books: It is true it was my own Fault for taking them, and my own Fault for letting my Nephew have them: But I did for the best. And now, Mr. Holt had the rest, I don't know how to get the Pay: Would it not have been hard now, if those Goods you sent for Mr. Hughes, after you had recommended them to my Care, I should have let Mr. Holt take them, as he desired, and he never paid me for them.[8] Would it not, I say, have been hard for me to pay you for them: and yet this I suppose would have been expected, tho' had he not already caus'd me to answer as well what he had of your sending, as well as those to Mr. Strahan, I should doubtless let him have them, tho' I believe he would never have paid me more for them than for the others, and this of Balfour's is just so. I told you before, I purposed to go to New-York in the Spring, God permitting: I observe what you say about the Office in the Custom-House: and indeed I think as you do about my Son:[9] But alas! he has been sick now above three Months, The 20th of last Month an Express arrived to me from him, that he lay a-dying, given over by the Doctors, I was unable to go myself having the Gout too hard upon me: My Wife and Daughter both went, tho' very cold Weather. They found him alive yet, but so low, as to have small Hopes: it has pleased God, however that the last News I had of him three Days ago, that there were some Hopes Still of his Recovery: The cold Weather sets in apace, and this River is so full of Ice there is no crossing, otherwise I expected to hear again as this Day: My Gout has held me the longest this Time that ever I had it: I mend now but very slow assoon as I am able I shall go to Philadelphia to proceed

8. On this other financial tangle in which Parker had unfortunately become involved, see above, XII, 355, 408. Hugh Hughes of New York (brother of BF's Philadelphia friend John), at whose request BF had shipped over an electrical machine and other goods under Parker's care, was staying close housed to escape the sheriff and imprisonment for debt, as Parker explains in the January 9 installment of the present letter.

9. The British Post Office officials had required that Parker, as comptroller in America, should reside in New York. To lessen the financial sacrifice the move would involve, BF had procured for him appointment as land waiter in the Custom House there; above, XII, 89–91, 111–12, 227–31, 275–6. Parker had suggested that the job be given to his son instead, though admitting Samuel's youth and the "Follies" he hoped the young man was outgrowing. BF had apparently expressed his doubts about such an appointment.

11

with your Business as far as I am able:[1] My Illness has detain'd me here upon Cost, or I had been with all my Family at Woodbridge by this Time; I have not but a Wench and three Young People with me: all the rest are at Woodbridge, tho' little or nothing going on, but Sickness. I wish I may know where to put these Materials[2] for your Pleasure, as I would leave them: If I can get to New York before the first of May, I will; but last Post, I had a Letter from New York, telling me a Rumour prevail'd there, that I was turn'd out or superseded in that Place in the Custom-House:[3] tho' I do not know what Grounds there are for such Report, yet as tis possible, I can't contradict it: Those who gave it, can doubtless take it away, and if it is so, I submit: If it is not so, I shall proceed to New-York assoon as I can, and know the Truth: I shall endeavour to execute it faithfully and honestly to the best of my Skill, that I may not disgrace your kind Recommendations. But if it is taken from me before I enter into it, neither my Ability or Integrity will ever be called in Question on that Account; I will go nevertheless, God Willing to New York and keep the Comptroller's Office there, for one year at least, or as long as I shall be intrusted with it: I wish I had not been engaged to this Job[4] I did here before I knew it, and then I Should have gone immediately, for I have made nothing of the Job, by Reason of Sickness and frequent Lets in the Way, which has kept me so long in doing it, as to eat up all my Profits. Two of my Boys has had long Sickness, and My Son, my Daughter and self have all had almost as long Doctor's Bills as Butcher's—And we are not well yet.

Jan. 7. This Day heard from Woodbridge, my Son then alive yet and some sanguine Hopes of his Recovery: I also received a Letter from Mr. Holt, in answer to one I wrote to him about Balfour, that part of it I send for your Perusal of it.[5] As the November Packet is

1. Parker managed to go to Philadelphia on January 16 to complete his work on the accounts of the Franklin and Hall partnership.

2. The press and other printing equipment that had once been Benjamin Mecom's and now belonged to BF.

3. No other reports of this rumor have been found. It may have originated in Lieut. Gov. Cadwallader Colden's charge that Parker had printed the *Constitutional Courant* against the Stamp Act in September 1765; above, XII, 287–8.

4. The printing of Samuel Smith's *The History . . . of Nova-Caesaria, or New Jersey,* at Burlington.

5. Not found.

expected, and may sail before I have warning, I write this before hand; and here it may not be amiss to say something about the Money you paid for me to Mr. Strahan.[6] When you went away I had near £100 Sterl. due in the Post-Office, and I purposed assoon as I heard of your Arrival in England to have tried to pay as far as it would go: The Beginning of March, I had not yet heard from you, but Mrs. Franklin wrote me Word, she had by Advise of your Friends, purchased a Lot of Land adjoining your House, for which a large Sum was to be paid down:[7] As I had not Money myself, I directly went off to New-York, and requested some of Mr. Colden, as I could not readily find any other, he with Difficulty let me have £100, which I immediately sent to her. It help'd a little to make up the Sum, but as I had not heard from you, I charged it as paid to you on the Post-Office Account. Some time after I received yours about the Payment of Strahan: I can't help confessing the Stile of that Letter was not pleasing: I never was nor never will be such a Hypocrite, as to speak contrary to my Mind, but I will let that drop: The first Money I got of the Post-Office Money, I paid Mrs. Franklin £172 10s. Phil[adelphia] at that Time £100 Sterl. and then gave her my Bond for £65-odd Sterl. being the whole of the Remainder, with the Interest from Feb 1. so that in that you get Interest for Interest of Some part of it, and this is what I tho't Right and Just: If it shall be proved otherways hereafter I will allow it, for I never wanted to wrong any Body, I have rather oftentimes wrong'd myself—and it always was a Maxim with me so to do.

Jan. 9. Now I have mentioned Mr. Hughes of New-York. He readily allowed the Goods you sent to be delivered to my Order,

6. In October 1764 Parker had asked BF to pay his debt to William Strahan and offered to pay BF interest on the amount advanced, BF complied, paying Strahan £163 13s. 7d. sterling on Feb. 1, 1765. Writing on June 14, 1765, Parker complained that BF required him to give bond for this debt and to pay interest on it, since he hoped to have much of it offset by money due him from the Post Office. He did, however, manage to pay off part of the loan, as he explains here, and gave bond to DF for the balance on Aug. 1, 1765. Three weeks after writing the first part of this letter he paid DF the equivalent of £25 sterling more, leaving an unpaid balance of about £40 sterling. Above, XI, 414, 470–1, 520; XII, 174–5, 226–7.

7. The Syddon lot, adjoining the Franklins' previously owned property; above, XII, 283–6.

but said he had not requested a 10th part of them and the Electrical Machine, he understood was not to exceed two Guineas: He has not yet surrendered up his Estate, but keeps close in his own House, and keeps a School, and is so situated as the Sheriff can't easily come at him: He has offered to deliver all he has up, but his Creditors won't accept it, in Hopes if he is sent to Goal, that his Brother would relieve him: This he says he will by no Means allow of.[8] Things remain so: Tho' would they take all he has got now, and let him go free he would he thinks soon get into a tolerable Way again, as he has a very good School: and he would then take some of the Goods you sent, and make Payment: but as it is, we are in Suspence about him: Were I able I would go to New York, and try to dispose of them, but in my present Illness and the Confusion of the Times, they must lay till something alters. I hope the Goods won't damage by being kept pack'd, tho' perhaps they may get no good by it, especially if they should have happen'd to be damp'd in the Passage, but as tis, I durst not trust them to be open'd out of my Sight, lest some of them melt, as I have known such Things happen.

Jan. 10. No News of the Packet this Post, but I had News from my Son, that he is somewhat better, and good Hopes of his Recovery. I hope it may be so: tho' he is represented to be quite low indeed, I think I am a little better myself to day, tho' far from being well.

Mr. Foxcroft is gone to Virginia again, tho' he said he would not Stay long: I suppose he wrote per last Packet,[9] and I have Nothing material farther about the Office: I fear the Cold Weather will detain him longer than he imagined. I told you in my last, it was thought most expedient to order Benny Mecom to pay half the Hartford Rider's Allowance, in Connecticut Money:[1] because it

8. In contrast to John Hughes, appointed stamp distributor of Pennsylvania, Hugh Hughes was an ardent Son of Liberty. This sharp difference in politics may explain why Hugh was unwilling to accept financial help from his brother, though personal pride could have been another reason.

9. No letters between Foxcroft and BF have been found from the period between BF's departure for England, November 1764, and February 1769. The complete disappearance of all the correspondence that must have taken place between the two deputy postmasters general for so considerable a period is difficult to explain.

1. Benjamin Mecom, BF's nephew, was serving as postmaster in New Haven.

would suit the Rider in that Money, when he Benny could not get New York Money to remit, at the same Time, it would keep the Ballance from running too high against Benny, and save the Sum in Mr. Colden's Hands,[2] who before paid it: I have not had Benny's Accounts since last March, tho' I have wrote to him often, and have last Post wrote more peremptorily to him than usual: He paid some of his first Ballances to the Post-Office, but he has not paid me a Farthing of a small Rent he was to allow me: nor indeed can I prevail upon him so much to get the better of his lethargick Indolence as for him to write to me, but very seldom; yet I don't find that any Fault is found with him lately about his Office or printing.

As to the Affair in New Haven of Mr. Holts', you know I begg'd to be excused the intermeddling with it, as its acting against my-self:[3] for I never can get it out of my Head, that he, or rather I, ought to have above £150 of that Money: but I submit to the Trial. I have not interfered, I have been told the Case was referred to Auditors, or Referrees appointed by the Court, but I have not heard what farther has been done, I suppose Mr. Ingersoll's present Troubles, of which No Doubt you hear, has prevented his pushing the Matter:[4] I rest in Patience, as I can't help myself any Way, not doubting, but the over ruling Hand of Providence, will work to me the best, at least in Reality if not to Appearance.

Jan. 12. Two Days past moderate Weather, the Ice almost thaw'd, but to Day cold again: the Ice fixed, but no crossing the River or expected to hear from Nyork, &c—Your Daughter in Burlington was to go home two Days ago, but no crossing the River: since; I still remain under the Jurisdiction of the Gout, tho' I am well Tired of the Confinement, as well as the Pain: It tyrannizes over me at a hard Rate, nor is my Situation the best suited for it, as it might be, but I can't get away, tho' I very much want to. Perhaps I have by

2. Alexander Colden was postmaster in New York.

3. John Holt, formerly associated with Parker in operating the printing office in New Haven and acting as postmaster there until Mecom took over in 1764, owed the American Post Office about £320 in December 1763, and at that time BF had directed Jared Ingersoll, as attorney, to attach any part of Holt's property he could locate in Connecticut and to bring suit against him in the King's name; above, x, 402–3.

4. Ingersoll's "present Troubles" were the unpleasant experiences resulting from his appointment as stamp distributor for Connecticut.

this Time almost tired your Patience, and as I hope the next News I hear will be the Arrival of the Packet, I will close this, to be ready to send it, and if any Thing happen material, I can add a Bit to it—With all Respects remain Your obliged Humble Servant

JAMES PARKER.

12 Clock. Just now hear the Packet is arrived, so close my Letter and send it off: Had none from you by it.

Jan 11, 1766[5]

For as much as I have asserted in the Letter, that I could not help thinking upwards of £150 of the Money, Mr. Holt is sued for at New Haven belongs to me you may Require some Reasons for my so asserting: The Case then is really thus:[6] Before the Year 1755, when I went to New-Haven, you know there was no Post-Office between New York, and New London, all Way-Letters from and to the Places between those two Towns were the Rider's Perquisites, and you can hardly help remembring that the Riders complain'd much of being deprived of them by the Means of Norwalk and New Haven Offices: But as to Middletown and Hartford, the Inhabitants whilst Living was cheap hired a poor little Man, to meet the King's Riders at Seabrook: All Letters from any Post-Office to those Places were accounted for, but any from the inter-

5. What follows here was written on both sides of a separate sheet, probably tucked in between the leaves of the folio containing the first installments of the letter, and from its date obviously written before the installment dated "Jan. 12," the signature, and the "12 Clock" postscript.

6. With reference to what follows it should be stated that the editors have been unable to determine precisely when the various post offices in colonial Connecticut were established. New London is the only place in the colony mentioned in the Postal Act of 1710; it probably had a post office at that time. Parker seems to be correct here in saying in effect that prior to his arrival in New Haven as postmaster in January 1755 the New London office was the only one in the colony, although "Way-Letters" might be carried to and from other towns on Long Island Sound by the postriders. By 1763 there were offices at Stamford, Norwalk, Stratford, and Guilford, as well as New Haven and New London, along the main route, which then traversed Rhode Island on its way from New York to Boston, and at Middletown and Hartford on a connecting route that also served offices at Springfield and Worcester in Massachusetts and likewise ended at Boston. See above, x, 418. No other offices are recorded among BF's papers as having been established in Connecticut during his tenure of office under the Crown.

mediate Towns, were the Rider's Profits: of which a good Number
went from New Haven: Upon erecting a Post-Office at New
Haven, the Inhabitants of Middletown and Hartford declined hiring their Rider any longer, and it was some Months in that Condition: I went there the Beginning of January, in April following, I
attempted to begin a News-paper and as it must be naturally concluded, that the most of my Customers would be off the Common
Post-Road, I was applied to, and induced to hire the little Rider,
(Brooker) to go between Hartford and New Haven. I wrote to you
to Philadelphia about [it] and you did give me some Encouragement in it:[7] Several of the Inhabitants of Hartford, were induced
to subscribe for the Papers, for the Benefit of the Riders coming
there: For the 8 or 9 Months that I was there and hired the Rider,
the whole of the Pay for the Papers taken by him would not pay
him, but I got something by the Letters received from thence and
expected as much by Letters sent thither, but of this last I was
entirely deprived: Matters continued so with Mr. Holt for near 6
Years longer, in all which Time, we paid more to that Rider, than
we ever got for the Newspapers he carried, being £40 a Year lawful Money, and allmost all the Money got for Postage of Letters
went to pay the Rider. Tho' had we not hired that Rider not a
Letter from any Post-Office would have gone to or come from
Hartford and Middletown: Mr. Holt declined settling, because he
was in Hopes you and Mr. Hunter[8] would have made an Allowance:
for we paid in that Time, £280 Lawful Money for a Rider, for
which all the News-papers he carried, were they all paid for, would
have fell short of the Pay: You may ask why we did it? But why
does any Body venture on unbeaten Tracks and often get ruin'd by
it, whilst others reap the Benefit of their Venture. When Mr. Holt
came to New York, he hir'd the Hartford Rider at £90 only per
An. for two Years—as we had a Prospect of a great Run of News
papers; and by him we did not lose so much proportionably as by
the others: yet as Mr. Hunter order'd Mr. Colden to keep that
Riders Returns separate, it to me is a Proof of what I know to be
true that Mr. Holt was to have some Allowance out of it: but it
pleased God to take Mr. Hunter away, and we were deprived of

7. Parker's letter on this matter and BF's reply have not been found.
8. William Hunter, BF's associate in the deputy postmaster generalship until
his death in 1761.

that: The hiring that Rider at first certainly did not answer the Purpose: as few such Adventures do at the Beginning, but it certainly will be advantageous in Time: However I believe in that we suffered in the two Years about £70 or £80 Loss. Now on the Whole, as Mr. Holt owes me, and this Money is the King's, so if he is compell'd to pay it, I lose it, because he has scarce much more than will pay the King: This makes him indifferent in the Matter, seeing if the King has it, I can't have it: and if the King don't take it, I shall: Altho' I have not interfered in this Trial one Word, only in my Applications to you and Mr. Foxcroft, both of which turn a deaf Ear: (for none so deaf as those who will not hear), yet I say I can't help thinking, nay I am morally positive that in strict Justice, we, or rather I myself, ought to be allowed above £150 Lawful Money, let the Judgment of the Auditors on Trial, be as it may: In a vacant Hour I have scribbled this, tho' I am resolved to suffer, patiently knowing that the Divine Providence can over rule all Things for the best: tho' my Follies make my Deservings very little or Nothing from it.

Endorsed: Mr Parker his Reasons about the Connecticut Post Office Acct.

"N.N.": On the Tenure of the Manor of East Greenwich

Printed in *The Gazetteer and New Daily Advertiser*, January 11, 1766.

This letter was the first of two that Goddard reprinted in the *Pennsylvania Chronicle*, March 2–9, 1767, the authorship of which William Franklin later also attributed to his father. It is part of his newspaper controversy with "Vindex Patriae" and the second in the series that he signed "N.N." His opponent's first letter, in the *Gazetteer* of Dec. 23, 1765, had stated that the Connecticut charter of 1662 had made that colony a part of England by a legal fiction, and its people constructively natives of England and hence represented in Parliament as all England was. Franklin replied briefly to this argument in his letter in the *Gazetteer* of December 28 (above, XII, 414–15), and "Vindex Patriae" responded with a long letter in the issue of January 3, a large part of which he devoted to this *"virtual representation"* of the colonists in Parliament. The New England charters, he pointed out, provided that the grantees should hold their lands "as of his Majesty's manor of East

18

Greenwich in the county of Kent," and by accepting these charters the colonists had solemnly accepted "the fiction in our law, *that New England lies within England.*" The writer held, in effect, that the New Englanders were virtually represented in the House of Commons by the members from the county of Kent. The present letter is Franklin's answer to the letter of January 3, and especially to its argument about the manor of East Greenwich.

Twentieth-century scholars have established beyond question that the references to East Greenwich in many of the colonial charters had nothing whatever to do with representation in Parliament, virtual or otherwise.[9] These clauses related specifically and solely to matters of land tenure. The underlying theory of English land law was that the King was the ultimate and paramount lord of all the soil in the *terra regis* and that all other individuals held their lands from him, either directly, or indirectly through a chain of tenurial relationships.[1] When the King made direct grants of land lying outside the physical boundaries of the realm of England, as in Ireland or America, that land was treated as belonging constructively to one of the existing royal manors or other properties. The Connecticut charter, and most of the others for the colonies that still existed as political entities in the 1760s, specified for this purpose the royal manor of East Greenwich,[2] and provided that the grantees should hold their land "in free and common soccage," which was the freest and least burdensome of all the tenures known to the ancient land law.

9. The most thorough treatment of this subject, which includes an excellent discussion of the historical background, is Viola F. Barnes, "Land Tenure in English Colonial Charters of the Seventeenth Century," *Essays in Colonial History Presented to Charles McLean Andrews by his Students* (New Haven, 1931), pp. 4–40. Andrews' own much briefer discussion is in *The Colonial Period of American History*, I (New Haven, 1934), 86–7 n.

1. In the case of Pennsylvania, for example, Charles II granted the lands of the prospective colony to William Penn, his heirs and assigns, by the charter of 1681/2, to be held of the King, his heirs and successors, "as of Our Castle of Windsor in Our County of Berks, in free and common Soccage." The charter then empowered Penn and his heirs to grant parcels of this land to other individuals "to be held of the said William Penn, his Heirs and Assigns, as of the said Seignory of Windsor . . . and not immediately of Us, Our Heirs or Successors."

2. The Maryland charter of 1632, like the later one for Pennsylvania, cited the castle of Windsor rather than the manor of East Greenwich. According to the argument of "Vindex Patriae," the inhabitants of those two colonies would have been "virtually" represented in the House of Commons by the members elected from Berkshire rather than by those from Kent.

To the PRINTER   Jan. 6, 1766.
I did not think to have given you any farther trouble, having already exprest my sentiments pretty fully, on the *impropriety* and *imprudence* of angry reflections on the Americans in the public papers, as more than half the trade of this country is with them; and that trade depends greatly on the regard they have for us, and in consequence for our fashions and fineries, which are by no means necessary to their subsistence; the Northern Colonies having among themselves the natural means of furnishing, by a little additional industry, every convenience and ornament of life; and to that industry I apprehended a resentment of harsh and contemptuous treatment might naturally provoke them.

But I cannot take leave of my antagonist VINDEX PATRIAE, without a few remarks on his letter of Friday last. All the mad proceedings of the mobs in America, however disapproved of by the sober and prudent part of the inhabitants, are charged to the account of the country in general, and the people are all involved in one common accusation. He remembers that your papers have informed us of the riots at Boston, but forgets that they likewise informed us, some of the rioters were apprehended and imprisoned, in order to be brought to justice; and that the body of the people detested these violences. It is true, they universally deem the stamp act an infringement of their rights, but then their assemblies have taken no violent measures to oppose it; they have only entered into resolutions among themselves, declaring their sense of these rights; and joined, as we are well assured, in dutiful petitions to the King and Parliament here, that the act may be repealed, and those rights preserved to them. Can more be expected from any subjects, how loyal soever, that think themselves aggrieved? Is it right to abuse all England as rebellious, because it has sometimes mobs of weavers, coal-diggers, &c.? Candour then should distinguish in this case fairly, between the proceedings of the assemblies there, and the actions of mobs; the latter are *certainly* wrong, the former *may* be so; but if they are, it is a mistaken judgment only of what they think their right; of this mistake they may possibly be convinced by reason; but I still doubt the argument of your correspondent, proving, or attempting to prove, "that they are represented in parliament, because the manor of East Greenwich in Kent is represented there, and they all live in that manor;" will hardly appear so intelligible, so clear, so satisfactory, and so convincing to the Americans, as it seems it does to himself.

I own it does not appear so to me; and that my plain understanding, unaccustomed to the subtle refinements of law, cannot easily conceive, that in the King's grants of territory in America to the colonists, the words, "to be holden of us, our heirs and successors, as *of* the manor of East Greenwich, in our county of Kent, in free and common soccage, and not *in capite,* or by knight's service;" do truly imply, that the lands so granted really lie *in* East Greenwich. I should rather have thought those words meant only to express, that the tenure should be of the *same kind* with that of the manor of East Greenwich. The countries held by this tenure, Sir, are perhaps as big as all Europe; and East Greenwich, in the county of Kent, in England, is at most but of a few miles circumference. I have read that the whale swallowed Jonah; and as that is in Holy Writ, to be sure I ought to believe it. But if I were told, that, in fact, it was Jonah that swallowed the whale, I fancy I could myself as easily swallow the whale as the story.

If *"New England lies within England,"* as your correspondent would have the New England men believe, and particularly in the manor of East Greenwich, a few questions must thence naturally arise, to which his law knowledge will probably furnish ready answers. As, What have these inhabitants of East Greenwich in Kent done, that they, more than any other inhabitants of Kent, should be curbed in their manufactures and commerce? Why are they restrained in making hats of their own beaver, nail rods and steel of their own iron, and cloth of their own wool? Why may not ships from East Greenwich carry its commodities to any part of Europe, and thence bring back others in exchange, with the same freedom that ships may go from any other part of Kent, or of England? And since it is agreed, that by our constitution, the King can raise no money *in England* but by act of parliament, how has it come to pass, that in consequence of requisitions from the crown, large sums have been raised for its service on these inhabitants of East Greenwich, in the county of Kent, *unauthorized by any such act,* particularly between three and four millions during the last war? And if this money was illegally taken, whether it ought not to be refunded, and the ministers impeached that advised the measure? These seem questions of some importance, and may possibly admit

21

of satisfactory answers; but to that end I doubt it will be found necessary, that these new inhabitants of East Greenwich in Kent, planted there by your correspondent, should be all sent back, and replaced in their native America.

In considering of these questions, perhaps, it may be of use to recollect; that the colonies were planted in times when the powers of parliament were not supposed so extensive, as they are become since the Revolution: That they were planted in lands and countries w[h]ere the parliament had not then the least jurisdiction: That, excepting the yet infant colonies of Georgia and Nova Scotia, *none of them* were settled at the expence of *any money* granted by parliament: That the people went from hence by permission from the crown, purchased or conquered the territory, at the expence of their own private treasure and blood: That these territories thus became *new* dominions *of the crown,* settled under royal charters, that formed their several governments and constitutions, on which the parliament was *never consulted;* or had the *least participation.* The people there have had, from the beginning, like Ireland, their separate parliaments, called modestly assemblies: by these chiefly our Kings have governed them. How far, and in what particulars, they are *subordinate* and *subject* to the British parliament; or whether they may not, if the King pleases, be governed as *domains of the crown,* without that parliament, are points newly agitated, never yet, but probably soon will be, thoroughly considered and settled. Different opinions are now entertained concerning them; and till such settlement is made by due authority, it is not criminal to think differently. Therefore, I wish the American opinion may, in the mean time, be treated with less acrimony.

As to VINDEX's accusation of the Americans, "that they run into their country divers commodities of the manufacture of France, to the *ruin* of Great Britain;" I fancy, they will be apt to answer, *Look at home;* and perhaps it will be found, that in this ruinous trade, the rest of the people of Kent, are not a whit behind-hand with the inhabitants of East Greenwich.   N. N.

Sir   [January 6, 1766]

I have attentively perus'd the Paper you sent me, and am of Opinion that the Measure it proposes of an Union with the Colonies is a wise one: but I doubt it will hardly be thought so here, 'till tis too late to attempt it.⁴ The Time has been when the Colonies, would have esteem'd it a great Advantage as well as Honour to them to be permitted to send Members to Parliament; and would have ask'd for that Privilege if they could have had the least Hopes of obtaining it. The Time is now come when they are indifferent about it, and will probably not ask it; though they might accept it if offered them; and the Time will come when they will certainly refuse it, But if such an Union were now establish'd, which methinks it highly imports this Country to establish, it would probably subsist as long as Britain shall continue a Nation. This People, however, is too proud, and too much despises the Americans, to bear the Thought of admitting them to such an equitable Participation in the Government of the whole. Then the next best thing seems to be, leaving them in the quiet Enjoyment of their separate Constitutions, and when Money is wanted for any public Service in which they ought to bear a Part, calling upon them by Requisatorial Letters from the Crown, according to the long establish'd Custom, to grant such Aids as their Loyalty shall dictate and their

3. The only clue the editors have to the identity of the addressee of this letter, other than the canceled name in the endorsement, is a passage which BF quotes in the body of the letter, which he attributes to a friend of the addressee. The passage appears with slight modifications in a letter published in the *Gazetteer*, Jan. 1, 1766, over the signature of "Amor Patriae," the nomme de plume of Thomas Crowley (below, p. 121 n), the London Quaker merchant who advocated Anglo-American union based on equitable American representation in Parliament. Therefore, the addressee of this letter may have been one of Crowley's friends among the London Quakers (although his relations with his co-religionists were far from satisfactory) or among the merchants; BF of course had many acquaintances among both groups. Crowley's letter to the *Gazetteer* is printed in his *Letters and Dissertations on Various Subjects* (London, [1776]), pp. 7–9.

4. At this point in the draft appears an uncompleted sentence that BF struck out before continuing: "No very extensive Empire can well be long maintained intire over People very remote from the Seat of Government, unless the Government is well in."

Abilities permit. The very sensible and benevolent Author of that Paper, seems not to have known that such a constitutional Custom subsists and has always hitherto been practic'd in America, or he would not have express'd himself in this Manner; "Tis evident, beyond a Doubt to the intelligent and impartial that after the very extraordinary Efforts which were effectually made by Great Britain in the late War, to save the Colonists from Destruction, and attended of necessity with an enormous Load of Debts in consequence; that the same Colonists now firmly secured from foreign Enemies, should be somehow induced to contribute some Proportion to wards the Exigencies of State in future." This looks as if he conceiv'd the War had been carry'd on at the sole Expence of Great Britain, and the Colonies only reap'd the Benefit without hitherto sharing the Burthen, and were therefore now indebted to Britain on that Account. And this is the same kind of Argument that is us'd by those who would fix on the Colonies the heavy Charge of unreasonableness and Ingratitude, which I think your Friend did not intend. Please to acquaint him then, that the Fact is not so; That every Year during the War, Requisitions were made by the Crown on the Colonies, for raising Money and Men that accordingly they made *more extraordinary* Efforts in proportion to their Abilities than Britain did; that they rais'd, paid and cloath'd for 5 or 6 Years near 25,000 Men besides providing for other Services, as building Forts, equipping Guard Ships, paying Transports, &c. and that this was more than their fair proportion, is not merely an Opinion of mine, but was the Judgment of Government here on full Knowledge of the Facts; for the then Ministry, to make the Burthen more equal, recommended the Case to Parliament, and obtain'd a Reimbursement to the Americans of about a £200,000 Sterling Every Year, which amounted only to about two fifths of their Expence,[5] and great Part of the rest lies still a Load of Debt upon them, heavy Taxes on all their Estates real and personal being laid by Acts of their Assemblies to discharge it, and yet will not discharge it in many Years. While then these Burthens continue; while Britain restrains the Colonies in every Branch of Commerce

5. Lawrence H. Gipson computes that by a series of nine acts Parliament granted the older colonies a total of £1,072,784 sterling as free gifts or as compensation for military expenditures, in addition to furnishing arms and provisions at Crown expense after 1757. *British Empire,* x, 50.

and Manufactures that she thinks interferes with her own; while she drains the Colonies by her Trade with them of all the Cash they can procure by every Art and Industry in any Part of the World, and thus keeps them always in her Debt: (for they can make no Law to discourage the Importation of your to them ruinous Superfluities, as you do the Superfluities of France; since such a Law would immediately be reported against by your Board of Trade and repeal'd by the Crown.) I say while these Circumstances continue, and while there subsists the establish'd Method of Royal Requisitions, for raising Money on them by their own Assemblies on every proper Occasion, can it be necessary or prudent to distress and vex them by Taxes laid here, in a Parliament wherein they have no Representative, and in a Manner which they look upon to be unconstitutional and subversive of their most valuable Rights; and are they to be thought unreasonable and ungrateful if they oppose such Taxes? Wherewith, they say, shall we show our Loyalty to our gracious King, if our Money is to be given by others without asking our Consent? and if the Parliament has a Right thus to take from us a penny in the Pound, where is the Line drawn that bounds that Right, and what shall hinder their calling whenever they please for the other nineteen shillings and eleven pence? Have we then any thing that we can call our own? 'Tis more than probable that bringing Representatives from the Colonies to sit and act here as Members of Parliament, thus uniting and consolidating your Dominions would in a little time remove these Objections and Difficulties; and make the future Government of the Colonies easy: But till some such thing is done, I apprehend no Taxes laid there by Parliament here, will ever be collected, but such as must be stain'd with Blood. And I am sure the Profit of such Taxes will never answer the Expence of Collecting them; and that the Respect and Affection of the Americans to this Country will in the Struggle be totally lost, perhaps never to be recover'd, and therewith all the Commercial and Political Advantages that might have attended the Continuance of that Respect and that Affection.

In my own private Judgment I think an immediate *Repeal* of the Stamp Act would be the best Measure for *this* Country; but a *Suspension* of it for three Years, the best for *that*. The Repeal would fill them with Joy and Gratitude reestablish their respect and Veneration for Parliament, restore at once their ancient and natural Love for this Country, and their regard for every thing that comes from it; hence the Trade would be renew'd in all its Branches, they would again indulge in all the expensive Superfluities you supply them with, and their own new assumed home Industry would languish. But the Suspension, tho' it might continue their Fears and Anxietys, would at the same time keep up their Resolutions of Industry and Frugality, which in two or three years would grow into Habits to their lasting Advantage. However, as the Repeal will probably not be now agreed to [from] what I think a mistaken Opinion, that the Honour and Dignity of Government is better supported by persisting in a wrong Measure once entred into, than by rectifying an Error as soon as it is discover'd; we must allow the next best thing for the Advantage of both Countries is the Suspension. For as to executing the Act by Force, tis Madness, and will be Ruin to the whole.

The rest of your Friend's Reasonings and Propositions appear to me truly just and judicious. I need therefore only add, that I am as desirous of his Acquaintance [*illegible*] as he was of my Opinion. I am, with much Esteem Your obliged Friend   B F.

Endorsed: Letter to [*name heavily canceled but may be* T. Crowley] Jan 6. 1766

"N.N.": Communicating Massachusetts Documents

Printed in *The London Chronicle*, January 7–9, 1766

This introductory note to the printer is attributed to Franklin chiefly because its signature, "N.N.," is one he certainly used for three other letters to the press in the winter of 1765–66 and continued to use from time to time during later years.[6]

With this communication Franklin sent copies of the instructions adopted by the Boston town meeting, Sept. 18, 1765, for the town's representatives in the Massachusetts General Court, the instructions for a similar purpose adopted by the Braintree town meeting, September

6. The index of Crane, *Letters to the Press*, lists nine letters with the signature "N.N." besides this one that may certainly or almost certainly be ascribed to BF. He states (p. xxix) with apparent justification that the printers reserved this signature for letters by BF.

24, and an extract from Machiavelli's *Discourses on Livy*. The *London Chronicle* printed the introductory note and the Boston instructions in its issue of January 7–9 and the other two pieces in its issue of January 9–11. The Boston instructions had been printed in *Boston Gazette*, Sept. 19, 1765, and reprinted in the *Pennsylvania Gazette*, Oct. 3, 1765. The Braintree instructions had been printed in the *Massachusetts Gazette. And Boston News-Letter*, Oct. 10, 1765, and reprinted in the *Pennsylvania Gazette*, Oct. 24, 1765. Franklin may have obtained his texts from the Philadelphia reprints.

The Boston instructions were written by Samuel Adams.[7] Firm in their opposition to the Stamp Act and vigorous in stating the colonial objections to it, they were nevertheless couched in "decent and respectful terms." They directed the town's representatives to use their "best endeavours" to see that "the *inherent inalienable* rights" of the province's people were "asserted and vindicated," so that posterity might "never have reason to charge the present times with the guilt of *tamely giving* them away." The Braintree instructions, written by John Adams,[8] were to the same effect and showed a similar regard for the opinion of "all future generations," but they were somewhat more outspoken in their criticism of the act and its effects, and in the people's resolve "that we never can be slaves." Both sets of instructions directed the representatives in guarded but emphatic terms to prevent any expenditure of public funds by the governor for the defense of the stamp officers or for the enforcement of the act.

To the Printer of the London Chronicle.   [January 7–9, 1766]
SIR,

Many People imagine that the opposition given by the Americans to the Stamp act, proceeds merely from a mean disposition, and an unreasonable fondness for their money.[9] Whoever is acquainted with their public conduct in general, and particularly

7. William V. Wells, *The Life and Public Services of Samuel Adams* (Boston, 1865), I, 65–66, prints an extended footnote on this authorship and Samuel Adams' priority over John Adams in the preparation of such instructions.

8. On John Adams' authorship, see L.H. Butterfield *et al.*, eds., *Diary and Autobiography of John Adams* (Cambridge, Mass., 1961), I, 265, and on the uncertainty of Samuel Adams' priority in authorship of the instructions for the Boston town meeting, see *ibid.*, III, 283 n.

9. Such criticisms of the Americans, among several in the English newspapers of this period, are to be found in the letters from "Tom Hint," published in the *Gazetteer*, Dec. 13 and 23, 1765, to which BF replied over the signature "F.B." in the issues of December 19 and 27, above, XII, 406–7; 410–13.

through the last war, must know, that niggardliness is no part of their just character. You have already printed some of the instructions from the people there to their Representatives; but the two following, from two of the principal towns in New England I have not yet seen in your or any other paper here: And I think it would be well to publish them at this time, as the chief objections to that act are fully explained in them. I send you also an extract from Machiavell's discourses on Livy;[1] as a due consideration of the sentiments it contains, may perhaps on this occasion be of some service. I am, your's, &c.   N. N.

To the Pennsylvania Assembly Committee of Correspondence

> Extract: printed in *Votes and Proceedings of the House of Representatives of the Province of Pennsylvania*, v (Henry Miller, Phila., 1775), 446, in the record of May 6, 1766; also as a broadside headed "Addendum," but taken from the Miller edition (n.p., n.d., copy in Yale University Library).

London, January 11, 1766

In Compliance with the Direction in the Committee's Letter,[2] I have procured, and now send you inclosed, authentic Office Copies of the Representation of the Board of Trade, dated September the Eighth, 1709, upon our Acts of 1705, referred to them, and of the

1. The quotation, printed in *London Chron.*, Jan. 9–11, 1766, is to be found in any edition of Niccolo Machiavelli's works in *Discourses on Livy*, bk. II, chap. xxiii. It recounts the appearance of the chiefs of the rebellious Privernates for sentencing by the Roman Senate. In response to questions, one leader proclaimed his people's desire to be free and gave assurance that a peace would be "firm and perpetual" if it were granted "upon good terms." Impressed that he had spoken "like a Man and like a Freeman," the Senate pardoned the rebels and granted them citizenship, declaring "That they deserved to be Romans, whose liberty was the greatest part of their care."

2. On Oct. 16, 1765, the Pa. Assembly Committee of Correspondence wrote BF and co-agent Richard Jackson, requesting them to search the Privy Council records and obtain a copy of the royal confirmation of a Pa. act, passed Jan. 12, 1705/6, an "Act to ascertain the Number of Members of Assembly, and to regulate Elections," as well as copies "of all such other Acts as were passed about that Time," and to send them to the Assembly. The committee was particularly interested in the act of 1705/6, declaring it to be "of great Importance to the Rights and Privileges of the People." See above, XII, 322–3.

Order of Council, October the Twenty-fourth, 1709, upon that Representation.[3] By these it appears, that our Act for regulating Elections, &c. which includes and confirms the principal Privileges of the Proprietary Charter, was duly laid before the Council, with the other Acts passed the same Session; that they were, on the Twenty-eighth of April, 1709, referred by the Council to the Board of Trade; that that Board reported upon them September the Eighth, proposing six of them as proper to be disallowed, and declaring that they had *no Objection* to *any* of the others, of which they give the Titles. Then the Order of Council shews, that no more were repealed by Her Majesty than were proposed for Her Disallowance by the Board of Trade: And this Order being on the Twenty-fourth of October, was within Four Days of the Expiration of the Six Months, after which all stand confirmed that were not before repealed. I suppose these Papers will be quite satisfactory on that Head.

From Deborah Franklin
ALS: American Philosophical Society

My Dear Child   Jan. the 12 [1766]
[As it] is verey Cold I did not go ought to day so was a writeing a letter to our Sister Janey in anser to one I had wrote to her sense the deth of her husband[4] I Cante helpe thinking the more trials shee do meet with the more shee shines I pray god to bless and kep her.
So this minit or with in this ower the poste Come in and the packit is arived and I have the pleshuer of a letter from you[5] which

3. The extract of BF's letter and the documents which he mentions here, authenticated by the secretary of the Board of Trade, John Pownall, were read before the Assembly on May 6, 1766, published in its journal under that date, and reprinted as indicated above. The Board of Trade on Sept. 8, 1709, recommended that only six of fifty Pa. acts be disallowed. Among the acts to which it had no objection was the election act of 1705/6, which was allowed to become law by lapse of time in accordance with the proprietary charter. See 8 *Pa. Arch.*, VII, 5861–7.

4. Jane Mecom had written DF on Sept. 28, 1765, announcing her husband's death. DF's answer has not been found. Van Doren, *Franklin-Mecom*, pp. 83–4.

5. Probably BF's letter of Nov. 9, 1765; see above, XII, 360–1.

never failes of giveing me graite pleshuer I will begin and tell you that Capt. Sparkes and Capt. Hammit arived safe and our friends Came in all in good helth I saw my Miss Grayham [Graeme] next evening as I did Mr. Evens I have not seen Mr. Petters yit[6] as I rely am So much taken up a visiting the sick it was on tusday that Capt. Sparkes arived and on friday night Capt. Roboson[7] and on satterday morning I reseved a letter from you[8] with a note from Mrs. Nelson.[9] I read them bouthe and got a verey desent young man to go down to the vesill for her but Capt. Roboson sente me word he wold bring her up and brakefaste with me So he did. Shee was but poorley but after drink a dish or two of tee I had a fier maid in the chaimber up one pair of stairs and shee wente to bead and got sum Sleep shee was better and I did all in my power to make a Straing plase agreabel to her which I hope I did. The Capt. meet with a good deal of trubel[1] so we did not get the things on shore so soon as I did expeckte but att severel times we did. I will tell you Mr. Evens Sente the pair of shoveles and tonges prodigously [rusted?] but he Cold not helpe it.[2] By Robison I have reseved the boyler with the things menshoned in your letter[3] the painted flore cloathe and the other mater which is verey good the set of Chaney quite whole the tee Pot and salte for which I give you maney thankes and if I live tell your Birthday[4] I think to fill it with punch

6. The *Mary and Elizabeth*, Capt. James Sparks, carrying the Rev. Richard Peters and the Rev. Nathaniel Evans and Miss Elizabeth Graeme, and the *Dragon*, Capt. Francis Hammett, arrived in Philadelphia on Thursday, Dec. 26, 1765. See above, XII, 420 n, and *Pa. Jour.*, Jan. 2, 1766.

7. The *Prince George*, Capt. James Robinson, arrived in Philadelphia on Friday, Dec. 27, 1765. *Pa. Jour.*, Jan. 2, 1766.

8. This letter, mentioned in his of Oct. 2, 1765, has not been found. See above, XII, 289.

9. Apparently an English woman whom BF had recommended for domestic service with a New Jersey family, possibly WF's. DF to BF, Oct. 19, 1767; BF to DF, Feb. 13, 1768, both in APS.

1. Captains Sparks and Robinson both brought stamped paper with them and on Dec. 28, 1765, they were forced to make public declarations that they would not deliver it to Stamp Distributor John Hughes, without first giving public notice to the local citizenry. Sparks and Robinson put the stamped paper aboard H.M.S. *Sardine*, Capt. Hawker, thereby satisfying the opponents of the Stamp Act in Philadelphia. *Pa. Gaz.* and *Pa. Jour.*, Jan. 2, 1766.

2. See above, XII, 290.

3. Probably the missing letter mentioned in a previous note.

4. January 17 was BF's sixtieth birthday.

and treet sum of your friends the Cambridg [scissors?] you sente I took one as you desined one for me but before thay Come on shore I told Mr. Rhodes[5] of them he semed plesed at hearing of such things and sed sumtimes he had bin put to a lose for wante of a meshuer so on freyday laste he Come to see me I shoud it to him and he was much plesd with it. I maid him a presant of it and I make no doute but you will say I did write. Now I will tell you sum thing of our one [own] buisnes firste a bought that land in Chester Countey[6] I never heard you say aney thing but what you wrote be for you lefte the Cape that I sente to Mr. Parker. He did the busnis but never sed one word to me a bought it nor I never knew aney thing tell one day I had bin to church when I Came home I found a letter on the tabel direckted to me it was from Amos Strutel Smarte and Shorte demanding of me 18 pound intreste money due on that plantashon. I wrote to Mr. Parker a line or two and in-closed his letter to me and took it to the ofis and I had not bin thair more then 2 minites when Strutel Come in. I told him I was quite a Strainger to the a faire but that letter that I had then brought to the ofis was to inquier of Mr. Parker a bought the afair and his [nos?] in it. He was verey shorte with me[7] so, parker thot he shold a told me sum thing a bought it but had let it slip his memerey and took the deades up with him but then sente them down to me and sed the money muste be paid so I wente down and paid him the 18 pounds and I raly think him one of the rudeste men I ever meet with. I have had one or two to hier the plase but then thair Comes sumbody and ses that thay air Roges and will spoyle the plase. I did inquier in whose Congruygash[on] it was in thay tell me in F Allisons[8] and that thair is none but roges all a bout. I paid ten

5. Samuel Rhoads (above, II, 406 n), who was supervising the construction of BF's house.

6. For an account of these lands which William Dunlap had assigned to the post office to pay debts incurred while he was postmaster of Philadelphia, see above, XI, 469 n. The roles of James Parker and Amos Strettell in this transaction are explained there.

7. Strettell's manner with DF may have been due in part to the fact that he was an active political opponent of BF. See above, XI, 390, 407 n, 412.

8. Francis Alison was a Presbyterian minister, vice provost of the College of Philadelphia, and a political enemy of BF. See above, II, 392 n; XI, 526 n. He had been the settled minister at New London, Chester Co., 1737–52, before moving to Philadelphia.

31

shillins tackes be for but Gorge Read of New casel[9] was to see me I spook to him to see if we Cold get a Chap[?] to sel it to for he ses that he thinkes it in the worste plase in all the Countey. So far on that head now for sumthing which I hope will be more plesing but Mr. Hughes ses he shall write to you a bought it as he Can tell you better then I can but this I have paid to wordes [towards] the land I beleve it is in NovaScosha or sum such plase but to be shorte I have paid 53 pounds to young Wain be fore the Deades is dun but he had borrowed the money of a man that was a going ought of town so you see that I am a raile Land Jober.[1] I tell Salley this is for Grandchildren[2] shee semed verey well plesed att it and thinkes we shall have sume in good time I hope I have dun as you wold have me or as you wold if you had bin at home your self.

The two Mrs. [Messrs.] Foxcroftes[3] air gon to Virjaney thees three weeks we have not heard from them indead I donte know wather aney poste has bin up sense that time. I shall deliver your mesages as you desier me. Poor Parker has bin verey ill a long time and so has his son[4] his wife has bin oblige to go twise to woodbridg as it was thought Sammey was deying but he Cold not stir with the Goute Shee and Jenkey is thair now. On twelef night[5] Jemey

9. George Read (1733–1798) was a lawyer who settled in Delaware after studying in Philadelphia. He was attorney general of Delaware, 1763–1774, member of the Assembly, 1765–1777, and a delegate to the First and Second Continental Congresses. He was a member of the Federal Constitutional Convention in 1787, where he was a conspicuous advocate of the rights of small states. He was one of Delaware's U. S. senators from 1789 to 1793, and from 1793 until 1798 was chief justice of the state. Read investigated the situation of Dunlap's land and sent DF a letter, Feb. 7, 1766, advising her to sell it or even let it lie waste rather than rent it, as the "Inhabitants of that Quarter are generally poor and worthless." APS.

1. For BF's participation in Nova Scotia land speculation, see above, XII, 345–50. "Wain" was "Mad Anthony" Wayne of Revolutionary War fame; early in 1765 he had been in Nova Scotia, surveying lands for a Philadelphia syndicate of which BF was a member. See *ibid*.

2. BF, however, devised "all the lands I hold or have a right to, in the province of Nova Scotia" to WF, although it is not clear that WF ever derived any benefit from them.

3. BF's colleague, John Foxcroft, deputy postmaster general for the northern district of North America, and his brother, Thomas, who was appointed postmaster of Philadelphia after Peter Franklin's death later in the present year.

4. For the illness of Parker and his son, see above, pp. 11–12.

5. That is, January 6.

Logan Came to aske Salley to go with him to Burlinton the next day.[6] Shee was gon to spend the evening att Mr. Roses [Ross's][7] so I sed shee was of aige shold anser for her self. Shee sed yis and next morning thay set ought in a Chariot and 4. He Came downe on freyday and left her be hind. I had no letter as shee was a cuming over with him so had not time to write. Our river is froze over. On monday morning laste it was 5 degres Colder then aney time laste winter. I have my poor Chin froste bit with the Cold. I was in hopes that our friend Mrs. Smith wold a got the better of her disorder but I have bin to see her this evening and found her verey ill shee ses shee muste dey.[8] Shee Cante bair aney bodey to speek to her shee is so low sperrited. It is thought bouthe the Mr. Norrises is verey near thair ende.[9] Our nabor Capt. Horrison[1] is dead and poor Henerey Pastick* was froze to deth and sum other man with him.[2] So far I wrote by Candelite. Mrs. Thomson[3] desiers that I wold give her love to you as doe every bodey that I have seen this day and thay are not a fhew. Remember me to Capt. Orrey[4] and Ladey and Miss. Salley has the sattin. Good old Master Beverag[5]

*The Porter he was a good father indeed.

6. James Logan, Jr., had obviously offered to take Sally to Burlington to visit WF.

7. Sally would have been visiting Margaret Ross, the daughter of BF's good friend John Ross.

8. Mrs. Mary Smith ("Goody" Smith), having suffered some time with the "numb Palsey," died on March 22, 1766. See below, p. 198, and Van Doren, *Franklin-Mecom*, p. 89.

9. Charles Norris (above, II, 376 n) died on Jan. 15, 1766. His brother Isaac, the speaker, died on July 13, 1766. *Pa. Gaz.*, Jan. 23, July 17, 1766.

1. Henry Harrison, former alderman and mayor of Philadelphia, died on Jan. 3, 1766. *Pa. Gaz.*, Jan. 9, 1766.

2. Bastick was frozen to death taking a load of fish to New Castle in an open boat, Dec. 30, 1765. See *Pa. Gaz.*, Jan. 16, 1766.

3. Charles Thomson's wife, a neighbor.

4. For Lewis Ourry, Bouquet's quartermaster and commissary officer, see above, VII, 62–3 n.

5. John Beveridge (1703–1767), a teacher for upwards of forty years in his native Scotland and in America, was appointed professor of Latin at the College of Philadelphia in 1758. In *Pa. Jour.*, Oct. 3, 1765, he invited subscriptions to an edition of his work that William Bradford published later in the year as *Epistolae Familiares et Alia Quaedam Miscellanea. Familiar Epistles, and Other Miscellaneous Pieces, Wrote originally in Latin Verse,... To which are added several Translations into English Verse, by different Hands, &c.*

was maid verey happey with that letter from Sir Robort Pringel.[6] The worthey Jentelman ascd me to give him leve to set you down as a Subscriber for his Book and I gave him leve.[7] I hope it was write and he has had one Bound and left for you Smith[8] has given the good man sum trubel a boute it he teles him the revewers will due sum thing to it but I for get what it is so leve it. I sente Gorge[9] to inquier hough your good old man and woman at paster [pasture] did.[1] He ses thay air well and was glad to hear from the Madam Gorge ses thay have not got a Child as he Cold see I had maney things more to say and if I live I will but the Packit Came before ites time and is to go at 12 a clock and it is near one. My love to all the good pepel that I know. Tell Mrs. Emson that it has plesed God to spair her Papey to his famely a littel Longer.[2] I was to see Brother and Sister[3] laste evening. Brother ses he is verey well but I never say aney body but Mr. Kinersly[4] look so thin as he dus. Sister Complains much but look verey well. All our nabors come in one after another to send Love to you. I have not heard one word from aney bodey att Burlinton so Cante tell hough thay due nor wather Mrs. Nelson got up well lets hope shee did. Debey sends her Duty to you Nancy sendes hers and Susanah hers. I am my Dear Child your afeckshonet wife   D FRANKLIN

6. Sir Robert Pringle (1690–1779) of Stichell, Roxburgh, Scotland, was the elder brother of BF's friend, Dr. John Pringle (VI, 178 n). G.E. Cokayne, *Complete Baronetage*, IV (London, 1904), 319. In a note to one of his poems Beveridge praised Sir Robert as "a gentleman of the greatest Virtue and fairest Reputation; to whom the Author is indebted for many obligations, which he gratefully acknowledges." The poem, which mentions the loss of Pringle's eldest son John (d. 1740), suggests that the young man may have been a pupil of Beveridge's in Scotland.

7. BF is noted as subscribing for two copies.

8. The Rev. William Smith.

9. An aged Negro servant.

1. BF owned a pasture on Hickory Lane (above, II, 310), which he evidently rented to an "old man and woman," not otherwise identified. See Penrose R. Hoopes, "Cash Dr To Benjamin Franklin," *PMHB*, LXXX (1956), 50.

2. Elizabeth Empson was the daughter of the Franklins' neighbor, Samuel Soumaine, the silversmith; both he and his wife had been seriously ill; above, XI, 190 n; XII, 272, 302.

3. Peter Franklin and his wife, Mary.

4. Ebenezer Kinnersley (above, IV, 192 n), BF's collaborator in many electrical experiments.

I did not forget for I hope I have a graitefull harte.

I thanke you for the fine tee Pott for the Carpetes and the verey fine brom. It is verey hansome. For the Salte which is verey excepeabel to me for I like it verey much indeed. For the butyfull Candel stickes[5] and for the Shoefels and tonges which is Cureyous [curious]. D FRANKLIN

From Joseph Galloway   ALS: American Philosophical Society

Dear Sir   Philada. Jany. 13. 1765 [1766].[6]

I received your favours of Sept. 26, and Novr. 9th.[7] We are Sensible of the many Obstructions and unavoidable Difficulties which you have met with in proceeding on our Petitions. And from the perfect Confidence we repose in you we have not the least doubt, but that every thing has been done for the Obtaining the Desirable Object, a Royal Government, should it be obtained or not. The Presentation of the Petitions gives us great Pleasure,[8] and we hope the full orders of the Present Assembly to prosecute them to Effect forthwith, will facilitate an Issue upon them, and remove any Difficulties that may remain with your worthy Colleague, tho by his Letters to the Committee of Correspondence as well as to my Self he Seems firmly resolved to unite with you in bringing this Affair to a Speedy Conclusion.[9]

I thank you Sincerely for the Notice you take of the Piece Signed Americanus.[1] Be assured I shall ever esteem your Approbation of

5. See above, XII, 248.

6. The contents of the letter and BF's endorsement make clear that Galloway's pen slipped when, early in the new year, he wrote "1765."

7. Neither of these letters has been found. Letters to Thomas Wharton and James Parker of September 26 are similarly lost.

8. A letter from Richard Jackson to the Committee of Correspondence dated Nov. 9, 1765, was laid before the Assembly on January 14. It reported that the petitions for a change in government had been presented. 8 *Pa. Arch.*, VII, 5828. Apparently BF's letter to Galloway of the same date made a similar report.

9. In earlier letters Richard Jackson had shown a desire for caution in proceeding with the petitions; apparently his more recent letters had expressed greater willingness to go ahead as Galloway and others wanted.

1. This was certainly the article printed in *Pa. Jour.*, Aug. 29, 1765, described above, XII, 269 n. Some writers have assumed that Galloway's "Piece

my Conduct among the highest Rewards. I have nearly finished a Pamphlet on the Same Subject. Entituled "Political Reflections on the dispute between Great Brittain and her Colonies respecting her Right of Imposing Taxes on them without their Assent." I shall show it when done to my Good Freind your Son, and not Publish it without his Approbation.[2] Something of this Kind Seems absolutely necessary to allay the Violent Temper of the Americans, which has been so work'd up as to be ready even for Rebellion itself. But the Difficulty will be in getting it Published; The Printers on the Continent having combined together to print every thing inflamatory and nothing that is rational and Cool. By which means every thing that is published is ex parte, the people are Taught to believe the greatest Absurdities, and their Passions are excited to a Degree of Resentment against the Mother Country, beyond all Description.

Our Assembly is now Sitting, and yesterday Ordered to be transcribed a Petition to the Commons for the Repeal of the Law Prohibiting Paper Money from being Lawful Tender in the Colonies.[3] I hope the Decency of it, will recommend it to the Attention of that House in these Violent Times as well as its merits. And I think If the Parliament duly weighs the Effects of granting us the Liberty prayed for, they will not Refuse it. Without Money Labour will be Low, and Manufactures may and must from Necessity be carried on In America which must diminish our Brittish Importations. Let us have Money and we shall never think of Manufacturing or if

Signed Americanus" was a different letter, though similarly signed, that was printed in *Pa. Jour.*, Jan. 9, 1766, but they have overlooked the fact that the *Journal* clearly identified this second letter as a reprint of one first appearing in the London *Public Ledger*, Oct. 9, 1765, which seems from its tone and content to have been much more probably written by an Englishman than an American, in spite of its signature. The earlier letter was reprinted as a pamphlet, *Americanus Examined, and His Principles Compared with Those of the Approved Advocates for America. By a Pennsylvanian* (Phila., 1774) with defensive commentary variously attributed to Jabez Fisher and to Galloway himself (Evans, 13277).

2. Apparently Galloway never published this pamphlet.

3. A committee to draft this petition was named, January 9, 1766; after consideration and some amendment, it was signed by the speaker, January 14, and ordered sent to the agents for presentation. 8 *Pa. Arch.*, VII, 5818, 5819–20, 5822, 5824–7. The petition carefully avoided any discussion of parliamentary power.

36

we do, we shall never be able to perfect it to any Degree.[4] I hope the Petition will be ready to come by this Conveyance.

We impatiently wait for the resolutions of the Brittish Parliament respecting the Stamp Act. For while on one part the Law is prevented from being Executed by the Mobs in the Principal Colonies of America, on the other No Buisiness is transacted in any of the Courts of Justice, which is attended with inexpressible Mischief.[5] A certain Sort of People if I may Judge from all their late Conduct Seem to look on this as a favorable opportunity of establ[ish]ing their Republican Principles, and of throwing of[f] all Connection with their Mother Country.[6] Many of their Publications justify the Thought. Besides I have other Reasons to think, that they are not only forming a Private union Among themselves from one End of the Continent to the other, but endeavouring also to bring into their union, the Quakers and all other Dissenters if possible. But I hope this will be impossible. In Pennsylvania, I am Confident it will. I am, my Dear Friend with Sincerest Wishes for your Happiness your truly Affectionate humble Servant   Jos. Galloway

Addressed: To | Benjamin Franklin Esqr. | Deputy Post Master General | of North America | in | Craven street | London | per Packet

Endorsed: Mr Galloway Jan. 13. 66.

4. Among other arguments the petition pointed out the probable curtailment of British imports if there were no "proper Medium of Trade" in America, but it did not even hint at a possible increase in colonial manufactures as this sentence to BF does.

5. Several letters from Philadelphians to BF during the last two months of 1765, printed in Volume XII, touch on the closing of the courts after November 1.

6. The third word in this sentence may have been intended as "Sect," not "Sort." If so, Galloway could have been alluding to Presbyterians and Congregationalists (often linked together) as advocates of "Republican Principles" in the colonies where these denominations flourished. In 1780 Galloway published in London his *Historical and Political Reflections on the Rise and Progress of the American Rebellion* in which (pp. 47–55) he gave a grossly over-simplified account of the development of intercommunication and organization within each of these denominations and between the two, that apparently were designed to defend civil as well as religious liberties.

37

"F.B.": Third Reply to "Tom Hint": Two Taylors

Printed in *The Gazetteer and New Daily Advertiser*, January 14, 1766.

This is the second of two letters that Goddard reprinted in the *Pennsylvania Chronicle*, March 2–9, 1767, the authorship of which William Franklin later also attributed to his father. In December 1765 "Tom Hint" and Franklin, the latter writing as "F.B.," had twice exchanged letters in the *Gazetteer* (above, XII, 406–7, 410–13), and a further exchange took place in January 1766. Franklin's opponent, who had earlier said he had spent several years in America, returned to his attack on the colonists in the issue of January 4, insisting that the late war had been fought primarily for the protection of the colonies and that the money the Americans had raised for the war had not in fact been a heavy burden on them. He also responded to Franklin's defense of the New Yorkers on the matter of the hospitality they had shown to the British troops. The reply printed here concluded this correspondence.

[January 14, 1766]

TOM HINT's virulence against the people of New York, has been in some sort accounted for by himself, in one of his former letters. It seems, tho' he lived several years in that country, they never extended to him any of that civility they generally shew to strangers. He now tells us, in your paper of Saturday, by way of fresh abuse on that *whole people,* that "he admires their wonderful sagacity in distinguishing the *gentleman* from the *scoundrel;* for in serious truth, it would be a difficult matter for an *old-country* man to make that distinction among them, after living with *them* for many years." This will excuse my remarking, that it appears this *old country* man has little of that sagacity himself, and, from the difficulty he supposed in making *such distinction,* might naturally conceive an opinion when he arrived there, that he should be able easily to pass upon those ignorant *new-country* men, as a *gentleman.* The event, it seems, did not answer his expectations; and hence he *had reason* to admire *their* sagacity, but still continues to be angry at its consequences. It puts me in mind of a short story, which, in return for his scraps of plays, I will take the liberty of telling him. Two journeymen *Snips,* during the season of little business, agreed to make a trip to Paris, with each a fine lac'd waistcoat, in which they promised themselves the great pleasure of being received and treated as *gentlemen.* On the road from Calais, at every inn, when they called for any thing hastily, they were answered, *Tout a l'heure, Tout a l'heure;* which not a little surprized them. At length, D— these French scoundrels, says one how *shrewd* they are! I find it won't do; e'en let us go back again to London. Aye, says 'tother, they must certainly deal with the devil, or dress'd as we are dress'd, they could not possibly all at first sight have known us to be *two taylors*.   F. B.

To William Strahan: Report on William Pitt's Speech in the House of Commons   AL: Pierpont Morgan Library

When Parliament reassembled on January 14 after a recess of about four weeks, the King delivered a speech from the throne recommending in deliberately indefinite terms that the members give attention to "the just Rights and Authority of the British Legislature" and the "Welfare and Prosperity of all my People." The king promised that his ministers would lay papers relating to the "American disturbances" before the House of Commons.[7] When the members of that body returned to their chamber after hearing the speech, Secretary of State Conway presented a selected group of such papers, and the customary motion was made and seconded for an address of thanks to the King for his speech. A memorable debate followed.

The most important speaker was William Pitt, who was present for the first time after a protracted illness. In the course of his speech he criticized the present ministry for its long delay in reporting to Parliament on events in the colonies, and he attacked much more severely the previous ministry, of which George Grenville had been the active head, saying that "every capital measure they have taken, has been entirely wrong!" Conway responded, agreeing in general with Pitt's expressed opposition to taxing the colonies and explaining that he and his colleagues had held back the first, rather vague reports coming from America until "more precise and full" information became available.

Grenville then spoke denouncing the disturbances in America, which had grown into "tumults and riots," now bordered on "open rebellion," and he feared would soon "lose that name to take that of Revolution." In response to Pitt's statements he declared that he could not "under-

7. The speech from the throne was printed in *London Chron.*, Jan. 14–16, 1766. It was also printed, together with the addresses from the two Houses of Parliament in reply, in *Pa. Gaz.*, March 27, 1766.

stand the difference between external and internal taxation," and that taxation was one branch of legislation and part of the "sovereign power."

Pitt regained the floor, accepted Conway's explanation of delay in presenting papers, but continued at considerable length in rebuttal of Grenville. In response to the former minister's use of the term "rebellion," Pitt declared flatly, "I rejoice that America has resisted," and he elaborated on the historic distinction between legislation and taxation. In his peroration he summed up his opinion by declaring "that the Stamp Act [should] be repealed ABSOLUTELY, TOTALLY, and IMMEDIATELY," and that Parliament "may bind [the colonists'] TRADE, confine their MANUFACTURES, and exercise every POWER whatsoever, except that of taking money out of their pockets without their consent!"

The fullest report of Pitt's speech, much of it given as direct quotation, with reports of the responses of Conway and Grenville to Pitt's criticisms and of interpolations by other speakers, is in a pamphlet entitled *The Celebrated Speech of a Celebrated Commoner*, published in London by Stephen Austin at an undetermined date in 1766, and in another pamphlet, printed almost entirely from the same type and in the same year, entitled *Political Debates*, but bearing an almost certainly false imprint: "A Paris Chez J. W. Imprimeur . . . ." No writer's name is given in either case. The summary and quotations given in the paragraphs above are taken from *The Celebrated Speech*. Under the heading of "Political Debates, &c." the April 1766 issue of *Gentleman's Magazine*, pp. 155–9, printed a slightly condensed version of the speeches as taken from the pamphlets. In the form of letters from London, the *Pennsylvania Gazette*, March 20 and 27, 1766, printed short reports on the debates in the Commons, January 14 and 15, on the address to the King, and in the issue of April 24 printed a long report in very nearly, but not precisely, the same words as *The Celebrated Speech*. The *Gazette* called it "Extract of a Letter from a Gentleman in London to his Friend in America, dated January 1766." Occasional use of the first person in describing what took place indicates that the writer of this letter wanted it to be believed that he was present and had heard the speeches himself, though he seems actually to have used the pamphlet version as his source.

Apparently William Strahan, among others, had found it impossible to gain admission to the gallery of the House of Commons; he wrote David Hall, April 6, 1766, that "This Winter especially, when the Stamp Act was canvassing in both Houses, none but Members were admitted, and any Account of the Debates which could be procured from those who heard them, was so very lame and imperfect, it was really good for nothing."[8] He wrote again, May 10, of having been "restrained

8. *PMHB*, x (1886), 95.

from hearing the most material Debates whilst the Stamp Act was under Consideration," but was pleased to see from the *Gazette* issue of March 27 that Hall had received reports of the debates from others, including members of the Committee of Merchants working for repeal of the Stamp Act "as well as from Dr. F. whose Assiduity upon the Occasion was superior to any Thing of the Kind I ever saw before."9

There seems to be no way of discovering whether Franklin's "Assiduity" had gained him admission to the gallery on January 14 (perhaps through the good offices of Richard Jackson, a member of Parliament), or whether the account printed below, written in Franklin's hand and sent to Strahan, was based on what Jackson or some other member had reported to him. Nor is it possible to say whether Strahan considered it one of the "very lame and imperfect" reports he had seen. Comparing Franklin's report with the pamphlet accounts, it is obvious that it is much shorter and omits a great deal of what Pitt said, including his expression of pleasure at American resistance and his flat statement at the end that the Stamp Act ought to be repealed, both quoted above. So far as it goes, however, Franklin's account is in the main consistent with the pamphlets, though there are some differences and the pamphlets do not include his report of Conway's expression of willingness to mount his horse and ride out of office when he should be superseded.

Franklin's report is undated. It seems appropriate to assign it the same date as that on which Pitt's speech took place.

[January 14, 1766]

Mr. Pitt spoke some time before one could divine on which side of the Question relating to America he would be; but beginning first to mention the Stamp Act by the soft Term of that *unhappy* Act, he went on, and every Time he had Occasion to mention it, it was by a Term still stronger, as *unconstitutional, unjust, oppressive,* &c. till he finally declar'd in express Terms that the British Parliament had in his Opinion *no Right* to raise internal Taxes in America, tho' it had to regulate their Commerce and even restrain their *Manu-*

9. *Ibid.*, p. 219. John Fortescue, ed., *The Correspondence of King George the Third*, 1 (London, 1927), 224–5, prints a list of the speakers on January 14, 1766, with brief summaries of what they had said. L.B. Namier's *Additions and Corrections* to the Fortescue edition (Manchester, 1937), p. 47, reports that this paper is in the hand of Henry Seymour Conway. The list gives the names of six members who participated in the debate in addition to those mentioned in the printed accounts or by BF, but none of the six seems to have made any major contribution to the discussion.

factures.[1] He said many Things in favour of America, particularly that they had always readily granted Aids to the Crown in all our Wars, on Requisitions made to their several Assemblies, and particularly in the last War far beyond their Abilities, which the Parliament here considering had made them some Compensation;[2] that the Act was therefore *unnecessary;* that no Minister before the last, (naming all the Ministers in order from the Revolution, and giving their Characters, some of whom were remarkable for their Firmness and Resolution, as well as their Understanding, had never thought fit or ventur'd to tax the Colonies; that he himself was sometimes represented as rash enough for any thing; and there had not been wanting some during his Administration that urg'd him to it as a thing that would have been acceptable to Gentlemen here, but they could not get him to burn his Fingers, with so unnecessary, so unjust, and therefore so odious a Measure: The Arguments of virtual Representation, of the Case of the Colonies being the same with that of Corporations in England, or of the Non Electors here, he treated with great Contempt as trifling, and insignificant and ridiculous; asserted that Representation in Parliament was originally and properly of *Landed Property;* that every 40s. a Year of landed Property in England still is represented by the Owner's having a right to vote in County Elections; but that tho' a Man in America had £1000 a Year in Land, it gave him no right to vote for a single Member of Parliament. That the Representation of the Commons, was not an original Part of the Constitution; the Owners of Lands only were call'd to Parliament and all the Lands in England were divided between the King, the Church, and the Barons. The Church, God bless it, had one Third at least. The Commons, were mere Tenants or Copy holders. But now the Case was greatly alter'd. The Church was stript of most of its Lands, and the Nobles had sold so much of theirs, that what remain'd in their Hands was but like a Drop of the Bucket compar'd to what was now in the Hands of the Commons. It was therefore on Ac-

1. In the pamphlets this statement (quoted almost in full in the headnote above) is the final sentence reported from the speech.

2. Here BF differs somewhat from the pamphlet accounts. He stresses the monetary contributions of the colonies during the intercolonial wars; the pamphlets cite Pitt's emphasis on the economic value of colonial trade to Great Britain.

count of their Lands properly that the Commons were represented in Parliament. As to the Representatives of Burroughs, it was wrong to suffer their Sitting in Parliament. It was the rotten Part of our Constitution, and could not stand another Century.[3] How could we with any Face maintain, that a Burrough of half a Dozen Houses ought to have a Representative in Parliament to take care of its Interests; and yet that three Millions of People in America with many Millions of Landed Property should not have a single Vote in the Election of any one Member.[4]

Mr. Grenville saying in Defense of the Act that he had before the Measure was entred into, call'd upon the House, and ask'd if there was any one Member that doubted the Right of Parliament to lay an internal Tax on America; and there was not one,[5] Mr. Pitt answered, that That by no means prov'd the Rectitude of the Measure: for that there had long been in the House a Tenderness of opposing Ministerial Measures, a kind of—what shall I call it— Modesty, that made the Members rather doubt their own Judgments. He wish'd therefore that the young Members would apply

3. This contemptuous reference to the "rotten boroughs" that sent members to the House of Commons, though their population was negligible or nonexistent, appears in the pamphlets in almost the same words.

4. Conway spoke next, as stated in the headnote, but BF does not report his explanation of the delay in presenting papers on America nor Pitt's subsequent acceptance of the explanation.

5. The pamphlets give Grenville's response at considerably greater length. They quote him as calling up the precedents of the counties palatine of Chester and Durham to show that they were taxed before being allowed representation and state that he had the preambles of the acts granting them representation read to the House to prove his point. In the second part of Pitt's speech the pamphlets quote him as saying that if he had been citing these precedents it would have been "to have shewn, that, even under arbitrary reigns, parliaments were ashamed of taxing a people without their consent, and allowed them representation." He added that "He might have taken a higher example in Wales; Wales that never was taxed by parliament, 'till it was incorporated." For BF's notes on these three precedents and the use of them by others during this period, see above, XII, 32–7. The pamphlets report that when Grenville ceased speaking Pitt was recognized, but one member raised a point of order that neither Pitt nor Grenville was talking to the matter before the House, namely, the address to the King. Another member declared that "nothing had been said, but what was fairly deducible from the king's speech," and the speaker ruled in Pitt's favor. Thereupon, amid cries from the House, "Go on, go on," he resumed his speech.

them selves more to the Study of Publick Affairs, and qualifie themselves better to judge of them. That their Silence should be no Proof of the goodness of a ministerial Measure, he reminded the House, that from Year to Year he had in the same Manner call'd upon the House, to know if any one dislik'd our then Continental Connections, and but one ever took the Freedom to speak his Mind on that Head, and he should like him the better for it as long as he liv'd; for he indeed said frankly, "that he did not like what he was pleas'd to call my German War."[6] But with the rest it went down glibly. That Oppositions were generally interested; but his Sentiments of this Act had always been the same, and he had ever dislik'd it as destructive to *Liberty;* a Word often made use of by ambitious Men only as a *Horse* on which they might *mount and ride into Preferment;* but he had no such Views. Mr. Conway remark'd on this, that the *Preferment* he was *in,* was not of his own seeking; and that whenever the honorable Gentleman, for whose Abilities and Integrity he had the highest Veneration, should be, as he sincerely hop'd he soon would be, appointed to supersede him, he should with great Pleasure *mount his Horse and ride out again.*

These are the Particulars you chiefly desir'd an Account of. 'Tis the best I can give you. But I am sensible the Expression is far short of that used by the Speakers.

Addressed: To | Mr Strahan | Printer | New street | Shoe Lane

"Homespun": Further Defense of Indian Corn

Printed in *The Gazetteer and New Daily Advertiser,* January 15, 1766.

This is the first of two letters Goddard reprinted in the *Pennsylvania Chronicle,* March 16–23, 1767, the authorship of which William Franklin later also attributed to his father. On January 2, writing as "Homespun," he had replied briefly to aspersions on Indian corn by "Vindex Patriae" (above, pp. 7–8), and that writer had responded with a letter in the *Gazetteer* of January 7. The first part of that long piece

6. The pamphlets identify this member as Sir Francis Dashwood (1708–1781), who had removed to the House of Lords in 1763 upon succeeding to the title of Lord Le Despencer. He was postmaster general from late in 1766 until his death, and later volumes of this edition will include documents on his official and personal relations with BF.

was a reply to another defender of the colonies. "Vindex Patriae" pointed out how much Scotland had benefited economically from the union with England; he declared that the laws, customs, and religion of New England were largely Scottish; and he viewed with alarm the possibility of an addition of colonial members to the House of Commons, who would, he believed, form a coalition with the Scottish members against the English interest. Then, in reply to "Homespun," he declared that the white Americans rejected Indian corn as a food for themselves but assigned it instead as a diet for their slaves. "Homespun's" answer, printed here, deals with both parts of the letter by "Vindex Patriae."

To the Printer.   [January 15, 1766]

JOHN BULL shews in nothing more his great veneration for good eating, and how much he is always thinking of his belly, than in his making it the constant topic of his contempt for other nations, that *they do not eat so well as himself.* The *roast beef of Old England* he is always exulting in, as if no other country had beef to roast; reproaching, on every occasion, the Welsh with their leeks and toasted cheese, the Irish with their potatoes, and the Scotch with their oatmeal. And now that we are a little out of favour with him, he has begun, by his attorney VINDEX PATRIAE, to examine our eating and drinking, in order, I apprehend, to fix some horrible scandal of the same kind upon us poor Americans.

I did but say a word or two in favour of *Indian corn,* which he had treated as "disagreable and indigestible," and this vindictive gentleman grows angry. "Let him tell the world, IF HE DARES (says he) that the Americans prefer it to a place at their own tables." Ah, Sir, I see the dilemma you have prepared for me. If I should not *dare* to say, that we do prefer it to a place at our tables, then you demonstrate, that we must come to England for tea, or go without our breakfasts: and if I do *dare* to say it, you fix upon me and my countrymen for ever, the indelible disgrace of being *Indian corn-eaters.*

I am afraid, Mr. Printer, that you will think this too trifling a dispute to deserve a place in your paper: but pray, good Sir, consider, as you are yourself an Englishman, that we Americans, who are allowed even by Mr. VINDEX to have some English blood in our veins, may think it a very serious thing to have the honour of our eating impeached in any particular whatsoever.

45

"Why doth he not deny the fact (says VINDEX) that it is assigned to the slaves for their food? To proclaim the *wholesomeness* of this corn, without assigning a reason why white men give it to their slaves, when they can get other food, is only satirizing the good sense of their brethren in America." In truth I cannot deny the fact, though it should reflect ever so much on the *good sense* of my countrymen. I own we do give food made of Indian corn to our slaves, as well as eat it ourselves; not, as you suppose, because it is *"indigestible* and *unwholesome;"* but because it keeps them healthy, strong and hearty, and fit to go through all the labour we require of them. Our slaves, Sir, cost us money, and we buy them to make money by their labour. If they are sick, they are not only unprofitable, but expensive. Where then was your *English good sense,* when you imagined we gave the slaves our Indian corn, because we knew it to be *unwholesome?*

In short, this is only another of Mr. VINDEX's paradoxes, in which he is a great dealer. The first endeavoured to persuade us, that we were represented in the British Parliament *virtually,* and by *fiction:* Then that we were *really* represented there, because the Manor of East Greenwich in Kent is represented there, and all the Americans live in East Greenwich.[7] And now he undertakes to prove to us, that taxes are the most profitable things in the world to those that pay them; for that Scotland is grown rich since the Union, by paying English taxes. I wish he would accommodate himself a little better to our dull capacities. We Americans have a great many heavy taxes of our own, to support our several governments, and pay off the enormous debt contracted by the war; we never conceived ourselves the richer for paying taxes, and are willing to leave all new ones to those that like them. At least, if we must with Scotland, participate in your taxes, let us likewise, with Scotland, participate in the Union, and in all the privileges and advantages of commerce that accompanied it.

VINDEX, however, will never consent to this. He has made us partakers in all the odium with which he thinks fit to load Scotland: "They resemble the Scots in sentiments (says he) their religion is Scottish; their customs and *laws* are Scottish; like the Scotch they Judaically observe what *they call* the Sabbath, persecute old women for witches, are intolerant to other sects, &c." But we must not,

7. See above, pp. 18–19.

like the Scots, be admitted into Parliament; for that, he thinks, would increase "the Scotch interest in England, which is equally hostile to the cause of liberty, and the cause of our church."

Pray, Sir, who informed you that our "*laws* are Scottish?" The same, I suppose, that told you our Indian corn is unwholesome. Indeed, Sir, your information is very imperfect. The common law of England, is, I assure you, the common law of the colonies: and if the civil law is what you mean by the Scottish law, we have none of it but what is forced upon us by England, in its courts of Admiralty, depriving us of that inestimable part of the common law, trials by juries.[8] And do you look upon keeping the *Sabbath,* as part of the Scottish law? "The Americans, like the Scots, (you say,) observe what *they call* the Sabbath." Pray, Sir, you who are so zealous for your church (in abusing other Christians) what *do you call* it? and where the harm of their *observing* it? If you look into your prayer-book, or over your altars, you will find these words written, *Remember to keep holy the* SABBATH *Day.* This law, tho' it may be observed in Scotland, and has been *countenanced* by some of your statutes, is, Sir, originally one of *God's Commandments:* a body of laws still in force in America, tho' they may have become *obsolete* in *some other* countries.

Give me leave, Master JOHN BULL, to remind you, that you are *related to all mankind;* and therefore it less become you than any body, to affront and abuse other nations. But you have mixed with your many virtues, a pride, a haughtiness, and an insolent contempt for all but yourself, that, I am afraid, will, if not abated, procure you one day or other a handsome drubbing. Besides your rudeness to foreigners, you are far from being civil even to your own family. The Welch you have always despised for submitting to your government: But why despise your own English, who conquered and settled Ireland for you; who conquered and settled America for you? Yet these you now think you may treat as you

8. Admiralty law, based on the Roman civil law rather than the English common law, was administered in England by a separate set of courts and with a specially trained corps of judges and lawyers. The High Court of Admiralty and the ecclesiastical courts (operating basically under canon law) were situated in Doctors' Commons on St. Bennet's Hill, south of St. Paul's Churchyard, London. Trials of violations of the Navigation Acts and the Stamp Act in the colonies were entrusted to Vice-Admiralty Courts without juries.

please, because, forsooth, they are a *conquered* people. Why dispise the Scotch, who fight and die for you all over the world? Remember, you courted Scotland for one hundred years, and would fain have had your *wicked will* of her. She virtuously resisted all your importunities, but at length kindly consented to become your lawful wife. You then solemnly promised to *love, cherish,* and *honour* her, as long as you both should live; and yet you have ever since treated her with the utmost contumely, which you now begin to extend to your common children.[9] But, pray, when your enemies are uniting in a *Family Compact* against you, can it be discreet in you to kick up in your own house a *Family Quarrel?* And at the very time you are inviting foreigners to settle on your lands, and when you have more to settle than ever you had before, it is [*sic*] prudent to suffer your lawyer, VINDEX, to abuse those who have settled there already, because they cannot yet speak "Plain English?" It is my opinion, Master BULL, that the Scotch and Irish, as well as the colonists, are capable of speaking much *plainer English* than they have ever yet spoke, but which I hope they will never be provoked to speak.

To be brief, Mr. VINDEX, I pass over your other accusations of the Americans, and of the Scotch, that we "Persecute old women for witches, and are intolerant to other sects," observing only, that we were wise enough to leave off both those foolish tricks, long before Old England made the act of toleration, or repealed the statute against witchcraft; so that even *you yourself* may safely travel through all Scotland and the Colonies, without the least danger of being persecuted as a churchman, or taken (up) for a conjurer. And yet I own myself so far of an intolerant spirit, that though I thank you for the box-in-the-ear you have given TOM HINT, as being, what you justly call him, "a futile calumniator," I cannot but wish he would give you another—for the same reason.[1]

One word more, however, about the *Indian corn,* which I began and must end with, even though I should hazard your remarking,

9. BF's own attitude towards the Scots had undergone an opposite change. Compare, for example, his criticism of Scots army officers in 1759 (above, VIII, 352–5) with the happy impression of the country and its people he formed as a result of his visit there later in the same year (above, IX, 3, 9–10, 375–6; X, 168n), and with his present criticism of the English for their treatment of Scotland.

1. At the close of his most recent letter "Vindex Patriae" had taken "Tom Hint" to task for having "basely" denied that the Americans were hospitable. For "Tom Hint's" criticisms, see above, XII, 406, 410, and this volume, p. 38.

that it is certainly "indigestible," as it plainly appears to *stick in my stomach*. "Let him tell the world, IF HE DARES, (you say) that the Americans prefer it to a place at their tables." And, pray, if I should DARE,—what then?—Why then—"You will enter upon a discussion of its salubrity and pleasant taste." Really? Would you venture to write on the salubrity and *pleasant taste* of Indian corn, when you never in your life have tasted a *single grain* of it? But why should that hinder you writing on it? Have you not written even on *politics?* Your's,   HOMESPUN.[2]

From Benjamin Kent[3]   ALS: American Philosophical Society

Dear Sir: Boston Jany: 19th: A.D. 1766.

With a pleasing pride I often recollect, your former complaisance in calling me Brother Ben and agreable to the Old saying non Animam Mutant, qui trans mare Currunt.[4] I still challenge the Honour of being your Friend: but I should be but a miserable private Friend, If I was not the Friend of all men: and it is from that, principle, as well an especial Love and Esteem I have of the *Patriot* that I [tell] you we have lately by An Indian discover'd a small wilderness Root which steeped in Madira Wine has not faild, on many tryals to carry off any fit of the Gout in a very few Hours time.[5]

2. The *Gazetteer*, Jan. 24, 1766, printed another letter from "Vindex Patriae" part of which was a reply to this one from "Homespun." BF did not carry the correspondence on dietary matters or the Scots any further, though as "N.N." he did reply once more on the issue of colonial representation.

3. For Benjamin Kent, a Boston lawyer and an ardent patriot during the Revolutionary War, see above, XI, 80 n. Since Kent was only two years younger than BF and a native of Charlestown, the two men may have known each other during their Boston boyhood and the sobriquet, "Brother Ben," which BF applied to Kent, may possibly date from that period.

4. Kent is applying and misquoting Horace, *Epistles*, Book I, XI, line 27: *Coelum non animum mutant qui transmare currunt*—"They change their sky, not their character, who sail across the sea."

5. In a letter of September 1766 Kent identified the root as Cauhouse, i.e., cohosh; see below, p. 431. The "Patriot" whom Kent esteemed was William Pitt, a famous sufferer from the gout. On Sept. 25, 1764, William Allen had sent Pitt some pine buds which, when brewed into a tea, were supposed to alleviate the gout. Lewis B. Walker, ed., *The Burd Papers Extracts from Chief Justice William Allen's Letter Book* ([Pottsville, Pa.], 1897), pp. 58–62.

This information I have from those persons of the very best credit, who have experienc'd it, and what is very wonderfull a couple of Glasses of this Wine will make the Part affected being well wrapped up to Sweat profusely while all other parts of the body are nowise affected. As to politick of which we are brim full and running over. I think it would be imprudent to give you my Thots on that Subject, and I can no more expect from you information of the political state of Afairs at home, than a passenger in a Storm at Sea, could expect the Captain shoul'd inform him of all the distresses of the Ship. Farewell Dear Sir I am,   BEN. KENT

Addressed: For, The Honble: / Benjamin Franklin / Esq; / In London / per Capt Scott

Endorsed: B Kent

From John Beveridge[6]   ALS: American Philosophical Society

Sir   Philadelphia Jany 20th 1766

Herewith you will receive three Copies of some familiar Epistles &c, which I have printed. Two bound to be delivered to Dr. Pringle,[7] and one on Common paper as they were Sold here for your self. I have given one bound in the same manner to Mrs. Franklin, which waits your return at your own house, but this common one is in order to shew to any of your friends, or the Book-sellers, if you please to try, for me, if they will undertake to sell some Number of the Copies but I hope you will take Care they do not serve me as Mrs. Franklin tells me they served you &c[8]—

6. For John Beveridge, professor of Latin at the College of Philadelphia and author of a recent book of letters and other occasional pieces, see above, p. 33 n. At Beveridge's request, DF had put BF down as a subscriber for two copies of his volume.

7. Beveridge, who had taught for many years in Scotland before emigrating to America, seems to have known the Pringle family there. In a note to his *Familiar Epistles* he acknowledged his "many obligations" to Dr. Pringle's elder brother, Sir Robert Pringle, although it is not clear precisely what those obligations were.

8. Perhaps DF had told Beveridge about BF's experience with James Logan's *Cato Major*, of which he had sent 300 copies to London in 1744 to be sold but for which he had, as late as 1781, received no account. Above, II, 404 n, 412; BF to William Strahan, Dec. 4, 1781, N.Y. Publ. Lib. (Berg).

or if you and the Dr. think fit, you may shew it to the reviewers. But I would not leave it long in their hands, lest by some means or other it should come abroad in London, as I have a view of re-printing it either there or rather at Glasgow &c.[9]

I have been advised by some to send several Copies more, to your Care, viz for Lord Halifax,[1] his Grace &c. of Canterbury[2] &c. but as they were not of my Acquaintance I thought it Presumption, and absolutely refused, unless you think it would answer some better purpose than I can forsee. I wish you all Happiness a Speedy and Safe Return, which is all at present from Sir Your very humble and most obedient Servant   JNO: BEVERIDGE

Pennsylvania Assembly Committee of Correspondence to Richard Jackson and Benjamin Franklin

Printed in *Votes and Proceedings of the House of Representatives of Pennsylvania . . .* , v (Philadelphia, Henry Miller, 1775), p. 454.

GENTLEMEN,   Philadelphia, January 21, 1766.
Inclosed is a Copy of our last, with a Duplicate of the Address to the House of Commons therein mentioned, on the Subject whereof, and the other Matters recommended to your Attention in the said Letter, we have nothing more to add.[3]

9. Beveridge's book was apparently neither reviewed nor reprinted in Great Britain.

1. Beveridge's Epistle xxx was dedicated to Halifax.

2. The Rev. William Smith, with whom Beveridge had consulted about his book (see above, p. 34), may have advised him to send a copy to the Archbishop of Canterbury.

3. The text of the Committee's "last" letter has not been found. On April 12, 1766 (below, p. 236), BF acknowledged receiving its letters of January 13 and 20, although he may have given each letter a date one day too early. On January 14 the speaker of the Assembly signed a petition to the House of Commons seeking repeal of the Currency Act of 1764 and restoration of the right to issue bills of credit that would pass as legal tender. The Assembly thereupon directed its Committee of Correspondence to transmit the petition to the agents in London "by the first Opportunity." 8 *Pa. Arch.*, VII, 5824–7. In response to an order of January 14, the Committee of Correspondence laid the present letter before the Assembly on the 21st and it was promptly approved. *Ibid.*, pp. 5828, 5837. Perhaps the Committee, anticipating favorable action, had in each instance prepared and signed its letter to the agents one day in advance of such action, in which case BF's dating would be correct.

We have laid Mr. Richard Jackson's Letter, of the Ninth of November, before the Assembly, now sitting,[4] who observing that he informs them, that the Petitions for a Change of this Government, from Proprietary to Royal, "may be dropped, by proper Instructions for that Purpose, notwithstanding they are presented," have directed us to assure you, that they are by no Means inclined to withdraw the Petitions; but, on the contrary, desire that you will prosecute them with the utmost Expedition to an Issue, provided it may be done with Safety to all those Rights and Privileges, to which the People of this Province are entitled, under their Charters and Acts of Assembly, agreeable to the Instructions heretofore sent you, a Triplicate whereof is also inclosed.[5] We are, with great Respect, Gentlemen, Your most obedient, and most humble Servants,

JOSEPH RICHARDSON,   ISAAC PEARSON,
JOSEPH GALLOWAY,   GILES KNIGHT.
THOMAS LIVEZEY,

"A Friend to Both Countries":[6]
More Arguments against the Stamp Act

Printed in *The Gazetteer and New Daily Advertiser*, January 23, 1766.

To the PRINTER.   [January 23, 1766]

THE sketch in your last Friday's paper, of the *arguments on both sides,* relating to the American stamp act, (signed *A Friend to my Country*)[7] is, I think, on the whole, a pretty fair one. There are, however, a few omissions in it, which I beg leave to supply.

4. The Committee of Correspondence laid Jackson's letter of Nov. 9, 1765, before the Assembly on January 14 immediately after the action mentioned in the note directly above, concerning the petition to the House of Commons. "After some Debate" the members ordered the Committee to draft "further Instructions" to the agents on the matter of the proposed change of government. 8 *Pa. Arch.*, VII, 5827–8.

5. See above, XII, 321–3.

6. Verner W. Crane first identified BF as the author of this piece on the basis of writing style and similarities between its contents and arguments which he used in his examination before the House of Commons in February. See Crane, *Letters to the Press*, pp. 52–4.

7. A letter in the *Gazetteer*, Jan. 17, 1766. It was reprinted, minus the first paragraph and signature, in *London Chron.*, Jan. 18–21, 1766, under the title, "A Short Sketch of the Arguments for and against the American Stamp Act."

On behalf of the colonies it is farther said, that, allowing the principle, which they do not, nor never did dispute, that they ought in justice to bear with other subjects their share of common burthens, yet the act was *unnecessary* whether we look backward or forward. As to what is *past*, they have in all wars exerted themselves fully equal to their abilities, and in the last, beyond them, which has been acknowledged by government here;[8] and that they still are under a heavy load of debt incurred by that war, for which all their provincial land-taxes, taxes on personal property, excises, poll-taxes, taxes on the profits of business, &c. &c. during many years to come, are mortgaged. And as to the occasions of expence that may *hereafter*, arise, the ancient *established* method of calling on their assemblies by requisitory letters from the crown, is sufficient to answer all purposes; since they always should, as they always have done, think themselves obliged in duty, on such requisitions, to grant aids suitable to their circumstances. That besides this, they actually pay great taxes to this country, in the accumulated price (occasioned by its taxes) of all the British manufactures they consume; and which, if it were not for the restraints on their trade, they might buy cheaper elsewhere. That the acts for regulating commerce and navigation, and the Post-office act, differ very materially from the stamp-act.[9] The former lay duties on the importation of goods, which people may buy or let alone, and the other fixes a rate for the carriage of letters, that is merely a *quantum meruit* for service done, and which every man may do in another way, if he thinks it cheaper and safer, i.e. he may send his letter by a special messenger, or by his friend. But the stamp act *forces* the money from the country under *heavy penalties,* and denies *common justice* in the courts, unless they will submit to part with it, and this without the consent of the legislative body, in which only the country has representatives. And though it is true, that the distance between session and session gave time enough for "pre-

8. For a fuller statement of this claim, see above, p. 24 n.

9. "A Friend to my Country" had argued that "the stamp act is not the first act of the British parliament which has extended to America. The act of navigation, and the post office act, very materially affect America; the latter in particular is an internal tax on her, and neither of these have been disputed; although if parliament had no right to pass them, they ought likewise to be rescinded."

paring proper arguments to oppose the stamp act"; yet that time was rendered of no use, the petitions that were sent over from the colonies, containing their reasons against it, not being *admitted,* or *so much as read,* because it was, it seems, contrary to an established rule, importing that petitions should not be received against a money bill. The parliament may have "asserted a right" to tax Ireland; but it is certain they have never practised it.[1] And though it should be allowed right neither to tax Ireland or the colonies by act of a legislature in which they have no representative, it does not appear how "all the counties in England could found a like claim on that principle," since they are all represented; there not being a landed freehold estate above 40*s.* per ann. in any county, that does not give its owner a right to vote for a member of parliament.

A FRIEND TO BOTH COUNTRIES.

"Pacificus": Pax Quaeritur Bello

Reprinted by Verner W. Crane, ed., *Benjamin Franklin's Letters to the Press 1758–1775* (Chapel Hill, [1950]), pp. 54–7, from *The Public Advertiser,* January 26, 1766.

While there is no certainty that Franklin wrote this piece, the probability is strong, as Verner W. Crane has pointed out in *Letters to the Press,* pp. 54–5. The satirical vein is characteristic of a good deal of Franklin's writing at this time, as is his use of inverted logic; references to the origins of the colonies appear in others of his papers, and the suggestion in the closing paragraph that the colonies might be repopulated by the importation of English felons reminds the reader strongly of his celebrated piece on "Felons and Rattlesnakes" in 1751 (above, IV, 130–3) and other references to the same subject. The use of the signature "Pacificus," somewhat comparable to his earlier "Pacificus Secundus" (above, pp. 4–6), is a deliberate theft of the pseudonym used by one of the more vehement advocates of strong measures against the colonists, and so furthers the satirical purpose of this paper.[2]

1. "If the British legislature have no right to tax America, they have none to tax Ireland, notwithstanding they have asserted it; and all the counties in England may claim an exemption from taxes, which the rescinding of this act will be encouragement for them to do." *Ibid.*

2. Most of these comments appear in the headnote and footnotes of Crane's printing of the text, cited above.

To the Printer of the Public Advertiser.   Jan. 23, 1766.

Pax quaeritur Bello.[3]

SIR,

THE very important Controversy being next Tuesday to be finally determined between the Mother Country and their rebellious American Children,[4] I shall think myself happy if I can furnish any Hints that may be of public Utility.

There are some Persons besides the Americans so amazingly stupid, as to distinguish in this Dispute between *Power* and *Right,* as tho' the former did not always imply the latter. The Right of Conquest invests the Conqueror with Authority to establish what Laws he pleases, however contrary to the Laws of Nature, and the common Rights of Mankind. Examine every Form of Government at this Day subsisting on the Face of the Globe, from the absolute Despotism of the Grand Sultan to the Democratic Government of the City of Geneva, and it will be found that the Exertion of Power in those Hands with whom it is lodged, however unconstitutional, is always justified. The Reign of the Stuarts might serve to exemplify this Observation. Happy it was for the Nation that, upon Trial, the superior Power was found to be in the People. The American Plea of *Right,* their Appeal to Magna Charta, must of course be set aside; and I make no Doubt but the Grand Council of the Nation will at all Hazards insist upon an absolute Submission to the Tax imposed upon them. But that they will comply without

3. The source of this quotation has not been found. It may be translated: "Peace is sought [*or possibly:* obtained] by war."

4. At the request of the House of Commons to the King, Secretary Conway had laid before the House a large number of papers relating to the disturbances in America in consequence of the Stamp Act. Many groups of British merchants also presented petitions concerning the drastic reduction of their trade to the colonies and praying for relief. On January 14 the House of Commons voted that on Tuesday, January 28, it would go into Committee of the Whole to consider these papers. On that date began the series of debates in committee that led to the critical vote, February 22, to repeal the Stamp Act. The resulting bill was introduced on the 26th, receiving its first reading, and was finally passed by a vote of 250 to 122 and sent to the Lords on March 4. After passage by the House of Lords it received the royal assent on March 18. These steps may be followed in the *Journals of the House of Commons,* xxx (Jan. 10, 1765-Sept. 16, 1766), 447–667, *passim,* though the *Journals* contain no records of the deliberations of the Committee of the Whole, where the principal debates and most of the critical votes took place.

coercive Measures, is to me a Matter of very great Doubt: For when we consider, that these People, especially the more Northern Colonies, are the Descendants of your Pymms, Hampdens, and others of the like Stamp, those outrageous Assertors of Civil and Religious Liberties; that they have been nursed up in the same Old English Principles; that a little more than a Century ago their Fore-fathers, many of them of Family and Fortune, left their native Land, and endured all the Distresses and Hardships which are the necessary Consequences of an Establishment in a new uncultivated Country, surrounded with a cruel Blood-thirsty Enemy, oftentimes severely pinched with Cold and Hunger; and all this to enjoy un-molested that Liberty which they thought was infringed: I say, however these People may be mistaken, they will not tamely give up what they call their natural, their constitutional Rights. Force must therefore be made use of.

Now in order to bring these People to a proper Temper, I have a Plan to propose, which I think cannot fail, and which will be en-tirely consistent with the Oeconomy at present so much in Vogue. It is so cheap a Way of going to work, that even Mr. G—— G——,[5] that great Oeconomist, could have no reasonable Objection to it.

Let Directions be given, that Two Thousand Highlanders be im-mediately raised, under proper Officers of their own. It ought to be no Objection, that they were in the Rebellion in Forty-five: If Roman Catholics, the better. The C——l at present in the P——ze Service may be at their Head.[6] Transport them early in the Spring to Quebec: They with the Canadians, natural Enemies to our Col-onists, who would voluntarily engage, might make a Body of Five or Six Thousand Men; and I doubt not, by artful Management, and the Value of two or three Thousand Pounds in Presents, with the Hopes of Plunder, as likewise a Gratuity for every Scalp, the Sav-ages on the Frontiers might be engaged to join, at least they would make a Diversion, which could not fail of being useful.[7] I could

5. George Grenville.

6. Probably a reference to Francis Mclean, an officer who had been sent to Portugal in 1762 to organize Portuguese defenses. He remained there "in the P[ortugue]ze Service" as governor of Almeida and later of Estramadura and Lisbon until 1778. Evangeline W. and Charles M. Andrews, eds., *Journal of a Lady of Quality* (New Haven, 1921), p. 238 n.

7. This passage anticipates in some measure General Burgoyne's expedition southward from Canada in 1777, in which Indian auxiliaries participated and

point out a very proper General to command the Expedition; he is of a very sanguine Disposition, and has an inordinate Thirst for Fame, and besides has the Hearts of the Canadians.[8] He might march from Canada, cross the Lakes, and fall upon these People without their expecting or being prepared for him, and with very little Difficulty over-run the whole Country.

The Business might be done without employing any of the Regular Troops quartered in the Country, and I think it would be best they should remain neuter, as it is to be feared they would be rather backward in embruing their Hands in the Blood of their Brethren and Fellow Subjects.

I would propose, that all the Capitals of the several Provinces should be burnt to the Ground,[9] and that they cut the Throats of all the Inhabitants, Men, Women, and Children, and scalp them, to serve as an Example; that all the Shipping should be destroyed, which will effectually prevent Smuggling, and save the Expence of Guarda Costas.

No Man in his Wits, after such terrible Military Execution, will refuse to purchase stamp'd Paper. If any one should hesitate, five or six Hundred Lashes in a cold frosty Morning would soon bring him to Reason.

If the Massacre should be objected to, as it would too much depopulate the Country, it may be replied, that the Interruption this Method would occasion to Commerce, would cause so many Bankruptcies, such Numbers of Manufacturers and Labourers would be unemployed, that, together with the Felons from our Gaols, we should soon be enabled to transport such Numbers to repeople the Colonies, as to make up for any Deficiency which Example made it Necessary to sacrifice for the Public Good. Great

---

during which one of the Indians was believed to have murdered a Loyalist girl, Jenny McCrea, to the great indignation of the inhabitants regardless of their political sympathies.

8. Probably a reference to General James Murray, governor of Quebec, whose arbitrary and illegal exactions from British merchants there and alleged favoritism to the French Canadians had led to a petition for his recall; above, XII, 392 n.

9. Many of BF's letters during the Revolution express particular indignation at the burning of colonial towns by British forces, for which he sought indemnity during the peace negotiations of 1782.

Britain might then reign over a loyal and submissive People, and be morally certain, that no Act of Parliament would ever after be disputed. Your's, PACIFICUS.

From Joseph Chew[1]   ALS: American Philosophical Society

My dear Sir   New London 24th Janry 1766

Since I wrote to you last[2] this Colony has Rather increased in the Confusion and distraction of the times then otherways. Meetings have been Called by the Populace &c. where the most Ext[raordina]ry Votes have Passed and our friend Ingersoll has been more then humbled. He has been so intimidated as to give up his Letters publick and Private[3]—almost Every moderate Man has been found fault with[4]—this Spirit has Prevaled more on the Eastern than on the western side of the River owing in my Opinion to our Near Neighbourhood of the good and Sanctified People of the Massachussets Bay. I have on many Accounts Endeavourd to keep my self as Clear of these disputes as Possible—and altho' I have in the most modest manner disaproved of the Stamp act yet because I do not joyn in the Extreem Methods which have been taken I am Looked upon with a Jealous Eye and Rather Esteem'd as a friend to those measures I would by Every Humble Remonstrance try to

1. For Joseph Chew, postmaster and merchant of New London, Conn., see above, XI, 109 n.

2. The present letter is the first from Chew to BF that has been found.

3. Jared Ingersoll (above, X, 112 n), the Conn. stamp distributor, was forced by a mob to resign his office at Wethersfield, Sept. 19, 1765, although a proclamation by Governor Fitch soon thereafter against the mob persuaded him to repudiate his resignation. The victim of threats and harassment throughout the fall of 1765, Ingersoll late in November was compelled to surrender his correspondence with British officials to the representatives of the Sons of Liberty of eastern Connecticut, who read it at their meetings and published distorted accounts of it in the newspapers. Early in January 1766 Ingersoll swore an oath before a justice of the peace never to execute the Stamp Act and formally resigned his commission to the appropriate officials in England. See Lawrence H. Gipson, *Jared Ingersoll* (New Haven, 1920), pp. 149–208.

4. Chew himself, as he wrote Ingersoll on Feb. 5, 1766, had become the object "of the attention of the Sons of Liberty who are desired by some of their western friends Closely to watch and observe my Actions and motions, for that I Carry on a very traterous and wicked Correspondence with you." New Haven Colony Hist. Soc. *Papers*, IX (New Haven, 1918), 377.

58

get Clear of. You will know that in New York Matters have been Carryed to the greatest lenghths so far as to Burn the Stamp Papers. By the Pacquet which arrived [*illegible*] Sundays agoe a Circular letter from Mr. Conway Secretary of State is Come over; that to the Governor of Rhode Island I have seen. Tis Couched in the Strongest Termes you Can Conceive and telling the Governor that his Majesty Can in no way Suffer his own dignity and the authority of the British Parliament to be Trampled upon—and Exorts him and all his Majestys Servants to Represent to the people the dreadfull Consequences that must inevitably attend the Forceable opposition to an Act of the British Legislature—and directs them to Call upon General Gage and Lord Colvile Commanders of his Majestys Naval and Land Forces in case Force is Necessary to maintain order and good Government.[5] As Very few have seen these Letters I Cannot tell you what impression they will make on the Minds of the People. But do assure you I tremble for the Consequences that may attend this matter—good God what a Situation is this unhappy Country in and how have the People been Raised to a Pitch of Inthusiasm by bringing themselves to believe that they are able to withstand the Force of great Britain. It will give me infinite Pleasure to hear from you and what you say will Remain with me alone. My Little Woman and Little Girl are Very well. We often think of you and I am with great Respect and Regard Sir Your Very Obedient Servant   Jos CHEW

Benja Franklin Esqr In London

I mentioned to you that the times were Very bad and that I had suffered so much by Bad Debts &c.[6] that I was put to sundry hardships and had met with a Very Poor Return for many Civilitys done at an Expencive Rate for People in New York—that if any thing

---

5. Conway's letter to Gov. Samuel Ward of Rhode Island, Oct. 24, 1765, is printed in J.R. Bartlett, ed., *Records of the Colony of Rhode Island,* VI (Providence, 1861), 471–2.

6. Later reference to Chew's financial troubles, leading to his bankruptcy in October 1771, are found in James Parker to BF, July 1, 1766 (below, p. 328), Chew to BF, Dec. 12, 1769 (APS), and Charles J. Hoadly, ed., *The Public Records of the Colony of Connecticut,* VIII (Hartford, 1885), 147–8, 190, 312–13, 440–2, 527–9. Apparently he got no recommendation from BF for another position during the latter's connection with the Post Office, but in 1774 Sir William Johnson appointed him secretary of Indian affairs.

should offer and you Could procure me a Place in any Department in this or any Other Colony on this side Carolina you would do an infinite Service to one who will on Every Occasion make the most Greatfull Returns. I do assure you I have met with the most Severe misfortunes and disapointments. I am Sure I need not Say more to you and am Confident that if you Can Serve a poor old friend a good Woman and Little Girl that it will give you infinite Pleasure.

I will write to you by the next Pacquet and am once more with wishing you Every good that a Virtuous good Man Merits Dear Sir Your obedient Humble Servant   JOS CHEW

James Parker: Valuation of the Printing Office

ADS: Columbia University Library

The partnership agreement between Franklin and Hall provided that at its termination Hall should "have the Preference of purchasing the said Printing-Presses, Types and Materials (if he shall be so disposed . . .) at their present Value, allowing for the Wear thereof what shall be judged a reasonable Abatement, considering the Time they shall have been used" (above, III, 266). In the power of attorney Franklin gave James Parker, Nov. 5, 1764, before going to England, he directed Parker to examine the accounts of the partnership "and also to value the Printing Presses Types and other Materials for printing belonging to me and now in the Use and Occupation of the said David Hall and which he has agreed to purchase of me at the rate of such Valuation" as Parker should make on Franklin's behalf (above, XI, 442).

Parker undertook this appraisal toward the end of January 1766, drew up this detailed account on the 27th, and incorporated its total as entry 72 in his financial report of February 1 (below, p. 98). In his letter of February 3 he described the worn condition of much of the type and the presses and explained the methods used in weighing the type. These methods, it may be added, are virtually unchanged today.

Quantity and Valuation of the Printing-Office, as taken Jan. 27: 1766. per J Parker

wt

383   Old Brevier,[7] much worn, and worth little
        more than Old Metal, at 8*d.* per lb.   £12   15   4

7. The type sizes mentioned in the first eleven entries approximate those in the present point system as follows: Brevier, 8 point; Burgeois, 9 point; long

60

282	Newer Brevier, 7 Years worn, valued at 1*s.* 3*d.* per lb.	17	12	6
663	Burgois, eight years worn at 1*s.* 3*d.*	41	8	9
436	Long Primer, well worn at 1*s.* 2*d.*	25	8	8
318	Small Pica, almost worn out at 10*d.*	13	5	0
421	Pica, Old, and much batter'd at 10*d.*	17	10	10
334	Old English, fit for little more than Old Metal at 8½	11	16	7
502	Newer English, near half-worn at 1*s.* 3*d.*	31	7	6
223	Great Primer, well worn at 1*s.* 2*d.*	13	0	2
158	Double Pica, pretty good, at 1*s.* 4*d.*	10	10	8
91	Double English Do at 1*s.* 2*d.*	5	6	2
70	Flowers[8] at 2*s.*	7	0	0
53	Figures, Planets, Space Rules, Black Letter,[9] at 2*s.* 3*d.*	5	19	3
63	Large and Title Letter, some old some good at 1*s.*	3	3	0
40	Quotations, Justifiers[1] &c. at 1*s.*	2	0	0
3	Crooked Letters, at 1*s.*	0	3	0

primer, 10 point; small pica, 11 point; pica, 12 point; English, 14 point; great primer, 18 point; double pica, 22 point; double English, 28 point. For purposes of comparison it may be stated that in the present edition indexes and most tabulations are set in 8-point type; editorial footnotes, such as this one, in 10-point; headnotes, original author's footnotes, and occasionally other material in 11-point; texts of documents, except most tabular matter, in 12-point; and the headings of documents in 13½-point. On some of the matters touched on in this "Valuation" Daniel B. Updike, *Printing Types Their History, Forms, and Use A Study in Survivals* (Cambridge, Mass., 1922) is helpful. Since most of the type in the Franklin and Hall printing office in 1766 had come from the foundry of William Caslon, the specimens of Caslon types reproduced by Updike in his second volume, following pages 102, 104, 106, and 107, are pertinent to this "Valuation." A useful introductory study of BF's type, though dealing mostly with the earlier years, is C. William Miller, "Franklin's Type: Its Study Past and Present," APS *Proc.,* XCIX (1955), 418–32.

8. Typographical ornaments originally in a floral design but, by extension of the term, in a variety of other designs as well.

9. Black letter is usually now called "Old English" or "Gothic."

1. Spacing material of varying widths to be inserted between words in the type to space out the line enough to even it with other lines and so "justify" the right-hand margin of the printing.

85	Cases,[2] some Old and shatter'd at 5s.		21	5	0
13	Frames[3] at 8s.		5	4	0
15	Chaces,[4] some large, some small, at 6s.		4	10	0
16	Letter-Boards,[5] only 10 of 'em good-for-any-thing		0	15	0
3	Folio Gallies[6] 8 Quarto, and 7 small Do		1	10	0
1	Letter Rack and one Case Rack		1	0	0
1	Lye-Trough, 1 Lye Tub, and one Wetting Trough[7]		1	10	0
6	Composing-Sticks,[8] one of which good-for-Nothing		1	10	0
2	Imposing Stones,[9] with their Stands		3	10	0
1	Old Book-Press much shatter'd		1	0	0
16	Poles for drying Paper[1]		0	16	0
2	Mallets, 2 Shuting Sticks, a Plainer, and some old Furniture[2]		1	0	0

2. Shallow trays divided into compartments to hold type, usually set up in pairs, the upper case containing capitals, small capitals, and numerals, the lower case containing small letters and marks of punctuation. Other characters in the font are divided between the two cases according to a standard arrangement.

3. Stands to support the type cases.

4. Rectangular metal frames (now spelled "chases") into which pages or columns of type are locked for printing.

5. Boards for the storage of composed type.

6. Galleys are long trays with upright sides to hold composed type. Since first proofs are usually pulled from type so held, these proofs are called "galley proofs."

7. After use, hand-set type is commonly cleaned in lye, then rinsed in water, before being distributed to the cases for future use.

8. A composing stick is a tray, usually of metal, that the compositor holds in his left hand and in which he sets the type. Journeymen printers who may move from one employer to another often own personal composing sticks.

9. Smooth flat stones on which pages of type are placed before being locked in the chase.

1. After printing, each sheet of paper must be dried before storage.

2. After the type has been placed in the chase, the blank spaces are filled with pieces of wood or metal, called furniture, of less height than the type. An instrument of wood or metal notched at one end, called a shooting stick, is then struck with a mallet to drive in quoins (wedges) to tighten the whole. At intervals during this process a smooth block of wood, called a planer, is laid on the type and tapped to level it in order that it may produce an even impression.

12	Cuts for Dilworth's Spelling-Books	3	o	o
2	King's Arms, 3 S's for Bills of Lading 3 or 4			
	Head & Tail piecs	2	o	o
	The Cuts for the Advertisements much worn	1	o	o
	Some Brass pieces of Rules, and other Rules[3]	o	12	7
		268	10	o
	Three Printing Presses, One much shatter'd	45	o	o
		£313	10	o

       Errors excepted
         Per JAMES PARKER.

Endorsed: Account and Valuation of D.H Old Printing Materials as taken Jan. 27. 1766.

"N.N.": Reply to Vindex Patriae on American Representation in Parliament

Printed in *The Gazetteer and New Daily Advertiser,* January 29, 1766

This letter was not reprinted in the *Pennsylvania Chronicle* among those attributed to Franklin, but the signature "N.N." is the same as that he had used in two earlier replies to "Vindex Patriae" on political and legal aspects of their controversy the authorship of which appears well established. The style is characteristically Franklin's as is the ironical twist toward the end of the third paragraph where he explains the American belief in the "venality and corruption" of both sides in the British political divisions. This letter responds to a longer one by "Vindex Patriae" in the *Gazetteer* for January 17 attempting to answer "N.N." on the tenure of the manor of East Greenwich and other matters touched on in the letter dated January 6, above, pp. 18–22.

To the PRINTER.   [Jan. 29, 1766]
    IN your paper of Friday last, VINDEX PATRIAE justifies his involving all the people of the colonies in the guilt of the late riots, because they were not prevented. He seems not to have considered that riots are sudden things, which often are not foreseen, and therefore cannot be prevented. Scarce a year passes, in which Eng-

3. Thin metal strips of the same height as the type, set on edge to print solid lines. They may be cut to the required length or set end to end when necessary.

land, and even London, how well soever governed, do not afford ample instances of this, which are therefore never, by reasonable people, imputed to the "whole community."[4]

His repeated arguments about "East Greenwich" and *"America in England,"* and the "total illegality of the power of assemblies to raise money," I pass over, as I do not find that any body is convinced by them, but himself, and I believe no one elsewhere will be. I would only remark another instance of his unacquaintedness with facts. He denies, that the people of New England are restrained (as I heard they were) in "working their own beaver into hats, their wool into cloth, or their iron into steel:" Let him but consult the statutes under the several heads, and he will see how much those operations are fettered in America, and perhaps be sensible of his mistake.[5]

His justification of the abuses with which he has treated the Americans, is curious. "I agree, says he, that reflections on the morals of the Americans ought to be shunned, *except when the Americans make it necessary to display their true character.* Had it never been proposed to subject us to America, by introducing Members from thence into our legislature, I had never touched that point; but when a proposal of this sort is made, it is necessary that their *true characters* should be looked into and published," &c. Now after affirming, from my certain knowledge of, and long acquaintance with both countries, that the "Morals of the Americans" in general, considered in the whole *as a people,* are much purer, much less corrupt, than the general morals of the English, a difference naturally to be expected, and always to be expected, between *young* countries and *old* ones; the remark of SWIFT being equally applicable to states as to single persons, when he said, he would venture great odds in a wager, that the *greatest* knave in England was the *oldest.*[6] I say, after affirming this of the Americans, and observing, that whatever might *"make it necessary* to display their

4. "Vindex Patriae" had argued, citing British precedents, that "the whole community" was legally liable when mobs attacked the persons or property of public officers.

5. "Vindex Patriae" seems to have been ignorant of the provisions of the Hat Act (1732), the Wool Act (1699), and the Iron Act (1750).

6. The editors have been unable to locate this passage in the writings of Jonathan Swift.

true character, nothing could make it necessary to give them a *false one "*; I would ask this gentleman, where is the foundation he mentions for supposing "The Americans made it necessary" to give them any character at all? Have *they* ever "proposed to introduce Members from thence into the legislature here? Has there ever been the least petition, memorial, or request to that purpose sent hither from America? Does he imagine the people there have the least inclination towards it? If he does, he never was more mistaken. There never was any danger to the public, which he had less reason to apprehend. For in the first place, the Americans not only *never have,* asked such a privilege, but, he may depend on it, *they never will;* for they have not the least conception that it could be of any use to them.[7] They are contented with their own little legislatures, if they may be permitted to enjoy the privileges belonging to them. They read the political papers and pamphlets of this country; they see that the parties, into which the great are continually divided, are for ever mutually accusing each other with the grossest *venality* and *corruption.* At so great a distance, they can be but little acquainted with the particular merit of personal characters, and therefore, to be impartial, they believe both sides. They could propose to themselves no advantage, if they did not send their best and honestest men; and those they are not willing to expose to the danger of being corrupted, or themselves to the *legal* mischiefs that might be the consequence of such corruption. In the next place, though I think it *highly* the *interest* of *this country* to consolidate its dominions, by *inviting,* and even (if it has a power) *compelling* the Americans as well as Irish to submit to an union, send representa-

7. For an extended commentary on BF's changing views as to the desirability of colonial representation in the House of Commons, see Crane, *Letters to the Press,* p. 72 n. In December 1754 he seems to have favored such representation, but only on condition that the colonies were allowed "a reasonable number" of members and "that all the old Acts of Parliament restraining the trade or cramping the manufactures of the Colonies were at the same time repealed" (above, v, 449). The second condition was politically quite unrealistic, as perhaps BF knew. Gradually he came to discard the idea of colonial representation, though he never completely and finally rejected it prior to the final break with the mother country. Some of his statements that seem on the surface to favor representation may be construed, not as advocacy of it, but rather as arguments against legislation for the colonies by a body in which they were unrepresented.

tives hither, and make one common p——t of the whole; yet I am persuaded that *will never be done,* as every ministry has already difficulty enough to satisfy those, who think they have a right to divide, or to recommend the division of all posts, profits and emoluments; and those who think they have such right, will never agree to increase their own number, by which the chance in favour of each would be diminished. Agreable to the shrewd remark of one of Sir Robert Walpole's friends, that of late he found their party increasing, which he did not like. How so, says Sir Robert. Why, z——ds, Sir, says he, don't we lie *two in a bed* already?   N. N.

Magna Britannia: Her Colonies Reduc'd

"Explanation" and "Moral" reprinted from William Temple Franklin, ed., *Memoirs of the Life and Writings of Benjamin Franklin, LL.D. F.R.S. &c.* (quarto edition, London, 1817–18), I, 219–20. Philadelphia "Explanation" reprinted from print in American Philosophical Society Library.

Among the methods Franklin used during the winter of 1765–66 to gain support for the repeal of the Stamp Act was the private circulation of a political cartoon. As his grandson, William Temple Franklin, explained this *"emblematical design"* many years later, it was "intended to represent the supposed state of Great Britain and her colonies, should the former persist in her oppressive measures, restraining the latter's trade, and taxing their people by laws made by a legislature in which they were not represented." The design was engraved on a copper plate, Franklin's grandson wrote, and the colonial agent "had many of them struck off on cards, on the back of which he occasionally wrote his notes. Copies were also printed on a half sheet of paper with an "Explanation" and an appropriate "Moral."[8]

A familiar symbol of British power was that of the female figure Britannia seated on the globe with a spear in one hand and a shield emblazoned with the Union Jack in the other. Franklin's cartoon depicted a very woe-begone Britannia on the ground beside the globe, her dismembered arms and legs strewn before her, each inscribed with the name of a colony or group of colonies, her shield lying flat beside her, and her spear, having first pierced the leg inscribed "New Eng," aimed at her own breast. Her eyes and the stumps of her arms are raised im-

8. WTF, *Memoirs,* I, 218–19.

The Condut, of the two B*****rs.

Figure 1. Britannia Dismembered and Disemboweled. 1749

Figure 2. The English Lion Dismember'd. 1756

Figure 3. Benjamin Franklin's Stamp Act Cartoon

Figure 4. Philadelphia Redrawing of the Stamp Act Cartoon

ploringly to heaven, and in the distance a fleet of merchant ships is tied up with brooms at their mastheads. A ribbon displays the motto: *Date Obolum Bellisario*, "Give a penny to Belisarius."[9]

Temple Franklin stated flatly that his grandfather had "invented" this somewhat gruesome design, and this originality was long accepted. In 1956, however, Wilmarth S. Lewis, editor of *The Correspondence of Horace Walpole*, discovered in the magnificent collection of eighteenth-century British prints he and Mrs. Lewis had brought together at their home in Farmington, Connecticut, a 1749 version of the dismembered Britannia, from which Franklin had clearly derived his idea. Later Mrs. Lewis found another print in the collection, this one of 1756, in which the British lion is suffering similar mistreatment. In the 1749 print (reproduced here as Figure 1), Britannia's arms, labeled "Cape Breton" and "Gibraltar," lie on the floor "and she is being disembowled for good measure." In the 1756 print (Figure 2) the lion has lost a paw labeled "Minorca," and will shortly lose two others identified as "Nova Scotia" and "Oswego."[1]

In recognizing Franklin's indebtedness to the creators of these two prints it should not be overlooked that as far back as 1754—almost certainly before he could have seen the Britannia cartoon of 1749 in England—he himself had used the pictorial device of a dismembered living body to symbolize a dismembered political community. His "Snake Cartoon," printed in the *Pennsylvania Gazette*, May 9, 1754, a few weeks before the Albany Congress began to consider a plan for intercolonial union, showed a dissected snake, whose segments were identified as the different colonies. Beneath the drawing Franklin admonished his readers succinctly: "Join, or Die."[2] The use of Britannia as the central figure of his Stamp Act cartoon, however, is strong evidence that his immediate source was the British print of 1749.

Franklin may possibly have had his engraving made and have started to use the prints before the end of 1765. No surviving document of that year, however, mentions the cartoon, nor indeed does any until nearly the end of February 1766. Probably its appearance and use should first be associated with Franklin's stepped-up newspaper campaign against the Stamp Act in January 1766 and with the generally increased tempo of activity shown by all opponents of the law in London after Parliament reassembled January 14 following the holiday recess. This account of

9. Belisarius, a famous Roman general during the reign of Justinian, achieved notable victories over the barbarians, but in his old age incurred the envy of the emperor and for a time was imprisoned and reduced to penury.

1. Wilmarth S. Lewis, *One Man's Education* (N.Y., 1967), pp. 455–6.

2. Above, V, 272–5.

the cartoon is therefore placed at the end of that month but without specific dating.[3]

The fullest study of Franklin's cartoon itself and of later reproductions of it is a paper by Edwin Wolf, 2nd, published in the *Proceedings* of the American Philosophical Society in 1955, and the present editors are indebted to Mr. Wolf for much of what follows here.[4]

Franklin seems not to have mentioned his cartoon in any letter to America until after the crucial vote in favor of repeal passed in the Committee of the Whole on February 22. Two days later in a postscript of a letter to David Hall he wrote: "I enclose you some of the Cards on which I have lately wrote all my Messages; they are to show the Mischiefs of reducing the Colonies by Force of Arms."[5] On February 27 he enclosed "a few of my Political Cards" with a letter to Deborah, and on March 1 he did the same to his sister Jane Mecom in Boston, explaining somewhat more fully that it was on these cards that "I wrote my Messages during the Time, it was debated here whether it might not be proper to reduce the Colonies to Obedience by Force of Arms: The Moral is, that the Colonies might be ruined, but that Britain would thereby be maimed."[6]

Franklin apparently sent copies of his cartoon to others in America, for Joseph Galloway wrote William Franklin on April 29: "I suspect the Print inclosed by Mr. Fn. to me and several others is his own. Quere. It is certainly a good one. Explains the Subject deeply. The Launce from the Thigh of New Eng. pointed at the Breast of Brittannica is striking, as is indeed every other Emblem. If you have not one inclosed to you keep it, if you have please to return it by the Bearer."[7]

Only one example of Franklin's original cartoon seems to have survived. This is neither a "card" in the usual meaning of that word, nor a half-sheet of paper with the "Explanation" and "Moral" printed on it as Temple Franklin described the alternative form his grandfather had used. It is an impression of the print alone, made on a piece of paper just over three inches high and almost an inch shorter than a page of the present volume is wide. The paper has the common *Pro Patria* watermark that appears on many of the letters Franklin wrote during these years. The Library Company of Philadelphia, the owner of the print,

3. Careful search of BF's account books for the years 1765 and 1766 reveals no entry that could be identified with any degree of confidence as representing payment to an engraver or a printer for the production of the cartoon.
4. Edwin Wolf, 2nd, "Benjamin Franklin's Stamp Act Cartoon," APS *Proc.*, XCIX (1955), 388–96.
5. Below, p. 170.
6. Below, pp. 176, 189.
7. Franklin Papers, XLVIII, 123, APS.

68

acquired it in 1785 in a folio scrapbook formerly belonging to the artist and antiquary, Pierre Eugène du Simitière (c.1736–1784). Notations in du Simitière's handwriting, obviously made during Franklin's lifetime, attest to the origin and nature of the print.[8] It is reproduced here as Figure 3.

Since this copy of the cartoon is not accompanied by the "Explanation" and "Moral" that Temple Franklin said appeared with many of the originals, those two paragraphs are reprinted here from the first Temple Franklin edition of his grandfather's works, the earliest version of their texts known to have survived.

Just as happened with Franklin's Snake Cartoon, his Stamp Act Cartoon was copied and used again several times. What may well have been the first such reproduction was done in Philadelphia, quite possibly, as Wolf suggests, in the late summer of 1767, after news of the Townshend Acts had reached the colonies, or during the next year or so, when Americans were discussing and adopting non-importation agreements. The drawing of the cartoon is a close copy of the original, the principal difference being that in the Philadelphia copy the ships in the background are shown in considerably more detail and the water in which they lie is fully indicated. This redrawing, reproduced from the copy in the American Philosophical Society, appears here as Figure 4. Not reproduced in the present illustration, however, are the very long "Explanation" and "Moral" printed on the same sheet. The "Moral" is almost word for word identical with that reprinted here from Temple Franklin, but the "Explanation" is so much longer and more elaborate that, although it was probably written by someone other than Franklin, it is reprinted here under the heading "Philadelphia 'Explanation.' "[9]

8. Above the cartoon du Simitière wrote: "NORTH AMERICA/November the First MDCCLXV," probably referring to the date on which the Stamp Act was supposed to go into effect. Below he wrote: "The Original Print done in England on the back of a Message Card, the / Invention and for the use of BENJAMIN FRANKLIN ESQ: LL.D. *Agent for / the Province of Pennsylvania, in London.*"

9. Another example of this version is in the Library Company. At the bottom of the APS example, below the "Moral," is a contemporary longhand inscription: "The above piece was invented by Benja. Franklin and a Number of them struck off on Card paper on which it is said, he used to write all his Messages to Men in power in Great Britain; he also employd a Waiter to put one of them in each Parliament Mans hand as he entred the house the day preceding the great debate of the Stamp Act—" Along the left side of the sheet in the same hand is written: "The meaning of the Spear from N England your own Sagacity will point out." Next to the cartoon is a later note, identified as in the hand of John Vaughan, referring to the William Duane edition of

Wolf has located and reproduced in his article three other versions of Franklin's cartoon, none of which, however, are illustrated here. The first is a very close copy printed as part of the frontispiece to *The Political Register for December, 1768*, facing p. 321.[1] Below the drawing of the dismembered Britannia is another cartoon in which Britannia, her "Weakness" exposed, is being stabbed in the rear by a Frenchman's sword. The two cartoons introduce an article violently attacking Lord North, especially for his allowing France to take Corsica. Of the other two versions known to have been made during Franklin's lifetime, one is a modified copy with a French inscription on the back stating that when Franklin departed from England in 1775 he left copies of the card with the ministers and other public figures to remind them of the dangerous course they were pursuing.[2] The last of these versions is a large Dutch adaptation, probably made in 1780 as part of an anti-British campaign of that year.[3]

I

[January 1766?]

EXPLANATION.

GREAT BRITAIN is supposed to have been placed upon the globe; but the COLONIES, (that is, her limbs,) being severed from her, she is seen lifting her eyes and mangled stumps to heaven; her shield, which she is unable to wield, lies useless by her side; her lance has pierced New England: the laurel branch has fallen from the hand of Pennsylvania: the English oak has lost its head, and stands a bare trunk, with a few withered branches; briars and thorns are on

Memoirs of the Life and Writings of Benjamin Franklin, facing I, 270, where the cartoon, "Explanation," and "Moral," as in the Temple Franklin edition appear: "See his Works Vol. 1. p. 270, a Copy of the Plate and a Short Explanation only."

1. This version, the one most often reproduced, can be identified by its script caption, "The Colonies Reduced," which is followed on the next line in smaller script letters by "Design'd and Engrav'd for the Political Register."

2. This version, located in Hist. Soc. Pa., is illustrated front and back and discussed in Frederick R. Kirkland, "An Unknown Franklin Cartoon," *PMHB*, LXXIII (1949), 76–9.

3. This version is an essentially new rendering of the theme; the mutilated Britannia sits on the ground at the right, chained to a rock; a British sailor stands at the left, chained to an anchor and a barrel; the ships are in the center at middle distance. Two copies, one colored, the other not, are in the Halsey Collection at the John Carter Brown Library. The print is listed in R. T. Haines Halsey, " '*Impolitical Prints*' *An Exhibition of Contemporary Cartoons Relating to the American Revolution*" (New York Public Library, 1939), p. 28.

the ground beneath it; the British ships have brooms at their topmast heads, denoting their being on sale; and BRITANNIA herself is seen sliding off the world, (no longer able to hold its balance) her fragments overspread with the label, DATE OBOLUM BELLISARIO.

THE MORAL.

History affords us many instances of the ruin of states, by the prosecution of measures ill suited to the temper and genius of their people. The ordaining of laws in favor of *one* part of the nation, to the prejudice and oppression of *another,* is certainly the most erroneous and mistaken policy. An *equal* dispensation of protection, rights, privileges, and advantages, is what every part is entitled to, and ought to enjoy; it being a matter of no moment to the state, whether a subject grows rich and flourishing on the Thames or the Ohio, in Edinburgh or Dublin. These measures never fail to create great and violent jealousies and animosities between the people favored and the people oppressed: whence a total separation of affections, interests, political obligations, and all manner of connections, necessarily ensue, by which the whole state is weakened, and perhaps ruined for ever!

II

[1767–1768?]

PHILADELPHIA "EXPLANATION"

The above Prophetical Emblem, of what wou'd be the Miserable State of Great Britain and her Colonies, Shou'd She persist in restraining their Trade, distroying their Currency, and Taxing their People by Laws made by a Legislature, where they are not Represented.

The Author with a Sagacity and Invention natural to himself, has compriz'd in one View, under the Character of Belisarius, the late Flourishing State of Great Britain, in the Zenith of Glory and Honour; with her Fall into the most Abject State of Disgrace Misery and Ruin. Belisarius was one of the Greatest Heroes of the Antients. He lived under Justinian the Emperor: He Gain'd a Victory over and concluded an Honourable Peace with Cabades King of Persia, Took Carthage and Subdued Gilimes the Usurper of the Crown of the Vandals, Overthrew Vitiges and refused the Throne of the Goths when offer'd to him; Rebuilt the Walls of Rome after they were distroy'd by Totila, and performed many other Military Atchievements too tedious to enumerate. In this Part of his Char-

71

acter is represented the late Succesful and Flourishing State of Great Britain, which Aided the King of Prussia against the Powerful Armies of Hungary and Russia; Supported Portugal against the Spaniards, and reduc'd France and Spain to the most Advantageous Terms of Accommodation.

By the latter Part of Belisarius's Life is represented the Unhappy and Miserable State of Great Britain, should the late Measures against America take Place. This General at length being Accused of a Conspiracy against Justinian, That Emperor barbarously Ordered his Eyes to be pulled out, which reduced him to the Greatest Poverty, and Obliged him to Subsist on the Alms of others. The Motto is also Stricking, and elegantly Expressive of this Truth DATE OBOLUM BELISARIO—Give Poor Belisarius a Penny.

View the Countenance of Great Britain under this Character, and you Percieve nothing but Abject Despondency: Her Eyes, and the Stumps of her mangled Arms raised towards Heaven in Vain. Behold her Colonies, the Source of Her Commerce, Wealth and Glory, Separated from her Body, and no longer Useful to her. The Famous English Oak Diprived of the Wide Extended Top and late flourishing Branches, save a few, and those with its Body witherd and Decay'd. The Ground Beneath it producing nothing but Bryars and Thorns, The British Ships, the Instruments of her Trade, with Brooms on their Topmasts, denoting that they are Advertized for Sale, being no longer either necessary or Useful to her People. Her Sheild which she is incapable of Weilding, laying useless by her. The Lawrel Branch droping from the hand of Pennsylvania, which She is renderd unable to retain. And in Fine, Britania herself Sliding of[f] the World, no longer Courted by the Powers of Europe; No longer Able to Sustain its Ballance; No longer respected or Known among Nations.

Fragments of a Pamphlet on the Stamp Act

Plan, notes, rough draft, and fair copy: American Philosophical Society

During the period of agitation and discussion before the repeal of the Stamp Act Franklin began to prepare a pamphlet to supplement his letters to the newspapers. No published pamphlet that he might have written has been found, and it is probable that, well before he had finished writing, the movement for repeal had gained enough headway to induce him to drop the project. Among his papers in the American Philosophical Society are several sheets that represent notes, rough drafts, and revised fair copies of segments of such a pamphlet. While these sheets are all bound in the volume designated as "L (ii)," they are scattered through that volume, sometimes placed with papers belonging to quite different writings. In Verner W. Crane's *Letters to the Press*, pp. 62–73, these sheets are brought together in an "attempted reconstruction" of the pamphlet to the extent that detailed study and arrangement appeared to make possible. The present editors have carefully reviewed this ingenious effort and have leaned heavily upon it in preparing the presentation that appears here. We fully agree with Crane's conclusions as to what papers belong to this proposed pamphlet and in most respects have followed the same order, though we have departed from it in a few instances and have organized the presentation in a somewhat different form.

The surviving papers that appear to relate directly to this projected pamphlet fall into five groups:

1. A one-page outline or general "Plan of the Pamp[hlet]." L (ii), 12, *verso* of one sheet; Hays, *Calendar*, III, 467 (part of the 4th entry).[4]

2. Three pages of what are here called "Topical Notes," jotted down as they occurred to Franklin and hence in no particular order. Most of them include in the left margin coded notations to show in which section of the plan he intended to treat them in full. L (ii), 46 (a), 46(b), 46(c); Hays, *Calendar*, III, 460 (parts of the 6th entry).

3. One page of an outline for development in full on the topic of smuggling. L (ii) *recto* of the page listed in no. 1 above.[5]

4. Two pages of rough draft for the latter part of the surviving text of section 2 and a fragment possibly for section 3 in the proposed pamphlet. L (ii), 30a; Hays, *Calendar*, III, 464 (part of the 5th entry); and L (ii), 27; Hays, *Calendar*, III, 452 (3rd entry).

5. Seven pages of fair copy for the text of sections 1 and 2 of the pro-

4. In *Letters to the Press*, p. 65 n, Crane has incorrectly identified this piece as being in L (ii), 13, and on p. 70 n has similarly erred regarding the *recto* of the sheet, listed below as no. 3. The *Calendar* incorrectly places this sheet with the draft of a letter on smuggling, separately printed in *London Chron.*, Nov. 21–24, 1767. Though the *recto* of this sheet also deals with smuggling, it is not a draft of part of the *Chronicle* letter, and the *verso* is certainly a general outline for the projected Stamp Act pamphlet.

5. While it cannot be certainly determined that this outline was intended for the Stamp Act pamphlet, its argument is appropriate to the pamphlet and the use of the *verso* for the "Plan" strongly suggests that the *recto* belongs here too.

posed pamphlet. L (ii), 13, fo. 7; Hays, *Calendar,* III, 452 (part of the 1st entry); and L (ii), 31, fos. 9, 13, 14, 15, 17, 18; Hays, *Calendar,* III, 465 (3d entry).[6]

In the presentation below, the "Plan of the Pamp[hlet]" is first printed in full to give the reader a general view of the intended whole. Then, under numbers corresponding to the six sections of the Plan, are printed the Topical Notes identified by symbols as intended for development in those sections, and in one instance what appears to be a more detailed outline for development of a particular topic (no. 3 above). Finally, within each section is printed whatever survives of the full text for a part of that section, taken when possible from the fair copy, and in one instance taken in part from the surviving rough draft and in part from a later newspaper letter that quoted it at greater length. The character of each of these units within a section is indicated in brackets where it begins. Footnotes locate the source of each printed segment.

It cannot be said that this presentation is in any complete sense a "reconstruction" of the pamphlet, for clearly only a small part of the projected text appears to survive among Franklin's papers, and this part is limited almost entirely to portions of the first two sections. Probably Franklin never completed even a rough draft of all he planned to write. However inadequate this presentation must necessarily be for a knowledge of the intended pamphlet, it may have value as an indication of the methods Franklin used, at least on one occasion, in planning and organizing an extended literary production.

These papers are placed with others of January 1766, an approximation of the time when Franklin may have been working on the pamphlet. Some of the views suggested here appear more fully developed among his letters to the press of about the same time.

PLAN OF THE PAMP[HLET][7]

[*Torn*]   [1. *Torn*] their Attachment to this Country, prior to the late unhappy Misunderstandings.

6. The first of these pages of fair copy was incorrectly bound with the surviving pages of the draft of the Canada Pamphlet of 1760 and that group was listed together in the *Calendar;* see above, IX, 47 n. The other six pages of fair copy (consecutive except for the loss of folio 16) are erroneously described in the *Calendar* as parts of an incomplete draft of a letter to the printer of the *Public Advertiser.* The reason for such an identification is not apparent.

7. The heading, placed here at the top, is written sideways in the left margin. The top margin and upper left corner of the sheet are torn, causing the loss of most of the first line and the identifying symbols for the first two numbered descriptions. The identifying symbol for section 1 (if BF had any, for there are no Topical Notes he certainly assigned to it) cannot be conjecturally

[C. o M.]   2. The several Causes that concurr'd to produce those Misunderstandings.

I. o M   3. The Impropriety and Unnecessariness of the Measures that produced those Misunderstandings.

M Co P   4. The Mischievous Consequences that must attend a Persisting in those Measures.

G E. D.   5. The good Effects of departing from them.

M. o Pr.   6. The Means of preventing such Misunderstandings for the future, and cementing the two Countries in a lasting Union.

I

[*Topical Notes:*[8]]

Services of the Colonies

Their readiness to contribute Canada Exp[editio]n Carthagena and all last War

[*In the margin:*] The last War not for the Colonies but for the Trade of Britain, Indian Trade being carried on with English Goods

They as Consumers contribute in the Price of Commodities. Encrease your Seamen.

[*Pamphlet text:*]

[*First part missing*[9]] "Compensation for the Expences incurred by the respective Provinces, in the Levying, Cloathing and Pay of

supplied; that for section 2 is supplied from the Topical Notes, "C. o M" standing for "Causes of Misunderstandings." The others, which appear in both the "Plan" and the Topical Notes are: 3. "I. o M," standing for "Impropriety of Measures"; 4. "M Co P," for "Mischievous Consequences [of] Persisting"; 5. "G E. D.," for "good Effects of departing"; and 6. "M. o Pr.," for "Means of Preventing." This "Plan" is in APS, L (ii), 12 *verso*.

8. This group of Topical Notes appears on L (ii), 46(c), near the top, a page marked at the top "B." There is no identifying symbol in the margin of this group, but a notation "See Page A" and the words shown here as being in the margin. Nothing on the page headed "A"—L (ii), 46b—relates to this material. Crane, *Letters to the Press*, p. 69, has placed these notes with section 3, because the next entry in the notes bears the symbol "I. o M." The present editors believe, however, that they are more appropriate to the subject matter of section 1, as indicated in the "Plan," and to the surviving text that both Crane and the present editors have assigned to this section.

9. The first paragraph here is from a page of the fair copy numbered 7. This is the page erroneously bound with the surviving fragments of the MS of the Canada Pamphlet in L (ii), 13. A considerable hole in the middle of the sheet has caused the loss of some words, supplied here conjecturally.

the Troops raised by the same, according as the *active Vigour and strenuous Efforts* of the respective Provinces shall justly appear to merit. G.R." On which Message the House of Commons did the next Day resolve, "That a Sum not exceeding £200,000 be granted to his Majesty on Account, to enable his Majesty to give a proper Compensation to the respective Provinces in North America, for the Expence incurred by them, in the Levying, Cloathing and Pay of the Troops rais'd by the same according as the *active Vigor* and *strenuous Efforts* of the respec[tive] Provinces shall be thought by his [Majesty] to merit." The same Message [followed] by the same Resolve was *repeated* [*torn;* each year?] during the War; by which it appears [that] these *"his Majesty's faithful Subjects"* exerted themselves with unremitting *Zeal* and *Vigour* to the last in Defence of his Majesty's "just Rights and Possessions"; and I know that the Honour of having their Conduct thus approved by their gracious Sovereign, and by that great Council for whom they ever had the highest Veneration [*remainder of passage missing.*]

[*First part of passage missing;*[1] de]fence, and for raising among themselves by common Taxes such Sums as would be necessary for defraying the Expence. This PLAN OF UNION, was sent to Government here, that if approv'd it might be carried into Execution. It was *not approv'd;* whether from a Jealousy that such an Union might make the Colonies in some degree formidable to the Mother Country as well as to the Enemy, or from what other good Reasons, I will not pretend to conjecture. It was however thought better to send Troops from hence, and they were sent accordingly, at first a few only, but many more afterwards than were either originally intended here or desired there, at an immense Expence to this Nation, which in my Opinion, and that of many Americans, might well have been spared; a Fleet only, to favour the Operations of an American Land Force under such UNION, and prevent Troops and Succours from France to Canada, being perhaps what alone was truly necessary. And yet, however great this Expence, as the War ended in the Reduction of Canada, and Cession to Britain of all the vast Country northward, southward, and westward to the Missisipi, wherein she may from time to time plant more Colonies out of the vast Increase of the present, thereby

---

1. At this point begins the page of the fair copy numbered "9." L (ii), 31.

76

extending her Empire in the most natural Ma[nner] and with it her Strength by Sea and Land, [*torn*] by Commerce and an ever-craving Demand [*remainder of passage missing.*]

2

[*Topical Note:*]
C. o M.   The manner they are represented by Governors and Officers.[2]

[*Pamphlet text:*]
[*First part missing*[3]] the various Causes that combin'd to produce it, are particularly attended to, we rather ought to wonder that it was not foreseen and prevented.

It is not my Purpose here to censure the Conduct of Ministers, whose Motives, whose Lights, Informations and Misinformations I am unacquainted with. They might intend all for the best, and yet be mistaken in the Means, as wise Men sometimes are, and wiser Men are always ready to acknowledge. They might be prejudic'd against the Colonies by the artful Misrepresentations of the Enemies of the Colonies: For Enemies the Colonies have, and bitter ones, as one may see by the rancorous Libels with which the Papers are daily fill'd against them, exciting this Country to imbrue its Hands in their Blood; and yet perhaps no People ever deserv'd Enemies less. What I shall put down therefore, as the Causes of this Change, I desire may be consider'd simply as a Relation of Facts; and I leave Censure to those who are better qualify'd to judge, and to whom it more properly belongs.

In the first Place, by posting Frigates all along the Coast, with armed Tenders and Cutters to run into every River and Creek, the Officers of which were all vested with Custom-house Powers, and who, especially those of the lower Rank, executed their Commissions with great Rudeness and Insolence, all Trade and Commerce, even the most legal, between Colony and Colony, was harass'd, vex'd and interrupted, by perpetual Stoppings of Boats, Rummagings and Searchings, Unladings and Detainings, on trifling Occasions, and Seizures of Vessels on the slightest Omission or

2. This is the only surviving Topical Note marked for section 2. It was inserted, apparently as an afterthought, in the lower left corner of L (ii), 46(c).
3. Here begins a series of three consecutive pages of the fair copy numbered 13, 14, and 15. L (ii), 31.

Irregularity of Papers, &c. extorting Compositions by terryfying the Owners with carrying the Vessels seized on Suspicion to Halifax, in which remote Place the great Court of Admiralty was establish'd. 2°. The Exacting rigorously at the same time a too heavy Duty on foreign Mellasses, an Article which our own Islands could not furnish in sufficient Quantities, and which was not only of great Consequence in the Distilleries, Fisheries and Guinea Trade, but in North America was become one of the Necessaries of Life, being the common Sweetning used in the Food of the poorer Sort, and universally a principal Ingredient in their common Beer, gave also a general Dissatisfaction. 3° The Trade too, which had been carried on with the foreign Plantations, (whence Money, and Commodities that being carried to Europe might be turned into Money, were usually procured, to discharge the Ballances continually growing due in England) was at the same time greatly embarrass'd, discourag'd and prevented, so that a *Scarcity of Cash,* and the Distresses such Scarcity always occasions in Trade, came on very fast. 4°. And what render'd that Scarcity of Gold and Silver less tolerable, was a new Act of Parliament, prohibiting the making any more *Paper Money* in the Colonies that should be a legal Tender. 5°. And then, when both Silver and Paper Money were daily diminishing, and in a Way of being totally annihilated, comes the fatal STAMP-ACT, demanding a *new* and *heavy* Tax; and this laid on by the very Power that had in a great degree taken away the means of paying *any* Tax at all; while every Province was groaning under the Weight of Taxes laid by its own Assemblies to discharge the Debts left by the last War. 6°. This Act too was render'd the more galling, by its taking away Trials by Juries for all Offences against it, and[4]
[*One page of the manuscript missing*]
it might take when it pleas'd the other nineteen so that in fact they had then nothing they could call their own. It was now that they recollected all the former Hardships imposed on them, which their Respect for the Mother Country had induc'd them to bear in Silence. The numerous and perplex'd Restraints on their Trade, many of them requiring *Labour in vain,* and *Expence to no purpose.* The Restraints on their Manufactures, those very few that their Situa-

4. The page of the fair copy numbered 15 ends here. Page 16 is missing. Following the indicated break two consecutive pages of the fair copy begin, numbered 17 and 18. L (ii), 31.

tion and particular Circumstances gave them some Opportunity of carrying on to Advantage: The Emptying by Law all the Goals of this Country into their Settlements; an Instance of sovereign cruel Insolence unexampled, with which no Nation before had ever treated even a Country they had conquer'd, made if possible still more grievous by that barbarous *Sarcasm*[5] in a solemn Report of the Bo—d of T—e, on a Plantation Act intended to prevent the Importation of Convicts, "that the Act for transporting them was necessary for the BETTER Peopling of his Majesty's Colonies!" And now while their Minds were in this disturbed State, came among them numberless ministerial Pamphlets and Papers printed here, arguing away all their Rights by the most sophistical Reasoning representing them in the most odious Lights, and treating them and their Pretensions to English Liberty with the utmost Contempt; one of those Pieces, too, said to be written by a Person in *high Office*, with much Wit indeed, but which a little more Wit would have induc'd him rather to suppress. Let any sensible[6] considerate Englishman put himself but for a Moment in this Situation of these People, and attend to his own Feelings, I am persuaded he will find himself dispos'd to pity (even while he blames) the Distractions and Extravagancies this Situation and these Apprehensions drove them into.

But why should it be thought strange that the Governing People here are usually prejudic'd against the Colonies?[7] Much has been

5. Here begins a page of the rough draft numbered 14. L (ii), 30a. The next few lines of text appear on both the rough draft and the fair copy.

6. This passage on page 14 of the rough draft ends with "Let any sensible, Yc. [from the preceding Page]," obviously a reference to a missing page 13 of the rough draft; apparently it contained the text of the rest of this paragraph.

7. A letter printed in *London Chron.*, April 7–9, 1767, signed "F.B.," transmits an "Extract of a Letter" said to have been "written here at the time of our last year's disputes, by one who had lived long in America, knew the people and their affairs extremely well—and was equally well acquainted with the temper and practices of government officers. Speaking of the opinion entertained in Britain of the Americans, he says." Then "F.B.," easily identified as BF, quotes from this projected pamphlet at this point. With a few changes, the text of the "Letter" in the *Chronicle* follows the surviving portions of the fair copy and the rough draft to the end of the text printed here as belonging to section 2 of the proposed pamphlet. For another possibly planned use of this passage, see below, p. 223.

said of a *virtual Representation*, which the Colonies are suppos'd to have here. Of that I understand nothing. But I know what kind of *actual Representation* is continually made *of* them, by those from whom Ministers chiefly have their Information. Governors and other Officers of the Crown, even the little Officers of the Revenue sent from hence, have all at times some Account to give of their own loyal and faithful Conduct, with which they mix some contrary Character of the People that tends to place that Conduct in a more advantageous Light. Every[8] good thing done there in the Assemblies, for promoting his Majesty's Service, was obtained by the Governor's Influence; he propos'd; he urg'd strongly; he manag'd Parties; there was great Opposition; the Assembly were refractory, and disaffected; but his Zeal and Dexterity overcame all Difficulties. And if thro' his own Imprudence, or real Want of Capacity, any thing goes wrong: he is never in fault; the Assembly and the People are to bear all the Blame; they are factious, they are turbulent, disloyal, impatient of Government, or, what is the same thing, disrespectful to *his Majesty's Representative*. The Custom House Officer represents the People as all inclin'd to *Smuggling*, Dutch and French Goods (by his Account) swarm in the Country, nothing else would be us'd if it were not for his *extream Vigilance;* which, indeed, as it takes up all his Time, he hopes will be considered in the Allowance of a *larger Salary*. Even the Missionary Clergy, to whom all Credit is due, cannot forbear acquainting the Bishops, and their other Superiors, here from whom they receive their Stipends, that they are very [dili]gent in their respective Missions, but that they[9] meet with great difficulties from the adverse disposition of the people: Quakers oppose them in one place, Presbyterians in another: *this* country swarms with thwarting hereticks; *t'other* with malevolent sectaries: Infidelity gains ground *here*, Popery is countenanced *there*. Their unwearied endeavours, which are never wanting, scarce suffice to prevent the colonists being

8. The last surviving page of the fair copy (numbered 18) ends here. A page of the rough draft, badly torn in the bottom portion and with its number missing begins here. L (ii), 27.

9. From here to the end of this passage the unnumbered page of rough draft is badly mutilated. Although parts of each line remain, it seems more satisfactory to print the remainder from the *Chronicle* version, which in any case probably represents BF's own revision and an expansion of the text.

overwhelmed with vice, irreligion, ignorance, and error![1] Then the Military Officer, who has served in the colonies, represents them as *abounding in wealth;* the profuse tables they used to spread for him in their hospitable entertainments convinced him of it; for these he saw daily when he din'd from house to house, and therefore he had reason to imagine it was their common way of living; (though in truth that was extreamly different and much more suitable to their circumstances.) But opulent as he supposes them, they must, in his opinion, be the meanest of mortals to grudge the payment of a trifling tax, especially as it is to maintain soldiers. Thus REPRESENTED, how can it be otherwise, but that the governing people in Britain should conceive the most unfavourable idea of Americans, as unworthy the name of Englishmen, and fit only to be snubb'd, curb'd, shackled and plundered.[2]

3

[*Topical Notes:*[3]]

I. o. M. The Stamp Act unnecessary. There was another and a regular Constitutional Method of getting Money from the Colonies.

England by Trade gets all their Superlucration beyond the Necessaries of Life. Shirley's Letters.

They have by their Hospitality given false Ideas of their Wealth.

I. o. M. Colonies consider'd too much in a Commercial Light.

[*Possible fragment for pamphlet text:*[4]]

And now let it be remarked, that the Stamp Act for extorting a

1. At this point in the rough draft occurs a very badly mutilated passage referring in some manner, impossible to determine exactly now, to the baptism of Negro children. The next two sentences, printed here from the *Chronicle* and relating to the "Military Officer" and his false impressions of colonial wealth, do not appear in the rough draft.

2. Both the page of rough draft and the quotation in the *Chronicle* end here.

3. The first three of these notes appear together at the top of L (ii), 46(a); the fourth appears in the middle of L (ii), 46(c), immediately following the notes the present editors have assigned to section 1, although Crane places them with section 3.

4. The sentence printed here appears in the middle of L (ii), 30a. It is set off by a brace and is sandwiched between passages of section 2, both of which appear also in the fair copy though this does not. The editors have followed Crane in assigning it tentatively to section 3.

Revenue from the Colonies against their Consent was as unnecessary as it was unseasonable and improper.

[*Outline for developed treatment:*[5]]
[*Vertically in the margin:*] Wrong to punish a whole Community for the Fault of a few.
Merchants but a small Part of the People.
Smugglers of European Goods into the Country but a small Part of the Merchants.
That Smuggling of no Service to the Body of the People, as the Smugglers put the Advantage into their own Pockets.
The Smuggling of English Goods out of the Colonies into the Spanish and Foreign Colonies vastly greater than the other.
If an Account could be stated of the Disadvantages and Advantages to Britain of both Sorts of Smuggling, the Ballance would appear vastly in her favour, perhaps 20 to 1.
The Smuggling of European Goods into the Colonies, [*torn*] of such as Britain cannot supply, as Linnens, and [*torn*] Loss to her by it is the Merchants [*torn*] the Manufacture. As to the Duties [*torn*] drawn back.
Coarse Teas indeed have been smuggled in grea[t Quantities?].
[*No extended text found for this section.*]

[*Topical Notes:*[6]]   4
M Co P. They think it matters little whether the arbitrary Power of Taxing them is vested in one Man or a 1000 if they have no Choice of Representatives.
          If this Power is insisted on, Americans can never conceive they have any Property left. Dangerous to reduce them to this Extremity.
          They can subsist without this Country or any Trade and being too weak to express their Resentments in any

5. This outline, on the *recto* of L (ii), 12, appears to belong to the projected pamphlet and, following the suggestion of Crane, is placed with section 3. It appears to relate most closely to the general subject of this section indicated in the Plan, even though none of the Topical Notes of this section specifically mentions smuggling.

6. The four groups of notes marked with the symbol for section 4 are found in L (ii) on 46(a) middle, 46(b) top, 46(b) bottom, and 46(c) top, respectively.

other Way it will be more strongly express'd in this.
[*In the margin here:*] Germany the Mother Country
of this Nation.

M Co P. The great Growth of America.
> Prudence to treat them now as you would wish a hun-
> dred Years hence that you had treated them.
> A Mistake that they emigrated from hence
>> that they are chiefly Irish Scotch and Foreign-
>> ers, (have more Merit) or Convicts.[7]
> They are the Offspring of good Families, &c. encreas'd
> in the Country.
> Mistake that they are unwilling to contribute.

M Co P They cannot be forc'd to submit to the Stamp Act but
> at an Expence greater than the Profit.
> Their Hearts will be lost and with it the Trade. Animosity
> and Hatred will succeed. Enemies will take Ad-
> vantage.
>> Spaniards and Portuguese
>> Genoese and Corsicans.
> The Empire weaken'd, and the Foundation laid of a total
> Separation.
> Mortification in the Foot.

M Co P Value yourselves on Trade, forgetful how much the Re-
> spect of People and Good Will contributes to it.
> [*No pamphlet text found for this section.*]

5
[*Topical Notes:*[8]]
G Eo D. Of great Importance to recover the Respect of so great
> a Body of Subjects.
> The Strength that will arise from a cordial Union.
> The great Growth of America.
> [*No pamphlet text found for this section.*]

7. The page on which this group of notes is placed—46(b)—is marked at
the top "A." At this point in the margin are the words "See Page B," an
apparent reference to the group of notes here assigned to section 1, which are
marked "See page A." The editors are unable to explain satisfactorily the purpose of these cross-references.
8. These Notes are found in L (ii), 46(a) bottom.

6

[*Topical Notes:*⁹]

M o Pr   Representation necessary to consolidate the Empire—to inform Government of the State of the remote Parts —and them of the Motives and Measures of Government.

        People in Colonies will never be convinced that they are virtually represented, &c.

M o Pr   See Letters to Shirley

        Ireland once would have been united. Now refuses. America will now accept but will probably not ask for Representatives—will hereafter refuse.

        [*No pamphlet text found for this section.*]

        [Conclusion¹]

[*Topical note:*]

        The true Politics regard the *Whole* Empire and not how to benefit one Part at the Expence of another.

        [*No pamphlet text found for this section.*]

From William Dunlap²   ALS: American Philosophical Society

Honor'd Sir   Falmouth, Febry. 1st. 1766

It is now upwards of a Twelve month since I sail'd from Philadelphia for Barbados, in order to inspect into the State of my Affairs there, and if possible procure some Kind of Subsistance on

---

9. The two groups of notes marked with the symbol for section 6 are found in L (ii), 46(c) bottom, and L (ii), 46(b) middle, respectively.

1. The Plan does not list a concluding section, as such, though BF would almost certainly have contemplated one, however brief. The single note printed here is found in L (ii), 46(c) lower middle; in the adjacent margin, where section symbols usually appear in the Topical Notes, the word "Conclusion" was written and then struck through.

2. For William Dunlap, husband of DF's niece and a printer at both Lancaster and Philadelphia, whom BF appointed postmaster of Philadelphia in 1757, see above, V, 199 n; VII, 168–9. In the fall of 1764 Dunlap was replaced in the postmastership by Peter Franklin, while still owing the post office a substantial sum of money; he charged BF and Foxcroft with "merciless Oppression" in trying to collect the debt. Above, XI, 418–22, 469 n.

the Spot that might Support my Family:[3] When I arriv'd, I found my little Interest on the Island badly regulated, and the Partnership Accounts in worse Order; the rectifying of which has been my Employment ever since: Tho' indeed the Place has hitherto produced scarce sufficient to maintain the Man who has had the Management of the Business in his Hands,[4] yet I am clearly convinc'd, that could I procure a Residence there, it might be brought to produce Something well worth the Attention: To this my Inclinations, with that of my Family, strongly lead me; but the Income of my Share of the Business there, will not be sufficient of itself to support us: There is a Vacancy at present, for the Office of *Searcher* of His Majesty's Customs, for the Port of Bridge-Town, in that Island, occasion'd by the Death of Mr. John Green, who last held the same, and who was burried on the 16th. of Novr. last. Could I be fortunate enough to procure that Office, it would effectually raise me above the Contempt and Distresses usually attendant on a State of Dependancy: The Sallary allow'd by the Crown is but about £70 Str: per Annum but the Perquisites make it at least £200 Barbadoes Currency: It is reckon'd a genteel Office, and requires but a very moderate Attendance: Mr. Green came from England about fore Months ago, and occupied his Office but about five Weeks before his Death: He told me it was to Lord Grenvill's[5] Interest he was beholden for his Promotion: As I cannot doubt your Inclination, so I am sure your Interest is sufficient to serve me effectually in this important Affair: Indeed I am the more sollicitous on this Head, as I have now a very Advantageous Offer with respect to the Disposition of my Interest in Philadel-

3. In 1760 Dunlap sent one William Brown, a former apprentice, to Barbados to manage a printing office at Bridgetown in which he had an interest. "No record remains of any printing done by Brown in Barbados. He left the island in 1763 and went to Quebec." See Douglas C. McMurtrie, *Early Printing in Barbados* (London, 1933), p. 13. Whatever other assets Dunlap may have had in the West Indies remain unknown, but he was able to take occasional leave of absence from his Virginia parish in later years to attend to his affairs in the islands.

4. Apparently a successor of Brown, not otherwise identified. A George Ismand is noted as having begun to print a newspaper in Barbados in 1762; perhaps he was Dunlap's partner. *Ibid.*, p. 13.

5. Dunlap obviously means George Grenville, first lord of the Treasury, 1763–65.

phia⁶ which if closed in with, will enable me in Time to pay off my Debts, and that sooner than I am sorry to say I can otherwise ever hope for: I inclose the Paper on which this Belief is founded, for your Inspection: After this, I need not enlarge: If you mean to serve me, however, there is no Time to be lost, as there are a Variety of Letters come in the Vessel that has brought me here, from different Hands, on the same Subject with this: One in particular to Lord Edgcomb,⁷ whom I am told is like to be the most Formidable: I know not in whose Gift this little Office is invested, but of this you will be at no Loss: I intended to have waited on you in Person with this Application, but not being innur'd to travelling, and my weaken'd Frame rendering it impossible for me to make that Dispatch that is realy necessary on such an Occasion, I concluded it most expedient to write: For God's Sake, Sir, do not fail me on this important Occasion, nor blame me in this Effort as Rash and Inconsiderate: There is nothing more natural than for a *drowning Man* to catch at the most distant Twig:⁸ I am, Honor'd Sir Your most obedient Humble Servant   W. DUNLAP

6. Perhaps Dunlap's nephew and former apprentice, John Dunlap, who took over his printing business in Philadelphia in 1768, had offered to do so at this time.

7. George Edgcumbe (1720–1795), M.P. from Fowey, 1746–61, was a naval officer who served with Boscawen at the capture of Louisburg in 1758. He succeeded his brother as 3d Baron Edgcumbe in 1761. Under the Rockingham ministry (1765–66) he served as a privy councillor and as treasurer of the Household. As Dunlap surmised, Edgcumbe's interest was "most Formidable" because, in addition to the offices which he held, he controlled "one of the greatest borough interests in Great Britain." Namier and Brooke, *House of Commons,* II, 379–80.

8. Dunlap's application proved ineffectual, either because BF refused to support it (perhaps he did not care to be called a "distant Twig") or because the post in the customs was already promised or filled; instead, the *"drowning Man"* caught hold of another twig and was ordained a deacon in the Church of England on February 22 and a priest the next day. See below, p. 176. In a letter to the Bishop of London, Dec. 18, 1766, the Rev. William Smith related that Dunlap had sought letters of recommendation for Holy Orders before leaving Philadelphia for Barbados, but had been refused "as he had no education but reading and writing" and because his role in a lottery a few years earlier, in which he was threatened with a law suit, was remembered against him. According to Smith, Dunlap procured the appropriate letters in Barbados, even though the clergy there could not have known him very well. Because of Dunlap's deficient education Smith believed that the Church in

P.S. I had form'd a Resolution to mak Application to the Secretary of the Treasury,[9] and not to have troubled you in the least; and had actually wrote the Letter which accompanies this, before I could bring myself to break through the Rule I had prescrib'd myself; but being diffident of his Interest, I have taken the Liberty with you I could have *wish'd to avoid:* I send the Letter that I intended for him cased, that you may open and act by it as may be most agreeable to you:

Addressed: To / Benj Franklin Esqr. / Craven Street / London

James Parker:
Final Report on the Franklin and Hall Account

ADS: Haverford College Library (2 copies), Historical Society of Pennsylvania (1 copy)

According to the agreement between Franklin and David Hall, Jan. 1, 1748 (above, III, 263-7), their printing partnership was to commence on Jan. 21, 1748 (new style), and continue for eighteen years. The agreement provided that Franklin was to furnish the presses, type, and other printing equipment; Hall was to assume direct charge of the business, including the "working Part of Printing," the "disposing of Work printed," and the collection of all money due, and he was to pay the costs of these operations. Charges for all such supplies as paper and ink, for "common Repairs" to the presses, the rent of the building, and all bad debts, and all monetary receipts were to be equally shared by the partners. At the end of the partnership Hall should have the right to buy the presses, type, and other materials, if he desired, "at their present Value," but allowing "a reasonable Abatement" for their wear during the period of use.

When Franklin was about to leave Philadelphia for England in November 1764 he gave a power of attorney to James Parker to examine all the books and other records in Hall's possession, to appraise the printing

---

Philadelphia would "suffer a little in the sight of her adversaries," all of whom, the Presbyterians in particular, had a learned ministry. William S. Perry, ed., *Papers relating to the History of the Church in Pennsylvania, A. D. 1680–1778* ([Hartford], 1871), pp. 412–13. He later obtained a parish in Virginia.

9. Charles Lowndes (1699?–1783) was secretary to the Treasury, July 1765–August 1767. Namier and Brooke, *House of Commons,* III, 55.

equipment (Hall had expressed a wish to buy it), and to "make a final Ending of all Accounts" between the two men (above, XI, 441-3). Parker was to send a preliminary report on his examination of the accounts to Franklin at least six months before the expiration of the partnership. Just how Parker was to be compensated for the time and labor he would spend on this business does not appear in any surviving paper.

Parker spent thirteen days on this task in February 1765 and three more in June, then sent Franklin a preliminary report covering the records he had so far examined. That report is printed above, XII, 176–82. In August 1765 he sent a second report that included a few additional entries, most of them merely carrying forward the summaries of Hall's receipts in specific categories since the report of June. The added entries are printed above, XII, 242.

On January 16, 1766, Parker was only just recovering from a severe attack of gout but managed to get to Philadelphia, and during the rest of the month he completed his detailed report and then sent it to Franklin in London. It is organized in the same general manner as the preliminary reports. On the left half of a large sheet are the entries of money for which Franklin should be debited, on the right hand those for which Hall was charged. Parker divided the entries on each side into sections or "Articles" to which he gave numbers. For convenience and easier reference the editors have here designated the sections as A-1, A-2, A-3, and B-1, B-2, B-3, respectively, in the same manner as was done in printing the two preliminary reports in the last volume. At the bottom of each half sheet of the final report Parker added a summary of the "Articles" above, showing the totals to be debited to each partner according to the terms of the agreement, and striking a final balance. Many of the entries in the "Articles" are repetitions of ones found in the two preliminary reports, and reference may be had to those documents for explanatory information in their appended notes. In a few instances the present full report clarifies matters not adequately set forth in its predecessors.

As drawn up and balanced, this account showed that Franklin owed Hall £993 11s. 6d. Parker accompanied his long report with a letter explaining some details (printed below, pp. 104–10). Franklin gave both papers careful study and then drew up a series of "Observations" (below, pp. 110–16), which the reader should use in connection with the report itself, since they show what Franklin considered to be the inadequacies of numerous entries. In April 1767 he promised to send this paper to Hall but never did so, and his long-continued absence from Philadelphia prevented the former partners from ever getting together to clear up questionable details. Hall died in 1772. The account between

Franklin and Hall's estate, printed as the next document after this one, starts off with the balance of £993 11s. 6d. shown by the present report as owned by Franklin; it includes no credits or debits caused by corrections of any of the entries printed in the present report. It seems probable that Parker's figures were never revised.

All the three copies of this report that have been found are in Parker's hand and bear his dating and signature at the bottom of the first column. There are a few variations in phraseology from copy to copy, none of any significance. In his letter of February 3 explaining the report Parker indicated that copies were going to England by two different ships. One of the two copies in the Haverford College Library is the only one of the three that bears an endorsement in Franklin's hand. Since this endorsement establishes that Franklin certainly received this copy, it is the one used for the present printing. The individual entries in it, however, are unnumbered, though they are numbered in the other two. In his "Observations" on the report Franklin referred to the entries by their numbers, showing that he also received at least one such numbered copy. For convenience in comparing Franklin's comments with the entries they concern, the editors have taken the liberty of prefacing each entry in the printed text below with the numbers found in the other two surviving copies.

As stated with the first of these reports, descriptions of several of the Franklin & Hall accounts that Parker used, are given above, III, 270–1, 276.

[February 1, 1766]
NUMB. 1. [A-1]¹

1	Account of Money paid by D. Hall: to B. Franklin, from March 1747/8. to March 1. 1765. as per several Receipts in B.F's own Writing appears, examin'd per J. Parker	7849	7	4¾.
2	Account of Money, paid by D. Hall for Bills of Exchange sent to England, to B.F. from June 1757. to February 1765, as per D.H's Accounts, examin'd per J. Parker	4776	19	6
3	Account of Sundries had in Mr. Hall's Shop, and Cash lent at sundry Times by D. Hall to B Franklin, as per Account, examined per J. Parker, March 1. 1765	541	2	1¾.

1. The first four entries in this section appeared in Parker's first report; entries 5–12 are new.

4 Account of 4000 Poor Richard's Almanacks
   sent to Rhode Island, by B. Franklin's
   Orders from 1752 to 1761. inclusive
   (stiching deducted)   62 13 4
   Ditto of 1900 Pocket Almanacks sent per
   Do as per Account   31 13 4
5 Account of Sundries had, in D. Hall's Shop,
   and Cash lent at sundry Times by D.H. to
   Mrs. Franklin from March 1. 1765. to Jan.
   28. 1766[2] examin'd per JP.   407 3 5
6 Account for the Book Noetica, being for Mr.
   Franklin,[3] which in the Work-Book is
   charged at   25 0 0
7 Account for 300 Young Men's Companion
   sent to Mr. Hunter, by B.F.[4] (the whole
   chargd at 4s.)   60 0 0
8 Account of Cash paid for Baskerville's Bible,
   for Miss Sally, Gilt and bound in Turkey
   charged at £6 5s.[5] Sterl. Exchange then at
   160   10 0 0
9 Account for Work done for the Post-Office,
   in 1752, 1754, and 1756. Paper included, as
   exam'd per JP.   11 3 6

2. Probably part of the money lent to DF during this period had been to help her make the down payment of £500 on the Syddon lot in September 1765; above, XII, 283–6, 351–2.

3. Samuel Johnson (of Connecticut), *Noetica: Or the Principles of Human Knowledge,* published by Franklin & Hall in 1752 with Johnson's *Ethices* under the general title of *Elementa Philosophica.* See above, III, 478 n; IV, 63, 71, 107, 108, 146, 261; V, 157. Apparently BF had originally assumed full financial responsibility for his friend's somewhat unprofitable book, rather than make it a partnership matter.

4. ["Mrs. Slack"], *The American Instructor: Or, Young Man's Best Companion... By George Fisher, Accomptant. The Ninth Edition, Revised and Corrected* was published by Franklin & Hall, 1748, and the Tenth Edition in 1753 (Evans, 6238, 7120). BF had apparently had 300 copies of one edition or the other sent to William Hunter in Williamsburg for sale there. In his "Observations" BF proposed that Hunter's account be examined to see if these copies had been charged to the Virginian.

5. For John Baskerville's folio edition of the Bible, see above, IX, 257 n.

10 Account for printing 300 Copies of a Petition
to the King, in 1764.⁶ fine Paper, and
Covering, the One Half of it, and Paper,
amounting to   2 19 9
11 Account of Money paid by D. Hall, on Mr.
Franklin's Account, to Mr. Strahan in
England, at Sundry Times, as exam'd per
JP. being £82 8s. 6d. Sterl. Exchange 170.
is   140   2   3
                                                        ¯¯¯¯¯¯¯¯¯¯¯¯¯¯¯
                                                        13918 4 7½

12 [NB.⁷ By a Receipt of B.F.'s writing, he acknowledges to have
had £26 13s. 6d. of D.H. on Account of Sally's Books Feb.
25. 1749. from whence it seems D.H. had some of her Books
for Sale: but no other Account appearing about it. J.P. can
say Nothing further: but D.H. thinks some of the Money he
paid to Mr. Strahan, was on the Account of those Books, and
possibly B.F. may have repaid him some of that Money back:
and therefore submits it to B.F.]

NUMB. 2. [A-2]⁸

13 Account of Money paid by D. Hall, for
Paper, to the several Paper Makers. and
to March 6. 1765, as per Receipts and
Vouchers, examin'd per J Parker   4298 9   0
14 Account of Money paid for 163½ lb.
Lampblack from 1749. to June 13. 1765,
examin'd by JP   40 17   6
15 Account of Incidentals paid by D. Hall. for
the Use of the Office, from 1749. to June
13. 1765. as per Account, exam'd JP.   584   1   2½
16 Account of Money paid by D. Hall, for
Printing-Ink, English News-papers, &c.
as per Book, examined per J. Parker
amounting to £172 5s. 7d. Sterl. Exchange
170, is   292 17   3

6. Above, XI, 145–7.
7. The brackets surrounding this note are in the original.
8. The first three entries in this section appear in Parker's first report; entries 16–20 are new.

17 Account of Incidents paid by D.H. for the
Office, from June 13. 1765. to January 28.
1766, examin'd per JP.   18   5   11
18 Account of Money paid by D.H. for Paper to
the several Paper Makers, from March 6.
1765. to February 1. 1766. as per Receipts,
examined per J Parker   524   6   6
19 Account of Writing Paper of different Sorts
furnished by D. Hall, for sundry Jobs
printed, as charged in the Leidgers, and
examin'd by J Parker   153 13   7
20 Account of Parchment, furnished by D.H.
for sundry Jobs, charged as above, and
examined per J Parker   52   7   6
                                                          _____
                                                          5964 18   5½

NUMB. 3. [A-3][9]
21 Account of Money received by B. Franklin
for printing Work, charged in the Leigders
from Jan. 26. 1748. to Feb. 1765. as
examined per JP.   219 18 11¼
22 Account of Money received by B. Franklin
for Gazette, from Jan. 1748. to July 15.
1749, as had his Name affixed exd per JP.   24   2   6
23 Account of Money received by B.F. in
Account with Th. Lightfoot, as per his
Account in settling with D.H. for Gazette   2 17   6
24 Account of Money received by B.F. for the
Gazette, after July 15. 1749. to 1765. as
exam'd per J Parker   448 10   3
25 Account of Money received by B.F. for Wm.
Ramsey's[1] Books, as per Mr. F.s Account,
examin'd per JP.   91   4   0
                                                          _____
                                                          786 13   2¼

9. The first three entries in this section appeared in Parker's first report, the
fourth in his second report; only entry 25 is new.

1. In BF's Ledger D, p. 126, is an account between BF and "Mr. Wm. Ramsey" running from 1742 to 1752. One entry, dated Jan. 16, 1749, records a
cash payment of £11 11s. ½d. by Ramsey "towards his book now printing," but the book has not been certainly identified. One William Ramsey

[Gen]eral [Ac]count

Dr. Benjamin Franklin. Esqr in Account with
David Hall

26 To the Whole of the above Account, Number 1	13918	4	7½
27 To the Half of the above Account Numb. 2	2982	9	2¾
28 To the Half of the above Account, Numb. 3.	393	6	7
	17294	0	5¼

Errors excepted Phila. Feb 1. 1766 per J PARKER.

NUMB. 1. [B-1]²

29 Account of Money received by D. Hall for
publick Work from Nov. 1756. to March
1765. as examined per J. Parker, (the
Publick work before Nov. 1756, had been
settled before)   2182 19 5½

30 Account of Money received by D. Hall, for
publick Work, from New Castle, Kent and
Sussex, from 1756. to 1764, as examin'd per
J. Parker (the work here before 1756. had
been settled)   242 16 8

31 Account of Money received by D. Hall for
Advertisements paid for when brought in,
in the Gazette, from Jan. 26. 1748 to
February 21. 1765. as examin'd per J
Parker³   3312 17 8

(d. 1785) is mentioned elsewhere as a founder and leading merchant of Alexandria, Va., and a Masonic friend of George Washington. Was Ramsey's book, perhaps, an anonymous work advertised in *Pa. Gaz.*, May 11, 1749, as "just published, and to be sold at the Post-Office," entitled *The Impenetrable Secret* (Evans, 6334; Hildeburn, 1131; Campbell, 418)? If so, the author's secret remains impenetrable, for no surviving copy of this publication has been found.

2. Entries 29–43 in this section were covered by entries in Parker's first or second report, or both, except that small amounts are here added to entries 34 and 39 to bring them down to Jan. 17, 1766. Entries 44–48 are new. By sheer coincidence Jan. 17, 1766, the terminal date of several of these accounts, was BF's sixtieth birthday.

3. The 12 surviving pages of this account as shown in entries 31, 32, and 45 are among the Franklin Papers, APS, and are briefly described above, III, 270, no. 1.

93

32 Do of the same, from Feb. 21. 1765. to
    August 22. 1765. as examin'd by J Parker   212 2 6
33 Account of Money received by D. Hall, for
    single Advertisements, Blanks, and other
    Work done in the Office, for ready Pay,
    from Jan. 26. 1748. to Feb. 16. 1765. as
    examin'd per J. Parker.[4]   484 14 9
34 Do of the same from Feb 16. 1765. to Jan. 17.
    1766. as examin'd per JP   14 16 6
35 Account of Money received by D. Hall, for
    printing Work, &c. charged in the
    Leidgers, from Jan. 21. 1748. to February
    25. 1765. as examin'd per J Parker[5]   2393 12 $8\frac{1}{4}$
36 Do of the same from Feb. 25 1765. to
    August 22. 1765. As examin'd per JP   513 5 0
37 Account of Money received by D. Hall, on
    Account of the Gazette, from July 15.
    1749, to March 1. 1765, as in the four
    Books examined by J Parker[6]   9683 15 $4\frac{1}{2}$
    An Error in the first casting it up, and
    carried to the End, makes it more   8 16 6
38 Account of Ditto, from March 1. 1765. to
    Aug. 22. 1765, as examined by JP   871 18 $11\frac{1}{2}$
39 Account of Money received by D. Hall for
    Entrance Money for the Gazette, from
    1748. to January 17. 1766. as examin per JP   1620 14 0
40 Account of Money received by D. Hall for
    Gazette, viz by James Hunter, Esqr
                   £72:9:2
  By Stratton Burton,
    Snowhill Post   43:0:0
  By John Wise, Do   37:5:0   152 14 2

4. The 22 surviving pages of this account as shown in entries 33 and 34 are among the Franklin Papers, APS, and are described above, III, 270, no. 2. The final page shows an additional 10s. paid on Jan. 28, 1766, and examined by Parker on February 1, but not shown in his report.

5. The 13 surviving pages of this account as shown in entries 35, 36, and 46 are among the Franklin Papers, APS, and are described above, III, 271, no. 3.

6. No detailed account of this entry or the remaining ones in Section B-1 (except entry 46) has been found.

41 Account of Almanacks printed and Sold by
   D. Hall, from 1752. to 1765. inclusive
   (those printed before 1752. has been settled)
   Poor Richards, 141,257 at 4*d.* (stiching
      deducted)   2213   0   8
   Pocket Ditto 25,735 at 6*d.*   643   7   6
   Jerman's Ditto[7] 5,197, at 3½ exclusive
      of Copy paid for and stiching   69 11   9½
42 Account of Primers printed by D. Hall from
   1749. to 1765.[8] being 35,100, at 2½*d.* each   365 12   6
43 Account of Blanks printed for the Shop, being
   109 Ream, and 18 Quire, (Paper deducted)
   as per Account examin'd per J Parker   482 18   6
44 Account of Money received by D. Hall for
   the Gazette, from Aug. 22. 1765. to Jan. 17.
   1766: as examin' per JP.   518 10   6½
   Do of Ditto, per John Jones[9] of the Lower
   Counties paid to D. Hall in July 1765   80   0   0
   Do of Ditto per Hunter and Glassel of
   Virginia,[1] paid D. Hall, Jan. 2. 1766   54   0   8
45 Account of Money received by D.H. for
   Advertisement paid in the Gazette, from
   Aug. 22. 1765. to Jan. 17. 1766. exam'd
   per JP.   114 12   0

7. John Jerman's almanac; above, XII, 181 n.
8. An apparently unique copy of *The New-England Primer Enlarged, For the more easy attaining the true Reading of English. To which is added, The Assembly's Catechism,* printed by Franklin and Hall in 1760, is in the Schwenkfelder Lib., Pennsburg, Pa. The editors are indebted to Professor C. William Miller of Temple University for this information. An apparently unique copy of the Franklin and Hall printing of 1764 is in Yale Univ. Lib. It is rather strange that of more than 35,000 copies of the *Primer* here reported to have been printed by Franklin and Hall, only these two can now be located. But *Primers* were cheap and received hard usage, and most were probably thrown away when the children in a family had outgrown them.
9. Identified by Hall in a later letter as one of the post riders.
1. An announcement by Franklin and Hall in *Pa. Gaz.*, June 6, 1765, repeated several times during the following months, directed all persons in Virginia owing money for the *Gazette* to make payment to "Messieurs Hunter and Glassel, Merchants in Fredericksburgh," who were furnished with the accounts and would give receipts. In some of the announcements the second name is spelled "Glassell."

46 Account of Money received by D.H. as
  charged in the Leidgers, from Aug. 22.
  1765. to Jan. 17. 1766. examin'd per JP.[2]   117 4 3
47 Account of Money received by D. Hall, for
  Books and Pamphlets, printed and sold in
  the Shop, from the Beginning to January
  18. 1766. as examin'd per J Parker   1118 14 4
48 Account of 2000 Primers printed by D.H.
  between March 1765. and February 1. 1766,
  at 2½d.[3]   20 16 8
49 Account of 4000 Catechisms,[4] (omitted
  before, chief Part unsold) at 4½   75 0 0
50 Account of Mr. Peters's Sermons sold by D.
  Hall, exclusive of those taken by the
  Academy[5]   14 11 4
51 Account for nine Half Sheets Dilworth's
  Spelling Books now done 2000, in Number
  (5 Half Sheets not done)[6]   83 6 8

2. This entry, which later puzzled BF because it is inadequately explained in the report, is a continuation of the account in entries 35 and 36.

3. Most of the standard bibliographies and works on the *New England Primer* list a 1765 edition by Franklin and Hall, apparently based on this entry in Parker's report, but without giving the precise title. No copy has been located.

4. At the back of the Franklin and Hall 1749 edition of Lord Bolingbroke's *Letters on the Spirit of Patriotism,* the printers advertised ten other recent publications, including *The Shorter Catechism of the Reverend Assembly of Divines* and Isaac Watts's *The Assembly's Catechism with Notes,* each retailing for 6d. Either one of these might be the work referred to here, or the entry might include both. The principal bibliographies list "A Catechism" published by Franklin and Hall in 1765, based on this entry in Parker's report, but without giving a precise title or locating a copy. The phraseology of this entry, however, suggests a large remainder of some earlier printing, though why so many copies should remain unsold in as large a center of Presbyterianism as Philadelphia cannot now be explained.

5. This entry probably refers to Richard Peters, *A Sermon on Education* (with which were included the Constitutions of the Academy and BF's "Idea of the English School," above, III, 421–8; IV, 101–8), published by Franklin and Hall in 1751.

6. Thomas Dilworth, *A New Guide to the English Tongue; in Five Parts* is listed by Evans (10284), Hildeburn (2210), and Campbell (727) as having been published by Hall in 1766, the first two with a notation, apparently taken from this entry in Parker's report, that 2000 copies were more than half printed at the time of the dissolution of the firm of Franklin and Hall.

52 Allowance for Sale of Votes, Laws, Indian Treaties, during the Partnership, (guess'd at)	200	0	0
53 Account for 9771 of Poor Richard's Almanacks for 1766,[7] at 4*d.*—and 1000 Pocket ditto, at 6*d.*	187	17	0
54 Account for a Pamphlet just printed, called Meditations, &c.[8] 500 done, but suppose one half may sell at 9*d.*	9	7	6
55 Account of printing Paper remaining in D.H.'s Hands, Feb. 1. 1766. with which the Partnership has been charged, exam'd per JP.	70	10	0
56 Account for 40 Ream of Waste Paper of Old News-papers &c. in D.H.'s Hands, as made out Jan. 22. 1766. exam'd per JP at 5*s.*	10	0	0
57 Account of Money received, from Jan. 17. 1766. to Feb 1. 1766. for News, Advertisements, the Leidgers, &c.	57	10	9
58 Allowance for 4400 of Moore's Almanacks[9] at 3½*d.* omitted above	64	3	4
	28266	0	3

NUMB. 2. [B-2][1]

Account of Paper furnished by B. Franklin, viz

59 638 Ream and 8 Quire of Propatria Size for Newspaper. From 1747/8. to Aug. 2. 1750, at 7*s. 6d.*	239	8	4
60 1475 Ream and 8 Quire of Demi. for Newspapers from Aug. 2. 1750. to January 1756 at 11*s.*	811	10	0

7. The use of the expression "for 1766" here establishes that the sales in entry 41 were of almanacs *for* the years noted, not of almanacs sold *during* those years.

8. [Thomas Letchworth], *A Morning and Evening's Meditation, or, A Descant on the Times. A Poem by T. L.* London, Printed. Philadelphia, Re-printed and Sold by B. Franklin, and D. Hall. 1766. It was advertised in *Pa. Gaz.*, Jan. 23, 1766, as "Just Published," and was the last book issued with the Franklin and Hall imprint.

9. See above, XII, 181 n.

1. This section was not included in Parker's first and second reports. In his letter of February 3 Parker said it was based on the work books.

61 178 Ream of Demi, for Almanacks from
     1752. to 1756. at 11s.   97 18 0
62 208 Ream of Pott—used for Primers, Sermons
     and Jerman's Almanacks—at 7s. 6d.   78   2 6
63 11 Ream 10 Quire of Law paper, for the
     Pocket Almanack at 10s.   5 16 0
64 192 Ream of Demi used in sundry Work, &c.
     at 11s.   105 12 0
65 70 Ream of Propatria Size, used in sundry
     Work at 7s. 6d.   26   5 0
66 21 Ream 2 Quire of Law-Paper used in
     sundry Work, &c. at 10s.   10 11 6
67 (All other Paper furnished by Mr. Franklin
     had been settled before with D.H. except
     some small Jobs, as Play-Bills &c. for
     which is allowd)   10   0 0
                                                              ————————
                                                             1385   3 4

NUMB. 3. [B-3]²

68 An Account of Books and Stationary, left in
     the Shop by B.F. at the Beginning of the
     Partnership, as examined by J Parker³   681   1 0
69 1754. June 17. Cash paid to D. Hall, by B
     Franklin, on Account, examin'd per JP   86   4 11
70 1758. June. A Bill of Exchange return'd by
     B F. to D.H.   162 10 0
71 A Ballance due to B F. on Th: Chalkley's
     Book as per Account in the Leidger, pag.
     326. examin'd per JP   15 15 10
72 1766. The Printing Materials an Account of
     which taken Jan. 27. 1766.⁴ and Valued by
     J Parker at   313 10 0
                                                    ——————————
                                                £1259   1 9

2. The first four entries in this section appeared in Parker's first report; entry 72 is new.

3. Only the first two pages of the account in this entry survive among the Franklin Papers, APS. They are briefly described above, III, 271, no. 4.

4. For Parker's detailed valuation of the printing materials, see above, pp. 60–3.

General Account

Contra   Cr.

73 By One Half of the above Sum from Numb. 1	14133	0	1½
74 By One Half of the Sum from Numb. 2	692	11	8
75 By the Whole of the Sum of the Account Numb. 3	1259	1	9
76 By Cash received by D.H. for Gazette and Sundries, before the Partnership began, and yet charged above in No. 1 of the Cr. side	123	2	1¼
77 By Do received by B.F. for Do. before the Partnership began, and yet charged in No. 3 of the Debtor side	92	13	3½
	16300	8	11¼
By Ballance due to David Hall, Feb. 1. 1766	993	11	6
	17294	0	5¼

Endorsed: Valuation between Franklin & Hall by J. Parker

[William Hall]: Account of Benjamin Franklin with the Estate of David Hall

AD: American Philosophical Society

After the partnership of Franklin and Hall had come to an end and James Parker had completed his examination of the books, as reported in the document immediately above, David Hall opened an account of his financial relations with his former partner. From time to time he sent Franklin a statement of the transactions shown in his records, but neither man seems to have made an attempt to settle the balance prior to Hall's death on Dec. 24, 1772. Following that event Hall's two sons, both trained in his shop, inherited his share in the printing firm of Hall and Sellers. The elder son, William, was then about seven weeks short of attaining his twenty-first birthday, sufficiently mature to carry his share of the business; David Hall, Junior, was not yet seventeen.

In January 1773 one of the sons—it must have been William—prepared a full record of the Franklin account as it then stood. It is printed here, immediately following Parker's final report of the partnership accounts, because its earliest entries involve the same date, Feb. 1, 1766, as that on which Parker signed his report, and because it carries forward without break the accounts between the former partners until the death of the junior member of what had been the firm of Franklin and Hall.

As customary in such accounts, this record consists of two columns, that on the left listing items for which Franklin was debited, that on the right those with which he was credited. The first entry in the debit column is for the £993 11s. 6d. which Parker's report had shown that Franklin owed to Hall. Twice during the period covered, William Hall struck a balance and entered a new amount due from Franklin (smaller each time) in the debit column. He did not strike a final balance after the date of his father's death, but it can easily be determined that, according to this account, Franklin still owed Hall's estate £459 6s. 2¼d.

Most of the debit entries relate to money paid out to Franklin, to his wife, or to others on his behalf. The credit entries are of two sorts: continuing payments of one half the income from the *Gazette*, the newspaper that, for all practical purposes, Franklin had founded in 1729 and in which he continued to claim rights; and payments of one half of all money belatedly received by Hall for printing work done during his partnership with Franklin.

Typographical considerations do not permit the printing of this account in parallel columns here, with the debit and credit entries belonging to each balance period placed side by side as in the manuscript. To show the two groups of entries for each of the three periods as closely together as possible, however, each debit segment is followed by the corresponding credit segment, and all are given italicized headings in brackets: [*Debit Column A*], [*Credit Column A*], [*Debit Column B*], etc.

The editors have found no records similar to this one for the later years. It appears that nothing was done to settle the account between Franklin and the Hall heirs during the twelve years that elapsed before Franklin returned to Philadelphia from France in 1785, for on March 5 of that year he wrote William Strahan, old friend of both the former partners, that when he got home in the following summer he would "have an old Account to settle there with the Family of our Friend Hall." Apparently the Hall sons had declined to recognize, as their father had done, Franklin's right to half the income from the *Gazette*, for Franklin told Strahan that there was "a particular Article of Importance, about which we were not agreed," but on which both parties wanted Strahan's opinion. That matter was "the Value of a Copy Right in an establish'd Newspaper," which Franklin described (with probably much exaggeration) as having had a circulation of 8,000 to 10,000 copies. He thought that a decision by Strahan about this publishing property would "be satisfactory to us both."[5] Strahan does not appear to have answered; he was probably in declining health, and he died about four months after Franklin wrote. The disagreement seems to have continued, for in the fall of 1789 Franklin asked James Parker's son-in-law, Gunning Bedford, to look for and send him the original partnership agreement between Franklin and Hall that he had left with Parker in 1764. That faithful friend had died in 1770. Franklin explained to Bedford that he had "now an urgent Occasion" for this document, almost certainly a reference to an attempted settlement of the issue with the Hall family.[6] Bedford found the paper and sent it to Franklin, Nov. 27, 1789,[7] but apparently nothing further was done in the matter of this long-standing account before Franklin, too, succumbed, five months later.

[February 1, 1766]

Benjamin Franklin Esqr; in account with the Estate of David Hall decd.

Dr.   *[Debit Column A]*

1766

Feby. 1.	To a Balance of Acct. due Decst. as per Mr. J.P. Settlement of this date See Letter Mar. 17, 1770.			993 11 6
	Sundries Sinc the above Settlement as per said Letter			
Mar. 8.	To Cash	£200 – –		
July 12	To Ditto	91 – –		
Novr. 25	To Ditto	50 – –		
Decr. 27	To Ditto	160 – –		
[176]8				
Jany. 8	To Ditto	100 – ·		
Sept. 1.	To Ditto	30 – –		
[176]9				
Mar. 16	To Ditto	45 – –		
	To Sundries out of the Shop	11 3 6½	687 3 6½	
			£1680 15 –½	

5. BF to Strahan, March 5, 1785, New York Pub. Lib. This was the last letter BF is known to have written Strahan.

6. BF to Gunning Bedford, Oct. 26, 1789, Lib. Cong.

7. Bedford to BF, Nov. 27, 1789, APS.

[Credit Column A] Cr.

1770

Feby. 16 By Your half of £1457
8s. Recd. for the Ga-
zette from Feby. 1st.   728 14 –
1766 to this Day

By your half of £318
5s. Recd. June 18,
1767 of Samuel   159 2 6
Preston Moore Esqr.[8]

By your half of Cash
Received for Work
done as Credited in
the Leidger in the   194 17 –½
above mentioned
Time Amounting to
£389 14s. 1d.

                                             1082 13 6½
Balance due this date and carried below   598 1 6

                                              £1680 15 –½

[Dr]   *[Debit Column B]*

1770

Mar. 16 To Balance brought down   598 1 6

1771[?]

Jany. 25. To Cash for purchasing a Bill of Exchange   £50 – –
for £30 – – Ster:

Augst. 16 To Cash pd. Balance
of an Acct. from the
Estate of the late Mr.   7 19 7½
William Branson[9]
against you by Order

8. Moore was provincial treasurer in 1767; this payment was probably for public printing. The editors have been unable to reconcile the figure given here with the total of various entries in the provincial accounts.

9. A well-to-do Philadelphia merchant.

	To my Part of Eleven years and three Quarts. Gazette discounted in Mr. Branson's Acct. against you	2	18	9	
Octr. 18	To Cash pd. Mrs. Franklin	24	–	–	
29	To Ditto pd. Robert Erwin by Mrs. Franklins Order	7	12	–	
Novr. 29	To Ditto pd. Mrs. Franklin for the purchasing a Lot of Ground for you of Mr. Parker	100	–	–	
	To Sundries had in the Shop	6	13	2	199 3 6½
					£797 5 –½

[*Credit Column B*]   [Cr.]

1772
Jany. 28   By your half of £358
13s. Recd. for the Ga-   179 6 6
zette from Feby. 17th.
1770 to this date
By your half of £183
17s. 10½d. Received
for Work done as
Credited in the   90 18 11¼
Leidger in the above
time mentioned
Amountg.   270 5 5¼
Balance due this date carried below   526 19 7¼
                                    £797 5 –½

[Dr.]   [*Debit Column C*]
1773
Jany. 28   To Balance brought down   526 19 7¼

103

[*Credit Column C*]   [Cr.]

1772
Decr. 31 By your half of £97
        0s. 10d. Recd. for the
        Gazette from Jany.
        28. to the 24 of Decr.   48 10 5
        following the time of
        my Fathers Decease
        By your half of £38
        6s. Receivd for Work
        done as Credited in
        the Ledgrs. in the   19 3   –
        above time mentioned   _____
        Amtg.   67 13 5

From James Parker

ALS (first and longer version): Columbia University Library; ALS (second and shorter version): New York Public Library

After completing his examination of the Franklin and Hall accounts and drawing up a report, James Parker wrote this letter to accompany one copy of the report he planned to send to Franklin by the New York packet. He then copied the first long paragraph that deals with the valuation of the printing materials and the account itself. This second version of the paragraph differs only trivially from the text as printed here. To this copied passage he added two much shorter paragraphs that repeat the substance of the second paragraph here, the mention of Foxcroft's journey to Virginia, and comment on the cold weather; he signed the second letter and then added a postscript repeating in essence, though not in phraseology, the first postscript here about Hall's employment of clerks. This second version of his letter he explained, he was leaving with Hall "to be sent with one Copy of the Accounts." Understandably, therefore, it does not include the three postscripts Parker wrote after returning to Burlington. Since this second version contains nothing not amply covered in the first version as printed here, except as noted below, and indeed omits nearly everything in it beyond what deals with the Franklin and Hall accounts and with Parker's and his son's ill health, it seems unnecessary to reprint any part of it here.

Honoured Sir   Philadelphia, Feb. 3. 1766.

This accompanies one Copy of the State of your Accounts with Mr. Hall, according to the best of my Skill and Judgment and the Quantity and State of the Printing Office:[1] And tho' I have endeavoured to mention every Thing as plainly as I could, yet possibly some Articles may need a little Explanation besides what is so set down: The Valuation of the Printing Materials seems smaller than I imagined it would be;[2] but as I examined all the Letter, and saw the whole weighed, I could not do otherways, for the greatest Part of the Letter is much worn; the Old Brevier fit for very little, and Mr. Hall purposes to throw it by as soon as he can, having got a new Fount himself already come over, to use in its Stead and indeed the Whole is worn much except the Double Pica and newest English, tho' neither of them are new. We weighed the Forms and Pages of Almanacks &c. with all the Rules in and about them, So that those Rules are charged in the Letter, the same as the Letter:[3] In weighing a Form we only took the Chace out of the Weight, and in Weighing the Letter in the Cases, we weighed two empty Cases first, and took their Weight always out of it. The Furniture and Rules not actually up in Forms, and weighed with the Letter, were but little and poor, and he must soon get himself more: One of the Presses is almost done its best, having been mended so often, as to be very patch'd and Shackled: On the Whole, I think I have valued it at what I thought was the Value of it, supposing no Advantage of one wanting to buy it or of one wanting to sell it, on either Side to be taken. Yet Mr. Hall says, if there be any Particulars in it, that you shall make Objection to, he is willing it should be rectified. With Respect to the Paper furnished by you he says, he had no other Rule to ascertain it, than by the Work-Books, which we carefully look'd over, and set down the Quantity used in every Job and News-paper.[4] As the Paper used for Publick Work before 1756, and sundry other Work, had

1. Above, pp. 87–99.

2. Above, pp. 60–3.

3. The parts of the almanacs that were reprinted unchanged from year to year were kept as standing type and not reset annually. C. William Miller, "Franklin's Type: Its Study Past and Present," APS *Proc.*, XCIX (1955), 426.

4. See B-2 of the report. In the document printed immediately below this one BF expressed the opinion (observation 13) that this was the proper procedure rather than that used for the accounts of paper furnished by Hall.

been settled and accounted for to you already, as by the Accounts he produced in your own Writing appears. Tho' we settled the Pocket Almanacks he sold at 6*d.* which is as he sold them whole-sale, yet he charges you with those sent to Rhode-Island but at 4*d.* which were part of those he charges himself at 6*d.* at.[5] The Money paid by him in England at sundry Times, as charged Sterl. we rekon'd Exchange at 170, as a Medium, as for some of that Money he gave above £180—and for some others, little more than 160,[6] And we have been as exact in reckoning every Thing as we possibly could. We had gone on very nigh finishing, when we recollected some of the Money, both of what you received, and what he had, was due to you before the Partnership began: This obliged us to have a new research, and a thorough new Examination of all the Books and Accounts, and discovered, that he had received the Sum of £246 4*s.* 2½*d.* of Money due to you before the Partnership began, which Sums being included already in the Articles of Numb. 1, on the Credit side, where by you are credited for One half of it, we Credited the other Half at the Bottom of the General Account, being £123 2*s.* 1¼*d.*[7] Again, we found of the Sums you had received, the Sum of £185 6*s.* 7*d.*, which belonged to you before the Partnership began, and as you had been charged with Half of that Sum in No. 3. Debtor side, so we have Credited the General Account for that other Half being £92 13*s.* 3½*d.*[8] This we thought the most eligible Way, as we had already enter'd, and cast up the Whole before: On your Considering this Matter, I think you will find this to be the right, and perhaps the best that could be, to set such blended Accounts in the clearest Light. There are some of the Books and Pamphlets printed in the Partnership unsold, some of which he has taken to himself, and allowed for them,[9] but some others which don't appear saleable, he has left, and if hereafter any of them sells, he will account for them: And upon the Whole, if any Mistake or Error shall be here-after discovered on either Side, he is willing it Should be rectified. If you should return home this Spring or Summer, you can examine

5. Entries 41 and 4 of the report; see also BF's observation on entry 4.
6. Entry 2 of the report, on which BF also commented in his "Observations."
7. Entry 76.
8. Entry 77.
9. Probably allowed for in entry 47.

any Thing you shall think wrong yourself: as I shall leave the final Passing of them, till I hear from you, or such Return to do it yourself.[1]

My last to you was from Burlington, the End of last December, and beginning of January.[2] I came down here, tho' scarce able to crawl,[3] the 16th Instant. I continued all the rest of the Month to proceed on with the Accounts, whenever I was able to stir, tho' I had a Relapse, or rather only an Increase of the Pain, a few Days after I came, that rendered me unable to walk for three Days, and am still but very poorly. I hope to be able to get back again to Burlington, as it is not comfortable to be sick from home, nor there neither, if it could be help'd. I have now been in the Joint three Months,[4] and have had it some Days in the Heart and Stomach so bad, I thought I could not live: My Son [has] been sick above three Months—and he is but poorly yet, tho' he is mending, and likely to get well: on the Whole, this Year past has been a distressed one with me. But God's Will be done.

Mr. Foxcroft is gone to Virginia, and I have not heard any Thing from him since his Departure: I wish I may hear from you, before the End of this Month, where I am to put the Printing-Materials of B. Mecom's that are now in Burlington:[5] I have no body there at Work, all my Boys being gone to New York and Woodbridge: and indeed, I have no Work for them to do, if they were there: I would immediately away to New York now, were I able to travel at any Rate but I even fear, I shall hardly be able to get back to Burlington only, as the Weather is uncomfortable:[6] but I will go assoon as I can. I think I wrote you before, I had secured the Goods you sent to Mr. Hughes, but they are unopen'd,

1. The other version concludes this paragraph: "or such Return enables you to do it yourself. (So far I copied from one to go per Packet.)"

2. Dec. 20, 1765, and Jan. 4–12, 1766; above, XII, 407–10, and this volume, 10–18.

3. In the other version of this letter Parker replaced "crawl" with "creep." Either way, it appears to have been a difficult, if short, journey.

4. Parker apparently meant that the gout had been afflicting his joints for three months. In the other version he does not mention the location of his pain.

5. On these printing materials, see above, XII, 87.

6. As in many ailments affecting the skeletal system, Parker's affliction was doubtless particularly distressing in inclement weather.

as I would be there myself.[7] I wrote also to Balfour, which I enclosed to you, and hope you will have received it: I don't know any Thing further material about Affairs wherein I am concerned. And those relating to the Publick you will doubtless have from abler and better Hands. I wrote to B. Mecom lately, but had but a short Answer that he would soon send me the Account &c. I have wrote again—But—I fear nothing can quicken his Sluggishness. I have told Holt[8] I intend to come to New York, and take my Printing Office again: I don't know what he designs: he keeps it secret from me: I heard the Gentlemen of Virginia were trying to get a new Printer, in Opposition to Mr. Royle,[9] because he declined going on, or was too much under the Influence of the Governor there: and as Green and Rind are parted, I imagine Rind is the Man,[1] and that they have bought the Office, that was Stretch's,[2] which by an Invoice I saw of it, was very compleat and good, so that if it be so, it will be bad for Billy Hunter, whether Royle lives or dies: It was reported Royle grew worse after his Return home but as we have not heard lately from thence, I can't say no more about it, and doubtless you will hear from thence from Mr. Foxcroft soon, who can give you a better Account of the Matter.

As I am necessarily to send you two Copies of the Accounts, &c. so another to the same Purpose as this, I shall leave in Mr. Hall's Hands to be forwarded to you with them. Therefore I think

7. On Parker's difficulties with Hugh Hughes of New York and John Balfour of Edinburgh (mentioned in the next sentence), see above, pp. 10–14.

8. John Holt, Parker's former associate, now independently active as a printer in New York.

9. Joseph Royle, who was carrying on William Hunter's printing office in Williamsburg for the benefit of Hunter's son Billy. His *Virginia Gazette* was taken over towards the end of 1765 by Alexander Purdy (sometimes spelled Purdie), who was joined in June 1766 by John Dixon, and Royle died in the early spring of that year. Clarence S. Brigham, *History and Bibliography of American Newspapers 1690–1820* (Worcester, 1947), II, 1159.

1. William Rind was a former apprentice of Jonas Green in Annapolis, Md., and briefly his partner there in 1765. In 1766 Rind moved to Williamsburg and in May started *Rind's Virginia Gazette,* the title of which he confusingly changed to *Virginia Gazette* in the fall of the same year, so that two newspapers with the same name were simultaneously published in the same town. Brigham, *American Newspapers,* II, 1161; Isaiah Thomas, *The History of Printing in America* (Albany, 1874 edit.), I, 321, 335-6; II, 164.

2. Not identified.

I can add no more, than all Respects &c. from Your most obliged
Servant   JAMES PARKER.[3]

PS. Mr. Hall made some Demands for hiring a Clerk: He says he
hired one at your Particular Request at one Time: that he had one
constantly from 1753: and for 18 Months two of 'em: never less
than 20s. a Week, and great Part of the Time 25.[4] He also must
keep one Still, to draw out Accounts and get in the Money due,
and thinks Part of the Expence should be yours: As the Articles
were silent on that Head, and my Power did not extend so far, I
could only refer it to you: Two Iron Fire places of yours are left,
and he having a Year or two ago, purchased two Cannon Stoves,
he keeps them himself as he bought them with his own Money.

Burlington, Feb. 10. I got as well home here as I expected: the
Gout not quite left me yet. As soon as my Strength will admit, I
shall set forward for NewYork: No Packet come in yet tho' momentarily expected: I shall send down B. Mecom's Printing Office
to Philadelphia, immediately, as Mrs. Franklin says she will see
Care taken of it.

Feb. 11.[5] I just now heard Mr. Holt has had an Execution levied
on his Goods: he does not tell me so himself, but I have heard it,
and fear its too true: I believe I shall be a far greater Loser by
him, than you were by B. Mecom: Its an easy Thing to behave
with Fortitude, when all goes generally well: But I must exert it
notwithstanding all may go against me: and indeed, I know I
can't command Success in my Affairs, but as far as Resignation,
and a Steady Diligence could deserve it, I have endeavoured it: I
have supported others and almost Starv'd myself: but I am thankful its no worse, and will still say, God's Will be done.

3. For this paragraph and closing the other version substitutes: "This is
wrote to be left with Mr. Hall to be sent with one Copy of the Accounts, as I
am to send another per Packet: therefore I shall add no more at present, but
with all Respects remain your most obliged Servant JAMES PARKER."
4. At the equivalent point of his statement of this matter in the other version Parker added: "and he took Mr. Jones the last Time at the Request of
Mr. Franklin." This Jones was possibly the ne'er-do-well Lewis Jones, formerly apprenticed to Parker and later employed by Hugh Gaine in New York;
above, x, 343–8.
5. Parker dealt with the subject matter of this and the next postscript at
tedious length in later letters. No editorial amplification seems necessary here.

Feb 20. Last Night heard the Packet was come in, but no Letter for me, so I now attempt to close: I am still poorly with this wretched Gout, or rather now a real Rheumatism, as it takes all my Bones. Hope only remains at the Bottom of the Box. I long for my Health to go to New York, but I must submit.

One Thing I forgot to mention, I must now note. One Box of Goods sent to Mr. Hughes came by Capt. Tillet, this I suppose is the Stationary: this I have in my Store at NewYork, but I have Advice of another come in Capt. Berton, which I suppose is the Electrical Machine: but as you have never sent a Bill of Lading for it either to Mr. Hughes or me, Capt. Berton won't deliver it without a Bill of Lading tho' I sent him Word I would indemnify him: so he keeps it in his Possession, and I cannot demand it without a Bill. &c.

All Mecom's Materials are sent down to Philadelphia. Adieu.[6]

Observations on Mr. Parker's State of the Account

AD: Haverford College Library

This undated document is placed here for convenience because it relates so closely to Parker's final report on the accounts between Franklin and Hall, Feb. 1, 1766 (above, pp. 87–99), and his letter of February 3 about that report (immediately above). Franklin could hardly have received the report and letter before the middle of March 1766, but they had reached him by April 6, as he told Parker in a letter of that date, now lost, that Parker acknowledged on June 11 (below, p. 300). Franklin had probably prepared these "Observations" by May 19, when he wrote Hall a letter, also now lost, raising a few of the questions indicated here. Hall replied on Aug. 19, 1766, acknowledging that letter and answering some of the questions asked (below, pp. 380–1).

From time to time in later correspondence the former partners alluded to matters to be found in these "Observations," and Hall asked for a copy of the entire document. Franklin promised to send it, but seems not to have done so at any time before Hall died the day before Christmas 1772. In fact, as indicated in the headnote to the account between Franklin and the Hall estate (above, p. 101), there seems to have been no

6. The other version has an address page inscribed "For / Benjamin Franklin Esqr. / Craven Street / London" and an almost illegible endorsement reading "Mr Parker's Letter about the State[?] of [the Printing?] Office."

final settlement of the account during the lifetime of any of the people directly concerned: James Parker, David Hall, and Franklin himself.

In considering these "Observations" reference should be had to the entry numbers added to the copy of the Parker account as printed above.

[Undated]
Observations on Mr. Parker's State of the Account between B F. and D Hall. Referring to the Articles as Numbred with Red Ink

No. 1. Article 1. Query, May not this Article contain Sums paid on Accounts settled, as Receipts were given on such Settlements, and the Sums then paid ought not to be brought into this Account.

2. Mr. Parker writes that the Exchange was settled at a Medium Rate. But the real Rate of Exchange is the best to settle this Article at, Mr. Hall can easily find what he paid for the Bills he sent me. If not, the Price of Bills at the Time each Bill was sent, may easily be known from any Merchant's Books. Mr. H. in his Letters frequently mention'd to me the Rate of Exchange.[7]

3. What is the meaning of Cash *lent?* When does the Account mention'd in this Article begin?

4. If the Almanacks sent to Rhodeisland are charg'd to me, which indeed I gave away as I us'd to do before the Partnership and never receiv'd any Pay for; then I ought to be allow'd for the Copy of the Almanacks which cost me Money, besides a good deal of Trouble of my own. And to which Copy I still have the Right.[8]

---

7. In his letter of explanation (immediately above) Parker told BF that he and Hall had taken the exchange rate for Hall's remittances to England at £170 Pa. currency for £100 sterling "as a Medium." Examination of Hall's letters accompanying these remittances (printed in vols. VII-X, above) shows that he mentioned the exchange rate for about two-thirds of the bills he sent. The average rate for the bills so described is just over £161 Pa. currency per £100 sterling involved. Probably, therefore, BF had been somewhat overcharged in the account.

8. This entry in the report covered *Poor Richard Almanacks* and *Pocket Almanacks* for the years 1752 through 1761. BF had prepared printer's copy for the first seven issues of *Poor Richard,* Hall for the last three. Almost cer-

5. —
6. Is there Credit given for Noetica's sold? Are there none remaining?
7. Examine Mr. Hunter's Account to see if these were ever charg'd to him.
8. —
9. Let this be charg'd to Post Office Account £11 3s. 6d.
10. —
11. Enquire of Mr. Strahan about this Payment of £82 8s. 6d. sterl. to see if it was on Account of Sally's Books.
12. Do. Copy these two Articles.
No. 2. 13. The Account of Paper should be taken from the Work book as mine was, and not from Papermakers Receipts.[9]
14. Lampblack is one of the Incidentals as well as Oil or Ink.[1] As there is no Article for Oil, I suppose it comes under the next Head of
15. Incidentals. What do they consist of, that they amount to £584 1s. 2½d. besides what is in the next Article
16. Ink, and *English Papers*. Quy. if the latter ought to be charg'd?
17. More Incidentals. What were they? £18 5s. 11d.
18. This Article like No. 13. should be made out from the Work Books, not from Receipts.
19. —[*Added later in this space in different ink:* Sent Mr. Hall

---

tainly BF had paid some mathematically inclined person (such as Thomas Godfrey during earlier years) to prepare the astronomical and other data for these almanacs by use of one of the available printed Ephemerides that gave calculations for several years ahead; these tables could be converted mathematically for application to a particular locality. Here and in the general observations at the end of this paper BF showed his belief that the basic rights in the almanacs belonged to him, not to the partnership.

9. In his explanatory letter Parker said that Hall "had no other Rule to ascertain" the value of the paper BF had supplied (shown in the report as "B-2") than by the work books, though in the account of paper supplied by Hall ("A-2") they had used the papermakers' receipts and vouchers. BF appears to have preferred use of the work books in both instances.

1. The partnership agreement had provided that "all Charges for Paper, Ink, Balls, Tympans, Wool, Oil, and other Things necessary to Printing, together with the Charge of all common and necessary Repairs of the Press and its Appurtenances" should be shared equally by the partners. BF was displeased at the somewhat unsystematic way in which these expenses were shown in entries 14–17 in the report.

20. — 300 Post the second Journals.—and some of the first.²]
No. 3. 21. What Printing Work? Was it not such as was settled?
22. —
23. —
24. Receiv'd by B.F. was this Sum? or received by D.H. and paid
  by him to B F. on Gazette Account? £448 10s. 3d.
25. Has Ramsey paid the rest?
Gen. Acct. 26.
27.
28.
2d Page. No. 1. 29.⎫ Was not the Old Body of Votes printed before
         30.⎬1756?³ How is that Work settled? Are there
            ⎭ not a great Number unsold?
31. —
32. This Article should extend to Jan. 26. 1766. See below Art. 45.
33.⎫The Sum of these two Articles seems very low. Is there no
34.⎭Mistake? Is there not some great Omission. The single Advertisements, Blanks, and other Jobbs, are chiefly ready Pay, and
  do not by this Account amount to more than £27 per Ann.
35. —
36. This Article ends Aug. 22. 1765, should be extended to Jan.
  26. 66.⁴

2. This comment is entered in the space made available by the absence of
comment on entries 19 and 20 and has no relevance to them. BF was referring
to the two journals by Christian Frederick Post on his mission to the Ohio
Indians in 1758, the first of which Strahan printed for BF as an appendix to
Charles Thomson's *Enquiry* in 1759 and the second of which he printed
separately in the same year. BF sent 225 copies of the first work to Hall and
300 of the second; above, VIII, 199–200, 298 n, 322, 453.

3. BF probably had in mind *Votes and Procedures of the House of Representatives of Pennsylvania, Beginning the Fourth Day of December, 1682. Volume
the First. In Two Parts.* Franklin and Hall, 1752 (Evans, 6908; Hildeburn,
1284; Campbell, 499); *[Ibid.] Beginning the Fourteenth Day of October, 1707.
Volume The Second.* Franklin & Hall, 1753 (Evans, 7087; Hildeburn, 1333;
Campbell, 515); *[Ibid.] Beginning the Fourteenth Day of October, 1726. Volume The Third.* Franklin and Hall, 1754 (Evans, 7286; Hildeburn, 1387; Campbell, 530); and possibly *Laws of the Government of New-Castle, Kent and Sussex, Upon Delaware. Published by Order of the Assembly.* Franklin and Hall,
1752 (Evans, 6835; Hildeburn, 1252; Campbell, 486).

4. As explained above, p. 96 n, additions carrying entries 35 and 36 down
to Jan. 17, 1766, appear in Parker's report as entry 46, but without being fully
identified there.

1766

37.
38.
39. —
40. —
41. Almanacks
42. Primers
43. Blanks, Query, how were they valued, how much per Quire?
44. Gazette
45. Advts.
46. On what Account is this Money received?[5]
47. What Books and Pamphlets?
48. Primmers. Quy. the Paper.⎫
49. Cats. Quy. Paper.   ⎬Are these reckond Paper and all.
51. Has not Dilworth been printed several times before?[6]
52. Was the Sale of the Body of Laws all Accounted for?[7]⎫left
    Quy. Testaments and Pamelas.[8]   ⎭
53.
54. —
55. See Article 18. near £500's worth of Paper per Ann.
58. Quy. the meaning of this Article? Moore's Alm[anac]s.[9] If sold
    for B.F. are they accounted for?

5. See the note immediately above.

6. BF had published what appears to have been the first American edition of Thomas Dilworth's *New Guide to the English Tongue* in 1747 (Evans, 1783 note), and five later editions by other printers are listed, but no others by BF, Franklin and Hall, or Hall alone are listed until the unfinished edition of 1766 cited in entry 51 of Parker's report.

7. *A Collection of All the Laws Of the Province of Pennsylvania: Now in Force. Published by Order of Assembly* (Phila., B. Franklin, 1742).

8. The mention here of "Testaments" may possibly be a reference to BF's 1744 printing of *The New-England Psalter; or Psalms of David,* with which were included the Proverbs of Solomon and the Sermon on the Mount (Evans, 5334; Hildeburn 888; Campbell, 300). None of the standard bibliographies list any English-language Testaments printed in the colonies before 1777, yet the list of books BF turned over to Hall in 1748 includes "15 Testaments Philadelphia Printing," valued at 1s. 6d. each. The same list includes 44 copies of *Pamela,* undoubtedly a reference to BF's 1744 edition of Samuel Richardson's *Pamela; or Virtue Rewarded.* Whatever "Testaments" BF may have had in mind, therefore, they were probably accounted for, as were the *Pamelas,* as part of the books for which Parker's report gave credit to BF in entry 68.

9. The editors are unable to clarify the uncertainty here.

114

No. 2 [*bracketed together with single comment:*] 59 60 61 62 63 65 66
67 Examine these Articles. They make the whole Quantity
of Paper us'd in 8 Years, while I found it, to amount only
to £1385 3s. 4d. which is but £173 per ann. See Article 55.
[*Added comment on 63:*] I think Pocket Almanacks used to be done
on fine Post.[1] Quy.
No. 3. Art. 68. Does this Account include Pensa. Law Books and
Newcastle with Testaments, Pamelas, Common Prayers, &c.[2]
69. Query the Nature of this Article, and on what Occasion.
70. Was Damages receiv'd.
71.
72. Flowrs cost 5s. Sterl. per lb. Book Press, the Screw worth
much more. Chaces too low. Several other Articles Ditto.
particularly Presses.
Gen. Acct. 73
74
75
76
77
Gen. Observations[3]
    No Valuation of my Copy Right to Poor Richard's Almanack
    Book and Pocket.
    No Valuation of my Copy Right to the establish'd Gazette.
    No Computation of the outstanding Debts, or Offer made for
    them.

1. Post paper, a sheet measuring 16 by 20 inches, is so called because it was
originally watermarked with a postman's horn.
2. The two surviving pages of the list of books BF turned over to Hall in
1748 include Testaments and *Pamelas*, as indicated in a previous note, but do
not include compilations of Pennsylvania or Delaware laws or the *Votes and
Proceedings*. These may have appeared on pages of the list that have been lost.
3. The final figures in Parker's report may have come as something of a
shock to BF, indicating as they did that he owed Hall almost £1000. As these
"General Observations" and some later correspondence show, BF believed
that he had unlisted offsetting claims of substantial value. He had what he
called his "Copy Right" to the almanacs and the *Gazette*, publishing properties
of importance that he had brought to the partnership and on which the income was to be evenly divided between Hall and himself during the continuance of the firm. If, as it appears, both men understood that Hall was to
continue to publish the almanacs and newspaper under his own name in the
future, BF felt that a "Valuation" should be put down to his credit in the ac-

[*Added in different ink:*] No Account of the Sale of 500 Reviews of the Constitution of Pensilvania, an 8vo of 5s. Sterl. sent. to Mr. Hall for Sale in July 1759.[4]

Endorsed: B. Franklin's Remarks on the Account settled by Mr. Parker. between Franklin & Hall

From Deborah Franklin

AL (incomplete)[5]: American Philosophical Society

[February 5–8? 1766][6]

[*First part missing*] as I am a lone [*torn*] down to Chat a littel with you all thow I have not aney thing extray[ordinary to say. I] have

---

count for the rights he would be surrendering to Hall, otherwise that some entry should be included to show his entitlement to a share in future income from these publications. The outstanding debts due to the firm, he felt, should also be shown, since he was entitled to one half of all that should later be paid, or else Hall should make some "Offer" for them if he was to keep all he might be able to collect. As the account with Hall's estate (above, pp. 99–104) shows, Hall did credit half the income of the *Gazette* and half the debts he collected during his lifetime to the reduction of his claim against BF, but he never credited his former partner with any income from *Poor Richard* or the *Pocket Almanack* in later years. What similar credit, if any, Hall's sons may ultimately have been willing to allow BF remains unknown.

4. Richard Jackson's *An Historical Review of the Constitution and Government of Pensylvania*, of which BF sent Hall 500 copies for local sale, but which Hall reported were selling very poorly; above, VIII, 292 n, 360–2, 402–3, 448.

5. Some words near the end are lost by a tear in the MS; they have been supplied from a partial reprinting of the letter in [William Duane, ed.], *Letters to Benjamin Franklin, from His Family and Friends. 1751–1790* (N.Y., 1859), pp. 21–3.

6. This letter can be dated by its references to James Parker's staying at BF's house for three weeks and to DF's advancing Samuel Rhoads £20 "this day" to pay a "Bricklair." From Parker's letter to BF of Feb. 3, 1766, we know that he came to Philadelphia to work on BF and Hall's accounts on Jan. 16, 1766, so that if he had been at BF's house for exactly three weeks and departed the day before this letter was written—DF said he left "yisterday morning"—the letter could be dated Feb. 7, 1766. As for DF advancing Rhoads £20 "this day" to pay a bricklayer, in Rhoads' accounts for building BF's house, kept by his son (see above, XI, 456), there is an entry, Feb. 6, 1766, of a payment of £20 by Rhoads to two of his employees for work done on BF's "Well Little House &c.," the "Little House" apparently meaning the "pente houses" whose completion DF mentions in this letter. Therefore, if DF advanced Rhoads

had Parker hear for 3 weeks under a viloant fitt of the Goute in [the limbs] and the Stumack he ses his harte I say it was the stamp ackte or the illnes of his Son but be it as it will he is better and went home yisterday morning. Indead he has had a sad time of it[7] in dead I can assure you and so I was a going to say but I ad no more than that thank God I am as well as yousual. Brother Petter I think is verey poorly[8] but as he is a dockter he Cures himselef maney times a day but look very miserabel in dead so that everey bodey that sees him telles me hough he looks. I was told within this week that he was un well. I wente over. he was in his chamber I wente up to see him. He wondered aney bodey Cold say that he was un well and began to administer or subscribe to me I sed I wished he wold be advise by me and live like me and look like my Papey and me but his knoledg is so superer to mine I Cold not porswaid him to follow my advise but to be as serious as I Can I never saw but only Mr. Kinersly look like him sense I knew aney thing. If he donte recover soon it is over with him. Sister[9] is verey well. Our poor Mrs. Smith Contineus verey ill still 15 or 17 weeks since shee was first taken ill and shee is not like to get beter.[1]

So far I wrote and then had the pleshuer of a visit from Mr. and Mrs. [*illegible*] thair marreyed Dafter Mrs. Rhodes the younger and Miss Rhodes.[2] Laste night Mr. Rhodes Came to see me he wanted twenty pounds for the Bricklair. I sent it to him this day.

---

the money the same day he paid his workmen, the present letter can be dated Feb. 6, 1766. Thus it appears to have been written on either Feb. 6 or Feb. 7, 1766, give or take a day or so.

7. In his letter of Feb. 3, 1766 Parker related that he had been ill for three months, his son for nearly four.

8. In her letter of Jan. 12, 1766, DF had remarked that Peter Franklin's physical appearance was distressing, he being, with Ebenezer Kinnersley, as thin as any man she had ever seen. On Peter's pretensions to medical knowledge, BF observed in 1763 that he was "touch'd a little in his Head with something of *the Doctor,* of which I hope to cure him." See above, X, 392.

9. Peter's wife, Mary Harman Franklin (C.9).

1. Mrs. Mary "Goody" Smith died, March 22, 1766; see below, p. 198.

2. The indecipherable name is a short one, of about four letters. Commas should probably have been inserted after the name and after "Dafter." The former of the two Rhoads women was apparently Sarah Pemberton Rhoads, whom Samuel Rhoads, Jr., married on June 27, 1765; the latter was Samuel Rhoads, Sr.'s, younger daughter, Hannah, who never married. *PMHB,* XIV (1890), 421; XIX (1895), 71.

He will write to you and tell you hough it is for my memery is not safe boute the pente houses is don.[3] I paid above tin poundes for shingeles and sume other thinges. So you see that when a house is dun thair is much to be dun after. I shold be glad if we Cold get the well duge but I am afraid it will not be dun this seson all thow I am told the awarde[4] is finish but it is seled up tell the Corte but when that is to be I no not so I Cante tel [*torn*] to due so I due nothing only I have had all the rubig of the lime Conveyed [to the farm] and sente Gorge to spred it over the pastur[5] with what ashes we have ma[de. Gorge is] for my [planting] an orchord at paster but we difer in senteyments [then he is] for my giting worke men and masonry to buld a bridg over the [run as it] will be more [easy] to [step] over. We difer in that all so indead his marraig [is of no] servis to him nor aney one eles but one thing I beleve thair is like to [be no] more Gorges which is sume Comforte to me. I ad no more on that [head.] Salley is gon to the Assembley to danse with a friend of Mager Smalls[6] so I have had my letter readey be for the packit Comes in as thair is not time to writ when he dus Come as the stay is verey shorte. [*Remainder missing.*]

[*In the margin of the last paragraph:*] this was wrote two weeks a go.

"A Lover of Britain":
Preface to Three Letters to William Shirley

Printed in *The London Chronicle*, February 6–8, 1766.

In the issue of Feb. 6–8, 1766, the *London Chronicle* printed three letters Franklin had written to Governor William Shirley of Massachusetts twelve years earlier, together with an introductory letter that Verner W.

3. They had been still unfinished in October 1765; above, XII, 298.

4. The award evidently concerned judgment on the title to a lot adjacent to BF's property on the west; see above, XII, 166–7 n. Apparently the Franklin well was going to be dug close to this boundary and DF wanted to clear the matter with the rightful owners before proceeding.

5. George was BF's Negro servant. For BF's pasture on Hickory Lane, see above, II, 310.

6. For Major John Small of the 42nd Royal Highlanders, who had carried to England the news of Bouquet's successful expedition against the western Indians in the fall of 1764, see above, XII, 42 n. The major's friend has not been identified, although he was probably a fellow army officer.

Crane has identified as being also written by Franklin.[7] His letters to Shirley, Dec. 3, 4, 22, 1754, have been printed earlier in this edition in their appropriate chronological positions, above, V, 443, 443–4, 449–51. In so far as they were a critique of an alternative to the Albany Plan of Union,[8] they would have aroused only academic interest in 1766. But since they also had the effect of refuting contemporary aspersions on both America and Franklin, they were of immediate interest to newspaper readers in both Britain and the colonies and were widely reprinted. They put publicly on record Franklin's repeated earlier expressions of opposition to proposals that Parliament tax the unrepresented American colonists. Having taken this position in 1754, he was able to deny the contentions of later critics, mentioned in the introductory letter, that American opposition to parliamentary taxation had developed only after the French were expelled from Canada and after the passage of the Sugar Act. Furthermore, by citing his position in 1754, he and his friends were able to refute charges raised in Pennsylvania that he was not averse to parliamentary taxation and had in fact been the author of the Stamp Act. As Joseph Galloway wrote in a covering note[9] to the republication of two of the letters in *Pennsylvania Gazette*, May 15, 1766, proof was now available that Franklin's "Sentiments, respecting Parliamentary Taxation of the Colonies, have been uniformly the same, for many Years past; and that he has been one of the first and warmest Advocates against it."

SIR,   [February 8, 1766]

IN July 1754, when from the encroachments of the French in America on the lands of the crown, and the interruption they gave to the commerce of this country among the Indians, a war was apprehended, commissioners from a number of the colonies met at Albany, to form a PLAN of UNION for their common defence.[1] The plan they agreed to was in short this; "That a grand council should be formed, of members to be chosen by the assemblies and sent from all the colonies; which council, together with a governor general to be appointed by the crown, should be empowered to

7. Crane, *Letters to the Press*, pp. 60–3. The present editors agree with this identification.

8. For the nature of this alternative plan, described at some length in the present letter, see above, V, 442.

9. Crane, at any rate, assumed that the author of this note, who signed himself "G. J.," was Galloway. See Crane, *Letters to the Press*, p. 61.

1. For BF's role at the Albany conference and in the formulation of the Plan of Union, see above, V, 335–8, 344–55, 357–64, 364–92, 397–417.

make general laws to raise money in all the colonies for the defence of the whole." This plan was sent to the government here for approbation: had it been approved and established by authority from hence, English America thought itself sufficiently able to cope with the French, without other assistance; several of the colonies having alone in former wars withstood the whole power of the enemy, unassisted not only by the mother country, but by any of the neighbouring provinces. The plan however was not approved here: but a new one was formed instead of it, by which it was proposed, that "the Governors of all the colonies, attended by one or two members of their respective councils, should assemble, concert measures for the defence of the whole, erect forts where they judged proper, and raise what troops they thought necessary, with power to draw on the treasury here for the sums that should be wanted; and the treasury to be reimbursed by a tax laid on the colonies by act of parliament." This new plan being communicated by Governor Shirley to a gentleman of Philadelphia, then in Boston, (who hath very eminently distinguished himself, before and since that time, in the literary world, and whose judgment, penetration and candor, as well as his readiness and ability to suggest, forward, or carry into execution every scheme of publick utility, hath most deservedly endeared him not only to our fellow subjects throughout the whole continent of North-America, but to his numberless friends on this side the Atlantic)[2] occasioned the following remarks from him, which perhaps may contribute in some degree to its being laid aside. As they very particularly show the then sentiments of the Americans on the subject of a parliamentary tax, *before* the French power in that country was subdued, and *before* the late restraints on their commerce, they satisfy me, and I hope they will convince your readers, contrary to what has been advanced by some of your correspondents, that those particulars have had no share in producing the present opposition to such a tax, nor in the disturbances occasioned by it; which these papers indeed do almost prophetically foretell. For this purpose, having accidentally fallen into my hands, they are communicated to you by one who is, not *partially,* but in the *most enlarged sense,* A LOVER OF BRITAIN.

2. Crane suggests that William Strahan probably added this encomium on BF. See *Letters to the Press,* p. 60.

From Thomas Crowley[3]

ALS: American Philosophical Society

Worthy Friend   Grace Church Street 8 feb 1766

Subsequent to our Conversation at or near the House of Commons, I was informd by one of the Committee[4] that he had been informd that I was the author of the Paragraph inserted in the Gazetteer 1 feb:[5] alledging that "by a Calculation of an Eminent American Merchant it appears that the whole Taxes in all the American Provinces, do not amount, upon an Average to more than eight pence per head on every individual person including, men, Women and Children whereas the Taxes to pay the Interest only of Money spent in great Brittain to defend America, amounts to twelve shillings per Annum on every individual in great Brittain." However the two annual sums may possibly have been somehow pickd, up in Conversation I cannot say; but I had no hand at all in such advertisement,[6] nor dont know, nor can guess,

3. Thomas Crowley (d. 1787?) was a scion of an English Quaker family long important in the iron trade. Crowley himself was apparently involved in exporting bar iron to America, although he quit the business by 1775. His relations with his co-religionists were most unsatisfactory; he was described as a "vexer of the brethen," his writings were "disapproved and testified against," and he was finally disowned by the meeting. Crowley deeply interested himself in the dispute between America and the mother country and in numerous letters to the newspapers tirelessly promoted the idea of a union between the two parts of the empire, based on equitable American representation in Parliament. The idea of a British-American union apparently became an obsession with him and in 1773 BF pronounced him "a little cracked upon the subject," a diagnosis which WF had made four years earlier. A selection of his letters on America and a variety of other subjects were collected and published (apparently by himself) in London in 1776 under the title of *Letters and Dissertations on Various Subjects.* On Crowley, see Norman Penney, ed., *Pen Pictures of London Yearly Meeting 1789–1833* (London, 1930), p. 111; Joseph Smith, *A Descriptive Catalogue of Friends Books* (2 Vols., London, 1867), I, 496–500; M. W. Flinn, *Men of Iron The Crowleys in the Early Iron Industry* (Edinburgh, 1962), pp. 74, 114–16; WF to BF, Jan. 31, 1769, APS; BF to WF, Sept. 1, 1773, Lib. Cong.

4. A committee of London merchants interested in the North American trade which was working for the repeal of the Stamp Act. Crowley was apparently a member.

5. The following paragraph also appeared in *London Chron.*, Jan. 30-Feb. 1, 1766.

6. In *London Chron.*, Feb. 20–22, 1766, Crowley, writing over his customary nomme de plume, "Amor Patriae," formally denied that he had inserted the

who put it in or Caused it to be so advertised, nor did I ever think or breach such insidious, unjustifiable Doctrine and I may add was never capable of such absurd Conduct. So much I have thought but necessary to prevent any unjust imputation, so far as it may happen to reach Your notice and while I have my pen in hand suffer me to say or Repeat That I think it highly behoves every Agent and Every particular of the Committee of Merchants to very Maturely Consider the Danger of Miscarrying in the Grand Point, if what the Ministry may deem unbecoming objections should be raised against Conciliating Measures, which do avowedly tend to answer both purposes of Saving the Honour of the Supreme Legislative power, and also of Saving the Right Claimd by the Colonies of not being Taxed without their Consent. I am ever for *Moderation* as being far the most likely means to produce *Reconciliation,* than allegations tenacious of Rigid Right does ever produce especially in Cases in their nature of a disputable kind—and not Capable of being in its utmost extent exercised fully in favour of either side, without prejudice to the other.

May therefore Every one whose Station and Abilities has in some degree made Arbiter of the Measures necessary to bring about the desireable end of Reconciliation, lend forth a hand of Aid, in that *Great, Good, and salutary Work.* I am very respectfully Your assurd ready Friend and Servant   THO CROWLEY

Addressed: To | Benja. Franklin Esqr | Prest

---

foregoing paragraph in the *Gazetteer* and requested the reader not to confuse it with a "scheme on the same subject inserted in the *Gazetteer* on the 3d of Feb. signed *Amor Patriae.*" Crowley's scheme of February 3 is published in his *Letters and Dissertations on Various Subjects,* pp. 18–20. It suggested that the Stamp Act be repealed in any colony which voluntarily taxed itself to raise the same sum it would have paid under the act. Having calculated each colony's share according to a table of population, Crowley concluded that all the American colonies would pay £63,000 which worked out to 8d. per capita. For purposes of comparison, Crowley estimated that the annual interest charges on the British national debt amounted to 12s. per capita. In his letter to the *London Chron.,* Feb. 20–22, 1766, Crowley suggested that his figures appeared in the paragraph of February 1 because the author of that paragraph had overheard them, misunderstood them, and misused them.

Privy Council: Referral of Franklin's
Application for a Land Grant MS Minutes: Public Record Office

Franklin's interest in Nova Scotia lands has been examined in the preceding volume, where documents were printed showing that, as a member of two land speculating syndicates headed by Alexander McNutt, he acquired in 1765 claims to thousands of acres in what is now the province of New Brunswick. See above, XII, 345–50. The petition summarized here differs from the earlier two in that Franklin made it individually and not as a member of a syndicate, and that he applied to the Privy Council in England and not to the governor of the province.

[February 10, 1766][7]

Upon reading this day at the Board the Petition of Benjamin Franklin L.L.D. humbly praying that His Majesty will be graciously pleased to grant him twenty thousand Acres of Land in such part of the Province of Nova Scotia as the Petitioner or his Agent shall choose upon the same terms and conditions on which Lands have been granted within the said Province, in order to make a Settlement thereupon. It is Ordered &ca. ut antea.[8]

[*In the margin:*]
Nova Scotia
Petn: of Benj: Franklin for Lands in this province.
Refd: to the Bd: of Trade

From Springett Penn[9] ALS: American Philosophical Society

Dear Sir   Dublin 12th Feby 1766
    I received Mr. Penningtons Letter you was so Kind to forward.[1]

7. *Acts Privy Coun., Col.*, IV, 817, notes this referral to the Board of Trade under this date.
    8. Like a number of similar petitions entered above this one, it was ordered referred to the Board of Trade for report. That body having reported favorably on May 28, 1767 (more than a year later), the Privy Council Committee approved the application, stipulating the conditions for the grant, June 12, and the Privy Council issued an order, June 26, 1767, directing the governor to grant BF 20,000 acres. Public Record Office.
    9. Springett Penn, William Penn's great-grandson through his first wife, whose claim to the proprietorship of Pa. BF had encouraged during his first mission but who seemed by 1766 inclined to make his peace with Thomas Penn; above, IX, 260–2, 315–17; X, 6; XI, 151, 532–3.
    1. Penington enclosed his letter to Springett, apparently dealing with the

I wrote to you a long time since to desire the favour of you to ask Mr. Life[2] for somuch Money (as he had some of my Mothers in his Hands) as would purchase a Lottery Tickett since which have not had the favour of a Line from you.[3] My Mother and myself join in Respects and good Wishes to you and your Family and Mrs. Stephenson. I remain Your Obliged humble servant.

SPRINGETT PENN

Pray Excuse this poor paper.

[*In the margin:*] Mr. Life wrote me that Mr. Jackson gave no hopes of succeding in my Claim to the Government at present.

Examination before the Committee of the Whole of the House of Commons

Text of the Examination printed in *The Examination of Doctor Benjamin Franklin, before an August Assembly, relating to the Repeal of the Stamp Act, &c.* [Philadelphia, Hall and Sellers, 1766]; Franklin's Notes, AD: Historical Society of Pennsylvania; Nathaniel Ryder's Notes, transcription of shorthand MS: Harrowby Manuscript Trust, The Earl of Harrowby, Sandon Hall, Stafford.[4]

During the sittings of the House of Commons as a Committee of the Whole to consider problems resulting from colonial opposition to the Stamp Act, that body devoted most of the sessions of February 11, 12, and 13 to the examination of witnesses. These men, who attended at the bar of the House, included English merchants, colonials, and others conversant with the attitude of the Americans and its effects on British

---

sale of Pennsbury Manor, in his letter to BF of Nov. 14, 1765; see above, XII, 370–2.

2. For Thomas Life, a lawyer whom BF employed to try to prove Springett's title to the proprietorship of Pa. and whom Springett's mother, Mrs. Ann Penn, considered his "adviser in business," see above, X, 369 n; XI, 151 n; *PMHB*, XXII (1898), 183.

3. Springett's letter to BF has not been found; neither has BF's response, if indeed he ever wrote one.

4. The editors wish to express especial thanks to the Earl of Harrowby for making available transcriptions of the notes on this Examination taken down at the time by his ancestor, Nathaniel Ryder, later 1st Baron Harrowby. These notes are more fully described below.

trade.[5] The principal witness on Thursday, February 13, was Benjamin Franklin. Because of his position as agent of the Pennsylvania Assembly, his office of deputy postmaster general of America under the Crown, and more especially his generally recognized familiarity with the colonies at large and his personal standing and reputation, his testimony was regarded as especially important.

At this time the clerk of the House of Commons was Thomas Tyrwhitt; the clerk assistant was John Hatsell, part of whose duty it was to attend the sittings of the Committee of the Whole and record its proceedings. A parliamentary resolution of 1738, however, forbade the publication of reports of debates, although the newspapers and other journals employed various subterfuges to evade the prohibition. On April 7 William Strahan wrote David Hall that the clerk of the Commons had promised him a copy of Franklin's "Whole Examination," and on May 10 he sent the American printer the document, "which I have at last procured with great Difficulty, and with some Expense." He added that he had generally inserted in the margins the name of the questioner "and where doubtful, whether he was a *Friend* or an *Enemy*."[6]

Strahan stressed to the Philadelphia printer the effect of Franklin's testimony: "To this very Examination, more than to any thing else, you are indebted to the *speedy* and *total* Repeal of this odious Law. The Marquis of Rockingham [first lord of the Treasury] told a friend of mine a few Days after, That he never knew Truth make so great a Progress in so very short a Time. From that very Day, the *Repeal* was generally and absolutely determined, all that passed afterwards being only mere Form, which even in Business the most urgent must always be regarded. Happy Man! In Truth, I almost envy him the inward Pleasure, as well as the outward Fame, he must derive from having it in his Power to do his Country such eminent and seasonable Service."

Strahan's enthusiasm may be explained in part by his warm friendship for Franklin and also by the hope he expressed to Hall that this "Proof of his Patriotism" would "forever silence his Enemies with you." Considerations of general expediency and of the virtual impossibility of enforcing the Stamp Act without the extensive and costly use of force, which might have provoked a general war, certainly weighed heavily in the parliamentary decision to repeal the "odious Law." Yet in the per-

5. In general, the most useful printed account of these sittings of the Committee of the Whole, which are never recorded in detail in the *Commons Journals*, is Lawrence H. Gipson, "The Great Debate in the Committee of the Whole House of Commons on the Stamp Act, 1766, as Reported by Nathaniel Ryder," *PMHB*, LXXXVI (1962), 10–41.

6. *PMHB*, (1886), 96–7, 220–1.

spective of history it is clear that Franklin had made an important contribution to the result and that the later widespread publication of his Examination greatly enhanced his reputation on both sides of the Atlantic.

Although Strahan suggested that Hall print the Examination as a pamphlet, Hall delayed doing so for some time, contenting himself with reading the manuscript to whatever groups would listen. Then in the *Pennsylvania Gazette* for Sept. 18, 1766, just in time for the annual election campaign, appeared an announcement that the Examination was "Just published, and to be sold by the Printers hereof. Price Sixpence, or Four Shillings per Dozen." Because of the parliamentary rule against such publications the sixteen-page pamphlet carried no title page or publisher's imprint, and, following Strahan's advice, Hall phrased the caption at the top of the first page of text to indicate that the Examination had taken place "before an August Assembly," without mentioning the House of Commons or using the names of any of the questioners that Strahan had supplied. The text of the pamphlet printed below is taken from the Hall and Sellers edition, the first of its many printings.

Very soon James Parker reprinted the Examination, his edition so closely following that of Hall and Sellers in type and pagination as to be distinguishable only in very minor particulars. Other reprints appeared during 1766 in Boston and Williamsburg, and Henrich Miller brought out a German translation in Philadelphia in the same year. The first pamphlet publication in England came in the summer of 1767, when John Almon issued it anonymously with the "August Assembly" in the caption changed to "Honourable Assembly." Almon probably took his text from one of the copies of the Hall and Sellers edition that Hall sent over to Strahan, though six minor verbal differences appear in it. Almon brought out a second edition in the same year, this time omitting even the cautious reference to the "Honourable Assembly."[7] The *London Chronicle*, July 4–7, and 7–9, 1767, and *Gentleman's Magazine*, XXXVII (July 1767), 368–72, both printed extended, but not identical, extracts from Almon's recently published first edition. In introducing them the magazine commented that "The questions in general are put with very great subtilty and judgment, and they are answered with such deep and familiar knowledge of the subject, such precision and perspicuity,

7. The most thorough bibliographical treatment of these early American and British editions is in Thomas R. Adams, *American Independence The Growth of an Idea* (Providence, 1965), nos. 31a–31g. Paul L. Ford, *Franklin Bibliography* (Brooklyn, 1889), nos. 287–95, 297, is also useful but somewhat confusingly arranged. It lists two Boston printings in 1766 and one in an extra issue of the *New London Gazette*, Oct. 10, 1766.

such temper and yet such spirit, as to do the greatest honour to Dr. Franklin, and justify the general opinion of his character and abilities." In later years the Examination was frequently reprinted, in English or in translations, in Great Britain, America, and the European Continent, often in conjunction with the text of Franklin's "The Way to Wealth" and others of his writings. No complete bibliographical study of the Examination has ever been made.[8]

The manuscript of the Examination that Strahan sent to Hall in May 1766, with some of the questioners identified, has long since disappeared. Three other early manuscript versions, however, are known to have survived into the twentieth century. One, among the Franklin Papers in the Library of the American Philosophical Society, consisted originally of a sixteen-page document in an unidentified hand but endorsed by Franklin "Copy of Examination of B.F." Two sheets are missing causing the loss of pages 1–2 and 9–10, and tears account for the loss of the tops of pages 7–8 and part of 15.[9] A second manuscript, in the British Museum, appearing as part of notes on the examinations of several witnesses before the Committee of the Whole, is a substantially condensed version of the text with both questions and answers often much shortened and some omitted altogether.[1] The third was advertised in a sale catalogue of 1929 as a manuscript of seventeen folio pages, stitched, with the first page reproduced in facsimile and sixteen selected pairs of questions and answers printed with the description of the document.[2] The editors have been unable to discover the present location of this manuscript.

At one time or another Franklin sent copies of the Examination to various friends. In one such instance, uncertain as to date or addressee, he undertook to identify, as completely as memory allowed, the members of the House who had asked each of the 174 questions recorded. The three pages on which he wrote the identifying notes with occasional further commentary are now in the Historical Society of Pennsylvania. At the top of the first page he wrote: "I have numbered the Questions for the sake of making References to them." No version of the Examination, in manuscript or in one of the printed editions, has been found with the questions so numbered in his hand. But because these identifications add so considerably to an understanding and appreciation of the

8. The editors regret that considerations of available time and space have prevented them from undertaking and including here such a study.

9. Franklin Papers, XLIX, 62.

1. Additional MSS, 33030, fos. 163–180, being pp. 35–69 of this set of notes.

2. American Art Association Sale Catalogue, The William W. Cohen Sale, Feb. 5–6, 1929. Item 88.

Examination, the editors have supplied the appropriate number in brackets before the "Q" of each question as printed here and have given Franklin's identification or comment as a footnote to the question number, or to the first of a series of question numbers with which he dealt as a group. By placing Franklin's notes in close proximity to the text passages in this manner, it is hoped that they will be more illuminating than if they were printed as a single document separate from the text of the Examination.[3]

It has sometimes been said that Franklin's appearance before the Committee of the Whole was a carefully staged affair with friendly members prepared in advance to ask precisely the questions that Franklin wanted to answer. His notes make clear that such was in part certainly the case and that some of his friends had been well armed with helpful questions. But his notes also establish that by no means all the questions came from advocates of repeal of the Stamp Act. Of the 174 questions recorded as being asked, he identified 89, or just over half, as coming from members of the Grenville ministry or some other "Adversary." One of the most interesting aspects of the Examination is the adroitness with which he parried some potentially embarrassing questions and the skill with which he turned other distinctly hostile ones to his own advantage.[4]

One other contemporary document sheds helpful light on the Examination and is printed here directly following the text recorded by the clerk assistant. Nathaniel Ryder (1735–1803), M.P. for Tiverton, took extensive shorthand cipher notes of the debates and proceedings in the House of Commons from the spring of 1764 to the spring of 1766. With some gaps, they are now bound in one volume in the Harrowby Manuscript Trust. The portion of these notes relating to Franklin's examina-

3. BF's notes were printed from this MS in Robert Walsh's life of BF in *Delaplaine's Repository of the Lives and Portraits of Distinguished Americans* (Phila., 1816–17), II, pt. I, 74–7, and have been several times reprinted. But because the notes seem never to have been associated in print with the full text of the Examination in which the questions had been numbered as BF had done with them, much of the utility of the document has been lost. A good many of the questions and answers, with the questioners identified, are printed in Van Doren, *Franklin*, pp. 336–52.

4. In addition to reprinting BF's notes from *Delaplaine's Repository*, Bigelow *(Works*, III, 453–4) prints a quite different list of questioners from marginalia added later to a printed text of the Examination, the location of which he does not indicate. Comparison of these attributions with the indicated questions shows that in several instances clearly hostile questions were assigned to known friends of BF and friendly questions to adversaries. For this reason the present editors have rejected this list of attributions as unworthy of credence.

tion, part of Document 64 in the series, deciphered and transcribed, has been most kindly made available for publication here.[5] As Ryder indicated, he missed the first part of Franklin's testimony, and the notes he took by no means cover all the answers he did hear. Footnotes at appropriate points indicate, by the numbers assigned in the longer record, the questions and answers on which he made notes. Quite often Ryder combined into one paragraph his summaries of Franklin's answers to two or more related questions, and twice he seems to have changed the sequence. Only once does his note depart significantly in substance from the longer report of Franklin's statement. In general, the two documents substantiate each other effectively, and in some respects Ryder adds usefully to what we would otherwise know of the Examination. Twice, for example, he definitely identified a questioner whom Franklin did not specifically name. Perhaps the most interesting feature of these notes is that they show what parts of Franklin's testimony impressed one thoughtful and painstaking auditor as being of such importance as to warrant recording for that auditor's own future reference.

[February 13, 1766]

The EXAMINATION of Doctor BENJAMIN FRANKLIN, before an AUGUST ASSEMBLY, relating to the Repeal of the STAMP-ACT, &c.

[1][6] Q. What is your name, and place of abode?

A. Franklin, of Philadelphia.

[2][7] Q. Do the Americans pay any considerable taxes among themselves?

5. Nathaniel Ryder was M.P. for Tiverton from 1756 to 1776, when he was raised to the peerage as Baron Harrowby. He took down these notes for his own use. They have been said to "contain the fullest reports yet found of the debates on the Stamp Act and the repeal of the Stamp Act." Namier and Brooke, *House of Commons*, I, 523. Documents 61–65, deciphered and transcribed by Dr. K. L. Perrin, were used extensively by Lawrence H. Gipson in the article cited in an earlier note to this headnote and in his discussion of the debates on repeal in his *British Empire*, x, chap. xvii. Further clarification of the notes has been made by D. H. Watson, and the portion relating to Franklin's Examination is printed here through the generosity of the Earl of Harrowby and with the cooperation of Professor Gipson.

6. BF: "Qu. 1. is a Question of Form; askd of everyone that is examin'd."

7. BF: "Qu. 2. 3. 4. 5. 6. 7. were askd by Mr. Hewit, Member for Coventry, a Friend of ours and were designd to draw out the Answers that follow, being the Substance of what I had before said to him on the subject, to remove a common Prejudice, that the Colonies paid no Taxes, and that their Governments were supported by burthening the People here. Qu. 7. was particularly

A. Certainly many, and very heavy taxes.

[3] Q. What are the present taxes in Pennsylvania, laid by the laws of the colony?

A. There are taxes on all estates real and personal, a poll tax, a tax on all offices, professions, trades and businesses, according to their profits; an excise on all wine, rum, and other spirits; and a duty of Ten Pounds per head on all Negroes imported, with some other duties.

[4] Q. For what purposes are those taxes laid?

A. For the support of the civil and military establishments of the country, and to discharge the heavy debt contracted in the last war.

[5] Q. How long are those taxes to continue?

A. Those for discharging the debt are to continue till 1772, and longer, if the debt should not be then all discharged. The others must always continue.

[6] Q. Was it not expected that the debt would have been sooner discharged?

A. It was, when the peace was made with France and Spain— But a fresh war breaking out with the Indians, a fresh load of debt was incurred, and the taxes, of course, continued longer by a new law.

[7] Q. Are not all the people very able to pay those taxes?

A. No. The frontier counties, all along the continent, having been frequently ravaged by the enemy, and greatly impoverished, are able to pay very little tax. And therefore, in consideration of their distresses, our late tax laws do expressly favour those counties, excusing the sufferers; and I suppose the same is done in other governments.

[8]⁸ Q. Are not you concerned in the management of the Post-Office in America?

---

intended to shew by the Answer, that Parliament could not properly and equally lay Taxes in America; as they could not by reason of their distance be acquainted with such Circumstances as might make it necessary to spare particular Parts." James Hewitt (1712–1789), M.P. for Coventry, a lawyer, later chief justice of Ireland, had opposed the passage of the Stamp Act in 1765 and in this year opposed the Declaratory Act. Identifications of members cited in BF's notes are from Namier and Brooke, *House of Commons.*

8. BF: "Qu. 8. to 13. ask'd by Mr. Huske, another Friend, to shew the Impracticability of distributing the Stamps in America." John Huske (1724–1773), M.P. for Maldon; see above, XI, 444 n.

A. Yes. I am Deputy Post-Master General of North-America.

[9] Q. Don't you think the distribution of stamps, by post, to all the inhabitants, very practicable, if there was no opposition?

A. The posts only go along the sea coasts; they do not, except in a few instances, go back into the country; and if they did, sending for stamps by post would occasion an expence of postage, amounting, in many cases, to much more than that of the stamps themselves.

[10] Q. Are you acquainted with Newfoundland?

A. I never was there.

[11] Q. Do you know whether there are any post roads on that island?

A. I have heard that there are no roads at all; but that the communication between one settlement and another is by sea only.

[12] Q. Can you disperse the stamps by post in Canada?

A. There is only a post between Montreal and Quebec. The inhabitants live so scattered and remote from each other, in that vast country, that posts cannot be supported among them, and therefore they cannot get stamps per post. The English Colonies too, along the frontiers, are very thinly settled.

[13] Q. From the thinness of the back settlements, would not the stamp-act be extreamly inconvenient to the inhabitants, if executed?

A. To be sure it would; as many of the inhabitants could not get stamps when they had occasion for them, without taking long journeys, and spending perhaps Three or Four Pounds, that the Crown might get Sixpence.

[14]⁹ Q. Are not the Colonies, from their circumstances, very able to pay the stamp duty?

A. In my opinion, there is not gold and silver enough in the Colonies to pay the stamp duty for one year.

[15] Q. Don't you know that the money arising from the stamps was all to be laid out in America?

A. I know it is appropriated by the act to the American service; but it will be spent in the conquered Colonies, where the soldiers are, not in the Colonies that pay it.

[16] Q. Is there not a ballance of trade due from the Colonies

9. BF: "Qu. 14. 15. and 16. by one of the late Administration; an Adversary."

where the troops are posted, that will bring back the money to the old colonies?

A. I think not. I believe very little would come back. I know of no trade likely to bring it back. I think it would come from the Colonies where it was spent directly to England; for I have always observed, that in every Colony the more plenty the means of remittance to England, the more goods are sent for, and the more trade with England carried on.

[17][1] Q. What number of white inhabitants do you think there are in Pennsylvania?

A. I suppose there may be about 160,000.

[18] Q. What number of them are Quakers?

A. Perhaps a third.

[19] Q. What number of Germans?

A. Perhaps another third; but I cannot speak with certainty.

[20] Q. Have any number of the Germans seen service, as soldiers, in Europe?

1. BF: "Qu. 17 to 26. by Mr. Huske again. His Questions about the Germans and about the Number of People were intended to make the Opposition to the stamp Act in America appear more formidable. He ask'd some others here that the Clerk has omitted, particularly one I remember. There had been a considerable Party in the House for saving the Honour and Right of Parliament by retaining the Act, and yet making it tolerable to America, by reducing it to a stamp on Commissions for Profitable Offices and on Cards and Dice. I had in conversation with many of them objected to this, as it would require an Establishment for the Distributors, which would be a great Expence for that the stamps would not be sufficient to pay them, and so the Odium and Contention would be kept up for nothing. The Notion of Amending however still continued, and one of the most active of the Members for promoting it, told me he was sure, I could if I would assist them to amend the Act in such a manner as that America should have little or no Objection to it. I must confess, says I, I have thought of one Amendment, that if you will make it, the Act may remain and yet the Americans will be quieted. 'Tis a very small Amendment, too, 'tis only a Change of a single Word. Ay! says he what is that? It is says I, in that Clause where it is said that from and after the first day of November *One* Thousand seven Hundred and sixty five, there shall be paid &c. The Amendment I would propose is for *One* read *Two*, and then all the rest of the Act may stand as it does: I believe it will give nobody in America any Uneasiness. Mr. Huske had heard of this, and desiring to bring out the same Answer in the House askd me, Whether I could not propose a small Amendment that would make the Act palatable? But as I thought the Answer He wanted too light and ludicrous for the House, I evaded the Question."

A. Yes,—many of them, both in Europe and America.

[21] Q. Are they as much dissatisfied with the stamp duty as the English?

A. Yes, and more; and with reason, as their stamps are, in many cases, to be double.

[22] Q. How many white men do you suppose there are in North-America?

A. About 300,000, from sixteen to sixty years of age.

[23] Q. What may be the amount of one year's imports into Pennsylvania from Britain?

A. I have been informed that our merchants compute the imports from Britain to be above 500,000 Pounds.

[24] Q. What may be the amount of the produce of your province exported to Britain?

A. It must be small, as we produce little that is wanted in Britain. I suppose it cannot exceed 40,000 Pounds.

[25] Q. How then do you pay the ballance?

A. The Ballance is paid by our produce carried to the West-Indies, and sold in our own islands, or to the French, Spaniards, Danes and Dutch; by the same carried to other colonies in North-America, as to New-England, Nova-Scotia, Newfoundland, Carolina and Georgia; by the same carried to different parts of Europe, as Spain, Portugal and Italy. In all which places we receive either money, bills of exchange, or commodities that suit for remittance to Britain; which, together with all the profits on the industry of our merchants and mariners, arising in those circuitous voyages, and the freights made by their ships, center finally in Britain, to discharge the ballance, and pay for British manufactures continually used in the province, or sold to foreigners by our traders.

[26] Q. Have you heard of any difficulties lately laid on the Spanish trade?

A. Yes, I have heard that it has been greatly obstructed by some new regulations, and by the English men of war and cutters stationed all along the coast in America.

[27]² Q. Do you think it right that America should be protected by this country, and pay no part of the expence?

2. BF: "Qu. 27. 28 and 29. I think these were by Mr. Greenville, but am not certain." George Grenville (1712–1770), M.P. for Buckingham; first lord of the Treasury, 1763–65, and father of the Stamp Act.

A. That is not the case. The Colonies raised, cloathed and paid, during the last war, near 25000 men, and spent many millions.

[28] Q. Were you not reimbursed by parliament?

A. We were only reimbursed what, in your opinion, we had advanced beyond our proportion, or beyond what might reasonably be expected from us; and it was a very small part of what we spent. Pennsylvania, in particular, disbursed about 500,000 Pounds, and the reimbursements, in the whole, did not exceed 60,000 Pounds.

[29] Q. You have said that you pay heavy taxes in Pennsylvania; what do they amount to in the Pound?

A. The tax on all estates, real and personal, is Eighteen Pence in the Pound, fully rated; and the tax on the profits of trades and professions, with other taxes, do, I suppose, make full Half a Crown in the Pound.

[30]³ Q. Do you know any thing of the rate of exchange in Pennsylvania, and whether it has fallen lately?

A. It is commonly from 170 to 175. I have heard that it has fallen lately from 175 to 162 and a half, owing, I suppose, to their lessening their orders for goods; and when their debts to this country are paid, I think the exchange will probably be at par.

[31] Q. Do not you think the people of America would submit to pay the stamp duty, if it was moderated?

A. No, never, unless compelled by force of arms.

[32]⁴ Q. Are not the taxes in Pennsylvania laid on unequally, in order to burthen the English trade, particularly the tax on professions and business?

A. It is not more burthensome in proportion than the tax on lands. It is intended, and supposed to take an equal proportion of profits.

[33] Q. How is the assembly composed? Of what kinds of people are the members, landholders or traders?

A. It is composed of landholders, merchants and artificers.

3. BF: "Qu. 30. 31. I know not who ask'd them."
4. BF: "Qu. 32 to 35. Ask'd by Mr. Nugent who was against us. His Drift was to establish a Notion he had entertain'd, that the People in America had a crafty Mode of discouraging the English Trade by heavy Taxes on Merchants." Robert Nugent (1709–1788), M.P. for Bristol, vice-treasurer of Ireland, 1760–65.

[34] Q. Are not the majority landholders?

A. I believe they are.

[35] Q. Do not they, as much as possible, shift the tax off from the land, to ease that, and lay the burthen heavier on trade?

A. I have never understood it so. I never heard such a thing suggested. And indeed an attempt of that kind could answer no purpose. The merchant or trader is always skilled in figures, and ready with his pen and ink. If unequal burthens are laid on his trade, he puts an additional price on his goods; and the consumers, who are chiefly landholders, finally pay the greatest part, if not the whole.

[36]⁵ Q. What was the temper of America towards Great-Britain before the year 1763?

A. The best in the world. They submitted willingly to the government of the Crown, and paid, in all their courts, obedience to acts of parliament. Numerous as the people are in the several old provinces, they cost you nothing in forts, citadels, garrisons or armies, to keep them in subjection. They were governed by this country at the expence only of a little pen, ink and paper. They were led by a thread. They had not only a respect, but an affection, for Great-Britain, for its laws, its customs and manners, and even a fondness for its fashions, that greatly increased the commerce. Natives of Britain were always treated with particular regard; to be an Old England-man was, of itself, a character of some respect, and gave a kind of rank among us.

[37] Q. And what is their temper now?

A. O, very much altered.

[38] Q. Did you ever hear the authority of parliament to make laws for America questioned till lately?

A. The authority of parliament was allowed to be valid in all laws, except such as should lay internal taxes. It was never disputed in laying duties to regulate commerce.

[39] Q. In what proportion hath population increased in America?

A. I think the inhabitants of all the provinces together, taken at a medium, double in about 25 years. But their demand for British

5. BF: "Qu. 36. to 42. Most of these by Mr. Cooper and other Friends with whom I had discoursd, and were intended to bring out such Answers as they desired and expected from me." Grey Cooper (c.1726–1801), M.P. for Rochester, secretary to the Treasury, 1765–82; above, X, 185 n.

manufactures increases much faster, as the consumption is not merely in proportion to their numbers, but grows with the growing abilities of the same numbers to pay for them. In 1723, the whole importation from Britain to Pennsylvania, was but about 15,000 Pounds Sterling; it is now near Half a Million.

[40] Q. In what light did the people of America use to consider the parliament of Great-Britain?

A. They considered the parliament as the great bulwark and security of their liberties and privileges, and always spoke of it with the utmost respect and veneration. Arbitrary ministers, they thought, might possibly, at times, attempt to oppress them; but they relied on it, that the parliament, on application, would always give redress. They remembered, with gratitude, a strong instance of this, when a bill was brought into parliament, with a clause to make royal instructions laws in the Colonies, which the house of commons would not pass, and it was thrown out.

[41] Q. And have they not still the same respect for parliament?
A. No; it is greatly lessened.

[42] Q. To what causes is that owing?
A. To a concurrence of causes; the restraints lately laid on their trade, by which the bringing of foreign gold and silver into the Colonies was prevented; the prohibition of making paper money among themselves; and then demanding a new and heavy tax by stamps; taking away, at the same time, trials by juries, and refusing to receive and hear their humble petitions.

[43][6] Q. Don't you think they would submit to the stamp-act, if it was modified, the obnoxious parts taken out, and the duty reduced to some particulars, of small moment?

A. No; they will never submit to it.

[44][7] Q. What do you think is the reason that the people of America increase faster than in England?

A. Because they marry younger, and more generally.

[45] Q. Why so?

A. Because any young couple that are industrious, may easily obtain land of their own, on which they can raise a family.

6. BF: "Qu. 43. Uncertain by whom."

7. BF: "Qu. 44. 45. and 46. by Mr. Nugent again, who I suppose intended to infer that the Poor People in America were better able to pay Taxes than the Poor in England."

[46] Q. Are not the lower rank of people more at their ease in America than in England?

A. They may be so, if they are sober and diligent, as they are better paid for their labour.

[47]⁸ Q. What is your opinion of a future tax, imposed on the same principle with that of the stamp-act; how would the Americans receive it?

A. Just as they do this. They would not pay it.

[48] Q. Have you not heard of the resolutions of this house, and of the house of lords, asserting the right of parliament relating to America, including a power to tax the people there?

A. Yes, I have heard of such resolutions.

[49] Q. What will be the opinion of the Americans on those resolutions?

A. They will think them unconstitutional, and unjust.

[50]⁹ Q. Was it an opinion in America before 1763, that the parliament had no right to lay taxes and duties there?

A. I never heard any objection to the right of laying duties to regulate commerce; but a right to lay internal taxes was never supposed to be in parliament, as we are not represented there.

[51] Q. On what do you found your opinion, that the people in America made any such distinction?

A. I know that whenever the subject has occurred in conversation where I have been present, it has appeared to be the opinion of every one, that we could not be taxed in a parliament where we were not represented. But the payment of duties laid by act of parliament, as regulations of commerce, was never disputed.

[52] Q. But can you name any act of assembly, or public act of any of your governments, that made such distinction?

A. I do not know that there was any; I think there was never an occasion to make any such act, till now that you have attempted to tax us; that has occasioned resolutions of assembly, declaring the distinction, in which I think every assembly on the continent, and every member in every assembly, have been unanimous.

[53] Q. What then could occasion conversations on that subject before that time?

8. BF: "Qu. 47. 48. and 49. by Mr. Prescot, an Adversary." George Prescott (c.1711–1790), M.P. for Stockbridge, a wealthy merchant.
9. BF: "Qu. 50. 51. 52 to 58. by different Members, I cannot recollect who."

A. There was in 1754 a proposition made (I think it came from hence) that in case of a war, which was then apprehended, the governors of the Colonies should meet, and order the levying of troops, building of forts, and taking every other necessary measure for the general defence; and should draw on the treasury here for the sums expended, which were afterwards to be raised in the Colonies by a general tax, to be laid on them by act of parliament.[1] This occasioned a good deal of conversation on the subject, and the general opinion was, that the parliament neither would nor could lay any tax on us, till we were duly represented in parliament, because it was not just, nor agreeable to the nature of an English constitution.

[54][2] Q. Don't you know there was a time in New-York, when it was under consideration to make an application to parliament to lay taxes on that Colony, upon a deficiency arising from the assembly's refusing or neglecting to raise the necessary supplies for the support of the civil government?

A. I never heard of it.

[55] Q. There was such an application under consideration in New-York; and do you apprehend they could suppose the right of parliament to lay a tax in America was only local, and confined to the case of a deficiency in a particular Colony, by a refusal of its assembly to raise the necessary supplies?

A. They could not suppose such a case, as that the assembly would not raise the necessary supplies to support its own government. An assembly that would refuse it must want common sense, which cannot be supposed. I think there was never any such case at New-York, and that it must be a misrepresentation, or the fact must be misunderstood. I know there have been some attempts, by ministerial instructions from hence, to oblige the assemblies to settle permanent salaries on governors, which they wisely refused to do; but I believe no assembly of New-York, or any other Colony,

1. For BF's objections to this scheme when he first heard of it in 1754, see above, v, 443–7. For Ryder's very different report of this answer, see his note.

2. Ryder indicated that Qs. 54–56 were asked by Jeremiah Dyson (?1722–1776), M.P. for Yarmouth, Isle of Wight, an opponent of repeal. The New York incident to which they refer occurred in 1710–11. BF, being about five years old at the time and never a resident of that province or concerned in its local politics, may perhaps be excused for never having heard of it.

ever refused duly to support government by proper allowances, from time to time, to public officers.

[56] Q. But in case a governor, acting by instruction, should call on an assembly to raise the necessary supplies, and the assembly should refuse to do it, do you not think it would then be for the good of the people of the colony, as well as necessary to government, that the parliament should tax them?

A. I do not think it would be necessary. If an assembly could possibly be so absurd as to refuse raising the supplies requisite for the maintenance of government among them, they could not long remain in such a situation; the disorders and confusion occasioned by it must soon bring them to reason.

[57] Q. If it should not, ought not the right to be in Great-Britain of applying a remedy?

A. A right only to be used in such a case, I should have no objection to, supposing it to be used merely for the good of the people of the Colony.

[58] Q. But who is to judge of that, Britain or the Colony?

A. Those that feel can best judge.

[59][3] Q. You say the Colonies have always submitted to external taxes, and object to the right of parliament only in laying internal taxes; now can you shew that there is any kind of difference between the two taxes to the Colony on which they may be laid?

A. I think the difference is very great. An external tax is a duty laid on commodities imported; that duty is added to the first cost, and other charges on the commodity, and when it is offered to sale, makes a part of the price. If the people do not like it at that price, they refuse it; they are not obliged to pay it. But an internal tax is forced from the people without their consent, if not laid by their own representatives. The stamp-act says, we shall have no commerce, make no exchange of property with each other, neither purchase nor grant, nor recover debts; we shall neither marry, nor make our wills, unless we pay such and such sums, and thus it is intended to extort our money from us, or ruin us by the consequences of refusing to pay it.

[60] Q. But supposing the external[4] tax or duty to be laid on the

3. BF: "Qu. 59 to 78. chiefly by the former Ministry."
4. Almon's editions of 1767 substitute "internal" for "external," an obvious error.

necessaries of life imported into your Colony, will not that be the same thing in its effects as an internal tax?

A. I do not know a single article imported into the Northern Colonies, but what they can either do without, or make themselves.

[61] Q. Don't you think cloth from England absolutely necessary to them?

A. No, by no means absolutely necessary; with industry and good management, they may very well supply themselves with all they want.

[62] Q. Will it not take a long time to establish that manufacture among them? and must they not in the mean while suffer greatly?

A. I think not. They have made a surprising progress already. And I am of opinion, that before their old clothes are worn out, they will have new ones of their own making.

[63] Q. Can they possibly find wool enough in North-America?

A. They have taken steps to increase the wool. They entered into general combinations to eat no more lamb, and very few lambs were killed last year. This course persisted in, will soon make a prodigious difference in the quantity of wool. And the establishing of great manufactories, like those in the clothing towns here, is not necessary, as it is where the business is to be carried on for the purposes of trade. The people will all spin, and work for themselves, in their own houses.

[64] Q. Can there be wool and manufacture enough in one or two years?

A. In three years, I think, there may.

[65] Q. Does not the severity of the winter, in the Northern Colonies, occasion the wool to be of bad quality?

A. No; the wool is very fine and good.

[66] Q. In the more Southern Colonies, as in Virginia; don't you know that the wool is coarse, and only a kind of hair?

A. I don't know it. I never heard it. Yet I have been sometimes in Virginia. I cannot say I ever took particular notice of the wool there, but I believe it is good, though I cannot speak positively of it; but Virginia, and the Colonies south of it, have less occasion for wool; their winters are short, and not very severe, and they can very well clothe themselves with linen and cotton of their own raising for the rest of the year.

[67] Q. Are not the people, in the more Northern Colonies, obliged to fodder their sheep all the winter?

A. In some of the most Northern Colonies they may be obliged to do it some part of the winter.

[68] Q. Considering the resolutions of parliament, as to the right, do you think, if the stamp-act is repealed, that the North Americans will be satisfied?

A. I believe they will.

[69] Q. Why do you think so?

A. I think the resolutions of right will give them very little concern, if they are never attempted to be carried into practice. The Colonies will probably consider themselves in the same situation, in that respect, with Ireland; they know you claim the same right with regard to Ireland, but you never exercise it. And they may believe you never will exercise it in the Colonies, any more than in Ireland, unless on some very extraordinary occasion.

[70] Q. But who are to be the judges of that extraordinary occasion? Is it not the parliament?

A. Though the parliament may judge of the occasion, the people will think it can never exercise such right, till representatives from the Colonies are admitted into parliament, and that whenever the occasion arises, representatives will be ordered.

[71] Q. Did you never hear that Maryland, during the last war, had refused to furnish a quota towards the common defence?

A. Maryland has been much misrepresented in that matter. Maryland, to my knowledge, never refused to contribute, or grant aids to the Crown. The assemblies every year, during the war, voted considerable sums, and formed bills to raise them. The bills were, according to the constitution of that province, sent up to the council, or upper house, for concurrence, that they might be presented to the governor, in order to be enacted into laws. Unhappy disputes between the two houses arising, from the defects of that constitution principally, rendered all the bills but one or two abortive. The proprietary's council rejected them. It is true Maryland did not contribute its proportion, but it was, in my opinion, the fault of the government, not of the people.

[72] Q. Was it not talked of in the other provinces as a proper measure to apply to parliament to compel them?

A. I have heard such discourse; but as it was well known, that the people were not to blame, no such application was ever made, nor any step taken towards it.

[73] Q. Was it not proposed at a public meeting?

A. Not that I know of.

[74] Q. Do you remember the abolishing of the paper currency in New England, by act of assembly?

A. I do remember its being abolished, in the Massachusett's Bay.

[75] Q. Was not Lieutenant Governor Hutchinson principally concerned in that transaction?

A. I have heard so.

[76] Q. Was it not at that time a very unpopular law?

A. I believe it might, though I can say little about it, as I lived at a distance from that province.

[77] Q. Was not the scarcity of gold and silver an argument used against abolishing the paper?

A. I suppose it was.

[78] Q. What is the present opinion there of that law? Is it as unpopular as it was at first?

A. I think it is not.

[79][5] Q. Have not instructions from hence been sometimes sent over to governors, highly oppressive and unpolitical?

A. Yes.

[80] Q. Have not some governors dispensed with them for that reason?

A. Yes, I have heard so.

[81] Q. Did the Americans ever dispute the controling power of parliament to regulate the commerce?

A. No.

[82] Q. Can any thing less than a military force carry the stamp-act into execution?

A. I do not see how a military force can be applied to that purpose.

[83][6] Q. Why may it not?

A. Suppose a military force sent into America, they will find nobody in arms; what are they then to do? They cannot force a man to take stamps who chooses to do without them. They will not find a rebellion; they may indeed make one.

5. BF: "Qu. 79 to 82. by Friends."
6. BF: Qu. 83. by one of the late Ministry."

[84][7] Q. If the act is not repealed, what do you think will be the consequences?

A. A total loss of the respect and affection the people of America bear to this country, and of all the commerce that depends on that respect and affection.

[85][8] Q. How can the commerce be affected?

A. You will find, that if the act is not repealed, they will take very little of your manufactures in a short time.

[86] Q. Is it in their power to do without them?

A. I think they may very well do without them.

[87] Q. Is it their interest not to take them?

A. The goods they take from Britain are either necessaries, mere conveniences, or superfluities. The first, as cloth, &c. with a little industry they can make at home; the second they can do without, till they are able to provide them among themselves; and the last, which are much the greatest part, they will strike off immediately. They are mere articles of fashion, purchased and consumed, because the fashion in a respected country, but will now be detested and rejected. The people have already struck off, by general agreement, the use of all goods fashionable in mournings, and many thousand pounds worth are sent back as unsaleable.

[88] Q. Is it their interest to make cloth at home?

A. I think they may at present get it cheaper from Britain, I mean of the same fineness and neatness of workmanship; but when one considers other circumstances, the restraints on their trade, and the difficulty of making remittances, it is their interest to make every thing.

[89] Q. Suppose an act of internal regulations, connected with a tax, how would they receive it?

A. I think it would be objected to.

[90] Q. Then no regulation with a tax would be submitted to?

A. Their opinion is, that when aids to the Crown are wanted, they are to be asked of the several assemblies, according to the old established usage, who will, as they always have done, grant them freely. And that their money ought not to be given away without their consent, by persons at a distance, unacquainted with their circumstances and abilities. The granting aids to the Crown,

7. BF: "Qu. 84. by Mr. Cooper."
8. BF: "Qu. 85. to 90. by some of the late Ministry."

is the only means they have of recommending themselves to their sovereign, and they think it extremely hard and unjust, that a body of men, in which they have no representatives, should make a merit to itself of giving and granting what is not its own, but theirs, and deprive them of a right they esteem of the utmost value and importance, as it is the security of all their other rights.

[91]⁹ Q. But is not the post-office, which they have long received, a tax as well as a regulation?

A. No; the money paid for the postage of a letter is not of the nature of a tax; it is merely a quantum meruit for a service done; no person is compellable to pay the money, if he does not chuse to receive the service. A man may still, as before the act, send his letter by a servant, a special messenger, or a friend, if he thinks it cheaper and safer.

[92] Q. But do they not consider the regulations of the post-office, by the act of last year, as a tax?

A. By the regulations of last year the rate of postage was generally abated near thirty per cent. through all America; they certainly cannot consider such abatement as a tax.

[93]¹ Q. If an excise was laid by parliament, which they might likewise avoid paying, by not consuming the articles excised, would they then not object to it?

A. They would certainly object to it, as an excise is unconnected with any service done, and is merely an aid which they think ought to be asked of them, and granted by them, if they are to pay it, and can be granted for them by no others whatsoever, whom they have not impowered for that purpose.

[94] Q. You say they do not object to the right of parliament in laying duties on goods to be paid on their importation; now, is there any kind of difference between a duty on the importation of goods, and an excise on their consumption?

A. Yes; a very material one; an excise, for the reasons I have just mentioned, they think you can have no right to lay within their country. But the sea is yours; you maintain, by your fleets, the safety of navigation in it; and keep it clear of pirates; you may have therefore a natural and equitable right to some toll or duty on merchandizes carried through that part of your dominions, towards

9. BF: "Qu. 91. to 92. by Mr. Greenville."
1. BF: "Qu. 93 to 98. by some of the late Ministry."

144

defraying the expence you are at in ships to maintain the safety of that carriage.

[95] Q. Does this reasoning hold in the case of a duty laid on the produce of their lands exported? And would they not then object to such a duty?

A. If it tended to make the produce so much dearer abroad as to lessen the demand for it, to be sure they would object to such a duty; not to your right of laying it, but they would complain of it as a burthen, and petition you to lighten it.

[96]² Q. Is not the duty paid on the tobacco exported a duty of that kind?

A. That, I think, is only on tobacco carried coastwise from one Colony to another, and appropriated as a fund for supporting the college at Williamsburgh, in Virginia.

[97] Q. Have not the assemblies in the West-Indies the same natural rights with those in North America?

A. Undoubtedly.

[98] Q. And is there not a tax laid there on their sugars exported?

A. I am not much acquainted with the West-Indies, but the duty of four and a half per cent. on sugars exported, was, I believe, granted by their own assemblies.

[99]³ Q. How much is the poll-tax in your province laid on unmarried men?

A. It is, I think, Fifteen Shillings, to be paid by every single free-man, upwards of twenty-one years old.

[100] Q. What is the annual amount of all the taxes in Pennsylvania?

A. I suppose about 20,000 Pounds sterling.

[101]⁴ Q. Supposing the stamp-act continued, and enforced, do you imagine that ill humour will induce the Americans to give as much for worse manufactures of their own, and use them, preferably to better of ours?

2. Ryder indicates that Qs. 96, 97, and 98 were asked by Welbore Ellis (1713–1802), M.P. for Aylesbury; secretary at war, 1762–65, and opposed to repeal of the Stamp Act.

3. BF: "Qu. 99 and 100 by some Friend, I think sir Geo. Saville." Sir George Saville, Bart. (1726–1784), M.P. for Yorkshire, and opponent of Grenville; he nevertheless declined to serve in the Rockingham administration.

4. BF: "Qu. 101 to 106. by several of the late Ministry."

A. Yes, I think so. People will pay as freely to gratify one passion as another, their resentment as their pride.

[102] Q. Would the people at Boston discontinue their trade?

A. The merchants are a very small number, compared with the body of the people, and must discontinue their trade, if nobody will buy their goods.

[103] Q. What are the body of the people in the Colonies?

A. They are farmers, husbandmen or planters.

[104] Q. Would they suffer the produce of their lands to rot?

A. No; but they would not raise so much. They would manufacture more, and plough less.

[105] Q. Would they live without the administration of justice in civil matters, and suffer all the inconveniences of such a situation for any considerable time, rather than take the stamps, supposing the stamps were protected by a sufficient force, where every one might have them?

A. I think the supposition impracticable, that the stamps should be so protected as that every one might have them. The act requires sub-distributors to be appointed in every county town, district and village, and they would be necessary. But the principal distributors, who were to have had a considerable profit on the whole, have not thought it worth while to continue in the office, and I think it impossible to find sub-distributors fit to be trusted, who, for the trifling profit that must come to their share, would incur the odium, and run the hazard that would attend it; and if they could be found, I think it impracticable to protect the stamps in so many distant and remote places.

[106] Q. But in places where they could be protected, would not the people use them rather than remain in such a situation, unable to obtain any right, or recover, by law, any debt?

A. It is hard to say what they would do. I can only judge what other people will think, and how they will act, by what I feel within myself. I have a great many debts due to me in America, and I had rather they should remain unrecoverable by any law, than submit to the stamp-act. They will be debts of honour. It is my opinion the people will either continue in that situation, or find some way to extricate themselves, perhaps by generally agreeing to proceed in the courts without stamps.

[107]⁵ Q. What do you think a sufficient military force to protect the distribution of the stamps in every part of America?

A. A very great force; I can't say what, if the disposition of America is for a general resistance.

[108] Q. What is the number of men in America able to bear arms, or of disciplined militia?

A. There are, I suppose, at least—[*Question objected to. He withdrew. Called in again.*]

[109]⁶ Q. Is the American stamp-act an equal tax on that country?
A. I think not.

[110] Q. Why so?

A. The greatest part of the money must arise from law suits for the recovery of debts, and be paid by the lower sort of people, who were too poor easily to pay their debts. It is therefore a heavy tax on the poor, and a tax upon them for being poor.

[111] Q. But will not this increase of expence be a means of lessening the number of law suits?

A. I think not; for as the costs all fall upon the debtor, and are to be paid by him, they would be no discouragement to the creditor to bring his action.

[112] Q. Would it not have the effect of excessive usury?
A. Yes, as an oppression of the debtor.

[113] Q. How many ships are there laden annually in North-America with flax-seed for Ireland?

A. I cannot speak to the number of ships, but I know that in 1752, 10,000 hogsheads of flax-seed, each containing 7 bushels, were exported from Philadelphia to Ireland. I suppose the quantity is greatly increased since that time; and it is understood that the exportation from New York is equal to that from Philadelphia.

[114] Q. What becomes of the flax that grows with that flax-seed?

A. They manufacture some into coarse, and some into a middling kind of linen.

[115]⁷ Q. Are there any slitting mills in America?

5. BF: "Qu. 107 and 108 by Friends." The brackets in the answer to Q. 108 are in the original.
6. BF: "Qu. 109 to 114. by Friends."
7. BF: "Qu. 115. to 117. by Mr. A. Bacon." Anthony Bacon (*c.*1717–1786), M.P. for Aylesbury, a London merchant who claimed to have opposed the Stamp Act in 1765. An army contractor during the last war, he had invested

A. I think there are,[8] but I believe only one at present employed. I suppose they will all be set to work, if the interruption of the trade continues.

[116] Q. Are there any fulling mills there?

A. A great many.

[117] Q. Did you never hear that a great quantity of stockings were contracted for for the army, during the war, and manufactured in Philadelphia?

A. I have heard so.

[118][9] Q. If the stamp act should be repealed, would not the Americans think they could oblige the parliament to repeal every external tax law now in force?

A. It is hard to answer questions of what people at such a distance will think.

[119] Q. But what do you imagine they will think were the motives of repealing the act?

A. I suppose they will think that it was repealed from a conviction of its inexpediency; and they will rely upon it, that while the same inexpediency subsists, you will never attempt to make such another.

[120] Q. What do you mean by its inexpediency?

A. I mean its inexpediency on several accounts; the poverty and inability of those who were to pay the tax; the general discontent it has occasioned; and the impracticability of enforcing it.

[121][1] Q. If the act should be repealed, and the legislature should shew its resentment to the opposers of the stamp-act, would the Colonies acquiesce in the authority of the legislature? What is your opinion they would do?

A. I don't doubt at all, that if the legislature repeal the stamp-act, the Colonies will acquiesce in the authority.

[122][2] Q. But if the legislature should think fit to ascertain its right to lay taxes, by any act laying a small tax, contrary to their opinion, would they submit to pay the tax?

heavily in 1765 in the iron industry of South Wales. For his attitude on other colonial issues, see above, XI, 176 n, 476 n.

8. Almon's editions of 1767 read: "I think there are three," perhaps a revision suggested by BF.

9. BF: "Qu. 118 to 120 by some of the late Ministry."

1. BF: "Qu. 121. by an Adversary."

2. BF: "Qu. 122. by a Friend."

A. The proceedings of the people in America have been considered too much together. The proceedings of the assemblies have been very different from those of the mobs, and should be distinguished, as having no connection with each other. The assemblies have only peaceably resolved what they take to be their rights; they have taken no measures for opposition by force; they have not built a fort, raised a man, or provided a grain of ammunition, in order to such opposition. The ringleaders of riots they think ought to be punished; they would punish them themselves, if they could. Every sober sensible man would wish to see rioters punished; as otherwise peaceable people have no security of person or estate. But as to any internal tax, how small soever, laid by the legislature here on the people there, while they have no representatives in this legislature, I think it will never be submitted to. They will oppose it to the last. They do not consider it as at all necessary for you to raise money on them by your taxes, because they are, and always have been, ready to raise money by taxes among themselves, and to grant large sums, equal to their abilities, upon requisition from the Crown. They have not only granted equal to their abilities, but, during all the last war, they granted far beyond their abilities, and beyond their proportion with this country, you yourselves being judges, to the amount of many hundred thousand pounds, and this they did freely and readily, only on a sort of promise from the secretary of state, that it should be recommended to parliament to make them compensation. It was accordingly recommended to parliament, in the most honourable manner, for them. America has been greatly misrepresented and abused here, in papers, and pamphlets, and speeches, as ungrateful, and unreasonable, and unjust, in having put this nation to immense expence for their defence, and refusing to bear any part of that expence. The Colonies raised, paid and clothed, near 25000 men during the last war, a number equal to those sent from Britain, and far beyond their proportion; they went deeply into debt in doing this, and all their taxes and estates are mortgaged, for many years to come, for discharging that debt. Government here was at that time very sensible of this. The Colonies were recommended to parliament. Every year the King sent down to the house a written message to this purpose, That his Majesty, being highly sensible of the zeal and vigour with which his faithful subjects in North-America had exerted themselves, in defence of his Majesty's just rights and possessions, recommended it to the house to take the same into consideration, and enable him to give them a proper compensation. You will find those messages on your own journals every year of the war to the very last, and you did accordingly give 200,000 Pounds annually to the Crown, to be distributed in such compensation to the Colonies. This is the strongest of all proofs that the Colonies, far from being unwilling to bear a share of the burthen, did exceed their proportion; for if they had done less, or had only equalled their proportion, there would have been no room or reason for compensation. Indeed the sums reimbursed them, were by no means adequate to the expence they incurred beyond their proportion; but they never murmured at that; they esteemed their Sovereign's approbation of their zeal and fidelity, and the approbation of this house, far beyond any other kind of compensation; therefore there was no occasion for this act, to force money from a willing people; they had not refused giving money for the purposes of the act; no requisition had been made; they were always willing and ready to do what could reasonably be expected from them, and in this light they wish to be considered.

[123][3] Q. But suppose Great-Britain should be engaged in a war in Europe, would North-America contribute to the support of it?

A. I do think they would, as far as their circumstances would permit. They consider themselves as a part of the British empire, and as having one common interest with it; they may be looked on here as foreigners, but they do not consider themselves as such. They are zealous for the honour and prosperity of this nation, and, while they are well used, will always be ready to support it, as far as their little power goes. In 1739 they were called upon to assist in the expedition against Carthagena, and they sent 3000 men to join your army. It is true Carthagena is in America, but as remote from the Northern Colonies, as if it had been in Europe. They make no distinction of wars, as to their duty of assisting in them. I know the last war is commonly spoke of here as entered into for

3. BF: "Qu. 123. by Mr. Ch. Townsend." Charles Townshend (1725–1767), M.P. for Harwich, paymaster general, 1765–66; chancellor of the Exchequer, August 1766-September 1767, had supported passage of the Stamp Act, but now favored repeal on the grounds that the colonies were unable to pay the tax and that means of enforcement were lacking.

the defence, or for the sake of the people of America. I think it is quite misunderstood. It began about the limits between Canada and Nova-Scotia, about territories to which the Crown indeed laid claim, but were not claimed by any British Colony; none of the lands had been granted to any Colonist; we had therefore no particular concern or interest in that dispute. As to the Ohio, the contest there began about your right of trading in the Indian country, a right you had by the treaty of Utrecht, which the French infringed; they seized the traders and their goods, which were your manufactures; they took a fort which a company of your merchants, and their factors and correspondents, had erected there, to secure that trade. Braddock was sent with an army to re-take that fort (which was looked on here as another incroachment on the King's territory) and to protect your trade. It was not till after his defeat that the Colonies were attacked. They were before in perfect peace with both French and Indians; the troops were not therefore sent for their defence. The trade with the Indians, though carried on in America, is not an American interest. The people of America are chiefly farmers and planters; scarce any thing that they raise or produce is an article of commerce with the Indians. The Indian trade is a British interest; it is carried on with British manufactures, for the profit of British merchants and manufacturers; therefore the war, as it commenced for the defence of territories of the Crown, the property of no American, and for the defence of a trade purely British, was really a British war—and yet the people of America made no scruple of contributing their utmost towards carrying it on, and bringing it to a happy conclusion.

[124]⁴ Q. Do you think then that the taking possession of the King's territorial rights, and strengthening the frontiers, is not an American interest?

A. Not particularly, but conjointly a British and an American interest.

[125]⁵ Q. You will not deny that the preceding war, the war with Spain, was entered into for the sake of America; was it not occasioned by captures made in the American seas?

A. Yes; captures of ships carrying on the British trade there, with British manufactures.

4. BF: "124. by Do."
5. BF: "Qu. 125. by Mr. Nugent."

[126]⁶ Q. Was not the late war with the Indians, since the peace with France, a war for America only?

A. Yes; it was more particularly for America than the former, but it was rather a consequence or remains of the former war, the Indians not having been thoroughly pacified, and the Americans bore by much the greatest share of the expence. It was put an end to by the army under General Bouquet; there were not above 300 regulars in that army, and above 1000 Pennsylvanians.

[127]⁷ Q. Is it not necessary to send troops to America, to defend the Americans against the Indians?

A. No, by no means; it never was necessary. They defended themselves when they were but an handful, and the Indians much more numerous. They continually gained ground, and have driven the Indians over the mountains, without any troops sent to their assistance from this country. And can it be thought necessary now to send troops for their defence from those diminished Indian tribes, when the Colonies are become so populous, and so strong? There is not the least occasion for it; they are very able to defend themselves.

[128]⁸ Q. Do you say there were no more than 300 regular troops employed in the late Indian war?

A. Not on the Ohio, or the frontiers of Pennsylvania, which was the chief part of the war that affected the Colonies. There were garrisons at Niagara, Fort Detroit, and those remote posts kept for the sake of your trade; I did not reckon them, but I believe that on the whole the number of Americans, or provincial troops, employed in the war, was greater than that of the regulars. I am not certain, but I think so.

[129]⁹ Q. Do you think the assemblies have a right to levy money on the subject there, to grant to the Crown?

A. I certainly think so; they have always done it.

[130]¹ Q. Are they acquainted with the declaration of rights? And do they know that, by that statute, money is not to be raised on the subject but by consent of parliament?

6. BF: "Qu. 126. by Mr. G. Grenville."
7. BF: "Qu. 127. by one of the late Ministry."
8. BF: "Qu. 128. by Mr. G. Greenville."
9. BF: "Qu. 129. by Mr. Wellbore Ellis late Secry. at War."
1. BF: "130 and 131 by the same."

A. They are very well acquainted with it.

[131] Q. How then can they think they have a right to levy money for the Crown, or for any other than local purposes?

A. They understand that clause to relate to subjects only within the realm; that no money can be levied on them for the Crown, but by consent of parliament. The Colonies are not supposed to be within the realm; they have assemblies of their own, which are their parliaments, and they are in that respect, in the same situation with Ireland. When money is to be raised for the Crown upon the subject in Ireland, or in the Colonies, the consent is given in the parliament of Ireland, or in the assemblies of the Colonies. They think the parliament of Great-Britain cannot properly give that consent till it has representatives from America; for the petition of right expressly says, it is to be by common consent in parliament, and the people of America have no representatives in parliament, to make a part of that common consent.

[132]² Q. If the stamp-act should be repealed, and an act should pass, ordering the assemblies of the Colonies to indemnify the sufferers by the riots, would they obey it?

A. That is a question I cannot answer.

[133] Q. Suppose the King should require the Colonies to grant a revenue, and the parliament should be against their doing it, do they think they can grant a revenue to the King, without the consent of the parliament of G. Britain?

A. That is a deep question. As to my own opinion, I should think myself at liberty to do it, and should do it, if I liked the occasion.

[134]³ Q. When money has been raised in the Colonies, upon requisitions, has it not been granted to the King?

A. Yes, always; but the requisitions have generally been for some service expressed, as to raise, clothe and pay troops, and not for money only.

[135] Q. If the act should pass, requiring the American assemblies to make compensation to the sufferers, and they should disobey it, and then the parliament should, by another act, lay an internal tax, would they then obey it?

A. The people will pay no internal tax; and I think an act to oblige the assemblies to make compensation is unnecessary, for I

2. BF: "Qu. 132 and 133. uncertain."
3. BF: "Qu. 134 and 135. ditto."

am of opinion, that as soon as the present heats are abated, they will take the matter into consideration, and, if it is right to be done, they will do it of themselves.

[136]⁴ Q. Do not letters often come into the post-offices in America, directed to some inland town where no post goes?

A. Yes.

[137] Q. Can any private person take up those letters, and carry them as directed?

A. Yes; any friend of the person may do it, paying the postage that has occurred.⁵

[138] Q. But must he not pay an additional postage for the distance to such inland town?

A. No.

[139] Q. Can the post-master answer delivering the letter, without being paid such additional postage?

A. Certainly he can demand nothing, where he does no service.

[140] Q. Suppose a person, being far from home, finds a letter in a post-office directed to him, and he lives in a place to which the post generally goes, and the letter is directed to that place, will the post-master deliver him the letter, without his paying the postage receivable at the place to which the letter is directed?

A. Yes; the office cannot demand postage for a letter that it does not carry, or farther than it does carry it.

[141] Q. Are not ferrymen in America obliged, by act of parliament, to carry over the posts without pay?

A. Yes.

[142] Q. Is not this a tax on the ferrymen?

A. They do not consider it as such, as they have an advantage from persons travelling with the post.

[143]⁶ Q. If the stamp-act should be repealed, and the Crown should make a requisition to the Colonies for a sum of money, would they grant it?

A. I believe they would.

4. BF: "Qu. 136. to 142. by some of the late Ministry, intending to prove that Postage was demanded where no service was done, and therefore it was a Tax."

5. Almon's editions of 1767 read: "accrued."

6. BF: "Qu. 143. by a Friend, I forget who." BF did not identify the member who asked no. 144; it was probably the same person.

[144] Q. Why do you think so?

A. I can speak for the Colony I live in; I had it in instruction from the assembly to assure the ministry, that as they always had done, so they should always think it their duty to grant such aids to the Crown as were suitable to their circumstances and abilities, whenever called upon for the purpose, in the usual constitutional manner; and I had the honour of communicating this instruction to that honourable gentleman then minister.[7]

[145][8] Q. Would they do this for a British concern; as suppose a war in some part of Europe, that did not affect them?

A. Yes, for any thing that concerned the general interest. They consider themselves as a part of the whole.

[146][9] Q. What is the usual constitutional manner of calling on the Colonies for aids?

A. A letter from the secretary of state.

[147] Q. Is this all you mean, a letter from the secretary of state?

A. I mean the usual way of requisition, in a circular letter from the secretary of state, by his Majesty's command, reciting the occasion, and recommending it to the Colonies to grant such aids as became their loyalty, and were suitable to their abilities.

[148] Q. Did the secretary of state ever write for money for the Crown?

A. The requisitions have been to raise, clothe and pay men, which cannot be done without money.

[149] Q. Would they grant money alone, if called on?

A. In my opinion they would, money as well as men, when they have money, or can make it.

[150] Q. If the parliament should repeal the stamp-act, will the assembly of Pennsylvania rescind their resolutions?

A. I think not.

[151] Q. Before there was any thought of the stamp-act, did they wish for a representation in parliament?

A. No.

[152][1] Q. Don't you know that there is, in the Pennsylvania charter, an express reservation of the right of parliament to lay taxes there?

7. See above, XI, 396–7 n, 425.
8. BF: "Qu. 145. by C. Townsend."
9. BF: "Qu. 146 to 151. by some of the late Ministry."
1. BF: "Qu. 152 to 157. By Mr. Prescot and Others of the same."

A. I know there is a clause in the charter, by which the King grants that he will levy no taxes on the inhabitants, unless it be with the consent of the assembly, or by act of parliament.

[153] Q. How then could the assembly of Pennsylvania assert, that laying a tax on them by the stamp-act was an infringement of their rights?

A. They understand it thus; by the same charter, and otherwise, they are intitled to all the privileges and liberties of Englishmen; they find in the great charters, and the petition and declaration of rights, that one of the privileges of English subjects is, that they are not to be taxed but by their common consent; they have therefore relied upon it, from the first settlement of the province, that the parliament never would, nor could, by colour of that clause in the charter, assume a right of taxing them, till it had qualified itself to exercise such right, by admitting representatives from the people to be taxed, who ought to make a part of that common consent.

[154] Q. Are there any words in the charter that justify that construction?

A. The common rights of Englishmen, as declared by Magna Charta, and the petition of right, all justify it.

[155] Q. Does the distinction between internal and external taxes exist in the words of the charter?

A. No, I believe not.

[156] Q. Then may they not, by the same interpretation, object to the parliament's right of external taxation?

A. They never have hitherto. Many arguments have been lately used here to shew them that there is no difference, and that if you have no right to tax them internally, you have none to tax them externally, or make any other law to bind them. At present they do not reason so, but in time they may possibly be convinced by these arguments.

[157] Q. Do not the resolutions of the Pennsylvania assembly say all taxes?

A. If they do, they mean only internal taxes; the same words have not always the same meaning here and in the Colonies. By taxes they mean internal taxes; by duties they mean customs; these are their ideas of the language.

156

[158]² Q. Have you not seen the resolutions of the Massachusett's Bay assembly?

A. I have.

[159] Q. Do they not say, that neither external nor internal taxes can be laid on them by parliament?

A. I don't know that they do; I believe not.

[160] Q. If the same Colony should say neither tax nor imposition could be laid, does not that province hold the power of parliament can hold neither?³

A. I suppose that by the word imposition, they do not intend to express duties to be laid on goods imported, as regulations of commerce.

[161] Q. What can the Colonies mean then by imposition as distinct from taxes?

A. They may mean many things, as impressing of men, or of carriages, quartering troops on private houses, and the like; there may be great impositions, that are not properly taxes.

[162] Q. Is not the post-office rate an internal tax laid by act of parliament?

A. I have answered that.

[163]⁴ Q. Are all parts of the Colonies equally able to pay taxes?

A. No, certainly; the frontier parts, which have been ravaged by the enemy, are greatly disabled by that means, and therefore, in such cases, are usually favoured in our tax-laws.

[164] Q. Can we, at this distance, be competent judges of what favours are necessary?

A. The Parliament have supposed it, by claiming a right to make tax laws for America; I think it impossible.

[165]⁵ Q. Would the repeal of the stamp-act be any discouragement of your manufactures? Will the people that have begun to manufacture decline it?

A. Yes, I think they will; especially if, at the same time, the trade is opened again, so that remittances can be easily made. I have

2. BF: "Qu. 158. to 161. by C Townsend." BF did not identify the member who asked the repetitious no. 162.

3. Almon's editions of 1767 read: "can lay neither?" BF may have suggested this correction.

4. BF: "Qu. 163 and 164 By a Friend: I think Sir Geo. Savile."

5. BF: "Qu. 165. By some Friend."

known several instances that make it probable. In the war before last, tobacco being low, and making little remittance, the people of Virginia went generally into family manufactures. Afterwards, when tobacco bore a better price, they returned to the use of British manufactures. So fulling mills were very much disused in the last war in Pennsylvania, because bills were then plenty, and remittances could easily be made to Britain for English cloth and other goods.

[166][6] Q. If the stamp-act should be repealed, would it induce the assemblies of America to acknowledge the rights of parliament to tax them, and would they erase their resolutions?

A. No, never.

[167] Q. Is there no means of obliging them to erase those resolutions?

A. None that I know of; they will never do it unless compelled by force of arms.

[168][7] Q. Is there a power on earth that can force them to erase them?

A. No power, how great soever, can force men to change their opinions.

[169][8] Q. Do they consider the post-office as a tax, or as a regulation?

A. Not as a tax, but as a regulation and conveniency; every assembly encouraged it, and supported it in its infancy, by grants of money, which they would not otherwise have done; and the people have always paid the postage.

[170] Q. When did you receive the instructions you mentioned?

A. I brought them with me, when I came to England, about 15 months since.

[171] Q. When did you communicate that instruction to the minister?

A. Soon after my arrival, while the stamping of America was under consideration, and before the bill was brought in.

[172][9] Q. Would it be most for the interest of Great-Britain, to employ the hands of Virginia in tobacco, or in manufactures?

6. BF: "Qu. 166 and 167 by an Adversary."
7. BF: "Qu. 168. by a Friend. I think."
8. BF: "Qu. 169. 170. 171. By a Friend."
9. BF: "Qu. 172. 173. 174. By another Friend."

A. In tobacco to be sure.

[173] Q. What used to be the pride of the Americans?

A. To indulge in the fashions and manufactures of Great-Britain.

[174] Q. What is now their pride?

A. To wear their old cloaths over again, till they can make new ones.[1]

Withdrew.

The END.

NOTES BY NATHANIEL RYDER

Feb. 13 1766.

Several evidences examined, principally merchants at Halifax, Manchester, and other trading towns in England. After this, Dr. Franklin was examined some time before I came in.

That he recollected before 1763 that the persons in Philadelphia had made a distinction between internal taxes and duties, particularly at time when a proposal was made for committee from assembly to meet and consider of the proportion to be raised by each particular colony; the general conclusion was that the Parliament would not lay internal taxes upon them because it was not right nor constitutional.[2]

That he never supposed a case where the assembly would not raise supply for the support of their own government. Dyson said that he knew there was the case where this had happened and the assemblies were only obliged to it by being threatened with an Act of Parliament to tax them if they did not tax themselves.[3]

That before their old clothes are worn out they will have new clothes of their own making.[4]

1. At the end of his notes BF added separately: "Mr. Nugent made a violent speech next day upon this Examination. In which he said 'We have often experienced Austrian Ingratitude, and yet we assisted Portugal. We experienced Porteguese Ingratitude, and yet we assistd America. But what is Austrian Ingratitude, what is the Ingratitude of Portugal compared to this of America? We have fought, bled and Ruin'd ourselves, to conquer for them; and now they come and tell us to our Noses, even at the Bar of this House, that they are not obliged to us! &c. &c.' But his Clamour was very little minded."

2. Answer, with important differences, to Q. 53.

3. Qs. 54–56, concerning the proposed parliamentary tax of New York in 1710–11, and parts of BF's answers to Qs. 55 and 56. On Dyson see the footnote to Q. 54.

4. Answer to Q. 62.

That there is a distinction between internal and external taxes, that a man is left to his option more in paying one than the other.[5] That the Americans have agreed to eat no lamb last year, which will increase the quantity of wool in that country very considerably. He thinks in three years there might be a quantity of wool raised in America sufficient to clothe all those who want clothing.[6]

That the Americans will think the resolution of both Houses unconstitutional but yet would be satisfied with a repeal of the Stamp Act because they would then consider themselves as in the case of Ireland over whom the Parliament has asserted that power but has never thought fit to exercise it.[7]

That he has heard of Maryland expressing an unwillingness upon a difference with their Governor to put a sum of money sufficient to raise their quota of troops for the war, and for one or two years did not contribute, but that the other provinces did contribute more than their proportion to make up that deficiency. And at this time there was a conversation among the other provinces that Maryland ought to be forced by Act of Parliament to contribute to the common expenses.[8]

That Governor Hutchinson was the promoter of a law restraining paper currency. That it was then a very unpopular law, but that it has become now much less so.[9]

That the Americans in general never disputed the controlling power of this Kingdom to regulate their trade.[1]

That he thinks the Stamp Act cannot be carried into execution, either with or without a military force. For if a military force was to be sent there, it would find nobody there in arms, but you cannot force them to take stamps if they refuse it.[2]

That in a few years they would be able to do without our manufactures. That the manufactures they take from us are of three sorts: necessaries, conveniences and superfluities, which last are much the greatest proportion. That they have already struck off

5. Answer to Q. 59.
6. Answers to Qs. 63 and 64.
7. Answers to Qs. 48, 49, 68, and 69.
8. Answers to Qs. 71–73.
9. Answers to Qs. 74–78.
1. Answer to Q. 81.
2. Answers to Qs. 82 and 83.

many superfluities and will strike off more, and are raising some necessaries of life as fast as possible.[3]

That regulation attended with an internal tax would be objected to.[4] That the Post Office is not so much a tax as a regulation, as it compels no person to send letters by it, as he may send it by a private messenger.[5]

That they would not object to duty laid upon importation as considering the sea as belonging to Great Britain, and anything passing that sea would be subject to Great Britain.[6] They would object to duty upon exportation if it lay hard upon their commerce and prevent sale in foreign parts, but they might object by expediency without calling the right into question.[7]

Ellis mentions several instances of duties upon exportation, particularly that upon tobacco exported coastwise of a penny per pound.[8]

That the people of the West Indies have in his opinion the same rights as the people of N. America.[9]

That there is a poll tax in Pennsylvania of 15 shillings per head upon every man unmarried above 21 years age. The poll tax and the tax upon land raise about £30,000 in Pennsylvania money and £20,000 in sterling.[1]

That if the inhabitants are dissatisfied with this country, they will use worse manufactures of their own, though dearer than the English, as they would pay as much to gratify one passion as another, to gratify their resentment as readily as to feed their pride or their vanity.[2]

That they have at present an administration of justice in criminal matters and would do without them in civil matters till they can find a remedy.[3]

3. Answers to Qs. 85–87.
4. Answer to Q. 89.
5. Answer to Q. 91.
6. Answer to Q. 94.
7. Answer to Q. 95.
8. Q. 96–98, apparently asked by Welbore Ellis, secretary at war in the Grenville administration.
9. Answer to Q. 97.
1. Answers to Qs. 99 and 100.
2. Answer to Q. 101.
3. No reference to criminal cases is found in any question or answer, but this response is otherwise implicit in the answers to Qs. 105 and 106.

That as the principal distributors have resigned their offices who would have the greatest profits, it is not probable that any sub-distributor would undertake.[4]

That in his own opinion he should sooner trust to debt of honour than take the stamps, and he believes this would be the general practice.[5] That he believes it would require a great force to be distributed about the country for the protection of the stamps and stamp officers.[6]

That gentlemen may in time by abolishing distinction between internal and external taxes teach them to change their own present opinion and abolish it likewise.[7] By the word taxes they have always considered internal taxes only, and when they mean external taxes they use the word duties.[8] By the word impositions are meant internal taxes or other charges such as billeting men.[9]

"Pacificus": On Chastising the Colonies

Printed in *The London Chronicle*, February 11–13, 1766.

The authorship of this piece has not been established with any certainty, and the editors can offer little evidence that Franklin wrote it. He often used anecdotes to support or illustrate his ideas, but he was by no means the only writer of the time to employ such a device. The *London Chronicle*, with which his friend William Strahan was closely connected, often served as a vehicle for his communications to the public, though most of his letters of recent weeks had appeared in other papers. He had cited the Duke of Alva's oppressions in the Netherlands in his Canada Pamphlet of 1760 (above, IX, 91), though other writers in England also used the duke as a symbol of tyranny. And the signature "Pacificus," commonly reserved for advocates of stern measures against the colonies, had been used ironically about two weeks earlier by one writer, probably Franklin, for a purpose similar to that of this letter. The piece is included here only as a possible contribution from Franklin's pen, and the reader may decide for himself whether it should be identified as one of his writings.[1]

4. Answer to Q. 105.
5. Answer to Q. 106.
6. Answer to Q. 107.
7. Answer to Q. 156.
8. Answer to Q. 157.
9. Answer to Q. 161.
1. Crane, *Letters to the Press*, p. 294, includes it only in his list of "Possible Franklin Pieces."

To the Printer. [February 13, 1766]
A Certain Judge, at an Assize, declared it from the Bench, as his Opinion, that every man had a *legal* right to chastise his wife, if she was stubborn and obstinate; but then he observed, that his right ought to be exercised with great lenity and moderation.

It seems our Lawyers are of opinion, that England has an indisputable right to correct her refractory children of North America. But then, as the Judge observed, it ought to be done with temper and moderation; lest, like an unskilful Surgeon, we should *exasperate* and *inflame* the wound we ought to *mollify.* It is an old maxim, but not the less true, that it is much easier to *lead* than to *drive.* If the Duke d'Alva had treated the people of the Netherlands with gentleness and humanity, they would never have revolted. Thank God, we have no Duke d'Alva in England.

The Great Commoner is, at least in the present instance, a *Friend to Peace,* and for *healing measures:* So are the late King's *old and faithful servants.*[2] The same Apostle who says, *Children, obey your Parents;* says also, *Fathers, provoke not your Children to wrath.*[3]

PACIFICUS.

From Amelia Evans[4]   ALS: American Philosophical Society

Dear Sir,   Tuesday 18 [February 1766][5] 12 o'clock
This morning I have had my difinitive answer from the family I

2. William Pitt, "the Great Commoner," and other opponents of George Grenville, though political alignments at the moment were highly confused.

3. Ephesians 6:1: "Children, obey your parents in the Lord, for this is right." Colossians 3:20–21: "Children, obey your parents in all things: for this is well pleasing unto the Lord. Fathers, provoke not your children to anger, lest they be discouraged."

4. For Amelia Evans, daughter of the cartographer Lewis Evans and goddaughter of DF, see above, XII, 64 n. As she relates in the present letter, she was just on the point of leaving England as a governess in the family of James Traill, the British consul-designate at Tunis.

5. This letter can be dated by the document immediately following. Writing on "Tuesday 18," Miss Evans here asked BF to appraise "the Copper plate" —the plate for Miss Evans' father's 1755 map, his *General Map of the Middle British Colonies in America* (see above, VI, 173)—and to advance her some money. The next day, Wednesday, Feb. 19, 1766, she gave BF a receipt for five guineas for the plate, showing that he had responded to her request im-

am in,[6] and am to go with them. The Ship in which they are to sail is now ready at Portsmouth and they only wait for the Consuls Credential letters which are hourly expected. The reason therfore Sir for my troubling you in this manner is to beg you will endeavour to have some estimation put on the Copper plate but I would most willingly refer that to you.

I have had a letter a day or two ago from my Guardian in Philadelphia[7] and am disappointed of receiving some money I have there but he says he expects to receive it very soon as it is at interest upon undoubted security. You do not Sir perhaps think the money I have due to me from the Estate in Boston secure enough to advance me anything upon it—if you do Sir and would oblige me so far I should esteem it as the greatest favor in the world,[8] as I am obliged to lay in many articles before I leave England there being very few things to be purchased at Tunis of wearables and I am to expect very little from my Uncle[9] than severity. The money I have due to me from the Boston estate[1] has been fully proved and the account acknowledged by the Executors of that Estate and perhaps my draught on them they will be obliged to answer.

If the above request you do not think proper to comply with I hope you will pardon the boldness of it and believe that nothing but the necessity of my situation could drive me to it therefore from the knowledge I have of Mr. Franklin I may flatter myself he will not only excuse but pity his most obliged and obedient Servant   AMELIA EVANS

Please to direct to me at Mr. Norris King street Golden square. I [would] have waited upon you Sir but had not the confidence upon such an errand.

Addressed: For / Benjamin Franklin Esqr. / Craven-street / Strand

mediately. Since Tuesday the 18th fell in February 1766, the present letter can be confidently dated Feb. 18, 1766.

6. The Traill family.

7. Thomas Gay had been appointed Miss Evans' guardian upon the death of her uncle, John Evans, in 1759.

8. The next day BF gave £11 11s., of which five guineas was in payment for the map plate and six guineas was a loan. Journal, 1764–1776, p. 7; Ledger, 1764–1776, pp. 5, 7, 21. The endorsement of her receipt for the five guineas shows that she repaid the loan in 1771.

9. Apparently a brother of Lewis Evans who remained in England.

1. Nothing is known about Miss Evans' property in Boston.

Amelia Evans: Receipt
DS:[2] American Philosophical Society

[February 19, 1766]

Receiv'd Feb. 19. 1766 of Benja. Franklin Five Guineas for the Plate of the American Map[3] made by my Father Lewis Evans and the Right to the Copy of the Book wrote by him to explain that Map. AMELIA EVANS

£5. 5. 0

Endorsed: No 73[4] Amelia Evans £11. 11. 0 Note, Herein is an Order on Mrs Strettell for £6. 6s. 0d.[5] Sent to Mrs Franklin Jan. 26. 1771

To Deborah Franklin
ALS: Yale University Library

My dear Child,   London, Feb. 22. 1766

I am excessively hurried, being every Hour that I am awake either abroad to speak with Members of Parliament or taken up with People coming to me at home, concerning our American Affairs, so that I am much behind-hand in answering my Friends Letters. But tho' I cannot by this Opportunity write to others, I

2. The entire document except the signature is in BF's hand.

3. See the document immediately above for an explanation for this receipt. After the publication of his *General Map of the Middle British Colonies in America* and his accompanying *Analysis* in Philadelphia in June 1755 Lewis Evans consigned several copies to Robert Dodsley for sale in London with instructions that in case his map was "hashed up in a New Form or pyrated" (which was exactly what happened) Dodsley should consult Thomas Pownall about "getting it Engraven at large and the Analysis published with it." The press of business prevented Pownall from bringing out an authorized edition of the map and there matters rested until 1766, when Amelia assigned her rights to the plate and copyright of the *Analysis* to BF as security for the loan of five guineas mentioned in this receipt. In 1776 Pownall published Evans' map in a new and enlarged edition, stating that the profits would go to Amelia and her children, a promise which both he and BF tried very hard to keep. See Evans to Dodsley, Jan. 25, 1756, *PMHB*, LIX (1935), 295–301. Evans' 1755 map and his *Analysis* are reproduced and reprinted in Lawrence H. Gipson, *Lewis Evans* (Phila., 1939), 141–76, and appendix.

4. The number assigned to the map transaction in BF's Journal, 1764–1776, p. 7.

5. The part of this endorsement from "Note" to this point was struck through and the remainder was added, apparently at a later date. Since BF sent the order on Mrs. Amos Strettell to DF for collection, he did not enter it in his own Journal and Ledger.

must not omit a Line to you who kindly write me so many. I am well; 'tis all I can say at present, except that I am just now made very happy by a Vote of the Commons for the Repeal of the Stamp Act.[6] Your ever loving Husband   B FRANKLIN

Monday, Feb. 24.

The above was wrote supposing the Packet would be dispatch'd that day. She is still detain'd, so I give it to Mr. Penrose[7] who was so obliging as to call and tell me of his going.

From Matthew Boulton[8]   Copy:[9] Assay Office, Birmingham

[Birmingham February 22, 1766]

The addition you have made to my happiness in being the cause of my acquaintance with the amiable and ingenious Dr. Small deserves more than thanks and theretofore I take this opportunity, of making my acknowledgements to you in the Same Sort of Coin by introducing to you, my Good friend Mr. Samuel Garbett,[1] who is an admirer of Mr. Francklin in particular, a Friend to Mankind in General, a Lover of his Country, a Zealous Advocate for Truth and for the rights, of your oppress'd Countrymen,[2] he is a Man

6. At about two o'clock on the morning of February 22 the Committee of the Whole House of the House of Commons voted, 275 to 167, to repeal the Stamp Act. See below, p. 168.

7. The Penroses were a Philadelphia shipbuilding family; it is not possible to ascertain which one of them carried this letter.

8. On Matthew Boulton, Birmingham engineer, associated with James Watt in the development of the steam engine, see above, x, 39 n.

9. On the same sheet with a letter from Boulton to Samuel Garbett of the same date, transmitting the original of this letter of introduction to BF.

1. Samuel Garbett (1717–1803), a Birmingham merchant and manufacturer, associated with John Roebuck in the production of sulphuric acid. In 1749 they established a plant at Prestonpans, near Edinburgh, and in 1760 they, with other partners, started the Carron iron works that BF visited in 1771. Having become a bankrupt, Garbett was living in Birmingham in 1788, when BF corresponded with him about a legacy to John Tyler (or Tiler), a relative of DF who had migrated to America. Robert E. Schofield, *The Lunar Society of Birmingham* (Oxford, 1963), p. 40 n.

2. In his letter enclosing this copy, Boulton had assured Garbett that he would be happy in the acquaintance of BF "as the disarmer of Jupiter and the British Parliaments." News of BF's appearance before the House of Commons,

who does honour to the Character of a Merchant, a Manufactorer, and of a Soldier, indeed he is of that Class of Men which I know you Love, and though I am Sensible your time is of Great value, yet I Shall make no apology for thus breaking in upon it, as youll thank me for his acquaintance. My engagements Since xmas have not permitt'd me to make any further progress, with my Fire Enguine but as the Thirsty Season is approaching apace, Necessity will oblige me to set about it in good Ernest.[3]

Query. which of the Steam Valves do you Like best.

Query. is it better to Introduce the Jet of Cold Water in at the bottoms of the receive[*sic*]. (which is about 3 feet from the top) or in at the top, Each has it adventages and disadvantages, my thoughts about the Secondary or Mechanical contrivences of it are too numerous to trouble you with in this Letter and yet I have not been Lucky enough, to hit upon any that are objectionless, therefore beg if any thought occours to you fertile Genius which you think may be usefull or preserve me from Error in the Execution of this Engine you'll be So kind as to comunicate it to me, and you'll very greatly oblidge your   M B

Having occasion to anneal a Steel Dye about 6 lb wt. the other Day, I put it (when moderatly Red Hott) into Some wood Ashes, which I consid'd as the best incombustible non Conductor of heat I know, those ashes were contain'd in a wooden Barrell which I wrapt up in Some Woolen blankets and left it in a Cold Garret (then Cover'd with Snow) w[h]ere it remain'd for 30 hours and then I open'd it in the presence of Dr. Small. I found a good deal of Steam condenc'd upon the Barrell and Blankets, which shew'd they were not dry enough For the Experiment. Yet neverthless the Dye was nearly as hot as boiling Water. There are a few other experiments which I want to make in this Way and then I intend to try if I Can't send you a 12 pounder red hot to London.

I Should be much oblig'd to you if you would Let the Servant order a Corker[4] to neal [nail] up the model of the Engine in the

---

February 13, on the repeal of the Stamp Act had apparently reached Boulton in Birmingham.

3. As the next passage and part of the postscript indicate, Boulton had sent BF a model of the steam engine in its then state of development. BF returned it in March.

4. A caulker is probably meant.

box again, and take it to the Birmingham Carrier at the Bell in smithfield the Expence of which you'll please to post in your Philosophical Account Book where your Debtor is not Distinguish'd from Creditor.

Benjm. Francklin Esqr

To Joseph Fox

ALS: Princeton University Library

Dear Sir,   London, Feb. 24. 1766.

I have now the Pleasure of informing you, that on Friday last, in a Committee of the whole House, Mr. Secretary Conway mov'd that it should be recommended to the House to give leave to bring in a Bill for repealing the American Stamp Act, which Motion was seconded by Mr. Cooper:[5] But an Amendment to the Motion being propos'd by the late Ministry, viz. instead of *Repealing* to say *explaining and amending*,[6] the Debate began, which lasted till two the next Morning, when it was carried for the total Repeal, by 275 against 167. Many of those who were for *explaining and amending* meant to reduce it to a Stamp on Cards and Dice only, and that merely to keep up the Claim of Right. The British Merchants trading to America have been extreamly zealous and hearty in our Cause; I hope they will receive the Thanks of the several Assemblies. The House will next proceed to reconsider all the Acts of

5. Henry Seymour Conway was secretary of state for the Southern Department and hence in general ministerial charge of colonial affairs. Grey Cooper (above, x, 185 n), M.P. from Rochester and secretary to the Treasury, was a personal friend of BF. Four members of the House of Commons, Nathaniel Ryder, Charles Garth, Horace Walpole, and Grey Cooper, have left accounts of the debates in the Committee of the Whole that led to the passage of the Declaratory Act and the repeal of the Stamp Act. For a description of these accounts, with citations to the last three, see Gipson, *British Empire*, x, 387 n, and on the debates themselves, *ibid.*, pp. 386–95. For another treatment by the same writer, based largely on the Ryder account and quoting extensively from it, see his "The Great Debate in the Committee of the Whole House of Commons on the Stamp Act, 1766, as Reported by Nathaniel Ryder," *PMHB*, LXXXVI (1962), 10–41.

6. The amendment was proposed by Charles Jenkinson, who had been secretary to the Treasury (Cooper's present post) in the Grenville ministry. Lord Rockingham to George III, Feb. 22, 1766, Sir John Fortescue, ed., *The Correspondence of King George the Third*, I (London, 1927), 275.

Trade, designing to give us every reasonable Relief.[7] I doubt not, but that if the Bill passes, a decent, dutiful, grateful Behaviour in us Americans will show that these Favours (for such they are thought here) are not ill bestowed. The present Ministry have been truly our Friends, and have hazarded themselves greatly in our Behalf. It would be a Pity if any future Misconduct of ours should turn to their Prejudice. With great Esteem, I am, Dear Sir, Your most obedient humble Servant   B FRANKLIN

Addressed: To / Joseph Fox Esqr / Speaker of the Honble. House of / Representatives / Pennsylvania / per favour of / Mr Penrose[8]

To David Hall   ALS: Salem County Historical Society, Salem, N.J.

Dear Mr. Hall,   London, Feb. 24. 1766
    The House of Commons after a long Debate, which lasted from Friday 3 aClock to 2 the next Morning, came to a Resolution to *repeal* the Stamp Act, 275 to 167, the Minority being for *explaining and amending.*[9] The Party of the late Ministry will give the Bill all the Obstruction and Delay possible, but there is reason now to believe it will pass both Houses which has long been rather doubtful. The present Ministry, who have been true Freinds to America in this Affair, purpose also to review the Acts of Trade, and give us every farther Relief that is reasonable. I hope therefore that Harmony between the two Countries will be restor'd, and all Mobs

7. Subsequent joint efforts by the merchants, the West Indian planters, and the colonial agents resulted in some favorable modifications of the trade laws, but no general revision took place. See Jack M. Sosin, *Agents and Merchants British Colonial Policy and the Origins of the American Revolution, 1763–1775* (Lincoln, Neb., 1965), pp. 81–6.
8. Which member of this family this might have been has not been determined. Speaker Fox laid BF's letter before the Assembly, June 5, 1766, after it convened following an adjournment of three weeks. 8 *Pa. Arch.,* VII, 5884. Very premature news of the "Repeal" of the Stamp Act in Irish newspapers had reached Philadelphia on March 24. *Pa. Gaz.,* March 27, 1766. Texts of the resolutions of the Committee of the Whole, including that for repeal, were printed in *Pa. Gaz.* and *Pa. Jour.,* May 1. The brig *Minerva* arrived on the 19th with the full text of the repealing act, which both newspapers printed as one-page supplements the same day. Their issues of May 22 reprinted the text and gave accounts of the local celebration.
9. See the notes to the document immediately above.

and Riots on our Side the Water totally cease. It will certainly become us on this Occasion to behave decently and respectfully with regard to Government here, that we may not disgrace our Friends who have in a manner engag'd their Credit for us on that head. We now see that tho' the Parliament may sometimes possibly thro' Misinformation be mislead to do a wrong Thing towards America, yet as soon as they are rightly inform'd, they will immediately rectify it, which ought to confirm our Veneration for that most august Body, and Confidence in its Justice and Equity. Great Honour and Thanks are due to the British Merchants, trading to America, who have all of them been our zealous and indefatigable Friends, particularly Mr. Trecothick and Mr. Capel Hanbury.[1] We had also many firm Friends in the House of Commons, viz. Mr. Pitt, Mr. Conway, Mr. Cooke, Mr. Dowdeswell, Sir George Saville, Sir William Meredith, Mr. Burke, Mr. Cooper, Mr. Jackson, Mr. Huske, with a Number of others too many to enumerate at present.[2] I am, as ever, Yours affectionately   B FRANKLIN

[The above for the Gazette I enclose you some of the Cards on which I have lately wrote all my Messages; they are to show the Mischiefs of reducing the Colonies by Force of Arms.][3]

Addressed: To / Mr David Hall / Printer / Philadelphia

Endorsed: Mr. Franklin February 24. 1766

1. Barlow Trecothick (*c.*1718–1775), London merchant and alderman, later sheriff, lord mayor, and M.P. for the city, spent his boyhood in Boston, and later became associated in business in London with the Thomlinsons and Apthorps. Capel Hanbury (d. 1769) was a London merchant trading to Virginia. A young man of the same name but of a different branch of the family married BF's great-granddaughter, Ellen Franklin, in 1818.

2. The men named here, with the constituencies they represented and the ministerial offices, if any, that they held at the time of these debates, were: William Pitt, Bath; Henry Seymour Conway, Thetford, secretary of state; George Cooke, Middlesex; William Dowdeswell, Worcestershire, chancellor of the Exchequer; Sir George Saville, Yorkshire; Sir William Meredith, Liverpool, lord of the Admiralty; Edmund Burke, Wendover, private secretary to the first lord of the Treasury; Grey Cooper, Rochester, secretary to the Treasury; Richard Jackson, Weymouth and Melcombe Regis; and John Huske, Maldon. Namier and Brooke, *House of Commons.* All but the last two were named on the 24th as members of the committee to prepare the repealing bill.

3. Brackets in the original. Hall did not print this letter in the *Gazette;* it may have reached him so late that the news it contained had become stale. Its ad-

From George Croghan

LS: Public Record Office; copy: Historical Society of Pennsylvania

Sir   Philada, February 25. 1766.

I did myself the Honour of writing to you, on the 12th. of December and inclosed you, a Copy of my Journal and Transactions, with the several Western Nations of Indians, that I met with, in my Tour to and from the Ilinois Country;[4] Since which I have had the Pleasure of hearing, that his Majesty's Troops have obtained, peaceable Possession of Fort Chartris.[5]

I beg leave now Sir, to present you, with the Copy of my private Journal. It is as descriptive, of the Territory, I passed thro', as the Embarrassments and Difficulties, I met with, from the French and Indians, would Admit of.

The Ilinois Country, far exceeds any other part of America, that I have seen—both as to Soil and Climate.

The French indeed, were so sensible of this and of its advantageous situation, both for enjoying the Benefits of a very extensive furr Trade and controuling, the numerous Nations of Indians, which surround it, that they a considerable Time ago, began to establish a Colony there; Which is now, in a very thriving Situation.

My Opinion is, that the British Nation ought immediately, whilst the Indians are friendly to us, and before the French can have Time, to Poison their Minds, To pursue their excellent Plan. And therefore, upon my Return from the Indian Country, I thought it my Duty, to communicate my sentiments, upon this Subject, freely, to Sir William Johnson. A Copy whereof, I pray leave to put under Cover, for your Perusal, and shall esteem it, a particular favor, if you will be pleased to afford me, your Thoughts upon it.

---

monition to seemly behavior, however, found parallel expression in several American newspaper pieces during the months that followed, and a number of the men BF singled out here for special gratitude were often hailed in the colonial press. The "Cards" he enclosed were probably copies of his "Magna Britannia her Colonies Reduc'd," above, pp. 66–72.

4. For Croghan's letter of Dec. 12, 1765, see above, XII, 395–400, and for his journals, mentioned in this and the next paragraph, see the first footnote to that letter. BF transmitted this letter, like its predecessor, to the ministry for its information.

5. Major Robert Farmer took possession of Fort Chartres, Dec. 2, 1765, though Capt. Thomas Stirling had reached there on October 9.

Sir William is entirely of my Opinion and has by this Month's Packett wrote very fully, to the Lords of Trade, concerning it.[6]

When I did myself the Pleasure of writing to you, on the 12th. of December, I took the Liberty of communicating to you, the Inclination and Desire of the Indians, To make the Traders, a satisfaction for their *Robbery's*. This, I thought then, as I do now, ought by no means to be refused, by his Majestys Ministers, As it is undoubtedly, a piece of Justice due to the sufferers and will be indulging the Natives, in a scheme of Retaliation, that may Ever hereafter, be rendered inexpressibly subservient, to his Majesty's Service.

I returned last Week, from a Visit to Sir William Johnson; When We frequently conferred, upon the above Subject. He is so thoroughly convinced, that it is a measure, which the Kings Ministers ought, immediately, to adopt (and especialy, as He has *finally* and *fully settled the matter* with the *six Nations*) That he has, by this Months Packett, (which I suppose, sailed the 16th Instant) wrote to the Lords of Trade and express'd to them, the Voluntary Offer of the Shawanese and Delawares, and that *the Six Nations,* had expressly Authorized him, to *confirm the Grant;* Wherefore he has earnestly desired, that he may have the Kings Orders to settle it, At the same Time, that he is Commanded to ratify a permanent Boundary, between the Colonies and *the Indians hunting Ground.* This certainly, is an Object of the greatest Consequence to these Provinces, as it will effectualy ascertain, a sufficient extent of Land for Colonization, and put an End, to dangerous Disputes, respecting our Frontier People's hunting, on their Ground; Therefore it is to be hoped, No Time will be lost, before Sir William is authorized to Compleat it. When I dare say, you will Joyfully seize that Opportunity, of doing our distressed Countrymen, so much essential Service, As to *back Sir Williams request,* That He may *then,* have his Majestys *clear* and *express Orders To confirm* the *six Nations Grant,* to the sufferers.

Indians are of a fickle, uncertain Temper, Wherefore their Offers ought always to be accepted, as soon as possible, after proffer'd, otherwise they are too apt, to construe a Delay, into a Contemptuous refusal.

6. Johnson's letter of Jan. 31, 1766, is printed in *N.Y. Col. Docs.*, VII, 808–10, and Alvord and Carter, eds., *The New Régime*, pp. 149–53.

It is also, as remarkable, that altho' they are thus Capricious, yet to their Honour, be it mentioned, that it was never known, they ever attempted to dissolve a Contract, justly and plainly, made with them.

Sometime next Month, I shall make another Visit to the Illinois &c. in Order to consolidate my last Year's Negotiations.[7] If anything material should occur, worthy your Consideration, I shall take the Liberty of communicating it, to you. I am with great Respect Sir Your Obledient humble Servant   GEO: CROGHAN

Benjamin Franklyn Esqr.

Endorsed: Letter from Col Croghan Feb. 25. 1766 His Sentiments of a Colony in the Ilinois Country And of the Indians making a Retribution in Lands to the Traders they robbed.[8]

To David Hall   ALS: Maryland Historical Society

Dear Mr. Hall   London, Feb. 26. 1766.

I wrote to you on the 22d Instant, via Maryland.[9] I now congratulate you again on the Prospect of having the Stamp Act repeal'd. The Grand Committee reported on Monday.[1] Mr. Conway mov'd that Leave should be given to bring in a Bill for repealing the American Stamp Act. The Motion being seconded and agreed to, one of the late Ministry mov'd, that a Clause should be inserted in the Bill, to prevent the Repeal taking Place till every Colony Assembly had eras'd out of its Minute Book the Resolves that militated against the Right of Parliament: The Debate lasted till one a Clock next Morning, when it was carried again the last

7. Croghan did not leave Philadelphia until May, arriving at Fort Pitt on the 22d. He left there for the Illinois Country on June 18, accompanied on the Ohio River by thirteen large bateaux with presents for the Indians and provisions for Fort Chartres. Nicholas B. Wainwright, *George Croghan Wilderness Diplomat* (Chapel Hill, [1959]), pp. 231–3.

8. This endorsement is in BF's hand. The copy, which Croghan retained, is endorsed: "Copy my Letter to Doctor Franklin Per Capt. Sparks who sailed Monday March 3d. 1766."

9. BF should probably have written "24th" (not "22d") in reference to the letter printed next but one above.

1. Rose Fuller (above, VIII, 132 n) served as chairman of the Committee of the Whole during the debates and so brought in its report on February 24.

Motion 240 to 133.[2] I write in great haste; but am as ever, Yours affectionately   B FRANKLIN
I received yours of Oct. 14 and Nov. 5.[3]

Addressed: To / Mr David Hall / Printer / Philadelphia / Mr P Campbell.

Endorsed: Franklin Feby 26. 1766.

From Ezra Stiles   Draft: Yale University Library

Dear Sir   Newport Febry 26 1766
     Permit me to request that you would perfect the inclosed List.[4] It is some Satisfaction to know the company into which one is associated. It would oblige me if Mr. Strahan would furnish a List of the Divines in Scotland now living and dignified with a Doctorate, I am told they are not numerous.[5] Among the Ten Thousand

     2. BF here somewhat confused the sequence of events. After the resolution asking leave to bring in a bill repealing the Stamp Act had been introduced, a motion to recommit the resolution was defeated 240 to 133. This was the decisive vote of the day on this matter. The House thereupon accepted the resolution, granted leave for the bill, and appointed a committee of twenty members to prepare it. Only then did William Blackstone, M.P. for Hinton, a supporter of the former Grenville ministry but not a member of it, move for an instruction to the committee to include a provision in the bill to require the expunging of the assemblies' offensive resolves. The Commons defeated Blackstone's motion without a division. *Journals of the House of Commons,* XXX, 602–3.
     3. For the first of these letters, see above, XII, 319–21; the second has not been found.
     4. Possibly a list of Americans who had been awarded doctorates by British universities, as Stiles himself had been by the University of Edinburgh the preceding year. See above, XII, 194–6, 384–5. On Aug. 28, 1767, BF wrote Stiles, inclosing "your List of Doctors, compleated as far as I can do it without the Help of my Friends." Filed with this letter in Dr. Williams' Library, London, is a list in Stiles's hand of "Episcopalians in America" who had received British doctorates. It is most unlikely that this list was copied from the one BF sent him on Aug. 28, 1767, because it contains the names of many New England divines who Stiles certainly knew held doctorates and whose names he would certainly have included on the list sent in the present letter. The list of "Episcopalians in America," which includes BF, must have been prepared by Stiles himself for reasons that are not now apparent. The list which BF sent him on Aug. 28, 1767, has not been found.
     5. There is no evidence to indicate that Stiles ever received such a list from Strahan; its compilation would have required an enormous amount of labor.

Clergy of the Church of England are there 2 or 300 Doctors? Pray oblige me with a List of those most eminent for Literature. The Dutch are said to have a Degree beyond the Superlative—these seem to be eruditissimi eruditissimorum such were Bacon, Selden, Newton Locke &c. In your last you mentioned a Correspondence with which I should esteem myself much honoud, if Dr. Watson should consent, which I shall know by receiving his Letter.[6]

I have seen lately seen an excellent and amiable Character of the Marquis of Rockingham as a Patron of Literature and real Merit, and a Judge of both.[7] I should share the pleasure with the rest of your New England Friends if this Nobleman, or some other of your Acquaintance would recommend you, my dear Sir, to his Majesty for the Honor of Knighthood: I wish you an heriditary Dignity and such I think is that of a Baronet:

I have somtimes wished, after you had digested such of your Letters and other Writings as you would desire to accompany your Name through all american Ages, that I might be charged with the publication of them, prefixing them with the history of your Life.[8] But this is an honor, to which among your numerous friends I can have no pretension. Confucius and his Posterity have been honored in China for Twenty Ages—the Electrical Philosopher, the American Inventor of the pointed Rods will live for Ages to come to live with him would please no one more than, my Dear Maecenas Your affectionate Friend and obedient Servant   EZRA STILES

Dr. Franklin London
Sent by Mr. Robt. Stevens Junior who saild March 9. 1766. on Board the ship America Capt. Osborn from Newport Rh. Isl. for Bristol in England, and Arrived at Bristol Apr. 17.

6. In his letter of July 5, 1765 (above, XII, 195) BF stated that he would attempt to persuade Dr. William Watson (above, III, 457 n), the eminent physician, naturalist, and electrician, to correspond with Stiles. The two men do not seem to have corresponded, however.

7. Charles Watson-Wentworth, 2d Marquis of Rockingham (1730–1782), was, of course, prime minister at this time. In England he was considered a patron of horse racing and of little else.

8. In July 1763 while visiting with BF in Newport, R.I., Stiles had collected facts about the honors which his friend had received, material which he could have used in preparing a biography. See above, X, 309–11.

To Deborah Franklin   ALS: American Philosophical Society

My dear Child,   London, Feb. 27. 1766.

I wrote you a few days ago by Mr. Penrose via Mary land, when I wrote also to the Speaker, to Mr. Galloway, Mr. Hughes and Mr. Hall.[9] I have now as little time as then to enlarge, having wrote besides to day so much that I am almost blind. But by the March Packet shall fully answer your late Letters. Let the Vaults alone till my Return:[1] As you have a Wood Yard, perhaps they may not be necessary. I send you some curious Beans for your Garden.[2] Love to Sally and all Relations; and to all the Ladies that do me the Honour to enquire after me. I congratulate you on the soon expected Repeal of the Stamp Act; and on the great Share of Health we both enjoy, tho' now going in Fourscore, (that is, in the fourth Score.)[3] Mr. Whitfield[4] call'd today and tells me a surprizing Piece of News. Mr. Dunlap is come here from Barbadoes, was ordain'd Deacon on Saturday last, and Priest on Sunday![5] In haste, but very well, I am, my dear Girl, Your ever loving Husband,   B FRANKLIN

Inclos'd are a few of my Political Cards.[6]

Addressed: To / Mrs Franklin / at / Philadelphia

9. For BF's letters to DF, Joseph Fox, and David Hall, see above, pp. 165–6, 168–9, 169–70. His to Joseph Galloway and John Hughes have not been found.

1. DF was evidently perplexed about the wisdom of constructing vaults in or near her new house. Apparently Samuel Rhoads had advised against it, arguing that they "will always be a harbor for Rattes and such Creeping things." See above, XII, 299.

2. One wonders if these were a different variety from "the Bush Beans, a new Sort for your Garden," which BF sent DF on April 6, 1766. See below, p. 234.

3. BF had celebrated his sixtieth birthday in January. Born in 1708, DF was not quite yet in her fourth score.

4. George Whitefield (above, II, 241 n), the evangelist. Whitefield had written Samuel Wharton about this time, praising BF's performance in his examination before the House of Commons. An extract in *Pa. Gaz.*, May 1, 1766, from "an eminent Clergyman in London," relating that BF "spoke very heartily and judiciously" before Commons, may have come from Whitefield's letter. Joseph Galloway to WF, April 29, 1766, APS.

5. See above, p. 86 n.

6. See above, pp. 66–72.

To Edward Penington

ALS: Historical Society of Pennsylvania

Dear Sir, London, Feb. 27. 1766

I received yours of Nov. 14.[7] with that enclos'd for Mr. Sp[ringett] Penn, which I immediately forwarded to him. He continues in Ireland I know not why. I hear from him sometimes, but to little purpose.[8] I think it not unlikely he may suffer him self to be finally impos'd on by his Uncle in the Affair of Pensbury, but shall endeavour to stir him up against it, and prevail with him to go over, or impower you to sell for his best Advantage. The Artifice you mention is a base one; but I hope you will defeat it, and secure the poor young Man's whole Right for him. I shall give him every Assistance in my Power. With great Esteem I am, Your most obedient humble Servant   B FRANKLIN

Mr Js. Pennington[9]

Addressed: Mr Edwd Pennington / Mercht / Philadelphia

Endorsed: Feby 27th 1766 from B Franklin
Second Endorsement: from B. Franklin

To [Hugh Roberts]

ALS: University of Pennsylvania Library

Dear Friend London Feb. 27. 1766

I receiv'd your kind Letter of Nov. 27.[1] You cannot conceive how much Good the cordial Salutations of an old Friend do the Heart of a Man so far from home, and hearing frequently of the Abuses thrown on him in his Absence by the Enemies that Party has rais'd against him.

In the meantime I hope I have done even those Enemies some Service in our late Struggle for America. It has been a hard one,

---

7. See above, XII, 370–2.
8. See above, pp. 123–4.
9. So written at the lower left hand corner of the letter, but the address furnishes indisputable proof that Edward Penington was the addressee of this letter. BF may have written "Js." with James Pemberton in mind, because on this same day Dr. John Fothergill had written Pemberton a testimonial, exonerating BF from complicity in the passage of the Stamp Act. Fothergill's letter is in Hist. Soc. Pa.
1. See above, XII, 386–8.

and we have been often between Hope and Despair; but now the Day begins to clear, the Ministry are fix'd for us, and we have obtain'd a Majority in the House of Commons for Repealing the Stamp Act, and giving us Ease in every Commercial Grievance.[2] God grant that no bad News of farther Excesses in America may arrive to strengthen our Adversaries and weaken the Hands of our Friends, before this good Work is quite compleated.

The Partizans of the late Ministry have been strongly crying out Rebellion, and calling for Force to be sent against America! The Consequence might have been terrible! but milder Measures have prevailed.

I hope, nay I am confident, America will Show itself grateful to Britain on this Occasion, and behave prudently and decently.

I have got a Seal[3] done for four Guineas, which I shall send per Friend.

My Respects to good Mrs. Roberts, and to your valuable Son. Remember me affectionately to the Junto, and to all enquiring Friends.

Adieu, my dear Friend. Your Integrity will always make you happy. Believe me ever Yours affectionately   B FRANKLIN

Mr. Neave[4] [has been] long in the Country.

To Charles Thomson

ALS: Library of Congress

London Feb. 27. 1766.

My good Friend and Neighbour,

I forget whether I before acknowledg'd the Receipt of your kind Letter of Sept. 24. I gave an Extract of it to a Friend, with an Extract of mine to which it was an Answer; and he printed both in the London Chronicle, with an Introduction of his own:[5] and I

2. For the various stages through which the effort to repeal the Stamp Act passed in the House of Commons, see above, pp. 55 n, 168.

3. For the Pennsylvania Hospital; see above, XII, 236, 386.

4. Samuel Neave; above, XII, 136 n.

5. Under a short introduction of his own, William Strahan printed extracts of BF's letter to Thomson, July 11, 1765, and of Thomson's reply, Sept. 24, 1765, in the Nov. 14–16, issue of the *London Chronicle*. For these letters, see above, XII, 206–8, 278–80.

have reprinted everything from America that I thought might help our common Cause. We at length, after a long and hard Struggle, have gain'd so much Ground, that there is now little Doubt the Stamp Act will be repealed, and reasonable Relief given us besides in our Commercial Grievances, and those relating to our Currency.[6] I trust the Behaviour of the Americans on the Occasion, will be so prudent, decent, and grateful, as that their Friends here will have no reason to be ashamed; and that our Enemies, who predict that the Indulgence of Parliament will only make us more insolent and ungovernable, may find themselves, and be found, false Prophets. My Respects to Mrs. Thomson. I have not had the Pleasure of hearing from you by any of the late Opportunities; but am so bad a Correspondent myself that I have no right to take Exceptions, and am nevertheless Your affectionate Friend and very humble Servant   B FRANKLIN

Mr. Cha. Thomson

Addressed: To / Mr Charles Thomson / Mercht / Philadelphia

Endorsed: Doctr B. Franklin Feby 26. 1768 [*sic*] a lett from B Franklin in London Feby 27 1766

From Joseph Galloway   ALS: American Philosophical Society

Dear Sir   Philadelphia Feby. 27. 1765 [1766][7]
I wrote to you by the Packet, inclosing a Copy of the Extract of a Letter from Thomas Penn Esqr. to his Nephew the Governor, which is inclosed in this Letter.[8]

6. BF was too sanguine about prospects for colonial relief from parliamentary restrictions on paper money. The Currency Act of 1764, which prevented the American colonies south of New England from issuing any more legal tender paper money, was not, as he apparently expected, repealed or extensively modified.

7. Galloway wrote 1765, but the body of the letter makes it unmistakably clear that this was a slip of the pen and that he meant 1766.

8. Although Galloway's letter to BF of Jan. 13, 1766 (above, pp. 35–7) went by the packet, he did not mention sending any accompanying enclosures. The extract from Thomas Penn's letter which he sent with the present letter was undoubtedly the first paragraph of one to his nephew, Governor John Penn, of Nov. 30, 1765: "In my last Letter . . . I told you Mr. Franklin had

This Account of the Petitions for a Change of this Government from Proprietary to Royal, has struck our Friends with the utmost Consternation.[9] And indeed I am not a little alarmed at the Consequences. For you well know the Assembly Party are the only Loyal Part of the People here, and are those very persons who have preserved the Peace and good Order of the Province, not only against the Paxton Rioters and Murderers, but also in these Times of general Tumult and Distraction; when all the Powers of this Government were asleep, and its Officers even Active in the Opposition. And they Conceive that this good Demeanor and remarkable Services to the Crown justifies their Claim of some Share of [the] Merit, and at Least entitles them to a Hearing of their Complaints.

But they say if this Extract be true, That his Majestys Privy Council, has rejected the Humble Petitions of their Representatives without even a Hearing. That they have not been permitted, when they have approached the Throne with the utmost Duty and Loyalty, to breath forth their Complaints against Proprietary Oppression and Injustice, which has often wounded their own Welfare and obstructed their essential Duties to the Crown. And that they have nothing now left, but to groan, if they dare to groan at all, under the Tyranny of a private Subject, without the least Hopes of Redress, the Royal Ear being Shut against the [a][1] Part of his Liege Subjects the most Dutiful and Loyal.

They further Say, what you well know, that the Laws are not, nor have been, for many Years Duly Executed. That no Justice is

---

presented the Petitions, I have now the satisfaction to inform you they have been considered by the King in Council, and resolved not to be proper for further consideration, but by his Majesty's order postponed, sine die, that is (to use my Lord Presidents own expression) for ever and ever; this is the most easy way of rejecting, and which they make use of when any considerable bodys of People Petition; so that you may be assured we shall not have any further trouble about them not any of the Council thought them proper to be referred to a Committee, as they prayed for a thing not in the King's Power to grant nor in the least in his will and not giving any good reason for their request." Penn Papers, Hist. Soc. Pa.

9. For the form of the Privy Council's rejection of the petition for royal government, see above, XII, 235–6 n.

1. The first page of the MS ends with "the" and the second page begins with "a." Either word would make sense; the reader may correct Galloway's slip to suit his own preference.

to be obtained against the Proprietors or their Adherents. That the most Flagetious Offenders, even Murderers and Rebels are travelling about the Country with Impunity.[2] And that they have no Protection of Life, nor Safety of Person or Property. These with many other Complaints are constantly issuing from the Hearts of the People. The Proprietary Dependants excepted, who greatly rejoice and even insult the Petitioners and their Friends, since the receipt of this incredible Letter, extracts whereof have been industriously Sent all over the Province, in order to Spirit up the Temper and violent Disposition of their Party.[3] I have left nothing in my Power unessayed among our Friends to oppose the Torrent and to prevail on them to discredit this Account, and to beleive that his Majesty will yet hear their Petitions and redress their Aggreivances—And I have been obliged, to give many Extracts of your Letter to me[4] respecting the State of these Petitions to convince them of my Assurances, which has in some Degree prevented their Despair, as they have been from thence induced to discredit the Extract.

Our Assembly, anxious to know the result of the Petitions have adjourned to the 6th. of May next,[5] who are inviolably attached to his Majesty, and firmly determined to become his immediate Subjects, if there are any Human Means left to Effect it. And Since

2. The Pa. frontiersmen, who, as the Paxton Boys, had terrorized and murdered Indians in 1764 and who, as the "Black Boys," had assaulted and forcibly interfered with Indian traders in 1765. See above, XI, 22–9, 42–69; XII, 92 n.

3. *Pa. Journal,* Feb. 27, 1766, published the following version of the extract: "By letters from England, of the best authority, we are advised, that, "the PETITIONS for and against the CHANGE of the GOVERNMENT of this Province, had been read twice before the KING and COUNCIL, when it was put off *sine die,* which, to use *the Lord President of the Council's* own words, is *for ever* and *for ever.* Thus we hope we have got rid of this unhappy bone of contention, and that now peace, good-will and brotherly love will take place."

4. Possibly a reference to BF's letters of Sept. 26 and Nov. 9, 1765, mentioned in Galloway's letter of Jan. 13, 1766 (above, p. 35). According to Thomas Wharton, BF was quite optimistic in one of these letters about the prospect of securing a royal government. See above, XII, 420.

5. On Feb. 8, 1766, the House adjourned to May 5, 1766. Galloway correctly anticipated that a quorum would not be present until May 6. 8 *Pa. Arch.,* VII, 5859.

the Assurances, that have been received that our Liberties will be preserved on the Change,[6] All their Constituents (the Proprietary Dependants and Presbyterians excepted) are determined to support them in the Attempt. And shoud this Account from the Proprietor prove true (which God forbid) that their Petitions are rejected without a *Hearing*, I fear their Consternation and Distress will be wrought still higher. For while the present Members are Continued, I am convinced, they will never cease Entreating his Majesty to rescue them from the Oppression of his private Subjects. And that there is a great Probability to presume their Continuance, will appear from the Accounts of the last Election, I transmitted you by Captain Friend.[7]

Wherefore, I hope, the Petitions, as you have wrote, and I have confidently declared, are not rejected, or laid aside, but will be Resumed when the more important American Affairs are Settled. Nothing less than a Change, I think will satisfy the People, certain I am a Dismission without a Hearing never can: But I fear will throw this already too unhappy Province in to equal Disorder and Confusion with its Neighbouring Colonies.

You will therefore be pleased, to inform me, in what state the Petitions are before his Majestys Council by the earliest Opportunity, That I may be enabled to Satisfy the People who rely on us, with Certainty. In the Mean Time be assured, that nothing in my Power shall be wanting to preserve the Peace, and render them Easy. Beleive me, Dear Friend, ever, yours most affectionately

JOS. GALLOWAY

Endorsed: Mr Galloway Feb. 27. 66 Petitions

"F.B.": The Frenchman and the Poker

First printing not located; reprinted in *The Pennsylvania Chronicle, And Universal Advertiser,* March 16–23, 1767.

This is the second of two letters Goddard reprinted in the *Pennsylvania Chronicle,* March 16–23, 1767, the authorship of which he attributed to

6. These assurances were contained in a letter from Richard Jackson to the Assembly, Aug. 9, 1765. See above, XII, 322.
7. Galloway is referring either to his letter of Oct. 8–14, 1765, or to another letter mentioned in it. See above, XII, 305–6.

Franklin. In a letter to his sister, Jane Mecom, many years later, Franklin acknowledged that he had "told" the story.[8] Goddard gave no source from which he reprinted the piece, though the fact that the first of the letters he reprinted in this issue came from the *Gazetteer* probably explains why Smyth *(Writings,* v, 14 n) stated that this one was also taken from that London paper. The editors have been unable to identify the journal from which Goddard took it.[9]

To the PRINTER.   [February–March 1766[1]]
It is reported, I know not with what Foundation, that there is an Intention of obliging the Americans to pay for all the Stamps they ought to have used, between the Commencement of the Act, and the Day on which the Repeal takes Place, *viz.* from the first of November 1765, to the first of May 1766; that this is to make Part of an Act, which is to give Validity to the Writings and Law Proceedings, that contrary to Law have been executed without Stamps, and is to be the Condition on which they are to receive that Validity. Shall we then keep up for a Trifle the Heats and Animosities that have been occasioned by the Stamp-Act? and lose all the

8. The story was later reprinted several times with embellishments, the first apparently being in Matthew Carey's *American Museum,* IV (Aug. 1788), 184, where the conversation was considerably expanded and where the Englishman twice ejaculated "damn your soul" and once "damn me." After reading this version, Jane Mecom wrote her brother, Nov. 11, 1788, complaining of such additions. He replied, November 26, that "as you observe, there was no swearing in the story of the poker, when I told it. The late new dresser of it was, probably, the same, or perhaps akin to him" who related a conversation between Queen Anne and the Archbishop of Canterbury during which, he said in effect, they had engaged in a swearing match. When questioned, the narrator had admitted that "that is only *my way* of telling the story." Van Doren, *Franklin-Mecom,* pp. 317, 319. Very similar but not identical versions of the poker story, with each "damn" discreetly changed to "d--n," appeared in the *Massachusetts Centinel,* Nov. 1, 1788, and the *Georgia State Gazette,* March 28, 1789.

9. Verner W. Crane has also indicated his inability to locate the initial printing. *Letters to the Press,* p. 76.

1. BF could not have written this piece before February 22, when the critical vote in the Committee of the Whole House in favor of repealing the Stamp Act took place, and he is hardly likely to have written it before the 26th, when the repealing bill received its first reading and when, in consequence, the effective date of the proposed repeal, May 1, would have become public knowledge. It is quite possible that he wrote the piece between February 26 and March 18, when the bill was finally enacted, and he almost certainly wrote it before the May 1 date of repeal he mentions in the first sentence.

Benefit of Harmony and good Understanding between the different Parts of the Empire, which were expected from a generous total Repeal? Is this Pittance likely to be a Whit more easily collected than the whole Duty? Where are Officers to be found who will undertake to collect it? Who is to protect them while they are about it? In my Opinion, it will meet with the same Opposition, and be attended with the same Mischiefs that would have attended an Enforcement of the Act entire.

But I hear, that this is thought necessary, to raise a Fund for defraying the Expence that has been incurred by stamping so much Paper and Parchment for the Use of America, which they have refused to take and turn'd upon our Hands; and that since they are highly favour'd by the Repeal, they cannot with any Face of Decency refuse to make good the Charges we have been at on their Account. The whole Proceeding would put one in Mind of the Frenchman that used to accost English and other Strangers on the Pont-Neuf,* with many Compliments, and a red hot Iron in his Hand; *Pray Monsieur Anglois,* says he, *Do me the Favour to let me have the Honour of thrusting this hot Iron into your Backside?* Zoons, what does the Fellow mean! Begone with your Iron, or I'll break your Head! *Nay, Monsieur,* replies he, *if you do not chuse it, I do not insist upon it. But at least, you will in Justice have the Goodness to pay me something for the heating of my Iron.*   F.B.

To Deborah Franklin

ALS (fragment):[2] American Philosophical Society

[February–March 1766[3]]

There is a brown Paper Packet for you directed but contains chiefly a Letter and Parcel of News papers for Billy, which pray send to

*A Bridge over the River Siene, leading to Paris.

2. Written on the obverse of the address page, this surviving paragraph was probably the postscript to a letter now lost.

3. There are two clues which help date this fragment. One is BF's statement that DF should open the packet to remove some beans which he was sending her; in his letter of Feb. 27, 1766 (above, p. 176) he had mentioned sending her "some curious Beans." The other is his notation that he was sending the letter from which this fragment survives by Captain Friend. *Pa. Gaz.,* June 5,

him directly. I mean the Newspapers. You need not indeed open the Pacquet, if it were not to take out a Letter or two for Neighbour Sumain,[4] and the Beans. But pray send him up the Papers directly before they are scatter'd and lost.

Addressed: To / Mrs Franklin / Philadelphia / Per Favour of / Capt. Friend / with a brown Parcel

From Joseph Priestley[5]

ALS (fragment):[6] American Philosophical Society

[February 1766]

[*First part missing*] myself so much as to think I am able to [carry to completion] this large plan. I only propose to do it [if I can

---

1766, records the entry of the *Carolina,* Capt. James Friend. If this vessel had a passage of between two or three months, long but not unusual, then the letter could have been written and sent at the end of February or in March 1766.

4. The silversmith Samuel Soumaine; above, VI, 113 n; X, 135 n. The letters may have been from his daughter Elizabeth Empson, who was in London at this time; see above, XI, 190 n.

5. Joseph Priestley (1733–1804), man of science and theologian, is so well known that he requires no extended biographical notice here. At this time he was a tutor at Warrington Academy. Following his custom, he visited London in the winter of 1765–66; there he met Richard Price, John Canton, William Watson, and BF and "was led to attend to the subject of experimental philosophy more than I had done before" and was encouraged to write a history of electricity. *Memoirs of Dr. Joseph Priestley, to the Year 1795* (London, 1806), p. 50. His new friends promptly nominated him for election as a Fellow of the Royal Society (above, VIII, 358). His *History of Electricity* appeared in 1767. Nearly all the surviving correspondence with these scientists in London concerning the preparation of the book is published in Robert E. Schofield, ed., *A Scientific Autobiography of Joseph Priestley (1733–1804)* (Cambridge, Mass., and London, [1966]), pp. 12–49. See also *DAB; DNB; Life and Correspondence of Joseph Priestley, LL.D., F.R.S.* (2 vols., London, 1831–32). Although only a fragment of this letter remains, it was probably in this communication that Priestley told BF in some detail of his plans for a history of electricity and solicited the help of BF and other London friends. This supposition suggests a February dating.

6. Only the lower right-hand segment of the last page survives. The first few words of each of the last six lines are also torn off. In an attempt to make the remainder readable, the editors have supplied in brackets what seems to be the sense, if not the precise words, lost from these lines.

leave] it to you and my other friends in Lon[don readily to sup]ply my deficiencies. In the mean time I should be glad to have your sentiment of it. [Asking your pardon for] trespassing so long upon your patience [I am with the greatest res]pect, Dear Sir your most obliged humble servant   J PRIESTLEY
[*Torn*] contents[7]
[*torn*]ent, to
[*torn*]

To Joseph Fox   ALS: William Logan Fox, Philadelphia (1956)

Sir   London, March 1. 1766
I wrote to you of the 22d past, via Maryland.[8] Inclos'd I send a Copy of the late Votes on the Affair of the American Stamp-Act. The Repeal is now in a fair way of being compleated, on which I congratulate you and the Assembly.[9] I am, Sir, Your most obedient humble Servant,   B FRANKLIN

P.S. An Act will pass at the same time with the Repeal of the Stamp Act, similar to that relating to Ireland pass'd in the Reign of George the first;[1] it will be call'd *an Act for the better securing the Dependency of His Majesty's Dominions in America, on the Crown and Parliament of Great Britain;*[2] This is merely to save Appearances, and to guard against the Effects of the Clamour made by

7. Too much of this postscript is lost to permit verbal reconstruction. Filed with this letter fragment in the Franklin Papers at APS is a scrap from another letter, possibly also by Priestley, though the handwriting and torn signature are less certainly his. It reads: "was sorry to have been out of the way [*torn*] called Yesterday, the inclosed have [*torn*] my Packet for you to which I [*torn*] Yours J. P. [*torn*] Saturday."
8. No letter to Fox of Feb. 22, 1766, has been found. BF may be referring to his letter of Feb. 24, 1766, above, pp. 168–9.
9. For a chronology of Parliament's repeal of the Stamp Act, see *ibid.* and above, p. 55 n.
1. The act relating to Ireland was 6 Geo. I, c. 5 (1719).
2. This is BF's first mention of the prospective Declaratory Act (6 Geo. III, c. 12) in which Parliament resolved that it "had, hath, and of Right ought to have, full Power and Authority to make Laws and Statutes of sufficient Force and Validity to bind the Colonies and People of America, Subjects of the Crown of Great Britain, in all Cases whatsoever." The decision to press for such an act was reached at a meeting of the Rockingham ministry

the late Ministry as if the Rights of this Nation were sacrificed to America: And I think we may rest secure notwithstanding such Act, that no future Ministry will ever attempt to tax us, any more than they venture to tax Ireland. But then it is suppos'd, that we shall be, as we have been heretofore, always willing and ready to grant such voluntary Aids to the Crown as are suitable to our Abilities, when duly call'd upon for that purpose.

Addressed: To / Joseph Fox Esqr / Philadelphia / via New York / per Packet / Free, B. Franklin

To Jane Mecom   ALS: American Philosophical Society

Dear Sister   London, March 1. 1766
I acknowledge the Receipt of your kind Letters of Nov. 12. and Dec. 20. the latter per Mr. Williams.[3] I condole with you on the Death of your Husband, who was I believe a truly affectionate one to you, and fully sensible of your Merit.[4] It is not true that I have bought any Estate here. I have indeed had some thoughts of re-purchasing the little one in Northamptonshire that was our Grandfather's, and had been many Generations in the Family, but was sold by our Uncle Thomas's only Child Mrs. Fisher, the same

---

on Jan. 17, 1766, and a resolution, requesting such a statute, was introduced in the Committee of the Whole, Feb. 3, 1766. On behalf of the Committee Rose Fuller reported a series of resolutions to the full House on February 24, the first of which was that Parliament had powers which were described in precisely the words, just quoted, which were incorporated in the Declaratory Act. The House agreed to the resolution the same day and ordered the drafting of a bill embodying it. Such a bill was presented to the House and read for the first time on Feb. 26, 1766, as was the bill for repealing the Stamp Act. Both bills were read for the second time on February 27 and on March 18 both received the royal assent. See *The Statutes at Large*, x (London, 1771), 152–3; *Journals of the House of Commons*, xxx (Jan. 10, 1765–Sept. 16, 1766), 602–67, *passim;* Morgan, *Stamp Act Crisis*, pp. 268–81.

3. Neither the letter of Nov. 12, 1765, nor the one of Dec. 20, 1765, has been found. For Mrs. Mecom's letter of Dec. 30, 1765, which BF may have misdated from memory December 20, see above, XII, 417–19. John Williams, a customs official and brother of BF's nephew by marriage, Jonathan Williams, Sr. (C.5.3), is identified above, XII, 193 n.

4. Jane's husband, Edward, a saddler, died Sept. 11, 1765. Van Doren, *Franklin-Mecom*, pp. 84–5.

that left you the Legacy.[5] However I shall not do it unless I determine to remain in England, which I have not yet done.

As to the Reports you mention that are spread to my Disadvantage,[6] I give myself as little Concern about them as possible. I have often met with such Treatment from People that I was all the while endeavouring to serve. At other times I have been extoll'd extravagantly when I have had little or no Merit. These are the Operations of Nature. It sometimes is cloudy, it rains, it hails; again 'tis clear and pleasant, and the Sun shines on us. Take one thing with another, and the World is a pretty good sort of a World; and 'tis our Duty to make the best of it and be thankful. One's true Happiness depends more upon one's own Judgement of one's self, on a Consciousness of Rectitude in Action and Intention, and in the Approbation of those few who judge impartially, than upon the Applause of the unthinking undiscerning Multitude, who are apt to cry Hosanna today, and tomorrow, Crucify him. I see in the Papers that your Governor, Mr. Barnard, has been hardly thought of, and a little unkindly treated, as if he was a favourer of the Stamp Act: Yet it appears by his Letters to Government here, which have been read in Parliament, that he has wrote warmly in favour of the Province and against that Act, both before it pass'd and since; and so did your Lieutenant Governor to my certain Knowledge,[7] tho' the Mob have pull'd down his House. Surely the N. England People, when they are rightly inform'd, will do Justice to those Gentlemen, and think of them as they deserve.[8]

Pray remember me kindly to Cousin Williams,[9] and let him

5. BF visited the Franklin ancestral home in Ecton, Northamptonshire, in the summer of 1758; he found it a "decayed old stone building, but still known by the name of Franklin House." The property had descended to his first cousin, Mary Franklin Fisher (A.5.2.1.1), whose husband had sold it to a third party. See above, VIII, 136. Upon Mrs. Fisher's death, Dec. 25, 1758, her remaining estate was divided among her American and English cousins. *Ibid.*, 224–5.

6. Almost certainly the same charges that were concocted in Pa., that BF was instrumental in the passage of the Stamp Act.

7. For the opposition of Francis Bernard and Thomas Hutchinson to the Stamp Act, see Morgan, *Stamp Act Crisis*, pp. 19, 60–1, 100, 129–30, 210–15.

8. On Dec. 9, 1766, the Mass. General Court passed an act compensating Hutchinson and others who had suffered damages from the Stamp Act mobs. See above, XII, 339–40 n.

9. Jonathan Williams, Sr., mentioned in the first note to this letter.

know that I am very sensible of his Kindness to you, and that I am not forgetful of any thing that may concern his Interest or his Pleasure, tho' I have not yet wrote to him. I shall endeavour to make that Omission up to him as soon as possible.[1]

I sent you some things by your Friend Capt. Freeman, which I shall be glad to hear came safe to hand, and that they were acceptable[2] from Your affectionate Brother   B FRANKLIN

My Love to your Children.

P.S. I congratulate you and my Countrymen on the Repeal of the Stamp Act. I send you a few of the Cards[3] on which I wrote my Messages during the Time, it was debated here whether it might not be proper to reduce the Colonies to Obedience by Force of Arms: The Moral is, that the Colonies might be ruined, but that Britain would thereby be maimed.

From Philip Syng[4]   ALS: American Philosophical Society

Dear Sir   Philada. March 1st. 1766

I received yours of the 26th of September last,[5] with your very agreeable Present Doctor Lewis's new Work.[6] You judged very right that I should find in it entertaining Particulars in my Way—

1. BF wrote Williams on April 28, 1766; see below, pp. 252–3.

2. Jane wrote DF, Feb. 27, 1766, that BF had sent her and her daughters "a considerable Present of Cloathing" by Captain Freeman. Each of them received "a Printed coten Gownd a quilted coat a bonit Each of the Garls a cap & some Ribons." Van Doren, *Franklin-Mecom,* p. 89.

3. See above, pp. 66–72.

4. For Syng, one of BF's oldest friends, see above, I, 209–10 n.

5. Not found.

6. Almost certainly William Lewis's *Commercium Philosophico-Technicum, or The Philosophical Commerce of Arts* (London, 1763–65). Lewis (1708–1781), M.B., Cambridge, 1731, was elected F.R.S. in 1745 and received the Copley Medal in 1754 for his work on platinum; he was also a member of the Society of Arts, whose gold medal he received for his studies of American potash. His *Philosophical Commerce of Arts* was a treatise on the possible industrial applications of metals and other raw materials. The first part of the book analyzed the physics, chemistry, and uses of gold, a subject of particular interest to silversmith Syng, as he notes later in this letter. For Lewis, see F. W. Gibbs, "William Lewis, M.B., F.R.S. (1708–1781)," *Annals of Science,* VIII (1952), 122–51.

the Management of Gold and Silver is treated of in it better and more particularly than I have met with in any Author.

The regard you have always shewn me requires my acknowledgment, which I wish to make by serviceable Actions, because they speak louder than Words, but I fear I shall die insolvent. The Junto fainted last Summer in the hot Weather and has not yet reviv'd, your Presence might reanimate it, without which I apprehend it will never recover. I am dear Sir your Affectionate Friend and obliged Humble Servant PHIL SYNG

Addressed: To / Benjamin Franklin Esqr / Post Master general of / North America / in London / per Captn Sparks

From Thomas Wharton   ALS: American Philosophical Society

Dear Friend.   Philada. March 2d: 1766.

About a week since, I wrote thee a few Lines per Capt. Robinson via Lisbon;[7] which Letter was principally to enclose thee an Extract of a Letter wrote by T. Penn to his Governor, respecting the assurances he had obtained that, there would be no change of Government:[8] This account filled the minds of our Friends with great concern, as we thereby—(if it be true) shall experience the in-attention of those in power, to our Prayers, and evince the proprietary Party here that they are capable of carrying every measure against the voice of the People; And when it is considered that, the People who have been for a Royal-Government are those, who in those tumultuous times have kept the Peace, or at least obliged the other Party to be more moderate, it would seem extreamly hard, that, they should be denied that security in their Persons and Properties which they hop'd for from this Change.

There are some of us, who since the receipt of thy Letter have stood their utmost Attacks, which were usher'd forth by the great *Giant*[9] with his usual vehemence; nay so sure are they of the mat-

7. *Pa. Ga*̄*.,* Feb. 27, 1766, reported the clearance of the *Prince George,* Capt. James Robinson; Wharton's letter has not been found.

8. Joseph Galloway also sent BF a copy of the extract of the Proprietor's letter of Nov. 30, 1765, with comments about its impact on Pa. politics. See above, p. 179.

9. William Allen.

ter having been finished in their favour, that, they have published it in our Papers, and that of the Dutch;[1] And all we have been able to urge is thy Integrity, Capacity, and Assurance that the Petitions are not rejected, and we find that the Doctrine, which is now directed by some of the *wiser and better sort of the People*, is that, as the affairs of the Petition are at an end, 'tis best for all Parties to be at Peace; thereby they hope to Lull us a sleep, and inch by inch get our privileges from us: But I hope the People will be watchful and guard every part from their secret, as well as open Attacks.

I think it my duty as a Friend, to inform thee of every part, which seems to wound thy Reputation—either in a private or public capacity, and for which reason I trust, thou'l not be displeased with me.

Thou well knows that there have been Men of the Court side, who have never failed to augment the least omission, and make it as far as in them lays—appear as a breach of Trust; so on the arrival of the December-Packet, they inquired whether the Committee of Correspondence had any Letters from the Agents, and it was answered in the negative; they soon found that our friend J. Galloway had rec'd two from thee, and one from R.J. this they declared was contrary to your Instructions &c. and leave no method un-essay'd to alienate the regard of Individuals of the Assembly from thee. It would give all of us great pleasure if thou would write the Committee as often as it suited: as I dont mean to go into a full detail of this matter, hope thou'l understand the foregoing hint.[2]

1. *Pa. Jour.*, Feb. 27, 1766, announced that the petition for royal government had been "put off . . . *for ever* and for ever." See above, p. 181 n. The German newspapers publishing in the province at this time were Henry (Henrich) Miller's *Der Wöchentliche Philadelphische Staatsbote* and Christopher Saur, Jr.'s *Germantowner Zeitung*.

2. On Feb. 17, 1766, the *Harriot* packet, Capt. Robinson, arrived at New York from Falmouth carrying the December mail including, as Wharton informs us, two letters from BF to Galloway and one from Jackson to Galloway. None of these letters has been found. When the Assembly reconvened in May, prodded evidently by the complaints of the proprietary party, it resolved, May 7, that the Committee of Correspondence acquaint BF and Jackson that henceforth they should address all letters covering official business to the speaker of the House and the committee. The next day the committee wrote the agents, expressing "some Uneasiness" that they had not written directly to it and ordering them to do so in the future. *N.-Y. Mercury*, Feb. 24, 1767; 8 *Pa. Arch.*, VII, 5870; below, pp. 267–8.

Our friend J.G.[3] and self did ourselves the pleasure yesterday—of spending a few Hours with Governor Franklin and his Spouse, who enjoy a good state of Health, and a great share in the Affections of the substantial Inhabitants of N. Jersey. The Governor requested me to forward thee the enclosed Packet.

My Father and Self have made all the enquiry we can respecting the Letter which was said to be read in the Dutch Church, and have rec'd for answer of Parson Millenburg, that to his knowledge no such Letter was read;[4] but that it was a Charter of Incorporation, they had received from the Proprietor; tho' some others assert that both this Charter and that Letter were read: He told my Father, that W. A.[5] had lately sent for him to know if there was any truth in the report, whom he informed there was not. But for our parts we rather conclude that the *sending for him;* was to give some directions, how the affair might be best conceal'd.

By the December Packet came an appointment to James Tilghman fixing him in the Land-Office;[6] consequently removing William Peters therefrom; which has given general satisfaction, and it's said there is £300 per ann. tack'd to the former Perquisites, under some particular Restrictions, respecting his not being concern'd in any Purchases &ca.

I am told that our Courts are to be open this week, and that it is determin'd not to go on with any old Business till *June* Term,[7] but that they will Issue Writs &ca. returnable to that term; not doubting but before then all Affairs will be terminated respecting the Stamp Act. I remain thy sincere friend   THO WHARTON

To Benja. Franklin Esqr.

3. Joseph Galloway.
4. See above, XII, 240, 365.
5. William Allen.
6. Tilghman, a staunch proprietary partisan, was appointed secretary of the Land Office; see above, XII, 301–2 n.
7. On April 17, 1766, however, *Pa. Gaʒ*. reported that Benjamin Baker was tried, convicted, and sentenced by the Pa. Supreme Court for spiking the guns at the battery at Wicaco.

From David Hall   Letterbook copy: American Philosophical Society

Dear Sir   Philadelphia March 3d. 1766
    I was in hopes of a Letter from you by the Packet,[8] but disappointed, was glad however to know from those that had, that you was well.
    Inclosed have sent you a Copy of the Accounts settled by Mr. Parker with me on your Account, which I hope will be Satisfactory, as, to the best of my Knowledge I think they are right;[9] tho', as I suppose he told you, if any Thing is wrong in them, it shall be rectified, either as to what might have been forgot, or as to the Valuation of the Office.
    Mrs. Franklin had Fifty Pounds Cash of me, the Tenth of January last, to purchase a Bill of Exchange of Mrs. Stevens.[1] The 18th of last Month, she had One Hundred Pounds; towards Payment of the Lot she purchased of Mr. Siddons;[2] and on the Tenth of this Month, I am to give her One Hundred Pounds more for the same Purpose. When she wants more, she shall have it; and any Service, I may be able to do her in that, or any other Way, you may depend upon it, shall not be wanting. I am Dear Sir Yours most Affectionately   D H
Addressed: To Benjamin Franklin Esq.

From John Free[3]   ALS: American Philosophical Society

Sir,   Newington Butts Mar. 4. 1766
    The Books inclosed in these Parcels, to wit;
    Dr. Free's Controversy with the Methodists
    His Petition to the King,
    His Petition to the H. of Commons, against the two Archbishops,
    His Speech at Oxford; and

8. The *Harriot* packet; see the notes to the document immediately above.
9. See above, pp. 87–99, 104–10.
1. BF recorded the receipt of a bill for £30 sterling, Stevens on Grant, on April 3, 1766. Journal, 1764–1776, p. 7; Ledger, 1764–1776, pp. 2, 15.
2. See above, XII, 283–6.
3. On Dr. John Free, clergyman, schoolmaster, and writer on a variety of subjects, see above, III, 389 n.

Voluntary Exile a Poem,[4]
are a Present from the Author, who lives at Newington Butts near Southwark
To an old Subscriber of his Mr. Richard Dunscomb of new York[5] and sent with a View, of being conveyed to him by the kind assistance of either Dr. Franklin or Mr. Kelly:[6] but if Mr. Dunscomb be dead or removed; they are then the Property of Dr. Franklin, if he pleases to accept of them.

In the Meantime Dr. Free would be glad of a Penny Post Letter to signify the Probability of their being conveyed.[7]

Addressed: For / Dr. Franklin of / New York. / with 2 Small Parcels

Endorsed: Dr. Free Dated March 4, 1766.

From Amelia Evans   ALS: American Philosophical Society

Dear Sir,   Portsmouth 6 March 1766

I write to beg ten thousand pardons for not having waited on you before I left town but having been excessively hurried with the necessary preparations for our embarkation I deferred seeing most of my friends till I found I was not mistress of a moment. But I hope you will pardon me Sir and allow me to intreat yours and Mrs. Stevensons wishes for success to the Æolus which is the Man of war we are to sail in. She is command by Capt. Gower brother

---

4. Free published a series of pamphlets attacking the Methodists in 1758 and 1759. Though he invited subscriptions in the latter year for a work on this subject, no copy or recorded date of publication has been located; perhaps what he was sending was a collection of the separate pamphlets. The other works on his list were: *A Genuine Petition to the King* (1762); *The Petition relative to the Conduct of the Archbishops of Canterbury and York* ... (1763); *The Speech of Dr. John Free* ... [on the British Constitution] (1753); and a poetical epistle intitled *The Voluntary Exile* (1765). See John Nichols, *Literary Anecdotes of the Eighteenth Century* (9 vols., London, 1812–15), V, 695.

5. While several Dunscombs are recorded in the New York registers of wills, 1749–76, there is no Richard among them. The editors have been unable to identify him.

6. Perhaps Dr. John Kelly, Regius professor of medicine at Oxford; above, x, 59 n.

7. No letter of acknowledgment has been found.

to my Lord Gower.[8] We are to have a prodigious number of passengers among the rest is Sir Thos. Erskin[9] who is I believe going to visit the remains of antient magnificence in the African world from whence I shall certainly (having your permission Sir) do myself the honor of writing to you.

If you will please to give yourself the trouble of sending to Mrs. Mistiviers french school at the Edinburgh Castle Drury lane you may get a Copper plate of my fathers of Pensilvania, New Jersey, New York and the Counties up the River Deleware.[1] It can now be of no use to me and possibly to nobody but I would not have it lost as it was my fathers and when you return to America it m[a]y chance to be of some use.

My respectful compliments wait on Mrs. Stephenson to whom I ought to appologize for not having waited on her but the excuse I have pleaded to you Sir I hope will entirely satisfy that Lady. With the greatest sincerity and respect I am Sir your most obliged Humble Servant   AMELIA EVANS

Endorsed: Amelia Evans

From Ezra Stiles   ALS: Yale University Library

Dear Sir   Newport March. 7th. 1766.

This waits upon you by Dr. Grant,[2] with whom I have had the pleasure of an acquaintance during his Residence in Newport the winter past. He was educated at Aberdeen and received the Finishings in Medical Literature at Edinburgh and Paris. Your Reputation in the learned World excites a Curiosity in Gentlemen of

8. John Leveson-Gower (1740–1792) commanded the *Aeolus* frigate in the Mediterranean, 1766–67. He was the half-brother of Granville Leveson-Gower (1721–1803), 2d Earl Gower, created Marquis of Stafford in 1786.

9. The editors have been unable to identify this gentleman among the several Erskine families of Scotland.

1. This was Lewis Evans' *Map of Pensilvania, New-Jersey, New-York, And the Three Delaware Counties,* published in 1749; above, III, 392 n, and this volume, p. 164.

2. In the absence of a first name it appears impossible to identify this person among the many Grants listed as having attended the University of Aberdeen. Stiles's *Literary Diary* and *Itineraries* mention no visitor to Newport named Grant during the winter of 1765–66.

Taste and Erudition to be known especially to one of your Humanity and Politeness. Permit me therefore to ask your kind Notice of my amiable Friend, in addition to the numerous Favors by which you have condescended to make me, my Dear Sir, Your most affectionate Friend and obliged humble Servant

EZRA STILES

To Dr. Benja. Franklin FRS. London

Endorsed: By Dr Grant who sailed on Board the America 9th. Mar. 1766.

From Mary Stevenson   ALS: American Philosophical Society

My dear Sir   Sunday Morning March 9. 1766

You will give us great pleasure if you will favour us with your company to day,[3] our dinner shall be ready at any hour you will appoint, four o'clock will be as convenient to us as any other time; say you will come and you make us happy. My mother gave us hope that you might come to day, and thought it was the only one you could. I will flatter myself that I shall see you both this day, which is one of the highest pleasures that can be enjoy'd by Your dutiful and affectionate   M STEVENSON

Addressed: To Dr / Franklin / Craven Street / in the / Strand

To Matthew Boulton   ALS: Assay Office, Birmingham

Dear Sir,   London, March 19. 1766

You will I trust excuse my so long omitting to answer your kind Letter per Mr. Garbet,[4] when you consider the excessive Hurry and Anxiety I have been engag'd in with our American Affairs. I thank you for introducing me to the Acquaintance of that very sensible worthy Man, tho' I could have but for a short Hour the Pleasure of his Company.

3. Mary (Polly) Stevenson, daughter of BF's landlady, was living with two aunts in Kensington.

4. For Boulton's letter of Feb. 22, 1766, to which this is a reply, and some of the matters discussed here, see above, pp. 166–8.

I know not which of the Valves to give the Preference to, nor whether it is best to introduce your Jet of Cold Water above or below. Experiments will best decide in such Cases.[5] I would only repeat to you the Hint I gave of fixing your Grate in such a Manner as to burn all your Smoke. I think a great deal of Fuel will thus be sav'd, for two Reasons. One, that Smoke is Fuel, and is wasted where it escapes uninflam'd. The other, that it forms a sooty Crust on the Bottom of the Boiler, which Crust being not a good Conductor of Heat, and preventing Flame and hot Air coming into immediate Contact with the Vessel, lessens their Effect in giving Heat to the Water. All that is necessary, is, to make the Smoke of fresh Coals pass descending thro' those that are already thoroughly ignited.[6]

I sent the Model last Week, with your Papers in it, which I hope got safe to hand.[7]

Please to make my Compliments acceptable to Mrs. Boulton, and present them likewise to our Friends Mr. and Mrs. Baskerville, and Mr. Small.[8] With great Esteem, I am, Dear Sir, Your most obedient humble Servant   B FRANKLIN

To Mr M: Boulton

Endorsed: Benjn: Franklin—19 March 1766.

5. At this point in the margin is a rough sketch of a rabbeted right-angle carpenter's joint, which appears to have nothing to do with any topic discussed in this letter.

6. At some time between 1771 and 1773 BF completed development of his smoke-consuming stove on the principle indicated here, and he reported in the latter year that he had used it effectively during the previous winter. This letter shows that he had established the theoretical basis of his invention as early as 1766, though he had not yet worked out all the practical details.

7. The model of a steam engine Boulton had asked him to return.

8. John Baskerville, the famous type designer, and his wife, the former Sarah Ruston (above, IX, 257 n), and William Small, a naturalist (above, XI, 480), residents of Birmingham.

From Sarah Franklin

ALS: American Philosophical Society

[Honoured][9] Papa   Philadelphia March th 23 [1766]

Our dear Friend Mrs. Smyth after an illness of 5 months and 6 days Expired Yesterday morning.[1] In the whole time she had not been out of bed a quarter of an hour at a time, so thankfull she was for any thing her friends did for her and patient to a Miracle. Poor Mrs. Dufield[2] and poor Mama are in great distress, it must be hard to lose a Friend of 50 Years standing, but when we saw her in such extreame pain it would have been selfish to wish her stay, when so much happyness await'd her.

Miss Greame has lost her only Sister Mrs. Stedman who died a Week or two ago.[3] I write the bad news first as it is upermost in my thoughts.

Brother and Sister[4] is to be in town next Monday and stay some time with us, they are both well he was in town last Saturday.

March 25

I meet Mr. Read of Burlington last evening he told me he had been down to Capt. Egdons Wreck and among the things he saw a parcel of nice Wax work fruit, which the Capt. told him was put on board by Dr. Franklin for his Daughter.[5] He then had a box

9. Tears in the upper left and lower right corners of the sheet have caused the loss of some words. These have been supplied in brackets from William Duane, ed., *Letters to Benjamin Franklin, from His Family and Friends. 1751–1790* (N.Y., 1859), pp. 28–9.

1. Mrs. Mary Smith, usually referred to as "Goody Smith" in letters between BF and DF from 1755 on, was a good friend of DF. The latter had mentioned Mrs. Smith's illness several times in recent months.

2. Mrs. Edward Duffield. Her husband advertised in *Pa. Gaz.*, April 17, 1766, calling upon all debtors or creditors of Mrs. Smith's estate to bring him as executor their payments or claims "without further Notice." Later he was also one of BF's executors.

3. Ann Græme Stedman, sister of Elizabeth Græme (whom WF had jilted; above, VII, 177 n), died March 3, 1766. Her husband, Charles Stedman, owned and operated an iron furnace in Lancaster Co.

4. WF and his wife Elizabeth.

5. Charles Read was secretary of New Jersey; above, X, 313 n. The new ship *Ellis*, Capt. Samuel Richardson Egdon, drove ashore in a storm at Absecon (or Absecum) Beach, near Egg Harbor, N.J., with a cargo valued between £20,000 and £30,000. Two lives and the vessel were lost. Although a large part of the cargo was saved, it was subjected to serious plundering,

made for it (for the things had been strangely hawld about) packed it Carefully and it was coming round. I told him I was much obliged to him for his kindness, but did not think it belonged to me, as I was sure you would have mentioned it, if you had sent it.

We have heard by a round about way that the stamp act is re-peal'd, the People seem ditermined to beleave it, tho it came from Ireland to Maryland.[6] The bells rang we had bonfires and one house was illumanited, indeed I never heard so much noise in all my life the very Children seem distracted. I hope and pray the news may be true. As your time is now taken up so [much] a short Letter will be more agreable than a long one. I beg leave therefore [to] Conclude with my love to Mrs. Stevenson and Miss, and my Love and [duty] to you. I am as ever Your Dutiful Daug[hter]   S FRANKLIN

Addressed: To / Benjamin Franklin Esqr / in / Craven Street / London / per Packet

Endorsed: Mrs Franklin and Sally, from Nov. 1765 to March 1766 —answered[7]

From [Joseph Priestley]

ALS (mutilated):[8] American Philosophical Society

Dear Sir   Warrington 25 March 1766.

I have received your letter, containing some remarks on my experiments, and a printed paper for the transactions which has given me very great satisfaction, and for which I think myself

and WF, as governor, issued a proclamation for the apprehension of the plunderers and the recovery of their loot. *Pa. Gaz.* and *Pa. Jour.*, March 13, 1766.

6. On March 24 (the day before Sally wrote this part of her letter) word reached Philadelphia of the arrival at Oxford, Md., of a ship with a Cork newspaper reprinting a paragraph from one published in Dublin that contained a letter of late January from a member of Parliament in London saying that American affairs were settled and "the Stamp-Act was repealed." *Pa. Gaz.*, March 27, 1766. The news was as premature as it was "round about"; the ship had a 40-day passage, so it must have left Cork even before BF's Examination in the House of Commons had taken place.

7. This endorsement probably applied to a small bundle of letters from BF's wife and daughter, of which three from DF and this one from Sally are now known.

8. The bottom of the folio has been cut off, causing the loss of one or more lines on each of the first two pages and the concluding lines and signature on the third.

much obliged to you.[9] I shall think myself very happy if the accounts you are pleased to permit me to send you of my imperfect experiments do but revive your attention to your once favourite study; for that seems to be universally acknowledged to be the great desideration to further discoveries.

Immediately upon the receipt of yours, I set about pursuing the hints you gave me, and I am impatient, little as I have done, to give you an account of it. My great ambition would be to act under your auspices in the business of electricity.

I carefully repeated the experiment with *condensed air* and could perceive no more cloudiness when it could not be excited than when it could, as I have written more at large to Dr. Watson, to whom I beg leave to refer you.[1]

I have this day tried the experiment with the *vanes,* and I believe I should have done it; tho not so soon, if You had not recommended it to me. I took a cork, and stuck into the sides of it (pointing directly from the center) thirteen vanes each consisting of half a common card. Into the middle of the cork I stuck a needle, by which I suspended [*passage missing*] glass stand, in contact with a pointed wire projecting some inches from the jar. In this situation it is evident, that for every spark that I took from the inside, one must enter at the point which communicated with the outside. I then held the vanes about two or three inches from the point of the wire, but a little on one side, that the streams of air (if there were any) might act to advantage, on the extremities of them; and observed, that all the time I was taking sparks from the wire communicating with the inside, the vanes turned, as if strongly blown upon by a current setting from the point. In a great number of trials they never failed to turn the same way, and even if they were made to turn as much as possible the contrary way, the stream never failed to fetch them back again, and make them turn as before.

To determine whether this effect was produced by any electrical attraction or repulsion, I placed a wire communicating with the ground, between the vanes and the point, to intercept the electricity, but the vanes turned as swiftly as before. The motion was sometimes so swift, that I could hardly distinguish the separate

9. BF's letter has not been found and the "printed paper for the transactions" has not been identified.
1. Schofield does not print the letter to Watson mentioned here.

vanes as they turned round, and the motion would continue a very considerable time.

As I never chuse to depend upon my own testimony, I called in Mr. Holt[2] to witness the experiments, and we repeat[ed *passage missing*] different principles, and very agreeable to the theory of negative and positive electricity.[3]

I shall make all the experiments you direct, and many more which I have thought of relating to *mephitic air*[4] when my apparatus is completed, and I have finished the greatest part of my treatise on Electricity. I have sent to Mr. Price *five numbers*, a quire each, and I shall send (if all be well) three more the beginning of the next week. You must only consider it as a very rough draught, but I think I have made the most of the materials I have at present. I am impatient to receive the books you are so kind as to procure for me, and wish you could likewise procure me the *histoire de l'electricité* you mention.[5] Desire Mr. Canton also to favour me with his *Gilbert*, and that piece of *Otto Gueric*, if he have it, which treats of electricity.[6] Please also to desire Mr. Johnson to send me a copy of *Theophrastus* for I have not the book, tho' I remember reading it formerly, I think, in an edition of Dr. Hill's.[7] I have this day been favoured with [a] letter from Mr. Price, for which I beg you would make my acknowledgments to him. After puzling myself to no purpose with some of *Mr. Wilson's experiments*, you will find that I have related them just as he published them himself, with very few remarks.[8] I thought that the most [*about five words missing*] directed by you what to do [*remainder missing*]

2. John Holt (d. 1772), a fellow tutor at Warrington Academy.

3. For BF's introduction in 1747 of this terminology and the basic concept it represents, see above, III, 130-2, 157-8, 162-3.

4. Carbon dioxide.

5. Probably Abbé de Mangin's *Histoire générale et particulière de l'électricité* (3 vols., Paris, 1752). Possibly, however, Priestley may have intended the *Histoire abrégée* that Thomas-François Dalibard prefixed to his translation of BF's *Exper. and Obser.* in both the 1752 and 1756 editions; above, IV, 302, 425.

6. William Gilbert, *De Magnete Magneticisque Corporibus* (London, 1760), and Otto Guericke, *Experimenta Nova Magdeburgica* (Amsterdam, 1672).

7. John Hill, *Theophrastus's History of Stones with an English Translation and Critical and Philosophical Notes* (London, 1746).

8. Dr. [Benjamin] Hoadly and Mr. [Benjamin] Wilson, *Observations on a Series of Electrical Experiments* (London, 1756). For BF's comments on this pamphlet, see above, VIII, 239–63.

Addressed: To | Doctor Franklin | at Mrs Stephens's, Craven-street, | in the Strand | London.

From Thomas Hutchinson

ALS: American Philosophical Society; letterbook copy: Massachusetts Archives, Office of the Secretary of State

Dear Sir,   Boston 26 March 1766

My son[9] being bound to London I give him a letter to you that he may have a better Pretence for waiting on you and Paying his own as well as my respects to you.

I expected to have gone my self some of my friends advising to it; others thought it best for me to remain here and that I should not recommend my self to the ministry by leaving the Province at this time although I had leave for it.[1] I hope my son will be of some service to me in my sollicitations for relief under my great sufferings which was my Principal inducement to consent to his voyage just at this time. I have cautioned him much against the snares and temptations of London. I hope he will be upon his guard. I am sure your advice will have great weight with him in every affair.[2] I am with great esteem Sir Your faithful humble Servant   THO HUTCHINSON

Doctor Franklin

Addressed: To Benjamin Franklin Esqr | London

Endorsed: Lieut. Govr. Hutchinson March 26. 1766

From James Parker   ALS: American Philosophical Society

Honoured Sir   Woodbridge March 27. 1766

My last to you was from Burlington, with the Accounts[3] from

9. Thomas Hutchinson, Jr. (1740–1811).

1. For Hutchinson's losses from the Stamp Act disturbances in Boston, his intended journey to England to seek compensation, and the ultimate action of the Massachusetts General Court on this matter, see above, XII, 339–40, 382, and accompanying notes.

2. Nothing about the younger man's contacts with BF in London appears in BF's correspondence.

3. Above, pp. 104–10.

whence I was soon after Summoned here on the Occasion of my Son's being, as was then thought, at the Point of Death: It pleased God however to spare him a little longer, and tho' he is not yet well Yet he is Stirring about, and has some hidden Disorder lurking in his Bowels, which we cannot investigate: I have been better since I returned Hither, but am not well recovered. I am preparing for New York with all the Expedition possible for me,[4] hoping as the Warm Weather approaches I shall get well. Mr. Foxcroft I told you was gone to Virginia, from whence he is expected at Philadelphia, the first of April. I had One Letter from him ordering me to issue the inclosed Letter,[5] which I have done: I have not the best Prospect of any one good End being answered with Mr. Holt: Royle is dead, and there were several Competitors so that Holt can't go to Virginia,[6] and tho' he is by Articles to deliver me up my Materials, yet I am informed privately, tho' he will not own it to me that he intends to continue his Paper, having engaged and got ready other Tools for that Purpose: What Truth there may be in it, 5 or 6 Weeks more will show: tho' I can get no Settlement or any Money from him.[7]

I told you, that your Box of Books &c. per Tillet, I paid the Freight for, and had put in my Store in York.[8] I have not been able to go there yet, as the Weather has been bad, and I not much otherways; but another Box per Capt. Berton supposed to be the Electrical Machine, we cannot get up, as you have never sent either Mr. Hughes or myself any Bill of Lading, and he won't deliver it up without, so it rests: If I can sell your Goods when I go at the Cost your Invoice mentions, I will otherways I must keep them and retail them myself: Perhaps you will think it best I should keep them, and pay you: This might be the best Way if I could readily pay them: and to pay Interest is almost too heavy for me, unless I could get what I think I am deprived of thro' Holt's Means which I have but very little Hopes of. Were my Strength equal to

4. To take up his post in the Customs.
5. Not identified.
6. On the competition for the printing business in Williamsburg, see above, p. 108.
7. Parker discussed his prospective rivalry with John Holt in greater detail in letters later this spring.
8. On these books and the electrical machine, mentioned in the next sentence, see above, pp. 10–11 and notes.

my Will, I would Still make one Push more—but I fear my Constitution is gone.

Benny Mecom continues I fear on the going-back Road,[9] I cannot get him to do any Thing hardly, and I should be much alarmed about him, but that he pays half the Hartford Riders Salary, which being £50 per An. I believe takes almost all the Money that may arise in his Post Office, but I have not received a penny yet on my own Account from him, nor can I make him reply to any Letters I send him, and I fear grows more torpid than ever.

I have not had the Pleasure of one Line from you these two Packets, but its no Consequence, except the Bill of Lading mentioned be so. As to publick Affairs, you get them from better Hands, than I can pretend to. So have Nothing more to add, than Respects from Your most obliged Servant   JAMES PARKER.

Endorsed: Mr Parker March 27. 66

Heads of a Bill to Authorize Paper Currency

MS not found; facsimile of AD: Parke-Bernet Galleries, Catalogue 223, The John Gribbel Sale, October 31, 1940, no. 252; photostat: American Philosophical Society

Franklin's belief that a viable system of paper currency was essential to the colonial economy goes back to 1729, when he published a pamphlet he called *A Modest Enquiry into the Nature and Necessity of a Paper-Currency.*[1] His most recent proposal was the scheme he and Thomas Pownall had presented to George Grenville in February 1765 as an alternative to the Stamp Act.[2] In March 1766 that act was repealed, and he and his friends and associates in England could turn their attention to other matters relating to the colonies that would require parliamentary action. High on his list of priorities was the repeal, or at least the considerable modification, of the Currency Act of 1764, which extended from New England to the other colonies a complete ban on issuing paper money that would serve as legal tender.

On Jan. 14, 1766, the Pennsylvania Assembly approved a petition to the House of Commons asking for the repeal of the Currency Act, and

9. Parker's troubles with BF's nephew, at this time postmaster in New Haven, have been mentioned often in previous letters.

1. Above, I, 139–57.

2. Above, XII, 47–59.

ordered the Committee of Correspondence to send the petition to the agents, Jackson and Franklin, in London.[3] The Committee's first letter of transmittal and instruction has not been found, but on April 12 Franklin acknowledged its receipt and reported the presentation of the petition.[4] In his letter he also told the Committee of Correspondence that "last Week at the Request of one of the Members" he had drawn a bill to repeal the Currency Act and provide a new system of colonial currency.[5]

The document in Franklin's hand printed below is undated, but it appears to fit the description he gave the Committee and is probably the outline of this proposed bill. It provides for the repeal of all the acts restraining colonial paper currency and substitutes a parliamentary authorization for such issues by the assemblies with what Franklin seems to have believed would be adequate safeguards against runaway inflation and with protection of the interests of British merchants. In strong contrast to the scheme he and Pownall had presented to Grenville the previous year, the proposed measure was permissive, not mandatory, and it did not assign to the British government the interest arising from loans of the bills of credit, but specified that this income was "to be applied to the current Service of the Year in each Colony." No one in America, therefore, could assert that Franklin was here offering a plan, however disguised, by which Parliament would impose internal taxes on the colonies against the will of the people as expressed through their elected representatives, or by which the money produced would go to support British troops in the colonies or any other service normally paid for from British revenues.

A motion was made in the House of Commons, May 14, for leave to bring in a bill for repealing the acts of 6 Anne, 24 George II, and 4 George III, relating to coinage and bills of credit in the colonies, and the Rates of Silver and Gold, in all Payments, in His Majesty's Colonies and Plantations in America," which sounds very much like the present proposal. The motion was negatived, however, without a record vote.[6]

3. 8 *Pa. Arch.*, VII, 5824–7. For the Committee's second letter, Jan. 21, 1766, transmitting a duplicate of the address, see above, pp. 51–2.

4. For BF's letter, see below, pp. 236–40. The *Commons Journal*, XXX, 676, records the receipt of this petition on March 20 and its referral to the Committee of the Whole already charged with considering colonial affairs.

5. The member who requested BF to draft the bill may have been his fellow agent, Richard Jackson. BF elaborated on the background of this proposal in his letter to Galloway, Oct. 11, 1766, below, pp. 448–50.

6. *Commons Journal*, XXX, 822.

[March 31–April 5, 1766][7]

Preamble, Necessity of an equal Currency for all America.

2. Acts of 6 Anne, 24 Geo. II. 3 Geo. III to be repeal'd after Sept.
1. 1766.[8]

3. All present P. Money to sink at its present Periods, no more to
be issued but as follows

4. After Sept. 1. 1766 it shall be lawful for any Colony Legislature,
to issue any Sum they find necessary for the Revenue, Trade
Business Agriculture of each Colony, each Bill to express
Sterling Money, or Silver at 5s. 2d. Gold at £3 17s. 10½d. per
oz., which Bills to be received in *any and every Colony* in all
public and private Payments. *Provided,* Taxations laid on all
Estates for calling in and sinking the same 1/6 per Annum.
Bills not brought in in 6 Years to be destroyed, void, after 3
Months. Deficiency in Taxes to be paid in Gold and Silver,
Bills to be redeem'd with Gold and Silver if brought in Time.
Profit of Bills lost to be applied to the current Service of the
Year. In Emergencies, War, &c. may issue to be sunk 1/12
each Year.

5. All Debts, Specialties &c. contracted or commencing after Sept.
1. 66 to be estimated in Gold and Silver at aforesaid Rates
and recoverable accordingly, payable in Bills equivalent at
the price of Gold and Silver at the Time, according to Certificate upon Oath of the Majority of any 5 of the most eminent
and judicious Merchants of the Town or Colony.[9]

6. Legislatures of each Colony may lend the Bills on Securities at
4 per Cent per Annum taking care to make the Colony re-

7. In his letter of Saturday, April 12, to the Committee of Correspondence
BF said that he had drawn the bill "last Week," which would place the date
between Monday, March 31, and Saturday, April 5.

8. These three acts were: An Act for Ascertaining the Rates of Foreign
Coins in Her Majesty's Plantations in America, 6 Anne, c. 57 (1707); An
Act to Regulate and Restrain Paper Bills of Credit in His Majesty's Colonies
or Plantations of [New England] and to Prevent the Same being Legal Tenders in Payments of Money, 24 Geo. II, c. 53 (1751); and An Act to prevent
Paper Bills of Credit, hereafter to be issued in any of his Majesty's Colonies
or Plantations in America, from being declared to be a legal Tender in Payments of Money; etc., 4 Geo. III, c. 34 (1764). In listing these acts BF gave
the regnal year of the last one incorrectly.

9. This clause appears to be the one BF told the Committee of Correspondence in his letter of April 12 that he had inserted to satisfy the British merchants.

sponsible by Taxation for the same in due and proper time, for all Deficiencies of Security. Interest to be applied to the current Service of the Year in each Colony.

7[1] To counterfeit, Death.

8 Governors contravening this Act, cashiered. Laws contrary to be void.

Marginalia in Protests of the Lords against Repeal of the Stamp Act

I. MS notations in the margins of a copy of *Protest against the Bill To repeal the American Stamp Act, of Last Session.* A Paris, Chez J. W. Imprimeur, Rue du Colombier Fauxbourg St. Germain, à l'Hotel de Saxe. 1766, in the collections of the New York Public Library. II. MS notations in the margins of a copy of *Second Protest, with a List of Voters against the Bill to Repeal the American Stamp Act, of Last Session.* A Paris, Chez J. W. Imprimeur, Rue du Colombier Fauxbourg St. Germain, à l'Hotel de Saxe. 1766, the property of Boies Penrose, Devon, Pa., 1968.

The second reading in the House of Lords, March 11, 1766, of the bill to repeal the Stamp Act carried by a vote of 105 to 71, including proxies on both sides. In accordance with a common practice in cases of highly controversial bills, some of the dissenting members prepared and signed a lengthy Protest, in which they stated and explained their reasons for opposing the action of the majority. In this instance a group of dissenters also prepared and signed a second protest following the third reading and passage of the bill on March 17. The next day the King gave his assent to several bills, including the repealing measure and its companion piece, the Declaratory Bill. The two Protests on the repealing bill were entered on the journals of the House of Lords, where they were ultimately printed.[2]

Meanwhile the Protests became public in another way. Two pamphlets appeared: the first contained the full text of each of the Protests, a list of the peers who had spoken on each side prior to the vote, and the names of those who signed the Protest; the second pamphlet contained a full list of the lords and bishops who had voted against the bill, personally or by proxy, at the earlier reading. In all these lists the names or titles of the individuals were given without any attempt at disguise, and

1. In the margin of the paper reproduced by photostat, next to the numbers 7 and 8, is drawn a conventional pointing hand, possibly added at a later date.

2. *Journals of the House of Lords,* XXXI, 303–5, 311–13.

in the last list information was even added as to the offices that some members held in the government, the armed forces, or the royal household. The titlepages of the pamphlets bear a Paris imprint; whether this was genuine or served as a cover for surreptitious printing in England is not certain.[3]

These pamphlets must have appeared within a very few weeks of the passage of the repealing act. The March 1766 issue of *Gentleman's Magazine*, published early in April, printed as its first article a piece entitled "A Summary of the Arguments against repealing the Stamp-Act."[4] Although the magazine never identified the article with Parliament in any way, it was in fact a condensation of the two Protests in the House of Lords. The condenser may have procured private copies from the clerk of the House; more probably he used copies of these pamphlets. It is certain that the pamphlets were available in England early in April. Franklin sent copies of both Protests to the Pennsylvania Committee of Correspondence on April 12.[5] David Hall and William Bradford printed the text of the first Protest in the *Pennsylvania Gazette* and the *Pennsylvania Journal* on May 29. The text they printed is unmistakably that found in the pamphlet, but both colonial printers were cautious enough to print only a few letters from each peer's name or title in the lists, connecting them with enough hyphens to represent the omitted letters. The *Journal* printed the second Protest on June 12, but the *Gazette* delayed until the 19th. Again the pamphlet was clearly the source, but by now both printers had become so bold as to give in full all the names in the lists of peers.

Franklin acquired copies of both pamphlets, read them with great care, and wrote numerous comments, both long and short, in the margins. The nature of some of his notations and the phraseology of others makes it virtually certain that at the time of writing these comments he contemplated getting out a pamphlet that would have been, in part at least, a reply to the Protests. Such a pamphlet, however, was never published.

Just when Franklin wrote these marginal comments is unknown. It is natural and tempting to suppose that he did so very soon after the

3. Yale Univ. Lib. contains two different printings of the First Protest, three of the Second Protest, and one pamphlet entitled *Correct Copies of the two Protests . . .* , all bearing the same Paris, 1766, imprint. The copy of the Second Protest in which BF's marginalia appear has an errata list not found in any of the Yale copies. It is perhaps significant that the Paris imprint on these Protests is the same as that on one of the pamphlets reporting Pitt's speech of January 14; above, p. 40.

4. *Gent. Mag.*, XXXVI (1766), 107–9.

5. Below, p. 240.

pamphlets appeared, that is, sometime in the spring of 1766. Probably he did, though a few of the ideas he expressed here will strike some readers as being rather too advanced to represent his general position this early in the great constitutional debate between Britain and her colonies. It is always dangerous to assume, without clear evidence, that marginalia such as these were written very soon after the publication of the work in which they appear. There are, for example, two other political pamphlets published in 1766, in copies of which Franklin wrote extended marginal comments. In his comments in one pamphlet he made an allusion to an event in 1768 and in the other an allusion to an event of 1770; clearly then, some years must have elapsed in each instance between the pamphlet's publication and Franklin's annotation of it.[6] Similar delay could have occurred in connection with these two Protests of 1766. Such little evidence as there is, however, suggests an early dating: the notes themselves show his intention to write a reply to the Protests, and such a pamphlet, to be most effective, would have to be published within a few weeks or months after the Protests had appeared. For this reason, therefore, and to conform to the general editorial policy of this edition, the pamphlets and Franklin's marginal comments are placed here at the end of March 1766, the earliest period during which he could have written his annotation. But the editors are not prepared to state unequivocally that he did so at this time.

Whatever the date of Franklin's marginalia may have been, these notes and the dissenting peers' statements with which they are connected form together a significant contribution to an understanding of the great constitutional debate. The lords who explained at such length why they opposed the repeal of the Stamp Act stated very clearly and forcefully the position many British political leaders held at this time and later. Franklin on his part, while not above scoring a few mere debater's points in his comments, succeeded repeatedly in bringing out basic issues that divided British and American views on the constitutional status of the colonies. In their arguments the dissenting peers repeatedly set forth constitutional concepts, referred to institutions of government, and employed terminology that dated back many decades,

6. In *Good Humor: or, A Way with the Colonies* . . . (London, 1766), p. 30, BF wrote: "There was no Posture of Hostility in America. But Britain herself in a Posture of Hostility against America: Witness the Landing of Troops in Boston. 1768." In Josiah Tucker's *A Letter from a Merchant in London to His Nephew in North America* . . . (London, 1766), p. 53, where Tucker had mentioned British troops in America to defend the colonies, BF exclaimed in the margin: "To oppress, insult and murder them, as at Boston!" How much after the events alluded to here BF wrote these comments it is impossible now to say.

or even centuries, to a time before the colonies had attained political or economic consequence, or to a period before they even existed. What the peers said was generally appropriate when stated with reference to the constitution of England itself, or to that of Great Britain after the union with Scotland. Franklin's quarrel was in considerable part with the unmodified application of those concepts, institutions, and terminology to a much larger and geographically scattered domain that embraced politically and economically advanced colonies as well as Great Britain itself. As he put the matter succinctly in one of his comments on the first Protest, "The Agitation of the Question of Right makes it now necessary to settle a Constitution for the Colonies." The provisions of such a constitution for the colonies became the central problem confronting the English-speaking world during the years immediately ahead.

Clear and adequate joint presentation of a printed text and its accompanying hand-written marginal comments raises some typographical problems, especially when, as in this instance, greater interest attaches to the words of the commentator than to those of the original text. The following statement explains the method used here:

The text of the Protest is printed full measure of the page without special identification. Words in the text that Franklin underlined are set in italics, and any word that he underlined twice for emphasis is printed in small capitals. With the exception of very short marginal notes, all Franklin's comments are printed in separate lines indented at the left margin and are preceded by an identifying "[BF:]." A line of the printed text of the Protest may be interrupted at any point for the insertion of a Franklin comment; the Protest text then resumes, flush left, after the insertion at the point where it had been interrupted. Very brief notes by Franklin are not printed in separate lines, but are inserted directly into the Protest text, preceded by "BF:" and the whole set in brackets. In some places the lords went on at length without expressing any new ideas or saying anything on which Franklin thought it worthwhile to comment. In such cases the liberty is taken of substituting for the full text a condensed summary within brackets.

It is hoped that this method of presenting these annotated pamphlets will do justice to both writers and at the same time make clear to the reader the relationship of the marginalia to the printed text.

I

[BF, *at the top of the titlepage, partly lost by trimming:*] Mean by a thorough Disquisition of the Point to procure a Settlement of Rights.

[BF, *on p. 2, where are printed lists of speakers against and for repeal:*] General Sent.[7]

We have submitted to your Laws, no Proof of our acknowledging your Power to make them. Rather an Acknowledgment of their Reasonableness or of our own Weakness.

Post Office came as a Matter of Utility. Was aided by the Legislatures. Mean to take Advantage of our Ignorance. Children should not be impos'd on: Are not, even by honest Shopkeepers. A great and mag. Nation should disdain to govern by Tricks and Traps, that would disgrace a petty fogging Attorney.

Settlement of the Colonies stated. Parlt. not consulted. Not taken Notice of for 40 Years. had no Participation not till after Restoration, except by Rebel Parlt.

[*Several lines illegible*] at least can grant no greater Power than he had himself.

[BF, *at the top of p. 3:*] Die Mercurii 11th Martii, 1766.

The Order of the Day being read for the second reading of the Bill, entituled, An Act to repeal an act made in the last session of parliament, entituled, An Act for granting and applying certain stamp duties and other duties in the British Colonies and Plantations in America, . . . Then the said Bill was read a second Time, and it being proposed to commit the Bill, the same was objected to. After a long Debate thereupon, the Question was put, Whether the said Bill shall be committed: It was resolved in the Affirmative.

Contents	73	
Proxies	32	105
Not Contents	61	
Proxies	10	71
Majority		34

[BF:] Comp[limen]t the Lords. Not a wiser or better Body of Men on Earth. The deep Respect imprest on me by the Instance I have been witness to of their Justice. They have been mislead by misinformation. Proof of my Opinion of their Goodness is the Freedom with which I purpose to examine their Protests.

---

7. What follows here may have been an outline for part of BF's contemplated pamphlet.

FIRST.

Dissentient,

Because, as this House has in this Session by several resolutions most solemnly asserted and declared, first, "That the King's Majesty, by and with the advice and consent of the Lords Spiritual and Temporal, and Commons of Great Britain, in Parliament assembled, *had, hath, and of right ought to have,* [BF: Neg.] full power and authority, to make laws and statutes of sufficient force and validity to bind the Colonies, and people of America, subjects of the Crown of Great Britain, *in all cases whatsoever:* "[8] [BF: Neg.] Secondly, "That tumults and insurrections of the most dangerous nature have been raised and carried on in several of the North American Colonies, in *open defiance of the power and dignity of his Majesty's Government,* [BF: Neg.] and in manifest violation of the laws and *legislative authority of this Kingdom:*" Thirdly, "That the said tumults and insurrections have been encouraged and inflamed, by sundry votes and resolutions passed in several of the Assemblies of the said Provinces, *derogatory to the honour of his Majesty's Government,*

[BF:] Neg. All acknowledge their Subjection to his Majesty.[9]

and destructive of the *legal and constitutional* dependency of the said Colonies, on the imperial Crown and *Parliament* of Great Britain": [BF: Neg.] Which resolutions were founded on a full examination of the papers on our table, manifesting a [BF *inserts:* daring] denial of the *legislative authority* of the Crown and *Parliament* of Great Britain,

[BF:] Thrust yourselves in with the Crown in the Governmt. of the Colonies. [*Struck out:* Do your Lordships mean to call the Parliamt. *imperial.*]

to impose duties and taxes on OUR *North American Colonies;* [BF: Not *our,* the King's][1] and a *criminal resistance* [BF: Qu.] there made

8. The chief substance of what became the Declaratory Act.

9. The first of several notes indicating that BF fully acknowledged the colonists' subordination to the Crown, although he denied similar subordination to Parliament.

1. Few small matters more seriously annoyed Americans in England than to have people there refer to the King's possessions overseas as "our" colonies, as if the colonies belonged to the people of Great Britain rather than to the common sovereign of both British and American subjects.

to the execution of the commercial and other regulations of the Stamp Act, and of other acts of parliament: we are of opinion, that the total repealing of that law, especially while such resistance continues, would (as Governor Barnarde says is *their intention*) "make the *authority of Great Britain contemptible* hereafter:" [BF: Not the King's] and that such a submission of King, *Lords, and Commons,* under such circumstances, in so strange and unheard of a contest, would in effect, surrender their *antient, unalienable rights of supreme jurisdiction,* [BF: They have no such Rights.] and give them exclusively to the subordinate Provincial Legislatures *established by prerogative;* [BF: Glad this is acknowledg'd.] which was never intended or thought of, and is *not in the power of prerogative to bestow;*

[BF:] Dispute this with the King my Lords, he has done it.

as they are *inseparable from the Three Estates* of the *Realm* assembled in Parliament.

[BF:] Quy, Agreed, *within* the Realm.[2]

SECONDLY.

Because the law, which this Bill now proposes to repeal, was passed in the other House with *very little opposition,* and in this *without one dissentient voice,* during the last session of Parliament, which we presume, *if it had been wholly and fundamentally wrong,* could not possibly have happened; as the *matter of it is so important,*

[BF:] Strange that a Matter of so much Importance should be pass'd over so lightly. Wise Men happening to get wrong do not therefore think it right to continue so.

and as the intention of bringing of it in, had been communicated to the Commons by the first Commissioner of the Treasury the year before, and a *resolution relating and preparatory**

*[BF:] Much has been said of this Notice given the Colonies.

to it was then agreed to in that House, without any division.†

†[BF:] Petitions not recd after made on the Part of Pensa. and other Colonies, not accepted.

2. An important part of BF's view was that the colonies were not part of the *Realm* of England (or Great Britain), hence were not subject to any authority that was operative only within that Realm.

[BF:] All this shows how very insignificant to the Colonies is the *virtual Representation* that has been so much talk'd of.

A thing wholly and fundamentally wrong may easily pass when it is not opposed, when it is not considered, when it is not debated. But after the full strong Opposition given to the Repeal, after repeated long Debates upon it in both Houses, where the fullest Consideration was given to it, the most able Statesmen and Lawyers arguing the Point on both Sides; if after all this a very considerable Majority voted the Repeal, Does not this Argument of your Lordships *revers'd* prove the Repeal fundamentally right?

THIRDLY.

Because, if any particular parts of that law, the *principle of which has been experienced and submitted to in this country,* without repining,

[BF:] The Principle differs when extended to America, *toto caelo.*

for near a century past, had been found liable to just and reasonable objections, [these might have been altered by a bill for the purpose, and had the Commons sent the Lords such an amending bill, it would have been our duty to give it] a most *serious consideration,* with a *warm desire of relieving* OUR COUNTRYMEN in America from any *grievance or hardship;*

[BF:] Applaud this. Thanks for the Acknowledgment that we are your Countrymen. We desire always to be considered as such, &c.

but with proper care to *enforce* their submission and obedience to the law so amended,

[BF:] This would have been wrong if the Law not well founded in Right.

and to the *whole legislative authority of Great Britain, without any reserve or distinction whatsoever.*

[BF:] This is encroaching on the Royal Power.

FOURTHLY.

Because, it appears to us, that a most *essential branch* of *that authority,* the *power of Taxation,* cannot be *properly, equitably* or *impartially* exercised, if it does not extend itself to *all the members of the state* in proportion to their respective abilities;

[BF:] Right, but we are different States, Subject to the King.

but suffers a *part to be exempt* from a *due share of those burthens,* which the public exigencies require to be imposed upon the whole:

[BF:] If we were Parts of the State, we are not exempt from a Share of the Burthen.

Repeat on this Head all that has been done and paid by America. King's Message, Parl[iamen]t, Grants, &c.

a partiality which is directly and manifestly repugnant to the *trust reposed by the people* in every legislature, and destructive of that confidence on which all government is founded.

[BF:] The Trust of Taxing America was never reposed by the People of America in the Legislature of Gr. Britain.

They had one kind of Confidence indeed in that Legislature, that it would never attempt to tax them without their Consent, the Law was destructive of *that* Confidence among them. No body of Men on Earth more worthy of such Confidence, i e, the Power of Taxing, &c. The Repeal shows it.

FIFTHLY.

Because, the *ability* of our North American Colonies, to bear without inconveniency the proportion laid on them by the Stamp Act of last year, appears to us most unquestionable, for the following reasons:

[BF:] Ability to pay gives no Right to demand.

First, That the *estimated produce of this Tax,* amounting to *sixty thousand pounds* per Annum, [BF: far too short] if divided amongst twelve hundred thousand people (being little more than one half of the subjects of the Crown in North America) would be only one shilling per head a year; which is but a third of the wages usually paid to every labourer or manufacturer there for one day's labour:

[BF:] Ship Money[3] might have been easily paid. Carrying the Money out of the Province where raised to the Prejudice of their Trade.

Secondly, That it appears by the accounts that have been laid before this House from the Commissioners of Trade and Planta-

3. A tax levied by Charles I in 1634–35 during time of peace, resisted by John Hampden and others, and proscribed by statute in 1640.

tions, that of the debt contracted by those Colonies in the last war, above £1,755,000 has already *been discharged* during the course of three years only, by the funds provided for that purpose in the several Provinces;

> [BF:] These Accounts defective and short. Much easier to discharge being done by Paying in their Paper Bills to be Burnt, no Silver as the Stamp Act requird.

and the much greater part of the remaining incumbrance, which in the whole is about 760,000 pounds, will be paid in *two years more:* [BF: A Mistake] We must likewise observe, that the *bounties* and advantages *given to them* by Parliament in 1764 and 1765,

> [BF, *at the top of a page, partly lost by trimming:*] the Dearness of Labour that you may obtain what you could not otherwise have.
> [BF:] Quy. The Principle of these Bounties. The Quantity. Why give with one hand to take away with the other?

and the duties *thereby lost* to Great Britain for *their service,* and *in order* to *enable them* the *more easily* to pay this Tax,

> [BF:] How? Strange Policy! Lay an odious Tax and give Bounties to enable People to pay it!

must *necessarily* amount in a *few years* to a far greater sum than the produce thereof. It is also evident, that *such produce* being *wholly appropriated* to the payment of the army maintained *by this Kingdom in our Colonies,*

> [BF:] The Stamp Revenue would necessarily have carried in Proportion. In the conquer'd Colonies. *Unnecessary.* Would cost as much at home. The Colonies will maintain as many as are necessary.

at the vast expence of almost a shilling in the pound land tax, annually remitted by us for *their special defence and protection;*

> [BF:] Unnecessary. Give a Civil Govt. to Canada.[4]

not only *no money* would have been *actually drawn by it out* of that country,

> [BF:] Drawn out of different Parts.

4. Quebec had no elective, representative Assembly at this time.

216

but the ease given by it to the people of Great Britain, who are labouring under a debt of *seventy millions, contracted by them* to support a *very dangerous* war, *entered into* for the *interest* and *security* of *those Colonies,*

[BF:] The fact deny'd. State the Cause and Effect of the War. The expensive Manner of Carrying it on &c.

would have redounded to the benefit of the Colonies themselves in their own immediate safety, by contributing to deliver them from the *necessary expence,* which many of them have *hitherto always borne,* in guarding their frontiers against the savage Indians.

[BF:] true; they have always borne it, and never desir'd you to bear any Part of it.

The frontiers still as open to Inds. as ever. Troops posted at Fort William in Scotland as useful to protect Travellers from Highwaymen on Hounslow Heath.[5]

SIXTHLY.

Because, not only the right, but the expediency and necessity of the *supreme legislature,*

[BF:] There is yet no such Thing. It is indeed wanted and to be wish'd for. But then it should be properly *qualified,* by Repn.

exerting its authority to lay a general tax on our American Colonies, whenever the wants of the public make it fitting and reasonable, that all the Provinces should contribute in a proper proportion to the defence of the whole, appear to us undeniable, from these considerations: First, that every Province being separate and independent on the others, and having no *Common Council*

[BF:] Why do you not give them a Common Council. They pland one.[6] You rejected it. They would have carried on the War without any Expence to you.

impowered by the constitution of the Colonies to act for all, or

5. Fort William is situated in Inverness-shire at the northeastern end of Loch Linnhe, near Ben Ness. Hounslow Heath, on the outskirts of London, is about 12 miles west-southwest of BF's house on Craven St. The two places are a little more than 400 miles apart, air line.
6. At the Albany Congress. To be strictly fair BF should have said that both the British government and the colonial Assemblies rejected the Albany Plan with its provision for a "Common Council."

bind all, such a tax cannot regularly, or without infinite difficulty, *be imposed upon them** at any time,

*[BF:] but they may as they did last War give voluntarily; Defend Marylanders.[7]

even for their immediate defence or protection, by their own provincial assemblies; but requires the intervention and superintending power of the Parliament of Great Britain. Secondly, That in looking forwards to the possible contingency of a new war, a contingency perhaps not far remote, the prospect of the *burthens* which the gentry and people of this Kingdom must then sustain, in addition to those, which now lie so heavy upon them, is so melancholy and dreadful,

[BF:] The Colonies will contribute voluntarily. Ask 'em. Why were they not ask'd before tax'd.

that we cannot but feel it, a most indispensible duty to *ease them* [BF: There's the Rub] as much as is possible, by a due and moderate exertion of that great *right,* which the *constitution of this realm has vested* in the Parliament, [BF: Neg.] to provide for the safety of all, by a proportionable charge upon all, equally and indifferently laid. We likewise apprehend, that a partial exemption of our Colonies from any exercise of this right by the British Legislature, would be thought so *invidious,* and so *unjust* [BF: If they paid no Taxes] to the other subjects of the Crown of Great Britain, as to *alienate the hearts* of these from their Countrymen residing in America,

[BF:] Great Pains has been taken to do this. The folly of it. As it will likewise necessarily alienate the Hearts of Americans.

to the great detriment of the latter, who have on *many occasions received,* and may again want assistance, from the *generous warmth* of their affection.

[BF:] England has on some Occasions received Assistance from America. Affection of America full as great, or greater.

SEVENTHLY.

Because, the reasons assigned in the public resolutions of the Provincial Assemblies, in the North American Colonies, for their

---

7. For BF's defense of the Marylanders in his Examination before the House of Commons, see above, pp. 141-2.

218

disobeying the Stamp Act, viz. "That they are not represented in the Parliament of Great Britain," *extends to all other laws,* of what nature soever,

> [BF:] It is so reason'd here, not there, but in time they may be convinc'd.[8]

which that Parliament has enacted, or shall enact, to bind them in times to come, and must (if admitted) set them absolutely free from any obedience to the *power of the British Legislature;*

> [BF:] but not to the Power of the Crown.

we likewise observe, that in a letter to Mr. Secretary Conway, dated the 12th of October 1765; the commander in chief of his Majesty's forces in North America has declared his opinion, "That the Question is not of the inexpediency of the Stamp Act, or of the inability of the Colonies to pay the Tax; but that it is unconstitutional and contrary to their Rights, supporting the independency of the Provinces, and not subject to the legislative power of Great Britain."[9] It is moreover affirmed, in a letter to Mr. Conway, dated 7th November, "That the people in general *are averse to Taxes of any kind;*

> [BF:] Never refuse to pay Taxes laid by their own Representatives.

and that the merchants of that place think they have a right to every freedom of trade which the *subjects* of *Great Britain* now enjoy."[1]

> [BF:] If Subjects of Great Britain, not merely Subjects of the King, Why not?

This opinion of theirs strikes directly at the Act of Navigation, and other subsequent laws, which from time to time have been made in the *wise policy* of that Act;

> [BF:] The Policy *wise* with regard to foreigners. Selfish with Regd. to Colonies.

8. This note echoes BF's answer to a question on much the same point in his Examination; above, p. 156.

9. This letter from Gen. Thomas Gage is printed in full in Clarence E. Carter, ed., *The Correspondence of General Thomas Gage with the Secretaries of State 1763–1775* (New Haven, 1931), I, 69–70.

1. Cadwallader Colden to Conway, Nov. 9 (not 7), 1765, *Colden Letter Books,* II (N.-Y. Hist. Soc. *Colls.,* 1877), 62.

and should they ever be encouraged to procure for themselves that absolute freedom of trade, which they appear to desire, our plantations would become, not only of *no benefit,* [BF: Quy.] but in the highest degree prejudicial *to the commerce and welfare* of their Mother-country;

> [BF:] Other Advantages of Colonies besides Commerce. Self-ishness of Commercial Views.

nor is it easy to conceive a greater encouragement, than the re-pealing of a law opposed by them on such principles, and with so much contempt of the *Sovereignty* of the *British Legislature.*

> [BF:] The Sovereignty of the Crown I understand. The Sov[ereignt]y of the British Legislature out of Britain, I do not understand.[2]

EIGHTHLY.

Because, the appearance of weakness and timidity in the *Govern-ment* and *Parliament* of this kingdom, which a concession of this nature may too probably carry with it,

> [BF:] *Govt.* and *Parlt.* seem here to be distinguish'd.
>
> The FEAR of being *thought weak* is a *Timidity* and *Weakness* of the worst Sort, as it betrays into a Persisting in Errors, that may be much more mischievous than the Appearance of Weakness. A great and Powerful State like this has no Cause for such Timidity. Acknowledging and correcting an Error, shows great Magnanimity. Small States and small Reputations [*remainder lost by trimming at the bottom of the page.*]

has a manifest tendency to draw on further insults, and by *lessening the respect* of all his Majesty's subjects to the *dignity of his Crown,*

> [BF:] Dignity of the Crown not concern'd in this.

and authority of *his Laws,*

> [BF:] It was upon Laws of Parlt.

throw the whole British empire into a miserable state of confusion

2. The peers and BF may have meant different things by the term "British Legislature" here. The peers may have meant King, Lords, and Commons acting together, while BF meant only the two Houses of Parliament. The distinction could be regarded as constitutionally important in the context of "sovereignty."

and anarchy, with which it seems by many symptoms to be dangerously threatned; and this is the more to be feared, as the plea of our North American Colonies, that not being represented in the Parliament of Great Britain, they ought not to pay Taxes imposed or levied *upon them* by the *authority thereof,* may by the same reasoning *be extended to all persons in this Island, who do not actually vote for Members of Parliament;*

[BF:] Case widely different, as has been often shown. But if wrong here, rectify it.

nor can we help apprehending, that the opinion of some countenance being given to such notions by the Legislature itself, in consenting to this Bill, for the Repeal of the Stamp Act, may greatly promote the contagion of a most *dangerous doctrine, destructive to all Government,*

[BF:] The Danger safely removed.

which has spread itself over all our North American Colonies, that the obedience of *the subject* is not due to the Laws and Legislature of *the Realm,* farther than he in his *private judgment* shall think it comfortable to the ideas he has formed of a free constitution.

[BF:] The Subject in America only. America not in the Realm of England or G.B. No Man in America thinks himself exempt from the Jurisdiction of the Crown and their own Assemblies —or has any such private Judgment.

NINTHLY.

Because, we think it no effectual guard, or security against this danger, that the Parliament has declared in the resolutions of both Houses, passed during this session, and now reduced into a Bill,[3] That such notions are ill founded; as men will always look more to deeds than words, and may therefore incline to believe, that the insurrections in our Colonies, excited by those notions, having so far proved successful, as to attain the very point, at which they aimed, the immediate repeal of the Stamp Act, without any previous submission on the part of the Colonies; the Legislature has in fact submitted to them, and has only more grievously injured its own dignity and authority, by *verbally asserting that Right,* which it substantially yields up to their Opposition.

3. The Declaratory Bill.

[BF:] It is to be wish'd it had not asserted it, or asserted it with some Limitation as when *qualified,* &c.

The reasons assigned for this concession render it still more alarming, as they arise from an *illegal and hostile* combination of the people of America,

[BF:] Surely there is nothing illegal in People's resolving to work for themselves. Every Man in Britain may do it.

to distress and starve our Manufacturers, *and to with-hold from our Merchants the payment of their just debts:*

[BF:] No such Combination to with hold the Payment of just Debts. The Ldps. are misinform'd and ought to be highly displeas'd with those who led them to give Countenance to so horrible a Calumny.

the former of which measures has only been practised in open war between two States; *and the latter, we believe, not even in that situation, either by the public or by individuals, among the civilized nations of Europe, in modern times.* If this unprecedented *plan of intimidation shall meet with success,* [BF: No such Plan.] it is easy to foresee, that the practice of it for other and still greater objects will frequently be renewed,

[BF:] It is pity to give such a Hint to the Colonies, that in your Ldps. Opinion, the Act was repeal'd on Intimidation.

and our *manufacturers* and merchants reduced to the like, and more permanent distress;

[BF:] The Merchts. may avoid Distress by not giving such extensive Credit. Hope they will. The Credit ruinous to the Colonies.

we cannot therefore but wish, that *some more eligible method,* consistent with their future safety and *our dignity,* had been taken *by Parliament,* to shew our tender concern and compassion for their sufferings, and to *discourage any other such unwarrantable attempts;*

[BF:] Query what can that be? Pride Force

which we are *fully persuaded* would have been very practicable, with due care and attention, and *at an expence* very inferior to the importance of the object.

[BF:] Charge of Troops to subdue the Colonies.
And do your Lordships really think Force and Bloodshed more eligible than rectifying an Error?

LASTLY.

Because, we are convinced from the unanimous *testimony of the Governors,* and other *officers of the Crown in America,*

[BF:] Strange Testimony to rely on. The Nature of it.

that if, by a most unhappy delay and neglect to provide for the due execution of the law, and arming the Government there with proper orders and powers, repeatedly called for in vain,

[BF:] Governors always complain for want of Power. Paint them.[4]

these disturbances had not been continued and encreased, they might easily have been quieted before they had attained to any dangerous height; and we cannot, without feeling the most lively sense of grief and indignation, hear arguments drawn from the progress of evils, which should and *might have been stopped* in their first and feeble beginnings, [BF: A Mistake] used for the still greater evil of sacrificing to a present relief the highest permanent *interests,* and the whole *Majesty, Power, and Reputation of Government:* This afflicts us the more deeply, because it appears from many letters, that this law, if properly supported by Government, would from the peculiar circumstances attending the disobedience to it, *execute itself* without bloodshed.

[BF:] It has executed it self;[5] that is, it has been *felo de se.* Observe how in some of the Colonies that there was no Occasion to *execute* their Laws, they died of themselves. A Law universally odious can never be executed in any Govt.

4. BF was walking on rather thin ice here, considering that his son was one of the governors. In *London Chron.,* April 7–9, 1767, however, he printed a piece in which he did "paint" the governors and other officers as being highly unreliable as reporters. He said in his first paragraph that what followed had been written the year before. It has been identified as a segment of his intended Stamp Act pamphlet; above, pp. 79–81. After he laid that project aside he may have thought of using it in the answer to the Protests. He finally settled for quoting it in his letter to the *Chronicle* in 1767.

5. BF's friend, the inveterate punster Hugh Roberts, would have liked the *double entendre* in this comment.

And it is said in one of the letters to Mr. Secretary Conway,[6] "That the principal view is to intimidate the Parliament; but that if it be thought prudent to enforce their authority, the *people dare not oppose a vigorous resolution of the Parliament of Great Britain.*"

[BF:] The People had indeed a high Respect for Parlt.

That vigorous resolution has not yet been found in the Parliament; and we greatly fear, that the want of it will certainly produce one of these two fatal consequences; either that the *repeal of this law will in effect annull and abrogate all other laws and statutes**

*[BF:] The Agitation of the Question of Right makes it now necessary to settle a Constitution for the Colonies.

relating to our Colonies, and particularly the Acts that *restrain or limit their Commerce,* of which they are *most impatient,*†

†[BF:] Restrictions should be only for the General Good. Endeavour to convince reasonable Creatures by Reason. Try your Hands with me.

or, if we should hereafter *attempt to enforce* the execution of those laws against their will,

[BF:] Never think of it. They are reasonable Creatures. Reasonable Laws will not require Force!

and by virtue of an authority, which they have dared to insult with impunity and success, that endeavour will bring upon us all those evils and inconveniencies, to the *fear of which we now sacrifice* the Sovereignty of the Realm;

[BF:] This should not have been suppos'd.

and this at a time when the strength of our Colonies, as well as their *desire of a total independence on the Legislature and Government of their Mother-country,* [BF: a Mistake] may be greatly augmented, and when the circumstances and dispositions of the other powers of Europe, may render the contest far more dangerous and formidable to this Kingdom. [*Here follow the names of 33 peers who signed the Protest.* BF *underlined the names of two Scottish representative peers, the Earls of Eglintoun and Abercorn, and that of the Earl of Ker, whose British earldom entitled the Scottish Duke of Roxburghe to sit in the House of Lords.*]

6. Colden to Conway, Nov. 9, 1765, as cited in a previous note.

[BF:] I observe two or three Scotch Lords Prot[estor]s. Many more voted agst. the Repeal. Colonies settled before the Union. Query. If the Parlt. had a Jurisdiction over the Colonies by the first Settlement Had they a Right to introduce new Legislators? could they sell or commute the Right with other Nations? Can they introd[uce] the Peers of Ireland, and Commons, and the States of Holland and make them Legislators of the Colonies. How could Scotland acquire a Right to any Legislation over English Colonies, but by Consent of the Colonies themselves.

I am a Subject of the Crown of Great Britain have ever been a loyal one, have partaken of its Favours:[7] I write here with Freedom relying on the Magnanimity of the Parlt. I say nothing to your Ldps. that I have not been indulg'd to say to the Commons. Your Lordps Names are to your Protest therefore I think I ought to put mine to the Answer. Desire what I have said may not be imputed to the Colonies. I am a private Person and do not write by their Direction. I came over here to solicit in Behalf of my Colony a closer Connection with the Crown. Burning Glass.

II
Die Lunae, 17° Martii, 1766

The Order of the Day being read for the third reading of the Bill, entituled An Act to repeal an act made in the last session of parliament, entituled, An Act for granting and applying certain stamp duties, and other duties in the British Colonies and Plantations in America, ... Then the said Bill was read a third Time, and it being proposed to pass the Bill, the same was objected to. After some Debate thereupon, the Question was put, Whether the said Bill shall pass: it was resolved in the Affirmative.

FIRST.

Dissentient, [because the protesting lords think that the Declaratory Bill passed last week] cannot possibly obviate the growing mischiefs in America, where it may seem calculated only to deceive

7. There appears to be no valid reason for questioning the sincerity of this statement. While in his comments on this Protest BF had repeatedly expressed doubts about the authority of Parliament in relation to the colonies, he had scrupulously refrained from challenging the authority of the King.

the people of Great Britain, by holding forth a *delusive* and *nugatory* affirmance of the *Legislative Right of this Kingdom,*

> [BF:] It is indeed a nugatory Affirmance and we Americans are oblig'd to your Lo[rdshi]ps for justifying our Esteeming it such.
> If you had such Right before it was unnecessary. If not, you could not give your selves a Right you had not, without our Consent.[8]

whilst the *enacting part of it does no more than abrogate* the Resolutions of the House of Representatives in the North American Colonies, [BF: It cannot abrogate them] *which have not in themselves the least colour of* AUTHORITY; and declares, that which is *apparently* and *certainly* criminal, only null and void [BF: neither].

> [BF:] I beg your Lps. Pardon. They are only declaratory of their own Opinion of their own Rights, and are certainly authentic; they may indeed like this Act be null and void or as your Lps. call it nugatory. But I should think by no means criminal.

SECONDLY.

[Because the particular objections made to the Stamp Act in America and adopted in the course of the debates on the repealing bill are contradicted by undeniable evidence before us] First, that all the money to be collected by this Tax was to be annually remitted hither, and that the *North American Colonies would thereby be drained of all their specie;*

> [BF:] Particular Colonies drained, all drained, as it would all come home. Those that were to pay most of the Tax would have least of it spent at home. It must go to the conquer'd Colonies. The View of Maps deceives.

and Secondly, That the institution of Vice Admiralty Courts in those Colonies, for the recovery of Penalties upon Revenue Laws without Juries, is a *novel practice,* [whereby the colonists would be deprived of trial by jury, "one of their most valuable Liberties," and would thereby be distinguished from fellow subjects in Britain;]

8. In answer to questions in his Examination concerning the "declaratory resolutions" of Parliament BF had said at one point that he believed the colonists would "think them unconstitutional, and unjust"; but a little later he said he thought the resolutions would give the colonists "very little concern, if they are never attempted to be carried into practice."

[BF:] Talk with Bollan on this Head.[9] Query, Courts of Common Law.

[In reference to the first of these objections, it appears that the Treasury had ordered that the revenue to be raised by the act was to be paid over directly] to the Deputy Pay-master *in America,* to defray the subsistence of the troops, and any military expences incurred *in the colonies.*

[BF:] America not a Village; may not England be drain'd by a War in Germany, tho' the Money still in Europe.

[In reference to the second objection, sundry acts of Parliament show that a jurisdiction has been assigned to the judges of the Admiralty Courts] for the recovery of penalties upon the Laws of *Revenue* and of *Trade,* without Juries for near a century past [and in some colonies these Admiralty judges] are the only Judges not elected by the people:

[BF:] All a Breach of the Constitution. Juries better to be trusted. Have rather an Interest in suppressing Smugglers. Nature of Smuggling. It is Picking of Pockets. All Oppressions take their Rise from some Plea of Utility, often in Appearance only.

[The Americans are far from being distinguished by being deprived of trials by jury, for the laws regarding stamp duties in Great Britain provide that penalties are to be] recoverable also without a Jury, before two *Justices of the Peace,* with the like Powers in both cases;

[BF:] Gentlemen of Property, and Character. No Profit. Arguing from one Evil to another.

[the Lords are glad to learn, moreover, that the Treasury reported on July 4 last a plan to erect] three different Courts of Vice Admiralty at the most convenient Places [in America], with proper

9. William Bollan (*c.*1710–*c.*1776), born in England, moved to Massachusetts as a youth, trained in law there, and was agent for the province in England, 1745–62. In the latter year the more radical leaders of the House of Representatives brought about his dismissal as agent for the colony, though he continued to act as agent for the Council. He was regarded as an able lawyer. *DAB.* Quite naturally BF would want to consult an American-trained lawyer on this matter of jury trial before dealing with it in a pamphlet.

Districts annexed to each; and to give the Judges sufficient and Honorable Salaries *in lieu of all poundage and fees whatsoever;*

[BF:] well intended.

[The Lords observe with concern and surprise that this representation was incorporated in a clause in the Stamp Act, and was expressly calculated to relieve the American subjects] from many unnecessary hardships and oppressions, to which they are now liable *by many other Laws* still subsisting

[BF:] Query, What were the particulars. Ask Mr. Cooper.¹

[but that this arrangement] should be totally disregarded for several months, and be suffered to remain unexecuted in every part of it even to this day; [and no notice of this plan has been sent to the governors, although the matter had been fully "opened and approved in Parliament" when the Stamp Act was proposed;] and as the total neglect of it *has given occasion to great Clamour and Dissatisfaction in the Colonies.*

[BF:] An Excuse however, for the Colonies. Repeat all the other Articles of Excuse.

[The Stamp Act was not to take place until November 1; if Parliament had been summoned early] their determinations, either for enforcing or repealing that Law, would probably have delivered the Merchants and Manufacturers here from all the difficulties and distress to which *they* have been for so many months exposed; nor would the *disorders in America,* where all government is prostrate, have risen to so great a height, or taken so deep a root.

[BF:] They were risen to the highest Pitch before any Advice of Parli[amenta]ry Proceedings could have reach'd them, tho' the Parl[iamen]t had met in Novr. as usual.²

THIRDLY.

[Because the argument is "extremely ill founded" that the experiment of a Stamp Act has failed; if it had been properly tried] with the same zeal for its success with which it was first proposed,

1. BF's friend, the barrister Grey Cooper (above, x, 185 n), who was M.P. for Rochester and secretary to the Treasury, and was therefore thoroughly familiar with "the particulars" of this Treasury plan. On the reorganization of the Vice-Admiralty Courts, see Gipson, *British Empire,* XI, 120–7, 130–5.

2. The Stamp Act disturbances had begun in August 1765.

it would not have failed in any of the Colonies: and that this was the *opinion* of the *greater part* of the *Governors* in North America;

[BF:] Their Opinion not to be relied on.

and of many of the most intelligent and respectable persons in those provinces [is evidenced by letters from the governors now on our table and from] the *latter having applied for, and accepted the Office of Distributor of the Stamps under that Act,* which they certainly would not have done [thereby exposing their lives and fortunes, had they considered the success of the act precarious:]

[BF:] Their Interest blinded them.

[and we have heard of no "impracticability" attending the act in Jamaica, Barbados,] and some other of the *West India islands, or in those of our Colonies in North America, where it has been executed.*

[BF:] West India Islands. Jamaica divided—Barbados weak. St. Kitts and some others burnt the Stamps. Canada, New Subjects and Soldiers, Halifax, few People. Georgia Ditto. Both Parl[iamentar]y Colonies.[3]

FOURTHLY.

Because, a Precedent of the two Houses of Parliament, lending their Power, from motives of Fear or Impatience under a present uneasiness, to overturn in one month a Plan of Measures, undertaken with their warmest Approbation and Concurrence, after the most *mature deliberation of two years* together,

[BF:] but one year and no Deliberation, no Debate in the Lords.

for the improvement of our Revenue, and the *relief of our People* [BF: Ay there!] will effectually *discourage all officers* of the Crown in America from doing their duty, and *executing* the *Laws of this Kingdom;*

[BF:] Likely, 'till those Laws are more reasonable or better founded.

and is enough to deter future Ministers, in any circumstances of distress or danger to their Country, from opposing their fortitude and zeal for the service of the Publick, to strong Combinations

---

3. Nova Scotia and Georgia were "Parliamentary Colonies" in the sense that the major parts of their governmental expenses were paid from parliamentary appropriations, not from locally voted taxes.

of private and particular Interests, to the *Clamour of Multitudes*, or the Malice of Faction [which will create such weakness as will soon end in the downfall of the State].

> [BF:] The Clamour of Multitudes. It is good to attend to it. It is wise to foresee and avoid it. It is wise, when neither foreseen nor avoided, to correct the Measures that give Occasion to it. Glad the Majority have that Wisdom.

LASTLY.

Because, the Repeal of this Law under the present Circumstances, will, *we fear*,

> [BF:] Do not fear, my Lords, this is an unnecessary Timidity.

not only surrender the *Honour* and *essential Interests* of the Kingdom now and for ever, both at home and abroad,

> [BF:] The Honour and essential Interests to be maintaind by Equity and Justice.

but will also deeply affect the *fundamental Principles of our Constitution;*

> [BF:] They are mistaken. Legislation over the Colonies is not one of them.

for if we pass this Bill against our Opinion, from the Threats and Compulsion publickly avowed in our Colonies, and enforced by the most unjustifiable means within Great Britain, we disclaim that Legislative Authority *over the subjects,* which we own ourselves unable to maintain.

> [BF:] over the Subjects within the Realm you have it. I do not disclaim. You are able to maintain it: for the People are willing you should.

[If the lords give assent to this bill without conviction that it is right, merely because it has passed the Commons,] we in effect annihilate this branch of the Legislature, and vote ourselves useless. Or if by passing this Bill, we mean to justify those, who in America, and even in Great Britain, have treated a series of British Acts of Parliament as so many Acts of *Tyranny and Oppression,*[4] which it is scarcely criminal to resist;

4. The italics here reflect the original typography, not BF's underlining.

230

[BF:] They are such when extended beyond the Realm to take Money without Consent.

[or to justify] those officers of the Crown, who, under the eye, and with the knowledge of Government, have taken upon themselves, whilst the Parliament was Sitting, without its Consent, to suspend the Execution of the Stamp Act, by *admitting Ships* from the Colonies, with unstampt Clearances, to an Entry, in *direct Violation* of it,

[BF:] Would you seize your own Property? Quy the Act.

[which appears to have been done;] we shall then give our approbation to an open breach of the first Article of that great Palladium of our Liberties, the Bill of Rights;* [which declares the suspending of laws without the consent of Parliament to be illegal].

*[BF:] Wish your Lordships had attended to that other great Article of the Palladium "Taxes shall not be laid but by *common Consent* in Parliament." We Americans were not there to give our Consent.

Lastly, If we ground our Proceedings upon the Opinion of those who have contended in this House, that from the Constitution of our Colonies they ought never to be taxed,†

†[BF:] meaning here. No body thinks they ought not to tax themselves.

even for their own immediate Defence, we fear that such a Declaration, by which near a fifth part of the subjects of Great Britain, who by the Acts of Parliament to restrain the Pressing of Seamen in America, are already exempted from furnishing Men to our Navy, are to be *for ever exempted from contributing their share towards their own support in money* likewise, will, from the flagrant *Partiality* and *Injustice* of it,

[BF:] No, no. they never did or will desire it. Fact wrongly Stated.

either depopulate this Kingdom, or shake the basis of Equality, and of that Original Compact, upon which every Society is founded; and as we believe, that there is no instance of such a *permanent Exemption* [BF: No Exemptions desired] of so large a body of the subjects of any State in any History, antient or modern, we are *extremely apprehensive* of the *fatal Consequences*

[BF:] too apprehensive. No bad Consequences will arise.

of this *unhappy* Measure [BF: rather happy]; to which, for these Reasons, in addition to those contained in the Protest of the 11th of this month, *our Duty to the King,* and Justice to our Country, oblige us to enter this our Solemn Dissent. [*Here follow the names of 28 members of the House of Lords who signed this Protest. As BF had done with the first Protest, he underlined the names of the Earls of Abercorn, Ker, and Eglintoun, as Scots of whose right to deal with colonial matters he had there expressed doubts.*]

> [BF:] My Duty to the King and Justice to my Country, will I hope justify me if I likewise protest, which I do with all Humility, in behalf of myself and of every American, and of our Posterity, against your Declaratory Bill, that the Parliament of Great Britain, hath not never had, and of Right never can have without our Consent, given either before or after Power to make Laws of sufficient Forces to bind the Subjects in America in any Case, whatever and particularly in Taxation.

[On the next three pages appears "A List of the Lords who Voted and Protested against the Repeal of the American Stamp Act, March 11, 1766," that is, at the second reading. The list includes the names of 71 individuals, 10 of whom acted by proxy. There were 7 dukes (including the King's brother, the Duke of York), 33 earls, 6 viscounts, 17 barons, and 8 bishops.]

> [BF, *on the final blank page of the pamphlet:*] I can only judge of others by myself. I have some little Property in America. I will freely spend 19 Shillings in the Pound to defend my Right of giving or refusing the other Shi[lling] and after all, if I cannot defend that Right, I can retire chearfully with my little Family into the Boundless Woods of America which are sure to afford Freedom and Subsistence to any Man who can bait a Hook or pull a Trigger.[5]

5. With such a conclusion as this all drafted, it is a pity that BF never completed and published his pamphlet.

To Deborah Franklin   ALS: American Philosophical Society

My dear Child,   London, April 6. 1766.

As the Stamp Act is at length repeal'd,[6] I am willing you should have a new Gown, which you may suppose I did not send sooner, as I knew you would not like to be finer than your Neighbours, unless in a Gown of your own Spinning. Had the Trade between the two Countries totally ceas'd, it was a Comfort to me to recollect that I had once been cloth'd from Head to Foot in Woollen and Linnen of my Wife's Manufacture, that I never was prouder of any Dress in my Life, and that she and her Daughter might do it again if it was necessary. I told the Parliament that it was my Opinion, before the old Cloaths of the Americans were worn out, they might have new ones of their own making.[7] And indeed if they had all as many old Clothes as your old Man has, that would not be very unlikely; for I think you and George[8] reckon'd when I was last at home, at least 20 pair of old Breeches. Joking apart, I have sent you a fine Piece of Pompador Sattin, 14 Yards cost 11s. per Yard.[9] A Silk Negligee and Petticoat of brocaded Lutestring for my dear Sally, with 2 Doz. Gloves, 4 Bottles of Lavender Water, and two little Reels. The Reels are to screw on the Edge of a Table, when she would wind Silk or Thread, the Skein is to be put over them, and winds better than if held in two Hands. There is also an Ivory Knob to each, to which she may with a Bit of Silk Cord hang a Pinhook to fasten her plain Work to like the Hooks on her Weight. I send you also Lace for two Lappet Caps, 3 Ells of Cambrick (the Cambrick by Mr. Yates) 3 Damask Table Cloths, a Piece of Crimson Morin for Curtains, with Tassels, Line and Binding. A large true Turky Carpet cost 10 Guineas, for the Dining Parlour. Some oil'd Silk; and a Gimcrack Corkscrew which you must get some Brother Gimcrack to show you the Use of. In the Chest is a Parcel of Books for my Friend Mr. Coleman,[1] and another for

6. On March 18, 1766.

7. Above, pp. 140, 159, 161.

8. BF's Negro slave.

9. Several of the things listed here fulfilled DF's requests of the previous October (above, XII, 296–7). BF had refrained from sending them while the colonial boycott of British trade continued.

1. William Coleman (above, II, 406 n), at this time a justice of the Pa. Supreme Court, was one of BF's oldest friends.

Cousin Colbert.[2] Pray did he receive those I sent him before? I send you also a Box with three fine Cheeses. Perhaps a Bit of them may be left when I come home. Mrs. Stevenson has been very diligent and serviceable in getting these things together for you, and presents her best Respects, as does her Daughter, to both you and Sally. There are too Boxes included in your Bill of Lading for Billy.

I received your kind Letter of Feb. 20.[3] It gives me great Pleasure to hear that our good old Friend Mrs. Smith is on the Recovery. I hope she has yet many happy Years to live.[4] My Love to her.

I fear, from the Account you give of Brother Peter that he cannot hold it long.[5] If it should please God that he leaves us before my Return; I would have the Post Office remain under the Management of their Son,[6] till Mr. Foxcroft and I agree how to settle it.

There are some Droll Prints in the Box, which were given me by the Painter; and being sent when I was not at home, were pack'd up without my Knowledge.[7] I think he was wrong to put in Lord Bute, who had nothing to do with the Stamp Act. But it is the Fashion here to abuse that Nobleman as the Author of all Mischief. I send you a few Bush Beans, a new Sort for your Garden. I shall write to my Friends per Packet, that goes next Saturday.[8] I am very well, and hope this will find you and Sally so with all our Relations and Friends, to whom my Love. I am, as ever, Your affectionate Husband,   B FRANKLIN

P.S. A Young Man, by name Joseph Wharton, came to me the other day, said he had been sick and was in distress for Money, and beg'd me to take a Draft on his Brother at Philadelphia for

2. Thomas Cuthbert; above, XII, 42 n.
3. Not found.
4. Mrs. Mary "Goody" Smith died, March 22, 1766; see above, p. 198.
5. Peter Franklin, who looked "very misarabel" to DF early in February, died, July 1, 1766; see below, 332 n.
6. Ephraim Brown, Peter's adopted son; see above, XII, 78 n.
7. The "Droll Prints" were satirical cartoons on the repeal of the Stamp Act. One of these portrayed the funeral procession of the act, with Grenville carrying a miniature coffin containing it, followed directly by Lord Bute. It is reproduced, among other places, in Gipson, *British Empire*, VI, facing p. 401.
8. Two letters which BF wrote on Saturday, April 12, are extant; see below, pp. 236–40, 242–3.

Twelve Guineas. I did not remember or know him, but could refuse nothing to the Name of my Friend. So I let him have the Money, and enclose his Bill. You will present it for Payment.[9]

From Ezra Stiles

Letterbook copy: Yale University Library

Dear Sir   Newport April 10. 1766.
I should not so soon have troubled you with another Letter, before I had known your receipt of my former ones,[1] but to oblige my Friend Capt. Fred Hamilton.[2] Mr. Swift Attorney at Law in Bo[ston][3] by a Letter to Capt. Hamilton last Winter, informed him that a Gentleman in London had, in the Name and at the desire of the "Lady of the Earl of Peterborough and her Sister" addressed to him an Inquiry after the Children of Mr. Andrew Hallyburton late of Bo[ston] in N. England. As Mrs. Hamilton is a Daughter of Mr. Hallyburton,[4] she has taken the Liberty of addressing a Letter to the Earls Lady; and that she may be certain of its reaching her hands, she begs you will do her the favor personally to present it. I know it to be intirely her own Composition. What were the Countesses Views in this Inquiry are not precisely known, yet suggest some flattering hopes.
This Evening for the first Time we saw a Comet in the Northwest. From a cursory View, with the assistance of a Celestial

9. BF entered this loan in his Journal, 1764–1776, p. 8, and in his Ledger, 1764–1776, pp. 7, 22, with a notation in the Journal that he had received a bill of exchange from the young man, drawn on James Wharton of Philadelphia.
1. For Stiles's letters of Feb. 26 and March 7, 1766, see above, pp. 174–5, 195–6.
2. Frederick Hamilton (1721–1772) was evidently the captain of a whaling vessel. James N. Arnold, ed., *Vital Records of Rhode Island*, VIII (Providence, 1896), 433; Franklin B. Dexter, ed., *The Literary Diary of Ezra Stiles, D.D., LL.D.* (New York, 1901), I, 88–9.
3. Samuel Swift (1715–1775), Harvard, B.A., 1735, was an active Son of Liberty who died while being held as a prisoner of the British. *Sibley's Harvard Graduates*, IX (1956), 580–3.
4. Abigail Hamilton was the daughter of Andrew Haliburton by his second wife, Abigail Otis of Scituate, Mass., whom he married on Feb. 22, 1730. The connection, if any, between Haliburton and the Peterboroughs is not clear. De Coursey Fales, *The Fales Family of Bristol, R.I.* (n. p., 1919), pp. 161, 169–72.

Globe I think it was in or below the Constellation Musca, and nearly in a Line from Pleiades to the first star of Aries.[5] It sat about VIIIh. 45'. P M. Your indefatiguable Assiduity for the american Interest we hear of with the sincerest Pleasure and Gratitude; but have not heard the success. I am Dear Sir Your most obliged and obedient Servant   EZRA STILES

Dr. Franklin in London

To the Pennsylvania Assembly
Committee of Correspondence ALS: The Rosenbach Foundation

Gentlemen,   London, April 12. 1766

I received your Letters of Jan. 13. and 20.[6] and communicated them to Mr. Jackson. The Petition, praying a Repeal of the Act of Parliament prohibiting the Paper Money of the Colonies being a lawful Tender, was immediately presented according to your Directions, and referred to a Committee.[7] We have for a long time been extreamly busy with our general American Affairs. I sometime since advis'd the Speaker of the Repeal of the Stamp Act.[8] The Regulations of our Trade came next under Consideration. On Monday next the Committee are to report on the American Commerce.[9] A Number of good Evidences have been thor-

5. Accounts of the observation of this comet at Paris, April 8–12, and at Kirknewton, England, April 9–10, were printed in *Phil. Trans.*, LVI (1766), 60–3, 66–7. Musca Borealis, the Northern Fly, is a minor constellation, just north of Aries.

6. The first of these letters not found; for the second and the dating of both of them, see above, pp. 51–2, and the first note to that document.

7. The text of the petition is printed in 8 *Pa. Arch.*, VII, 5824–7. It was presented to the House of Commons on March 20 and referred to the Committee of the Whole. *Commons Journal*, XXX, 676.

8. BF had written Speaker Fox on February 24 and March 1 reporting the progress and almost certain passage of the repealing bill (above, pp. 168–9, 186–7), but no letter to the speaker announcing its final enactment has been found or is reported in the *Votes*.

9. While discussion of the repeal of the Stamp Act was going on during January and February, the Commons had referred to its Committee of the Whole numerous petitions from British merchants relating to colonial trade. After the repeal of the Stamp Act the Committee continued to sit from time

oughly examined on that head before the House, and it is now seen in a Light much more favourable for us than ever heretofore. We have a Ministry extreamly well dispos'd towards us, from whom, if they continue, and become firmly established, we may hope every thing we can reasonably expect. But there is a strong Opposition against them, which makes them cautious of going all the Lengths at once which they wish to go in our Favour. It is now intended to reduce the Duty on foreign Mellasses to 1*d*. per Gallon; to permit Duty-free the Importation into North America as Articles of Commerce, to be stored in King's Warehouses, and afterwards exported to Europe, all foreign Sugars, Coffee, &c. and to Britain, Cotton, Indigo, &c.—and such Sugars as are consum'd in America, tho' clay'd and fine, to pay a Duty of 5*s*. per hund. only. The Reducing the Muscovado Duty to 2*s*. 6*d*. was talk'd of; but that is yet doubted.[1] A free Port is also intended at Dominica, and if it succeeds, another or two more may be made next Year, at Jamaica and Pensacola.[2] The direct Importation of

---

to time to consider what ought to be done to improve this trade and to modify the existing legislation controlling it. The Committee was scheduled to sit (and, according to BF, to report) on Monday, April 14. On that day, however, the sitting was postponed for a week, and later postponed again. *Commons Journal*, xxx, 724, 759. Five sessions of the Committee did take place in late April and early May, however, at which additional petitions were considered and witnesses heard, before the Committee reported on May 9. *Ibid.*, pp. 783, 800–1, 804, 805, 811.

1. The first three of these changes were included in the resolutions of the Committee of the Whole reported to the Commons on May 9, and in An Act for repealing certain Duties . . ., 6 Geo. III, c. 52, which received the royal assent on June 6, 1766. The proposal BF mentions regarding muscovado sugar was not mentioned in the resolutions or the act. The important change in the duty on molasses was that, in contrast to previous legislation, it was to apply to all molasses and syrup imported into a British colony, that produced in another British colony as well as that of foreign origin. This general application of the duty was intended to simplify the enforcement of the duty. In return the British West Indies received concessions on the direct exportation of sugar to Europe. For this act and the part played by the Rockingham Ministry in initiating and passing it, see Dora Mae Clark, *The Rise of the British Treasury Colonial Administration in the Eighteenth Century* (New Haven, 1960), pp. 151–4.

2. The resolutions of the Committee of the Whole proposed the establishment of such free ports, and An Act for opening and establishing certain Ports in the Islands of Jamaica and Dominica . . ., 6 Geo. III, c. 49, also

Wine, Oil and Fruits from Portugal and Spain to America is also to be allow'd, if it can be carried in the House; but that meets with particular Opposition, and may possibly fail, tho' I rather think it will be carried,[3] as Mr. Grenville's Party seem daily diminishing. As to the Paper Currency I last Week at the Request of one of the Members drew a Bill for Repealing the Act of 1763 relating to legal Tender, which he intends to bring in after considering it with Mr. Townsend.[4] The principal Point was to satisfy the Merchants, who obtain'd that Restraining Act, they having suffer'd in Virginia by the Depreciation of the Currency there in which their Debts were paid: I therefore inserted a Clause to make Sterling Debts due to British Merchants and payable here, recoverable according to the Rate of Exchange at the Time, which I think is no more than we have always practis'd in the Courts of our Province. What Alteration will be made in the Draft it is impossible to say; and I doubt whether if a Bill be brought in, it will be compleated this Session; the Ministry being inclin'd to consider the Affair of Paper Money more extensively, and therefore to leave it to another Year; which, if they do, I hope will not be attended with any great Inconvenience, as we have still a considerable Sum extant that is legal Tender. I shall however use my best Endeavours to get it compleated now.[5] There is a Bill also under Consideration relating to Admiralty Courts and other Admiralty Affairs in America, on which I have had several Conferences with the Ministry: It is among other Things propos'd that the Act made 19 Geo. II. to prevent the Impressing of Seamen in the Sugar Colonies for the King's Ships, unless with Consent

enacted June 6, 1766, provided for two free ports in Dominica and four in Jamaica. The purpose of this measure was to legalize and encourage trade with the Spanish Caribbean possessions that provided a mutually beneficial exchange of commodities and was the major source of the importation of bullion into the British colonies. Grenville's attempted strict enforcement of earlier laws had hampered this trade. *Ibid.*, pp. 151–2, 159.

3. No legislation on this trade was adopted in 1766.

4. See above, pp. 204–7. "Mr. Townsend" was probably Charles Townshend, at this time paymaster general, who became chancellor of the Exchequer in July 1766. BF's "1763" for the Currency Act was a slip of the pen; the act was 1764.

5. As stated in the headnote to BF's outline of the bill, the House of Commons refused on May 14 to permit the introduction of such a measure at that time.

of Governor and Council, be extended to North-America.[6] And on a Suggestion that had been made to the Admiralty, that the Men were entic'd from the King's Ships by the Merchants, and that the Governors and Councils of some North American Colonies would probably refuse to give their Consent, whatever might be the Necessity, a Clause was drawn to direct an Application to be made to them for Men when wanted, and that in case of their Refusal or Neglect to provide a sufficient Number, *it should be lawful for the Officers of the King's Ships to impress, &c.* I oppos'd this strongly, in a long Conversation with my Lord Egmont, who is at the Head of the Admiralty Board; and he was so obliging as to say he was satisfy'd with my Reasons, and the Power of Impressing should be omitted. It appear'd to me a terrible Thing to establish such Violence by a Law, however necessary it may be in some Cases; and I conceiv'd it a Power not fit to be given the Officers of the Navy, who might use it greatly to the Oppression and Injury of particular Colonies.

The Merchants trading to America have been of great Service to us in all our late Affairs, and deserve the Thanks of the Colonies.[7] I hope the Behaviour of the Colonists on the Repeal, will be decent and grateful to Government here, which will greatly strengthen the Hands of their Friends the present Ministry, as very different

6. No legislation relating to the colonial Admiralty Courts or to the impressment of seamen in the colonies was enacted at this time. An act of 1708 had forbidden naval officers to impress seamen in the colonies, but in 1740 the law officers of the Crown declared that it had expired at the conclusion of the War of the Spanish Succession in 1713. Colonists and some people in Great Britain denied the validity of this interpretation, but naval officers resumed their activity whenever circumstances seemed to require it. When maritime warfare, especially in the West Indies, resumed in the 1740s, British merchants and planters complained so strongly at the resulting interference with their commerce, that in 1746 Parliament passed an act, 19 Geo. II, c. 30, forbidding naval officers to impress seamen in the Sugar Islands. The mainland colonies received no such protection, then or later, and the issue remained one of their grievances until the Revolution. Dora Mae Clark, "The Impressment of Seamen in the American Colonies," *Essays in Colonial History Presented to Charles McLean Andrews by his Students* (New Haven, 1931), pp. 204–24.

7. All accounts, contemporary and recent, of efforts to repeal the Stamp Act and bring about remedial legislation emphasize the close cooperation between the colonial agents and the British merchants interested in American trade. On some issues, however, differences developed between those concerned with the continental colonies and the "West India interest."

Things are prognosticated. I send you the Lords Protests;[8] and also the best Account we have of the Debates on the Repeal; but it is very short and imperfect, Mr. Pitt having spoke in the whole near three Hours. Our particular Provincial Petitions remain ready to be proceeded on, as soon as these other Affairs are out of hand.

Please to present my Duty to the Assembly and believe me, with particular Esteem, Gentlemen, Your most obedient humble Servant

B Franklin

Committee of Correspondence.

Petition to the House of Commons

Draft: Library of Congress

At the request of members the House of Commons ordered to be read aloud on Friday, April 11, 1766, part of an act that provided for the transportation of felons from England to the American colonies. Thereupon the House granted leave to bring in a bill extending to Scotland the system of transporting felons to America.[9] Within a few days Franklin had drawn up a petition against the proposed measure and had given it to Richard Jackson for presentation. As Franklin explained when sending a copy of the petition to Joseph Galloway six months later, it would have needed "some Alterations" if it were actually to be presented to the Commons; Jackson understood Franklin's intentions and went no further than to show the paper "among the Members, and it occasion'd some Laughing."[1]

Readers of these volumes will at once recall Franklin's previous writing on the same general subject, when in 1751 he proposed in the *Pennsylvania Gazette* that, as "*suitable Returns*" for the felons England insisted on sending to America, the colonies send back quantities of rattlesnakes for the parks and gardens of the mother country.[2] It will be

8. See above, pp. 207–32.

9. *Commons Journal*, xxx, 718. The act of 1717 was 4 Geo. I, c. 11, An Act for the further preventing Robbery, Burglary, and other Felonies, and for the more effectual Transportation of Felons.

1. Below, p. 450.

2. Above, IV, 130–3. BF certainly remembered his earlier effort while he was drawing up this petition. He drafted a short paragraph, which he later struck out, in which he pointed out "That several of the Colonies, and particularly the Province of Pensilvania, have heretofore made Laws to lay a discouraging Duty on the Importation of Felons: but the same have been repealed by the Crown." See also, above, VIII, 351.

observed that Franklin showed rather more subtlety and finesse in the petition than he had in the *Gazette* piece. Perhaps the difference shows a development of his skill in satire; more probably it reflects his recognition that a paper intended to be read by members of the British governing elite called for greater delicacy of touch than had been necessary or even desirable in a communication directed to the generality of readers of a colonial newspaper.

It would be pleasant to report that Franklin's petition won over enough votes to defeat the bill in the House of Commons. But amusement among the members did not prevent the smooth passage of the bill through both Houses; it received the royal assent on May 14, 1766.[3]

[April 12–15, 1766][4]

To the honourable the Knights Citizens and Burgesses of Great Britain in Parliament assembled,

The Petition of BF. Agent for the Province of Pensilvania,
Most humbly Sheweth,

That the Transporting of Felons from England to the Plantations in America, is and hath long been a great Grievance to the said Plantations in general.

That the said Felons being landed in America, not only continue their evil Practices, to the Annoyance of his Majesty's good Subjects there, but contribute greatly to corrupt the Morals of the Servants and poorer People among whom they are mixed.

That many of the said Felons escape from the Servitude to which they were destined, into other Colonies, where their Condition is not known and wandering at large from one populous Town to another commit many Burglaries Robberies and Murders, to the great Terror of the People, and occasioning heavy Charges

---

3. *Commons Journal*, XXX, 732, 739, 754, 776, 795, 820. The act became 6 Geo. III, c. 32. BF did not forget this petition or his resentment at the insistence of the British on sending felons to the colonies. In 1787 (a date determined by internal evidence) he drafted a letter to *Pa. Gaz.*, that he signed "A.Z.," in which he planned to quote this petition in full, and in which he proposed a requirement that every English ship arriving in America with goods for sale give bond to "carry back to Britain at least one [American] Felon for every Fifty Tons of her Burthen." Lib. Cong.

4. Mention in the petition of the granting of leave to bring in the bill on "Friday last" fixes the date of composition as after Friday, April 11. Failure to mention the actual introduction of the bill indicates that BF wrote the draft no later than the 15th, when the bill was introduced.

for the apprehending and securing such Felons, and bringing them to Justice.

That your Petitioner humbly conceives the Easing one Part of the British Dominions of their Felons by burthening another Part with the same Felons, cannot increase the common Happiness of his Majesty's Subjects; and that therefore the Trouble and Expence of transporting them is upon the whole altogether useless.[5]

That your Petitioner nevertheless observes with extream Concern, in the Votes of Friday last, that Leave is given to bring in a Bill, for extending to Scotland the Act made in the 4th. Year of the Reign of King George the First, whereby the aforesaid Grievances are (as he understands) to be greatly increas'd by allowing Scotland also to transport its Felons to America.

Your Petitioner therefore humbly prays, in behalf of Pensilvania and the other Plantations in America that the House wou'd take the Premisses into Consideration, and in their great Wisdom and Goodness repeal all Acts and Clauses of Acts for Transporting of Felons; or if this may not at present be done, that they would at least reject the propos'd Bill for extending of the said Acts to Scotland; or, if it be thought fit to allow of such Extension, that then the said Extension may be carried farther, and the Plantations be also by an equitable Clause in the same Bill permitted to transport their Felons to Scotland.

And your Petitioner, as in Duty bound shall pray, &c.

To [Joseph Galloway[6]]

MS not found; extract printed in *Pennsylvania Gazette,* June 19, 1766

April 12, 1766.

Our Friends here are in Pain, lest the Condescension of Parliament, in repealing the Stamp-Act, will encourage the Americans

5. Appreciation of the jest in the concluding lines of this petition should not lead the reader to overlook BF's emphasis here on the essential unity of all the British dominions and his obvious belief that there was—or ought to be—such a thing as "the common Happiness of His Majesty's Subjects." Like other colonial leaders BF had a greater sense of the community of interest of all the English-speaking world at this time than did many, if not most, of the leaders in Great Britain.

6. BF's friends often published extracts of his letters in *Pa. Gaz.* It appears

to farther Excesses; and our Enemies, who have predicted it, hope to see their Prophecies fulfilled, that they may disgrace the present Ministry; but I hope we shall behave prudently, and disappoint them, which will establish the Ministry, and *thereby effectually secure* the American Interest in Parliament.[7] Indeed I wish this Ministry well, for their own Sakes, as well as ours, as they appear to me to be really very honest worthy Men, with the best Intentions; by no Means deficient in Abilities, very attentive to Business, and of Course daily improving in their Acquaintance with it.

The Proposal of free Ports in America, has been attended to, and one, for a Trial, will be established at Dominica.[8]

From Joseph Priestley   ALS: American Philosophical Society

Dear Sir   Warrington. 13 Ap. 1766

I this day received your favour of the 10th instant, and the day before yesterday another letter, with several parcels of books, containing all that are mentioned in your letters.[9] At the same time

---

probable that this extract was taken from a letter to Galloway. On June 16, 1766, Galloway wrote (below, p. 316) that he had received BF's letter of April 12 and had sent David Hall an extract in which BF had praised the members of the present ministry. It is not impossible, of course, that BF had written some other friend—including Hall himself—to the same effect on the same day.

7. Even as this letter was written, the Rockingham ministry was in the process of disintegrating over personal differences, not issues. It was replaced, July 23, by an administration headed by William Pitt. See Gipson, *British Empire*, XI, 70–82.

8. Hearings on such a bill were held, April 7, 1766. Although William Pitt opposed it when it was first introduced in Parliament, he later withdrew his opposition and the bill, establishing free ports in Dominica and Jamaica (6 Geo. III, c. 49), was passed and received the royal assent, June 6, 1766. See Ross J.S. Hoffman, *Edmund Burke, New York Agent* (Phila., 1956), pp., 343, 347, 350, and above, pp. 237–8.

9. Neither of BF's letters mentioned here has been found. Many of the persons, books, and experiments discussed in the present letter have received editorial comment in the notes to Priestley's letter to BF of March 25, 1766; above, pp. 199–202. It should be read in conjunction with this letter. These letters and those of the same period to other electricians in London are conveniently printed as a group in Robert E. Schofield, ed., *A Scientific Autobiography of Joseph Priestley (1733–1804)*, (Cambridge, Mass. and London, [1966]), pp. 12–49.

I received a parcel from Dr. Watson, containing, among others, the same history of electricity which you have sent me.[1] I shall immediately apply myself to the purusal of them all, with the greatest attention, and I make no doubt but from these, and other books which I hope you will be able to procure me, I shall make many valuable additions to my history. I need not tell you, that you will find it, in the condition in which it comes into your hands, very imperfect. It contains indeed every[thing] that the materials I then had by me [could furnish?], but [some?] very important articles have already [fallen] my way [torn]. When Mr. Canton sends me his Gilbert, [I shall] not fail to enrich my work with a particular account [of] all that he did in electricity. If I cannot get Otto Gueric, I must copy what is said of him in the history you have sent me.

I shall be very glad to hear your remarks on my experiment with the *vanes*, tho' I am quite satisfied, that it is perfectly agreeable to your general theory. You will find some additional experiments with the vanes in my letter to Mr. Canton.

Since I sent my last two numbers to Mr. Price, I have neither written a line on the subject of electricity, nor made any experiments of consequence, having been wholly employed in constructing an electrical machine upon a new, and, I think, in many respects, an improved plan. I propose to give a particular description and a cut of it in the book.[2]

I have not repeated my experiments with *condensed air* since I wrote to Dr. Watson, but in a piece of Boulanger[3] which he has sent me I find that the same experiment had been made before, and with the same success. This author adds, that the impossibility of exciting a tube in which air is condensed cannot be owing to moisture, as some suspect; for if a drinking glass full of water be poured into the tube, and poured out again, it will not destroy its

1. Perhaps the "histoire de l'électricité," by either Abbé de Mangin or Thomas-François Dalibard, which Priestley requested in his letter of March 25.

2. Part v of Priestley's *History of Electricity* is devoted to electrical machines. His own machine is described on pp. 530–4 with an accompanying plate.

3. A work described in Priestley's *History*, facing p. 736, as "Boulanger's Traité de la cause et des phenomenes de l'electricité, 1750, Paris." Priestley noted that he had "seen no more than one part of this treatise, which I had of Dr. Watson. How many more parts there are of the whole work, I have not been informed."

electrifying power so effectually as the condensed air. He adds, in another place, that Marcassites[4] are incapable of being excited, chiefly on account of the condensed air that is in them. This last is certainly a very gro[u]ndless supposition. I think, with you and Dr. Watson, that the effect is, some way or other, owing to moisture. Mr. Boulanger did not know, that when the [air] was heated it might be excited, though it did contain [torn]. This is not the first or second time [in] which [I have found] myself anticipated in experiments which I imagi[ned h]ad been originally my own. The blast from electrified [poin]ts and even the blowing of the candle I find mentioned by Nollet.[5] But he did not pursue the experiment, and he argues very weakly from it. I am ashamed when I think of the experiment with *mephitic air,* but I made use of every precaution I could think of, and others were deceived as well as myself.

I was yesterday favoured with a letter from Mr. Canton. Please to present my compliments to him. Tell him I thank him for the curious particulars it contains, and that I shall, with great pleasure, make the use of them that he desires, as well as strictly conform to every thing else that he requests of me. I sincerely ask his pardon for my hasty misapprehension of his observations on *hot air,* but I think he will find that I have not made that mistake in the history.[6] When I have made some more experiments on *hot air* and on *effluvia,* I will write to him again.

I shall not forget the motto of your seal.[7] I consider Mr. Wilson's performance in the same light that you do.[8]

If electrics naturally contain more of the electric fluid than other bodies, should not red hot glass, as it cools, draw the fluid from

4. Marcasites: crystallized iron pyrites.

5. Jean-Antoine Nollet, one of BF's earliest and most notable scientific antagonists; see above, IV, 423–8. Priestley cited his "Conjettures sur les causes de l'electricité des corps, Paris, 1745" and his "Essai sur l'electricité des corps, 1746, 1754, Paris" in the bibliography to his *History.*

6. For Canton's experiments on the relationship between heat and the conductivity of electricity in which he differed with Edward Delaval, see above, X, 23–6, 74–5. Priestley summarized the Canton-Delaval controversy in his *History,* pp. 237–45.

7. The Franklin arms, above, II, facing 230, contained the motto: "Exemplum adest ipse homo"—the example presents the man himself.

8. BF must have considered Benjamin Wilson's electrical work incomprehensible, as Priestley confessed that he had in his letter of March 25; see above, p. 201.

the bodies with which it is in contact? I placed a piece of red hot glass and let it cool upon a very smooth piece of insulated copper, without perceiving any such effect.

I hope you will be able to procure me Beccaria.[9] I am sorry that Wilke's piece[1] is not complete. I greatly admire Æpinus.[2] I hope you will make very free with the blank page of my MSS. I shall be sorry if I find but little in it. I am much obliged to [torn] explanation of two latin terms. If [torn] take of that kind, I hope you will [torn] sometime inclused French words in brac[kets] doubtful of my rendering of them. I am, with the greatest gratitude and re[spect] Dear Sir Your most obliged humble servant   J Priestley

Addressed: To / Do[ctor Frankli]n / at Mrs Stephens's in Craven street / in the Strand / London

From George Read[3]

MS not found; reprinted from William T. Read, *Life and Correspondence of George Read* (Philadelphia, 1870), p. 23.

Sir,   New Castle, April 14th, 1766.

From your known goodness, and the knowledge you have of me and my family, I have presumed to beg the favor of you to apply to the Lords Commissioners of the Treasury on my behalf, for the appointment of Collector of the Port of New Castle, made vacant by the death of Mr. William Till yesterday morning.[4] My preten-

9. Giambatista Beccaria, professor of experimental physics at Turin, and one of BF's defenders in his controversy with Nollet; see above, V, 395 n. In the bibliography to his *History*, facing p. 736, Priestley noted that BF had sent him a copy of Beccaria's *Dell' elettricismo artificiale e naturale* (Turin, 1753).

1. Johanne Carolus [Johan Carl] Wilcke, *Disputatio physica experimentatis de electricitatibus contrariis* (Rostock, 1757).

2. Franz Ulrich Theodor Aepinus, professor of physics at St. Petersburg; see above, VIII, 393–5; X, 204–5, 266–7.

3. For George Read, at this time attorney general of Delaware, see above, p. 32 n.

4. In 1763 Read had married Gertrude Ross Till, widow of William Till's son, Thomas. Read's wife was a half-sister of BF's good friend John Ross and the "knowledge" which Read claimed BF had of him may have come from this connection. William T. Read, *Life and Correspondence of George Read* (Phila., 1870), pp. 20, 60; Charles P. Keith, *The Provincial Councillors of Pennsylvania* (Phila., 1883), pp. 194–5.

sions to this post are solely founded on your good offices in my favor, for which I shall have no other return to make than a grateful remembrance of the service done me, and this, I am well assured, will be satisfactory to your generous mind. Should this appointment be obtained for me,[5] I am persuaded I can give very satisfactory security for the due execution of the office in the city of Philadelphia. Among others, I can venture to name Mr. Rees Meredith and Captain John Mease,[6] whose very independent fortunes, I do suppose, you are well assured of.

Good sir, pardon the freedom I have taken to address you on this occasion, and you will much oblige your most obedient, humble servant,   GEORGE READ.

To Dr. Franklin.

To Thomas Ronayne[7]

MS not found; reprinted from William Temple Franklin, ed., *Memoirs of the Life and Writings of Benjamin Franklin, LL.D. F.R.S. &c.* (Quarto edition, London, 1817–18), III, 364–6.[8]

London, April 20, 1766.

I received your very obliging and ingenious letter by Captain Kearney.[9] Your observations on the Electricity of Fogs, and of the air in Ireland, and of the several circumstances attending a thun-

5. It was not. On Nov. 14, 1766, Samuel Wharton wrote Read that "Dr. Franklin writes that he had an absolute promise of it from the Marquis of Rockingham; but when he was in Germany there was an unfortunate change in the ministry, and Alderman Trecothick applied to the Duke of Grafton, and obtained it for Mr. Walker." Read, *Life and Correspondence of George Read*, pp. 24–5.

6. Meredith, a Philadelphia merchant, and Mease have been mentioned in earlier volumes of this series. See above, II, 376 n; III, 215 n, 223, 296; V, 329; XI, 315.

7. For Thomas Ronayne, an Irishman whose interest was "atmospheric Electricity" and who had corresponded with BF on the subject as early as 1761, see above, IX, 350–2.

8. A French translation of this letter was printed earlier in Jacques Barbeu Dubourg, ed., *Oeuvres de M. Franklin, Docteur ès Lois* (Paris, 1773), I, 265–8. William Temple Franklin probably printed from a retained copy of the letter, though he may possibly have made a retranslation from Dubourg's French text.

9. Ronayne's letter has not been found.

der-storm, are very curious; and I thank you for them. I have endeavored to get Father Beccaria's book for you, but find it is not to be had here: 'tis in 2 vols. 4to. in Italian, printed at Turin.[1] In my opinion no part of the earth is, or can be, in a negative state of electricity naturally; and though an inequality may in some circumstances be occasioned, an equality would soon follow, from the extreme subtilty of the electric fluid, and the good conductors the moist earth is filled with. But yet I think when a highly-charged positive cloud comes near the earth, it repels and drives inward the natural quantity of electricity in the superficial parts, and in buildings, trees, &c. so as to bring them into a real negative state before it strikes. And I think the negative state you often find your balls in that hang to your apparatus, is not occasioned always by negative clouds, but often by positive clouds having passed over it, which, in passing, have repelled and driven out part of the natural quantity of electricity that was in the apparatus; so that when they are passed, the remainder diffusing itself equally in the apparatus, the whole is in a negative state. If you have read my experiments in pursuance of those made by Mr. Canton (they are in vol. 40 of the Transactions), you will easily understand this.[2] But you may readily make some experiments that will show it clearly. Make a common wine-glass warm by the fire, that it may keep quite dry for some time; set it on a table, and place on it Mr. Canton's little box, the balls hanging from the box a little beyond the edge of the table. Rub another warm wine-glass with a piece of black silk, or even a common silk handkerchief, so as to excite it. Then bring the glass over the box at the end farthest from the balls, at three or four inches' distance, and you will see the balls diverge, being then electrified positively by the natural quantity of electricity that was in the box, driven to that end by the repelling force of the atmosphere of the rubbed glass. Touch the box near the balls (the rubbed glass remaining as at first), and the balls will come together, your finger taking away the quantity driven to

1. BF did manage, however, to obtain a copy of Beccaria's *Dell' elettricismo artificiale e naturale* for Joseph Priestley who requested it in his letter of April 13, 1766. See above, p. 246 n.

2. The experiments to which BF here refers were published in volume 49 of *Phil. Trans*. See above, v, 516–19. Dubourg's translation omits the words in parentheses, substituting a footnote cross reference to his own edition.

that end. Then withdraw finger and glass at the same time, and the quantity left in the box diffusing itself equally, the balls will diverge again and be negative. While in this state, rub your glass afresh, and pass it over the box without coming too near, and you will see, as you approach it, the balls first close; they are then in a natural state: as the glass comes nearer, they open again; they are then positive. When the glass passes and begins to leave them, they close again, and are then in the natural state. When it has quite left them, they open again, and are then negative. The rubbed glass may represent a positively charged cloud, which you see is thus capable of producing all the changes in the apparatus without the necessity of supposing any negative cloud at all. But yet I am convinced there are negative clouds; because they will sometimes drink at and through the apparatus a large full bottle of positive electricity, of which the apparatus itself could not have received and retained the hundredth part. And, indeed, it is easy to conceive how a strongly charged large positive cloud may reduce smaller clouds to a negative state, as it passes over or near them, by driving their natural quantity out of them to their under side, whence it strikes into the earth, or to their farther end, whence it strikes into neighboring clouds; so that when the great cloud has passed or removed farther, they are left in a negative state, like the apparatus; they being, as well as it, often insulated bodies, not in contact with the earth or one another. And in the same manner it is equally easy to conceive how a large negative cloud may make others positive. The experiment you mention of filing the glass is similar to one I made in 1751, or 1752.[3] I had supposed in my letter[4] that the internal pores of glass were less than those near the surface, and so denied a passage to the electric fluid. To try whether this was so in fact, I ground one of my phials on one side extremely thin, passing a good way beyond the middle of the thickness, and very near to the other side, as I found on breaking it after the experiment. It charged as well after grinding as before; which satisfied me that my hypothesis was in that particular wrong. It is hard to conceive where the additional quantity on the charged

3. BF described this experiment in a letter to Dr. John Lining, March 18, 1755; see above, v, 522–3.

4. Presumably his "Opinions and Conjectures," [July 29, 1750]. See above, IV, 25–34.

APRIL 20, 1766

side of glass is deposited, there is so much of it. I send you my meteorological paper, which has lately been printed here in the Transactions,[5] following a paper of Mr. Hamilton's on the same subject.[6] I am, &c.   B. FRANKLIN.

From Thomas Wharton

ALS: American Philosophical Society

My Dear Friend.   Philadelphia April 26. 1766.

I had the pleasure of writing thee, on the 25th. Ulto,[7] since when We have not had the satisfaction of receiving any of thy Favours.

Various have been the Reports spread through the Continent, respecting the Repeal of the Stamp-Act; and as often as they arrived sometimes in favour and other times against Us, we were acted upon, by our Fears, and different views of this matter;[8] But about 10 Days past we received via Ireland, a certain Account; the Vote of the House of Commons, with Secretary Conway, W. Pitt, Grey, Cooper and several other Patriots, their speeches in our favour; which has greatly relieved us:[9] and I hope the March Packet will give the joyful News—that the King and Lords have accorded therewith: From whence I hope also We shall see at least for some time—Peace restored. Not that I beleive but a certain Sect,[1] or at least some among them—have by means of the

5. See above, IV, 235–43.
6. Hugh Hamilton (1729–1805), professor of natural philosophy at the University of Dublin, was a cleric and a writer on scientific subjects. *DNB*. His "A Dissertation on the Nature of Evaporation and several Phaenomena of Air, Water, and boiling Liquors" was read before the Royal Society, May 16, 1765, and published in *Phil. Trans.*, LV (1765), 146–81.
7. Not found.
8. For the repeal of the Stamp Act, March 18, 1766, see above, p. 55 n.
9. *Pa. Gaz.*, April 17, 1766, printed reports, brought by a Captain Keith from Londonderry in 31 days, of the deliberations in the House of Commons through Feb. 25, 1766. These reports affirmed that the House had resolved to bring in a bill to repeal the Stamp Act. The next week's issue of the *Gazette*, April 24, 1766, carried an extended account of William Pitt's famous speech proposing repeal of the Stamp Act. On May 1 both *Pa. Gaz.* and *Pa. Jour.* carried texts of the resolution of the Committee of the Whole House, Feb. 22, 1766, to repeal the Stamp Act, while on May 19 both papers issued special supplements printing the full text of the repealing act.
1. The Presbyterians.

250

Opposition given to this Act, been capable of ascertaining their Numbers; which must amount to many Thousands on the Continent. I think it would be of great advantage could the Bishop of London, (or Those to whom the Power belongs)—think of some easier and less expensive way of Ordaining their Clergy, than that of going to London.[2] We know the Synod performs this part —twice in every Year; and by this means joined with the uncommon Diligence of this Sect of People, to establish Places of Worship—even where there are but a few Families seated together; their society encreases extreamly: And in many Instances at the Loss of the Church, for they don't regard whether the generality of the Persons be of their society or the Church, if they have not a more convenient Place of Worship to attend; by these means however the Parents sentiments may be retained to the Church of England, Yet, their Children become fixed in the other Principles: And the Church sustains a Loss from the rising Generation. I am confidently assured that We have but Eight Churches belonging to the Church of England; when there are Eighty or upwards of the Presbeterian Meeting Houses—in this Province. I dont mean by this to persecute any Sect; But could wish to see that Religion bear the Reins of Government throughout the Continent, whose Sentiments are founded on the most Catholic-Principles—I mean the Church of England. However I am clear— that unless some speedy and just Methods be taken to set this Affair right; it does appear to me that in a few years it will scarce be worthy of the notice of those at the Helm. I got into this train of thought without the least premiditation—and which perhaps it will be best to quit lest it tire thy patience.

We have but little News among Us; Our Trade greatly stagnated: And unless the Parliament allows the Continent a general and free Trade—I cannot see how we can possible pay our Debts to or continue our Trade with Great-Britain.[3]

---

2. With no Anglican bishop resident in the colonies, candidates for ordination in that church had to travel to England. Proposals for an American bishop were causing agitation at this time. From what follows it appears that Wharton, a Quaker, favored the idea as a means of reducing defections from the Anglican Church to the Presbyterian.

3. For reforms in the laws of trade, written into bills which received the royal assent, June 6, 1766, see above, p. 237 n.

The Factory[4] has bought this spring 20,000 lb. Weight of Flax in Connecticut; and the Poor receive great advantage from that Institution: We pay about £25 a fortnight to the Poor-Women for Spinning, and I think there are near 200 employed, who find it a great Relief.

It pleased Providence this day fortnight to grant my Wife the happy delivery of a fine son; Governor Franklin and his Spouse were then in this City. I waited on thy spouse and them, and requested to know if they thought it would be agreable to thee, and was so to themselves, that, I should call his Name Franklin Wharton, to which they kindly answered in the affirmative; In consequence of which—we have undertaken to place that Character on him:[5] And hope it will not afford my Friend a disagreable sensation—as I do assure him it arises from the strict Regard—I bear you.

Thy Family are all well, I remain thy real Friend

THO WHARTON

Addressed: For Benjamin Franklin Esqr / Deputy Post master General / of North America / In / Craven street / London / per Cap. Johnson / via Liverpool

To Jonathan Williams

ALS: American Philosophical Society

Dear Cousin   London, April 28. 1766

I have received several of your kind Favours since my Arrival in England, the last by your good Brother,[6] the Subject not in the least disagreable as you apprehend, but in Truth it has not been at all in my Power to do what you desir'd; if for no other Reasons, yet for this, that there has been no Vacancy.[7]

4. A Philadelphia linen factory, established in 1764, in which BF was a shareholder; see above, XI, 314–16.

5. The child died in July and was buried, along with his brother Joseph, aged 6, on August 1. See below, p. 338.

6. None of Williams' letters has been found. His brother, John, had been in Philadelphia in the summer of 1765; he was appointed inspector general of customs under the American Board of Customs Commissioners, established in 1767. See above, XII, 193 n.

7. It is not clear what position Williams asked BF to procure or for whom he wanted it; possibly the candidate was his brother John.

I congratulate you on the Repeal of that Mother of Mischiefs the Stamp Act, and on the Ease we are like to obtain in our Commerce. My time has been extreamly taken up, as you may imagine in these general Affairs of America, as well as in the particular ones of our Province; yet I did not forget the Armonica, for Cousin Josiah:[8] but with all my Endeavours I have not yet been able to procure one. Here is only one Man that makes them well,[9] his Price no less than 34 Guineas, asks 40. I bid him 100 Guineas for three; he refus'd it. I then agreed to give him the 34 Guineas for one. He promis'd to make it now a 12 month since, I have call'd on him often 'till I am tir'd, and do not find he has yet done a Glass of it. If I could have got this, Josiah should have had it, or mine. But I fear it will not be got at all. And I hope his waiting till my Return, tho' it may seem long, will be no Disadvantage, as all his Improvement on the Organ in the meantime will go towards his better playing on the Armonica when he gets it.

I rejoice to hear of the Welfare and Increase of your Family.[1] I pray God to bless them and you, being Your affectionate Uncle

B FRANKLIN

Sister Mecom speaks very affectionately of you, and gratefully of your kindness to her in her late Troubles.[2]

The Bearer Mr. Sears,[3] is entring into Business as a Merchant here. He is a Friend of mine, and I recommend him to your Acquaintance and Civilities.

Addressed: To / Mr Jonathan Williams / Mercht / Boston / per favour of / Mr Sears.

Endorsed: Apl 28 1766
April 26 1766

8. On Nov. 3, 1764, BF promised to send Williams' blind son, Josiah, an armonica from London. See above, XI, 426–7 n.

9. Probably Charles James "of Purpool, near Gray's Inn, London" about whose lethargy BF had complained in 1763. See above, X, 118 n, 235.

1. On Feb. 27, 1766, Jane Mecom wrote DF that Williams' wife, Grace, was expecting a baby, perhaps the child named Sally who died in September 1767. Van Doren, *Franklin-Mecom,* p. 90; Williams to BF, Oct. 19, 1767, APS.

2. Jane's husband, Edward, had died on Sept. 11, 1765; see above, p. 187 n.

3. Not identified.

From James Johnson[4]

MS not found; reprinted from George Everett Hastings, *The Life and Works of Francis Hopkinson* (Chicago, [1926]), p. 122.[5]

[April 28, 1766]
The Bishop of Worcester presents his Respects to Dr. Franklin and begs the favour of Him to let the Inclos'd to Mr. Hopkinson go in his Packet when He has an opportunity of sending to Philadelphia.

From William Franklin   ALS: American Philosophical Society

Honoured Father   Burlin. 30th April, 1766
   Your Favour of the 25th. of Febry. is just come to hand. The one you mention to have sent me on the 16th. I have not receiv'd.[6] Perhaps it was on Board that unfortunate Vessel from Bristol which was lost on our Coast.[7] If so, and you have kept any Copy do favour me with it for I should be very loath to lose any of your Letters.
   You cannot conceive the Satisfaction which the Accounts of your Examination at the Bar of the H. of Commons have afforded your Friends. Dr. Fothergill and Mr. Whitefield have mentioned your Behaviour on the Occasion in high Terms.[8] I am told that

4. For James Johnson, Bishop of Worcester, whose kinship to the Hopkinson family of Philadelphia BF helped establish in 1765, see above, XII, 124 n, 200, 288–9, 401.
   5. Hastings indicated that the MS of this letter was owned by Mr. George O. G. Coale of Boston, but its present whereabouts has not been discovered.
   6. Neither BF's letter of February 25 nor that of the 16th has been found.
   7. On Sunday, April 6, 1766, the snow *Nancy*, bound from Bristol to Philadelphia, was wrecked in a northeast storm on Hereford Bar, about twelve miles north of Cape May. Twenty-five persons lost their lives, including Richard Smith, brother of the Reverend William Smith of Philadelphia. *Pa. Gaz.*, April 10, 17, 1766.
   8. *Pa. Gaz.*, May 1 and 8, 1766, printed extracts from several letters from England relating to the favorable prospects for repeal of the Stamp Act. Six of these praised BF's services particularly. One, dated February 27, from John Fothergill, identified as "a Gentleman, who, though never in America, has for many Years, proved himself a disinterested firm Friend to her true Interest," after extolling BF at some length and citing his examination, added: "He has been an able, useful Advocate for America in general, and the Province of Pennsylvania in particular, during his Stay here, of which you will have

the latter says America owes the Repeal of the Stamp Act to the assiduous Endeavours of Alderman Trecothick, Capel Hanbury and Dr. Franklin. I can't learn however that any of the Merchants have mentioned your Services at all. It would appear by their Letters that each of them would willingly have his Correspondents think that he alone by his Interest and Management had done every Thing that was done in favour of the Colonies. If you obtain a Copy of your Examination, pray send it me.[9] The N.Y. Mercury of Monday, contains a very sensible judicious Letter from the Committee of Merchants in London but you will see notwithstanding our Advertisement directly counter to their Advice, and I really fear our People's Indiscretion will be such as to [frustrate?] all endeavours to serve them.[1] However, I shall strive to get our Assembly to address the Parliament in the manner you [mention?].[2]

I don't wonder at your disapproving my mentioning in my

received from many Persons undoubted Information, as well as this." A copy of the entire letter is in Hist. Soc. Pa. Another letter of the same date "from an eminent Clergyman in London" (probably George Whitefield) said: "Doctor Franklin spoke very heartily and judiciously, in his Country's Behalf, when at the Bar of the House of Commons." Another of the same date, addressed to a person in New York, singled out for praise Pitt and Camden among the politicians, and Trecothick and Hanbury among the merchants, then added: "Our worthy Friend, Mr. Franklin, has gained immortal Honour by his Behaviour at the Bar of the House; the Answerer was always found Equal, if not Superior, to the Questioner. He stood unappalled, gave Pleasure to his Friends, and did Honour to his Country." Galloway and other Philadelphia supporters were undoubtedly responsible for printing some of these extracts.

9. Strahan sent a copy of the Examination to Hall in May; after reading it aloud to friends during the summer, Hall printed it as a pamphlet on Sept. 18, 1766; above, pp. 125–6.

1. The merchants' letter was probably one reprinted in *Pa. Gaz.* and *Pa. Jour.*, May 1, 1766, dated London, Feb. 28, 1766. What the "Advertisement" to which WF referred may have been is not clear; but he may possibly have known of a long letter by "A Son of Liberty" that appeared in the Supplement to *Pa. Jour.*, April 10, rehearsing in strong terms the history of the Stamp Act and the colonial opposition it produced. The writer called the present ministry "wise and prudent," but warned that "if an ill-chosen determination of forcing an observance of a parliamentary taxation should be the result of their deliberations, we shall then have to consider what will be a suitable conduct on our part."

2. WF was successful in this effort. *Pa. Gaz.*, June 19, 26; 1 *N.J. Arch.*, IX, 555–63.

Speech the villainous Reports of the Proprietary Officers.[3] It is impossible for you at so great a Distance to be acquainted with every Circumstance necessary to form a right Judgment of the Expediency or Inexpediency of particular Transactions. I have all the Evidence the Nature of the Case will admit, that They had taken their Measures so effectually with the Presby[terians] and the Sons of Liberty in this Province, that had it not been for the Paper I publish'd in Answer to the Lodge-Paper, I should have had my House pull'd down about my Ears and all my Effects destroy'd. I did not think the Notice I took of this in my Speech to be concerning myself with the Affairs of Pensylvania, all I intended by it was to fix a Brand of Infamy on the Transactions of the Officers of that Government within this Province, and I should have done the same had the Officers of New York, or any other Colony, given the like Occasion. All my Friends in every Part of the Province have approv'd my Conduct, and I have ever since experienc'd the good Effects of it; having, by thus removing the Prejudices of the People, render'd abortive every successive Attempt of my Adversaries to hurt me. For my Part I always think it best to nip in the Bud every Report which may tend to hurt a Man's Character or Interest; and that no Man should deem such Reports *below* his Notice. Governor Hutcheson, for Instance, knew very well that his Enemies had by their Intrigues spirited up the Populace against him, and made them believe, among other Things, that he was a Promoter of the Stamp Act. But he thought it beneath him to take any Pains to undeceive the People, in Consequence of which the Reports gain'd Credit, his House and Effects were destroy'd, and his Life endangered. It is possible that the Province will be obliged to make him some Reparation but great Part of his Loss is irreparable. On the whole, I am of Opinion, that it is best at all Times, but more especially in Times of Ferment and Confusion, for a Man to *lower himself* a little, rather than let *others lower* him.[4]

3. On this affair and WF's published defense, see above, XII, 367–8 and accompanying notes.

4. This passage suggests a considerable temperamental difference between father and son and may help to explain why, when the Revolutionary crisis came, the son followed such a different course from that of the father. On BF's attitude when under attack, see for example his letters to Jane Mecom, March 1, 1766 (above, p. 188), and March 2, 1767, Univ. of Va. Lib.

Enclosed are two Applications for Favours from the Ministry, One from Col. Croghan, and the other from Mr. Geo. Reed of New Castle.[5] They are both our Friends, and, I doubt not, but if you can that you will serve them. Croghan is highly incens'd at the Treatment he has received from the Proprietary Officers in Pensylvania and has been a means of bringing Sir Wm. Johnson and Genl. Gage to think favourable of the Assembly Party, and to wish them Success. A few of us, from his Encouragement, have form'd a Company to purchase of the French settled at the Illinois, such Lands as they have a good Title to, and are inclined to dispose of.[6] But as I thought it would be of little Avail to buy Lands in that Country unless a Colony was established there, I have drawn up some Proposals for that Purpose, which are much approved of by Col. Croghan and the other Gentlemen concerned in Philadelphia and are sent by them to Sir Wm. for his Sentiments; which when we receive, the whole will be forwarded to you. It is proposed that the Company shall consist of 12 now in America, and if you like the Proposals, you will be at Liberty to add yourself, and such Gentlemen of Character and Fortune in England, as you may think will be most likely to promote the Undertaking. Mr. Galloway has met with a Pamphlet at Mr. Hall's, on the Subject, which I wish I had seen before I had drawn up the Proposals, as it might have afforded some Hints.[7] However, as I

5. To just what Croghan's application related is unknown; it may have concerned the proposed western land company, though it sounds more like some personal matter. For Read's desire to be appointed customs collector at Newcastle, see above, pp. 246–7.

6. On March 29, 1766, ten partners—WF, Sir William Johnson, George Croghan, John Baynton, three Whartons, George Morgan, John Hughes, and Joseph Galloway—entered into an agreement to form what was at first called the Illinois Company, to acquire 1,200,000 acres or more from the Crown in the Illinois country for the settlement of an English colony. The text of the agreement is printed in Alvord and Carter, eds., *The New Régime*, pp. 203–4. This event marks the formal beginning of the speculative venture in western lands, later developed into the Vandalia Company. Correspondence relating to these projects will occupy considerable space in later volumes of this edition.

7. This pamphlet must have been *The Expediency of securing our American Colonies by settling The Country adjoining the River Mississippi, and the Country upon the Ohio, Considered* (Edinburgh, 1763). It is reprinted, with the titlepage reproduced in facsimile, in Alvord and Carter, eds., *The Critical Period, 1763–1765*, pp. 134–61.

believe you have not seen it, it being printed, and I believe wrote, in Scotland, I send it enclosed. You will find your Name mentioned in it, page 52.[8] Pray did you receive the Carolina Pamphlet I sent you.[9]

I would not have you stop the Chronicles coming from the G.P.O. unless you can contrive some other cheaper Way for me to get them.[1] But the Gazette and Magazines I would have stopp'd immediately. In the last Pacquet they missd sending me No. 1429, of the Chronicle. I wish I had it, as the Want of it spoils my Set. Betsy desires me to return her most cordial Thanks for the Notice you have taken of her Nephew.[2] Enclosed is a Letter for him, which please to send, and let that for Miss Clarke be put in the Penny Post Office.[3] Upon an Invitation from my Mother we have been at Philadelphia and spent a Fortnight very agreeably. I intended to have copy'd this, but some Gentlemen from Philadelphia are just come in which prevents, and indeed hinders me, from adding several other Matters. Betsy joins in Duty with your dutiful Son   WM: FRANKLIN

8. The pamphlet cites "the ingenious Dr. Franklyn" among others who were familiar with the western regions and who gave assurance that goods could be conveyed to and from inland America in boats and canoes "by great navigable rivers and fresh-water lakes communicating with one another," requiring only small portages here and there. The reference is to the Canada Pamphlet, above, IX, 81.

9. Apparently mentioned in some previous letter now lost, this pamphlet has not been identified.

1. Under dates of Feb. 12 and July 12, 1766, and from time to time thereafter BF's Journal, 1764–1776, pp. 7, 8, etc., and Ledger, 1764–1776, pp. 7, 9, record payments to Samuel Potts for "Chronicles" or "newspapers" charged to WF's account.

2. So little is known of the family of Elizabeth Downes Franklin that this nephew has not been identified, and he is not mentioned by name in any located correspondence.

3. Miss Mary Clarke appears to have been a London woman who bought shoes and other articles for WF's wife. She is mentioned in several letters from WF to William Strahan, 1763–65, *PMHB*, XXXV (1911), 430, 437, 438; BF recorded in his Journal, 1764–1776, p. 13, a payment of £20 to Mary Clarke that he charged to his son's account.

From David Hall   Letterbook copy: American Philosophical Society

Dear Sir,   Philada. May 1. 1766.
    In mine of the Third of March,[4] Via Belfast, by Captain Henderson, I told you Mrs. Franklin had of me Fifty Pounds, for the Purchase of a Bill from Mrs. Stevens. On the 18th of February One Hundred Pounds, towards paying for the Purchase of the Lot; and that on the Tenth of March I was to give her One Hundred Pounds more, for the last mentioned Use, which she has received. Also Twenty Pounds since, which she wanted for some other Use. And I have told her often, that what she wants at any time, she shall be most readily supplied with by me; and she has as often told me, she will apply, when there is Occasion.
    My Landlord, Mr. Grace, is dead, and I am told Mrs. Grace has her Life in the House, to whom I have applied, to rent it of her, when the Time of your Lease is out, but have not yet received her Answer. I make no Doubt you wrote to Mr. Grace in my Favour, according to Promise, with respect to the Preference of renting the House, when your Time was expired.[5]
    The Double Demy Paper was returned to Unwin[6] by the Philadelphia Packet, Captain Powell; but as I understand that Gentleman is dead, no Doubt you or Mr. Strahan, have made some Enquiry about it. The large Moulds must also be returned by the first Ship, as we have no Use for any of their Size in this Country.
I am, Dear Sir, Yours, &c.   D.H.

To Benjamin Franklin Esq;
Sent by Captain Sparks to London.[7]

4. See above, p. 193.
5. See above, XII, 170 n, and below, p. 331.
6. Henry Unwin (d. 1765), a stationer of Paternoster Row. See *London Mag.*, XXXIV (1765), 679. See also William Strahan to Hall, May 10, 1766, *PMHB*, X (1886), 217–18.
7. Hall's letter to BF of March 3 was apparently sent by Sparks, who cleared that week, as Strahan on May 10 acknowledged receiving a letter from him of that date sent by Sparks. The present notation may mean, however, that Hall had returned the "large Moulds" by Sparks.

From James Pemberton[8]

Draft:[9] Historical Society of Pennsylvania

My Worthy Friend   Philad. 1. 5 mo. may 1766

It is not with a view to add to the number of thy Correspondents, and thereby encrease thy trouble of writing; but from a motive of regard that I Send this. Conscious of thy integrity abilities and firmness to Serve thy Country I rest fully Satisfied in respect to myself but Observing with Concern every occasion however frivolous is taken to keep alive the flame of prejudice which Envy has raised against thee I take the liberty to give thee a hint that the Committee of Correspondence not having for some time received particular information from thee of the State of public Affairs [*struck out:* of the province under thy Care] is made use of in aggravated terms of [objection?] by some without doors, and a blunderer within up[b]raiding thy Friends with it as a neglect of design. I therefore wish that altho nothing material may occurr in respect to our Provincial affairs thou wouldst satisfy the discontented by writing to that Committee as frequently as the packet or a direct Conveyance offer;[1]

I am well pleased to find the Speaker has a letter from thee per the packet, with the minutes of Parliament,[2] as thou knows he is not a Scribe pray to Excuse his neglect of acknowledging the receipt of the several he has heretofore received from thee.

The Intelligence brought per this packet gives universal Joy, as

8. James Pemberton (1723–1809), brother of Israel; merchant of Philadelphia, philanthropist, and politician. He was one of the Quaker members of the Assembly who withdrew in 1756 on the issue of military support; above, VI, 456–7 n. For his readmission as a member from the city in a runoff election in 1765, see above, XII, 292 n. He was a close friend of Dr. John Fothergill, mentioned in this letter. *DAB.*

9. The draft contains many interlineations and crossed out words; some passages are indecipherable.

1. BF's tendency to write on public affairs to Joseph Galloway, rather than to the speaker and the Committee of Correspondence (of which Galloway was merely one member), caused much criticism within the Assembly and led to the repetition of standing instructions to the agents a week after Pemberton wrote this letter; see below, pp. 267–8.

2. BF's letter to Fox of March 1, 1766; above, pp. 186–7. His earlier letter of February 27 had gone by the hand of a private individual and did not arrive until later.

there is a danger of it's being carried by many imprudent people to an immoderate degree.[3] On receiving account of the final determination of the very important affair, I hope no pains will be spared to press the necessity and good policy of keeping within due bounds; I have a very judicious Letter from our truly valuable Friend Dr. Fothergill on this subject worthy the strictest attention which I hope may be of great Service as far as I can give it an [*illegible*]. I am likewise much pleased that he has furnished me with such authentic intelligence, as must tend to confute the charge industriously propagated of thy being a promoter of the Stamp Act or Convince the unprejudiced it is base and groundless, and that thy Endeavors in obta[in]ing a repeal of it have been indefaticable and upright.[4]

The Assembly meets the 5. Inst. when I hope the most Cool, and deliberate Consideration will take place of the part. It will be the duty of this Province to act in decent and thankfull acknowledgement to the Parliament &ca. for their Lenity in favour of the Colonies.[5]

Thou has doubtless received Information of the proceedings of the last Sitting that I need not now repeat it. A comendable harmony prevailed except now and then some [*illegible*] I shoud like to have [*illegible*] exceptions and the business transacted with

3. *Pa. Gaz.*, May 1, 1766, carried reports brought to New York by the packet that the betting in London was 275 to 167 in favor of the repeal of the Stamp Act and that the odds would soon increase. The same issue printed the resolves of the House of Commons, Feb. 24, 1766. Extracts from private letters urged restraint in the colonists' response.

4. A copy of a letter from Fothergill to Pemberton, Feb. 27, 1766, in Hist. Soc. Pa., declares categorically that BF had "uniformly opposed" the Stamp Act "to the utmost of his Abilities; that in a long Examination before the house of Commons within these few Weeks, he asserted the Rights and Privileges of America, with the utmost Firmness, Resolution and Capacity." Another passage from this letter is printed above, p. 254 n. Both appeared in *Pa. Gaz.*, May 8, 1766.

5. Although the Assembly met for a few days in early May, it took no action concerning the Stamp Act, but waited until its June sitting, after the governor had transmitted a letter from Secretary of State Conway of March 31 reporting officially the passage of the Declaratory Act and the repeal of the Stamp Act. On June 6 the Assembly approved, and the speaker signed, a grateful and thoroughly dutiful address to the King. 8 *Pa. Arch.*, VII, 5859–76, 5877–79, 5881, 5884–85.

good dispatch. Pray do not omit every favorable opportunity of warmly soliciting our Address in favour of paper Currency,⁶ the province is so much involved in debt the pub[lic] Credit must suffer unless we are releeved in this respect, and I hope Every Endeavor will be used to obtain a Confirmation of the Laws passed last Sitting particularly that for the better Employment of the poor &ca.⁷

Please to Excuse this freedom, and believe me to be very Sincerely thy respectfull Friend   J P

If thou hast opportunity please to present my kind respects to D. Fothergil. I cannot answer his very acceptable letter per this packet. Shall write him in a few days &c.

Endorsed: 5 mo. 1. 1766 Letter to Benj Franklin Esqr

From James Parker

ALS: American Philosophical Society

Honoured Sir   New York, May 6. 1766.

Agreeable to your Requisition and Opinion, in yours to me of the 11th of May, and 8th of June last, I am now come up to this City: and been accepted to the Exercise of the Place of Land-Waiter here the 3d of this Month:⁸ and an Account with the Bond executed, and a Certificate of the Matter would be sent with this

6. See above, pp. 51–2, 236, 238.

7. This act, approved by the governor on Feb. 8, 1766, was pushed through the Assembly largely by the efforts of Quakers and other compassionate citizens of Philadelphia. Pemberton was a member of the committee that drafted the bill. It substituted for the old and inadequate Alms House a new building called the Bettering House, partly supported by charitable donations, in which the indigent residents able to work were employed in light labor. The Privy Council considered the measure and allowed it to stand. In an account of the Bettering House Carl and Jessica Bridenbaugh have commented that "Nowhere in the then world, perhaps, did the indigent receive more efficient and generous treatment." *Rebels and Gentlemen Philadelphia in the Age of Franklin* (N.Y., [1942]), pp. 232–5. The text of the act is in *Statutes at Large, Pa.,* VII, 9–17.

8. Neither letter found. BF had procured for Parker the office of land waiter in the New York Customs House to compensate him for the necessity of moving to that city for the conduct of his duties as comptroller of the North American Post Office. Parker's previous letters had been filled with lamentations over having to make this move.

Packet, but the Surveyor-General, Mr. Stewart, who is at philadelphia, having wrote the Collector here Word, that he would be
here in a Day or two, the sending him the Bond and Certificate
was delayed, and he being the Officer directed to send them home,
they will probably not be sent till next Packet. I had been let to
know, a considerable Deal of Trouble and Fatigue was expected
to be the Share of this Office, and I am fully satisfied it is so: but
I am resolved to do my Endeavours to the best of my Ability to
give Satisfaction, more from a Principle of honouring my Recommender, than from any great Benefit or Advantage by the Office.
I thank God, I am pretty well in Health now, and while that continues, I hope all will go well, but as that is precarious, I know
not what will be the Case, if that fails me again.

With respect to the resuming the Printing Business here I have
a Press here, and some Letter, and shall do any Work that offers,
that my Hands are capable of:[9] but from the most deliberate Consideration, and consulting my own Mind, I think it not quite
expedient to print a News-Paper myself yet a While: and for
these Considerations: In the present unhappy Times, when the
Sons of Liberty carry all before them, Mr. Holt has gained very
great Popularity, and being back'd by them, seems to have a Run
of Business:[1] his Brother Royle being dead, who had purchased
the Printing-Office that was Mr. Stretch's, and which was never
Used, Mr. Royle's Right in it was disposed of, and Mr. Holt's
own Brother in Virginia, aided by the Sons of Liberty has purchased it for him.[2] With those Tooles, if I take mine from him, he
disigns to set out another Paper. Now, as he will be supported by

9. Most of the rest of this letter is taken up with discussions of Parker's
plans for resuming the printing business in New York, his long-standing
difficulties with his former associate John Holt, and other troubles involving
Hugh Hughes and BF's nephew, Benjamin Mecom. Readers with sufficient
interest and patience will find these matters (already dealt with in many
previous letters) explained in so much detail in Parker's very long letter of
June 11 (below, pp. 300–12) that extended annotation here seems unnecessary.

1. On Holt's popularity with the New York Sons of Liberty, see Arthur
M. Schlesinger, *Prelude to Independence The Newspaper War on Britain 1764–
1776* (N.Y., 1958), pp. 72, 77, 83; Beverly McAnear, "James Parker versus
John Holt," N.J. Hist. Soc. *Procs.,* LIX (1941), 89.

2. On the printing situation in Virginia, see above, pp. 108, 203.

the Sons of Liberty here, who are all-prevalent, and who look with bad Aspect upon every King's Officer, and in particular on those of the Customs and Post-Office, I apprehend I should scarce be able to Stem the Torrent, and while he and I, like two Dogs, were fighting for a Bone, the Third would run away with it: Therefore, as he is desirous to keep on good Terms with me, if I will let him carry on the Paper alone in his present good Prospect, so I apprehend, as he owes me a great Sum, that it must be the only Way for me to get my Money; for tho' I might be able to distance him in Time, which in the present Circumstances of Thi[ngs is] very doubtful, yet it would probably be at my own Ruin: These Considerations see[m to] weigh with me, but whether you will or can conceive them in the same Light, is w[hat I] am not so clear in: However, I submit it.[3] I have been a Father to him for he [could] neither have carried on his Business or held it at any Rate but for my Help. [The] Office of Stretch's, by the Invoice I have seen, is very compleat, full and good, and the Price Royle gave was but £209 Sterl. and I doubt whether Holt's Brother gave that: and in that is included two Presses and a Quantity of Ink: whilst mine that Holt has is almost entirely wore out, at least all the Common Used Small Letter: which would make the Match the more unequal against me, if I engaged. Should I arrest Holt for what he owes me, it might look like Spite too much, and he might take the Benefit of the present Act of Insolvency here, and be afterwards set up and supported by the Sons of Liberty, as they are called. It is possible nay probable that Times may alter, and if I shall ever be able to procure two or three Fonts of new Letter of the common small Sort, I might then be able to encounter with better Hopes and better Strength: Also, I

3. On May 29, 1766, upon hearing that Parker intended to publish a newspaper in New York, John Holt changed the title of his paper from *The New-York Gazette; or, the Weekly Post-Boy* to *The New-York Journal, or General Advertiser;* but when he found that Parker did not intend to publish a paper at this time, Holt reverted to the former title with the issue of June 5. On Oct. 16, 1766, however, Holt relinquished the *Gazette* to Parker, its former publisher, and brought out a new paper with the title he had used for one issue in the spring. Clarence S. Brigham, *History and Bibliography of American Newspapers 1690–1820* (Worcester, 1947), I, 635–6, 654–5. In spite of what he writes here, Parker changed his mind in October and resumed his old paper under its old name.

think Weyman[4] is still declining, and if we quarrel, he will recover Strength, which I am not very desirous of contributing to, tho' I shall never attempt to hurt him on Principle, yet I had rather avoid benefiting him. I am preparing to fit up my Shop, and to put the best Foot foremost that I can. I just opened your Box of Goods, and find they are not damaged. I have offered them to two or three at the most moderate Terms from the Invoice, but tis said some of the Articles come too high charged, and none would purchase for Cash: Holt would have taken them on Trust, but I could not betray mine in that, so I think I must take them myself, and make the best of them I can, and am willing to allow you Interest from the Day I take them, which is this present: if I could do better for your Satisfaction and Interest, I would. I have not the Electrick Machine yet for Want of the [Bill of Lading] and Mr. Hughes keeps close himself, tho' he is one of the Sons of Liberty. He desired [*torn*] your kind Offer of the Loss of it.

The New-Haven Affair with Mr. Holt is not yet determined: for tho' the Sons of Liberty have been so powerful, yet in Fact, little or no Business has been done in any place in the Law Way. The Courts indeed begin to open now: Benny Mecom pays one of the Hartford Riders which I suppose to be nearly what his Office produces, otherways my Hopes of him wax fainter and fainter.[5] I have repeatedly wrote and pressed him, but he renders [abortive] all I can do: He has never paid me one Farthing Rent yet, tho' he promises me some this Month, and promises all his Post-Office Accounts also, so that I hope by the next Packet, to give you a more favourable Account of him: God grant it may be so!

I have not heard from Mr. Foxcroft for two or three Weeks past, he has been above a Month expected from Virginia, whence he went in the Winter. I don't know any Thing very material on the Head of the Post Office, but this: That the Sons of Liberty

4. William Weyman had been Parker's partner in New York from 1753 to 1759, when he separated and began to publish *Weyman's New-York Gazette*, a title from which he soon dropped his own name. Presumably because of the impending Stamp Act and financial difficulties, issues of this paper appeared only sporadically between June 10, 1765, and the following November 25, when Weyman resumed regular publication. *Ibid.*, p. 638.

5. On problems arising from the postal service to Middletown and Hartford, Conn., see above, pp. 16–18. Benjamin Mecom was now in charge of the New Haven post office in succession to Holt.

finding themselves the Ruling Party, begin to take upon themselves the governing part also: Mr. Colden tells me they make the Captains of Vessels deliver their Letters at the Coffee-House after their old accustomed Manner, tho' against the Captain's Wills, except now and then one who happens to get in unperceived or in the Night, and he durst not say any Thing against it, nor does the Collector refuse to enter them:[6] It is surprizing to see the Influence they have, and the Dread every one is Under of Opening their Mouths against them.

Tho' we have had a very mild Winter, we have had the coldest and most backward Spring I think that ever I knew. There has not been but one warm Day properly speaking since the Month of February, and it is so cold now, that I am obliged to keep by the Fire: The Fruit I believe will be much affected by it. Trade and Business seems very dull in this City in Comparison to what it us'd to be, and yet Provisions as well as every Thing else, are excessive dear and indeed scarce.

I received yours of Feb. 26.[7] by this Packet, and observe the Contents thereof, but as there is nothing more material to say in Answer to it, than what is already wrote, I have only to add respectful Complements and remain Your obliged Humble Servant
JAMES PARKER.

Holt has never settled any Accounts with me, I shall try now to get 'em done amicably while I [let?] him to continue the Paper, perhaps I may get it better than if we differ first.

To Dr B Franklin.

Endorsed: J Parker May June and July 1756[8]

6. On the new regulations for the delivery of letters brought to colonial ports by merchant ships, see above, XI, 342–3. Apparently the Sons of Liberty, or at least those in New York, were forcing the ships' captains to violate the act of 1765, perhaps in order to keep a check on incoming mail from England. Alexander Colden was the postmaster of New York.

7. Not found.

8. Probably an endorsement covering a group of Parker's letters bundled together.

Pennsylvania Assembly Committee of Correspondence to Richard Jackson and Benjamin Franklin

Copy: Library of Congress

When the Assembly reconvened in May after a recess of about three months, "A Member of the Committee of Correspondence," undoubtedly Joseph Galloway, presented letters from Franklin "addressed to that Member only, and not to the said Committee, though relative to the Business of the Public." When the letters had been read the House resolved that the Committee "do acquaint the Agents for this Province, that the House enjoin and direct that their Letters, respecting the Business committed to their Care by the Assembly, whether jointly or separately wrote, be addressed to the Speaker and Committee of Correspondence," in order that these letters might come "with proper Authority" before the House. The Committee was directed to send a copy of this resolve to the agents.[9]

Gentlemen   Philadelphia May 8th. 1766

We transmit you herewith all the Laws. passed by the Present Assembly at their late Sessions in January.[1] The Proprietaries no doubt will in Convenient time lay them before his Majesty in Council agreeable to the Directions of Royal Charter. In that Case the House Request, should Any Objections be made Against them, That you will Exert your Utmost Interest and Abilities to remove such Objections, and Obtain their final Conformation. The Law entitled, "An Act for the better Employment Relief and Support of the Poor &c," is of the Utmost Importance to the City of Philadelphia and the Neighbouring Townships thereby United with it, And will we have not the least Doubt for this reason Obtain your Particular attention and Industry to save it from a repeal.[2]

The not receiving any Letter from you Directed to the Committee of Correspondence, Agreeable to the late order of the

9. MS extract from the Journals, May 7, 1766, attested by Charles Moore, clerk, APS; also printed in *Votes*, 1765–66, p. 49.

1. The texts of the ten acts to which the governor gave his assent on Feb. 8, 1766, are printed in *Statutes at Large, Pa.*, VII, 5–44. All were considered by the Privy Council, Feb. 11, 1767, and allowed to stand by expiration of the time limit prescribed by the charter.

2. On this act see above, p. 262 n.

House Communicated to you by Us, has given the House some Uneasiness which has induced it to make a new order which we Inclose You here with, In Pursuance whereof, in future you are Desired to Direct your Letters Respecting the Publick matters Committed to Your Care, To the Speaker and Committee of Correspondence for the reason in the order mentioned. We are with Esteem, your Assured Friends, and Humble Servants

Jos: Fox	Thos. Livezey
Jos. Galloway	Isa: Pearson
Jos. Richardson	Giles Knight

Copy. Origl. per Capt.Boggs Via. Dublin

To Richard Jackson. and Benjamin Franklin Esqrs.

Endorsed: Commee. of Correspe. May 8. 1766

To Cadwalader Evans

MS not found; reprinted from Samuel Hazard, ed., *Hazard's Register of Pennsylvania* XVI, No. 5 (August 1, 1835), 65.

Dear Sir: London, May 9, 1766.
    I received your kind letter of March 3,[3] and thank you for the Intelligence and Hints it contained. I wonder at the Complaint you mentioned. I always considered writing to the Speaker as writing to the Committee. But if it is more to their Satisfaction that I should write to them jointly, it shall be done for the future.[4]
    My private Opinion concerning a union in Parliament between the two Countries, is, that it would be best for the Whole. But I think it will never be done. For tho' I believe that if we had no more Representatives than Scotland has, we should be sufficiently strong in the House to prevent, as they do for Scotland, any thing ever passing to our disadvantage; yet we are not able at present

3. Not found.
4. On March 2, 1766, Thomas Wharton informed BF of proprietary party criticism that he was violating his instructions by writing directly to individual members of the Assembly's committee of correspondence (Joseph Galloway was meant) rather than to the full committee; see above, p. 191 n. See the document immediately above for a formal order to the agents to direct their letters henceforth to the committee and speaker of the House jointly.

to furnish and maintain such a Number, and when we are more able we shall be less willing than we are now. The Parliament here do at present think too highly of themselves to admit Representatives from us if we should ask it; and when they will be desirous of granting it, we shall think too highly of ourselves to accept of it.[5] It would certainly contribute to the strength of the whole, if Ireland and all the Dominions were united and consolidated under one Common Council for general Purposes, each retaining its particular Council or Parliament for its domestic Concerns. But this should have been more early provided for. In the Infancy of our foreign Establishments, it was neglected, or was not thought of. And now, the Affair is nearly in the Situation of Friar Bacon's Project of making a brazen Wall round England for its eternal Security. His Servant Friar Bungey slept while the brazen Head, which was to dictate how it might be done, said *Time is,* and *Time was.* He only wak'd to hear it say, *Time is past.* An explosion followed that tumbled their House about the Conjuror's Ears.[6]

I hope with you, that my being here at this Juncture has been of some Service to the Colonies. I am sure I have spared no Pains. And as to our particular Affair,[7] I am not in the least doubtful of obtaining what we so justly desire if we continue to desire it: tho' the late confus'd State of Affairs on both sides the Water, have delay'd our Proceeding. With great esteem, I am, Dear Friend, Yours affectionately,   B. FRANKLIN.

5. BF had sketched this argument in his plan of a pamphlet on the Stamp Act; see above, p. 84.

6. The usual version of this ancient tale has the philosopher Roger Bacon (1214–1294?) and a fellow Franciscan, Thomas Bungay, who like Bacon was reputed to be a magician, constructing a brazen head for the purpose of revealing the secret of defending England. A negligent servant is supposed to have permitted the two friars to nap while the contrivance revealed its strategy. A.G. Little, ed., *Roger Bacon Essays* (Oxford, 1914), pp. 359–72.

7. The securing royal government for the province of Pennsylvania.

To Francis Hopkinson   ALS: Historical Society of Pennsylvania

Dear Friend   London, May 9. 1766

I have been so busy that I have not had time to go to the Cus-
tomhouse about your Salary, since mine of Feby. 26.[8] (but will
now do it soon) nor to write to you since I saw the Bishop,[9] which
was some time after he receiv'd your Letters. He express'd a
Pleasure in hearing of and from his Relations, enquir'd in what
manner he could send Letters to you, and said he hop'd you would
not think his Slowness in corresponding was from any want of
Regard; this he desir'd me to mention when I should write to you.
I told him, that if he sent his Letters to me, I would forward them
to you with Pleasure, and I took the Opportunity of saying every
thing of you that Friendship and Truth dictated. He ask'd concerning your Views in Life, mention'd your Inclination to come
over to England, and said he should be glad to show you a proper
Regard here, if it suited you to come.[1] I told his Lordship, that
his Countenance to you and introducing you to the Knowledge
of Persons of Worth, as well as your having such an Opportunity
of seeing the World a little, might be of great Use to you. He
invited me very politely to come and see him in Worcestershire.
The other Day his Lordship call'd when I was not at home, and
left a Packet for your good Mother, which I send by this Opportunity. I suppose from the Contents, she and you can judge better
how proper it may be for you to make a Visit here, than from anything I can say; so I do not take upon me to advise.

I deliver'd your Present to Mr. Burrow,[2] who returns his Thanks;

8. Not found. Hopkinson had been appointed collector of customs at
Salem, N.J., in November 1763; apparently in a letter to BF which has not
been found he had asked help in getting the salary either increased or paid
more promptly. *Pa. Gaz.*, Nov. 17, 1763.

9. James Johnson, Bishop of Worcester, whose kinship to Hopkinson BF
had helped to establish in 1765.

1. Before this letter could have reached Philadelphia, Hopkinson had sailed
for England on May 22, 1766, hoping to obtain some position through the
bishop's influence. Finding his prospects dim, he returned home in the summer of 1767. George E. Hastings, *The Life and Works of Francis Hopkinson*
(Chicago, 1926), pp. 123–49.

2. James Burrow, master of the Crown Office at the Court of King's Bench,
who had supervised the research which had established Hopkinson's kinship
to Bishop Johnson; above, XII, 124 n, 401.

but the Apples were rotten, all to 4. I paid Freight and Porteridge, which I shall receive with the other Charges I have been at, when I see Mr. Barclay.[3]

I am oblig'd to you for the Concern you express at the Abuses I receive from unreasonable People. They are a sort of Things that are *more blessed to receive than to give*. I must, with much better Men, take my share of them, if they were harder to bear than they are.

I will see about Hogarth's Works, and get them for the Library if they have not been sent.[4] I am, my dear Friend, Yours affectionately   B FRANKLIN

F. Hopkinson Esqr.

Addressed: To / Francis Hopkinson Esqr / Philadelphia / via N. York / per Packet / B. Free FRANKLIN[5]

Endorsed: 12a Dr. Frankl[in] 1766

To Mary Hopkinson

ALS: Dr. Myron Prinzmetal, Beverly Hills, California (1956); copy: Historical Society of Pennsylvania

My dear Madam,   London, May 9. 1766
    I received your Favour of Oct. 1.[6] with the Order on Mr. Barclay,

3. On Oct. 1, 1765, Hopkinson's mother had sent BF an order on the Barclay merchant house to pay his expenses in pursuing the genealogical researches for her family; above, XII, 289.

4. On May 14, 1764, the directors of the Library Company had voted that their secretary, Francis Hopkinson, should ask David Hall to send to England for a complete set of William Hogarth's works. Apparently Hall had failed to get the material before the artist's death, Oct. 25, 1766, and Hopkinson had later asked BF to attend to the matter with Hogarth's widow. While Hopkinson was in England the two men carried out the transaction; Hopkinson delivered the prints upon his return to Philadelphia late in 1767; and BF paid Jane Hogarth £14 11s. on Feb. 5, 1768, charging this amount to the Lib. Co. account. Lib. Co. Minutes, May 14, 1764, Dec. 14, 1767; BF's Journal, 1764–1776, p. 15; Ledger, 1764–1776, pp. 19, 29.

5. This franking, and that on the letter of the same date to Mrs. Hopkinson immediately below, are the earliest instances the editors have found of the punning form of BF's official frank used as a substitute for the normal "Free B FRANKLIN." This punning form appears from time to time, though not regularly, on surviving address pages of letters written during the controversial years ahead.

6. See above, XII, 288–9.

of which I have not yet made any Use, but shall when I next see him; Tho' it was not necessary for you to take Notice of those small Expences till my Return. Your Acknowledgements are far beyond the Occasion, and bring me in your debt. I had a Pleasure in the Success of my Endeavours, that sufficiently repaid me for the little Trouble they gave me. Pray present my Respects to your new Son-in-law Dr. Morgan, whose Letter[7] I have receiv'd but cannot now write to him. I thank him for his Book which is well spoken of here. I congratulate him and you on his Marriage, and wish for you and your whole Family all Sorts of Prosperity. Being with sincerest Esteem and Respect, Dear Madam, Your affectionate Friend, and most obedient humble Servant   B FRANKLIN

Mrs. Hopkinson

Addressed: To / Mrs Hopkinson / at / Philadelphia / via New York / per Packet / B Free FRANKLIN

Endorsed: Letter from Doctr Franklin 1766

From Thomas Wharton   ALS: American Philosophical Society

My Dear Friend.   Philada. May 9. 1766
    I had the pleasure of writing thee a few Lines per Packet.[8] Since which our Assembly met and have this day adjourned to meet the 2d of June next. It is with great pleasure that, I acquaint thee, that the reason for this short Adjournment is, that they may take the earliest Opportunity of returning to the King, Lords and Commons their unfeigned Thanks for the Repeal of the Stamp-Act. The Account of which (its not doubted) will reach this by that time. I understand the New York Assembly stands prorogued to the 20th. Instant for the same good end; and I have not a doubt but the New-Jersey House will chearfully prosecute the same Steps.
    We have taken the lead to publish in our Papers, several Pieces tending to excite a prudent behaviour in the Inhabitants of the Continent on their receiving the Account of the Repeal, and I

7. That of Oct. 10, 1765; see above, XII, 307–8.
8. Not found; Wharton's letter of April 26 was sent by a ship bound for Liverpool, not by the packet.

doubt not but that our People will conduct themselves well on the occasion.[9]

And rest assured my Friend, that the publication of sundry Paragraphs of Letters from London, respecting thy Conduct, and the emminent Services thou has done the Continent in general and this Province in particular has so effectually silenced the calumniating Principles of the Party that, they know not what to say.[1]

I find Doctr. Fothergill's Letter to W.A. has had a good effect;[2] as I am assured he has taken some pains to instruct their People, that it would be prudent not to be over zealous on the occasion.

Our worthy Friend G. Ashbridge[3] has spared no pains to acquaint the Country Members of every thing which could tend to rivet their Affections for thee; And through the concuring Circumstances which we were enabled to acquaint them with the storm which was threatned by the Party vanished. Even the Giant[4] himself could scarce find anything to vent his sentiments on; but was obliged to introduce it by asking if the Committee had Letters, and what they contained—to which he was so fully answered that he did not attempt to reassume the subject.[5]

9. Several such letters were printed, in full or in extract, in *Pa. Gaz.*, and *Pa. Jour.*, May 1 and 8, 1766. The text of the repealing act reached Philadelphia on the *Minerva*, Capt. Thomas Wise, on the morning of May 19. Both *Pa. Gaz.* and *Pa. Jour.*, issued supplements containing the text of the act the same day, and in their issues of May 22 described the local celebration. Both papers stressed the propriety and restraint of the demonstrations, the *Journal* commenting that "notwithstanding the great and glorious cause of our present rejoicings, not one single instance of that kind of triumph so much dreaded by our friends and wished for by our enemies in England, has escaped the warmest son of liberty in this city."

1. In its issues of May 1 and 8, 1766, *Pa. Gaz.*, printed extracts from six letters particularly praising BF's services; the same issues of *Pa. Jour.*, printed three of these extracts.

2. Though not specifically identified in print as to writer or recipient, the letter from Fothergill to William Allen may have been one of those mentioned in the second note above.

3. George Ashbridge of Goshen, Chester Co., was a member of the Assembly, 1743–73.

4. William Allen.

5. On the criticism of BF for failing to write directly to the speaker and Committee of Correspondence, see above, pp. 260–2, 276–7.

I find J.F. is much pleased with receiving a Letter from thee,[6] and altho' it would be right for him to make returns therefor, yet, I hope my Friend will not discontinue his Correspondence with that Gentleman.

G. Croghan set off on the 4th Inst. for Pittsburgh and the Illinois in order to complete the great and salutary Work of fixing those numerous Tribes of Southern Indians in the English Interest.[7]

On the 5th Inst. came on the election of Managers for our Hospital, when the same sett were elected, except A. Strettell and D. Roberdeau in the stead of H. Harrison deceased and T. Gordon removed into the Country.[8] We have admitted this last Year 454 Patients and our Expences have amounted to upwards of £1600. A Sum far superior to our Income! Yet from the charitable Disposition of our Inhabitants and some with you—especially the benevolent Doctr. Fothergill—our Fund is not lessened;[9] but if we could receive the Interest arising on the Money which in the Year 1770 We are to receive from the London Land Company. it would be of particular Service.[1]

6. Probably BF's letter of March 1 to Speaker Fox, sent by the packet, not that of February 24, sent by a private individual.

7. George Croghan's trip to conciliate the Indians had been approved by Sir William Johnson and General Gage. It was part of Johnson and Croghan's plan that he should lay the groundwork for a settlement in which they and other land speculators were interested.

8. Amos Strettell, an assemblyman, was a political opponent of BF. Daniel Roberdeau, a former assemblyman politically allied to BF, had served as a Hospital manager, 1756–58. Henry Harrison, former mayor of the city, died Jan. 3, 1766, *Pa. Gaz.*, Jan. 9, 1766. Thomas Gordon (above, VII, 392 n) advertised in *Pa. Jour.*, June 26, 1766, that a quantity of his household furniture was to be sold and that his house in Lodge Alley was available for lease.

9. The Hospital annual report was printed in *Pa. Gaz.*, July 10, 1766. It showed £1591 9s. current operating expenses. New contributions of £709 12s. 4d., included a gift of £250 from Dr. Fothergill, and legacies received totaled £380 8s. 4d. Other sources of what may be called current income appear to have produced a total of £1190 16s. 7½d.

1. Certain lands granted by William Penn in 1699 had passed into the hands of individuals who formed a company called the Proprietors of the Pennsylvania Land Company in London, and in 1720 the rights were divided into 8,800 shares. By 1760 most of the land had been sold but claimants to some of the shares could not be found. In 1760 Parliament passed an act establishing a group of trustees, headed by Dr. Fothergill, who were to hold the unclaimed shares and place the money due them in the Bank of England,

Thy family are all well. I remain with sincere respect thy real friend   THO WHARTON

P S I am pleasd to hear that my Friend Cowley has Acted so much in our favour. I have receivd a Letter from Him, wherein He mentions thee with great respect, I intend shortly to write Him.[2]

Addressed: For / Benjamin Franklin / Esqr. / Deputy Postmaster General / of No. America / In Craven street / London / per / Via Ireland

To Baynton, Wharton & Morgan

> Extract: reprinted from Clarence W. Alvord and Clarence E. Carter, eds., *The New Régime 1765–1766,* in *Collections* of the Illinois Historical Library, XI (Springfield, Ill., 1916), 338.[3]

This is the first of three brief extracts from letters by Franklin, the originals of which cannot be found, expressing approval of the proposed western settlement.[4] All three have been tentatively dated May 10, 1766. The present extract and that to Galloway are contained in a letter from Baynton, Wharton & Morgan to Sir William Johnson, July 12, 1766, where they are said to have arrived "by the May Packet," and the merchant firm wrote Franklin on August 28 acknowledging his letter of May 10. The extract to William Franklin was first printed by

---

distribute the amounts due to individuals whose claims could be proved, and retain the rest until June 24, 1770, at which time the remaining funds were to be paid over to the Pennsylvania Hospital. A decision of the lord chancellor was recorded in the minutes of the Hospital Managers, May 26, 1766, authorizing the investment of the funds—by then amounting to nearly £6500 sterling—in 3 percent bank annuities. Thomas G. Morton and Frank Woodbury, *The History of the Pennsylvania Hospital 1751–1895* (Phila., 1895), pp. 250–4.

2. On Thomas Crowley, eccentric London Quaker, see above, p. 121 n. In *PMHB,* XVII (1893), 212, is printed a letter from Crowley, Feb. 24, 1766, to an unidentified correspondent, in which he warmly praises BF's services in promoting repeal of the Stamp Act. This may well be the letter to which Wharton has reference.

3. A footnote on p. 338 of *The New Régime* states that Mr. Carter had copied the letter in which this extract appears from the MS in the New York State Library at Albany before it was destroyed in the disastrous fire of 1911.

4. For WF's report to BF on the formation of a company to get a grant for such a settlement, see above, pp. 257–8.

Jared Sparks, who gave it the specific date of May 10.[5] William's letter
to his father of about July 13 mentions receiving "your Letter per the
Packet of May 10."[6] Probably all three letters were written on the same
day. The member of the firm who wrote the letter to Johnson added,
after the quotations, that "Upon the first thoughts of the Scheme, Mr.
Galloway and I wrote to Dr. Franklin, so that he might essay it, with
the Ministry."

[May 10, 1766]
I join fully in opinion with you, that a western Colony, would
be highly advantageous and *very easily settled.*

To William Franklin

Extract:[7] reprinted from [Jared Sparks, ed.,] *A Collection of the Familiar
Letters and Miscellaneous Papers of Benjamin Franklin* (Boston, 1833),
p. 275.

May 10th, 1766.
I like the project of a colony in the Ilinois country, and will
forward it to my utmost here.

To Joseph Galloway

Extract: reprinted from Clarence W. Alvord and Clarence E. Carter, eds.,
The New Régime 1765–1766, in *Collections* of the Illinois Historical
Library, XI (Springfield, Ill., 1916), 338.[8]

[May 10, 1766]
I think that a strong Colony in the Illinois Country, is a most
desirable measure. The Proposal is much listened to here.

5. *A Collection of the Familiar Letters and Miscellaneous Papers of Benjamin
Franklin* (Boston, 1833), p. 275, where it is the first of a series of extracts
under the heading "Walpole's Grant."

6. Below, p. 333. WF probably meant "your Letter of May 10 by the
Packet." Packets were usually referred to by the month, not by the day
of sailing, which was often unknown to the recipient.

7. The original letter has not been found. On the relationship between this
extract and those immediately above and below, see the headnote to the one
above. BF could not have received by May 10 WF's letter of April 30 reporting
the actual formation of a company of land speculators for western settlement.
His knowledge of the detailed scheme was certainly derived from earlier
letters not now to be found.

8. On the source and dating of this extract see the headnote and footnotes
to the document next but one above.

To Deborah Franklin

ALS: American Philosophical Society

My dear Child   London, May 18. 1766.

I wrote to you pretty fully per the Packet,⁹ and shall write again by some of our Ships: But Capt. Cruikshanks¹ kindly offering to carry a Letter to you, I write just to let you know I am well, as I hope you any [and] my dear Sally and all our Relations and Friends continue to be. Mrs. Stevenson is getting something to send you,² and presents her Compliments. Capt. Robinson is arriv'd.³ I am, Your affectionate Husband   B FRANKLIN

Addressed: To Mrs / Fran[klin] / [Philadelphia] / per favour of / Capt. Cruikshanks

From Charles Thomson

MS not found; reprinted from *Collections* of the New-York Historical Society for the Year 1878 (New York, 1879), pp. 15–16; extracts: printed in *The London Chronicle*, Sept. 6–9, 1766.⁴

MY WORTHY AND MUCH ESTEEMED FRIEND,   May 20, 1766.

I sincerely and heartily congratulate you on the repeal of the Stamp act, and from my heart thank you for the pains you have

9. Not found; probably dated about May 9 or 10.

1. Possibly Charles Cruikshank, a Scottish gentleman who had served in the British Army and had settled in Pennsylvania, buying the estate called "Clifton Hall" (later "The Grange") in what is now Delaware Co. He returned to Scotland in 1783. *PMHB*, VI (1882), 109; XXIII (1899), 77, 80.

2. Her bill of lading for "One Case," July 10, 1766, is in APS.

3. The ship *Prince George*, commanded by BF's friend James Robinson, had cleared Philadelphia for Lisbon near the end of February. *Pa. Gaz.*, Feb. 27, 1766. Presumably it had gone from Lisbon to England, but mention of its arrival there has not been found in *London Chron.*

4. *London Chron.* omitted from "and from my heart" in the first sentence to the end of the first paragraph, also the closing words of the letter from "I am," and the signature; that is, it left out everything that could be considered personal. The newspaper headed the document: "Extract of a Letter from a Gentleman in Philadelphia, to his Friend in London, dated May 20, 1766." BF wrote Thomson, Sept. 27, 1766, that "That Part of your Letter which related to the Situation of People's Minds in America before and after the Repeal was so well exprest, and in my Opinion so proper to be generally read and understood here, that I had it printed in the London Chronicle. I had the Pleasure to find that it did Good in several Instances within my Knowledge."

taken to bring that happy event. Your Enemies at last began to be ashamed of their base insinuations and to acknowledge that the Colonies are under obligations to you. I was exceeding glad at the Publication of your Letter to Governor Shirley.[5] That, joined to what you have done of late, shews such uniformity of Sentiment and Conduct that malice itself is almost struck dumb. For my own part whether you succeed or whether you miscarry in the first design of your agency[6]—I shall ever deem it a kind dispensation of Providence that brought you to London at this most critical conjunction.

It is impossible for me to describe the situation of People's minds on this Continent during the late debates in Parliament. Almost every vessel that arrived brought different accounts; and every different account excited different sensations and emotions. Determined in their own mind what part to act should matters come to extremities, the sensible and judicious waited the event with patience and temper, tho with much anxiety and distress of mind; while the turbulent and weaker spirits (of which there are but too many in every State) giving way to the sallies of their passions expressed their Resentment or Joy in acts which Cannot be justifyed, tho they may be excused. The Justice and tenderness of the mother Country (of which the late repeal is so striking an Instance) will, I am confident, distinguish and not impute to a whole people the acts of some individuals provoked to madness and actuated by despair.

I can with great Confidence assure you and all the Friends of America in England that they need be under no uneasiness about our Conduct on account of the Repeal. Our hearts are still towards Britain, our love and allegiance to our King is entire and unshaken, and I am sure never did a dutiful and Affectionate Son feel more

5. BF's letters to Governor Shirley of Massachusetts, Dec. 3, 4, and 22, 1754 (above, V, 443–7, 449–51) were printed in *London Chron.*, Feb. 6–8, 1766, with an extended introductory note (above, pp. 118–20), and the first two letters were reprinted with the introductory note in *Pa. Gaz.*, May 15, 1766. Thomson's use of the singular ("Letter") is clearly a reference to the long communication to Shirley of Dec. 4, 1754, in which BF had vigorously opposed parliamentary taxation of the colonies or any scheme which gave power to the governors and councils at the expense of the assemblies. Publication of this letter in Philadelphia more than a decade after it was written would certainly demonstrate BF's long-held views to people in his home city, where his enemies had accused him of promoting the Stamp Act.

6. The proposed change from proprietary to royal government in Pennsylvania.

sincere pleasure from a Reconciliation with a much loved parent unjustly offended at him, than the Americans feel at the prospect of re-establishment of harmony, peace and Concord between Great Britain and them.

I wish those Enemies of Britain and her Colonies who have so unworthily exerted their abilities to make a misunderstanding between them to the Ruin of both could but have seen in what manner the news of the repeal was received—Joy there was to be sure—a heart felt joy—seen in every Eye read in every Countenance; a Joy not expressed in triumph but with the warmest sentiments of Loyalty to our King and a grateful acknowledgement of the Justice and tenderness of the mother Country[7]—and what man who has the feelings of humanity (not to mention more) but rejoices that an affair which might have had such terrible Consequences is thus happily accommodated. May there never arise a like occasion! I am, with most sincere esteem and respect, Dear Sir your Affectionate. CHA. THOMSON.

To Benjn Franklin, Esqr.

From Isaac Hunt[8] ALS (mutilated):[9] American Philosophical Society

Worthy Sir   Philada. [May 21, 1766]
It is with great Reluctance that I trouble you with [*torn*] at a

7. It is to be observed that Thomson wrote the day after the receipt in Philadelphia of official news of the repeal of the Stamp Act. As both local newspapers did in describing the celebrations in their next regular issues, he stressed the dutiful and loyal atmosphere that prevailed.

8. Isaac Hunt (*c*.1742–1809), author, lawyer, and clergyman, graduated from the College of Philadelphia in 1763 and briefly held a tutorship there. During and after the election campaign of 1764 he published a series of satirical attacks on proprietary supporters, aiming his *Exercises in Scurrility-Hall* and other pieces especially at William Smith, Francis Alison, and others closely associated with the College; above, XII, 83 n. These writings served as the basis for the denial of his M.A. degree, about which he complains to BF in this letter. Five years later, however, he was allowed to receive the degree. He studied law and became a successful member of the Philadelphia bar. Attacked as a Tory during the Revolution, he made his escape to England, where he took Holy Orders. He was the father of Leigh Hunt, the essayist, critic, and poet. *DAB*.

9. The upper right corner of the leaf has been torn off, causing the loss

time when you must be busily engaged in Affairs of the [*torn*] to Great Britain and her Colonies. I hope however you will pardon [*torn*] indulge me in a Freedom which I do and ever shall esteem a great [Favour?].

One of the Medals which Mr. Sargent sent to the College[1] [was awarded at] the last anniversary Commencement to Dr. Morgan for the best [essay on?] the reciprocal Advantages of a perpetual *Union* between Great [Britain and] her American Colonies. There was but Eight that enterd the [*torn*] among whom I was one, and although I fell, yet I hope to rise [again.][2] Some who heard Doctor Morgan read his Performance at the Commencement are of Opinion that he has not done the Subject Justice. Be that as it may I cannot but think that a Peice wrote by a Gentleman of Doctor Morgan's Sense, Age, Advantages and Connections, and approved by Men of such *eminent Abilities* as our Trustees and Professors are must be vastly superior to any Thing of the like Nature that a Person of my Years and slender Abilities should attempt. The Determination of this matter I must leave, and would be glad to be *honored* with your Sentiments when you have read both Performances, which I propose sending you by the Packet. This much I would beg Leave to observe that I could not expect to

---

of the date (supplied from BF's endorsement) and several words in the top lines of both pages.

1. On John Sargent's gift of these medals through BF, see above, X, 143–4. One of the medals was to be for a discourse or essay "on the reciprocal Advantages arising from a perpetual Union between Great Britain and her American Colonies," open to all graduates.

2. The winner was Dr. John Morgan, above, IX, 374 n. The names of the writers were under sealed covers when the Trustees of the College read the essays. Two essays in addition to Morgan's were deemed worthy of publication and a fourth was added later. They were published together under the title *Four Dissertations on the Reciprocal Advantages of a Perpetual Union between Great-Britain and her American Colonies. Written For Mr. Sargent's Prize-Medal.* . . . (Phila., 1766) (Evans, 10400; Hildeburn, 2213). The medal was presented to Morgan at the commencement exercises, May 20, with a laudatory address by Provost Smith that was included in the publication of the essays. Hunt's piece was not included among those honored by publication, but he brought it out himself in 1775 with the title *The Political Family: Or a Discourse pointing out the Reciprocal Advantages, Which flow from an uninterrupted Union between Great-Britain and her American Colonies* (Philada., 1775) (Evans, 14123; Hildeburn, 3223). An account of this essay competition is in Montgomery, *Hist. Univ. Pa.*, pp. 367–71.

receive Honors from Men to whom I am so obnoxious. This is evident from the ill Usage I have very lately received. According to custom I made Application for my Master's Degree, an Honor which I had not forfeited and was therefore entitled to. The Trustees after sending for my Printer and strictly examining the poor, ignorant Man with respect to the Political Pamphlets I had wrote, without hearing what I had to say, rejected my Application and refused to give me my Master's Degree.³ There are no Honors for me, this Side the Water unless your patriotic Endeavors for a Change are crowned with Success. Had I not so great and sincere a Friend as you are, good Sir, I candidly confess that my Ambition would have been greatly checked by this cruel Behaviour, *cruel* because it flows from the poisoning Fountain of Faction and Revenge.

I beleive by Advice of my Friends I shall publish the Essay I wrote for the Medal. Gratitude great Affection and perhaps a little Selfishness will induce me to dedicate it to the justly respected Patriot and Agent of Pennsylvania.⁴ I hope I shall not give offence by taking so great a Freedom without first obtaining Permission. Excuse me when I say that your Name will be [*illegible*] [*torn*] Travellers, and tempt them to taste of my coars fare [*torn*.]

[*Torn*] to write fuller by the Packet. I had very little Time [*torn*] [opport]unity, and therefore should make an Appology for my rude [*torn*] of your great Candor and Goodness.

[Ameri]cans are all rejoicing at the agreeable News of the Stamp [Act being repeal]ed. Due Honors are paid our honored Agent for his great Activity in [behalf of the?] Colonies by all in Pennsylvania who have Honor, Honesty and [*torn*] those whose bad Hearts will not permit to give Merit its Due [*torn*] put to Confusion when we had the glorious Account in sundry [*torn*] of your so honorably nobly and satisfactorily acquitting yourself in our Be[half before?] the House of Commons.

3. See the first note to this document. In accordance with the English practice, graduates of at least three years standing who had paid their fees and were in good repute could apply for the M.A. degree and it was usually voted with a minimum of formality.

4. When Hunt finally printed his essay (somewhat revised) in 1775 he did not dedicate it to BF, but "To the Worthy Merchants, Farmers, and Mechanics of the Province of Pennsylvania, in Testimony of Esteem and Friendship," a much safer and less controversial form of dedication for an incipient Loyalist.

God give you all true Blessings and preserve you long for the Sake of dear Pennsylvania. I am, Worthy Sir, With great Faithfulness, Your Affectionate and oblig'd Humble Servant.

ISAAC HUNT.

Endorsed: Mr Isaac Hunt May 21: 1766 concerning his Competition for the Medal

From Thomas Wharton   ALS: American Philosophical Society

My Dear Friend.   Philada. May 22, 1766

I had the pleasure of writing thee, on the 9th Inst. via Ireland to which please to refer.[5]

On the 19th. by a Vessel from Pool we received the truely joyous and satisfactory News of the Repeal of the Stamp-Act; which diffused such universal pleasure that, it was easily to be seen in the Countenance of every Person. On which some Friends waited on all the chief Magistrates of the City, and requested they would use their Influence with the People to moderate their Joy on the Occasion; and that every Step, which might be taken should evince our sincere Acknowledgements to the Parliament for the Repeal: which they severally promised to do. The 20th. in the Evening being fixed for the Illumination, it was conducted with great Prudence: The Recorder, and several other Magistrates appeared and kept the Peace. Yesterday a handsome Dinner was provided at the Stadt-House and concluded with much decency.[6] It was there unanimously agreed, that all those, who (from a Patriotic Spirit) had procured Suits of Cloaths made of this Country Cloth, should give them to the Poor; and on the King's Birth

5. Above, pp. 272–5.

6. Other letters to BF from Philadelphia describe the celebrations and emphasize the decency and moderation with which they were carried on. Galloway's account, in the letter immediately below, differs in some particulars from Wharton's. Both *Pa. Gaz.* and *Pa. Jour.*, May 22, 1766, carried extended accounts of the celebration and the official dinner. Since the governor and other "Officers of Government" attended the dinner and it was presided over by the mayor, it is not surprising that among the 21 toasts offered, BF was not specifically mentioned among the individuals honored, though his friends present may have silently included him among those to be remembered in Toast No. 11: "AMERICA's Friends in Great-Britain."

Day appear in new suits of Broad Cloth made in England.[7] We hourly look for the Packet and I think the Adjournment of our Assembly will answer very well. 'Tis intended by a few of Us to introduce in the Address (after setting forth our Willingness to comply with the King's Requisitions) to declare that, nothing can bar the good Inclinations of the People of this Province, from chearfully answering such Requisition, unless it be Proprietary-Instructions; which have generally prefer'd private Interest to Public Good. It is not [to be doubted] but that, this will meet with an opposition from a few in the House; But as [torn] some Pains herein—there's no doubt it will be done.[8] We dispatched a [rider to Gov. Fran]klin with the News of the Repeal assoon as it was received.[9]

I hope what I have now to mention will not give thee Offence and should it not square with thy judgement to make application therefor—Please not to prosecute it.

I make no Doubt, thou art apprized that Springet Penn[1] stands possess'd in right of his Father of a Chain of Lotts, which lay between the second Street of the City and the River Schuylkill; Bounded on the South by Cedar, or south Street; on the West by Schuylkil River; on the North by Lotts belonging to the Proprietaries and others; and on the East by Second Street: Which Lotts we have been informed he inclined to sell; but as its not determined what Width on Second street and Sch[uylkil he] has a Right to leaves us at a loss how to make an Offer: We understand—He claims three f[ourths] parts of 204 Feet—and Thos. Penn says it is but ¾th. of 102. We cannot yet find in the Office such Papers as will set this matter in a clear Light. There are five of Us here, who intend to be concerned, and should thou and Governor Franklin think well of the Scheme—we shall be glad of your join-

7. This pledge is mentioned in the newspaper accounts of the dinner. The birthday of George III was on June 4, when he became twenty-nine.

8. See Galloway's letter of June 7 (below, pp. 292–6) on this plan and its failure.

9. *Pa. Gaz.*, May 29, 1766, carried an account of the celebration at Burlington on the 24th, at which 19 toasts were drunk, including one to "Doctor Franklin." *Pa. Jour.* ignored the New Jersey celebration.

1. Springett Penn was the great-grandson of William Penn through his first wife; above, XI, 315 n. He died in the fall of 1766 and nothing appears in BF's correspondence with him or his mother concerning the Philadelphia city lots that Wharton discusses here.

ing us. If on trial thou should find him willing to dispose thereof, it may be prudent to get something from under his Hands—which shall oblige him to comply on our agreeing to his Price. He has also a Right to Pennsborough Mannor in Bucks-County, which we should be glad to know if he will dispose of, and at what price:[2] 'Tis said that T. Penn claims 2000 Acres of what used [to] be called part of this Mannor; which will (as I am informed) reduce his quantity to about 4000.

Have inclosd the News Paper of the day. The Election for Managers for the building &c. of the Work house came on the 12th Inst.[3] when J Fox, H Roberts, J Wharton senr. P. Syng, J Lewis, A James, J. Palmer, S [*illegible*] L Morris, E Story, W Masters and J Redman were chosen and Jeremh. Warder Treasurer. They intend the buildings about 400 feet Long by about 60 feet Wide and its proposed to Erect them, on the Square next but One to the Hospital on the West; And having Purchased the Square next Westward of the Hospital that is to be left Open for the Accomodation of both the Institutions.

Thy family are well, my Father desires his sincere Respects paid to thee, Please to Accept the same from thy Real friend

THO WHARTON

Endorsed: Mr Th [Wharton] from April 24 to July 29. 1766 Speak to Dr Fothergil about Interest Money   Write to S. Penn abt Lotts and Pensbury

From Joseph Galloway   ALS: American Philosophical Society

Dear Friend   May 23d. 1766. Philada.
    I have now the inexpressible Pleasure of informing you that we have, Via Poole, the great News of the Royal Assent to the Repeal of the Stamp Act. Upon its Arrival agreable to your Advice, Our

2. On Pennsbury Manor and the interest of Edward Penington, a distant relative of Springett Penn, as agent for its possible sale, see above, XII, 370–2, and this volume, p. 123 n.

3. On the philanthropic plan to replace the old Alms House with a new structure called the Bettering House, see above, p. 262 n. *Pa. Gaz.* and *Pa. Jour.*, May 1 and 8, 1766, published notices of a meeting of the contributors to the scheme for May 12, but neither paper carried in a later issue an account of the meeting or a list of the persons elected officers and managers.

Friends exerted their utmost Endeavours to prevent any indecent Marks of Triumph and Exultation. We opposed the Intended Fire Works Illuminations, firing of Canon &ca. and Advised more Temperate and Private rejoicing on this great Occasion. The Chief Justice Mayor and Recorder with several other of the Majistrates were Spoke to, but to no Purpose,⁴ The City was illuminated by the P---y Party, Our friends refused to join with them but [were?] constantly Patroling the Streets in order to preserve the Peace; Which prevented any Great Mischief. And I find this Morning an Indiscreet Puff in Mr. Halls paper on the Occasion.⁵ However, I hope, the Indiscretion of a Small Part of the People of this City will not fix the Complexion of the whole Province.

Our Assembly meets on, the second of June when you may be assured, They will Send over to his Majesty and his Parliament a most Dutiful Address of Thanks for their Attention to the Ease and Happiness of the Colonies &ca. I have fixed the Measure with all the members our Friends whose Hearts cannot utter the Gratitude they Owe to the Present Virtuous and Worthy Ministry for the Infinite Trouble and fatigue they have undergone in the Arduous Task of Repeal. I have now no doubt that all Discontent will Subside in America, for altho I am every Day more and more Convinced, that [torn] Peoples Views, went further than a Repeal, and even wishd it might not take Place, in order to furnish them with a Pretext for other Designs, Yet their Number is so comparatively Small, that they will, I beleive, generally withdraw their Intentions.

The Numerous Accounts we have of my Dear Friends Integrity and Address in procuring the Repeal give us all the greatest Pleasure, and has open'd the Eyes of Many who entertained a Contrary Opinion of you, from the wicked Calumnies of your Enemies. Some few there are yet, who with unwearied Industry are endeavouring by their Malevolent Falsehoods to injure your Good Name. But it will be without Effect—The Prop[rietar]y Party never

4. In the letter immediately above, Thomas Wharton reported that "The Recorder, and several other Magistrates appeared and kept the Peace."

5. In its account of the evening of the illumination *Pa. Gaz.*, May 22, 1766, commented: "It was very remarkable, that the City was not disturbed by any Riot or Mob, as is common on such Occasions, but the whole was begun, continued and ended, to the universal Satisfaction of the Inhabitants." Precisely the same comment appeared in *Pa. Jour.*, May 22, 1766.

will desist from their Abuse of you.[6] Tho they are Dayly put to Shame on that Account.

As I expect to write you in a few Days by the Packet which is hourly Expected, and as I fear I shall Miss my Opportunity I conclude with the sincerest wishes for your Happiness and am Dear Sir yours Affectionately   J. GALLOWAY

Addressed: To / Benjamin Franklin Esqr. / Deputy Post Master General / of No. America / in Craven street / London / per Favor / Mr. Hopkinson

To Giambatista Beccaria

MS not found; retranslated from a translation into Italian printed in Guiseppe A. F. G. Eandi, *Memorie istoriche intorno gli studi del padre Giambatista Beccaria delle Scuole Pie professore di fisica sperimentale nella R. Università di Torino ec.* (Torino, 1783), pp. 146–8.[7]

Reverend Sir,   London, May 29. 1766.

It gives me pleasure to transmit to you herewith the thanks of our society for your most ingenious paper on electrical matters,* and permit me to add to them my own [thanks].

*[Footnote in Eandi:] The paper spoken of here is the one entitled *Novorum quorundam in re electrica experimentorum specimen, quod regiae Londinensi societati mittebat die 11 ianuarii anni 1766 Ioannes Baptista Beccaria ex scholis piis.* Printed in Turin by Fontana in fol., and then, with a few addenda and with illustrations, in the LVI volume of the *Transactions.*[8]

The note of thanks of the Royal Society to Father Beccaria, enclosed by Franklin in his letter, is as follows:

Viro ornamentissimo, et φιλοσοφικοτάτῳ [most philosophical] *Joanni Baptistæ Beccariæ ex scholis piis, et regiæ societatis Londinensis socio*

6. Attacks on BF continued in the June session of the Assembly and in the election campaign of the early fall.

7. The editors are grateful to Robert S. Lopez, Durfee Professor of History, Yale University, for making the retranslation printed here. Another retranslation, taken from the same Italian text, is in Smyth, *Writings,* IV, 457–9. Footnotes below call attention to the only two significant differences between these retranslations. The translator of the original English text into Italian was Count Prospero Balbo.

8. Beccaria's paper, read before the Royal Society on May 1, 1766, was published, with the Latin title printed here, in *Phil. Trans.,* LVI (1766), 105–18.

In conformity with your wishes, it had been shown to me before it was presented to the society, and I recommended it as well deserving the society's attention.

Before it is printed in the *Transactions* I should like to know whether there is not some mistake in that part of the table where you say:

Pili leporis accipiunt a tibiali albo pauculum; and then: *Tibiale album dat pilis leporis* plurimum; and following: *Tibiale album accipit a tibiali nigro* pauculum; next: *Tibiale nigrum dat tibiali albo* plurimum.†

If these are not writing mistakes, but agree with facts, I should like to know what circumstances in the experiments you think may account for [the fact] that in the reciprocal rubbing[1] of those substances one of them does not supply the same quantity as the other receives.

I ought to have thanked you before now for the favor you did to me some time ago by sending me your books on electrical matters, and for your mentioning me honorably in them.[2] Rest assured that I have read no other work on this subject that has given me so much pleasure. A new edition of my writings, with many additions, is being printed here; when it is finished I shall beg you to

----

C. Morton soc. reg. Londin. secret. et synedrus et academiar. imperial. Leopoldinæ S.C. et Petropolitanæ socius S.P.D.

Elegans, et doctissimum opus tuum de aliquibus circa rem electricam experimentis *Societati regiæ Londinensi in comitiis suis ordinariis hodie recitatum fuit, quo nomine gratiæ societatis tibi publicæ statutæ sunt. Datum ex ædibus societatis maii 1. 1766.*

†[Footnote in Eandi:] Both in the edition of Turin and in the *Philosophical Transactions* it reads as follows: *Pili leporis accipiunt a tibiali albo* pauculum. *Tibiale album dat pilis leporis. Tibiale album accipit a tibiali nigro. Tibiale nigrum dat tibiali albo.*[9]

9. That is, the unitalicized Latin words at the ends of BF's second, third, and fourth quotations were erroneous and do not appear in either of the eighteenth-century printed texts of the paper.

1. The Italian of this phrase is *nel vicendevole stropicciamento,* which Smyth renders as "in the alternate friction."

2. For the books and papers Beccaria sent to BF, see above, V, 395; VII, 300, 315. For an earlier letter of thanks, see above, X, 126.

accept a copy.[3] A small paper on meteorology which was read to the society some time ago, but not yet printed in the *Transactions*, is appended to it.[4]

Since I came back here from America in 1765 I have found only one new thing about electricity: this is that, if a spark is sent into the dark around bodies which *imbibe light*[5] (as I believe I must express myself), these bodies shine briskly for a few minutes thereafter. It is not necessary for electric fire to go through the body; a spark that passes at a two- or three-inch distance is sufficient. I suppose that Bologna[6] stone may be used for this experiment. Here we use an artificial compound of calcined oyster shells, burned in a crucible with sulphur.[7] A spark of your *fulminating table*[8] would give a long lasting light. I am sending you a small piece of wood covered with a little of this compound, which was given me, and made by Mr. Canton, a member of our society. The discoverer of this effect of electricity was Mr. Lane,[9] who also has devised an elegant method, by means of a screw, to give exactly equal shocks of a certain determined strength for medical objects, as the bottle will always discharge when it has received the quantity of fire that will hit at the distance determined by the screw.

I am pleased to hear that you read English, although you do not write it. I am in the same case with Italian. Hence we can cor-

3. This appears to be BF's first mention of the fourth edition of his *Experiments and Observations on Electricity,* presumably then in the early stages of preparation. Although it bears a 1769 imprint, it was published Dec. 5, 1768. *London Chron.,* Dec. 1–3, 3–6, 1768.

4. Above, IV, 235–43.

5. The Italian here is "che s' imbevono di luce," which Smyth renders as "that live by light." Eighteenth-century discussions of the phenomenon discovered by Lane and referred to here suggest that the bodies in question were those with the attribute of luminescence, and more particularly of fluorescence or phosphorescence.

6. A variety of the mineral barite, first discovered near Bologna; it is phosphorescent when calcined.

7. John Canton described the production of this compound in *Phil. Trans.,* LVIII (1768), 337–44.

8. In his paper for the Royal Society Beccaria described this contrivance, calling it "abacus fulminans." *Phil. Trans.,* LVI (1766), 115–16.

9. Timothy Lane (*c.*1734–1807), F.R.S., and one-time master of the Apothecaries' Company. Priestley described Lane's experiment in *The History and Present State of Electricity* (London, 1767), pp. 312–13, but Lane seems never to have reported it in print.

respond, if this pleases you, more easily if each of us writes his own language. I shall thus more often take the opportunity of expressing to you through my letters the great esteem, and the respect, with which I am, Reverend Sir, Your most obedient and most humble servant   B. FRANKLIN.

To Benjamin Waller[1]   ALS: Yale University Library

Dear Sir,   London, June 6. 1766
I hear with Pleasure from Philadelphia, that Billy Hunter behaves well and improves in his Learning;[2] but I am concern'd to hear that Mr. Royle is dead, who manag'd the Printing house jointly for his Account, and that Mr. Holt, whom I wish'd to succeed there, as one from whom a greater Care might be expected of the Child's Interest, does not incline to leave New York.[3] If this is the Case, and no other Person is yet engag'd, I would recommend to you Mr. Towne, a young Printer now going to America, who is extreamly well recommended to me by Mr. Strahan one of the principal Printers here, and by Sir John Cust, Speaker of the House of Commons, and who is willing to undertake the Partnership, and execute it on the same Terms that Mr. Royle did.[4] My

1. For Benjamin Waller of Williamsburg, Va., executor of the estate of William Hunter who had been BF's former colleague in the Post Office, and for BF's concern about Hunter's young son Billy, see above, X, 317–18 and accompanying notes.

2. The Hunter boy had been living in the Franklin house while attending school in Philadelphia. In October 1765 DF had reported that "Billey Hunter grows a fine Boy indead" (above, XII, 304); other letters, now lost, had probably also commented favorably on his behavior and progress in school.

3. Joseph Royle, who had been carrying on Hunter's printing business and newspaper in Williamsburg for the benefit of Billy Hunter, died in the spring of 1766. From time to time James Parker had sent BF reports on the confused situation in Williamsburg that had developed from Royle's long illness and death; above, XI, 415–16, and this volume, pp. 108, 203. He reported further on May 6, but BF had probably not yet received that letter when he wrote Waller. In his reference to John Holt, a relative by marriage of Hunter, BF discreetly omitted any mention of Parker's highly critical comments.

4. Benjamin Towne (d. 1793), printer and journalist. He did not get a position in Williamsburg but worked briefly for David Hall and later for William Goddard on the *Pennsylvania Chronicle*. In 1775 he started his own paper, the *Pennsylvania Evening Post*, which began as a tri-weekly but was published

Respects to Mr. Everard,[5] and believe me, with great Esteem, Dear Sir, Your most obedient humble Servant   B FRANKLIN

B. Waller Esqr

Pennsylvania Assembly Committee of Correspondence to Richard Jackson and Benjamin Franklin

LS: Library of Congress

Gentlemen   Philadelphia June 6. 1766

Our Assembly now sitting, having purposely adjourned, in May last, to this Time, have their Expectations joyfully gratified by receiving an authentic Account, in Secretary Conway's Letter to the Governor, of the Repeal of the Stamp Act,[6] which has been the Occasion of great Distress and Anxiety to the Colonies for Several Months past; We are ordered by the House to transmit to you, the inclosed Address to his Majesty, expressing the grateful Sense they entertain of his Wisdom and Clemency, and the Justice of his Parliament, in Releiving the Colonies from the distressing Consequences, which must have attended the Execution of that Law, which, as Soon as you receive, you will lose no Time in presenting, as the House, is desirous that this Province may be the foremost in a Testimony of their Loyalty and gratitude on that Occasion.[7]

somewhat irregularly; it changed sides during the Revolution depending on which army occupied the city. In 1783 it became the first daily in America but did not flourish and it ceased publication in 1784. *DAB;* Ward L. Miner, *William Goddard, Newspaperman* (Durham, N.C., 1962), p. 72; Clarence S. Brigham, *History and Bibliography of American Newspapers 1690–1820* (Worcester, Mass., 1947), II, 931–2. On Sir John Cust, see above, X, 32 n. He was a Lincolnshire man as was Towne.

5. Thomas Everard of York Co., Va., was co-executor with Waller of the Hunter estate; above, X, 252 n.

6. Conway's letter to Governor Penn of March 31, 1766, transmitting copies of the Declaratory Act and the act repealing the Stamp Act is printed in *Pa. Col. Recs.,* IX, 310–11, and in 8 *Pa. Arch.,* VII, 5878–9. It was read in both the Council and the Assembly on June 3.

7. On the same day that Conway's letter was read the Assembly appointed a committee of fourteen members to prepare an address to the King. Nine of these men had voted for the reappointment of BF as agent the previous

We have the Satisfaction to inform you, that amidst the rejoicings of the People here, on the Arrival of this Interesting News, such Moderation and Decorum, have been preserved, that we hope they will not occasion, the least Uneasiness to the Friends of America in England.

The House have omitted in this Address a Declaration of their readiness to comply with the Demands of the Crown in granting such Sums of Money, for the general Safety of the Colonies, as our Circumstances will admit, jud[g]ing it improper to blend Complaints of our Grievances with our grateful Acknowledgments to his Majesty and Parliament. You may however perceive, by their Resolve inclosed, which you will Communicate to his Majestys Ministers, in such Manner as your prudence may Suggest, That we are authorised to instruct you to give the strongest Assurances, that it is their full Determination to do every thing in their Power to answer such Requisitions, as may be made, consistent with the present distrest Circumstances of the Province.[8]

You cannot be insensible of the Impediments which have heretofore, prevented the Grants of former Assemblies, and the disagre-

---

October, four had voted against, and one had not yet been elected to the Assembly. The committee presented its draft on June 5, when it was approved "after some Alterations," and it was signed on the 6th. 8 *Pa. Arch.*, VII, 5882. BF was on his trip to Germany when this letter arrived in London, but he wrote the speaker and Committee of Correspondence, August 22 (below, p. 384), that Jackson had presented the address to Lord Shelburne, the new secretary of state, that Shelburne had presented it to the King, and that it was "graciously receiv'd, and printed in the Gazette."

8. Although supporters of the proprietary party were only a minority of the drafting committee and of the Assembly, they were able to get Galloway's declaration of "readiness to comply with the Demands of the Crown in granting such Sums of Money," removed from the address, on the floor of the House, but they could not prevent its adoption as a separate resolution. See Galloway's letter immediately below. The resolution, dated July 6, 1766, and sent to the agents, reads as follows: "Resolved, That whenever His Majesty's Service for the future shall require the Aids of the Inhabitants of this Province, and they shall be called on for that purpose in a constitutional Way, this House, and we doubt not all future Assemblies, will think it their indispensible Duty to grant such Aids to his Majesty, as the Safety of the Colonies requires and the Circumstances and Abilities of this Province may permit, unless the Proprietaries Instructions to their Deputy Governors respecting Proprietary private Interest shall continue to interfere." This copy was made and attested by BF. APS.

able Contests arising thro the Interuption of Proprietary Instructions to their Governors. And as you have, already, full Directions, to Solicit a Redress of these Grievances under which the Province has long laboured, We hope and request, that you will Omit no Opportunity or Argument to Obtain, the much desired Relief, in the manner and under the Limitations formerly Prescribed. In full Confidence of your Care and Attention to this Important Business, We are Gentlemen your Assured friends and humble Servants

GILES KNIGHT   JOS: FOX
THOS: LIVEZEY   JOS: RICHARDSON
JOS. GALLOWAY   ISA. PEARSON

Richard Jackson and Benjamin Franklin Esquires

Endorsed: Committee of Correspe. June 6. 1766 Enclosing Address, Pressing the Change

From Joseph Galloway

ALS: American Philosophical Society

Dear Sir   Philada. June 7th. 1766

I transmit you, herewith, a Letter from the Committee of Correspondence,[9] inclosing An Address from the Assembly to his Majesty, agreable to the Hint you gave me, in your's of the 27th. of February.[1] Our Assembly adjourned yesterday to the 8th of September, after Sitting 5 Days, during which Time my Fatigue was uncommon, The Court and Assembly both requiring my Attendance. The first had indeed very little Share of it, as the Proprietarians Seized every Opportunity in my Absence, of proposing Something, that might injure the Embassy you were Sent over upon. The Message to the Governor published in this Weeks Paper, carries the Face of Harmony, between our two Branches of the Legislature, and was obtained one Morning in my Absence, and as I much Suspect, to prove this to the Ministry.[2] But upon Perusal of the

9. See the document immediately above.

1. Not found.

2. John Penn's message to the Assembly of June 3 transmitting Conway's letter about the repeal of the Stamp Act and the Assembly's response to Penn of the same date were printed in *Pa. Gaz.*, June 5, 1766. Neither document appeared in *Pa. Jour.* Among other things, Penn said that he "took the earliest Opportunity to do justice to the good People of this Province, which

Committees Letter and the Resolve inclosed,[3] you will perceive
it was no more than a meer Compliment which they coud not
politely Avoid; And that they still Continue firm in their Resolution
never to be easy under a Government which Admits of the Intervention of a Private Subject between their Sovereign and them.
And indeed shoud any Use be made of this Address against us, I
think it may be justly replied, that it only proves, that the Assembly
do not Act on any personal resentment against the Proprietaries as
the Address Plainly proves, but that their Objection rests alone on
the unhappy Form of Government, which has so much injured the
Service of the Crown and the Safety of the People.

Great Opposition was given to the Resolve, and many Arguments used, by the Chief Justice and five more of the Proprietary
Friends, among others, they alledged, that we ought not, to give
his Majesty Assurances of granting Aids for the Defence of the
Colonies when required because they contended that the Assembly
were the Sole proper Judges when Aids were Necessary. To which
I replied, That it was obviously our Duty to Contribute towards
the Protection and Security of a Pro[v]ince which remain'd so
naked and Defenceless as this does. That the Power of Defence
was lodged in the Crown, and therefore it was the Province of its
Ministers to determine when Aids were Necessary, and that it was
unreasonable to suspect Supplies would ever be demanded, when
there was no Occasion for them. And shoud that be the Case, ever,
it woud be Time enough then, to determine the Right of Refusal
on just Terms. And indeed every Argument which the Party cou'd
Form either in or out of the House was made use of to prevent this
Assurance to the Crown. I had inserted it in the Address, but for
the reasons mentioned in the Committees Letter, it was taken

---

their Conduct merited, by representing to the King's Ministers the Moderation
and Decency with which they have behaved, under the Dissatisfaction and
Uneasiness universally prevailing in America, on Account of the Stamp Act."
He also quoted Conway's assurance of his Majesty's "Approbation of the
wise and prudent, as well as dutiful Behaviour, which the Province of Pennsylvania has held amidst the too prevailing Distractions, which have so
generally agitated the other Colonies." The Assembly's answer to Penn
thanked him for the report he had sent to England of the colony's "Moderation and Decency." These documents, including Conway's letter, are printed
in 8 *Pa. Arch.*, VII, 5877–9, 5881.

3. See the last footnote to the document immediately above.

out—And at length, passed in a Resolve by a Majority of 18. there
being 24. for and 6 against it.[4] The Letter from the Committee was
also read and Approved of in the House by the same Majority.

I was, at first reading of Secretary Conways Letter, to the Governor, not a little Surprized, to find his Majesty approved of his
Conduct,[5] but when I observed, that it was an Answer to the
Governor's Account of his own Behaviour, my Surprise Vanished.
No doubt he assured the Secretary of his having been instrumental
in Preserving the Peace of the Province &c. But if he did, nothing
coud be more untrue. For be assured, Nothing was left unessayed
by the Majestracy, to incite the People to Acts of Violence, which
coud be done, without publickly joining with the Mob and exposing themselves. Instead of being Silent on the Occasion, they were
the loudest in proclaiming the Inequity of the Law and their Ab-
horence to it. And when the Mob were invited in the Morning to
meet in the Afternoon at the State House to Oblige Mr. Hughes to
resign, The Governor Mayor Recorder and all the Majestrates save
Mr. Shoemaker went out of Town, and Had not our Friends Acted
with uncommon Resolution and firmness, and been ready in different Parts of the Town to preserve the Peace, infinite Confusion
woud have ensued, In short, three Different Attempts, were made
by the Proprietary and Presbyterian Party to Hang up Effigies
&c. &c. and they were as often Prevented, not by the Governor
or his Officers, but by the resolution of our Friends.[6] From whence

4. The Assembly Journal gives no hint of the vigor of this debate, merely
stating that the address to the King was agreed to "after some Alterations."
The text of the resolution follows immediately that of the address. *Ibid.,*
pp. 5884–5.

5. At the end of Conway's letter to Penn, after his favorable comments on
the behavior of Pennsylvania, he added that this behavior "reflects on your
Administration; and I have the Satisfaction to inform you, that your own
Conduct meets with his Majesty's Approbation."

6. For reports to BF on these events, see above, XII, 264–6, 269–71, 291–2,
301–2, 306, 315–17. In one of Penn's letters to Conway relating to the Stamp
Act, dated Feb. 19, 1766, the governor omitted all mention of the mob that
had assembled and threatened Hughes. He said that when the stamped papers
first arrived, Hughes had refused to accept them "under pretence that he had
not received his Commission or had any Authority to take them into his
possession." Thereupon Penn had ordered the papers placed on board H.M.S.
Sardoine. When Hughes resigned (there is no suggestion that he did so under
pressure), the governor committed all later shipments to the same custody,

it is plain, His Honour has deceived Mr. Conway by an Elogium on himself which he did not deserve.

The C. Justice's Malevolence against you never will end but with his Breath. He publickly Asserted in the House that you were the greatest Enemy to the Repeal of the Stamp Act, of all the Men in England. This Declaration filled your Friends with that Indignation and Resentment which it deserved. Mr. Ashbridge Pemberton, Livezey, Humphrys, &c. and my Self—called on him to make out his Charge, or to take Shame to himself—And the Consequence thereof would I think have been an Expulsion of the Accuser, had he not made good his Accusation, and that we had not the least Suspicion of, if the Speaker had not very Abruptly adjourned the House, for which he is not a little Censured by the Members.[7] And so high is their Resentment at length worked up, That they Seem resolved to call on him again to make good his Accusation, in the Beginning of the next Sitting.

Be assured, my Dear Friend, The Assembly entertain the most grateful Sense of the Firmness and Integrity with which you have Served your Country on this very important Occasion—And will not be Wanting in their Demonstrations of it on your Return. I have thought it my Duty, to insert the Extracts of the several Letters from London to our friend wherein honourable mention has been made of your Name, and from thence had them translated

---

until orders should arrive from England. The impression his letter gives is that the only performers on the Pennsylvania stage during that troubled period had been Hughes, the governor, and the captain of the warship. *Pa. Col. Recs.*, IX, 299–300.

7. Again, no hint of these proceedings appears in the Journal of the Assembly. News of Chief Justice Allen's charge that BF had worked against repeal, however, reached London. *Pa. Gaz.*, Oct. 2, 1766, printed an extract of a letter dated Aug. 2, 1766, from the London merchant firm of Sargent, Chambers, and Co. (formerly Sargent Aufrere; above, IX, 959 n) saying "We are very much concerned to hear Mr. Franklin's Character is called in Question, on Account of the Part he acted the last Session of Parliament; so far from being an abettor of the Stamp-Act, his Evidence, at the Bar of the House, was allowed to be one of the strongest, and most satisfactory, in Favour of the Repeal, and of the Colonies; and we are firmly persuaded, his utmost Endeavours were at all times exerted to that End, having been Eye-witnesses of his Assiduity, in attending the Committees of the Merchants, and of his publick Behaviour at different times, in the last two Sessions of Parliament."

into Millers[8] for the Satisfaction of the Dutch, who are now generally come over to the Assembly Party, and have lost their former Prejudices. Every Day Adds to the number of the People who Wish for the immediate Rule of their soverign, and in my Opinion Nothing Less will satisfy them.

You will perceive by the before mentioned Resolve, which you are directed to lay before the Ministry, that the House, tho Sincerely disposed to grant Aids, when required, that they have no Expectations of being able to do it, unless the Government is Changed, And Proprietary Influence removed. Their Abhorrence to the Proprietary Government Seems as deeply rooted, as their Dislike to the Stamp Act, and it is my firm Opinion, were requisitions now made, of the two Proprietary Provinces, the Crown woud not receive a Farthing from them. Maryland you know gave Nothing in Times of the greatest distress and altho Pennsylvania did, yet when that Necessity is over, it is not reasonable to Expect it. But coud these Provinces grant them on just Terms, They never woud be denied. This Consideration founded on the Safety of the People certainly points out the Policy and Wisdom of Changing both these Governments from Proprietary to Royal.

I Sincerely Thank you for the Many Letters I have received from you, notwithstanding your late Hurry. Beleive me, my Dear Friend, with the Sincerest Wishes for your Happiness, yours very Affectionately   JOS. GALLOWAY

I had the Pleasure of Seeing your Worthy Son Yesterday in Good Health in this City.

The Assembly, who, now, do not Suspect that their Petitions are rejected, Seem very Desirous they should be urged to a Determination with all prudent Expedition. As they are now much in Debt for the Common Exigencies of Government, and can think of no Means of discharging it, but what Proprietary Instructions will prevent A Hard Distressing Case indeed!

Did you receive a Letter from the Committee of Correspondence by Cap. Bogs via Dublin?

8. Henrich Miller's *Der Wochentliche Philadelphische Staatsbote.*

To Baynton, Wharton & Morgan

Extract: reprinted from Clarence W. Alvord and Clarence E. Carter, eds., *The New Régime 1765–1766*, in *Collections* of the Illinois Historical Library, XI (Springfield, Ill., 1916), 366.

[June 8, 1766][9]

I approve much of the Preposal of a strong Colony at the Illinois.[1] It is well listned to here; But all affairs, except what immediately relate to Great Britain are laid aside, until the Season of Publick Business comes on and until the Ministry, are a little better settled.

To the Pennsylvania Assembly Committee of Correspondence[2]

ALS: William Logan Fox, Philadelphia, Pa. (1956)

Gentlemen,   London, June 10. 1766

I wrote to you pretty fully by the April Packet.[3] The Parliament have since been continually agitating the Affairs of America, which has oblig'd us to constant Attendance. All the new Regulations I mention'd as like to take place, are now carried into Acts, except that relating to the Portugal Trade, which, together with the Paper Currency, is postpon'd, but I should have little doubt of their being obtain'd another Year if this Ministry continues, and no farther Imprudencies appear in America to exasperate Government here against us. The present have incurr'd a good deal of Abuse from

9. So dated because in their letter to Sir William Johnson of August 28, 1766, Baynton, Wharton & Morgan identified the extract as being from the last letter received from BF by the June packet. That must have been BF's letter to the firm of June 8, which Baynton, Wharton & Morgan acknowledged receiving in their letter to him of Aug. 28, 1766 (below, p. 395).

1. For similar statements of approbation for this project, see above, pp. 275–6.

2. Speaker Fox laid this letter before the Assembly on Sept. 9, 1766; 8 *Pa. Arch.*, VII, 5886. The journal particularly mentions BF's request for leave to return to Philadelphia the following spring.

3. Above, pp. 236–40. See the notes to that letter on the activities of Parliament relating to colonial commerce and paper currency discussed in the first two paragraphs of the present letter.

the Opposition, for the Favour they have shown us; and great Advantages will be taken of them next Session if that Favour should not appear to have been properly received.

With this I send you Copies of two of the Acts relating to America, and I congratulate you on the Reduction of Duties by another, not yet printed, and on the Establishment of Free Ports which I hope will prove so useful as that more may be obtained, some on the Continent.

Mr. Jackson, by his close Attendance in Parliament and with the Ministry, has been exceedingly serviceable to us; and is likely to be soon in a Station that will give him still more Weight, if it continues.[4] But all ministerial Dispositions are extreamly fluctuating.[5] The Duke of Grafton has lately quitted the Ministry; and Mr. Conway, who was Secretary of State for the Southern Department, which included America, is now gone into the Northern, and the Duke of Richmond is made Secretary for the Southern. America is now to be a separate Department, and Lord Dartmouth, first of the Board of Trade, is to have it: But all is yet unsettled, and all American Affairs, even the Granting of Lands, are now at a stand, and will probably be so for some time, 'till the Season of Business returns. The frequent Changes that have happened, and the general Opinion even among the Ministers themselves, that more will happen, disposes People generally to lie awhile upon their Oars; till the Ministry have so establish'd themselves, as that they can afford Attention to Affairs, which not being

4. It is uncertain what post of "still more Weight" may have been under consideration for Jackson at this time when many changes were taking place in the Ministry. There may have been rumors that he was to become counsel to the Board of Trade, a position he actually did receive in 1773.

5. The situation in the government was indeed in a state of flux. The absence of William Pitt from the Ministry and the decrease of agreement and mutual confidence among the leading members of the Rockingham administration were among the causes of weakness. Augustus Henry Fitzroy, 3d Duke of Grafton, secretary of state for the Northern Department, told the King on April 28 that he wanted to resign; on May 23 Henry Seymour Conway (above, XII, 209 n) changed from secretary of the Southern Department to Grafton's post, and Charles Lennox, 3d Duke of Richmond, became secretary for the Southern Department. Plans for the establishment of a third secretaryship, that for the colonies, were considered at this time but were put off until 1768, when the Earl of Hillsborough was named to that office. A new administration under Pitt took over at the end of July.

of national Concern they think may well be postpon'd: And indeed 'tis a kind of Labour in vain to attempt making Impressions on such moveable Materials; 'tis like writing on the Sands in a windy Day.

As to myself, finding a Summer Journey, to which I have been so many Years accustomed, and which I omitted last Year, necessary to my Health, of late sensibly impair'd, I am about to make a little Tour for Six or Eight Weeks, which I hope will re-establish it. At my Return I shall apply myself diligently to what concerns the Interests of our Province; and if the present Ministry should be confirmed, as I sincerely pray they may, I hope another Winter will bring our Affairs all to a happy Conclusion. At least I think they may be put in such Train as that my Continuance here will be no longer necessary, and I now request that I may have leave to return in the Spring.[6]

By all Accounts there is great Prospect that the Peace of Europe will not soon be disturbed. France is said to be perfectly well-dispos'd to be quiet, and Spain too much disturb'd with internal Commotions to prosecute its Views on Portugal. Commerce and Manufactures engross the Attention of other States; and the Empress of Russia is bent on increasing the Population of her Country, improving its Laws and farther refining its Manners. The King of Prussia too, tho' frequent in reviewing his Troops, seems rather intent on repairing the Damages of the last War, than projecting new ones. So that we may reasonably expect a Tranquility of some Duration.[7]

Be pleased to present my best Respects and Duty to the Assembly, and believe me, with sincere Esteem, Gentlemen, Your most obedient humble Servant   B FRANKLIN

Committee of Correspondence.

6. The Ministry did not continue in office and BF did not return home in the following spring. In May of 1767 Charles Townshend, chancellor of the Exchequer, presented to the House of Commons his scheme for an American revenue and a new crisis in the relations of the colonies and Great Britain impended.

7. A letter from London dated June 11, printed in *Pa. Gaz.*, Aug. 21, 1766, carried similar assurances of the continued peace of Europe, especially in view of the domestic disturbances in Spain. It concluded with a comment that "in Times of Tranquility, all commercial States must flourish."

From Baron Behr[8]

AL: American Philosophical Society

Cleveland Row St. James's 10. Juin 1766.
Baron Behr presente ses complimens à Mr. le Docteur Franklin, et souhaitant un heureux voyage, lui remet les incluses.
Addressed: To / Dr. Franklin / *Baron Behr*

From James Parker

ALS: American Philosophical Society

Honoured Sir,   New York, June 11 1766.
   Yours of the 6th. of April last[9] via Philadelphia, I received here but had none from you per the Packet, which arrived since: In my last to you of the Beginning of May,[1] per Packet, I told you of my coming here, and my Reasons for not immediately printing a News paper: Since that I having deliver'd my Certificate and Bond to the Surveyor General of the Customs, I am told he has sent them Home by a Man of War, that sailed soon after he got them.
   I am glad you got the Letter with the State of the Accounts:[2] I don't doubt but there are Mistakes in it, I had no Thoughts of closing them: Altho' such State as it was possible to make by the Time mentioned was sent home, and I would now willingly put up with One Hundred Pounds Loss were but as good a State for Settlement—that is as perfect from Errors, made between Holt and I;[3] but that I fear is not possible. I am so far from thinking it needful for me to close Yours that I don't think any Thing beneficial, that I have done, but that you and Mr. Hall might have

8. The Hanoverian minister in London, who had obviously been informed of the impending visit of Pringle and BF to Germany. In a letter tentatively dated June 15, 1770, to an unidentified correspondent at Walthamstow, possibly Anthony Todd, BF expressed great pleasure at the prospect of seeing at his correspondent's home "that excellent good Man Baron Behr." APS.
   9. Not found.
   1. See above, pp. 262–6, for Parker's letter of May 6, 1766.
   2. For Parker's letter of Feb. 3, 1766, covering a statement of BF's account with David Hall, Feb. 1, 1766, see above, pp. 104–10.
   3. This letter itself is one of the fullest accounts of the troubled and tangled dealings between Parker and John Holt. See also Beverly McAnear, "James Parker versus John Holt," N.J. Hist. Soc. *Procs.*, LIX (1941), 77–95, 198–212, and above, pp. 263–5.

done it to more Satisfaction to both Sides than I have or could do: As I have been as *unjustly* treated by Mr. Holt, as its possible I could be, and am so much a Sufferer by him. At the same time, whether by his Superior Cunning or by Accident, Col. Hunter[4] only being bound for performance of Agreement, while Holt is in that Affair clear, I must beg Leave tho' I may only be found a Fool for my Pains, to lay as concise a State of the Affair before you in Hopes you may lay it before Col. Hunter himself, that if I can any Way have some Justice done me, if its only so much as to save me from impending Ruin.

You know the first Acquaintance or Knowledge I had of Holt was from your and Mr. Hunter's[5] recommending him to me, requesting me to teach him the Printing-Business: It was enough for me that you recommended him: What I could do on that Head I did: Before I began a News-paper at New-Haven,[6] I offered him that Printing-House, on the same Terms I had it of you, but he declined it quite: on my own Strength I began a News paper in April, hired a Rider at my own Expence to carry them up to Hartford* and continued it Six Months, before it was sufficient to quit any Costs, being before that greatly out of Pocket. We are short-sighted Mortals, and don't know when we go too fast, or too slow. Holt who was with me all the While, seeing such a Prospect of Success, became then desirous of the Place: As I had before offered it, I did not love to be worse than my Word: tho' after I had run the Risk and beat the Road, it could not appear so eligible in him to ask it, And indeed, I should never have attempted to beat

---

*On a Post-Master being appointed at Hartford and Middletown just before I went to New Haven, the People refused to hire a Rider to Seabrook. Whereupon the Rider applied to me to hire him. I did, to my great Loss, to the Benifit of the Post-Office. This I can make appear.

4. Col. John Hunter (above, VI, 223 n), a Virginia merchant who had moved to England by 1766, was in some way related to William Hunter (above, V, 18 n), BF's former colleague as deputy postmaster general of North America, and to William's sister or half-sister, who was Holt's wife. In 1756 Col. Hunter had supplied the money for Holt to buy into partnership with Parker and had signed a bond guaranteeing Holt's performance of his obligations. McAnear, "Parker versus Holt," pp. 80–1.

5. William Hunter, mentioned in the note immediately above.

6. Parker began publishing the *Connecticut Gazette* at New Haven in April 1755; above, V, 441 n.

the Way as I did, but for a Prospect of providing a Place for my Nephew[7] (I believe you Sir, once designed a Favour for your Nephew but was disappointed as well as I).[8] He then was with me, and Mr. Holt seemed pleased much with his Disposition. After discoursing the Matter, Mr. Holt took the Heads of our Proposals, to consult his Friends: He went to Virginia: They approved of them: He returned, and drew the Articles himself, according to his own Conceptions and Will. The Books and Stationary, that were mine and there were one Half to be paid for to me at 112½ tho' I gave 125—and the other Half to be accounted for to me when Sold at the Retail Price. By these Articles, Accounts were to be remitted to me every three Months at least. Besides my Nephew, he had my Apprentice,[9] which under the Circumstances he came to me upon, was very disadvantageous to me, as the Lad's Parents were to find him Cloathes the first three years and I the last: those first 3 years I let Holt have him at his Intreaty, tho' against the Inclination of both the Boy and Parents. Quarter after Quarter pass'd and tho' continually requested, no Accounts sent. Mr. Holt had a fine Hand at parrying a Dun, or making an Excuse. When my Nephew had lived with him little more than one Year, I had continual Complaints of his Dissatisfaction with Holt and he being near free, absolutely disliked the Place: I had designed to give him my Half of the Tools, if he had merited it, and liked the Place: On the Expiration of the Term for which we had agreed, and for which Col. Hunter was bound, I wrote to Holt, as the Substitute appointed by Col. Hunter, to give him the Refusal of buying or selling. His Answer was He should not chuse either but would rather, if I would consent, continue as we were for some Time longer (perhaps a double Meaning was in this, that is to continue without accounting or paying, tho' I understood it on the Terms of the Agreement only) I consented but at the same Time pressed the

7. Samuel Parker, who was apprenticed to his uncle from 1752 to 1758. Upon the expiration of his term, part of which he served with Holt and with William Weyman, James Parker set him up in business in New York. Failing to prosper, Samuel began drinking heavily and in 1760 absconded to the West Indies. See Beverly McAnear, "James Parker versus William Weyman," N.J. Hist. Soc. *Procs.*, LIX (1941), 10 n, 15–16.

8. For BF's plans to establish his nephew James Franklin, Jr. (C.11.4), in New Haven and their failure, see above, v, 82, 422 n, 440–1 n.

9. Not identified.

Settlement of the Accounts, and Promises were not wanting: Shortly after this Col. Hunter pass'd our Way, and hinted, that if Holt could make it out, and was minded to purchase, he would try to do it for him: Here I was short in not pressing and inviting him to do it, which I repented of ever after. From his Kindness to Holt, I was more inclined to have a good Opinion of him, and thought the chief Reason of his delaying to account, was want of getting in his Pay which I knew in the News Paper Way is slow: As I supplied him with Paper and Ink, for which he remitted me the full Ballance, and did not run into my Debt any farther, I was easy, in Hopes it would come some time or other. When Weyman[1] and I parted Holt had made me some Offer of coming to assist me, which I took kindly, but thought it most eligible to decline it, and put my Nephew in at New York: for some Months he behaved tolerably: and I thought he would mend with Years and Experience, but he took to drinking immoderately and I saw he would soon run to Wreck and Ruin. I then wrote to Holt, told him my Case:[2] that I would either With draw my Printing House from New York, and Cease my Connection with him also, as I should chuse to bring my Matters into a less Compass, unless he inclined to take that at New York, that if he chose it, he might try a Year or two, and if it did not answer, he should be at Liberty to return, without paying a Farthing for the Use of the Tools, or if it answered, that he Should purchase the Half, and be on the same Terms as we were at New Haven, that as he frequently complained that he could not get a Clerk there to assist in settling the Accounts, I told him, if he came to New York he might easily get one: (In order as he says to get his Accounts in Readiness he delayed coming from February to July). He accepted the Proposal and came: I spared him my Hands, my Help, my House and my Advice. He hired a Book keeper 6 Months while there, but I never could get any Accounts. This at last brought on almost an open Rupture: It would be endless to reccount all the Arguments and Disputes we had. You know part of them, and Col. Hunter, who came along

1. William Weyman (d. 1768), Parker's partner in New York, 1753–59. A quarrel and then a law suit terminated their relationship. See McAnear, "Parker versus Weyman," pp. 1–23.
2. McAnear dates Parker's proposal to Holt in early 1760. See his "James Parker versus John Holt," p. 82.

about that Time knows also of my Complaints of that Matter. Mr. Hunter dying that Year,[3] the Sound of £1000 left Mrs. Holt, made a great Noise in his Favour, and I was threatned how Strong he would be, if I sued him, or he should set up against me tho' I wanted nothing of him but a Settlement but I never could get any, or a Sight of his Books. At last he told me he could not attend to keep new Accounts as they went on, and settle the old, but he would hire the House and Business of me for four Years if we could agree, and that then he should not be necessitated to keep Accounts of Partnership, but would apply to the settling the Past ones. As we had before discoursed about the Place and Business, I supposed the Business and Tools to be worth £800, that if he purchased the Half, as we at first proposed, and to go on in Partnership, he should for the Half the *Tools* and *Business,* give me £400, and thereupon I told him, that as the Tools wore out fast, and the Business was good at that Time, that the four Years Purchase was worth the Half the Whole, which was £400, that if he would pay me £400, down, he should have it at that Price. Mrs. Holt was then in Virginia, and I would not agree till she returned because the Money was to come from thence. When she came, she consented, tho' a little to my Surprize, because she had often desired to return to New Haven: but it seems that was only outside: The Money was to be paid the first of May according to the Agreement of the Beginning of the Hire:[4] but when it came to, I never got but £80, in Cash, and his Bond for £320, which has lain over since: During these four Years, I have wrote and pleaded many a Time for my Accounts, and he had a Clerk or Book Keeper near 3 whole Years, and yet I can never get the sight of an Account: I have extorted small Sums of Money from him for Sugar Tea, Flour, and sundry such Things at the Worst Rate conceivable, and he has wrote me more Paper to excuse the not sending them, than would have held them but he is a great Writer as an Author, but not as an Accomptant. (I wish to God Sejanus or Anti-Sejanus[5] had him

3. William Hunter died in August 1761. See above, IX, 363 n.

4. Holt leased Parker's house and business from May 1, 1762, to May 1, 1766.

5. The pen name of the Rev. James Scott (1733–1814), a prolific and scurrilous anti-American writer in the London *Public Advertiser.* Fred J. Hinkhouse, *The Preliminaries of the American Revolution As Seen in the English Press 1763–1775* (N.Y., 1926), pp. 70–3.

in England to write for them there, he then perhaps might be in his Element). Besides the Partnership, he had all the Books left in my Shop, great Part of which were those, I had of you, Sir, which arrived here in June 1760, and Holt came the Beginning of July following and for which I now stand bound to you: to these were added all those which you paid for me to Mr. Strahan besides the greater Part of those from Hamilton and Balfour of Scotland, for which I am threatned with a Suit[6] and all this exclusive of sundry Things had of me, for which I have scarce in my Opinion got Half the Pay. Upon your recommending to me last Summer to resume my Business in New-York, &c. I wrote to New-York to Holt, telling him my Purpose, and that as my Conduct to him, had been always candid and open, I had a Right to expect such Treatment and begg'd to know what he proposed to do. He answered, he had formed no Plans at all, nor should he he believed, but when the Time was up, he would deliver up the Tools, and would then settle his Accounts and other Affairs, collect in his Debts, and see how he stood with the World, for that he found himself unable to go thro' the Task in the Business he was in. This Answer made me a little easy, because I thought it was candid, and the best could be done for both of us, and accordingly made the necessary Preparations, tho' I had heard it hinted that when Mr. Royle[7] was up here last Fall, he had tried to purchase those Tools of him, that were Mr. Stretch's but Royle would not trust him, and he could not raise the Money: I heard no more of it, till after Royle's Death, when it was again hinted to me, that he was about purchasing 'em, but I had not a very great Concern about it, because he had so often pretended his *honest* Intentions to me: His many Equivocations, and Quibbles, had indeed given me but a mean Opinion of him, but I had not quite so bad as he turns out: During the late Troubles he was arrested as I am told for some Books he bought[8]

6. For Parker's indebtedness to Strahan (which BF assumed) and to Hamilton and Balfour, see above, XII, 174–5, 226–7; this volume, pp. 10, 13.

7. Joseph Royle had printed the *Virginia Gazette* at Williamsburg until the end of 1765; he died in the spring of 1766. See above, p. 108 n.

8. "In the fall of 1765, Timothy Hurst, a New York merchant, gained judgment against Holt for £440 in payment of a debt incurred by the purchase of a lot of books." The New York Sons of Liberty with whom Holt was very popular, paid this debt to keep him out of jail. McAnear, "Parker versus Holt," pp. 89–90.

just before you and Mr. Foxcroft got the Post-Office Books of him,[9] He having acquired some Reputation with the Sons of Liberty, and telling them (as I hear) that if he went to Jail, his Paper would Stop, they paid that Money for him, and probably with what Money he had provided towards paying for those Books he has purchased Stretch's Materials.

When I came here the first of May, he in his Smooth tongued Manner, told me his Brother in Virginia, had been so good as to buy them there for him and lend them to him, pretended he had now got into great Vogue, and could not drop such a Living: that he would be glad to live in Friendship with me, and he had Work enough, and would recommend me, &c. *very generous* thought I, only my Accounts and settlement is wanting! He said if he could get somebody to take Care of his Business for him on good Terms, he would set about the Accounts: At his Request, I sent to B. [*sic*] Goddard[1] whose Attempts at Providence had not answered, and who had wrote to me to help him to some Birth: He came, but Holt would not agree to what I thought not the most favourable to Goddard: finding they could not agree, I determin'd to arrest Holt and print a Paper: He thereupon issued a New Paper without any Notice to me:[2] I next Morning wrote the inclosed printed Piece[3] but before it was done he sent for Goddard twice, and consented to his first Proposals: I who want Nothing more than a Settlement, have sacrificed every Thing to That Consideration, if he will settle in three Months. I will not do a Newspaper in a Year, if not, I shall be obliged to do one in my own Defence[4]—tho' I suppose I shall hardly be able to make my Way good under the

9. These books may have been obtained by the threat of legal action, for BF and Foxcroft had directed Jared Ingersoll to bring suit against Holt in 1763 for debts he owed the post office. See above, x, 402–3.

1. William Goddard, formerly an apprentice of Parker and printer, 1762–65, of the *Providence Gazette;* see above, XII, 287 n.

2. Holt did this on May 29, 1766; see above, p. 264 n.

3. A broadside entitled "An humble Address to the Publick," dated New York, May 30, 1766. A copy is now at APS. McAnear (p. 91 n) suggests that Parker did not issue the broadside to the public, a statement that is apparently confirmed by Parker's endorsement on the APS copy: "Suppressed on Mr. Holt's engaging to settle in 3 Months tho' I doubt his Compliance then." The "humble Address" was a slashing attack on Holt's integrity and business ethics.

4. Parker revived his *New York Gazette* in October; see below, p. 454.

present Circumstances, yet I believe it will greatly hurt him, and if I arrest him, I may not be able ever to get a Settlement, or to get any Thing of him, but his Ruin, which I do not Want, if I can get any Thing without. As Green[5] at New Haven delayed all Accounts to me, and I could not sue Holt on that Account, I attach'd the other Half of the 6 Years worn Tools, at the Time B. Mecom surrendered up: I offered them to Mecom, on his own Terms. He profferd £10, for the first year, £20 for the 2d—and 30 for the 3d—so as to make it £20 per Ann. which was but one Half of what Goddard gave for Green's. I have trusted him with about £20, also, but I can't get one Penny of Mecom and begin to fear, I never shall.[6] I have wrote pressingly, but all won't do: I can't get the Post-Office Accounts of him, tho' as he pays one of the Riders £50 York per An. believe he can't be much behind-hand there: but otherways believe he is irrecoverable, and I the Sufferer on all Sides.

Perhaps you will say, what is all this Rig ma roll to you or Col. Hunter? Why, I don't know, unless you or he shall suggest it something, it is nothing, but a Story. I there leave it. Since my Return to this City, I have had no Opportunity of getting the Electrical Machine,[7] the Captain who brought it not being at home, and no delivering was to be had of him without a Bill of Lading, which he says he signed. Mr. Hughes keeps close yet, tho' the Person for whom he is bound walks at Liberty like a Gentleman, for as he has Nothing they don't trouble him, but think to get it of Hughes. I told him what you said, he thank'd you kindly, and when the Captain comes home, we shall try to get it. Tho' the Gout threatens me, yet I have had but little of it since I have been here, but if I am violently attacked, I don't know what I shall do: for I am obliged every Day to walk from one End of the Town to the other, along the Wharfs, they being determined I shall do the Utmost Duty.[8] And I comply with the more Alacrity, as I won't disgrace

5. Thomas Green (1735–1812), who at this time was publishing the *Connecticut Courant* at Hartford; see above, X, 403 n.

6. Throughout the year Parker complained about Benjamin Mecom's business difficulties.

7. The machine was ordered from BF by Hugh Hughes; Parker finally took possession of it in October. See above, XII, 355 n; this volume, below, p. 475.

8. As a land waiter in the customs.

the Recommender if I can help it, tho' God knows, I shall well earn the Allowance for it. We are sworn to take no Fee or Reward &c. and I know not that there is any one Perquisite or Allowance for any Thing: If the Parliament should take off some of the Duties &c.—it may make the Service something easier, unless it pass as I have seen it hinted, of Sugars being Stored in the King's Store Houses,[9] and then it will be worse for me. However better or Worse, I will try to make the best of it: I am sorry to find the Bulk of the People still disputing the Authority from home. They think and find the Parliament have given Way in one Affair of Grievance, they begin to imagine both the Post-Office and Custom-House are like Grievances: With Respect to Custom-House Officers they were always look'd on as such, but never disputed, till now: The Post-Office has only in Part been look'd on as such, and that is still so: for Notwithstanding the late Acts of Parliament, direct every Captain of Vessel to carry his Letters to the Post-Office and order the Collector not to enter the Vessel till a Receipt is brought from the Post-Master, yet Nothing of this is regarded here:[1] The Moment a Vessel comes in, the Letters are seized by Force, and carried to the Coffee-House, where they are cried out, and delivered even before Mr. Colden's[2] or my Face, and the Collector durst not, or will not refuse to enter any: I spoke to the Surveyor General and to the Collector[3] about it, but could get no Satisfactory Answer: *They are,* I should have said, *we are* all afraid of the Populace—for the Tail is where the Head should be: The Spirit of Independance is too prevalent, it does not subside much, and but little real Gratitude appears yet. The Assembly both here and at New Jersey sit this Day, and perhaps they may remove

9. Such an act, "An Act for repealing certain Duties, in the British Colonies and Plantations . . . and for further encouraging, regulating, and securing, several Branches of the Trade of this Kingdom, and the British Dominions in America" (6 Geo. III, c. 52), passed Parliament in 1766. It allowed foreign sugars to be stored in American ports without the payment of duties, if they were re-exported within a year.

1. Parker had complained of the violation of the Post Office Act of 1765 in his letter of May 6, 1766; above, p. 266.

2. Alexander Colden (above, VI, 113 n) was postmaster at New York as well as surveyor of the Customs there.

3. These officials were, respectively, Charles Steuart and Andrew Elliot. See above, XII, 228 n.

some of the Prejudices subsisting—Mean while I must sing small. I have no Work, my Tools all worn out or rather destroyed, and I not able to purchase, now, or even help myself: Whether my *ill-Nature*, of which I am accused of having a great deal, or my *good Nature*, of which I have but little, hath brought these Calamitous Circumstances on me, must be left to the World to judge here, and to my Maker to punish me for hereafter: However, I never had any Reason to doubt that the good Providence of God, which has hitherto preserved me, will now leave me: I have had your Favours at Times, which I always endeavoured to retain a grateful Sense of: I have met with many Crosses and Adversities, whether they proceed from my *ill Nature*, or not, I shall not determine: Before I had any Friends or Favour from any, I lived, I owed no body, nor wronged any. I did work, I could work, and I was always resolved to work, The greatest Troubles I ever met with might make me fretful and waspish, but they never shall make me *unjust* nor *idle:* I can Struggle thro' Misfortunes, and brave Adversity itself, but unkind Returns of Friends, or those I thought so, and have been friendly to, cuts me deep. The Losses from Heaven or Accident, of which I have had as many as my Neighbours, neither dejects or dismays me, but it seems hard to see other Persons eat, drink and go well in Cloaths, with my Sweat and Blood, and I in real Want my self: This you may call *Envy*, or what ill-Names it may deserve, but its a Trial few can patiently bear. I will try to do it.

I am now come to this City, in Conformity to the Injunctions of the Post-Master General.[4] The same Duty that I have hitherto done in the General Post-Office, I continue to do: If there be any different or peculiar Service, Method, or Transactions for me to do on that Head, or Matter or Conduct different, required of me, I shall be very glad to know it, and if in my Power to do it, shall comply: Whatever I know to be my Duty in that Office, I strive to do, but I may be ignorant of some part of it: Mr. Colden is my Superior in the Custom-House, whatever he may be in the Post-Office, and I never assumed any Authority over him, tho' I have perhaps often faulted his Conduct. Indeed, I have sometimes

---

4. In the winter of 1765 Parker had learned that post-office officials in Great Britain expected him to move to New York or lose his position as comptroller. See above, XII, 89–90.

thought he has been above his true Business, and assumed more than was consistent with his Duty, but he is a Worthy Man I believe: He enjoys other Offices of good Value, and being much on the Gentleman-Order, does not give that Attendance in the Post-Office that the Publick expects or desires, tho' he has a Right I believe to do it; that is, he will not attend at all Hours, but only at such as are or may be called Office Hours: He keeps two Clerks, but they will not attend at all Times, The Merchants I have heard complain of him, but whether justly or not, I can't farther determine. What ever Money I get in, I send to Mr. Foxcroft, from whom doubtless you hear particularly; and any Orders or Directions I receive from him, I endeavour strictly to obey.

I must touch again a little on B. Mecom:[5] I have lately had some Letters pass'd between us: for till lately very few pass'd; tho' I frequently press him, to see if it be possible to move him; He lives Still in the House that is yet Holt's, and I hear has paid him no Rent: The Trial of that Affair is not yet determined,[6] but I am told, it is to be done the following August, when Holt is to go up there: I have never interfered in that Dispute, as I am a Party as it were concerned I wish it was determined, because if there was any Thing left, I would try to get something. But this was not what I purposed when I began upon Mecom's Affair. The Thing was, I suppose Col. Hunter may justly come upon me, for half the Profits of that Printing-Office ever since I took the Possession of it: now two years. Now, tho' I have never received one Farthing from Mecom, yet upon making me full Satisfaction, and a Settlement for my Part there in the former Time. I am willing he should have his Dues: The Books and Stationary, that I left there, and for which I had given you Bond for, and paid you Interest for near upon 7 Years I have never been paid for, nor any Account rendered: tho' the very Interest of them, would be nearly equal to what I should get of Mecom, if he paid me, which I think he never will: On the Whole, unless I have some Relief some where, which I can't at

5. Benjamin Mecom had been a subject of Parker's complaints throughout 1765 and 1766.

6. On BF's orders, transmitted to Jared Ingersoll, Dec. 19, 1763, a suit was brought against John Holt for debts due the post office from his tenure as postmaster at New Haven; in January 1764 Holt's house and property there were attached in connection with this suit. See above, x, 402–3 n; McAnear, "Parker versus Holt," pp. 82 n, 201.

present conceive, should I keep it entire, I shall be a very great Loser for the whole Printing Office there now as it stands is not worth £200 our Money, the Business there being sunk, and the Letters worn out, some more and some less than others: [*In the margin, keyed to approximately this point:* With regard to the printing Material at New Haven, if Col. Hunter or his Substitute, will do me the Justice in settling and paying me according to the Tenor of the Articles, he shall have my Half for £90 York Money, or I will allow £90 for his Half, which he pleases, only settled and cleared first, is all I want: and had rather sell for £90, than buy.] I hardly think Benny will make both Ends meet, even were I to give it him, and his Rent into the Bargain, Whether Holt made any Thing by it, when he had 3 Times the Work that Mecom has, is not for me to say, as I can get no Accounts from him, but Green having a Paper at Hartford, and his Brother one at New-London,[7] as it were Split all the Business there to pieces. Indeed, Living of all kinds here seems so much altered, and the Business of printing so small a Demand, that I have now been here Six Weeks, and I have not had the Proposal of one Job, or so much as a single Advertisement. Indeed, it will cost me and my Hands two Months work to get the Office to rights, as the whole is in wretched Order worse than a Heap of Pye, and one Half of it battered to pieces; so that unless I get some new Letter, which I am not able to do, I shall never make any great Hand of it here: However, I may fret at it, I do not dispair: for if it please God to give me Life and Health, I shall never be afraid of a Subsistance one Way or other, and a Door may open, that I see nothing of yet.

As you propose to return this Summer, I heartily wish you a safe Voyage of it. It is probable, that it will be needless for me to write any more to you there, As you may be set off before any more comes: I have told you, I took the Things you sent for Mr. Hughes, I opened the Shop, and have advertised in Holt's Paper, but exclusive of a few Things that Mr. Hughes took of me, I have not sold but one single blank Book, now six Weeks: Trade in general is dull, but of Books and Stationary sellers, there are so many here, that a poor Beginner stands no Chance at all. And so many better sorted that there is little Inducement for any to come to me.

7. Timothy Green (1737–1796), younger brother of Thomas, mentioned above, published the *New-London Connecticut Gazette.*

I apprehend you will be now weary of reading this, if you read it all at once, as I am almost of writing: But as the Jersey Assembly is sitting and I purpose to go to Amboy next Week early, and may not come back till the Packet sails, I chuse to finish before I go: If I come back sooner, and have any Thing material, I may write again, tho' I don't imagine it, of any Importance, especially if it should be mixed with any further complaining, which I could wish to have Room to avoid, as it can be no Pleasure to you: I thank God, my Son is almost recovered of his long Sickness, and I hope begins to think seriously of the Station he Stands in, in the World; his Afflictions and Sickness has been long and grievous, but I hope they will work in him the Effects, I believe, a gracious Providence designs when it sends such: My Daughter has had a good deal also of Sickness, but we are now all Stirring about. With all our humble Salutations, remain Your most obliged Servant

JAMES PARKER.

From [Alexander] Small[8]   AL: American Philosophical Society

June 11th 1766

Mr. Small presents his Complements to Dr. Franklin, is glad Sir John Pringle[9] is to be happy in so agreable a Fellow Traveller, and begs leave to trouble him with the inclosed Letter and Bill, in case they take Hague in their way. If not the Dr. may burn them. Mr. Johnson[1] is a very polite Man, and will, I dare say, be very ready to do Sir John and Dr. Franklin any Service in his power. Mr. Small sincerely wishes them a pleasant Journey, and happy return.

Endorsed: June 11th. 1766   Birmingham

8. The endorsement, added at the bottom of the note, possibly in BF's hand, suggests by the word "Birmingham" that the writer was William Small, now resident in that city; above, XI, 480. The handwriting of the body of the note, however, is distinctly different from that in letters signed by William Small, and is very close to, if not identical with, that of letters by Alexander Small, the Scots army surgeon in London (above, IX, 110 n), who was on terms of familiarity with both BF and John Pringle.

9. Dr. John Pringle had just been created a baronet, June 5, 1766.

1. Not identified, but possibly an army surgeon attached to the Scottish regiment stationed at The Hague.

To George Read

MS not found; reprinted from William T. Read, *Life and Correspondence of George Read* (Philadelphia, 1870), p. 24.

Dear Sir,   London, June 12th 1766.

I received your letter of April 14th,[2] and immediately made an application in your favor. It will be a pleasure to me if it succeeds. But the Treasury have so many to provide for that we must not be surprised if we are disappointed. My regards to your good mother,[3] and believe me, with sincere regard, your assured friend and most humble servant,   B. FRANKLIN

George Read, Esquire.

From Thomas Wharton   ALS: American Philosophical Society

My Dear friend   Philada. June 12. 1766

I wrote thee on the 9th[4] which sent by Express after Capt. Egdon, but He not reaching the Vessell have deliverd them to Capt. Falkner, by whom thou'l receive this.[5]

We on the 10th. had the Pleasure of finding thou had wrote a Letter to the Commitee of Correspondence,[6] which at once Stoppd the Virulence of the P--ry P--ty and gave them reason to Apprehend, that thy great and Unwearied Endeavours, would, to their great Mortification, and our Joy, be crownd with Success.

I have enclosd thee, a News Paper of this date, in which thou'l find, that We rejoice, but not in Such a Manner as can Give our Ennemies a handle Against Us, and that my Friend is not forgot by a respectable Part of the People, I mean the Free and Independant in Judgement.[7]

2. See above, pp. 246–7.

3. Mary Howell Read (d. 1784).

4. Not found.

5. *Pa. Gaz.*, June 12, 1766, reported the clearance of the *Ellis*, Capt. Samuel Egdon; on June 19 it reported the clearance of the *Elizabeth*, Capt. Nathaniel Falconer.

6. For BF's letter to the committee, April 12, 1766, see above, pp. 236–40.

7. *Pa. Gaz.*, June 12, 1766, reported that on June 4 "a large Number of reputable Inhabitants of Philadelphia" celebrated the King's birthday with a mammoth public dinner on the banks of the Schuykill River followed by a

Hinton Brown and Doctr. Fothergill have wrote to Jas. Pemberton, a Letter, wherein they Express such sentiments of thy Integrety, Joind with the Important services thou has renderd to this Continent, as will (if possible) more Endear thee to the Freemen Amongst Us;[8] Which We intend to Publish.

Have also sent thee *an Address &c.*[9] which is said to be wrote by John Dickinson.

The Piece wrote by Doctr. Fothergill relative to the Stamp Act, does Him great Honor, being by Us Esteem'd a well done Performance.[1] I remain thy real friend   THO WHARTON

Addressed: For / Benjamin Franklin Esqr / Deputy Post Master General of No America / In / Craven Street / London / per favour of / Capt Falkner

Endorsed: Mr Thos Wharton June 12. 66

To Deborah Franklin   ALS: American Philosophical Society[2]

This letter is of interest because it contains the first specific information about Franklin's trip to Germany.[3] During his first mission to England he had made a habit of traveling to various parts of the British Isles in the summer for health and pleasure, and now he was renewing the practice, accompanied by his friend, John Pringle, to the spa of Bad Pyrmont in the principality of Waldeck-Pyrmont in the north central part of present-day West Germany. Information about this trip is sparse, so that the gaps in the chronology presented here are unavoidable:

---

fireworks display. Seventeen toasts were drunk at the dinner, one to "our worthy and faithful Agent, Doctor Franklin."

8. For Fothergill's letter of Feb. 27, 1766, refuting the accusation that BF had been a promoter of the Stamp Act, see above, p. 261 n.

9. Dickinson's *An Address to the Committee of Correspondence in Barbados* (Phila., 1766), an attack on the Stamp Act and a remonstrance to the Barbadians for not opposing it.

1. Probably a reference to Fothergill's *Considerations Relative to the North American Colonies* (London, 1765).

2. Also in APS is another almost identical ALS marked at the top by BF "Copy. Origl per Packet." It lacks the address page and has a few unimportant differences in phraseology.

3. A short but useful discussion of this journey is in Hans Walz, "Benjamin Franklin in Hannover 1766," *Hannoverische Geschichtsblätter,* Neue Folge Band 21, Heft ½, pp. 61–5.

June 15 :[4] Franklin and Pringle leave London.
June 22–July 5?:[5] The two men take the waters at Bad Pyrmont.
July 9: Franklin and Pringle visit the Royal Library at Hanover. While at Hanover they visit the scientist Johann Friedrich Hartman and observe him performing electrical experiments.[6]
July 19–21: Franklin and Pringle at Göttingen; both are formally admitted as members of the Royal Academy there, Pringle having been elected in the spring.[7]
July 22?–August 16: The two men travel through Cassel to Frankfort and to Mainz, then down the Rhine to Holland and on home to London.[8]

My dear Child,   London, June 13. 1766
  Mrs. Stevenson has made up a Parcel of Haberdashery for you, which will go in Capt. Robinson.[9] She will also send you another Cloak in the room of that we suppose lost in Capt. Kerr.[1]
  I wrote to you in Capt. Sparks,[2] that I had been very ill lately. I am now nearly well again, but feeble. To-morrow I set out with my Friend Dr. Pringle (now Sir John)[3] on a Journey to Pyrmont,

4. In the present letter BF speaks of his date of departure as "To-morrow," i.e., June 14. In a note in APS, however, in which he listed the dates of his trip to Germany and his French trips of 1767 and 1769 he gave his departure as June 15, a dating supported by a letter from William Strahan to David Hall, June 14, 1766, *PMHB*, X (1886), 228.
  5. These dates are conjectural, since there is no information about how long BF and Pringle stayed at the spa.
  6. Visitors' Book, Hannover Landesbibliothek, entry of July 9, 1766. *Göttingische Anzeigen von Gelehrten Sachen* (Göttingen, 1766), part II, 921; Hartman to BF, Oct. 1, 1767, APS.
  7. Beatrice M. Victory, *Benjamin Franklin and Germany* (in *Americana Germanica*, No. 21, Univ. of Pa., 1915), pp. 48, 53; below, p. 345.
  8. Though the travelers certainly visited Trier and Cologne, their itinerary during this part of their journey is not wholly clear; see below, p. 384 n.
  9. *Pa. Gaz.*, Oct. 2, 1766, reported the arrival at Philadelphia of the *Prince George*, Capt. James Robinson.
  1. *Pa. Gaz.*, April 10, 17, 1766, reported the loss of the snow *Nancy*, Captain Kerr, from Bristol, on April 6 on Hereford Bar, "about four leagues to the Northward of Cape-May."
  2. London shipping seems to have been very slow at this time; *Pa. Gaz.* did not report the arrival of the brig *Mary and Elizabeth*, Capt. J. Sparks, until the issue of Aug. 21, 1766. The letter from BF to DF that it carried has not been found.
  3. Pringle was made a baronet on June 3, 1766. *London Chron.*, June 3–5, 1766.

where he goes to drink the Waters; but I hope more from the Air and Exercise, having been us'd, as you know, to make a Journey once a Year, the Want of which last Year has, I believe, hurt me, so that tho' I was not quite to say sick, I was often ailing last Winter and thro' this Spring. We must be back at farthest in Eight Weeks, as my Fellow Traveller is the Queen's Physician, and has Leave for no longer as she will then be near her Time.[4] I purpose to leave him at Pyrmont, and visit some of the principal Cities nearest to it, and call for him again when the Time of our Return draws nigh. My Love to Sally, &c. I am, my dear Debby, Your affectionate Husband   B FRANKLIN

Addressed: To / Mrs Franklin / Philadelphia / via New York / per Packet / B Free FRANKLIN

From Joseph Galloway   ALS: American Philosophical Society

Dear Sir   Philada. June 16th. 1766
    I wrote to you, by Captains Falkner and Egdon last Week,[5] Since which I have received your Favor of the 12th. of April.[6] I now do, what I ought to have done long before, Sincerely Thank you, for the frequent Intelligences which I have received on publick Affairs. And altho a Continuance of that Favor will ever be very grateful to me, yet I am not so unreasonable as to desire, you will in the midst of your very important Engagements, take the Trouble of answering all my long and tedious Scrawls. They were intended to give you Information of what passed here, not to draw particular Answers which must engross too much of that Time, which you have ever employed for the Interest of your Country and the Benefit of Mankind.
    I have Sent to Mr. Hall an Extract of your letter which justly Characterises those Worthy Men now at the Head of public Affairs. I pray God they may long Continue in their Stations. Noth-

4. The Queen gave birth to a daughter, Charlotte Augusta Matilda (1766–1828), on September 29. In 1794 the princess married Prince Friedrich Wilhelm Karl of Würtemberg, who succeeded his father the same year and was made King of Würtemberg by Napoleon in 1806. *DNB.*
5. For the departures of Falconer and Egdon, see above, p. 313 n.
6. See above, pp. 242–3 n.

ing has been or shall be wanting in my Power, to impress the Minds of the People here with a just Sense of their Integrity Prudence and Justice. For this Purpose, I have Inserted many Extracts of Letters from Time to Time in the Publick Papers, mentioning their Virtues and Good Disposition towards America.[7]

It greatly revives the People here, to find, by your Letter to the Committee of Correspondence,[8] that our Petitions for a Royal Government, will be proceeded on, as soon as the general Affairs of the Colonies are Settled. The Proprietor T.P. in the Winter, wrote so positive and circumstantial a Letter respecting it's being laid aside, forever,[9] that it greatly dismay'd them, till your Letter to the Contrary was made known. This rendered them more easy.

I do not think the House will proceed to expel the Ch. J.,[1] but from their present Temper, I think they will transmit his Character to posterity, on record, in a Light which will not reflect much Honor on his Children. At our last Sitting he positively charged you, with being one of the greatest Enemies to the Repeal of the Stamp Act, in England, and that he coud prove it. But this happening in the Midst of a warm Debate, respecting the resolve about granting Requisitions to the Crown, and the Obstructions thereto occasioned by Proprietary Instructions, the Speaker called to Order, and so the Matter drop'd for that Time. But this infamous and Groundless Charge has filled the Members as well as the People out of Doors, with so much resentment, that they all Cry out, "it is Time, his Calumnies had met with the Censures they Deserve". And as the House is determined to resume the Matter in September next I wish you woud Favor me, if you Approve, with your Ex-

7. It seems likely that Galloway was responsible for inserting an extract of a letter from London of Feb. 25, 1766, in the May 8 issue of the *Gazette,* wherein the "present Ministry" was praised for its "Steadiness, Ability, and Application," and various individuals, including BF, were highly praised for their efforts.

8. For BF's letter to the committee, April 12, 1766, see above, pp. 236–40.

9. A reference to Thomas Penn's letter to his nephew, Gov. John Penn, Nov. 30, 1765, in which he related that the Privy Council had postponed consideration of the Assembly's petition for royal government "sine die, that is (to use my Lord Presidents own expression) for ever and ever." See above, pp. 179–80.

1. William Allen; for his attack on BF, discussed in this paragraph, see above, p. 295. There is no record of the House having pursued the matter in its September session, as Galloway believed it would.

amination in the House of Commons by the Earliest Opportunity;[2] Perhaps it woud be well to have it Certified by the Clerk.

I am greatly rejoiced at the intended Regulations of the American Commerce, and particularly at the Design of making Dominica a Free Port.[3] The most extensive Advantages will flow from the taking off every Incumbrance on the Trade with the Spaniards. And perhaps will in some Small Degree relieve us from the Distress we suffer, for want of a Medium of Trade of our Own. But I fear it will not effectually do it, as the Gold and Silver we may Smuggle from the Spaniard, will like the Birds of Passage Continue but a Small Time among us, and take their Flight to the Mother Country in Lieu of her Manufactures. A Currency of our Own, permanent and fixt in its Value, seems therefore Necessary to our Commerce, and will inable us with less reserve to Ship Home the Money we receive from Abroad. I wish the Colonies coud be gratified in this Matter this Year, because it would enable them to pay not only their Colony debts with more Punctuality as well as those to Brittain—which at present they are really not able to do, without breaking up a Multitude of Good Livers and reputable Families. But my Dear Friend, so much has been done, for us, this Year, That our Hearts ought to be filled with Gratitude instead of Murmurs. And what remains to be done shoud be waited for with a Decent and respectful Patience.

Powel not being Arrived, I have not received the Power from Governor Dennys Executors—When it comes [nothing] shall be wanting on my Part, to fulfil the Trust they shall repose in me with our Friend Mr. Hughes.[4]

It may not be amiss to inform you, That The Proprietary Party give out, that they have Assurances from the Proprietors, that they never will Consent to a Surrender of the Government, without

2. For the transmission and publication of this document, see above, pp. 125–7.

3. BF mentioned this and efforts to repeal the Currency Act of 1764, discussed later in this paragraph, in his letter to the Assembly's Committee of Correspondence, April 12, 1766; above, pp. 236–40.

4. Powell, a ship captain, was apparently bringing Galloway and John Hughes power of attorney from the executors of Col. William Denny, the former governor of Pa., who died toward the end of 1765. Galloway and Hughes offered Denny's house and property for sale on Jan. 1, 1767. Above, XI, 426 n; *Pa. Gaz.*, Jan. 1, 1767.

giving their Friends 12 Months Notice, that they may provide for themselves, I suppose, by obtaining All their Commissions during Good Behaviour, which I conclude will not be agreable to the Crown. I am, as ever, my Dear Friend yours Affectionately

JOS. GALLOWAY

Benja. Franklin Esqr.

Addressed: To / Benjamin Franklin Esquire / Craven Street / London

From John Read[5]   ALS: American Philosophical Society

Dear Brother   Philada: 17th June 1766

Inclosed I send You a Copy of a letter to reinstate me again into the Kings service how long it may last I know not I have agreed to go to Execute that business, under the disadvantages ariseing from the great Expence of traveling in hopes I may be allowed something at London for former Expencies as per my letter to You of the 21st May which I hope You have received.[6] If You can serve me it Will lay me under great obligations to You.

Mr. Franks here tels me he wrote to Mr. Franks one of the Contractors in London very warmly recomending me to him,[7] to get me apointed Commissary for the South West Districkt otherwise cauld the Pennsilvania Districkt and If posoble to Obtaine rank in the Army [*torn:* such as p]uts one upon a futing [footing] to do business with Officers, &ca.

5. DF's brother. He had served as a wagonmaster under Braddock in 1755 (above, VI, 221–2) and as deputy commissary under Bouquet later in the war. DF reported to BF early in August 1765 that he had returned from New York to Philadelphia; above, XII, 226.

6. Neither the letter enclosed with this one nor the letter to BF of May 21 has been found.

7. David Franks (1720–1793) and William Plumsted (above, XII, 45 n, 240 n) had been mercantile partners in Philadelphia until Plumsted's death in 1765. They had acted as agents for the London contractors for army supplies, Colebrook, Nesbitt & Franks. A member of the London firm was Moses Franks (1718–1789), brother of the Philadelphia merchant. Their father was the New York merchant Jacob Franks. There is much scattered material on this family in Edwin Wolf, 2nd, and Maxwell Whiteman, *The History of the Jews of Philadelphia from Colonial Times to the Age of Jackson* (Phila., 1957).

I have wrote several letters formerly[8] but Supose You have much other buseness upon Hands but should be glad to have a line or two to Know if any aplications have been made or If it be posoble any can be made. Mr. Leake[9] thinks a frind in England could Easely get me upon the Establisment Espetialy for One who has served so long and Don so much publick business as I have.[1]

Mr. Allin has Roundly Asserted and that in the House that You was the great Cause of Bringing on the Stam[p] Act, it makes a good Deal of noise. I hear a Number of Your Frinds and some that loves You very well say they Hope and wish You will fall upon some method of Convincing the Publick of the falshood of his Assertions.[2] Docter Smith has Said Somthing in religous Polliticks that has greatly Iretated the Prisbetearen Clerge the Sinod at New York have nominated Some Wits of the laiety to handle him it relats to the haveing of an American Bishop of which Smith has great Hopes of the apointment.[3] I am Dear Sir Your Loving and Efechonate Brother   JOHN READ

Addressed: To / Benjamin Franklin Esqr: / Craven Street / Lond[on]

Endorsed: Bror J. Read June 17. 1766 Wants Rank &c

8. None of Read's earlier letters to BF has been found, but BF acknowledged the receipt of one in the fall of 1765; above, XII, 360.

9. Almost certainly Robert Leake (*c.*1720–1774) commissary general for stores for the British Army in America.

1. No reply by BF to this request has been found and the editors have discovered no evidence as to the success of Read's application for army rank.

2. Several letters from Galloway, Wharton, and others earlier in the year had reported Allen's charges against BF and the "noise" they made. The circulation and later publication of BF's Examination before the House of Commons provided a helpful response to the attacks.

3. To a large degree Read's account here represents rumor and gossip rather than the solid facts of "religious Polliticks" at the time he was writing. Certainly Provost William Smith was active in the effort to get Anglican bishops appointed for the colonies, and there were suspicions—not wholly groundless, perhaps—among both Anglicans and Presbyterians that he himself hoped to be named a bishop if and when such prelates should be established. On the other side there was a considerable effort to effect a union between Presbyterians and Congregationalists—partly to strengthen the opposition to the Church of England—but at the Presbyterian Synod of May 1766 there appears to have been no move to nominate "Some Wits of the laiety to handle" Provost Smith or to attack him personally in any other manner. On some aspects of the situation at this time, see Carl Bridenbaugh, *Mitre and Sceptre* (N.Y., 1962), pp. 266–7, 271–4.

From George Wythe[4]

ALS (mutilated):[5] American Philosophical Society

Sir.   [June 23, 1766]

If our attorney gen[eral shall become speake]r of the house of
burgesses, and thereby h[is post is vacant, as in] all probability
will be the case, the govern[or will propose me] to succeed him;
and that recommendation, I [am very sure] will be more effectual,
were some of those great per[sons] to whom it must be addressed,
to know that such a promotion would be in any degree pleasing
to doctor Franklin.[6] If you incline to honour me with your patronage in this competition, you will perhaps be partly instrumental in producing that rare phaenomenon a contented mind, at least
in the article of fortune; and you shall find an exception to that
observation of Tacitus: "Beneficia eo usque laeta sunt, dum videntur
exsolvi posse: uti multum antevenere, pro gratia odium redditur."[7]
I am Sir, Your most obedient servant.   G. WYTHE.

Doctor Franklin.

Endorsed: Mr Wyth June 23. 1766

4. George Wythe (1726–1806) was an eminent Virginia lawyer, statesman,
and patriot. He was a signer of the Declaration of Independence and held the
first professorship of law in an American college, being appointed to that
position at William and Mary in 1779 through Jefferson's influence. *DAB.*
He and BF had almost certainly met each other in Williamsburg in 1756 and
again in 1763.

5. A large tear at the top of the sheet has caused the loss of the date line
and some words in each of the first five lines of the text. The date is supplied
from the endorsement and the missing words supplied conjecturally from a
consideration of the context.

6. Attorney General Peyton Randolph (*c.*1721–1775) became speaker of the
House of Burgesses in November 1766. As Wythe anticipated, Gov. Francis
Fauquier recommended him to the Board of Trade and to Lord Shelburne,
secretary of state for the Southern Department, as Randolph's successor, but
Randolph's younger brother, John, received the position in 1767. What part,
if any, BF played in these negotiations is not known. See *Board of Trade
Journal,* 1764–67, pp. 369–70, 418, and *DAB* (under both John and Peyton
Randolph).

7. "Obligations are pleasant to one, as long as it seems possible to repay
them; where they much exceed [that point], hatred is the return instead
of gratitude." Tacitus, *Annales,* Book IV, c. 18.

From William Franklin

ALS: American Philosophical Society

Honoured Sir   Perth-Amboy June 27, 1766

I wrote to you a few Days ago by the Packet, since which I have receiv'd Mr. Kearny's Opinion on the State of the Case sent over by Sir Alexr. Dick, and now enclose it. I sent you Mr. Smyth's Answer to the Queries before.[8]

I sent to you by Capt. Falconer[9] for some Table China, but as I have since purchas'd some from Capt. Wms. who is going to England which match mine extremely well,[1] I should be glad you would not send any over, unless you have already bought it. I must beg you to send me over two more Silver Bottle Sliders to match those you sent before, and a Silver Cross for the Table of a middling Size.[2] [I have] bought some Silver Salts of Capt. Wms. and he has promised to get me a Pair more in England to match these, and deliver them to you. If he should please to pay him the Cost on my Account. I am likewise in Want of Tea, and should be glad you would speak to Miss Smith to send me Nine Pound of the best Green Tea, in 3 lb. Canisters, and pay her for it.[3] I'll send you a

---

8. In 1765 BF had sent WF a letter and memorandum, transmitted to him by Sir Alexander Dick on behalf of his fellow Scotsman, John Swinton, requesting information about lands in New Jersey and Pa. to which he, Swinton, believed he was entitled; see above, XII, 156–7, 197. WF had submitted Swinton's case to two eminent N.J. lawyers, Philip Kearny (1721–1775) and chief justice Frederick Smyth (the Mr. Smyth may possibly have been John Smyth of Perth Amboy, however), had obtained their opinions and, as he here states, sent them to his father in London. See 1 *N.J. Arch.*, x, 420–2; XXXIV, 281–3; N.J. Hist. Soc. *Colls.*, x, 203–4; W.A. Whitehead, *Contributions to the Early History of Perth Amboy* (N.Y., 1856), pp. 90–1.

9. *Pa. Gaz.*, June 19, 1766, reported the clearance of the *Elizabeth*, Capt. Nathaniel Falconer, for London.

1. Capt. John Williams of the Engineers advertised in both *Pa. Gaz.* and *Pa. Jour.*, July 3, 1766, the sale of his household goods, plate, china, and other effects.

2. On Aug. 19, 1766, BF paid £4 14s. 6d. for "Bottle Stands" for WF. An earlier entry, May 29, 1766, recorded the payment of £1 4s. for a "Dish Cross" for WF, but no record of a further purchase of such an article for WF appears in BF's accounts. Journal, 1764–1776, pp. 8, 9; Ledger, 1764–1776, pp. 7, 9, 20. Simply described, a "dish cross" is a stand consisting primarily of two crossed bars raised on feet. At their intersection is a spirit lamp to keep warm the contents of a dish placed on the stand.

3. BF does not record paying Miss Susannah Smith for nine pounds of tea

Bill as soon as I return. Please to let me know how young Temple does, and his present Situation.[4]

The Assembly are upon the Point of breaking up, and I am excessively hurried.[5]

Sally and Betsy[6] join in Duty with Your dutiful Son

WM. FRANKLIN

Endorsed: Billy. Amboy June 27. 66
Sends Kearney's Opinion on Swinton's Affair.
Wants
A Silver Table Cross
Two Bottle Sliders
9 lb of Tea.—in 3 lb Canisters

From [Henry] Hope   LS: University of Pennsylvania Library

Gentlemen   from home Wednesday. [June? 1766][7]

We humbly ask your pardon for not waiting on you ourselves, if it had been possible for either of us, it would not have been ommitted; That however we may enjoy the happiness of your agreable Company, we kindly begg the favour of Seing you att dinner to morrow, your cordiall acceptance will very much

for WF until May 23, 1767, the charge being £5 14s. Journal, 1764–1776, p. 12; Ledger, 1764–1776, pp. 9, 28.

4. This appears to be the first mention of William Temple Franklin, WF's illegitimate son, in the Franklin correspondence, although in his Journal, Nov. 9, 1765, BF records paying Mr. Small, probably his friend, Dr. Alexander Small, £10 10s. for inoculating the boy. Journal, 1764–1776, p. 5; Ledger, 1764–1775, pp. 7, 9.

5. The N.J. Assembly adjourned June 28, 1766, having been in session since June 12. 1 *N.J. Arch.*, IX, 555–63, 567; XVII, 448–53.

6. BF's daughter and daughter-in-law.

7. On their way to or on their return from Germany this summer, BF and Sir John Pringle received "Civilities" from the Hopes of Amsterdam, one of Europe's great merchant families; see below, pp. 386–7. This dinner invitation, probably from Henry Hope, a Boston-born member of the family, may therefore have been written at either the beginning or the end of the trip; it is placed here at the earlier of the two possible dates.

oblige Gentlemen, Your most obedient humble Servants

[THE?] HOPES[8]

We dine att 2 aClock

Addressed: To Benjamin Franklyn Esqr

Endorsed: Messrs Hope Amsterdam

From Samuel Wharton

ALS (incomplete): American Philosophical Society

[June 1766][9]

[*First part missing*] That the Proprietors must have lost their Interest, Otherwise Mr. F, could not have got, that Obnoxious Man, John Hughs appointed[1]—Indeed! To do them Justice, I verily think, They believe it is all Over, with Them, for your Old Acquaintance Dr. Thomas Bond told Me last Night, They were extremely Mortified and disappointed. God Grant! This may Only, be a preparatory *Shock*, To the grand One, Which you, I ardently hope have secured for Them.

I am straitened very much in Point of Time, and therefore cannot send you the Particulars of the Conference, held by Mr. Croghan at Fort Pitt, The beginning of this Month; But you may

8. The signature is virtually a stylized scrawl. Were it not for the endorsement the deciphering of any part of the name would be nearly hopeless.

9. Dated thus because of the mention in the second paragraph here of George Croghan's conference with the Indians at Fort Pitt "The Beginning of this Month." The conference having ended, Croghan left for the west on June 18, 1766. Samuel Wharton, who had been at Pittsburgh at the time, was back in Philadelphia sometime before July 5. *Pa. Gaz.*, July 10, 1766, carried a brief statement of the success of the Indian conference. Alexander C. Flick, ed., *The Papers of Sir William Johnson*, V (Albany, 1927), 304; Nicholas B. Wainwright, *George Croghan Wilderness Diplomat* (Chapel Hill, [1959]), p. 233.

1. This passage harks back in part to events of the spring of 1765. When Grenville asked BF rather than Thomas Penn to suggest someone to be stamp distributor for Pa., it was believed on both sides of the ocean that this action showed BF as having greater influence with the government than the Proprietor had. See above, XII, 146 n; Morgan, *Stamp Act Crisis*, p. 246. What had been the case with Grenville would presumably be even more so now with Rockingham. As to Hughes, by this time his ineptitude and tactlessness in responding to attacks on his behavior had made him "Obnoxious" even to some members of his own political party.

depend upon his having settled the Peace, upon the most secure Conditions and That He will safely reach the Illonois and conciliate the Minds of the Indians, in that Neighbourhood. The particulars of the Treaty will, dubtless, be forwarded by the General to the Ministry and Therefore there is the less Necessity of my troubling you, with it.

The Post is just going off, Therefore I must abruptly conclude, with my best Wishes for your Success and a Continuation of your Health. I am Dear Sir, with sincere Regard your Obliged and affectionate Friend   SAML WHARTON

From James Parker   ALS: American Philosophical Society

Honoured Sir,   New York, July 1. 1766

You had a long Letter from me by the Packet a Week or two ago,[2] which I hope you will have received, and referring to that, I shall have the less to enlarge upon here: The Assembly of New-Jersey are broke up, and I hear Govr. Franklin is this Day at Newark, Miss Sally with him, but I don't learn that they are coming over here. The Commotions excited by the Stamp-Act are not yet quite subsided: We have just now heared of some Rioters about Lands between Albany and the New England Governments having been disturbed, the Lives of Some were lost on both sides, but the Particulars or the real Occasion I have not yet learnt:[3] I told you before that Letters were still continued to be openly delivered at the Coffee-House: nor is it safe yet to make Opposition to it: I informed you also, that I had given a Certificate from the Governor here, of his qualifying me into the Office of Land-Waiter, to Mr. Stewart, the Surveyor General, who has transmitted it home to the Commissioners of the Customs, and I have exercised it ever since. There is not a Day since, (but when

2. Above, pp. 300–12.

3. Earlier troubles between landlords and tenants in New York had a history of at least a decade, and violence broke out (and continued to do so) from time to time. The best general treatment is Irving Mark, *Agrarian Conflicts in Colonial New York 1711–1775* (N.Y., 1940). On the disturbances on and near the Van Rensselaer estates and in Dutchess County to which Parker refers here, see *ibid.*, pp. 131–55, and brief reports in *Pa. Gaz.*, July 10, 17, 1766.

I have been absent) but what I walk in that Exercise at least two Miles, and sometimes four: This City has increased in Length very much for Years past, and it is my peculiar Business to go from One End to the other every Day once or twice, and see that no Vessel load or unload without Permission &c. There is not the least Fee or Reward belonging to it, without being look'd upon with an evil Eye be a Reward: tho' that is no Discouragement to me, my highest Ambition being to do my Duty in whatever Station it shall please God to call me, I know I fall Short in many Things: And tho' there seems to be a moderate Salary attending it, I am convinced I shall dearly earn the Pay:[4] which however, whilest Providence gives me Strength to do, I am no Way concerned; but God knows, if I am taken with the Gout, what I shall do, and I am threatned with it every Day. I grow old and feeble in Body, and Shall fall Short: I have been here now two Months, in which Time I have had my Health; but have neither sold in my Shop to the Amount of 20s. nor have I had as much printing Work, as would come to 40s. more, exclusive of some Blanks for the Shop: I shall wait two Months longer, in Hopes of getting some Settlement with Holt,[5] tho' I begin to doubt much of his ever doing it, and I shall then be compelled to the Law, and perhaps get Nothing. I think I can say Holt has eat and drank my Sweat and Blood; but I endeavour to be resigned: I have been always ill natured and cross, but good Humour in such Fortune as mine, is like Patience in the Gout, much easier preach'd than practised: If lamenting Things past would do good, how would I cry, O God, why was I ever a Printer to be choused[6] and duped as I have been, why was I not a poor Labourer or Farmer, in which if I was choused or duped, I should not have had Sensations to resent it, but this I know is vain: I have Nothing left but to make the best of a bad Market, which had I but Strength equivalent to my Spirit, I should not be cast down in the least; but now in my old Age to be obliged to Struggle thro' Such Difficulties, seems hard: I believe

4. Later letters indicate Parker's uncertainty as to when and how he was to be paid.

5. Parker's letter of June 11, mentioned in the first sentence above, deals at such length with his trouble with Holt and Mecom, that editorial comment and further cross-referencing here seem quite superfluous.

6. To chouse: colloquially, to cheat or trick.

I have my Deservings, and try to practise the Patience I know it is my Duty to do: Every Day I now walk out my Round or Cruise, and by 11 or 12 o Clock come home, and fling myself into my Chair, scarce able to live. Judge you then the Comfort I feel from Rest; and this would be my Pleasure, did not my aching Bones convince me, I am drawing nigh to my great Change. Anxiety to leave the World as clear as I found it, without Injury to others, is the greatest of my Concern, And this I have long in Vain tried to be ready for, and can't but think had I but common Justice done me, from those I have most befriended and served, I might have done. In the Midst of all, I still have a strong Reliance on that Providence of God, which has so often delivered and supported me, and to whom, I try to have a chearful Resignation. No Prospect yet what Business in general may be in the printing Way: but my Tools are worn out, and I unable to get a Supply of new. I told you all Holt's Treachery, which I leave to Heaven to avenge: B. Mecom I told you also, I had less and less Hopes of: In the Post-Office, by his Accounts just come to Hand, there is a Ballance due of near £40, to the 6th of last April; tho' he pays a Rider (that to Hartford) £50, per An. and I imagined that would be almost all the Amount of his Office, but the £40, is above that in the whole, and I have continually press'd him for those Accounts, and the Ballance; those I have at last got, but the Ballance I fear; because I have wrote about my own Dues sundry Times very pressingly, and never could get one Penny. We have had some sharp Letters pass'd between us, but tho' I have Tried him, as the Seamen term it, upon every Quarter, I find it all as Vain, as washing the Blackmoor white: I threaten him, with removing him, that is taking away those Materials from him, but nothing can quicken his Motions any more than a dead Man's: What I shall do with him, I know not. It is hard for me, who can hardly keep myself above Water, under a Complication of Sickness, Infirmities and Wrongs, to support others also. Yet do I bear as quietly as I can every Thing, knowing that God has bore long with me: and that my Tresspasses are more against him, than those against me. The Office I yet Sustain in the Post-Office, I endeavour to execute to the best of my Power and Ability: and if any Thing more than I have hitherto done in it, be necessary or required, shall be glad to know it: That is now my chief Dependance, and whilst I have that, the others ill Usage Shall not make me despond: 'Tis true, I could wish, as Matters are circumstanced and obliged to live in this City, where every Thing is excessive high and dear, the Salaries attending that, or the Land-Waiter, were a little more adequate to the Expence of Living here: in one of which Mr. Foxcroft did tell me, he would use his Interest to obtain, as there are continual new Post Offices erecting, and much Writing to do; that almost my whole Time is taken up between the two; that I could have but little Time to attend other Business, if I had it, which as yet a while, I seem not to be in much Danger of; However I try to be as contented as I can.[7]

I suppose Mr. Foxcroft acquaints you with the General State of the Post-Office, whatever Money I get, I pay to him: which has been above £500, since I came to this City: Business is excessive dull in general throughout these Colonies, so that the Post-Office must be something affected, by such a State of Affairs: To what its owing to, I can't determine: Perhaps some may think it the Dregs of the Stamp-Act, but I rather think, that during the War, Money being plenty, Many abounded in Luxury, over-run the Constable, and thinking every Day alike, never thought a Day of Reckoning would come: and so Law-Suits and Ruins ensue. Apropo, Mr. Chew of New London, is reported to be near this State:[8] I have not been able to get many Accounts and no Money from him since you saw him at Philadelphia, tho' as he pays a Rider yearly, it is thought no great Matter can be behind, yet there is some Ballance due: I am trying to get a Settlement with him, and hope to accomplish it.

In the Ship, Capt. Davis, with whom I purpose to send this, comes many Passengers, possibly you may see some of them, or the Papers which will inform you of the publick News better than I can write: As you may probably be on the Preparations to return, I shall heartily pray God to send you a safe Passage, which is all I can do: With all our Complements remain Your most obliged Servant   JAMES PARKER

Addressed: For / Benjamin Franklin, Esqr / Craven-Street / London / per Capt. Davis

7. Foxcroft and BF did increase Parker's post-office salary by £20 later in this year.
8. See above, pp. 59–60.

From Sarah Broughton[9]   ALS: American Philosophical Society

Sir.   Philada. July 3 1766
    I hope you will pardon me as I am really sorry to find myself
Obliged to trouble you On this Occasion but as I have tryed every
Other way in my power and found them Enefectual I will not
doubt your Usuall Candor will plead My excuse and now to take
Up No More of your Usefull time I must inform you that I have
had An Account Running on with Mrs. Franklin for More than
Seven Years and which it Never was in My power to prevail on
her to settle till the last spring My Brother waited On her and
proposed two of our Neighbours should Examine the Affair. She
Consented and Choose one, and I another and they dertimined
that she was in My debt Thirty one pounds fourteen Shillings and
Nine pence Exclusive of a Bed which she bought of me Near two
Years Ago And Now Insists that I should take it Back. Her true
reason for this I know is because the price of feathers is fallen
from three Shillings and four pence to twenty pence a pound But
Notwithstanding the loss I must have been at I Agree'd to take it
Back in Case it was not Damaged. Now you'll Observe there Is
a Nighbour of Ours that had A mind for the Bed before Mrs.
Franklin bought it And Did look at it, And Now has by Mrs.
Franklins permission Reaxamined it And she Declares that it is
not now As good as it was at the time Mrs. Franklin had it. I then
wrote the inclosed Note[1] To Mrs. Franklin in hopes she would
send Me the Money which is seven pounds seven Shillings but she
sent me back the Note and sent Me for Answer that she Did not
know Me [and] that I might write to you she was An hege[hog.]
Now sir I Dont think her A hegehog but In reallity she has shot
a great Many Quills at Me but thank Heaven None of them has,
Or Can hurt Me as I doubt not that your known Justice will
Induce you to Order the Above sum of Seven pounds Seven shillings payed. To Sir your very humble Servant SARAH BROUGHTON

    9. Apparently a Philadelphia neighbor and possibly a tradeswoman of some
sort. In a letter of Dec. 13, 1766 (below, p. 520) BF referred to a "Mrs. Broughton"
as if she might have been an occupant of one of the Franklin tenant houses.
Nothing is known of her dispute with DF beyond the contents of this letter
and the comment in BF's endorsement.
    1. Not found.

NB that I have received thirty one Pounds fourteen Shillings and nine pence And gave a Receit for that sum and noted in the Receit that the Bed is not paid for.

Addressed: To / Docter Franklin / London / per favour of Capt/ Freind

Endorsed: Mrs Broughton   July 3. 1766   a silly Complt.

From Sir William Johnson

Draft: American Antiquarian Society; copy: Massachusetts Historical Society

Sir   Johnson hall July 10th 1766[2]

At the Request of your Son Govr. Franklyn, and several Gentlemen of Pensilvania, I now enclose you a Scheme proposed for establish[in]g a Colony at the Ilinois, together with my Letter to Mr. Secretary Conway in favour thereof, which the proposers desired might be transmitted thro' your hands. I have accordingly sent it under a flying seal, and must request you to forward it as Addressed.[3]

I daily dread a Ru[p]ture with the Indians occasioned by the Licentious Conduct of the frontier Inhabitants who Continue to Rob, and Murder them. I am imediately to meet Pondiac with the Western Nations, at Ontario and wish I may be able to satisfy them.[4]

Altho' I have not had an Opportunity of Cultivating your Acquaintance I shall always be Glad to render you, or yours any Service as I am &c.

2. This letter is printed twice in *The Papers of Sir William Johnson*, v (1927), 336–7, and XII (1957), 140. The first time it is dated July 18, the second July 10. The nineteenth-century copy in the Mass. Hist. Soc. is dated July 18. The editors of the present volume believe, however, the July 10 is the correct date, the "10" in the draft being a contemporary correction, written over an "8", giving it an erroneous impression of being "18."

3. Both the scheme for establishing an Illinois colony, written by WF, and Johnson's letter to Conway, July 10, 1766, are printed in *Johnson Papers*, v, 319–30. The expression *under a flying seal* is "Said of a letter with a seal attached but not closed, so that it may be read by a person who is requested to forward it to its destination." *OED*. See below, p. 414, for BF's forwarding of this letter to the secretary of state.

4. Johnson conferred with Pontiac and other western chiefs at Ontario (Oswego), July 23–31. *N.Y. Col. Docs.*, VII, 854–67.

To Benjn. Franklyn Esqr.

Endorsed: Johnson hall July 10 1766 To Benjn. Franklyn Esqr
London, with proposals for a Colony at Ilinois, &a Letter to Mr
Secy Conway thereon

From David Hall   Letterbook copy: American Philosophical Society

Dear Sir.   Philadelphia July 12th. 1766
I receiv'd your kind letter of May the 9th[5] by the Packet, for
which I am much obliged, and observe what you say as to the
Accounts; but, as you are pleased to express your Satisfaction,
with respect to my Desire of settling every thing right, and my
Sentiments are exactly the same as to you, we can not, as you
remark, have any Difference: However, I should have been glad
to have known what Articles you did not understand, and likewise
those you thought there were Mistakes in, which might have been
rectified before your Return; but of those, no Doubt, I shall hear,
when you have more Leisure.[6]
    I am much obliged for your Indulgence, in allowing Mr. Strahan
to send my News Papers, Via Boston and New-York, under your
Cover.[7] I never thought of asking it with respect to Letters.
    I acknowledge your Favour in writing to Mr. Grace in my
Behalf and doubt not its having the desired Effect with his Widow.[8]
    Mrs. Franklin as I wrote you formerly, may always command
any small service, it may be in my Power to do her. The Account
shall be presented to Mr. Bradford.[9]
    As to the publishing these Encomiums on you; It is true, I did

5. Not found.
6. The reader may learn (as Hall could not do at this time) the nature
of BF's questions concerning Parker's final report on the Franklin & Hall
accounts by consulting BF's "Observations," above, pp. 110–16.
7. On May 10, 1766, William Strahan wrote Hall that he was about to send
the newspapers by Boston and New York vessels, as well as directly to
Philadelphia, addressed to BF. *PMHB*, X (1886), 217. By having the papers
sent to BF, Hall would be saved the charge for postage.
8. Hall had asked BF's help in effecting a renewal of the lease of the Grace
property in which the printing office was situated; above, XII, 170, and this
volume, p. 259.
9. An unpaid account from the Post Office; below, p. 381.

shew some of my Letters from London to your particular Friends; who all, as well as myself, thought what we did was right, in order to do Justice in some Degree, to your traduced Character; but as I find it is disagreeable to you shall observe your Directions for the future.[1] Mrs. Franklin was well this Morning. Sally is at present in the Jerseys. I heartily condole with you on the Loss of your worthy Brother; but as he was an antient Man, and has been long in a declining State, the Shock must have been the less to his Family.[2]

I paid Mrs. Franklin this day Fifty one Pounds, towards purchasing a Bill of Mrs. Stevens;[3] and about the Time of your Brother's Death, she had Twenty Pounds which is all I have paid her, besides what I have already informed you of. My Wife, and Children who are all a little grown up now, send you their best Wishes. And you may believe me to be, Dear Sir Yours most Affectionately   D H

Pray remember me kindly to Mr. Strahan and tell him, I am much obliged to him for his Favour by the Packet.[4]

Per the Packet
To Benjamin Franklin Esq

1. In the issues of Feb. 27 and March 27, 1766, *Pa. Gaz.*, printed extracts from letters by Strahan to Hall praising BF by name for his services in the crisis. BF could not have yet seen copies of the May 1 and May 8 issues containing even more laudatory reports from London.

2. BF's brother, Peter (C.9), died July 1, 1766, aged 73. He had long been in the habit of doctoring himself, a practice that BF and DF had strongly criticized; above, X, 392; and this volume, p. 117. Hall printed a highly complimentary obituary notice in *Pa. Gaz.*, July 3, 1766.

3. BF's Ledger, 1764–1776, pp. 2, 15, under date of Aug. 13, 1766, records receipt of a bill of exchange from DF for £30 sterling from Stevens on Grant. He failed to record its receipt in his Journal, 1764–1776, p. 9, however, until October 4.

4. This must be Strahan's long letter of May 10, 1766, printed in *PMHB*, X (1886), 217–25. It contained much useful discussion of public affairs and was accompanied by the copy of BF's Examination before the House of Commons that Hall read aloud to many Philadelphians that summer and printed in September.

From William Franklin   ALS: American Philosophical Society

                            Suppose about July 10. or 11.
Honoured Father,   [July 13, 1766]⁵
    I have just returned from Amboy, and have received your Letter
per the Packet of May 10.⁶ Mr. Wharton's Clerk has this Moment
call'd on me to let me know he is going Express to N.Y. in hopes
of overtaking the Packet. I have stopt him that I might send you
an Extract of Sir Wm.'s last Letter relative to the Colony.⁷
    I before sent you an Answer to the Enquiry made by Sir Alexr.
Dick.⁸ Mr. Pennington informs me that he has sent Mr. Penn an
Account of the Land he enquir'd about in N. Jersey; nor can I
obtain any other Account of it but the same Mr. Pennington has
received. He is afraid of young Penn selling the Manor to the
Proprietor for much less than it could be sold for here, and wishes
you would caution him against it.⁹
    There has been lately several Murders of Indians in the different
Provinces. Those committed in this Province will be duely en-
quired into, and the Murderers executed, as soon as found guilty.
They are all apprehended and secured in Gaol.¹

    5. WF apparently failed to date this letter when he wrote it, and the tentative
dating may be in BF's hand. The correct date, however, appears to be July
13. WF mentions having "just returned from Amboy," and before he sent
off the letter he crowded in a statement that Lord Hope was coming to visit
him "Tomorrow." DF's letter (immediately below), the first part of which
must have been written on the 14th, relays Sally's report that she and her
brother, whom she had been visiting, had returned "on Satterday night,"
which would be July 12, and that Lord Hope was to be at Burlington to dine
"this day," that is, the 14th.
    6. For the brief surviving extract from this letter, see above, p. 276.
    7. Either Johnson's letter to WF of June 20 or that of July 8, both of which
relate to the proposed western colony; they are printed in *Johnson Papers,*
XII, 107–8, 136.
    8. See above, p. 322. It is not clear whether the land in N.J. Edward Pen-
ington was inquiring about for Penn (mentioned in the next sentence) was
the same land Dick was interested in or some wholly different tract.
    9. Several letters from Penington to BF had expressed the fear that Thomas
Penn was taking advantage of young Springett and that he, Penington, would
lose a substantial commission if the sale of Pennsbury Manor from one Penn
to another were to go through.
    1. On June 26, 1766, two well-known Indian women were murdered near
Moore's Town, Burlington Co., by two men traveling to New York. The

                                    333

I congratulate you on the Resolutions of Parliament relative to Commerce.[2] They are in general much approv'd. I am in hopes that the People of the Colonies, particularly Persons of Property, will conduct themselves so as to give great Satisfaction to the present Ministry. In New York there has been some Riots on Account of Lands in the Great Manors; but they are now quell'd, and their Chief, one Pendergrass, taken Prisoner.[3]

All the Provinces seem in quiet, except Virginia and Massachuset's Bay. The Governor of the first won't let his Assembly meet, as he understands they are disposed to pass a Bill of Rights, and act otherwise in such a Manner as to keep up the Spirit which they kindled before.[4] In the latter, the Assembly, by the Influence of that Firebrand Otis, has imprudently turn'd out all the Crown and other Officers out of the Council.[5]

I have come off with Flying Colours in the Brush I had with

---

authorities quickly arrested one of the suspects in New Jersey and the other later in Philadelphia. Each accused the other of the murders, but both were convicted and hanged. "A few of the principal Indians of Jersey" accepted an invitation to witness the double execution, "and behaved with remarkable Sobriety." *Pa. Gaz.*, July 10, 17; Aug. 7, 1766.

2. For BF's report to the Pa. Assembly on the prospective actions by Parliament, see above, pp. 236–40. The resolutions actually adopted by the Commons committee on May 9 were printed in *Pa. Gaz.*, July 10, 1766.

3. See above, p. 325 n.

4. Lieutenant Governor Francis Fauquier dissolved the Virginia House of Burgesses, June 1, 1765, after the adoption of the Resolves opposing the Stamp Act, and by a series of prorogations prevented the new House from meeting and organizing until Nov. 1, 1766. This action and the exchanges that then took place are discussed in Gipson, *British Empire*, XI, 7–9.

5. When the new House of Representatives of Massachusetts met at the end of May, it elected James Otis speaker and Samuel Adams clerk. Governor Bernard rejected Otis, as he had a right to do, but the House substituted Thomas Cushing, a strong supporter of the Otis faction. In the annual election of the Provincial Council, the House of Representatives turned out the governor's principal allies, including Lieutenant Governor Hutchinson, Secretary Andrew Oliver (the erstwhile stamp distributor), his brother Judge Peter Oliver, and Attorney General Edmund Trowbridge, replacing them with much more radical leaders. Reporting on these actions, John Adams commented in his diary: "What a Change! . . . Thus the Triumph of Otis and his Party are compleat." L.H. Butterfield *et al.*, eds., *Diary and Autobiography of John Adams* (Cambridge, 1961), I, 313.

my Assembly.[6] In order to get the better in the Dispute, they asserted a Number of downright Falsehoods, and finding themselves embarrass'd by this means, and that they had given me great Advantage, they fairly yielded and desired me to proceed no further in the Affair. I had them to be sure prodigiously in my Power; but however like a generous Enemy, upon their crying out *They had got enough,* I witheld my hand. For the future I believe they will be more cautious. I have just heard that Lord Hope is coming here Tomorrow on a Visit to me.[7]

Before this reaches you you will probably hear of Uncle Peter's Death.[8] We are much concern'd at it, particularly as it happen'd so unexpectedly, he having been lately better to all Appearance than for many Months before. I have not heard how the Post Office is dispos'd of, but I wish Coz. Davenport had it.[9]

The Proprietary Party give out that Col. Wm. Skinner (Brother to our Attorney General) is coming over Governor of this Province.[1]

6. The editors have found nothing in the records to explain the contents of this paragraph in so far as they may relate to the session of the Assembly that convened on June 19. If the reference is to events of the previous year, WF's boast of success seems a little late.

7. This sentence is crowded in at the end of the paragraph and was obviously added after the rest of the letter was completed. Charles Hope (1740–1767), as the son and heir of the 2d Earl of Hopetoun, had the courtesy title of Lord Hope. Because of ill health he undertook a long sea voyage, visiting several of the American colonies. He returned to England in the spring of 1767 but died at Portsmouth "after a tedious illness" a few days after landing. *London Chron.,* June 6–9, 1767.

8. See the document immediately above.

9. Josiah Franklin Davenport (C.13.4), BF's nephew, mentioned often in these volumes. BF apparently had less confidence in his business capacity than did WF, and steadfastly declined to appoint him to any place in the postal service (see BF's draft letter to Davenport, Feb. 14, 1773, Lib. Cong.). In any case, BF had previously agreed with John Foxcroft that the Philadelphia postmastership should go to the latter's brother, Thomas Foxcroft, when it next became vacant.

1. William and Cortlandt Skinner were sons of the Rev. William Skinner of Perth Amboy. Cortlandt studied law, rose to become attorney general of N.J., entered the Assembly in 1761, and was elected speaker upon Robert Ogden's resignation in 1765. William entered the provincial military service during the Seven Years' War, transferred to the British Army in 1757, and served with distinction in European campaigns. He was in England when WF wrote this letter. He never received any appointment as a provincial governor. 1 *N.J. Arch.,* IX, 8–9, 14–15, 277–9, 449–50 n, 548.

He has an Interest with Col. Fitzroy, the D. of Grafton's Brother, who married his Relation Miss Warren.[2] The Governor of Barbados has Leave to return Home for a 12 Month, when he expects to resign.[3] In Haste Your dutiful Son   WF

From Deborah Franklin

AL (incomplete): American Philosophical Society

My Dear Child   [July 14–August 15?, 1766][4]
On Satterday I wrote to you and in Closed a bill to you[5] gave it to Mr. Foxcrofte to send as I did not know wather the Packit wold not Saile before this poste. Laste evening I reseved a line and halef from Salley to let me know that thay was returnd on Satterday night and was well the reste was a bought getting things for them as Lord Hope was to be thair to dine this day[6] so for fair [fear] I shold not get up soon anevef [enough] I did not sleep all night and was up and ought att for [four] a Clocke for to helpe get things. Suppose when Mr. Foxcrofte returnes I shall have a letter or Salley will Come home.
You menshon that our Polley is a ging to be marreyed[7] I hope

2. The interlocking connections between these and some other Anglo-American families of considerable prominence are perhaps too complicated to justify exposition here.

3. Charles Pinfold (c.1717–1788) had been governor of Barbados since 1756. He left the island for England May 27, 1766, and the next governor, William Spry, judge of the Admiralty Court at Halifax, was commissioned in August 1767. *Annual Report,* Amer. Hist. Assn., 1911, I, 410, 415. If WF was hoping that he might succeed Pinfold, it was probably because the Barbados governor's salary and perquisites were certainly more than double those of the New Jersey governor.

4. Isaac Norris died on Sunday, July 13, 1766, and was buried the next day; *Pa. Gaz.,* July 17, 1766. DF's statement in the second paragraph that the rain coming down while she was writing would prevent her attending the burial fixes the date of the first section of this letter as July 14. The first sentence of the third paragraph confirms that she was writing on a Monday. For the dating of other sections of the letter see later notes.

5. DF's letter not found. The bill of exchange was doubtless the one David Hall mentioned in his letter to BF of that Saturday; above, p. 332.

6. See WF's letter immediately above and its accompanying notes.

7. BF's letter reporting Polly Stevenson's prospective marriage has not been found. On June 22, 1767, BF wrote that the match was "quite broke off." The man has not been identified.

it is one that is deservin of her and one that Shee likes and her friend like also. It raines now and I fair will be a guste or else I shold go to our old friends Buriel Isack Norris he is bureyed from his Sister Debbeys. Mr. Finley is near his end and has bin as dead for several days.[8] I thinke I did tell you that Joseph Shipen of Jormantown bureyed his only Son on Satterday.[9]

Yister day I wente with Sister[1] to meeting and in the evening I sett more then an ower with her and this morning I was it her house. Shee is in a verey poor staite of mind. When Salley Cumes home I hope it will be better as shee will be with her or I shall be more so. I donte like to be from home as we air still open to the Stabel[2] and abundans of pepel is going too and frow but we air in a fair way of geting of it dun as the brickes is a holing [hauling] to day and laste Satterday.

I am to tell you that my maid Susanah[3] is a larning to Spin now that shee has not so maney arontes [errands] to go on. I wish that when you Come home you wold bring her sume litel thing to in-Carraig her. Maney ladeys old and young to inquier hough you due on Satterday Mrs. and Miss Suel.[4] Senes I wrote the other Side I have had a deal to due amoungest our old friendes.[5] Mr.

8. *Pa. Gaz.*, July 24, 1766, reported the death on July 16 of the Rev. Dr. Samuel Finley (1715–1766), president of the College of New Jersey; above, x, 224 n. An unusually long and laudatory obituary notice accompanied the announcement.

9. Joseph Shippen of Germantown (1706–1793), known as "Gentleman Joe," had seven daughters and one son, Joseph, who died unmarried, July 12, 1766, at the age of 22. Charles P. Keith, *The Provincial Councillors of Pennsylvania* (Phila., 1883), pp. (88)–(89).

1. Mary Harman Franklin, whose husband Peter Franklin (C.9) had died on July 1.

2. On the Franklins' western property line, where building of the wall to shut off the stables of the Indian Queen tavern had been delayed pending the settlement of a dispute over the land title. DF had often mentioned her concern about the matter.

3. In the previous fall DF had mentioned that her maid Susannah shared her bedroom; above, xii, 296.

4. Probably the wife and daughter of either Stephen or Robert Shewell.

5. This sentence begins a fresh page in the ms. It and the rest of this paragraph must have been written on or after August 9, when some of the deaths mentioned in it took place, but before the 14th, when Mary Franklin died. The deaths DF reports here were as follows: Joseph Wharton, 6 years old, and Franklin Wharton, less than 4 months old (named for BF, above, p. 252)

Thomos whorton has loste his eldest son and the younges he fol-
lowd them bouth to the Grave to gather. Mr. Crose is dede allso
as is good old Passon Cammill and a Duch Poson all three lad
Dead to gother and now I am to tell you that our Sister Franklin
layes verey ill with the Same disordor and if shee dos not get
relefe verey soon shee cante Live long. I have as much to dew as
I Can dew att this time for I have but Jeste raised poor Gorge so
as to set up a littel. He has bin verey ill a bove two weeks and
handeled verey severly in deaid. I muste Say abought poor Sister
that shee is so verey low [s]perrited that I thinke it will be as much
as aney one can thinke shee will sirvive it and the wather is So
verey warme that I Can hardly stir and you know I donte ofen
Complain of the wather but the going back words and for words
is all moste two much for me and I Cante be all way thair on a
Counte of Gorge and Salley is much with Pegey Ross att Peel
Hall[6] poor dear child shee is all moste gon it is a wonder shee is a
live I have bin to see her ones and shold go agen but Cante for I
have not time I wonder I keep up and well god is verey good to
me indead.

Poor Dear Sister is dead shee never was well of her harte in
faling down staires and when dead that side of her showed shee
had sufered much.[7] Shee was bureyed in the same grave with

----

were both buried on Aug. 1, 1766. *PMHB*, I (1877), 455. The Rev. Robert
Cross (1689–1766), pastor of the First Presbyterian Church in the city,
1737–58, died August 9. The Rev. Colin Campbell (1707–1766), Anglican
missionary at St. Mary's Church, Burlington, N.J., since 1738, also died
August 9. The "Duch Poson," the Rev. Frederick Rothenbuehler (above,
XI, 201 n) of St. George's Church in the city, died August 7. On these three
clergymen, see Frederick L. Weis, "The Colonial Clergy of the Middle
Colonies," *Proc. Amer. Antiq. Soc.*, new series, LXVI (1956), 167–351, under
individual names. The deaths of Cross and Campbell were reported with substantial notices in *Pa. Gaz.*, Aug. 14, 1766.

6. Margaret Ross, daughter of BF's friend and political associate John Ross,
and a friend of Sally's, of nearly the same age. She died August 20. *Pa. Gaz.*,
Sept. 4, 1766.

7. Peter Franklin's widow, Mary, died on August 14 in her 70th year. *Pa.
Gaz.*, Aug. 21, 1766. This sentence and the remaining portion of the letter
must have been written on the 14th, or more probably, a day or so later.
Nothing further is known of the fall the effects of which contributed to her
suffering. Ephraim Brown, Peter and Mary's adopted son, mentioned later
in this paragraph, wrote BF, Aug. 25, 1766, that Mary Franklin had died
of "the Bloody Flux" (dysentery). DF's earlier statement that Mary suffered

Brother and Mr. Galloway and T Whorton ofred to Carrey her
and get the other Jentelmen that Carreyed Brother I thanked them
but declined it as not thinkin it safe but thay was at the buriol
which was plaine. I shold tell you that for 8 nights I had not fore
owers reste a nighte and the laste night I set all nighte all thow I
had a Nuorse the laste 4 days as it was imposabel I Cold doe my
selef aney longer for I was not abel to bair my waite on my feet.
Billey Come down to the buriol and with his helpe I maid shifte
to go. Capt. All[8] wente with Salley and our relashons all Come to
the bureyal and our good friends paid their laste regardes to her
memerey. Shee had not don aney thing as to Brothers afaires all
thow I ofen advised her to it and shee wold say that shee hope
shee was amoungest her friends.[9] I all ways ansered I hoped shee
was and as to my parte I Cold a shuer her shee was and I have
the satisfackshon to say I did all in my power to oblige and serve
her and shee did me the Jestis to say to several of the good folkes
that visited her after Brothers Deth that shee found her sister a
mother.[1] You know that I am quite a Strainger to thair Sir Cumstans
in everey respeckte but I know that funereal Charges and Hous
rente muste be paid and I know that as soon as the house is let
that will leve near 20 shilins a week so I have had the house clened
and shall let it as soon as posabel and as we have not rume to take
in the [lumbring?] goods I thinke it beste to sell them but not
Books nor what small mater of plaite and such as I Can packe up.

from "the Same disordor" as that which had carried off several other Philadelphians, suggests that an epidemic form of dysentery was present in the city
at this time. If so, it would account for DF's unwillingness, mentioned in the
next sentence here, to allow old friends to act as her sister-in-law's pallbearers,
since the actual means of transmission or dissemination of this and other
diseases were not understood.

8. Isaac All, a sea captain originally from Newport, R.I. (above, XII, 31 n),
had married Elizabeth Franklin (C.11.6), niece of Peter Franklin and BF.

9. Peter and Mary Franklin's adopted son, Ephraim Brown, told BF that
by Peter's will he had left all his property to Mary, but that, her last illness
having followed so soon after her husband's death, she had not even made
her own will; below, pp. 390–1.

1. Peter and Mary Franklin had been living in Philadelphia only about two
years, and before that time Mary and DF had had virtually no personal contact
beyond occasional letters. Mary was the elder of the two women by about
ten years; for her in her period of bereavement to speak of her sister-in-law
as "a mother" testifies to the kindliness and warmth of DF's heart.

Sister had given to Ephrem all Brothers Close and to her maid
her one [own] morning and as thay behave verey well to me I sed
I had not the leste obieckson to her maid shee gave a small bead
and all that belonged to it.[2] Shee is a going home in a week or
two as is Ephrem but Comes back a gen. The littel Boy[3] is to stay
att your house tell his Brother retuerns a gen as he ses he knows
his mother Cante maintaine him [*remainder missing.*]

From James Parker   ALS: American Philosophical Society

Honoured Sir   New-York. July 15. 1766
On a Supposition that this may find you not embarked yet, on
your Return home, I adventure to write once more: to acknowledge the Receipt of yours of May 9th.[4] I think I told you in my
last per Capt. Davis,[5] my Reasons for delaying yet to print a
News-paper, that is in Hopes of getting a Settlement with Holt,
which he has promised to get done in three Months, tho' indeed
he has so often failed in his Promises, that I have not the Strongest
Faith, that he will perform; but my Word is given to Wait that
Time, and tho' he breaks his Word, it is not right that I should, if
it be possible to keep it. I think I told you some other Reasons
which induced me to delay it a While at least till the Commotions

2. Writing to DF, Nov. 24, 1766, Jane Mecom expressed suspicion that
Mary Franklin's maid, perhaps with the connivance of Ephraim Brown, had
taken more than she should have of these possessions. Van Doren, *Franklin-
Mecom*, pp. 96–7. Later, DF seems to have sent some of Mary Franklin's
clothing to Jane Mecom. DF to BF, Oct. 19, 1767, APS.
3. Possibly a younger brother of Ephraim Brown, but the editors can offer
no explanation for this sentence.
4. Not found.
5. See above, pp. 325–8; in that letter and in Parker's letter of June 11,
1766 (above, pp. 300–12), many of the people and episodes mentioned in the
present letter are discussed at great length: John Holt, Benjamin Mecom,
William Weyman, and Alexander Colden, with all of whom Parker was having
financial, occupational, or personal difficulties; his debts to the Scottish firm
of Hamilton & Balfour; his complaints about his positions of landwaiter in
the Customs and comptroller in the Post Office; his assumption of responsibility for an electrical machine sent by BF to Hugh Hughes; and his observations about the violation of the Post Office Act of 1765 in New York. Those
letters should be consulted for the pertinent information about these matters.

here subside a little more: And at present every Thing in general looks but dull and gloomy here; tho' it is hoped the Regulations expected to be made by this Time on Trade, may have some good Effects; yet I think that is not the real Ground of our Distress, but the City is too large for the Country, and Idleness and Luxury too abounding; for as all the real Necessaries of Life are very dear here, it is to me plain, there are not Country Labourers enough in Proportion to the trading Part: for if Country Produce were cheaper more of it might be sent abroad. But why do I trouble you with my silly Reflections.

In Answer to yours, I never did *desire* any Thing of you and Mr. Foxcroft, with Relation to the Post-Office Affairs at New Haven, that I thought *unjust;*[6] but inasmuch as you might not think favourable of it, as we were both Parties, I should be willing to submit my Claim to indifferent Persons: this is sometimes done in Disputes, but then Law being costly, I put up with Wrong often, rather than try a Remedy worse than the Disease, yet Equity, if it could be procured without too much Cost, is certainly the most agreeable Thing in the World. I thank you sincerely for your promising "that when we meet again, all my Reasons shall be duly weigh'd and considered," Tis all I can equitably desire—Here let that rest.

With Regard to Mr. Hall's Accounts, I apprehended it needless for me to take any Notice of the Debts outstanding, of which there certainly is very considerable:[7] but inasmuch as you both lose your Part of what is never paid, so whatever is paid, will be accounted for by Mr. Hall as tis received: This be it more or less is half yours. Mr. Hall is under the same Obligations to act honestly in this, as in all the rest; he is trying to collect it in, tho' as Money is really scarce and Bankruptcies every Day, it is not possible to ascertain what he will receive, or what he will not: Here according to my Conception, we acted right: for he does not attempt to divide the Debts, to give you the bad and him the good, or vice

6. Parker had been appointed postmaster at New Haven in 1754 and had run the office for a time with the assistance of John Holt. See above, v, 441 n; vi, 113 n. For his claims on BF and Foxcroft, see above, pp. 14–18.

7. In his "Observations" on Parker's statement of his accounts with Hall, above, p. 115, BF had complained that Parker had made "No Computation of the outstanding Debts, or Offer made for them."

versa, but lets both have equal Chance—How happy should I have been, if any one of those I have been concerned with, had acted so by me; they on the Contrary took the Money paid to themselves, and would leave the Outstanding Debts, that perhaps will never be paid, for me to get if I can, and even this would have some Shew of Justice, had they divided those Debts with me; but they first get in all they can themselves, keep that to themselves, and then such as they can't get in, they would discount as Pay to me: But is this *Justice* and do I desire any Thing *unjust* in refusing such Concessions.

I wrote you before, that I had taken the Box of Stationary,[8] and am content to pay you Interest from the Day I open'd them, tho' I sincerely declare, I have not sold as much of them in Value, as will pay only the Interest: This however, I believe chiefly owing to the Dulness of the Times in General; but excepting their Lying long on Hand, I don't think I can be a great Loser by them, because the Paper and Books being the most material will sell one Time or other. But the Electrical Machine we have not got yet, they refusing to deliver it without the Bill of Lading, and the Captain who brought it, not being at home, we cannot help it: He is expected home this Summer. Mr. Hughes here continues to keep close, and to keep a good School also; I believe he would come to some Composition with his Creditors, but the greatest of them being absent in the West-Indies, he says, it cannot be done till he returns. In this I can't say much about it.

Your Advice for me, to push bravely, and to endeavour to possess a placid Temper, I take exceeding kindly. It is a little like Balm to a Wounded Mind But I have long experienced one Truth; that it is far easier to preach that Doctrine, than to practise it: I confess myself too subject to a fretting Temper, and it has been my constant Struggle to overcome it: I have Strove hard against the Current, and never was dejected for any Length of Time for assoon as Reason and Consideration could assume the Reins, I have submitted tho' it has been to those Hardships and Crosses which a Soul at Ease, can know but little of: You have known me long, and, I think, believe, I never desired to wrong any Body or

8. This was evidently part of a parcel of goods which BF sent Hugh Hughes and which Hughes was unable to dispose of; see above, pp. 13–14.

disire to do them Injustice, but when by my Folly, Weakness or Kindness to others, I am cruelly dealt with; when I see others eating and drinking my Sweat and Blood, and myself as it were really in Want of some of it, this is hard—indeed it is hard: I hope and believe you never felt much of the kind—and yet I believe you have a little: All Men don't rub thro' the World alike; tho' all do rub thro' somehow; (for none Stick in it long) yet it would be more pleasant, either to be more insensible of the Crosses I meet with, or less of them attack me; but every One are not to be alike in this Case: I believe even you will allow some have sharper Trials than others: their own natural Tempers and Faults excluded: However, I do not pretend to teach you: I am obliged to you for your Expressions of Kindness and Assistance. I will endeavour to follow your Advice, tho' indeed, my poor Carcase is weak and infirm; Tho' as far as I am a Judge, could my Body keep any Degree of Pace with my Mind I might yet recover all my lost Way: I do not dispair, but I find myself more and more feeble, and yet more Occasion for Strength, than ever I had, because the Difficulties I have to encounter are more.

I told you, I had taken all the Steps requisite in the Office you were so good to procure for me, of Land Waiter: I am in the constant Exercise of it. I shall endeavour to give Satisfaction in it; tho' in the Manner it is expected to be performed, the Salary will be well earned: and it is apprehended the new Regulations will make it more weighty: It is a Place in Reality of the most or heaviest Duty and the least Salary in the Custom-House: and tho' I should be glad if some larger Allowance could be made, yet I will be content with it if I can but give Satisfaction, tis the utmost of my Wishes.

In the Post-Office Affairs, I presume Mr. Foxcroft and your Friends relate every Thing needful except it relates particularly to me: I told you I continued to exercise that Post here: and if any Thing different or particular be necessary, I shall be glad of Instruction: It will give me a peculiar Pleasure to give Satisfaction also in that and as there are several new Offices appointed, which increases the Business I have, as well as the Revenue I should be very glad if I should be thought worthy of a little better Allowance on that Head; for every Thing here is very dear indeed.

In the printing Business, my Types are almost all worn out,

343

especially the common sort: I saw Holt's Invoice of his Original Cost of Scots Types which are very good, I think almost equal to Caslon's, and much cheaper. I wish I could get two or three Fonts of them: could you help me to such? I had rather owe all my Debts to you than others, and indeed I can say, could I get Holt to finish Hamilton' & Balfour's Business, that I owe No body else, put all together, the Value of £50, in the World, but what I owe you, and if I live to *push* thro', you will be paid, and if I do not, there will be enough left to pay you all. A little new Letter will go a great Way in such a Dispute with respect to Work, when my Antagonists have all new themselves, for Gaine[9] and Holt have both new Types, but mine are bad. Weyman continues yet, but I am credibly informed, he owes more than he is worth, and every Thing he has is under Execution, but they let him go on as they can't do any Thing better.

Benny Mecom, I told you also continues and he promises too but performs Not any Thing material. I will try every Movement of his Soul; but my Faith fails every Day in relation to him: He must live, and yet I know not what to do with him.

I told you also, that Masters of Vessels coming in here, do not comply with the Act of Parliament in delivering their Letters, but as usual cry them off at the Coffee-House; nor does the Collector decline any Entring on that Account: Indeed it is thought till Matters grow more settled that tis yet not practicable here: Nor is it otherways at Philadelphia. I want not to injure any Man and yet from many Complaints I have heard, Mr. Colden is rather too much of a Gentleman for the due Execution of the Post-Office: It would be more beneficial to the Revenue, were he a little more on the Plebean Order: It is true, he keeps Clerks: but they do not give the best Attendance, nor will they at all Hours: but no Man is perfect: I believe he is otherways a good Officer. But now I am here, I can't see any Benefit I am to the General Office in this Place more than I was at Woodbridge—But I will have done lest

9. Hugh Gaine (1727–1807) had come to New York from Belfast in 1745 and worked for Parker until 1752, when he began publishing the *New-York Mercury*. In 1768 he became public printer to the province of New York. During the British occupation of the city he turned his paper into a royalist sheet. Although he stopped newspaper publishing in 1783, he continued as a printer until 1800. *DAB*.

344

you grow more tired of reading, than I am of writing, or say, I write only to fill my Paper.

My Son as I told you grows stronger and I hope will recover his Strength, at least in part again: I have sent down my Hands to Woodbridge to help him do the Votes and Acts passed last Session there, not having any Thing here for them to do yet, not having had a single Job yet offered, except the Shop-Blanks: We hope for better Times. My Daughter is with me here: We are all as well as can be expected: and with all our Salutations to you and Prayers for your safe Return, I take Leave to subscribe myself Your most obliged Servant   JAMES PARKER.

To Rudolph Erich Raspe[1]   ALS: Landesbibliothek, Kassel

Memo.   Göttingen, July 21. 1766
I had a Bill on Messrs. Michael David, & Fils,[2] for 526 ⅓ Reichs Thalern. I receiv'd 50 Ducats in Specie, and a Bill on Franckfurth for 134 Ducats, making in all but 184 Ducats. I request the Favour of Monsr. Raspè to speak of it to Monsr. David, and to get the Mistake rectified, receiving and retaining in his Hands the Money still due to me, to pay for such Books as he may hereafter send[3] to his Humble Servant   B FRANKLIN

1. Rudolph Erich Raspe (1737–1794), whom BF had met at Hanover in July (see above, p. 315), was at this time librarian of the Royal Library at Hanover and a member of the Academy of Science at Gottingen. In 1767 he was appointed keeper of the Landgrave of Hesse's collection of antique gems and medals as well as professor at the Collegium Carolinum at Cassel. Because of the discovery of his thefts from the Landgrave's collection, he fled Germany for England in 1775. There he published various works on science and travel and became assay master at the Cornish mines; on the darker side, because of his misadventures in Germany he was expelled from the Royal Society to which he had been elected in 1769. In 1785 he published anonymously the collection of Baron Munchausen's travels, a famous anthology of tall tales. *DNB;* John Carswell, *The Prospector Being the Life and Times of Rudolph Erich Raspe (1737–1794)* (London, 1950); Rudolph Hallo, *Rudolph Erich Raspe Ein Wegbereiter von Deutscher Art und Kunst* (Stuttgart, 1934).

2. A well-known Hanover banking house. See Robert L. Kahn, "Three Franklin-Raspe Letters," APS *Procs.,* XCIX (1955), 397.

3. See below, p. 407.

Gottfried Achenwall:[4] Some Observations on North America from Oral Information by Dr. Franklin

Translated from "Einige Anmerkungen über Nordamerika, und über dasige Grosbritannische Colonien. (Aus mündlichen Nachrichten des Hrn. Dr. Franklins.)," *Hannoverisches Magazin,* 17tes, 18tes, 19tes, 31tes, 32tes Stücke (Feb. 27, Mar. 2, 6, Apr. 17, 20, 1767), cols. 257–96, 482–508[5] (Princeton University Library).

During the visit of Franklin and Pringle at Göttingen in July 1766 one of the professors of the University, Gottfried Achenwall, found opportunity to interview the American at length about the English colonies in the New World. Whether Achenwall's questions and Franklin's replies all occurred at a single session or were spread over several meetings or social gatherings it is impossible now to say.[6] Unless Achenwall

4. Gottfried Achenwall (1719–1772), a professor of jurisprudence at the University of Göttingen, had studied at Jena, Halle, and Leipzig, receiving his degree at Leipzig in 1746. He taught history, statistics, and law at Marburg for two years, then became a professor at Göttingen. His main field of interest became statistics, and he was sometimes called in Germany "the father of statistics." *Allgemeine Deutsche Biographie* (Berlin, 1967), I, 30.

5. An English version of these "Observations," translated by J. G. Rosengarten, was printed in *PMHB,* XXXVII (1903), 1–19. Comparison of this rendering with the original German text reveals, however, that the translator felt free to make substantial unannounced cuts in several places or to summarize in a sentence or two much longer passages in which, presumably, he thought his readers would have little interest. The present English version has been prepared by Helen C. Boatfield, Assistant Editor of this edition. She has used the Rosengarten text where it was serviceable, but has provided an entirely new translation of the German whenever that appeared necessary for completeness or accuracy. Rosengarten used a reprint of the work, published as a pamphlet: *Herrn Hofrath Achenwalls in Göttingen Anmerkungen über Nordamerika . . . aus mündlichen Nachrichten des Herrn Dr. Franklins* (Frankfurt und Leipzig, 1769). A later printing, *Einige Anmerkungen über Nord-Amerika und über dasige Grosbrittannische Colonien . . . verfaszt von Hrn. D. Gottfried Achenwall* (Helmstedt, 1777), included, continuously paged, a translation of John Wesley's *A Calm Address to Our American Colonies* of 1775. For other editions and translations of Achenwall's "Observations," see the discussion and notes in James R. Masterson, " 'A Foolish *Oneida* Tale,' " *American Literature,* x (1938–39), esp. 56–9.

6. On the circumstances surrounding Achenwall's gathering of material for this account the most useful discussion is in Edmund J. James, "A Neglected Incident in the Life of Dr. Franklin," *The Nation,* LX (April 18, 1895), 296–7. James quotes from the writings of Germans who entertained BF or met him at other friends' houses during this journey.

346

had an unusually retentive memory, it seems probable that during at least part of their time together the German was able to take written notes on what Franklin told him. Since Franklin could not converse in German, the two men must have talked in English. The use of this language is confirmed by Achenwall's repeated introduction of English technical terms into his report.

At the time of Franklin's visit there were few cultivated residents of the German states who had any first-hand acquaintance with America, or, indeed, had even met or conversed extensively with any knowledgeable and articulate Americans. Achenwall seized his opportunity. He was obviously interested in a great variety of topics relating to the English colonies, and he appears to have "pumped" Franklin to good advantage, moving from one subject to another in a somewhat unsystematic but still effective way. Much of what Achenwall learned must have been entirely new to him personally, as well as to the readers of the report that he put down on paper during the next six or seven months after the visitors had left Göttingen.

In reprinting these "Observations" here the editors recognize that this document is not, strictly speaking, one of the Franklin Papers. It is a report at second hand of conversation conducted in English, written down in German, and here translated back into English. Franklin's original thought, as well as his specific statements, may well have suffered during this passage. Yet the paper does tell us something about one of Franklin's important contacts while in Germany; more significantly, perhaps, it lets us know what information and what views one well-educated German learned by talking with Franklin and then passed on to some part, at least, of the reading public in the state of Hanover.

The nature of this account makes almost inevitable the inclusion of some factual errors for which one or the other of the two men may have been responsible. Some of these misstatements are pointed out in editorial footnotes, but a complete and detailed analysis of the document's accuracy does not seem to be necessary here.

The method used in presenting some passages in the text requires explanation. Achenwall seems often to have been in doubt whether a German word or phrase accurately represented the English term Franklin had used. In such cases he inserted the English word or words in parentheses after his German phraseology. The present printing has retained both the German wording, set in italics, and Achenwall's English words placed as his were in parentheses and in roman type. When Achenwall gave no German wording but only a non-German expression (English or very occasionally Latin), the words he actually used are reprinted but placed within quotation marks. In some other places it seems desirable, in the interests of accuracy and precision, to let the reader know

Achenwall's actual German phraseology for which the nearest English word or words may not have exactly the same connotation. In such cases the German original is given in a footnote.

Some Observations on North America, and the Colonies of Great Britain There.
(From Oral Information by Dr. Franklin.)

The most complete work on the British Colonies in North America is the *Summary historical and political* by William Douglas, of which the second improved edition was published in London, 1760, in two octavo volumes.[7] This physician collected material for many years in America itself, and gives valuable intelligence, especially of the colonies he visited, but his book is not a systematic work. He wanted to make one out of it, but he began to drink too much brandy in his old age, so lost the power to do it.

Professor Kalm has much that is good in his travels in North America, and often cites Franklin, but did not always understand him accurately enough.[8] Mr. Franklin had not become acquainted with Kalm's book before he saw the German translation in Hanover.

The east coast of North America, where the British Colonies lie, is generally colder than the countries in the same zone in Europe, nor has it been observed that owing to the decay of forests and cultivation the climate is becoming noticeably milder. Natural scientists have observed that generally eastern coasts are colder than western, so, as with the English coast settlements, Kamchatka is colder than the western coast of America.[9]

7. William Douglass, *A Summary, Historical and Political of the First Planting, Progressive Improvements, and Present State of the British Settlements in North-America* (2 vols., London, 1760). For a brief account of the early publishing record of this work, see above, IX, 70 n.

8. On the Swedish botanist, Peter Kalm (1716–1779), see above, III, 300 n. The original Swedish version of his travels in America was published in three volumes at Stockholm, 1753–61; two German translations began to appear in 1754, and a first English translation was published in 1770–71. The most authoritative English version, from which citations will be made here, is the two-volume work translated and edited by Adolph B. Benson, New York, 1937. For Kalm's accounts of conversations with BF, see above, III, 53–63.

9. BF had commented in 1762 on the relative temperature of eastern and western coastal regions in his favorable analysis of the spurious report of De Fonte's voyage from the west coast of Canada to Hudson's Bay; BF had specifically mentioned Kamchatka; above, X, 90–1.

Almost the whole eastern coast of North America is sandy, many little islands along the coast are sand banks, thrown up gradually by the sea.[1] The coast of Florida is sandy and unfruitful, but the interior is good land.

The native Indians, the aboriginal inhabitants of this country, consist of many small nations, each with its own language, quite different from that of their neighbors. But all these tribes, from Davis Strait to Florida, are of one appearance. They are as if descended from a common ancestor, all brown in color, with straight black hair, eyes all of one color, and all beardless. They call Europeans the bearded nations. We are all brothers, they say to one another, when two of different tribes meet and compare themselves with Europeans. They live in the wilds, except a few that have been gathered in villages and are partly civilized. They live on plants and by hunting, without farms or cattle, chickens, horses, etc.

Before the arrival of Europeans, their important plants were Turkish corn or maize;[2] a sort of beans; tobacco. Maize and tobacco are found only in America, and were brought from the New World to the Old. Maize and beans they cook and use bear fat in place of butter as dressing, but no salt. Smoking tobacco is an old custom, especially at their national gatherings.

These three plants they look on as a special gift of heaven. According to an old tradition among them, an American [Indian] once found a beautiful young woman seated on a hillock.[3] When

1. BF had never traveled along the North American coast further north than Portsmouth, New Hampshire. Had he ever visited the coastal regions between the Piscataqua and St. Lawrence Rivers, he might have modified this statement.

2. Achenwall: "türkisches Korn oder Mays." The 1952 edition of Jacob und Wilhelm Grimm, *Deutsches Wörterbuch*, traces back to as early as 1543 the use of "turkisch Korn" for what Germans more commonly call "Mais" and Americans call "Indian corn" or simply "corn."

3. What follows here is one of the earliest of several differing versions of a purported Indian legend printed in English, German, and French texts between 1751 and 1784. BF appears to be primarily responsible for Achenwall's version, and he was certainly directly responsible for a considerably different and longer form of the story included in his bagatelle of 1784, *Remarks concerning the Savages of North-America*. For extended and helpful discussions of how this myth first reached the attention of white men and of the differing textual versions, see James R. Masterson, " 'A Foolish *Oneida* Tale,' " *American Literature*, X (1938–39), 53–65; and Alfred O. Aldridge, "Franklin's Deistical Indians," APS *Proc.*, XCIV (1950), 398–410.

he had shown his reverence for her by a deep bow, she informed him she had come here from above, and that after a year he should come again to this hill. He followed her bidding, found her again sitting there, so that at her right hand maize, at her left hand bean-plants, and under her backside tobacco was planted.[4] And these three she left as a gift for the American Indian. Before the arrival of Europeans, they had no other kinds of grain but maize; neither wheat, rye, barley, etc., were known. All these grains, as well as domestic animals, were first brought over from Europe, and just like the European people have increased themselves unbelievably.

One can judge from this, how little to be trusted are the accounts of the conquest of the kingdom of Mexico, by the Spanish historian Antonio de Solis, who represents the city of Mexico as a populous and powerful city.[5] The Mexicans were savages, and without all arts and crafts, how could they create so great a city? How could they secure so many provisions, since they carried on no agriculture and no stock raising, and how could they bring provisions and other necessities into the city, since they had no draft animals at all, because domestic animals were unknown to them?

The weapons of the savages in North America are bows and arrows, the oldest arms of all. They shoot with the teeth of wild animals. They recognize some of the principles of natural law and observe them even with their enemies. Their scalping usually is not done until they know their enemy is dead. Then with a sharp instrument they cut a round piece, an incision about a hands' breadth wide, at the crown of the head of the slaughtered enemy, draw the skin off, and carry it as a sign of their victory. Sometimes such scalped men revive and recover. There are some such in

4. Achenwall: "und unter ihrem Schoosse Taback gepflanze war." The word "Schoosse" usually means "lap" or "bend of the body," and Rosengarten, ignoring the "unter" and the verb, translates these words simply as "on her lap." Most of the other versions of the story indicate that the tobacco grew from the ground at or behind the spot on which the maiden had sat.

5. Antonio de Solis (1610–1686), playwright and historian, published his *Historia de la conquista de Méjico* in 1684; an English edition appeared in 1724, a copy of which was in Lib. Co. Phila. by 1741. What follows in this paragraph shows how little English colonials such as BF could realize the great differences between the Indians they encountered in the north and the much more advanced societies, such as those of the Maya, Aztec, and Inca, in the areas occupied by the Spanish further south in the New World.

Pennsylvania, for scalping is not in itself fatal. That the savages fight on foot is understandable; they have no horses, and if they did they would be wild because they have no tame stock.

The savages living in western Pennsylvania were called by the French Iroquois. The English call them the Five Nations or the *vereinigten Nationen* (Confederate Indians). They stand in a close union with each other, which they had formed long before the English settled here. The Mohawks first united with another nation and others joined later. Now there are seven altogether so united.[6] They have their regular stated meetings and their great council considers the general good. The members are distinguished only by their different languages. They are called subjects of the King, but they are not subject to British laws, and pay no taxes, but rather the colonists pay them a tribute under the name of presents. The number of savages generally does not increase in North America. Those living near the Europeans steadily diminish in numbers and strength. Their two sexes are of a cold nature, for the men find that the women refuse to sleep with them as soon as they become pregnant. For they believe that makes childbirth difficult. Further, they suckle their children for two and a half or three full years and for the whole time they refrain from sleeping with men. The long nursing, they say, is because they have no pap or soft vegetables to nourish the children as Europeans do, and so must nourish them with mother's milk until they can eat and digest meat. The savages who are neighbors to Europeans, have lost amazing numbers through smallpox, a disease not previously known there, and the rest have become so addicted to brandy or sugar brandy, that is, rum, a very heating drink; for this they exchange their skins and peltries and with this they all, men and women, drink themselves quite mad.

The settlement of the English in North America went on much more slowly than in the West Indies or so-called Sugar Islands. Here they settled much later, where they came about 1640, and in twenty years had flourishing colonies, such as Barbados. In North America the colonists came sixty years before, but at the

6. The Iroquois at this time included six, not seven nations. In 1722 the Tuscarora joined the previously federated Five Nations: Mohawk, Oneida, Onondaga, Seneca, and Cayuga. The Delaware were dependents of the Six Nations, but not part of them.

end of the seventeenth century were small in number and exports. The causes of this difference are probably to be found, among other things, in the richer products of the Sugar Islands, which attracted more men, the lesser obstacle to settlement by the savages, few of whom are to be found in these islands, and in the easy and profitable contraband trade with the Spanish. Now since the colonies in North America have gained a foothold and struck root, the increase in the present century has grown unbelievably, and if it continues its present progress, the Sugar Islands will fall far behind, even if they themselves show some increase. This disproportion between the two groups of colonies will be more considerable the longer it goes on.

Mr. Franklin has shown, in a separate writing of 1751,[7] that people in the North American colonies, excluding the foreigners who settle there, double in 25 years, and this doubling in some provinces, with the addition of foreigners arriving, is accomplished in 18, in 16, even in 14 years. This increase and multiplication of the human race will continue so long as arable land is available in excess. This excess will continue unlimited, moreover, because of the recent conquest of Canada and Louisiana. It was reckoned in 1750 about 1 million souls in North America. Shortly after Douglas counted 1,051,000 without blacks or soldiers. On that basis in 1775 there will be 2 millions, and at the close of the present century, 4 millions.[8]

To attract foreigners, an Act of Parliament granted English citizenship to every Protestant after seven years' residence, (I understand by this, that he must not only stay there seven years, but must be settled there for so long.) This right in England can only be obtained with great expense and trouble by a special Act of Parliament. The certificate of the provincial authorities costs only a few shillings and is good through all England.

Near the coast and some miles beyond, all the Middle Colonies are settled, and new improvements are extending deeper in the interior. In Pennsylvania, where the Penn family own all the land, any one who wants to improve the land, chooses a piece, pays

7. "Observations concerning the Increase of Mankind"; above, IV, 225–34.
8. The census of 1800 gave a total of approximately 5,300,000 people in the United States. This figure, of course, did not include the populations of Mexico or the Canadian provinces.

the landlord for 100 acres the local equivalent of 10 Pound sterling,[9] and binds himself to pay an annual rent of half a penny for each acre, he then becomes absolute owner, and the little ground rent can never be increased against his or his heir's will.

Frequently the settlements in this province are advanced in the following way. Among the colonists are many hunters, who follow hunting as their trade. These settle on a particular hunting track in the forest. Here the first thing is to build a wooden cabin. So that is done. The hunter invites 20 or 30 neighbors: they cut down for him the required trees, lay them at right angles on each other, fill the cracks with mud, add the needed roof and openings, in short they build him a wooden house, and for that he treats them with a *Stübchen* (Gallon) of brandy, and stands ready to do his neighbor the same service in the like case. By his cabin he lays out now a small garden and field, as much as he needs for himself and his family. This land is mostly woodland. Then he cuts out the underbrush around, in the beginning cuts only the tops of the large trees and strips off the bark, so he can plow and sow, as the stripped trees die and do no damage to land and crop. Many hunters like this are settled in the remotest areas of the colonies close to the woods, or not far away, or even in the forest itself. Some years after this first cultivation, poor Scots or Irish come, who seek a place to settle. This they find in this half-improved condition. They buy from the hunters, get a patent[1] from the Proprietors, paying the usual charge. The hunter did not have this. His place was only temporary, and he moves further on, builds himself a new cabin, and cultivates another piece of land. The Scot or Irishman completes the half-finished task, builds a better house of sawed timber. The old hut remains standing and now becomes a stable. Some years later, he builds himself a comfortable and complete house of brick, and his extra house becomes a kitchen or an out building. The German often buys out the Irishman or Scot. This nation (of whom there are 90 to 100,000 in

9. Achenwall: "Pfund Sterling dortiger Währung." In 1764 BF had stated specifically that the sale price of unimproved land in the colony was £15 10s. per 100 acres; above, XI, 140. Given a rate of exchange varying from 125 to 175 percent, £15 10s. Pa. currency would correspond fairly closely to £10 sterling.

1. Achenwall: "einen Erbbrief (Chartre)." It is certain that BF never called such a document a "charter."

Pennsylvania), believes it is better to put their cash into land hold-ing rather than turn it over. The Scots or Irish find their profit in selling, and know they can find more land to improve, so they sell, so in the end the German generally remains the real proprietor of the new estate in land.

In Pennsylvania there is no law to prevent cutting up a farm into very small holdings nor to forbid the purchase of very large bodies of land. There is no danger from either course, for there is land enough for rich and poor, and the former prefer the larger profits from trade to the small return from land, so in this province no land leases have yet been introduced, but the estate which each possesses, he farms himself. In New England there are some leased estates. For there are many well-to-do inhabitants who own large and extensive properties in land. The same is apparently true in the Carolinas. In general, I suppose that in those two colonies, and probably in others, individual rich persons can become pro-prietors of a whole village, or of several villages, if they undertake the settlement of a certain area of land of 10, 20, or more thousands of acres, and bring in new colonists to improve it, at their own expense. In this way, owners of pieces of a colony may become proprietors of whole colonies. Mr. Kalm shows something similar in New York in his Travels in North America Vol. II, p. 411.[2]

When an owner of land dies intestate, and there are many chil-dren to inherit the father's landed estate, it is generally taken by the eldest son, and the younger children get in money their share of its appraised value: the eldest son gets two shares, the other children, be they sons or daughters, only one apiece. When a father has many children, and sees that the division of his property on his death will be too little, he usually sells his property for a good price, and with that he buys a larger piece of improved land from the Proprietor, and brings it into cultivation; then he can provide for his children and they can remain near each other.

In the New England colonies, new settlement is not so capri-cious as in Pennsylvania, but has its own regulated form. Here whole towns are laid out at once and restricted, as far as possible, to the nearest unimproved areas. As soon as sixty families agree to build a church and support a minister and a schoolmaster, the provincial government (for the New England provinces are inde-

2. Kalm, *Travels* (Benson edit.), I, 143.

pendent of any hereditary proprietary) gives them the required privilege, carrying with it the right to elect two deputies to the legislature, from the grant of six English square miles. Then the town or village is laid out in a square, with the church in the center. The land is divided and each works his own, leaving however the forest in common, and with the privilege of laying out another village in time.

In this way new settlements grow in New England in regular order and succession, every new village touching on an old one, and all steadily increasing in wealth and numbers. Nothing of this kind is done in Pennsylvania, where the Proprietor wants only to sell much land and as much as any one wants and wherever he likes. The mistake of this was shown in the Indian wars. Here on the border were many scattered houses and estates, which could give each other no help; they were surprised one by one, plundered, and destroyed, or, to prevent this, the people had to flee back to the colony, to which they became a burden.

Blacks are found in Virginia, Maryland, and the two Carolinas in large numbers, but very few in Pennsylvania and further north. In Pennsylvania, on principle they were prevented coming as much as possible, partly because there was no such hard work as they were fitted for in raising tobacco, rice, and indigo. In Pennsylvania, every Negro must pay a tax of 10 pounds sterling and this the master who brings him must pay.

These Negro slaves enjoy, as subjects of the state, in all the colonies, the protection of the laws as much as the free inhabitants. A colonist, even if he is the owner, who kills a black man, is also sentenced to death. If he overworks or ill treats his slave, the latter can complain to the judge. Then in their own interest the masters are obliged not to give their slaves excessive tasks or insufficient food, for their death is a loss. The Negro slaves have all, in short, the general rights of humanity except freedom and property, neither of which they possess.

Free servants in the colonies are of two classes. The one is, in the European way, man- and maid-servant, hiring themselves out for a half or full year, and the term is voluntary on both parts. The other part is quite different. Frequently poor Scots, Irish, Germans go to America, to seek there the fortune they do not believe they can find in the Old World. They have themselves transported without being able to pay the ship's captain. In return he has the right to find them a master who will pay him the money, and whom the immigrant must serve for some years for his mere living without wages: only for a fixed term, not for life.

There is often a case like the following: if a whole family, which is poor, ships to America, and have no assured prospects, the father sells one or several children to a master. They serve him in the aforesaid way, that is for their support, and are taught a trade, farming, handicrafts, cooking. This service lasts until the children attain their majority, that is, with the boys 21, and with the girls 18. In some cases it lasts eight years, but not longer. Then the children are by law free, and their master is bound to give them the needful articles for housekeeping, a cow, farming implements, tools etc. In this way all poor children have the hope of establishing themselves on their majority in freedom. The poor fathers find their comfort in this expectation, are relieved of the care of their children in the interval, and know that they are learning something useful and will start out in life with money in hand without having to pay anything to the master. The masters in turn are satisfied with the cheap service. This law has been introduced to cure the old need of servants and apprentices.

There is a special class of servants in the colonies, between peasants and slaves. That is, transported convicts. In Great Britain such people as have no property are for certain offenses sentenced to *transportation*, usually for 7 or 14 years. It is an exile from Great Britain, under the condition that the criminal may not return there within that fixed term, under penalty of the gallows; if he does, it needs no more than proof of identity to hang him.[3] Such an offender is sold by the courts to a ship's captain who takes him to the colonies and sells him as a slave for a limited period. That over, he is free. Formerly such servants were welcomed on account of the demand for laborers, but now they are no longer needed in the populous colonies. They remain for the most part good-for-nothings and malefactors, who usually are hanged for new offenses in the first months after their coming over.

As for the constitutions of the British colonies in America, I must preface the account by the observations that because of the

3. Achenwall: "so ist weiter nichts als *identitas personæ* zu erweisen, um ihn würklich aufzuknüpfen."

variety of the colonies, they are very differently organized, and that the English writers divide them into three main classes: 1) *die Königliche Regierungsart;* 2) *die eigenthümliche; und* 3) *die freye oder privilegirte* (the Royal- proprietary and Charter- Government). In the British Statutes of the Realm this division is thus expressed: "Plantations under proprietors, under Charters, under his majesty's immediate Commission, Stat. 6. Ann. cap. 30. sect. 2." The first class one could also call the English form of government. For it is organized on the model of the English constitution. This consists of a governor, who represents the King, and in two *"Collegiis,* 1) the Council,"* which one may call the *Staatsrath,* 2) the representatives of the different communities that belong to a colony. These two *Collegia* are comparable to the two Houses of the British Parliament, and so the Council is also called the Upper House, and the Body of Representatives of the people the Lower House. In these three branches are vested the law-making powers of the Colony, but subject to the Crown, hence the meeting of the governor with the two Houses of the colony is not the Parliament but merely the *Versamlung* (Assembly), although the name Assembly is often assigned to the two Houses exclusive of the governor or to the representatives of the commons alone.

The King appoints the governor and recalls him at pleasure. The councilors are also royal officers and depend on the King, as to individuals and term of exercise of the office; they are however chosen from the most considerable residents of the colony; likewise the most important legal and fiscal offices as well as military posts in this type of colony are filled by the King. Governor and councilors enjoy certain perquisites and incidental fees; the governor has a considerable salary established by law, which the colony is obliged to raise, thus the governor of Barbadoes has £2000, the Governor of Virginia £1000.

The popular representatives are elected annually and receive a fixed per diem allowance. They look after the rights and privileges of the people, just as do the Council and the governor after those of the Crown. Every measure approved by the three bodies becomes a law, but only *ad interim.* For it must be sent to the King for confirmation. The King can also annul the law. But if this is not done within three years, or when the actual confirmation is received, the act of the Assembly has complete validity.

357

This is the usual rule for colonial governments, (with some local exceptions) in all the West India Islands, New York, New Jersey, Virginia, both Carolinas, New Georgia, Nova Scotia, New Hampshire, and I believe Quebec, East and West Florida, and the newly acquired Caribbean Islands,[4] and the English consider it the best way of securing the rights of the Mother Country, that is, Great Britain.

The 2d class, that of hereditary Proprietors, once more common, is today to be found only 1) in Pennsylvania and 2) in Maryland. In the former, as mentioned above, it is the English family of Penn, in the latter the House of Baltimore of the Irish peerage, who are the hereditary proprietors of the whole land. To these proprietorships the hereditary government is also attached. As lords paramount the heads of both families are entitled to a certain quitrent annually from each land settler in proportion to the number of his acres, and all improved land must be purchased from them at a fixed price. Both purchase price and quitrent are indeed low, but the great extent of both colonies has made both families rich and of consequence. Lord Baltimore has the right of patronage of all churches in Maryland. As hereditary Proprietors both appoint their lieutenant governors, who are confirmed by the King and reside in the provinces. In both colonies there are assemblies, that in Maryland consists of the lieutenant governor, the Council, and the House of Commons, and subject to the right of the Proprietor, has the same jurisdiction as that of any other colony. Of Pennsylvania we shall speak more particularly below.

The third kind of government is the privileged, which may also be called the free government. This comes nearest to a democracy and is also less dependent on the Crown. This form of government exists especially in the three colonies of New England, completely in Connecticut and Rhode Island, but in Massachusetts with certain restrictions. The two first named colonies have the right to elect all their own officers, including the governor and Council, and to make all needful laws in their own right, without having to

4. The "I" of "I believe" in this sentence was probably Achenwall. As BF may well have known, neither Quebec, East Florida, nor West Florida had in 1766 been as yet allowed an elective Assembly, while Grenada had only just received this privilege a few months before BF visited Germany. *Acts, Privy Coun., Col.,* IV, 742–4.

seek royal confirmation. Also there is no appeal from the judgment of their courts. There are some particular differences; for example, in Rhode Island each congregation can dismiss its minister annually, which amounts to this, they keep their minister on a yearly salary.

Well-populated Massachusetts Bay formerly had these almost-royal privileges, but because of abuses they were annulled, with all their other rights and liberties, by the King's Bench under Charles II, and under William III only a few of their liberties were restored by a new Charter. Since this time the King appoints to the governorship, to the most important judgeships and treasury places, and to all military posts. The representatives of the people have indeed the right to elect the councilors, but the governor has a veto.[5] This election in Massachusetts as well as in Connecticut and Rhode Island, is made by both Houses, annually, because the members of the Council hold office only for a year. Laws passed by the Assembly must have royal approval to receive the force of law, and in cases involving over £300, there is an appeal to the Privy Council in London.

However, the royal governor in Massachusetts receives no standing salary, but one is granted him by the Assembly for a year at a time. (Kalm says the same of the governor of New York, in his Travels in North America, II, 401.)[6] He must therefore be popular with the Assembly or the King will replace him by another likely to be so. This uncertain tenure is unpopular in Europe because it affects unfavorably the interests of the colony and makes that of Great Britain dependent on the colony. The colonists however object that the governors with permanent salaries would usually be distinguished gentlemen who would not take up residence in the colonies but would remain in England and send out a substitute (lieutenant governor) and would trouble themselves very little about the welfare of the colony.

According to Mr. Franklin, the constitution of Pennsylvania has its own special feature. As has been mentioned above, Penn 1) as hereditary Proprietor of the land exacts annually from every acre of improved land, the local equivalent of a half penny sterling, and when any one wants to buy a piece of as yet unimproved land to

5. Achenwall: "aber der Statthalter hat dabei ein *Votum negativum.*"
6. Kalm, *Travels* (Benson edit.), I, 137.

cultivate, Penn sells 100 acres for £10 with the reservation of the annual half penny as his quitrent.

2) As hereditary governor, he appoints his deputy governor, whom he pays, and all judges; but ministers are chosen by their own congregation in all *Distrikten* (Counties).

The Assembly of the Pennsylvania legislature does not consist of two Houses, because there are no state councilors, but of one House only, the representatives of the different counties.[7] These are elected annually by the communities on the first of October, being elected for one year, and as follows: Pennsylvania is divided into certain counties.[8] Each county on that date holds its own meeting. In this meeting each colonist has a seat and a vote, who has £50 in possessions, and has resided twelve years in the colony. These meetings choose eight deputies each for the Assembly.[9] Every elector is eligible, but mostly well-to-do citizens are elected. The county gives its representatives six shillings a day, but this daily allowance now does not go far, and thus the deputies have to spend more out of their own pockets. There is no bribery. Every voter deposits a written ballot, all tickets are thrown together into a whirligig[1] and the persons who have the highest number are declared elected. The purchase of votes would be very unsafe, as the voter could always write another name on his ballot.

This House of Commons of all the counties now, in its session, with the concurrence of the governor, exercises the law-making power. But the governor is in some degree dependent on the Assembly, just as in Massachusetts Bay. He enjoys no fixed salary; but the House grants him one usually only for one year. If the Assembly is dissatisfied with him or the Proprietor, it grants him nothing for the following year. So the salary depends each year on the good will of the Assembly. This is the present situation in Pennsylvania. The Assembly is at odds with the Proprietor and for six years has granted no salary to his deputy. In this way the representatives can defy their Proprietor, but the country suffers for

7. Achenwall: "Distrikte."
8. Achenwall: "gewisse Counties."
9. In fact, only the three original counties elected eight representatives; those later formed chose from four down to one each. There is no mention here of the two members who represented the city of Philadelphia.
1. Achenwall: "in einen Topf."

it. Because the lieutenant governor has too little to live on, the respect his high office calls for is diminished. The controversy of the Assembly with the Proprietor lies in the demand that he contribute his share to the burdens on the country, especially the extraordinary war expenses, in proportion to his property and rents. The controversy can properly be decided by no one but the King in the Privy Council. Should the Assembly wish to appear as a complainant, a case could take place before the King's Bench.[2] The right of the Proprietor as governor to appoint all provincial judges is very important, as it has the consequence that in all sorts of conflicts between him as Proprietor and single colonists, he is often plaintiff and judge in his own case.

Moreover, it is to be noted that the newer colonies have arrangements based on acts of Parliament for Georgia, Nova Scotia,[3] &c., but the older colonies have charters from the King alone, for himself and his successors, and not from Parliament. Many in these colonies claim to be subject to the King, but not to Parliament, at least not to its arbitrary power, like the newer colonies, which owe their existence to Parliament. So these colonies are often called in the Statutes of the Realm "his Majesty's Plantations" and counted among the "Plantations within his Majesty's dominions beyond the Seas."

The system of justice in the colonies, it is to be said, is based on the English. For it is part of the English liberties of the subject, which the colonists enjoy. In all private affairs *das schriftliche, als das herkomliche Englische Recht* (Statutes Law *und* Common Law) prevails. The Roman law is introduced only in *den Seegerichten* (Courts of Admiralty). The decision of the twelve *geschwornen*

2. Achenwall: "Solte jedoch die Landesversamlung den Kläger abgeben wollen, so könte solches auch vor der königlichen Bank geschehen." The professor seems to have seriously misunderstood or misinterpreted something BF said. No case arising in a colony could be carried by complaint or appeal to the Court of King's Bench in Westminster; certainly no appeal lay from the Privy Council to the King's Bench, as Rosengarten's translation makes this sentence say. Appeals lay from the colonial courts to the Privy Council, just as BF had pointed out a few paragraphs earlier in relation to Massachusetts; King's Bench had nothing whatever to do with the administration of justice in the colonies or with the grievances of a colonial Assembly.

3. Achenwall's names for these two colonies are "Neugeorgia" and "Neuschottland."

Männer (the Jury) is required here in all civil and criminal cases, as in England. It was one of the complaints of the colonies against the Stamp Act that the disputes arising over it were to be tried without the jury by a special court.

Most of the colonists of English descent are Presbyterians.[4] There is not one bishop of the Established Church in America, though here and there congregations of the Anglican Established Church are to be found. These are all under the Bishop of London, and every one of their clergymen must be examined and ordained in England, at a cost of at least £40 to £50, but their stay in England helps their education. Since the bishops have spiritual jurisdiction, there are no ecclesiastical courts in the colonies,[5] and matters pertaining to them are settled partly by secular judges, partly by the Assemblies. The spiritual lords have proposed to establish a bishopric in the colonies, but the latter would find it hard to accommodate themselves to receiving one, because the name bishop has been hated in the colonies since the times of Charles I.

There are some Catholic congregations in Pennsylvania as well as in Maryland, in the former because freedom of religion is universal, in the latter because the Baltimore family, the Proprietors, were formerly Catholics; none are found in the other colonies.

There are Jews in Pennsylvania and New York, in the latter there is a synagogue, in the former only some schools.

Pennsylvania has especially grown and flourished through the universal religious equality (equality is more properly used than toleration)[6] established at the very beginning of the colony. Roman Catholics are however excluded from all offices and from the As-

4. If by "English descent" BF (or Achenwall) meant "English-speaking," thereby including the Scotch-Irish, and if by "Presbyterians" he meant "Calvinists," thereby including most New Englanders, this statement might be called literally correct, though as put here it would give a rather false impression of the sectarian distribution of the colonists.

5. It is true that there were no permanently established ecclesiastical courts in the colonies; but if BF made the statement as given here, he might well have remembered that his friend George Whitefield had been summoned to an ecclesiastical court specially called by Commissary Alexander Garden of South Carolina in 1740. After Whitefield failed to prosecute an appeal in England, Garden's court suspended him from office a year later. No other ecclesiastical court is known to have been held in the Continental Colonies before the Revolution.

6. Achenwall: "(Gleichheit ist eigentlicher gesprochen als Duldung)."

sembly, because they cannot take the usual religious oaths and subscribe to the Test Act. These oaths must be taken here as well as in England, as well as that against the Pretender. All other Protestant faiths enable the members to hold office.

For instruction in the arts and sciences[7] there has long been an academy[8] in Boston, the capital of Massachusetts, and there is another founded in 1749 in Philadelphia, the capital of Pennsylvania. Mr. Franklin made the proposal and with great pains brought it to pass, so is its founder. The money was raised partly by subscription, partly by provincial grants. Most of the endowment consists of land, not very productive, but of value hereafter. This university has a president with £250 salary, and four professors, two with £200, two with £150, besides fees for private instruction. They have no free lodging as yet, because no *Collegium* has been built. This academy has the right to create *Magistros philosophiae*. In 1764 a medical faculty was established and Mr. Franklin hopes the university will gain the right to make doctors of medicine. It does not have a public instructor of law yet, and it would find it very difficult ever to establish a professor of theology. The university was chartered by the Assembly for the general good of the colony, but as there are so many religious faiths, all of which enjoy equal rights and none of which dominates, so theology is excluded and every one may be instructed in his own faith in the schools of his own sect.

Farming, stock-raising, and fisheries flourish in all the North American colonies, and what the forests can supply is available everywhere for livelihood and industry; yet there are greater or less differences in the means of subsistence among the individual colonies, as they are very different.

Cultivation of vines can be carried on in Carolina and farther south; grape vines are to be found wild in some forests. But their cultivation has not been found very profitable because the excellent wines from the Canary Islands can be had very cheaply. In this same region there is good hope for silk, as mulberry trees can grow even in New England. The bounty for silk culture continues.

Cod-fishing in the colonies is far more valuable than a great

7. Achenwall: "in den Wissenschaften." In its present-day connotation "science" alone seems too narrow for Achenwall's context.
8. Achenwall: "Hohe Schule."

silvermine would be, for it affords industries of many kinds, especially shipping, and attracts a throng of able seamen. New England, Nova Scotia, and the island of Newfoundland are most largely interested in it. Colonists have the same fishing rights in these waters as Englishmen. Taking fish and carrying it are equally free. The greatest profit is drawn from Spain and Portugal. These Catholic countries are, because of Lent, very profitable to the colonies, so many of them often bless the Pope. What did they formerly do with all the fish? The French fisheries since the recent peace have greatly diminished in extent, but the French take a good deal of the trade, as their own consumption is supplied by French fishing fleets. In Portugal, Spain, Italy, and elsewhere the English and colonials always have the advantage because they can deliver the fish cheaper. The importance of the design to drive the French out of the fishery, exists more in imagination than reality.

The membranes of the cod are now utilized in America and a very good isinglass is made, for which formerly much money was paid to Russia. For some years whale fishing has flourished. In the little island of Nantucket off the coast of Connecticut fully a hundred ships go out yearly for this fishing. This sea beast is hunted in the spring in the Gulf of St. Lawrence, followed through the northern straits towards Greenland, on towards the Grand Bank, south in the fall to Florida. Also there is found in the waters off New England another sort of whale without baleen or whalebone,[9] which produces the best *Sperma Ceti,* the chief use of which is to burn for light.

Beasts of prey now do little harm to the colonists, though formerly they did more. There are bears and wolves, but if they are not provoked, they attack nobody. Not only the bear's-fat, but its flesh too, is used for food. The bear meat, for which the savages have a great liking, has indeed a good flavor, and a bear-ham is considered in the colonies very good game. The claws are left on the meat when it is cooked, to show that it is a bear's-leg.

Mr. Kalm gives an exaggerated account of the wood-lice: that they were a great plague in Pennsylvania and New Jersey, that they were found in unspeakable numbers under the leaves of trees in the woods and cause great pain, without there being found a means to destroy them. (In *Transactions* of the Swedish Academy

9. Achenwall: "ohne Barten oder Fischbein."

of Sciences, XVI, 30.) Wood lice did sometimes attack cattle, as was reported from Maryland, in some regions, but they soon disappeared of themselves.[1]

Deer are found in fair numbers. The colonists often shoot them, but only for the skin. To bring the meat to market is too long a trip from the woods. In the woods are many buffalo-bulls, rather larger and stronger than ordinary cattle, as wild animals usually are, compared with domesticated. Their flesh is quite palatable, and they have on back and shoulders a fine wool, which they shed yearly, about 15 pounds from each buffalo. Perhaps these animals might be tamed and then could be of good service as draft-animals. Certainly they are tamed in Asia Minor, Persia, Egypt, Ethiopia, and the East Indies and used as draft animals with great advantage.

Mr. Kalm praises the *Zuckerhorn* (Mapletree) in North America very highly, and probably brought some young trees to Sweden.[2] By cultivating the sugar maple, he says, West Indian sugar could be given up. Because of its weak wood, this tree cannot be used for building but through an incision one can in fact extract a sweet juice and by long cooking prepare from it something like sugar. Poor people in the colonies do that, but on the whole it is of no importance, because of the neighborhood of the West Indies Sugar Islands.

The *Ermunterung* (Bounty) given for the production of pearl- and pot-ash creates a good industry. In the American colonies there is now produced annually over 1000 tons (of 20 hundred weight each). The Englishman calls pearlash the sediment or salt which remains in the vessel after boiling ash-lye. When this sediment is boiled down still more fine, it becomes potash. Potash is better and more costly than pearlash. It is called potash because it is prepared in vessels or pots.

Ship building is growing greatly in the North American colonies. Ships are all built of oak, some for use at home, others for sale in England.

Pennsylvania maintains itself mainly by farming and cattle breed-

1. Kalm dealt with this subject briefly twice in his *Travels* (Benson edit.), I, 218, 364, and both times referred his readers to a "separate article" on the subject in the *Transactions* of the Swedish Academy of Sciences, 1754, pp. 19–31.

2. In the *Transactions* of the Swedish Academy for 1751, pp. 143–59, Kalm published a treatise on maple sugar: "Hura socker göres i America af lönnes saft." See Kalm, *Travels* (Benson edit.), II, 774.

ing, like most of the states in Germany. It carries on little fishery, as it has only a small area of land on the seacoast, and has no particular land-product by which it could develop especial strength in commerce. The great prosperity of most of the other colonies is gained from such exclusive kinds of trade, for example, fisheries, tobacco, rice, indigo. As soon as a colony realizes it can raise a special product by particular cultivation and wider activity, so it is assured of its superior advantage, and this advances it. Pennsylvania offers the best example, that a colony can become populous and prosperous by the most natural and general practice of agriculture and cattlebreeding.

Raising horses is carried on in some colonies, more than is profitable. Oxen are more useful for plowing fields, for they can be used for twelve years, and then slaughtered or sold. It is found that those colonies are better off which use oxen instead of horses for plowing.

The colonial farmer, like the English, lives on what his industry creates and enjoys the fruits of his labor. He does not live extravagantly but is frugal, yet denies himself nothing that he thinks necessity, true comfort, neatness, and customary decency demand. Every farmer has the consequence of a *Gentleman*, so he treats his wife, his children, his servants, even his stock well; nothing of his must starve. One must also see, from his servants and his cattle, that he is a man who has a good competence. In fact everybody in the colonies lives well in his own way, every decent head of a household saves something each year, and so the wealth of the colonies increases every year, if not in hard money, yet in abundant property, worth even more than money.

Generally they do not live in the North American colonies with the magnificence of the English Sugar Islands; however in Pennsylvania living is more frugal than in most of the other North American plantations.

Besides the craftsmen needed for every day necessities, there have already been set up in the different colonies all kinds of manufacturers, in wool, flax, hemp, iron, steel, copper. Even firearms are made, guns for hunters, and iron cannon are cast. As yet no gunpowder is made; but it can be. Generally, up to this time the colonies are not restrained by law in manufacturing what pertains to the consumption of each province.

The object of Great Britain, to confine the productive activity of the colonies within certain limits, is directed principally only to foreign trade, for example, no colony can export woolen goods and hats into another for sale, much less to a foreign country. The law is so strict as to hats, that even English hats may not be brought from one colony into another, so that under this pretext hats from colonial workshops may not be sneaked in. This prohibition has seemed necessary for the protection of the English hat makers because the English must get the chief material for fine hats, beaver fur, from the colonies, and the latter could supply their own hats much more cheaply.

Many English look on the trifling manufactures of the colonies as extremely dangerous for Great Britain and fear from their spread and increase the decline of their own trade. But this fear is under present circumstances groundless, at least of no importance. First, the preference for farming and cattle as the most common, most familiar, and safest and simplest way to establish a family, has the upper hand. Second, most of the goods manufactured in the colonies will be more expensive than what can be had from England where they have long been made. Manufactures are hard to establish in the colonies, and just as hard to maintain for any length of time. So long as the vast excess of unimproved land is available, so long will craftsmen be scarce, not only masters for the above-mentioned reason, but even more, journeymen, from whom skillful new masters can first come. And other laborers, peasants and day laborers, are not so easily to be had as in Europe. For as soon as a man has earned a few pounds, he would rather buy a piece of land for a farm than earn his bread by further service. So he becomes his own master and can marry and set up his own household. (Herein one sees another cause for population increase. The large family,[3] if I may venture the expression, is an advantage to the parents. With the children's aid, one can do more field work, improve more acres, and gain a larger property. Working people are scarce, and one's children are not only the most dependable, but generally the only workers one can find.)

In the third place, even if some manufacturers arise little by little, meanwhile the increase in numbers from year to year is so great, that England, besides finding its home-made goods are find-

3. Achenwall: "Die Vielkinderey."

ing a greater sale at home, will also find that prosperity and wealth in the colonies are enabling everybody to buy more because he can spend more. (This last condition is very important, for it has been shown that in Pennsylvania the population has in 34 years increased fourfold at most, but in the same period the importation of English goods into Pennsylvania has risen from £16,000 sterling to more than £268,000 sterling, that is, 17 times greater. In 1723, the value of imports was £16,000, in 1757, £268,426. It might be concluded that four times as many people would use only four times the goods but four times the people take seventeen times as much; plainly because this larger number of people are also four times richer.)

Fourth and last, certainly it will in time be necessary to establish some manufacturers in the colonies. For with the growth of the North American colonies lasting for centuries, Great Britain and Ireland, as islands of limited resources (e.g., their wool production cannot be increased proportionately or without limit) will in the future find it beyond their power to supply from their output, the quantity of goods required by the colonies.

The three largest cities, centers of trade and seaports, in British America, are Boston in New England, New York in the province of that name, and Philadelphia in Pennsylvania. About 1720, Boston was as large as the other two cities together, but since that time New York and Pennsylvania [sic] have grown far more than Boston. For in New England there are many seaports, but the other two are the only ports in their respective provinces, as these have only a small coastal area. So both these cities are the common markets for their whole province and grow more in proportion to the province and have the hope in consequence of becoming the largest cities in America. Philadelphia has more than 3000 houses and more than 20,000 inhabitants. The city is regularly laid out, the streets are all at right angles; they are extended every year and new houses are always being built beyond the first boundary. The houses are almost all of brick, like most of those in London.

All the American colonies have their cities and villages; but Virginia has the fewest villages and only one small city, Williamsburg, where the governor resides and the provincial Assembly and the courts meet. In this province the colonists are scattered and distant from each other, each on its own tobacco plantation. This is because of the nature of the country. Chesapeake Bay runs deep into the land, and many navigable streams flow into it. By these streams the colonists send down their tobacco in barges to the Bay, where the seagoing vessels load it. This transport is the easiest and cheapest, especially for a product taking up as much room as tobacco. Virginia is cut up by as many naturally navigable streams, as Holland by artificial canals.

New York has excellent advantage for the trade with the savages. It ships its goods up the Hudson River, to the city of Albany. Hence they are sent by other streams, and because of waterfalls, here and there partly by land several English miles, on to Oswego on Lake Ontario. Here the fairs for Indian trade are held. Lake Ontario is connected by water through the greater lakes lying inland with the *Obersee* (Lake Superior). The savages easily bring their skins and hides from the interior in their boats to Oswego. In this trade Pennsylvania has no share, as New York would not allow it. On the other hand, the trade of Pennsylvania profits by the commerce of New Jersey, as this by the convenience of the Delaware River is mostly directed to Philadelphia.

The English colonies lack salt and rarely make it for themselves. They import it from Spanish South America. There it is produced naturally, as in the Cape Verde Islands and Senegal. When the tide is high, it flows over the sand banks in certain valleys, and the heat of the sun makes salt. The colonies import it in 50 or 60 ships a year.

The colonies are generally restricted in all their foreign trade, and even more in their shipping in all sorts of ways. Nevertheless the continental colonies particularly maintain a considerable shipping trade of their own. Many products, particularly those for ship building and raw materials suitable for manufactures: mast trees, ship timber, iron, copper ore, hemp, flax, cotton, indigo, tobacco, ginger, tar, pitch, rosin, potash, skins and furs, they may not export. These are reserved for the British realm, must be bought by British merchants, and carried by British ships and sailors. In areas where an English company has the exclusive trade, they may not trade, for example, the East Indies. In 1765, trade also was prohibited with the West Indies colonies of the French and Spanish. But this prohibition had bad results, and has been lifted.[4] To the

4. Strict enforcement of existing laws, ordered by George Grenville while in office, had harmfully curtailed a profitable trade with the foreign West Indies, and the Rockingham Ministry abandoned this policy.

Portuguese Sugar Islands they may carry all sorts of food stuffs, such as grain, flour, butter, meat, and cattle for butchering, wood and timber for house building and farm use, and in return bring back chiefly molasses, from which rum is made. Trade with the Spanish in America is a mere contraband trade; the Spanish government requires the confiscation of the goods and enforces the law by its coastguard ships. But the colonist risks it because he can bring back specie, which is so rare in the colonies.

Great Britain has now, 1766, established two free ports in the West Indies, one in Jamaica and one in Dominica.[5] Other nations had formerly done so, the French a port in St. Domingo, the Dutch in St. Eustatius, an unproductive island, the Danes in the island of St. Thomas. Great Britain has done so to enjoy the same advantages, and particularly to reduce the contraband trade with the Spanish. Yet there are restrictions on this new arrangement: all foreigners can buy all goods there[6] duty free, but for cash, not in exchange for goods.

That the shipping trade of their own which the colonies carry on, is so important rises partly from the trade referred to with the Spanish and French West Indies, partly from the intercolonial trade by exchange of their marketable over-production, especially between the continental colonies and the English Sugar Islands, partly from their great off-shore fisheries.

After the West Indies, the chief trade of the colonies goes to the regions lying south of Cape Finisterre. They traffic directly (in their own products and in their own ships) to Africa, the Canaries, and other islands in the ocean; as also in their own wares but in British ships to Portugal, Cadiz, Malaga, Marseilles, Leghorn, and Naples. They can in this way even trade to Turkey, but up to now have not. Hither they export their surplus, especially fish, grain, and flour, timber, also sugar and rice, and bring back their price partly in hard cash. The trade with Portugal has special restrictions. They can export their products there, but cannot bring back Portuguese wine for that must be carried by way of England. So they usually in return bring back salt as ballast. Sugar is the only product which the colonist can export as his own property, though in British ships, to all Europe and sell directly.

5. By 6 Geo. III, c. 49; see above, pp. 237–8 n.
6. Achenwall: "alle dortigen Güter," which could mean "all local goods," but the terms of the act in question call for the phraseology used here.

The greatest part of American goods are taken by the English, as they ship their manufactures to America. In general, no foreign nation is permitted to go to the colonies to buy their products and carry them away, much less to send their own goods over; both export and import remain a privilege for British subjects or especially for inhabitants of England. The import of English goods into the colonies increases as they grow. England sells annually to the colonies in North America and the West Indies more than three million pounds sterling of its own products, chiefly manufactures, and including Scotland and Ireland over five million pounds sterling. This is what was estimated in the British Parliament, at the beginning of this anomalous year 1766, as probable, for it is so impossible to calculate quite accurately.

Hard money, as said before, is still scarce in the colonies, and more so in North America than in some of the Sugar Islands. So specie stands at a higher value than in Europe, and hence arises the difference between the English standard of coinage and the *Currentfuss* (Currency) which circulates in the colonies. For example, an English shilling in the colonies is worth, not 12 pence as in England, but 18 pence. This lower rate prevails in all the American colonies. (A similar condition exists in the French colonies.) A guinea is valued at 34 shillings. This is higher than its rate of value to the English shilling; but because of the convenience of this coin in transmission and acceptance in England it has acquired the higher value. The coinage most current in the colonies in business is the Spanish pieces of eight and Spanish gold pistoles. The first are worth in England 4s. 8d., in the colonies 7s. 6d. The latter are worth only 27s. They would be higher, but generally they are so clipped and cut that their value has fallen.

A bill of exchange on London usually is paid at 175 percent, that is, one English pound sterling at £1¾ in the *Landfuss* or "Currency." But this rate rises and falls. Par is really 100: 133⅓, but it is satisfactory if it is not over 166⅔. During the last war the rate fell for a time to 125, because England made great remittances for the war and English soldiers brought over much hard money.

The currency is not of the same kind in all the colonies. In Jamaica, the island being rich by its produce and contraband trade, it is nearer the English standard. In some of the North American colonies, it varies much more from it than in Pennsylvania.

But there are also in the colonies *Papiergeld oder Geldzettel* (Paper-bills, Bills of Credit, Paper-Currency). These bills can be issued only by the authority of an act of Assembly, and then pass in trade as money. They have credit because the province supports them. Usually such bills are issued as notes of no higher than £5 denomination, but they can be issued for all sorts of lower value down to one shilling, all as currency. But such bills are acceptable only in that province by whose Assembly they were authorized; in other colonies they have no value, much less in England.

This paper money is of two kinds, for different purposes.

The first kind is for the purpose of providing for the chief expenses of the colony, which cannot be postponed and must be paid. For example, in the war with France each colony decided to maintain a certain number of troops, so money had to be raised to levy, arm, clothe them, etc. This sum is sometimes raised in bills. The Assembly gives the governor the sum granted for the war in such bills, which he can at once use as cash throughout the province. No one refuses to accept them as money, because the province stands back of them, and redeems them at the public treasury. Meanwhile the sum granted is recorded as a public debt. As soon as the bills have run their term, they are called in and destroyed. What specie has been received, will be used to redeem that amount of bills; what bills still circulate, will be cancelled as ordered and the paper bills destroyed. So the debt of the province goes on discharging itself. This procedure was learned from the mother country (where the guarantee by act of Parliament was introduced in the reign of William III) but with the difference that the English "Exchequer-Bills" pay their holder a daily interest from the date of issue to the day of redemption, but the paper-bills of the colonies pay no interest.

The second sort of paper money has chiefly the object of encouraging domestic trade and industry. On the provincial authority a certain sum, for example £50,000 local currency, is issued in paper money, and it is proclaimed that whoever in the colony needs a loan, can get it in paper from the government as a loan at 5 percent annual interest on good security. So many who need money are assisted. Generally there is included a condition that the new debtor shall repay one tenth of the capital annually. The usual rate of interest in the colonies is 6 percent, but the government, for the good of the people, is content with 1 percent less. So the advantage of the province and its citizens are united. The government can by the interest of these loans meet some public outlays without laying new taxes. And since specie is very scarce, and these bills circulate as money, by these loans many poor colonists are put into position to acquire the necessary cattle, farm equipment, etc., and to cultivate their fields properly. Without money they could undertake nothing or accomplish little. By this means land improvement in the colonies has developed to an astonishing degree. The annual payment of ten pennies of capital[7] secures the credit of the bills, and frees the government of the risk of going into debt, because in a period of ten years the bills are redeemed and the debt discharged. A splendid discovery! The bills in circulation like other paper, sometimes rise, sometimes fall a few percent, according to circumstance. Their great usefulness is, that they can be increased. This increase was carried too far in some colonies. So they were issued too frequently, sank in value and fell 15, 20 percent or more. This instrument must be used with caution and moderation. When paper money is increased carefully, it does not lose credit, but by experience the limit is easily fixed. The bills can be increased a little each year and so long as they do not fall to a great degree, they remain stable. So long they are useful; otherwise they are harmful. All the colonies introduced paper money; when in some its sinking created disorder, its use was limited by British laws, and for each colony a sum for bills in circulation was prescribed, which it could not exceed. This sum is fixed more or less according to the different circumstances of the colonies. The trade of the mother country suffered by the fall of the paper money. The colonist pays the English seller in paper money at its full value; the Englishman, who cannot use it in England, buys with it a draft on London, and can only get it accepted at the rate of exchange and so loses. The uncertain value of the paper is to his disadvantage. When received, such a bill might be at full value, a few weeks later, when paid out, its worth might have

---

7. Achenwall: "Der jährliche Abtrag des zehnten Pfennigs vom Capital." These words appear to be a somewhat clumsy locution meaning "an annual payment of ten percent of the capital [loan]." The text had made clear a few lines above that the new debtor was to repay one tenth of his loan annually, an arrangement confirmed by the remainder of the present sentence.

dropped 6 to 10 percent. Pennsylvania has avoided this inconvenience by a provincial law that at payment so much exchange shall be added to keep specie and bills at par.

Most English have been of the opinion that *Paper* Currency is bad for the colonies and the Crown, and want it wholly abolished.[8] On the contrary the colonies maintain it is to the benefit of them and the Crown if the use of paper money is not restrained by act of Parliament, but the decision as to how much paper money shall circulate is left to the free determination of each colony. In fact they have made representations to this effect in England (and public report says that in the present session of Parliament greater liberty will be granted, but on what conditions I do not know).

Taxes in the colonies are still very light. In several provinces, as said above, a quitrent is imposed on improved lands but it amounts to only a half penny local money per acre. In Virginia this quitrent goes to the Crown as Proprietor of the whole colony. In other governments settled inhabitants are free of a quitrent and are *völlige sogenannte Freyhalter ihren Landgüter* (Freeholders).

All other taxes must be laid by the Assembly. Each colony taxes itself as its needs call for, *"in quanto* als *in modo."* The usual base is a land tax (as in England) there 6, 12, 18 pence up to half a crown, i.e., $2\frac{1}{2}$ shillings for each pound of income from the land. This is laid also on income from a profession or office. Tolls on imports and exports with an excise tax do not exist in North America.[9] There is only a small tax on shipping for the support of lighthouses on the coasts. There is no enforced labor tax at all. Everybody is wholly a free man and master of all his property, immovable and movable.

The stamp duties roused universal opposition. They touched the colonies in the right to dispose of their own money, a capital point of their liberty and indeed their darling treasure.[1] All other parlia-

8. It is a curious circumstance that nowhere in this discussion is specifically mentioned the question of whether the bills of credit should be legal tender— the central point of disagreement between British and colonial attitudes.

9. This statement overlooks the existence in Virginia and Maryland of an export duty of 2 shillings per hogshead on tobacco; this tax had been in force since the seventeenth century and was a significant factor in the economy of both provinces. Since the statement related to the colonies on the mainland only, it was proper to omit mention of the duty of $4\frac{1}{2}$ percent on all "dead" commodities exported from Barbados and the Leeward Islands.

1. Achenwall: "in ihren Lieblingsneigung."

mentary laws and restraints on their trade and manufacturing they had borne without resistance. By these their liberty had indeed been curtailed, but never so sensibly as in this instance which touched their purses directly.

The colonists would not concede to Parliament the right of taxation. They say they have the rights of English citizens. No English community can be burdened with a tax without its own consent, i.e., without the agreement of the Lower House, where each community is represented. The colonies, however, have in the Parliament of Great Britain no representatives, as for example the Scots have, but only in their own Assemblies. Here and nowhere else can taxes on the colonies lawfully be laid. So they maintain that the British Parliament cannot claim to dispose of their purses, but they will exercise this right themselves. So far from having the income of the stamp duties applied to paying the British national debt, the colonists believe they have the greater obligation to take care of the payment of their own debts. The last war had put all the colonies in debt. This they should pay off first. The colonies supported at their own expense 25,000 men against the French, which cost individual colonies annually, 20, 30, 50 thousand pounds and more. If these debts are paid, the Crown might always claim the right to propose the same contribution in the Assemblies.

On these fundamentals all the colonies were of one mind, and so they decided on a general congress, to avert the storm. Such a congress of delegates from all the North American colonies had never been voluntarily called before, and the common decision not to accept the stamp taxes and to work for their repeal by united strength, was a significant agreement. The colonies based themselves on the right belonging to every English subject, when he thinks himself injured, to make *Vorstellungen* (Petitions) against the act. Many can do this together, and the number is not limited by law, whether 2 or 100, or 100,000, or more, who are affected, can agree to act together.

There are few fortified places in America. Philadelphia is quite open to attack, and has only one battery on the river, to protect the city against invasion. Here and there are a few forts to protect the settlers from the Indians. The provinces have their own militia, maintained at their own cost. The King appoints the officers. New England has the largest body of militia, and the little forts are manned by these troops under the King's commanders. There are English regiments in North America garrisoning the large forts; these are paid by the Crown. The English like to serve in America, for they are paid not in local currency but according to the English standard and are supplied by the local authorities with provisions.

The conquest of Canada is advantageous alike to the English nation and to the colonies, for much of the expense of maintaining troops and forts is no longer required. During the last war England supported 25,000 men in the colonies, and the colonies as many more. The royal rule in America, when in harmony with the colonies, is inexpensive in the older colonies, for the King's Cabinet rules by the stroke of a pen.

The colonies are well pleased that France handed New Orleans over to the Spanish. The Indians are sworn foes of the Spanish, who are neither so intriguing nor so industrious as the French, and hence England can keep on better terms with the Indians.

The general agreement of the colonies as shown in relation to the Stamp Act, is the more noteworthy, as the colonies have generally been jealous of one another. There are many disputes between them as to their borders, rivers, trade, etc. If the colonies were entirely independent, they would soon be at war with one another. Only the protection of the King and his authority prevent open outbreaks. This jealousy increases with the growth of the colonies. Pennsylvania gets along best, for it leaves all trade, both import and export, open to all other colonies, only making such restriction in its own favor as may be needed to meet restrictions laid on its trade by other colonies, but all laws of this kind require the royal approval.

Postscript[2]

Here concludes the account of Dr. Franklin, which for the greatest part I received as answers to my questions. I believe I have quite understood his ideas, although I cannot write all his words and expressions exactly as he spoke. Here and there I have inserted something for explanation, and that includes, too, what is inclosed in parentheses. Should there be some deviation of my copy from

2. This "Nachschrift" was omitted from the pamphlet reprint of 1769. In the 1777 pamphlet it reappears at the front, headed "Vorbericht" (Preface), with a small verbal change in the first sentence, and signed with Achenwall's full name rather than merely his initials.

the original, this does not affect any essential or important particular. At any rate, the example mentioned above of the distinguished Mr. Kalm may serve me as an excuse, since he, I think, had more months than I had hours of time to hold conversations with Dr. Franklin. I do not doubt that other men of letters in this country have enjoyed the conversation of this honored man just as much as I. If by this I could encourage them to publish the noteworthy items of his talk, it would certainly please the public. Indeed I found in him not only every readiness to answer my questions, but he even expressed a special pleasure that people here were not less eager to learn something of the New World than he, who came from there, was to become acquainted with the Old.

I could add various useful and weighty considerations to these remarks. For the present I leave every reader to his own reflections, and I offer only the observation which a passage of the Greek historian Thucydides suggests to me. I take it from the recent *Programma* of the well-known Professor Heyne.[3] As the British colonies felt themselves injured by the Stamp Act they declared themselves of the opinion agreeing completely with that of the Corcyreans once expressed to their mother city Corinth as the principle of all colonization. As Thucydides, I, 34, records them saying: Every colony respects its founders, if it is well treated; but if it feels injured and despised, it is alienated. Colonies are not sent out to be slaves, but as lawful equals to those who remain at home.[4]　　　　G. A.

From James Balfour[5]　　ALS: American Philosophical Society

Sir,　　　　Virginia Little England August 1st. 1766
Permit me leave to thank you for your kindness to me when in London and to wish you with unfeignd sincerity health, happiness, and Sucess in all you wish or desire.

3. Christian Gottlob Heyne (1729–1812), philologist and professor at Göttingen, edited editions of several of the classics.
4. Achenwall: "Omnis colonia, *sagen sie beym Thucydid.* I. 34. honore prosequitur suam patriam, si bene erga se animatam videat; at si iniuriosam et contumeliosam in se videat, ab ea abalienatur. Non enim mittuntur coloniae ea conditione, ut sint servae, sed ut cum iis, qui domi relinquuntur, aequali iure sint."
5. A Virginia planter and merchant, whom BF had first met in 1756; above, VI, 428 n. He had been in England during the winter of 1766 and was one

I must leave you for the news of the Country to my worthy friend Colo. Hunter.[6] Believe me Sir, I have, and shall continue with a persevering warmth to sett forth your late services done America. Facts, Stuborn facts shall force even Mallice itself to do you Justice. I have had some severe battling with some Gentlemen lately from Pensilvania in publick Company on your Account, the facts to my own Knowledge, made them declare they began to see you were much Injurd. I am ready to sign and swear to those facts in the most public manner if it should be necessary. I have wrote my friends in Maryland.

I am well asured that Mr. Wolstenholme will interest himself on this occasion[7]—every disinterested man ought to do it. I wish my Abilities were equal to my inclination, the world should be made acquainted with the ungreatfull treatment you have mett with. The greatest abilitys and Love towards mankind has been for a while abused through you Great Sir, but in spite of party the Divil and all their Adherents, I hope to see your Superiour Worth and Ability and Your real inate honesty Blaze forth with a Lustre to confound Your ennimies and hand your name and Goodness of heart down to posterity with assurance and respect.

I beg you will be pleas'd to return my thanks to that obliging polite friendly Woman Mrs. Stevenson for the Civilitys she shewed me when I had the happiness to call on you. I am Great Sir with much respect Your obligd Humble Servant   JAMES BALFOUR

Addressed: To / Benjamin Franklin Esqr. / Craven Street / London

Endorsed: Mr Balfour Augt. 1. 1766

---

of the colonial witnesses who appeared before the House of Commons on February 13, testifying about Virginia conditions. For brief excerpts from his testimony, see Lawrence H. Gipson, "The Great Debate in the Committee of the Whole House of Commons on the Stamp Act, 1766, as Reported by Nathaniel Ryder." *PMHB*, LXXXVI (1962), 33.

6. Another Virginia planter and merchant; above, VI, 223 n. He and Balfour were jointly associated with the London firm of Thomlinson & Hanbury. Hunter had moved to England and settled there late in 1765 or early in 1766.

7. Daniel Wolstenholme, a merchant of Annapolis, Md., was also associated with the Hanburys of London; above, VII, 277 n. Balfour was doubtless aware of BF's specific defense of the people and Assembly of Maryland in his Examination before the Commons on the same day that Balfour testified. See above, p. 141. Information of this defense, passed along to key Marylanders, would certainly help BF's reputation in general.

Gunning Bedford:[8]
Insurance Survey of the Franklin House

ADS: The Philadelphia Contributionship for the Insuring of Houses from Loss by Fire

Since Franklin had been one of the principal founders and the first president of Philadelphia's earliest fire insurance company, it was natural that his new house should be insured with that mutual organization. The deed of settlement of The Philadelphia Contributionship for the Insuring of Houses from Loss by Fire, dated March 25, 1752 (above, IV, 283–95), made reference to the formal surveying of a house as a preliminary to the issuance of a policy for its insurance. Although Deborah Franklin moved into the new home in the spring of 1765, several details of the construction remained unfinished for some time, and it was not until the summer of 1766 that Gunning Bedford, acting for the Contributionship, completed and recorded his survey among its records.

Bedford's description helpfully supplements the sketches of the floor plans and Deborah's description of the rooms printed above, XII, 293–8. The most interesting feature of the survey, perhaps, is the information

8. Gunning Bedford (d. 1802, aged 83), house carpenter, alderman of Philadelphia, 1792–96. *PMHB*, XXIV (1900), 208. He was, most regrettably, one of four men of the same name who flourished in the Middle Colonies in the eighteenth century. One Gunning Bedford of Pens Neck, Salem Co., N.J., died in 1725 and his estate was administered by his widow Mary. 1 *N.J. Arch.*, XXIII, 33. They may have been the parents of the Gunning who made this insurance survey and of his brother William, a farmer of Delaware. Each of these two brothers had a son whom he named Gunning. William's son (1742–1797), being the elder of the two, was sometimes called Gunning Bedford, *Senior*. He married Mary Read, sister of George Read (some of whose correspondence appears in the present volume), served as an officer in the Continental Army, in the Delaware legislature and Senate, in the Continental Congress, 1782–85, in the Delaware Convention to ratify the Constitution, and as governor of the state, 1796–97. The house carpenter Gunning's son (1747–1812) was sometimes called *Junior* to distinguish him from his cousin, five years older. Gunning's Gunning graduated from the College of New Jersey in 1771, studied law, and set up practice in Delaware. He married Jane Parker, daughter of BF's friend and long-winded correspondent. He served, as did his cousin, in various state offices and also in the Continental Congress, 1785–86, in the Annapolis Convention, 1786, the Federal Constitutional Convention, 1787, and the Delaware Ratifying Convention. He was attorney general of the state, 1785–89. Both these Gunning Bedford cousins are treated in *DAB*.

it gives of the decorative treatment of the interior walls and the chimney pieces. The rooms on the first floor, and especially the large dining room on the east, must have been very handsome.

Surveyd. Augt. 5th 1766   No. 1148

A house house [*sic*] Belonging to Benjamin franklin, Situate on the South Side of high Street Between third and fourth Streets where his familys dwells.

34 feet Square—3 Storys high—14 and 9 inch walls—3 Rooms on a floor—pertitions in the Eastermost part of the house 9 inch Brick wall to the Garet floor is in the westermost part Studed and plasterd. East Room[9] below wainscuted, with frett Cornish all Round, four pedements with frett Bedmolds A Rich Chimney peice, fluted Cullums and half pilasters with intabliture—the other other [*sic*] Rooms and passage below wainscuted pedistal high, with frett and dintal Cornish throughout one of sd. Rooms has a Chimney peice with tabernacle frame pediment &c. All the Second Story wainscuted pedistal high, frett dintal and plain duble Cornish through the whole, a Chimney peice in one of the Rooms with tabernacle frame pediment &c.

Chimney Brests Surbass [surbase] Scerting and Single Cornish throughout the third Story—Garet plasterd. a way out on Roof—two Storys of Stairs Rampd. Brackited and Wainscuted—one do [ditto]—Brackited—painted inside and out—Modilion Eaves—2 Large painhouses[1] with trusses at each end—all New—kitchen in Celler.   GUNNING BEDFORD

£500 a[t] 30s. per Cent or if
any higher Sum to be at 32s. 6d.

From David Hall   Letterbook copy: American Philosophical Society

Dear Sir.   Philadelphia August 19th. 1766

Your Favour of May 19th.[2] by Captain Cruikshanks I received for which I thank you, and shall act as you desire, with respects to the Contents of it.

9. The dining room.
1. Penthouses; extensions of the front and back roofs at the eaves along the north and south walls.
2. Not found.

I presented the Account from the Post-Office to Mr. Bradford,[3] who seemed surprised it was not paid, as he said he had given Orders for the Payment, and has told me since, that he has desired a Person to pay the Money.

There was no Mention made in the Accounts of the Amount of the Outstanding Debts, due to our Partnership, nor did I make any offer as to purchasing them.[4]

The Reason, as to the Sum was, that as I was still to keep a Regular Account of the Monies Received, and to Account to you as before, for your Share, thought there was no Occasion to give the Amount. And as to purchasing the Debts of you, you may remember, that when there was something hinted about them, you thought it could not well be done, as there was no ascertaining what bad Debts there might be. And since the Expiration of our Partnership, when the People have been more pressed, the more Danger appears to be in purchasing, as a great many, who I should have had no Doubt of, turn out to be bad; so that I believe the safest Way to both of us, is to account for the Money as it comes in. In the Money owing in Virginia and Maryland, and, in short, in all at a Distance, there will be a prodigious Loss, and even of what is owing in the City, and near it, the Deficiency will be greater than could have been thought.

As Mrs. Franklin never misses any Opportunity of writing you, I need not say any Thing about your Family. No News here, but what you will find in the Papers which are sent you, I am, in Haste, Dear Sir, Yours most Affectionately,   D H

per Capt. Golley[5]
To Benjamin Franklin Esq.

3. William Bradford (above, II, 315 n), printer of the *Pa. Journal*. Precisely why Bradford was indebted to the Post Office is not known; perhaps post riders had been carrying his newspaper and he had not paid them sufficiently.

4. BF had evidently complained to James Parker about this matter in a lost letter of May 9; see above, p. 341.

5. The brig *Elizabeth*, Capt. A. Golley, was reported as having cleared Philadelphia for London in *Pa. Gaz.*, Aug. 21, 1766.

"Americanus": On Obstructions in the Thames

Reprinted in Verner W. Crane, ed., *Benjamin Franklin's Letters to the Press 1758–1775* (Chapel Hill, [1950]), pp. 77–8, from *The Public Advertiser*, August 22, 1766.

In accepting Verner Crane's tentative attribution of "this pleasing little piece" the present editors cannot do better than to endorse his explanation, wherein he gives more weight "to the signature, and to general impressions of style, than would be justifiable if the stakes were higher. The features which 'Americanus' exhibits are recognizably Franklin's: his fondness for the water, his ironic tone toward lawyers, his improving spirit, his American measure for English natural objects."

Sir,   Aug. 22, 1766

I Am an American Gentleman, and as yet not entirely acquainted with the Customs of my dear Mother Country, and therefore apply to the Public for Information what to do as a Redress of a Grievance I lately met with.

Being fond of the Water, I took a Pair of Oars at Westminster Bridge to go to the Temple, thinking to save Ground, but to my great Surprise the Waterman landed me two thirds across the River at the End of what he called a Causeway, and called that landing me at the Temple, taking Sixpence for his Fare. Now, Sir, what vexed me was, that I had near as far to walk to get to the natural Shore as if I had walked all the Way.[6] At first I thought of applying to the Benchers of the Temple; but I remember an old Friend of mine, Mr. Gulliver, a great Traveller, told me that the Lawyers of this Country understood nothing else but Law; in other Respects they were of no real Use to Mankind.[7] I then thought it my Duty

6. Perhaps it is too bad to spoil the fun, but it should be said that the writer was guilty of gross exaggeration here. The Thames takes a right-angle bend between Westminster Bridge and the Temple, and a person walking along the left bank would go about a mile between these points. A boatman rowing in as straight a course as possible between the west end of the bridge and Temple Stairs would cover a distance two or three hundred yards less. If he landed his passenger instead at a causeway projecting two-thirds of the way across the river from the Stairs, the passenger would have to walk about two hundred yards to reach "the natural Shore," not the mile he would have traversed if he "had walked all the Way."

7. The passage referred to is in Swift's *Gulliver's Travels*, Part IV, "A Voyage to the Country of the Houyhnhnms," Chap. 5, the final paragraph.

to wait upon the Trinity House, or the City Conservators,[8] to know why I was not properly landed according to Agreement, but was advised to apply to the Public.

We Americans have the same Contempt for the Thames as the Inhabitants of Gravesend have for Fleet Ditch,[9] and much wonder that as the Thames is so mean a River, any Causeways, Shoals, or accumulated Points should be suffered, as the Preservation of the City entirely depends upon it's Navigation. I am, Sir, Your humble Servant,   AMERICANUS.

To the Speaker and Committee of Correspondence of the Pennsylvania Assembly   ALS: Yale University Library

Gentlemen,   London, Augt. 22. 1766
In mine of June 10th.[1] I acquainted you that I was about to make a Journey for the Establishment of my Health. I accordingly went to Pyrmont, where I drank the Waters some Days; but relying more on the Air and Exercise of Travelling, I proceeded to Hanover, and from thence thro' Cassel to Frankfurt and Mentz, thence down the Rhine to Cologne, and so thro' Treves to Holland,

---

The second half of this chapter is a vitriolic attack on the English law, the courts, and the legal profession.

8. The Elder Brethren of Trinity House had jurisdiction over lighthouses, beacons, buoys, and other aids to navigation, and over the dumping of ballast, rubbish, ashes, and soil in the Thames. Ancient charters and statutes created the Corporation of the City of London as conservators of the Rivers Thames and Medway, and vested in the lord mayor as "bailiff and conservator" and his "under or deputy water-bailiff" jurisdiction over all encroachments on the river and its banks, including the installation of poles, wharves, causeways, and stairs. P. Colquhoun, *A Treatise on the Commerce and Police of the River Thames* (London, 1800), pp. 301–2, 329–30, 352–5.

9. Gravesend, on the lower Thames, was the chief station for East Indiamen and a major victualling point for other oceangoing ships outward bound from London. The Fleet or Fleet Ditch, a stream arising in Hampstead and Highgate and emptying into the Thames at Blackfriars, had long since become virtually an open sewer, in spite of efforts to protect and develop its lower course for barge traffic. Part was covered over in 1737 and the section between Fleet Street and the Thames was similarly hidden from the public's eyes and noses in 1765.

1. Above, pp. 297–9.

from whence I returned here again on the 16th. Instant, well and hearty, my Journey having perfectly answered its Intention.[2]

Changes in the Ministry, which I mention'd as apprehended, have since taken Place:[3] But we have the Satisfaction to find, that none of those whom we look'd upon as Adversaries of America in the late Struggles, are come into Power; and that tho' some of our Friends are gone out, other Friends are come in or promoted, as Mr. Pitt, Lord Shelbourne, Lord Cambden, &c. So that we have reason to hope the farther Points we would obtain relating to our Commerce and Currency, may in the next Session of Parliament meet with a favourable Attention; in the Prosecuting of which no Endeavours of mine shall be wanting.

Mr. Jackson is still in the Country, but had communicated the Assembly's Address to Lord Shelbourne, who as Secretary of State, presented it. It was graciously receiv'd, and printed in the Gazette.[4]

2. For the chronology of this journey, so far as it can be determined, see above, p. 315. The route as reported here offers some difficulty. From Bad Pyrmont to Hanover was a trip of about 35 miles to the northeast; from Hanover the course was generally southwesterly some 200 miles through Göttingen, Cassel, and Frankfort to Mainz, where BF and Pringle reached the Rhine. From this point, according to BF, they went 100 miles or so down the Rhine to Cologne "and so thro' Treves [Trier] to Holland." But to get from Cologne to Trier they would have had to retrace their route up the Rhine as far as Coblenz and then go up the Moselle to Trier, a combined distance of over 100 miles; and at Trier they would have been about six miles from the Luxemburg border and a long distance from Holland. It seems probable that BF got the sequence wrong in his letter and that they visited Trier after leaving Mainz but before going down the Rhine as far as Cologne. After reaching Cologne from Trier, in that case, it would have been an easy matter to keep right on down the Rhine through Holland to their port of embarkation for England. *London Chron.*, Aug. 16–19, 1766, confirms the date of the travelers' return to London.

3. The Rockingham ministry ended on July 30 and a new ministry headed by William Pitt as lord privy seal took its place. Simultaneously, Pitt accepted a peerage as Earl of Chatham and so departed from the House of Commons, to the Lords to the dismay of many admirers in Great Britain and the colonies. Among others in the new ministry the Earl of Shelburne was secretary of state for the Southern Department (Conway remaining in the Northern Department); the Earl of Camden became lord chancellor; the Duke of Grafton, first lord of the Treasury; and, most importantly for future colonial relations, Charles Townshend became chancellor of the Exchequer.

4. For the transmission of this address from the Assembly's Committee of Correspondence to the agents, see above, p. 290. *London Chron.*, Aug.

And I was yesterday told by Lord Egmont, whom I met with at Court; that the dutiful Sentiments express'd by our Province and the Jerseys gave great Pleasure to all the Friends of America here. Lord Shelbourne was also so good as to express to me his Regard for America, and to assure me of his Inclination to do every thing in his Power that might promote our Interest jointly with that of the Mother Country.[5] As soon as Mr. Jackson returns to Town we shall concert together the Steps to be taken in the Affairs of our Province, and proceed in them with our joint Industry and Application, agreable to the Orders of the House and your Letters of the 8th of May and 6th of June.

Please to present my Duty to the Assembly, and believe me with sincere Respect and Esteem, Gentlemen, Your most obedient and most humble Servant   B Franklin

Speaker, and Commee. of Correspondence

Endorsed: Benja: Franklin Esqr. to the Speaker and Commee. Augt. 22d. 1766

To ———: Two Letters of Recommendation

ALS: American Philosophical Society

These two drafts of documents appear on the same badly torn and stained sheet, both have the same date, and both are written on behalf of other persons. It seems appropriate, therefore, to present them together, especially since the addressee of neither letter is certainly known.

The first document, apparently intended as a certificate of character for George Spencer, may have been intended for the Society for the Propagation of the Gospel or its secretary, the Reverend Daniel Burton, since Spencer received ordination in 1766–67 and the Society then sent him to New Jersey. Franklin had recommended Spencer to Strahan for

9–12, 1766, reported that "Last Saturday's Gazette" contained the addresses of thanks to the King on the repeal of the Stamp Act from governmental bodies of Pa., Del., Mass., and N.J.

5. On William Petty, 2d Earl of Shelburne, see above, x, 348 n. As secretary of state for the Southern Department in the new ministry he had direct responsibility for colonial affairs until January 1768, when the new office of secretary of state for the colonies was created and given to Lord Hillsborough, who had been president of the Board of Trade, 1763–65 and 1766–68.

a job in 1762, but on both occasions his appraisal of the man's character seems to have been unduly optimistic, for within a year after Spencer began his ecclesiastical duties in New Jersey the Society dismissed him as "disreputable."[6]

The persons introduced in the second document have not been identified, but the friend addressed was certainly a resident of Amsterdam. Quite probably he was one of the members of the Hope family of British merchants in that city—either Thomas or Adrian or, since Franklin signed himself as "your affectionate Countryman," their nephew Henry Hope, said to have been born in Boston. The Hopes had entertained Franklin, his son William, and Richard Jackson in Amsterdam in 1761.[7] The last paragraph of this letter suggests that, either on the way to Germany in the summer of 1766 or on the return, Franklin and Pringle had passed through Amsterdam and had experienced the Hopes' "Civilities" together on that occasion.

I

London, Augt. 22. 1766

This may certify, that I have known Mr. George Spencer many Years as a Merchant of Credit in Philadelphia and New York, during which time, as far as I have ever heard, his Life and Conversation have been orderly [*torn*] with a constant Attachment to the [*torn*] Land.   B FRANKLIN

II

London, Augt. 22. 1766

The Bearers [*blank*] and [*blank*] Mamy[?][8] Inhabitants of Pensilvania, are going to Amsterdam in quest of an Inheritance. As they will be Strangers there I beg leave to recommend them so far to your benevolent Notice that if they should meet with any Difficulty you would advise them in the Steps they are to take and the Persons proper to be apply'd to for Assistance.

I remember when [*illegible*] of promenading with you along the Cingle[9] some [*illegible*] Population in America. I take [*illegible*] sending you a little Piece of mine on that Subject contain'd [*illeg-*

6. For the recommendation to Strahan and on Spencer's character, see above, x, 104–5 and note.

7. Above, IX, 367 n; see also this volume, pp. 323–4.

8. These letters, possibly forming a proper noun, leave the editors mystified.

9. Probably a reference to the Singel Gracht, or "girdle canal" of Amsterdam.

ible] publish'd here a year or two before the [*illegible*] made the retaining of Canada.[1] I hope it will be agreable to you.

Sir John Pringle is well. We din'd together yesterday and remember'd with Pleasure the Civilities we receiv'd in Holland. Be pleas'd to present my best Respects to the other Gentlemen of your House and believe me, with sincere Esteem Your affectionate Countryman and most obedient humble Servant   B F.

From Charles Thomson   Draft: Library of Congress

Philada. Aug 24 1766

I do not know whether the intimacy with which you have honoured my acquaintance gives me a right to introduce any to your notice with out first having your leave; yet as I have knowledge enough of the goodness of your heart[?] to be assured of the pleasure it will give you to encourage rising genius I am induced to recommend to your notice, Ben. R[2] a native of this Town going to Edinburgh, to finish his studies. I should not have taken this Liberty had not Doctr. J. Redman[3] whose character you know, called and informed "that Benj had lived with him Six years during which time his moral character behaviour and application was such as a father would wish that of a favourite son to be, and that his Skill and abilities promised him to be a very useful Member of society in his profession."

As his design in going abroad is wholy for the sake of acquiring medical knowledge, he is Ambitious of being under your patronage,

1. Apparently BF and his host had been talking during their walk about the rapid growth of population in the colonies and BF was now sending him a copy of his Canada Pamphlet, published in April 1760 (above, IX, 47–100), to which was appended a nearly complete reprinting of his 1751 pamphlet, *Observations concerning the Increase of Mankind* (above, IV, 225–34).

2. Benjamin Rush (1746–1813), physician and humanitarian, one of the most distinguished American members of the medical profession in his time. *DAB;* George W. Corner, ed., *The Autobiography of Benjamin Rush His "Travels Through Life" together with his Commonplace Book for 1789–1813* (Princeton, 1948); L.H. Butterfield, ed., *Letters of Benjamin Rush* (2 vols., Princeton, 1951); Carl Binger, *Revolutionary Doctor Benjamin Rush 1746–1813* (N.Y., 1966).

3. John Redman (above, V, 356 n), whose apprentice Rush had been.

and should think himself extremely happy if by a line from you he could be introduced to the Notice of Men of Letters especially such as are eminent in Physick, Nothing I can say would have equal w[eigh]t with that which Doctr. Redman (who spoke a great deal in his favour) said that any recommendation of that sort would be a service done to Society. He goes accompanied by Jonathan, (a Son of your old friend John Potts);[4] in whose behalf you doubtless will have letters from his Friends. I am Sir with the greatest esteem and respect Your affectionate Friend and very humble Servant

Doct. B. Franklin

To Deborah Franklin

ALS: American Philosophical Society

My dear Child,   London, Aug. 25. 1766
    I have scarce time to write to any body by this Ship, but must acknowledge the Receipt of yours of July 7.[5] with the Account of my dear Brother's Death, which was very affecting to me.[6] I can now only say, that I approve of what you have done on that Occasion, and recommend our desolate Sister to the Continuance of your tender Care and Kindness.[7] Mr. Foxcroft's appointing his Brother is agreable to what was formerly concluded on between us when my Brother was first appointed:[8] What I wrote to you was when there was an Appearance that young Mr. Foxcroft might go into some other Business. My Love to Sister, and tell her I will write to her per Packet. Love to our Children and Friends concludes from Your ever affectionate Husband   B FRANKLIN

4. John Potts (above, XI, 484 n), a member of BF's political party, who failed of reappointment as J.P. for that reason in 1764. His son Jonathan (1745–1781), Rush's companion, received his medical degree at the College of Philadelphia in 1768, and served actively with the American forces, 1776–80. *DAB*.

5. Not found.

6. For Peter Franklin's death, July 1, 1766, see above, p. 332 n.

7. DF's letter in which she reported Mary Franklin's death indicates that such a recommendation from BF to his wife would have been unnecessary in any case.

8. Peter Franklin had become postmaster of Philadelphia in 1764; see above, XI, 230 n, 253, 417–18. His successor was Thomas Foxcroft.

Postscript, Aug 26.

As I apprehend Sister may be under Concern about her Living, and her adopted Son, Mr. Brown has express'd to me his Readiness and Willingness to do all in his Power to assist her; I desire you would offer them the Use of the little Printing House that Mr. Parker return'd from Burlington,[9] and let them if they chuse it, set it up in the old House next the Street, to be carried on by him for their joint Profit. I hope you can by a little Repair of the House and Fences, soon make it fit for Sister to live in.

There is a Mohogany Press and some Letter in Casks I brought from England, which I would not have meddled with at present. They may be taken into a Garret in the House. And also the Stationary that is in the great Chest.   B F.

Addressed: To / Mrs D. Franklin / at / Philadelphia / per Capt. / Chancellor.[1]

To William Franklin

Extract: reprinted from [Jared Sparks, ed.,] *A Collection of the Familiar Letters and Miscellaneous Papers of Benjamin Franklin* (Boston, 1833), p. 275.

August 25th. 1766.

I can now only add, that I will endeavour to accomplish all that you and our friends desire relating to the settlement westward.[2]

From Ephraim Brown[3]   ALS: American Philosophical Society

Respected Sir   Philada. Aug. 25, 1766

By Capt. Friend I wrote you an Account of the Decease of

9. This printing equipment had belonged to Benjamin Mecom; see above, p. 107. Because of Mary Franklin's death and Ephraim Brown's departure for London (see the document next but one below) it was not used by either of them. Later in this year WF suggested that the projected *Pa. Chronicle* use it. See below, p. 501.

1. *Pa. Gaz.*, Nov. 6, 1766, reported the entry of the *Ann and Elizabeth*, Capt. S. Chancellor.

2. The scheme for establishing an Illinois colony in which WF was one of the principal movers. See above, pp. 257 n, 330 n.

3. The adopted son of Peter and Mary Franklin; above, XII, 77–8.

your worthy Brother; now I am sorry to inform you of the Death of his dear Wife, who departed this Life on Thursday the 14th Instant, after a short Illness in the Bloody Flux, by which I am bereaved of the best of Parents, and sincerest Benefactors;[4] and should look upon myself as a poor unfortunate destitute young Fellow, were it not for the Confidence I put in the good Mr. Franklin, whose Friendship has been always my Study to preserve, and I hope shall never forfeit. With a grateful Heart I now return you Thanks for all past Favours, and beg a Continuance of them. I shall always acknowledge your generous offer in putting me into a Printing Office in London for my Improvement;[5] and as I have now nothing to hinder me from embracing it, shall be glad to see you in London, if you please to write me a Line. I mention'd to Mr. Hall my Inclination of going to London, and he approv'd of it, and offer'd me Letters to his Friend Mr. Strahan, which I took very kind. I am now going to resign the Post-Office to Mr. Thos. Foxcroft, after doing the Business of two Years (I hope to Satisfaction)[6]—Mr. Foxcroft appears to be a very good Man, and much of a Gentleman, and I doubt not will fill the Vacancy with Judgment and Honour. I intended to have work'd with Mr. Hall till I had a Letter from you; but there is a young Man just arriv'd from London, with a Recommendation from Mr. Hall's Correspondent,[7] so there is at present no Room for me; but Mr. Hall says that the Man has wrote to Virginia, and if he meets with proper Encouragement, will set up his Business there: If so, he will employ me.

After your Brother died, your Sister shewd me his Will, wherein he left all he had to her. She told me that all her Relations were dead, that she should leave what she had, to me, and hop'd I

4. On the death of Peter Franklin, see above, p. 332 n; and on that of Mary, pp. 338–9.

5. BF may have made this offer orally before leaving for England in November 1764. Brown did go to London in the early months of 1767.

6. As BF mentioned to DF in his letter of this same day, he and John Foxcroft had agreed that the latter's brother Thomas should be the next postmaster of Philadelphia. Brown appears to have done much of the actual work in the Philadelphia office during his foster father's tenure.

7. Probably Benjamin Towne, whom BF recommended to Benjamin Waller of Williamsburg, June 6, 1766, (above, pp. 289–90), and whom Strahan mentioned to Hall in a letter five days later (*PMHB*, x, 226).

should make a good Use of it; but She was taken ill in so short a Time, before she had administered, or settled any of her Business, that she made no Will, and became delirious, before she scarce knew her Danger; by Reason of which I am deprivd of a Matter, which (tho' small) might have been of Service to me.[8] In about 4 Weeks Time I shall go to New England, and shall be gone about 7. Mrs. Franklin, and Miss Sally are well, and I suppose write.

I have no further to write, so beg leave to subscribe myself, Your most obliged Humble Servant   E Brown.

To Benja Franklin, Esqr

To Mary Franklin[9]   ALS: American Philosophical Society

Dear Sister   London, Augt. 26. 1766

It has pleased God at length to take from us my only remaining Brother, and your affectionate Husband, with whom you have lived in uninterrupted Harmony and Love near half a Century.[1]

Considering the many Dangers and Hardships his Way of Life led him into,[2] and the Weakness of his Constitution, it is wonderful that he lasted so long. It was God's Goodness that spared him to us. Let us, instead of repining at what we have lost, be thankful for what we have enjoyed.

Before this can reach you, every thing that can be said to you by way of Consolation, will have been said to you by your Friends, or will have occurred to your own good Understanding. It is therefore needless for me to enlarge on that Head. But as you may be under some Apprehensions for your future Subsistence, I am desirous of making you as easy and comfortable in that respect as I can. Your adopted Son Mr. Brown, has wrote to me, very prop-

8. If Peter and Mary Franklin had never formally adopted Brown, as may well have been the case, he would have had no legal claim to any part of Mary Franklin's intestate estate.

9. Of course BF could not know, when he wrote this letter to his recently widowed sister-in-law, that she too had died twelve days before he wrote.

1. Since Peter and Mary are recorded as having been married Sept. 2, 1714, they must have been in the 52d year of their marriage when he died.

2. Peter Franklin appears to have been a ship's captain at one stage of his career.

erly, "that he shall always think it his Duty to stand by and assist you to the utmost of his Power."[3] He is yet young; but I hope he has Solidity enough to conduct a Printing-House with Prudence and to Advantage. I shall therefore put one into his Hands to be carried on in Partnership with you; and if he manages well, I shall hereafter farther encourage him. I have not time to write to him now; but shall by the Packet. I have however desired my Wife to deliver to you and him the Press and Letters that were B. Mecom's, which Mr. Parker us'd at Burlington;[4] and to let you go into the House where I suppose they are, as the Rent of that you are now in is heavy.[5] I can now only add that I am as ever Your affectionate Brother   B FRANKLIN

Sister Franklin

From James Parker   ALS: American Philosophical Society

Honoured Sir   New York Aug 27. 1766

Tho' I have not the Pleasure of One Line from you by this last Packet, and have but little new to acquaint you of, but what I have wrote about before,[6] or your Friends will inform of, yet I will not forfeit my Charter by not writing, and wish I could say any Thing that would be pleasing. This has been for the greatest Length of Time the warmest Summer I know: And the fore part of it being pretty wet has caus'd a great deal of Sickness in many Places; my Son, who never got thoroughly well since last Winter, has had another hard Spell, but having got better about 10 Days, so as to be able to go about, he is thinking to take a Small Voyage to Sea, in Hopes that may help restore his Health:[7] and Six Days

3. The letter containing this dutiful undertaking has not been found.

4. Parker's letters of 1765–66 contain many references to the Mecom printing equipment he had used at Burlington and had sent to Philadelphia before moving to New York.

5. In her letter informing BF of Mary's death, DF indicated that the Peter Franklins had been paying 20s. a week rent.

6. One of Parker's most accurate statements; see his several most recent letters, above, 262–6, 300–12, 325–8, 340–5, for extended discussions of the principal topics found in this letter.

7. Samuel Parker had been seriously ill the previous winter. His prospective sea voyage was a visit to North Carolina.

ago, I was taken with a violent Fever, which reduced me very low, but by God's Blessing, upon the Medicines used, the Fever has left me, and I am recovering, and just able to write. I yet print no Paper, because I am yet in Hopes to settle Some how with Holt, which is promised to be the first of next Month, tho' my Hopes are but small, seeing his often Promises were never minded, nor have I any well-grounded Assurance of its being better now but I have promised to wait so long.[8] In the mean while Nothing is done with Hamilton and Balfour's Business[9]—and I am afraid of a poor Account from thence, so that at the last I shall suffer in that Affair: and I shall be glad if I should suffer no more: for I would freely lose all that to have a full Settlement and Payment on all other Matters: but alas! I fear after a Settlement, if such a Thing Should ever be effected, that I shall get little or nothing: for he will plead his New Printing Materials are his Brothers, tho I never could learn his Brothers were ever a Bit more generous than himself, or would ever help him before but were willing enough he should live upon me, and eat me up, and when an Opportunity offered to do it more effectually they would do that, or rather he found them my Money for them to do it for him; but thus it is, and I must Still use the Same Remedy I do in the Gout. I have not had the Pleasure of one single Six pence worth of Work since I been removed here, nor done any for Pay except what I did for the Jerseys at Woodbridge last Month.[1] What I have done here is part of an Almanack which I am now about, but have Stood Still a little for some Paper I daily expect:[2] Mean while Living in this City is excessive high. Every Body complains *No Money*, yet every One asks such Prices for Things, as if we had the Potosi Mountain within a Mile of us: By my Computation it takes every Farthing of my Allowance for only Victuals, Drink, and Taxes and Firewood so we must all go naked

8. It is perhaps unnecessary to say that poor Parker failed to achieve a settlement with Holt in September.

9. The Edinburgh firm, often mentioned, that had been trying for some time to collect a debt from Parker.

1. At Woodbridge this year Parker printed *The Acts of the General Assembly* and *Votes and Proceedings of the General Assembly* (Evans, 10412, 10413).

2. Later in the year Parker brought out *Poor Roger's American Country Almanack* for 1767 and *Poor Roger's Universal Pocket Almanack* for 1767 (Evans, 10396, 10397).

and pay no Debts, unless Providence sends us some Work otherways; and in my Charges I have not included the Doctor's Bill: I have yet Hopes that that good Providence, which never entirely left me, will not leave me now; but indeed, Sir, if the Post-Master General will have their Comptroller of these Offices live in New-York, I humbly think they Should be willing to allow him the other £20 per An: I do not desire your exorbitant or overgrown Allowances but Time and Places should be considered, and indeed there are many more small Offices to look after, and write to than there were a few years ago: tho' the additional Riders and Expences of Times, together *with* the Lowering of the Postages, to which may really be added, the Deadness of Trade at present makes it so that the Revenue is not much enlarged; but it is a growing Thing, and tho I have as much real Trouble now, as a Comptroller with double the Revenue and the same Quantity of Offices, yet I don't doubt but a succeeding One will be allowed more: But I submit. The Office in the Custom-House as I am obliged to act in it, has really not an Adequate Allowance, and I don't see by the new Laws, that I am like to have any Less to do in it, but rather more: I have no Merit to plead for me, but wish those Gentlemen of the Customs would think that £10 more, per An. would draw a little more of my Blessings on them: I know well the Nation is already too much Burdened with Pensioners, but apprehend those real Burthens are of a much larger Measure than mine, and too often Sinecures, which is not the Case with this; tho' perhaps it might have formerly been a little on that Order. But if I can but do my Duty to Satisfaction,—a hard Thing!—I shall be satisfied and a little more, like a Spur to an old Horse, would help somewhat in the Way.

You see I find something to fill up two Sides of Paper at the same Time have little or Nothing to say: Our Friend Hughes here Still keeps close, and still keeps a School. Thank God he is well, which is one Comfort he has in his Troubles. It seems there was one Comfort left even in Pandora's Box. But we have never got the Electrical Machine yet, nor shall we without the Bill of Lading, or at least till the Captain returns, who is still abroad. I believe I have sold 40 or 50s. worth of Stationary in my Shop since I opened it, and that is as much as I can say: There are so many flourishing Stationers here to what there were formerly, that I stand but a poor Chance among them: Rivington, Noel and Gaine, are Tip-tops:[3] there are several others of smaller Note; yet I think, had I not been so shamefully circumvented by Holt this last Time, that I could have got in for a Sharer with them; tho' as tis, I have not had the Offer of So much as a single Hand-Bill, &c. Indeed few of those are done here.

Benny Mecom, goes on in the usual Road, now-and-then a Promise: but that is all: Had he paid the Riders sooner, it would have been better: for the Ballances in the Post-Office since he paid them, are but small. Our Friend Chew[4] of New-London seems to me to be in much such a Box: He is the compleatest Parrier of a Dun, that I have any Occasion to treat of:

Now, my Honoured Sir, if I have not wrote as an agreeable Letter to you, as many of your Friends will have done by this Packet, yet I can assure you, there are two Things in my Letters generally not deficient; those are Length and Truth, which they possibly vye with any: but for other Matters I can't say much in their Praise, they may however besides, if you will permit them, assure you, that I beg all our humble Salutations may be acceptable, and that I am still Your most obliged Servant

JAMES PARKER

PS. Tho' I am but poorly, yet this is the 7th Letter I have wrote to Day, and but only this one to go beyond Sea:

Endorsed: Mr Parker Augt. 27, 1766

From Baynton, Wharton & Morgan   LS: Library of Congress

Dear Sir   Philadelphia Augst. 28th 1766

We are now to acknowledge the Receipt of your very kind Favors, of the 26th February, the 10th of May and the 8th of June;[5] and at the same Time, to do Ourselves the pleasure of heartily thanking you, for your many and great Kindnesses to Us.

3. These top stationers and booksellers were: James Rivington (1724–1802), Garrat Noel (c.1707–1776), and Hugh Gaine (1727–1807). Rivington and Gaine were also active printers.

4. The financial troubles of Joseph Chew, postmaster at New London, have been mentioned several times earlier.

5. BF's letter of February 26 has not been found; for the surviving brief extracts from the letters of May 10 and June 8, see above, pp. 275–6, 297.

It was with inexpressible Joy We received your Congratulations on the Repeal of the Stamp Act; and found the several agreable Alterations, in the Commercial Laws. These are Events, which will undoubtedly restore the Affections of the Americans, to the Mother Country; As They clearly demonstrate On her part, An Inclination to act justly and equaly, with her Children.

Our Enemys, on your Side the Atlantic, will find Themselves much disapointed, in their Expectation, That the Repeal of the Stamp Act will incite fresh Demands, from the Colonists and aggravate their intemperete Behaviour. Be assured it has had and will have, a very contrary Effect.

America has been fortunate, in having her Liberties, Rights and Commerce fully and firmly explained; And We shall ever esteem it, very Providential, That you was called to the Bar of the House of Commons, As We are convinced, Its Members were in a great Measure Strangers, to the true Interest of Great Britain, Until you so wisely and firmly delineated it to Them; For Which, both that Kingdom and her Colonies, are Under the strongest Obligations to you.

Your Friends received the highest Gratification in the perusal of your Examination and They anxiously looked for the Arrival of the last Packet, As They flattered Themselves, They should have One, They could print; But They are greatly disapointed. The One Mr. Hall has—He has been very industrious, in the reading to different large Companys; and the Demand for it, from all Parts of the province, is beyond Conception.[6]

Your Enemys acknowledge—That if it is genuine—You have been the great Defender of their Liberties—But They affect to doubt its Authenticity, As it is not signed, by the Clerk of the

6. For Strahan's sending the copy of BF's Examination to Hall on May 10 and its later printing in Philadelphia, see above, pp. 125–6. On Sept. 12, 1766, Governor John Penn sent his uncle, Thomas Penn, "a thing just printed said to be the Examination of Mr. Franklin before the house of Commons. It has been handed about in manuscript for some time past in a private manner, and is now published by the party. I suppose to prepossess the minds of the people in favor of Mr. Franklin at the ensuing election. It is thought to be patch'd up here to answer the present occasion, as many of the answers contained in it, appear to be calculated to deceive and I think he would not have ventured to have answerd the questions put to him in that manner, however I may be mistaken." Penn Papers, Hist. Soc. Pa.

House. They are, as Mr. Pope says "Willing to wound, But yet afraid to strike"[7]—It has had a very happy Effect, In confirming the wavering, awakening the Neutrals and dividing Our Opposites. Our Mr. Wharton returned last Month from Fort Pitt.[8] He was there, during the Treatys, Which Mr. Croghan held with the six Nations, Shawanese and Delawares. And We assure you, it was happy for these Provinces, That this Gentleman went thither, As the Natives were greatly incensed, at the repeated Murders of their Relations. We know you are truly interested, in the Welfare of America and Therefore for your Amusement, We will give you a Detail, of What passed at the Treaty. The Indians remonstrated to Mr. Croghan, That Out of Pity, to their Women and Children and Not from Fear, They had agreed to preliminaries of Peace, with Colonel Bouquet. That They had sent Hostages to Sir William Johnson to ratify the same. That as a proof of their Sincerity, They had appointed some Chiefs to attend Him (Croghan) last Year, to the Illinois; That some of those, had *fallen* in Our Service and That No One Instance could be adduced, of their having violated the Terms of the Pacification, Although They had received reiterated provocation, by the Butchery of their People. They also urged, That We boasted of Laws to regulate Our Inhabitants; Wherefore Our Wise Men was, in their Opinion, answerable for their Conduct; But as to Them, They had no Influence Over their Warriors, more than what their Advice and Address could effect and Therefore They were apprehensive, a Rupture would soon insue between Them and Us, unless some speedy and effectual Measures were made Use of, to restrain Our frontier People from settling On Lands, Not yet sold by Them and from killing their Hunters and Warriors, as They passed thro' it.

They very justly added. That if an Indian killed an Englishman, The News was instantly communicated to all the Goverments; and the Frontier Inhabitants stood ready, to kill the first Native They saw. They also Observed, That They had evinced by their Behaviour, How well disposed They were to keep the Peace and

7. "Willing to wound, and yet afraid to strike." Alexander Pope, *Epistle to Dr. Arbuthnot,* line 203.

8. Early in July Samuel Wharton returned from Fort Pitt with letters reporting Croghan's successful negotiations with the Indians. *Pa. Gaʒ.,* July 10, 1766; *Johnson Papers,* V, 304.

That if They had been actuated, by the same principles, as The *White Men,* They would 'Ere then, have ballanced the Account of Murder. They concluded, by representing in the most pathetick and cogent Terms, The absolute Necessity of a permanent Boundary, being fixt between Them and Us—Over Which, no *White* Man should be suffered to hunt.

If Unhappily Orders should not soon be received by Sir William Johnson, for the purchasing this *Boundary*—We tremble for the Consequence, As the Indians will not Only consider Themselves triffled With, in respect to it (as so long Time is elapsed, since Sir William, in the Spring 1765 called Them together, by Order of the Lords of Trade and obtained their Consent to the Sale of it)—But They will consider all those, who have seated Themselves, On the West side of the Allegany Mountain, as Intruders on their Country; Whilst the Settlers, confident in their Numbers, It is to be feared, will persevere in their Murders—Wherefor Hostilitys may be justly expected the approaching Fall or Winter, The fatal Consequences of Which, all the Middle Colonies must soon feel, As We know from melancholy Experience, That tho' Indians, may at first, direct their Resentment, to its proper Objects—Yet They soon forget, the partial Provocation, and quickly involve all *White Men,* in One general Predicament. We would fain hope, This will not occur, As We trust, before Now, Orders are transmitted, for the purchasing this *Boundary.*

If this was once done—The present great Cause of Quarrels, between the Indians and Us would be fully removed; For at present, there are about Two hundred Families settled on unpurchased Land On *Red Stone* and *Cheat* Rivers, in Virginia.[9] The Natives conceive Themselves, very ill treated by this Settlement; Wherefore frequent Disputes, happen between their Warriors (When on their Rout to, or returning from War, against the Cherokees) and the Settlers. An unhappy Instance of Which is the killing, ten six Nation Indians, On the 10th of June.

9. Tributaries of the Monongahela River. Redstone Creek, in Pennsylvania, enters at Brownsville; the Cheat River, almost entirely in West Virginia, joins the Monongahela at Point Marion, just north of the state line. Following receipt of representations on these settlements from General Gage, Governor Penn issued a proclamation, Sept. 23, 1766, ordering these squatters to depart and forbidding such settlements in the future. *Pa. Col. Recs.,* IX, 321–3, 327–8; *Pa. Gaz.,* Oct. 2, 1766.

By Order of General Gage, a party of Twenty Soldiers with a Lieutenant, accompanied by two Mingo Chiefs, went from Fort-Pitt On the 18th of June, to desire these Intruders, to remove from thence—But their Errand was fruitless. They declared, They would not retire.

Our Hearts are impress'd with the liveliest Sense of Gratitude, for the unwearied Pains, you have taken, in respect to the *Indian Grant*[1] and We have not the least Doubt, But your Friendship for Our Families, will not lose Sight of so great an Object, for Us. We have expended a vast Deal of Time and Money, to bring Matters to the Issue, We took the Freedom of mentioning, in March last; Wherefore if We should be disapointed, It will be realy, very distressing to Us; But We cannot suffer such a Thought to exist, with Us, When We reflect upon the Justice of Our Application and the policy of gratifying the Indians, in making Recompense, for their Robberys.

This Subject is of so very interesting and important a Nature to Us—That We trust your Goodness will rather smile, than frown at us—If Our Anxiety should impel us, to dwell so circumstantialy, Upon it, As now to Mention, What perhaps We have repeated before. We will however, be as brief, as possible.

Sir William Johnson has been and is very desirous, to do us an essential Piece of Service, in respect to Indian Losses and Therefore When He was directed, to treat with the six Nations, About a *Boundary,* He took that Opportunity, of requiring Them to grant a Part of the Country, within that *Boundary* by way of Retribution for their Robbery. Which They agreed to; That is, When the Treaty is to be held, for the ascertaining and paying for the Land, *within it,* They will acquaint Sir William, That They will Not receive any Pay from the Crown, for such a particular part of the Land, Within the Boundary (Which We shall take Care to be limited, by Natural and immoveable Bounds)—As They give it, to the INDIAN TRADERS, As a Restitution for the Goods, They stole from Them.

You will please therefore, Good Sir, to Observe That the Order

1. See above, XII, 397–9, and later correspondence, for George Croghan's proposal (in which this firm, Sir William Johnson, and others were interested) that the Indians cede a tract of land as compensation for the losses they had caused the traders.

to Sir William, for purchasing *this Boundary,* is the Basis, On Which, We can Only Obtain the Indian Grant; for Unless, that is ordered to be purchased, The Indians cannot give Us the Land, Which They are willing to present Us, with. We are afraid, We are tedious; But We hope the great Significance of the Subject, will apologize, for any seeming Tautology.

When the *Boundary* is Obtained, We apprehend it will be indispensably Necessary; That the respective Goverments should immediately pass Laws, declaring, That any Person Who shall hunt On Lands, to the Westward thereof, shall suffer Death and That all Offences committed in any Frontier County, On Indians Or their Property, shall be tried in some of the interior Ones; For without something of this sort is done, We are convinced, from the Temper and Practise of the Frontier People, No Example will be made of the Aggressors, As They are generaly, so *religiously* infatuated, as to esteem it a Virtue, to extirpate the Heathen. Of Consequence frequent Causes of just Complaint will be made by the Natives. After Mr. Croghan had satisfied, The six Nations Shawanese and Delawares at Fort Pitt, in respect to the Murder of their Bretheren—He acquainted Them, That He was going to the Illinois, to treat with the Numerous Nations in that Country, and it would be agreable to Him, If They would appoint a Deputation of their Chiefs and Warriors, to accompany Him; That so the Tribes below, might know from Themselves, That all the Northern Indians, had renewed the Covenant of Peace, with their Fathers, the English.

They made a most friendly Answer to his Speech and told Him —They much approved of his Errand and That They had appointed Deputys to attend Him; and More would join Him, at the Mouth of Sciota.

He left Fort Pitt on the 18th of June, accompanied by Our Partner, Mr. Morgan[2] and about 120 six Nation Chiefs and Warriors.

He arrived safe at Sciota—held a very satisfactory Treaty with the Indians in that Country and On the 7th of July, set Off, for

2. George Morgan (1743–1810), brother of Dr. John Morgan, and son-in-law of the firm's senior partner, John Baynton. Max Savelle, *George Morgan Colony Builder* (N.Y., 1932). For letters to his wife, Mary, while on this expedition, see Alvord and Carter, eds., *The New Régime,* pp. 311–17.

the Illinois attended with the above Chiefs and Warriors and a very respectable Deputation from the Shawanese Delawares &c.

The French notwithstanding the specious Covering of surrendring New Orleans to the Spaniards, are very industrious, in making their Settlement, On the West Side of the Missisipi and have gone great Lengths, in poisoning the Minds of the Indians, against Us; But We apprehend, Mr. Croghan will now essentialy weaken their Interest, As He takes with Him, such a powerfull Representation, from the Northern Tribes; Who are esteemed by those, below, as judicious Councellors and great Warriors:

At the same Time, That He is treatying at the Illinois—Sir William is gone to Meet Pondiac and a Number of the Western Chiefs at Oswego. And happy would it be for Great Britain and her Colonies, if She was immediately to counteract the French; by establishing a civil Goverment in the Illinois Country.

Such a Goverment, if the Governor was a person well esteemed by the Natives and accustomed to Indian Affairs, would soon have a considerable Number of Inhabitants, Whereby the British Garrisons in that extensive Country, would be *certainly* and *cheaply* supplied with Provissions (and not subject to be starved Out, Whenever The Indians thought proper, to intercept Our Convoys.) The Natives regularly and cheaply furnished with Goods and the Indian Police, conducted with Spirit and Address, Which upon its present Establishment, is impossible; As Sir William and Mr. Croghan reside at too great a Distance from the numerous Tribes, Who inhabit on the Waters emptying into the Missisipi.

We are truly thankfull to you, for the kind assistance you gave Mr. Neave, in respect to Our Insurance down[?] the Ohio.[3] We are certain it contributed Much to the effecting it, from the just Opinion, Which the Gentlemen Underwriters, had of your great Knowledge and probity.

We have the pleasure of informing you, That Our Batteaus are

3. Richard Neave and Son of London. The matter referred to here had probably been discussed in the missing letters mentioned in the first paragraph above. Writing to his daughter, Mary Morgan, July 11, John Baynton reported that by the last packet he had learned to his great satisfaction that Neave had insured the firm's first divisions of batteaux at a very reasonable rate, and that BF had been "not a little instrumental in getting our Insurance perfected." *Ibid.*, p. 337.

all safely arrived. They had ten Days passage from Fort Pitt to the Mouth of the Ohio and ten Days from thence to Fort Chartres.

They met several partys of Indians, On their passage; Who were all friendly to Them.

The Trade was just beginning, as Our Messenger came away And it had a very favorable Appearance.

We esteem it, a Mark of the Friendship, you honour Us With, in recommending Mr. Sevells[4] to Us. Be assured We shall make it a point, to render Him all the Assistance in Our Power.

We are entirely of Opinion with you, That the brewing of London Porter, As He is perfectly acquainted, with it, will be attended with great Advantage, As it is a Liquor, much esteemed both here and in New York.

The many Changes in the Ministry have been a vast Delay to your Negociations, But We live in Hopes, That 'Ere the Spring, We shall experience a happy Relief from proprietary Despotism. We ardently pray, That your Excursion to Germany will restore your Health and That you may return with Vigour. With the sincerest Respect and Regard We Are Dear Sir your Much Obliged Servants   BAYNTON WHARTON & MORGAN

Benjamin Franklin Esqr.

Endorsed: Baynton Wharton & Morgan. Augt. 28. 1766. Very importunate about the Boundary. to be urged with the Miny.

From Anthony Tissington[5] ALS: American Philosophical Society

Dear Sir   Alfreton 30th. Augt. 1766

By this time I expect you are returned to London from your German Tour, which I hope has been pleasing to you, and usefull to Sir John Pringle.

By keeping out of the Smoak I was got pretty well by the 4th of July, when I left London; and a Journey into the North, from whence I am Just return'd, has set me right, and I am now as well as ever in

---

4. Not identified.

5. For Tissington, who lived at Swanwick, near Alfreton, Derbyshire, and whose nomination to the Royal Society BF had recently supported, see above, VIII, 358; IX, 42 n.

my life: but my Wife[6] continued very bad in Town, and since, tho'
the Prescriptions of Dr. Morrice[?][7] have been of great use to her.
I have still a great opinion of Dr. Dom [*illegible*]'s[8] Practice
of bathing and sta[r]ving; and think him very Ingenious, but not
as Judicious as I could wish. He risques too much; and I think, if
I had not interfered, and put a Stop to the Process, my Wife must
have sunk under it: He aim'd at obtaining what Nature has pro-
hibitted; and continued to persist in it, when He gave Pains nearly
equall to those of Child Birth without Effects: But I still beleive,
tho' my Wife will not, that it has been of use to her; It forced the
Blood thro' the necessary passages, which gentle means wou'd not,
perhaps, have obtain'd; and for the last fortnight, her pains have
been less, and she is in the road to do well.

My Paper on the Mineral Customs,[9] left [with Mrs.] Stephenson,
I hope you've got. Mr. Ro[lles has] not yet proceeded against us;[1]
the Crown [*torn*] us; the Country in high Spirits; and [*torn*] shall
at last do well.

When you've got over all that Arrears of Writing, which your
absence must have created, I shall hope to hear from you; And
when Heaven inspires you with the good Resolution of giving
the greatest, friendly Pleasure, in your power; to see you here—
'till when, and allways, I am with the greatest Esteem My Dear
Friend Yours most Affectionately   ANTH TISSINGTON

Endorsed: Mr Tissington Augt. 30, 1766

6. Anthony Tissington, widower, married Mrs. Margaret Bunting, July 14,
1763, at Alfreton. *Derbyshire Parish Registers, Marriages,* XV, 110.
7. Possibly Michael Morris, M.D., F.R.S., of the Westminster Infirmary.
8. A dark stain in the MS renders this name illegible.
9. Tissington's only known published writing was *A Letter to a Friend on
the Mineral Customs of Derbyshire. In which the Question Relative to the Claim
of the Duty of Lot on Smitham is Occasionally Considered. By a Derbyshire
Working Miner* (London, 1766). A curious MS note in the British Museum
copy reports the assertion in 1794 that BF had written the pamphlet while on
a visit to Tissington. The author of the note, who signed it "A.W.," put little
stock in the assertion, which, as Albert H. Smyth pointed out, merely em-
phasizes the extent of BF's scientific reputation. *Writings,* I, 56–7.
1. In 1761 the Duke of Devonshire successfully asserted his right under the
Crown to receive duties on *smitham* (or *smeddum:* ore in fine particles) and
other low-grade lead ores in parts of Derbyshire; his success led a Mr. Rolles
to assert, and later to establish, a similar right elsewhere in the county. James
Pilkington, *A View of the Present State of Derbyshire* (Derby, 1789), I, 114.

From Samuel Wharton

ALS: American Philosophical Society

Dear Sir   Philada. August 30 1766

The Bearer hereof is Dr. Jonathan Potts son of your Friend John Potts Esqr. He pays Europe a Visit for an Improvement in the Duties of his Profession.[2]

He has requested me to mention his Name to you; Which I am persuaded, is all, that is Necessary, to introduce Him to Gentlemen of the first Character in the Physical Class. I did myself the Pleasure to call at your House a few Days ago and Miss Sally (Who this Moment passed my Window On Horse Back) was complaining She had missed the Packet—I therefore took Charge of the within Letter.[3]

My Partners and self are writing you a Letter to go by this Conveyance; But I am fearful We shall be too late.[4] I am with the [since]rest Esteem and Respect Dear [Sir Your] Obli[g'd Friend] &c   SAML WHARTON

Benjamin Franklin Esqr.

Addressed: To / Benjamin Franklin Esqr. / Deputy Post Master General / of North America / in Craven Street / London / per favor of / Dr. Jonathan Potts

From Joseph Galloway

ALS: American Philosophical Society

Dear Sir   [August, 1766][5]

The Bearer hereof Mr. Jonathan [Pot]ts son of our worthy Friend Mr. John Potts, served his Apprenticeship with Dr. Phineas

2. On Jonathan Potts, his traveling companion Benjamin Rush, and their journey to Great Britain to pursue medical studies, see above, pp. 387–8. Young Potts had only just reached Edinburgh when he learned that his fiancée, Grace Richardson, was very ill, so he returned to Philadelphia at once. She had recovered by the time he reached home. They were married in the spring of 1767; he completed his medical studies at the College of Philadelphia, and she became the mother of his seven children. *DAB.*

3. No letter from Sally to her father of about this date has been found.

4. Presumably the letter of August 28, the next document but one above.

5. So dated because of the recommendation of Jonathan Potts, who was traveling to Edinburgh to pursue his medical studies. On Aug. 24 and 30, 1764, Charles Thomson and Samuel Wharton had written BF on behalf of Potts and his companion, Benjamin Rush, both of whom were about to embark for Britain.

Bond[6] of this City. His Intention is to complete his Studies in England. He is here esteemed [to be a] sensible worthy Young Man. I am Convinced, that a bare Mention of his Connections will be a sufficient Recommendation of him to your Notice and Friendly Advices, whenever he shall stand in Need of them, during his Stay in England, and render any other unnecessary from Dear Sir your very Affectionate humble Servant   JOS. GALLOWAY

Addressed: To / Benjamin Franklin Esqr / In Craven / Street / London / per Favr / Dr. Jona Potts / p post paid

From George Read

Draft: Library of Congress

Sir   [August? 1766][7]

I now return you my most sincere thanks for the immediate Application you were so good as to make at the Treasury on my behalf, as I am informed by your Letter of the 12th. of June[8] and shou'd the event be otherwise than successful to me it will not prove a matter of much disappointment.[9] I am but little troubled with that Passion for Offices so generally prevalent. This is the first I ever sought after, the Execution of which answering my Situation tempted me to rely on your well known disposition to assist those you may think worthy. My Mother desires her best Compliments may be made to you for your kind remembrance of her and I am your much obliged and most obedient Humble Servant   GEO: READ

Doctor Franklin

Endorsed: Drt. of a Ltr to Doctor Franklin in London—1766

6. Above, II, 240 n.

7. Read might have received and answered BF's letter of June 12 before the end of July, but August seems a more probable month for the writing of this letter.

8. On April 14, 1766, Read had written BF asking that he apply to the Treasury for Read's appointment as collector of the port of Newcastle. BF had replied on June 12 reporting that he had made immediate application as Read had asked. Above, pp. 246–7, 313.

9. The change in the ministry during July was probably a major reason for the failure of the application. BF's extended absence in Germany may also have been a factor.

From William Sturgeon[1]   ALS: American Philosophical Society

Dear Sir   Philadelphi Sepbr. 1 1766
    I tacke the Freedom to trouble you with a few Lines hoping you may have Leasure to give them a persual: I would acquaint you that my Health has been So much on the Decline as obliged me to retire into the Country, and as the Mission of Burlington is vacant by the Death of Mr. Campbell,[2] I would request the Favour of you to interpose with the Society in my Behalf.[3] It would be a great Kindness to my Small Family if they Should grant me the Refusal of it. Form [from] the repeated Acts of FriendShip you have done me makes me thus apply. I long to hear from you and wishing you Success I am dear Sir yours   Wᴍ Sᴛᴜʀɢ[ᴇᴏɴ]

Addressed: To / Doctor Franklin / Agent from Pennsylva / London

To Rudolph Erich Raspe   ALS: Landesbibliothek, Kassel

Dear Sir,   London, Sept. 9. 1766
    I received your obliging Favour of Augt. 28.[4] with the Paper enclos'd for the Monthly Review, which I shall communicate to the Managers of that Work, and imagine I shall prevail with them to do you better Justice.[5]

    1. For the Rev. William Sturgeon, curate and assistant minister at Christ Church and St. Peter's, Philadelphia, and catechist of the school for Negro children supported there by the Associates of Dr. Bray, see above, VII, 252 n; X, 298. He had resigned his positions, July 31, because of ill health.
    2. The Rev. Colin Campbell, Anglican missionary at St. Mary's Church, Burlington, N.J., had died on Aug. 9, 1766. See above, pp. 337–8 n.
    3. See below, p. 483, for BF's letter recommending Sturgeon to the secretary of the Society for the Propagation of the Gospel for the position at Burlington or one at Trenton.
    4. Not found.
    5. The appendix to *The Monthly Review,* XXXIII (probably published in January 1766), contained a review article, pp. 497–505, on Raspe's Latin and French edition of Leibnitz's posthumous philosophical papers. The review was for the most part a discussion of the differences between the metaphysics of Locke and Leibnitz. Some phraseology apparently gave Raspe reason to think that he was being criticized for "disrespectful treatment of Mr. Lock's memory," and he wrote the letter to the "Managers" that BF here acknowledged. In the appendix to the *Monthly Review,* XXXV (published in

I am oblig'd to you for the Trouble you took in the Affair of my little Bill.[6] As the other Bankers beside the Jew, have satisfy'd you that it was fully paid, I am sure I ought to be satisfy'd, tho' I do not understand it.

I thank you for reminding me of the Promises I made in your Country, some of them might otherwise have escap'd my Memory, as it must be a considerable time before I can possibly perform them, the Seeds, Mohawk Grammar, and Pensilvania Laws being all to come from America, at least 3000 Miles from hence.[7] I deliver'd your Letter to Dr. Knight, who will write to you when he has receiv'd the Box of Fossils you sent him,[8] which is not yet come; being put in the Package we made up at Frankfurt, of Books bought there and those brought from Göttingen, which we left in the Hands of a Merchant, to be sent to us by way of Holland, and it is not yet arrived. Mr. Canton also will write to you as soon as he can. His House is just now repairing, and full of Confusion with Workmen, which he desired me to mention as his Excuse at present. Mr. Michell lives in the Country,[9] and I shall hardly see him till Winter, when he commonly spends some time in Town. I will then communicate to him your Book, and make him acquainted with you.

January 1767), appeared a short statement, p. 569, acknowledging Raspe's communication, expressing regret at his displeasure, and stating that the passages that had displeased him had not referred to his publication "but to another work, the natural produce of our own country." Later correspondence suggests that Raspe was not wholly mollified.

6. See above, p. 345.

7. Nothing is known of any attempt by BF to send American seeds to Germany. At this time there was no grammar of the Mohawk language in print, though John Christopher Pyrlaeus (1713–1785), a Moravian preacher, had begun the study of that language in 1744, became a teacher of it, and may by 1766 have compiled one of the MS grammars later deposited in Hist. Soc. Pa.; Amer. Antiq. Soc. *Proc.*, new series, LXVI (1956), 294. The volume of Pennsylvania laws BF was to send was probably his own edition of 1742; above, II, 391.

8. Gowin Knight (1713–1772), whose book on magnetism BF had sent to Ezra Stiles in 1755; above, VI, 103, 178. Raspe's first published work, *Specimen Historiae Naturalis Globi Terraquei* (Amsterdam and Leipzig, 1763), had dealt with fossils.

9. John Michell (1724–1793), the English astronomer and geologist; above, VII, 357 n; XI, 480–1.

The Map of the British Northern Colonies I send you herewith,[1] as also Dr. Knight's Book, which he desires you to accept from him. My own is yet in the Press; as soon as it is finished, I shall do myself the Honour of presenting you with a Copy.[2]

It would be a great Pleasure to me to see you here or in America, or in any Place where I could see you happy; but I would not have you hasty in Resolutions of Removing. Merit like yours continually increasing by fresh Acquisitions of useful Knowledge, cannot much longer remain unnotic'd and without due Encouragement where you are. Here Strangers labour long under Obscurity and Difficulties before they can establish themselves; and, except in one way, I see no Opening for you in America: For you would hardly chuse to turn Planter, and plough for a Living. The Way I mean is the Practice of the Law in our Courts; and that too, if I mistake not, would hardly be agreable to your Inclination; tho' I think the Foundation you have laid in the Civil Law would greatly facilitate your Study of our English Law and the particular Laws of our Province. If you think you could seriously apply yourself to this Profession, I believe America would do well for you, especially as your Knowledge of the German Language would qualify you particularly to do the Business of those People. But in any other way, I do not see how I can encourage you to go thither.

When the Books from Frankfurt arrive, I shall see what I have, and what I still want, of the Lists given me at Göttingen.[3] I shall then take the Liberty of troubling you with my Commissions.

Be so kind as to present my respectful Compliments to the good Baron Munichausen,[4] and assure him that I have the most grateful

1. This map may have been either the one by John Mitchell (d. 1768) entitled *Map of the British and French Dominions in North America* (London, 1755), or Lewis Evans' *General Map of the Middle Colonies in America* (Phila., 1755); above, II, 415 n; V, 448; VI, 173 n.

2. The fourth edition of *Exper. and Obser.* was not completed and published until the winter of 1768–69.

3. BF had visited both Frankfort and Göttingen during his recent journey.

4. Probably Baron Gerlach Adolph von Münchausen (1688–1770), privy councilor, first minister of the Electorate, and promoter and curator of Göttingen University; not Baron Hieronymus Karl Friedrich von Münchausen (1720–1797), of Bodenwerder in Hanover, a member of a junior branch of the same family. The younger man is generally the better known; diverting stories of his exploits as a cavalry officer fighting with the Russians against the Turks

Remembrance of the Civilities I receiv'd from his Excellency at Hanover, and thro' his Recommendation at Göttingen. Remember me also respectfully to Mr. Munichausen his Nephew, to the Veldt Marshal, to Mr. Brander, to Doctor Wichtman, and to Mr. Young, when you occasionally see them.[5] I never think of the Time I spent so agreably at Hanover, without wishing it could have been longer. Remember me also affectionately to the Professors at Göttingen, whose Learning and Politeness impress'd me with the highest Esteem for them: I wish every kind of Prosperity to them and their University. With sincerest Regard, I am, Dear Sir, Your affectionate Friend and most obedient humble Servant

B FRANKLIN

M. Raspe

Endorsed (following the date line at the top): resp. d. 10. Febr. 1767.[6]

From James Parker

ALS: American Philosophical Society

Honoured Sir   New York, Sept 11 1766

You I hope are well: tho' I have not the Pleasure of one Line for two Packets past and two Merchantships: Upon which Account I have perhaps the less to write because I don't know well

---

probably served his friend Raspe as inspiration for a small book, *Baron Munchausen's Narrative of his Marvelous Travels and Campaigns in Russia* (London, 1785). Later editions, "enlarged" by other writers, converted the former soldier into the legendary European counterpart of the American teller of "tall tales" of the frontier. BF's use of "his Excellency" certainly suggests the high ranking officer of state, not the retired soldier.

5. This untitled younger Münchausen cannot be positively identified. The "Veldt Marshal" (field marshal) may have been Johann Ludwig, Count von Wallmoden-Gimborn (1736–1811), an illegitimate son of George II residing in Hanover. "Mr. Brander" was Georg Friedrich Brandes (1729–1812), owner of a large library and later secretary of the University of Göttingen. Johann Ernst Wichmann (1740–1802) was a distinguished physician in Hanover, a widely traveled translator of English medical works into German. "Mr. Young" may have been Johann Heinrich Jung (1715–1799), chief librarian of the Hanover Royal Library. The editors are indebted for most of these identifications to Robert L. Kahn, who has edited and published this and other letters in "Three Franklin-Raspe Letters," *Proc.*, APS, XCIX (1955), 397–400.

6. Raspe's reply of Feb. 10, 1767, has not been found.

what to write:[7] If you have got all my late Letters, you will learn, First that being so great a Sufferer by Holt, I am in Hopes Col. Hunter will think I have some Call upon him for a Settlement: Next, I told you, I had promised to stay till the first of this Month with Holt for a Settlement he had promised by that Time: but as I feared, it does not appear to be any nearer now, than 5 Year ago. I am told he is sick with the Gout, but I think now he is a—Villain. I am now (only) applying to a Lawyer to sue him a Task I undertake very reluctantly: but what to do I know not: Both my Boys are sick with a bad Fever, so I am not able to begin a News-paper, nor does it appear to me to be a very proper Season to do it: Trade is excessive dull; every Thing very dear, no Money, and yet Nothing to be got without: We have had a hot Summer, and great Sickness prevails at this Time both at Phila. and here. I have not had Six pence worth of Work for this Province since I came. I am doing an Almanack, as usual,[8] if happily I may get as much by it, as will find my Winter's Firing, I shall be happy on that Score. I left this City in a wrong Time, when Money would have been to be got, and I come to it at as wrong a Time, when None is to be got. If I can but rub along the little Time I have to stay, I shall be thankful: but my Doctor's Bills being equal to the Butcher, fall heavy on me:

We have never got your Electrical Machine, nor I think shall not, unless you send the Bill of Lading.

Sept. 13. 1766

Here I was going to conclude but considering, that if I sent you so much Paper as to make a Letter, it might as well be filled up, because you could but burn it when you had done, or before you read it, if you pleased.[9] I may first inform you, that all Masters of Vessels that come in here, do with their Letters as they usually did nor is any Measure taken to make them conform to the Act of Parliament, nor do I see that any Measures can with Safety be taken about it, for the general Bent of the People being against conforming, it does not seem possible for the King's Officers to do

7. Virtually everything in this letter has been said before in several of Parker's letters of this spring and summer and need not be explained again.

8. *Poor Roger's Country Almanack*.

9. This remark appears about three-quarters of the way down the first page of the MS. As can be seen, Parker kept bravely at it; he filled three full pages of the sheet and about half of the fourth.

any Thing against them: I have done what I could, but Nothing have I got by it, but a little Sour Looking, and perhaps some Contempt.

The Office you was so good as to procure for me in the Custom House I have now executed about four Months, and every Day when my Health permits make a Tour or two the whole Length of the Town Wharves: I have never ask'd nor ever was told when or how any Pay was to be had for it, nor shall I, but I hope you know, and that if it be to be paid there, that you would let me know how you may be indemnified for the Trouble and Expence you have been at: The Business I do is really as much as the Salary is worth; tho' I wish the Salary had been a little more adequate to the Trouble. You mentioned at first that the Execution of this office might open a Door for something better in this Branch: but I never heard a Land-Waiter here was ever advanced any higher in that Branch at all, so I dont expect it, because I have not the least Pretension of Friends or Merit, in the Way: However, were this and the Post-Office a Certainty for Life, I would retrench my Family and live small: for not having done 6d. worth of Work all this Time, and a Family to maintain in the dearest Place I believe on this Continent, besides Taxes very high my single Lot being £6 per An. besides some City Charges, makes it so that I can hardly Square the Yards.[1]

Was I to deviate from this Affair, what shall I treat of: I am afraid Ben Mecom will not make both Ends meet at any Rate: I have wrote and disputed with him, till I have both affronted him and tired myself: but I durst not tell you all that has passed between us, because some of it has been unreasonable. What I shall do with him I know not. What Pity he and Holt had not happened to be connected as I was, because his Soul and Holt's seems to have a good deal of Resemblance: I was compleately unfortunate to have to do with either of them as their Tempers are cool, indifferent, and think more of themselves than of others, whilst mine is a warm, fretful Disposition, more fond of doing good to others than myself, and can but illy brook such Impositions as they seem fond of laying on me: In short, I would follow the Golden Rule of doing to all, as I would they should do unto me, whilst I think

1. It would appear that Parker's duties with the shipping at the New York wharves had begun to introduce nautical expressions into his formerly land-based vocabulary.

they are trying to make every Body do to them as they would have them, without being at the Pains of doing one right Thing to them again, unless a few good Words, which never yet filled a hungry Man's Belly.

The Post-Office at Quebeck seems to turn out some Profit to the General Office, when it was thought it would hardly bear its own Expences. There are three Offices in Canada,[2] and all help a little: These add something to my Trouble: but the many other Offices now erected, and the very bad Pay, or Backwardness of accounting by many of them: keeps me pretty well employed in writing to them, and pressing them to their Duty; Shall I tell you our Friend Chew keeps behind-hand the most, and there is a Report, that he is worse than Nothing, but as he pays one Rider, he can't be very largely behind-hand: I write to him, but he stands it too well, to regard it. Tho' I do not begrudge my Labour wherever I am successful, yet I should rather wish a little addition, could be made to my Allowance agreeable to Mr. Foxcroft's Opinion also, which would render it much more agreeable in this dear City, where all I have hitherto cleared by it won't buy me a new Hat.

The Publick News, the Papers will better inform you of: and I durst not venture on a Publick Paper, with my old batter'd Types and almost batter'd Fortune, not to add batter'd Reputation, but the Worst of all is a batter'd Body: almost unable to stand the Shocks of Time, and to which I must at last yield.

My Son I told you having been sick now near a whole Year, I tho't it would conduce to his Health to send him to Sea: accordingly about 12 Days ago, he sail'd from this Place, to go to the Northern part of Carolina, where my Brother still lives, if so be the Sea-Air may help him: I have not heard from him. Since his Departure, his Wife and Child have both been down with Fevers, and are yet so: tho' its no more than Neighbour's Fare, as its very sickly throughout. My unhappy Nephew,[3] who went to Cape

2. Quebec, Three Rivers (Trois Rivières), and Montreal.

3. Samuel Parker (above, p. 10 n), not to be confused with Parker's own son, Samuel Franklin Parker, mentioned earlier in this paragraph. Andrew Steuart, a printer, went to Wilmington and started the *North-Carolina Gazette* probably in September 1764. Clarence S. Brigham, *History and Bibliography of American Newspapers 1690–1820* (Worcester, 1947), II, 782.

Fear with Andrew Stewart, tis said is dead there: tho' I have no positive News of it, yet it seems direct, and I believe tis so. Our Friend Hughes here keeps close, and keeps a School yet: he is full of Concern himself, being one of the Sons of Liberty, at the general Odium cast upon his Brother in Philadelphia by Reason of some printed Letters there. Thus every one has his Troubles: only some has more than others: I have the most contrary one of all, that is Gout and Poverty at once: Are they not inconsistent? Yet I thank God, I have now been five Months without one, at the Time I seem threatned hard with both by-and-bye, Indeed, I have had a bad Spell about 6 Days with the Fever and Ague, but happily it has left me a little while, and I hope it will be like Apollyon to Christian, sped away, that I may see it no more. And wish the Gout would go along with it, to somebody who can make it more wellcome.

Thus, tho' I had nothing to write, at first, I have filled up three Sides with just—Nothing. I confess I was in Hopes, to have heard from you per this Packet for your Opinion what You thought I had best do in the Case with Holt: but in Hopes of Col. Hunter's making me some Satisfaction, and of your Opinion, Advice, or Orders in some Matters or other, I shall at this Time conclude, for tho' I might expect you were on your Return, yet as I have not heard that is likely to be this Fall, I am determined to write on something till I hear farther: Nothing now remains, but all our sincere Respects and affectionate Salutations wishing you Health and a safe Return to your Family is the real Wishes of my Family and in particular those of Your most obliged Servant

JAMES PARKER.

PS. On looking this over, it look'd so much like complaining, that I was almost determined not to send it: I confess it wrong, and could I but go into some Business again, or in Likelihood of Work, I have full Reason to be thankful thankful it is no worse; since I see vastly many in worse Boxes, tho' I doubt whether they have been so befool'd, or bam'd [sic] as I have been: I am thankful that I am not quite ruined, as I might have been long ago.

Endorsed: Parker

413

To William Franklin

MS not found; extract reprinted from [Jared Sparks, ed.] *A Collection of the Familiar Letters and Miscellaneous Papers of Benjamin Franklin; Now for the First Time Published* (Boston, 1833), pp. 275–7.

[September 12th, 1766]

I have just received Sir William's open letter to Secretary Conway,[4] recommending your plan for a colony in the Ilinois, which I am glad of. I have closed and sent it to him. He is not now in that department; but it will of course go to Lord Shelburne, whose good opinion of it I have reason to hope for;[5] and I think Mr. Conway was rather against distant posts and settlements in America. We have, however, suffered a loss in Lord Dartmouth, who I know was inclined to a grant there in favor of the soldiery, and Lord Hillsborough is said to be terribly afraid of dispeopling Ireland.[6] General Lyman[7] has been long here soliciting such a grant, and will readily join the interest he has made with ours, and I should wish for a body of Connecticut settlers, rather than all from our

4. See above, pp. 330–1.

5. Conway had shifted from secretary of state for the Southern Department, the ministry in charge of American affairs, to secretary of state for the Northern Department on May 24, 1766. When the Chatham administration took office in July 1766 he retained this position, the Earl of Shelburne becoming the new secretary for the Southern Department. For ministerial changes in the summer of 1766, see above, p. 384 n.

6. William Legge, 2d Earl of Dartmouth (above, XII, 362 n), was replaced as president of the Board of Trade in the new Chatham administration by Wills Hill (1718–1793), holder at this time of the Irish title, the Earl of Hillsborough, which he also received in the British peerage in 1772. Hillsborough had been president of the Board of Trade from 1763 to 1765. From 1766 to 1768 he was one of the joint postmasters general and in the latter year was appointed the first secretary of state for the American Department, in which capacity he served until 1772. Hillsborough was one of the largest landholders in Ireland and was keenly interested in developing the linen industry in that country. *DNB*. Namier and Brooke, *House of Commons*, II, 626–7.

7. Phineas Lyman (1715–1774) was a Connecticut officer who served with distinction in the French and Indian War. In 1763 at Hartford he and some fellow officers and soldiers formed the Company of Military Adventurers and joined with the subscribers to Samuel Hazard's project of 1755 (above, VI, 87 n) to seek a land grant in the Mississippi Valley. After years of lobbying in London he succeeded in 1770 in obtaining a grant of 20,000 acres for himself near Natchez in West Florida, where he died in 1774. Delphina L.H. Clark, *Phineas Lyman Connecticut's General* (Springfield, Mass., 1964).

frontiers. I purpose waiting on Lord Shelburne on Tuesday, and hope to be able to send you his sentiments by Falconer, who is to sail about the twentieth.[8]

A good deal, I imagine, will depend on the account, when it arrives, of Mr. Croghan's negotiation in that country.[9] This is an affair I shall seriously set about, but there are such continual changes here, that it is very discouraging to all applications to be made to the ministry. I thought the last set well established, but they are broken and gone. The present set are hardly thought to stand very firm, and God only knows whom we are to have next.

The plan is I think well drawn, and I imagine Sir William's approbation will go a great way in recommending it, as he is much relied on in all affairs, that may have any relation to the Indians. Lord Adam Gordon is not in town, but I shall take the first opportunity of conferring with him.[1] I thank the Company for their willingness to take me in, and one or two others that I may nominate.[2] I have not yet concluded whom to propose it to; but I suppose our friend Sargent[3] should be one. I wish you had allowed me to name more, as there will be in the proposed country, by my reckoning, near sixty-three millions of acres, and therefore enough to content a great number of reasonable people, and by numbers we might increase the weight of interest here. But perhaps we shall do without.

8. For an account of BF's interview with Shelburne, see below, pp. 424–5.

9. George Croghan arrived in New York, Jan. 10, 1767, by ship from New Orleans, having sailed down the Mississippi to that port at the end of his negotiations in the Illinois country. He gave General Gage a full report of his talks on Jan. 16, 1767, and about the same time sent BF a copy of it. See Croghan to BF, Jan. 27, 1767, William L. Clements Lib.

1. In a letter to WF, May 3, 1766, Sir William Johnson had suggested that Lord Adam Gordon be included among the promoters of an Illinois colony. Gordon (1726?–1801) was a military officer and M.P. for Aberdeenshire, 1754–68, and for Kincardineshire, 1774–88. In 1764–65 he had traveled from Jamaica, where his regiment was stationed, and toured extensively on the North American continent, visiting Johnson at Johnson Hall and becoming interested in speculation in American lands. *DNB*. Namier and Brooke, *House of Commons*, II, 510–12.

2. See above, p. 257.

3. John Sargent, the London banker (above, VII, 322 n), who had been interested with BF in earlier schemes of land speculation; see above, X, 209, 214, 366, 369.

To Sir William Johnson   ALS: Historical Society of Pennsylvania

Sir   London, Sept. 12. 1766

I am honoured with yours of the 10th. of July, just come to hand, with that for Mr. Secretary Conway under a flying Seal, which I have clos'd and forwarded.[4] He is now in another Department, but it will go of course to Lord Shelbourne, who I think is rather more favourably dispos'd towards such Undertakings.

I have long been of Opinion that a well-conducted western Colony, if it could be settled with the Approbation of the Indians would be of great National Advantage with respect to the Trade, and particularly useful to the old Colonies as a Security to their Frontiers.[5] I am glad to find that you, whose Knowledge of Indian Affairs and the Temper of those People far exceeds mine, entertain the same Sentiments, and think such an Establishment in the Ilinoias Country practicable. I shall not fail to use my best Endeavours here in promoting it, and obtaining for that purpose the necessary Grants; and I am happy that this Occasion introduces me to the Correspondence of a Gentleman whose Character I have long esteemed, and to whom America is so much obliged.[6]

It grieves me to hear that our Frontier People are yet greater Barbarians than the Indians, and continue to murder them in time of Peace.[7] I hope your Negociations will prevent a new War, which those Murders give great Reason to apprehend; and that the several Governments will find some Method of preventing such horrid Outrages for the future. With sincere and great Regard, I have the Honour to be, Sir, Your most obedient, and most humble Servant   B FRANKLIN

Sir William Johnson

Endorsed: London Septbr. 12th. 1766 Benjmn. Franklin Esqrs. Letter

4. For Johnson's letter of July 10 and mention of its accompanying letter to Secretary Conway, see above, pp. 330–1.

5. BF had written in 1754 in favor of the establishment of two western colonies (above, v, 456–63) and in a letter to George Whitefield in 1756 had mentioned his daydream of a colony on the Ohio which they might jointly found (vi, 468–9).

6. BF and Johnson had first met each other, as far as is known, at the Albany Congress of 1754. Though both were now interested in the proposed western colony, they never became regular correspondents.

7. In his letter Johnson had mentioned the "licentious conduct" of the frontier inhabitants towards the Indians.

From Ann Penn[8] ALS: American Philosophical Society

Sir   Dublin septbr the 16 1766

I hope you are Recoverd. from your late fatigue and indisposition,[9] my dear Springett has been very Ill of a fever I had 2 the most Eminent Physicians to attend him. He is better, but is very weak. I have him in the Country for the air, he would write to you himself but it would fatigue him to much,[1] but joyns with me in in our best wishes for your self and family your Humble servant   A Penn

Please to direct as usuall.

Please to give our Compliments to mrs. Stephenson who I hope with her daughter is well.

Addressed: To / Benjamn. Franklin Esqr. / att Mrs Stephensons, / In Craven Street In / the Strand / London

Endorsed: [Mrs.] Penn Sept. 16. 1766

From Hannah Walker[2] ALS: American Philosophical Society

Most Dear and Honoured Sir   Westbury Sep th 17 1766

I received your kind Letter on the 13th with greater joy than I can express and to hear as you with your good Family are all [in] Perfect health and by my Cousins[3] account [your?] good Brother

8. Ann Penn (d. 1767), widow of William Penn, 3d, and mother of Springett Penn; above, IX, 260–2.

9. Possibly a reference to BF's illness in the late spring; above, p. 315.

1. Springett Penn died of tuberculosis in early November, less than two months after his mother wrote this letter; *PMHB*, XXII (1898), 183.

2. The last surviving letter before this one between BF and his first cousin once removed, Mrs. Hannah Farrow Walker (A.5.2.3.3.1), was hers of Oct. 21, 1765; above, XII, 337–9. That letter was in part a humble apology for some offense she, or more probably her husband, had committed. Whether BF had replied at that time is not known, but the present letter makes clear that she had been much concerned by a long silence on his part, broken only a few days before she wrote by a letter from him, not now to be found. The MS of the present letter is badly torn along one margin; the resulting loss of words, together with Mrs. Walker's somewhat difficult handwriting, makes the accurate rendering or interpretation of some passages very doubtful.

3. Eleanor Morris (A.5.2.8.1), first cousin of BF and first cousin once removed of Mrs. Walker, who lived with the Walkers. She is mentioned by

it is not to be questioned is [*torn*] is only to a Better Place which I was sorry [to] hear of your Loss and our Consolation was so g[reat to?] hear from you that I almost was overcome [*torn*] known of such along journey we need not have [*torn*] your Silince long but my Cousin would be Poss[*torn*] Nothing but you was ill. Honoured Sir [*torn*] your long Silence was because I thought I had [incurred?] your Displeasure upon those things Past[4] and [*torn*] Express the uneasiness I have conceived because [it?] was so against my will and I hope you will Pa[rdon] me for that was the only Reason as I know so [*torn*] your Incumberance in Business is so great and [*torn*] do and will observe every word you write to be of [great?] Service to me and I for my Part will always be as frugal and Industrious as it Lies in my Power and [*torn*] I can assure you with Pleasure that my Hus[band] has followed his Trade closer within this [time?] than ever he had Done before Since I [knew him. I was?] Extreamly Sorry to hear your Loss of Late [*torn*] will be Providence to Retrieve it again [*torn*] is and shall be the Hearty Prayers of [*torn*] Suppleant for the health and Prosper[ity of you?] and yours, which is the Least I can do to so [great a?] Friend and kind Benefactor.

[*Torn*] only Friend in the world in which my Dependence [*torn*] Else I must In Eveatibly have Sunk in my Trouble [which?] I could wish you knew what I have gone thro but I hope through Gods mercy and your generous Donation[5] to be able to Support my Family in a very [com]fortable manner. Honoured Sir I Humbly [beg] the Favour of your acceptance of a few [*torn*] hearts and beg mrs. Stevensons acceptance of a little [*torn*] Loaf of this New Corn if you send John to [the] Oxford Arms in Warick Lane on

---

name later in this letter. Apparently she had received word, directly or indirectly, of the recent death of BF's brother Peter.

4. Presumably a reference to the matter that incurred her apology the previous October. The sense of this long and confusing passage seems to be that they would not have been so concerned over BF's long silence had they known of his journey to Germany, but so far as she could know his silence might be due to serious illness or to his continued displeasure over the episode of the previous year.

5. In 1759 BF had divided his inheritance of £11 8s. 4d. from a mutual relative equally between Mrs. Ann Farrow (Mrs. Walker's mother), and Eleanor Morris; above, VIII, 325 n. Obviously he had given Mrs. Walker further financial help, but how much and at what time or times cannot be determined from his financial records.

418

Friday next.[6] My cousin Morris and we are all well I bless God for it and She joyns me with my Husband [in] all joy to hear from you in which She with my [wh]ole Family joyn in begging the acceptance of all [our?] Humble Duties to your self and all your dear Family from your most Humble and most obedient Servant

HANNAH WALKER

P.S My cousin Morris [my hu]sband and I all joyn in Begging the Favour [of our] Humble compplements[7] [*torn*] She is in good health.

Addressed: To / Benjmin Franklin Esqr. / at Mrs Stevensons in / Craven Street near / the Strand / London

Pennsylvania Assembly Committee of Correspondence to Richard Jackson and Benjamin Franklin

LS: Library of Congress

Gentlemen,   Philadelphia Septemr. 20th. 1766

By this opportunity we acknowledge the Receipt of a Letter of the 10th. May from Richard Jackson Esqr. and of another of the 10th. of June, from Docr. Franklin,[8] inclosing two Acts of Parliament, pass'd the last Session, relating to the Trade of America, which we have laid before the Assembly.

The House upon considering the "Act for Repealing certain Duties in the British Collonies and Plantations &ca."[9] Observe

6. Just what these gifts were is not clear; one appears to have been a loaf of some special sort of bread or cake made from grain of the new harvest. BF's servant John was to pick them up at an inn well known in that century among literary circles, though this fact would hardly have mattered to Mrs. Walker.

7. The message was probably intended for Mrs. Stevenson.

8. Jackson's letter has not been found. For BF's letter, which Speaker Fox laid before the Assembly on Sept. 9, 1766, see above, pp. 297–9; 9 *Pa. Arch.,* VII, 5886.

9. This act, 6 Geo. III, c. 52, received the royal assent, June 6, 1766. It was not one of the acts a copy of which BF had sent with his letter of June 10, for, as he explained there, it had not yet been printed. The London Merchants' Committee did send copies of this and two other laws that were enacted on the same day to the Philadelphia Merchants' Committee with a letter, dated June 13, 1766, and printed in *Pa. Gaz.* and *Pa. Jour.,* Aug. 21, 1766. The *Journal* printed the text of this act in full in its issue of August 28, but the *Gazette,* explaining that it had been crowded out then, printed it only in the

that after the 1st: of January next Bond and Security are directed to be given at the Several Ports in America, that non enumarated Goods, Shiped from the said Plantations, shall not be landed at any part of Europe to the Northward of Cape Finisterre, *except in Great Brittain.*[1] By which it is Evident the Trade of the Collonies with Ireland, is expressly prohibited, unless it be through some part of Great Britain. This the House conceives to be so highly prejudicial to the true Interest of the Mother Country, and her American Colonies, that they are induced to conclude, that this clause has been inadvertently extended farther than the real intent of the Parliament.

It therefore appears necessary when bills are under consideration of Parliament relating to the Colonies, that particular attention should be given thereto, by the respective Agents, and we request that on future occasions of this Sort, you would make timely application to prevent grievances, which for want of this care we may be subjected to.

We are therefore ordered by the House to desire you will make Application to the Parliament, as early as possible in their next Session for a repeal of such parts of the said Act, as tend to restrain the Trade aforesaid, and if possible to obtain such repeal, before the Act takes place.[2]

The House apprehends this matter to be of so much importance

---

issue of September 4. These printings made possible the discovery of an obscurely placed provision, not mentioned in the London Merchants' letter, that provoked the urgent instructions in the present letter. While BF had sent the Assembly a preliminary report on this impending measure in April (see above, pp. 236–7), this obnoxious provision may not have been in the bill at that time, or if it was, it may have wholly escaped the notice of BF and other colonial agents until the final printed text became available after the bill's enactment.

1. This phraseology, which caused all the trouble, appears to have been an unintentional error, as the later amending act virtually admitted. The wording should have been "except in Great Britain or Ireland," thereby leaving unchanged the existing right of the colonists to ship non-enumerated products to Ireland.

2. The Assembly had voted this order to the Committee of Correspondence on the preceding day, September 19; 8 *Pa. Arch.*, VII, 5399. The offending provision of the act was to go into effect Jan. 1, 1767. BF wrote, Nov. 8, 1766 (below, p. 486), that the chancellor of the Exchequer had ordered a bill prepared to repeal the exclusion of Ireland and had promised to introduce it himself as soon as Parliament met. The repealing measure (7 Geo. III, c. 2) received the royal assent Dec. 16, 1766; *Commons Journal*, XXXI, 11, 15, 18, 20–1, 22, 27, 46.

to the real Wellfare of the Colonies, that they have warmly recommended it to the Succeeding Assembly, from whom you will probably hear on this occasion,[3] in the mean time, we have not the least doubt, but you will Exert yourselves in obtaining Redress in this very important point.

You have heard so fully from us respecting a paper Currency,[4] and the distress this Province is under for want of it, that we need only renew our Desire that you will Endeavour to obtain it at the next Meeting of Parliament if Possible. We are with esteem Your Assured Friends, &c   Jos: Fox
                                                    Jos: Richardson
                                                    Isa. Pearson

To Richard Jackson and Benja. Franklin Esqrs.

From Joseph Priestley   ALS: American Philosophical Society

Dear Sir   Warrington 21 Sepbr. 1766.
I wrote to Mr. Price last post, in which I desired him to remind you of your promise to procure me *Beccaria's work*, which you said you thought you could do of Mr. Delaval.[5] Fearing he might not see you soon, I write to desire you to get it for me, if possible, without loss of time. Otherwise, I must reserve his experiments for an *Appendix*, for, by the references I meet with to them, I find my book absolutely must not come abroad without them. I am in such haste, as we have already begun to print, and have done five sheets. The whole work will make betwixt 400, and 500 pages 4to, and we shall not have done quite so soon as Christmas.[6] For

3. See below, p. 466.
4. See above, p. 51 n.
5. Richard Price, William Watson, John Canton, and BF were giving help and criticism to Priestley in the preparation of his *History of Electricity*. It is not certain which of Beccaria's works Priestley wanted at this time: either *Dell' elettricismo artificiale e naturale* (Turin, 1753) or *Dell' elettricismo: lettere* (Bologna, 1758); see above, V, 395–6, 428; VII, 315. The former was probably the one desired, though Priestley cited both often in his book. On Edward Hussey Delaval of Pembroke College, Cambridge, from whom BF was to procure the book, see above, VIII, 360–1 n.
6. The main text of the book, not including front matter, "Additions and Corrections," or index, runs to 733 pages quarto. The book was advertised as just published in *London Chron.*, March 31–April 2, 1767.

the same reason, I must beg you would also send me, as soon as you conveniently can, the two last numbers of the work, which I left in the hands of Dr. Watson, to be transmitted to you.[7] I am now wholly employed in revising and correcting. I defer drawing up the account of my own experiments, till I have some more in pur[s]uance of them, and several others.[8] In about a week I shall betake myself to experiments in good earnest, but I have no expectation of doing much more than I have done. Upon Mr. Price's letter, I sent the mark that was actually made by a chain when a discharge was sent thro it.[9] I have several times since I came home got *three,* and almost always *two* concentric circles, upon the metal knobs with which I make discharges.[1] If I verify your experiments on the *electrified cup,* and *animal fluids,* may I publish them as yours, in *some proper* place in my work?[2] I shall soon go about them. Have you procured the *list of books* written on the subject of electricity, or the remainder of *Wilke's treatise.*[3] Dr. Watson has

7. Priestley probably meant the last two installments of the text as he had written it and left it in Watson's hands for criticism.

8. In Part VIII (pp. 573–733) Priestley presented "an account of such new experiments in electricity as this undertaking has led me to make." His reports are written in the first person, and many are given specific dates.

9. On this matter see Priestley's postscript to this letter and its accompanying notes and illustration.

1. Priestley described this and related phenomena in his *History,* pp. 660–71, with the dates of June 13–28, 1766, assigned to his experiments.

2. Priestley described experiments with an electrified cup, Dec. 21, 1766, acknowledging that he had "little to boast besides the honour of following the instructions of Dr. Franklin." *Ibid.,* pp. 731–3. He had reported on p. 212, Beccaria's experience with the bursting of the blood vessels of small birds killed by electric shocks, and added that BF found animal fluids to conduct better than water. In his "Additions and Corrections," p. 835, Priestley admitted that the reference to BF had been added from memory as "more accurate information" had reached him too late. But BF had told him that Ebenezer Kinnersley and others in America had found blood and urine and the sinews of newly killed animals to be better conductors than water.

3. BF may have promised to try to look up and send a copy of the list of books on electricity Pieter van Musschenbroek had sent him in 1759; above, VIII, 329–33. Johan Carl Wilcke (1732–1796) published his *Disputatio physica experimentalis de electricitatibus contrariis* (Rostock, 1757) in four parts, but Priestley admitted in his bibliography that the copy he had used contained only the first three parts. "It was that [copy]," he explained, "which the author sent to Dr. Franklin, before the remainder was printed."

...hain was returned, it was thrown back as...

...have tried the same several times since,

...half of a chain parallel to the other,

...exactly how far it reached upon...

...about an inch and

...a sudden jerk had been

...Indeed it was manifest,

...the links with the marks,

...link had moved a little.

...that have been effected by

...pulling one another, while

...was passing? Is not the paper really burnt.

...chain made superficially hot, and does

...entire shock pass chiefly over the surface...

Joseph Priestley's Electrified Chain

sent me a curious tract of *Johannes Franciscus Cignas* which I am now digesting.[4] In your notes [on] one of my former Numbers you say, you question whether Æolipyle[5] will turn the same way whether it draw in [or] throw out the water. I had tried it before I wrote [the] paragraph, you may depend upon the fact. I hope to find more of your excellent remarks upon the two numbers in your hands. I am, Dear Sir, your most obliged humble servant

J PRIESTLEY

Since I wrote the letter, I have made a discharge, through a chain that lay on this side of it.[6] At the moment of the discharge, the whole appeared like a bright flame. From (a) when the chain was returned, it was thrown back as far as (b).[7] I have tried the same several times since, laying one half of a chain parallel to the other, and marking exactly how far it reached upon the table; and always found the middle part pulled back about an inch and a half [as] if a sudden jerk had been given [to] it. Indeed it was manifest, by comparing the links with the marks, that every link had moved a little. Must not that have been effected by the links repelling one another, while the shock was passing? Is not the paper really *burnt*? Was not the chain made superficially hot? and does not the electric shock pass chiefly over the surfaces of bodies? so that small bodies will be melted, because they have most surface in proportion to their bulks. NB The fa[int] marks, at a distance from the rest, are not made [by] handling. They are just as the discharge

4. Gian Francesco Cigna (1734–1791), a nephew of Beccaria, later professor of Anatomy at Turin, published a piece, *De novis quibuidam experimentis electricis*, in the *Memoirs* of the Academy of Turin for 1765; see below, p. 453.

5. An Aeolipile or aeolipyle is described as an apparatus in which a globe or cylinder may be made to revolve by the discharge of jets of steam from projecting bent tubes. It has been called the first steam engine. The word is sometimes also used for a blowpipe. The editors confess their inability to understand Priestley's use of the word here or to find any reference to such an apparatus in his *History*.

6. All of this postscript appears on the third page of the folio, which is somewhat torn at the right edge and where the seal on the address page (the other side of this leaf) had been ripped away. This explanatory postscript fills the whole page except for the space occupied by the marks of the chain Priestley used in the experiment; these are shown in the accompanying illustration.

7. That is, the apex of the "V" retracted from "a" to "b."

left them. Indeed, you will find they are not easily effaced. NB The wire of the chain is not so thick as the marks.[8]

Addressed: To / Doctor Franklin / at Mrs Stephens / in Craven Street in the Strand / London

To William Franklin

MS not found; extract reprinted from [Jared Sparks, ed.,] *A Collection of the Familiar Letters and Miscellaneous Papers of Benjamin Franklin* (Boston, 1833), pp. 277–9.

[September 27th, 1766]

I have mentioned the Ilinois affair to Lord Shelburne.[9] His Lordship had read your plan for establishing a colony there, recommended by Sir William Johnson,[1] and said it appeared to him a reasonable scheme, but he found it did not quadrate with the sentiments of people here;* that their objections to it were, the distance, which would make it of little use to this country, as the expense on the carriage of goods would oblige the people to manufacture for

*I fancy, but am not certain, that his Lordship meant Lord Hillsborough, who, I am told, is not favorable to new settlements.

8. In his *History* Priestley described experiments he performed in September 1766 with a brass chain through which he sent an electrical discharge while it lay on a piece of white paper. He found that it made black marks on the paper, and lost a little weight. He then continued his account under date of September 21 (the date of this letter) as follows: "In making the mark above-mentioned, on part of the sheet of paper, on which I had written an account of the experiment to Dr. Franklin, I happened to lay the chain so as to make it return at a sharp angle [at the point marked "a" in the illustration], in order to impress the form of a letter on the paper; and observed that, upon the discharge, the part of the chain that had been doubled was displaced, and pulled about two inches towards the rest of the chain [to the point marked "b" on the illustration]. At this I was surprised, as I thought it lay so, as that it could not slide by its own weight. Upon this I repeated the experiment with more accuracy. I stretched the whole chain along a table, laying it double all the way, and making it return by a very sharp angle. The consequence always was, that the chain was shortened about two inches, and sometimes more; as if a sudden pull had been given to it by both the ends." *History of Electricity*, pp. 672–5 (quotation is on pp. 674–5, and is followed, pp. 675–84, with further experiments and discussion of the phenomena observed).

9. See above, pp. 414–5.

1. See above, pp. 330–1.

424

themselves; that it would for the same reason be difficult both to defend it and to govern it; that it might lay the foundation of a power in the heart of America, which in time might be troublesome to the other colonies, and prejudicial to our government over them; and that people were wanted both here and in the already settled colonies, so that none could be spared for a new colony.[2] These arguments, he said, did not appear to him of much weight, and I endeavoured by others to invalidate them entirely. But his Lordship did not declare whether he would or would not promote the undertaking; and we are to talk further upon it.

I communicated to him two letters of Mr. Croghan's, with his journal, and one or two of yours on that subject,[3] which he said he would read and consider; and I left with him one of Evans's maps of the middle colonies,[4] in the small-scale part of which I had marked with a wash of red ink the whole country included in your boundaries. His Lordship remarked, that this would coincide with General Lyman's project,[5] and that they might be united.

To Joseph Galloway   ALS: Yale University Library

Dear Friend,   London, Sept. 27. 1766
Since my last of the 12th Instant,[6] I have been told that one Williamson of Pensilvania[7] who is here, reads Letters at the Coffee-

2. These arguments were stressed in a "Plan for the West," drafted on May 10, 1766, by William Wildman Barrington, 2d Viscount Barrington (1717–1793), at this time secretary at war. Namier and Brooke, *House of Commons*, II, 55–9. Barrington's plan is printed in Clarence W. Alvord and Clarence E. Carter, *The New Régime*, pp. 234–43.

3. See above, XII, 395–400, 403–6; and this volume, pp. 171–3, 257–8.

4. Lewis Evans' *General Map of the Middle Colonies in America*, published in 1755. See above, VI, 173 n.

5. See above, p. 414 n.

6. Not found.

7. Hugh Williamson (above, X, 266 n), author of several attacks on BF and his party, including *What is Sauce for the Goose* (above, XI, 380–4). He had been abroad for medical study, returning to Philadelphia in December 1766. *Pa. Gaz.*, Dec. 11, 1766. Williamson was probably responsible for sending to Philadelphia the letters to and from John Hughes relating to the Stamp Act printed in *Pa. Jour.*, Sept. 4, 1766, Supplement, and the extract of a letter from Galloway to BF, Sept. 20, 1765, printed in the same issue and reprinted in the issue of Sept. 11, 1766 (above, XII, 269–70).

house, said to be from you to me, or from me to you, I know not which, nor have I been told the Import of them, so I cannot judge whether they may not be Forgeries. He is going over, and probably you may hear more of the Matter there than I can yet learn here. One thing only I would mention to you, which is, that I recollect several of my Friends Letters, and your particularly, sent to me at several Times by the North of Ireland, appear'd to me to have been very clumsily open'd and dabb'd up again, as if done with a hot Poker, all Impression of the Seal being destroy'd, and a great deal of coarser Wax added: For which Reason I would wish you to write no more to me by that Course, as I apprehend some Scoundrel may be employ'd there in the scandalous Office of prying into, and perhaps making bad or false Copies of our Correspondence. Williamson has spent some time in Scotland since he came over; I know not whether he was in Ireland.

The Parliament will sit down in November, when the great Officers of State will be more generally in Town. Till then I can have little to say to the Committee, and beg you will excuse to them my not Writing. Mr. Jackson is still in the Country.

I purpose by the Meeting of Parliament to publish, (with a few Additions and Alterations which you have given me Leave to make) your excellent Piece on the Necessity of an Union between the Mother Country and her Colonies. And I think the other also.[8] With constant Regard and Esteem, I am, my dear Friend, Most affectionately yours,   B FRANKLIN

Jos. Galloway Esqr

Addressed: To / Joseph Galloway, Esqr / Philadelphia[9]

Endorsed: Doctr. B. Franklin Sept. 27. 1766

8. Galloway's "Americanus" piece and a pamphlet he mentioned on Jan. 13, 1766, as then being written, but which he apparently never finished; above, XII, 218–19, 269 n; and this volume, pp. 35–6. BF does not appear to have carried out his proposed reprinting in England.

9. The following notes, apparently in Galloway's hand, appear on the address page: "depth of Chimney 1. foot. 9. Inches Width of Chimney 3. feet—Suppose the new formed Walls to be of the thickness of a Brick, make the Plates accordingly/Hugh Roberts, thin Iron Plates 15 Inches high, to keep fire from fallg on floor/Hewlings the Bricklayer at Burlington."

To David Hall   ALS: Salem County Historical Society, Salem, N.J.

Dear Mr Hall,   London, Sept. 27. 1766
    I have before me your Favours of May 1. and July 12.[1] and
thank you for the Readiness with which you have supplied Mrs.
Franklin from time to time.[2]
    Here is a dead Calm of Politicks at present, the Publick being
tired with the Invectives against Lord Chatham,[3] and no fresh
Game started for the political Beagles to hunt down; and probably
none will start till the Meeting of Parliament, which 'tis said will
certainly be on the 11th. of November.[4]
    I condole with you and Cousin Molly on the Death of your Brother
at Barbadoes, of which unhappy Event Mrs. Franklin inform'd me.[5]
    Mr. and Mrs. Strahan have been in the North some Weeks, and
are but just return'd. She is laid up with a most severe Fit of the
Gout, which I hope will prove salutary to her, by giving a new
Turn to her Constitution. He had desired me to mention his
Absence, and excuse his not Writing to you per last Packet; but
thro' Hurry I omitted writing to you myself.
    My Love to your Wife and Children, to whom with yourself I
wish all Prosperity, being Dear Friend, Yours affectionately
                                                B FRANKLIN
Addressed: To / Mr David Hall / Printer / Philadelphia
Endorsed: Mr. Franklin, Septr. 27. 1766

Stoughton[6]

1. See above, pp. 259, 331–2.
    2. In both of these letters Hall mentioned supplying DF with money. Now
that the partnership was ended such advances could not be considered merely
as payments on account of BF's share of the firm's income, as they had been
in previous years.
    3. The newspapers had been full of "political squibs" directed against Pitt
for accepting a peerage. One of the milder pieces was a quatrain in *London
Chron.*, Aug. 2–5, 1766, entitled "On a late Promotion"; it read: "The Court,
to please old talking WILL,/Whose Tongue was always at 'em,/For ever
more to keep it still,/Has made him Earl of Ch----m."
    4. Hall reprinted this paragraph in *Pa. Gaz.*, Dec. 18, 1766.
    5. In her missing letter of July 7 DF had probably told her husband of the
recent death of Mary Hall's brother, Samuel Leacock (F.2.2.6), a clockmaker
of Bridgetown, Barbados.
    6. Not identified.

To Charles Thomson

ALS: Library of Congress

Dear Friend and Neighbour   London, Sept. 27. 1766

I received your very kind Letter of May 20.[7] which came here while I was absent in Germany. The favourable Sentiments you express of my Conduct with regard to the Repeal of the Stamp Act, give me real Pleasure; and I hope in every other matter of publick Concern, so to behave myself as to stand fair in the Opinions of the Wise and Good: What the rest think and say of me will then give me less Concern.

That Part of your Letter which related to the Situation of People's Minds in America before and after the Repeal, was so well exprest, and in my Opinion so proper to be generally read and understood here, that I had it printed in the London Chronicle.[8] I had the Pleasure to find that it did Good in several Instances within my Knowledge.

There are Claimers enow of Merit in obtaining the Repeal. But if I live to see you, I will let you know what an Escape we had in the Beginning of the Affair, and how much we were obliged to what the Profane would call *Luck,* and the Pious *Providence.*[9]

You will give an old Man Leave to say My Love to Mrs. Thomson. With sincere Regard, I am, Your affectionate Friend

Mr. Thomson   B Franklin

Addressed: To / Mr Charles Thomson / Mercht / Philadelphia

Endorsed: Letter from B F. Sept. 27. 1766

7. Above, pp. 277–9.

8. BF reprinted virtually all but the first paragraph of Thomson's letter in *London Chron.,* Sept. 6–9, 1766.

9. The reference here is probably to a proposal following the adoption by the Commons, January 14, of the address to the King, to print all the papers received from America rather than a selected group of them. Edmund Burke wrote on the 18th that this awkward proposal, dangerous for some Americans who were mentioned in the papers, had been made in "a thin house" when many of the friends of the government had already left. A motion to discharge the order for printing carried on the 17th. *Commons Journal,* XXX, 451, 463; R.J.S. Hoffman, *Edmund Burke New York Agent* (Phila., 1956), pp. 329–30.

428

To Daniel Wister[1]

ALS: James W. Wister, Philadelphia (1955)

Dear Friend,   London, Sept. 27. 1766.

I received your Favour of June the 7th. with the German Paper enclos'd.[2] I am exceedingly oblig'd to my Friends for the constant Care they take of my Good Name in my Absence in defending it from the Slanders of my Enemies. Among the rest, I beg you would accept my thankful Acknowledgements for the generous Part you have always taken in that kind Work, and that you will be assured I shall never forget your Kindness.

I travell'd a good deal, for my Health, in Germany this Summer, which I found a very fine Country, and seemingly not so much hurt by the late War as one might have expected, since it appears every where fully cultivated, notwithstanding the great Loss it sustained in People. It should seem their Numbers are inexhaustible; since the Empress of Russia is now inviting into her Country such Germans as are willing to leave their own, and obtain'd no less than Forty Thousand of them last Year, who are to settle on the Volga, near the Caspian Sea. She bears all the Charges of their Journey.[3]

I cannot comprehend what Mr. Allen could mean by charging me with opposing the Repeal of the Stamp Act.[4] The contrary is well known here to everyone that knows me; and in Truth, besides opposing the Act before it was made, I never in my Life labour'd any Point more heartily than I did that of obtaining the Repeal.

I thank you for your good Wishes, which I pray may be fulfill'd sevenfold on you and yours, being, with real Regard and Esteem Dear Friend, Yours affectionately   B FRANKLIN

1. On Daniel Wister, a young German merchant, see above, XII, 277 n.

2. Wister's letter not found. The enclosed German paper was almost certainly an issue of Henrich Miller's *Der Wochentliche Philadelphische Staatsbote*. Galloway told BF, June 7, 1766, that he had inserted in the papers extracts of letters from London praising BF "and from thence had them translated into Millers for the Satisfaction of the Dutch." Above, pp. 295–6.

3. *London Chron.* and other English papers of this year contained several reports on the efforts of Catherine the Great to attract German settlers to the Volga region.

4. On Chief Justice Allen's charges against BF in the Assembly see above, p. 295 and note.

My Respects to your good Father and Mother.

Mr. D. Wister

Addressed: To / Mr Daniel Wister / Merchant / Philadelphia

From William Heberden[5] AL: William Pepper, Philadelphia (1956)

[Before September 29, 1766][6]

Dr. Heberden sends his compliments to Dr. Franklin and desires the favor of his company at dinner on monday next (Sept. 29th.) at half an hour past three.

To William Franklin

MS not found; reprinted from extract in [Jared Sparks, ed.,] *A Collection of the Familiar Letters and Miscellaneous Papers of Benjamin Franklin* (Boston, 1833), p. 279.

[September 30th, 1766]

I have just had a visit from General Lyman, and a good deal of conversation on the Ilinois scheme.[7] He tells me, that Mr. Morgan,[8] who is under-secretary of the Southern department, is much pleased with it; and we are to go together to talk to him concerning it.

5. On Dr. Heberden, distinguished physician, for whose pamphlet on smallpox inoculation BF had written the preface, see above, VIII, 281.

6. Since the invitation was for "monday next (Sept. 29th.)," it must have been written during the previous week. September 29 fell on a Monday during BF's English years only in 1760 and 1766, and BF was on a journey to Coventry, Worcester, and Birmingham from about September 17 to November 1 in 1760 (above, IX, xxvi, 231 n), hence this invitation is assigned to 1766.

7. See above, p. 414.

8. Maurice Morgann (1726–1802), Shelburne's private secretary and at this time under-secretary of state for the Southern Department. He obtained the post of secretary of New Jersey in 1767, discharging it by deputy, first Joseph Reed, then Charles Pettit. In 1773 he suggested to BF that he would be willing to replace him as N.J. agent. In 1782 Morgann again served as under-secretary to Shelburne, who at this time was conducting the peace negotiations with America as first lord of the Treasury. In 1783 Morgann was one of the secretaries to the embassy for ratifying the peace treaty with the United States. In 1777 his *Essay on the Dramatic Character of Sir John Falstaff* established his reputation as a literary critic. *DNB;* 1 *N.J. Arch.,* X, 1–6, 133–5; Franklin B. Wickwire, *British Subministers and Colonial America 1763–1783* (Princeton, 1966), pp. 96–7; BF to WF, July 14, 1773, Lib. Cong.

From Benjamin Kent[9]   ALS: American Philosophical Society

Much Honour'd and Blov'd Sir   [c. September, 1766][1]
    I Assure you I am not so mercinary as to expect the undeserv'd
favour of A Line from you; but agreable to An old Observation,
on which I much rely viz Non animam Mutant qui trans mare
Currunt[2] I shall make my self as free with you, as when you used
to flatter me, with the kind appellation of, "Brother" Ben.[3] And
If these should Interrupt your grand Concerns and Entertainment,
you may thank your Self, for your own former freedoms which in
my oppinion intitles me to this. I wrote you Some time Since (from
the Love as well as veneration I bear to Mr. Pitt, now Lord
Chatham[4]) that we have found a root, call'd by the Indian (who
communicated its virtue to us) Cauhouse[5] which being Steept, in
good Madira or in good Jamaica Spirit, taking about a Jill, at once
infallibly carrys off any fit of the gout. I have this assurance from
several Gentlemen who have try'd it. Our Secretary Oliver's oldest Son[6] last Month informed me that it never fail'd him, but very
lately he was determin'd to make a more thoro' tryal. The fit came
on, his foot greatly inflamed, but he bore the pain, untill he was

9. On Benjamin Kent of Boston, see above, XI, 80 n. This letter follows up
his shorter recommendation of a remedy for the gout, above, pp. 49–50.
    1. Early in this letter Kent refers to "Mr. Pitt, now Lord Chatham." News
of the peerage conferred on the "Great Commoner" did not reach the colonies
until the last week or ten days of September 1766. In accordance with the
editorial practice in this edition of placing an undated document at the earliest
justifiable date, this letter is printed here.
    2. Kent repeats here, and with the same error, a line from Horace that he
had quoted in his letter of January: "They change their sky, not their character, who sail across the sea."
    3. Again a repetition from his earlier letter; Kent seems indeed to have been
flattered to have BF call him "Brother Ben."
    4. Pitt's gout had been notorious; perhaps the deep concern Kent and other
Americans showed for it is striking, if unusual, evidence of their esteem for
the man.
    5. Probably one of the several varieties (white, black, red, blue, etc.) of a
medicinal plant known usually as "cohosh" or "baneberry."
    6. Andrew Oliver (1731–1799) was the eldest surviving son of Andrew
Oliver (1706–1774), secretary of Mass., and stamp distributor in 1765. DAB
mentions his suffering for thirty years from "a distressing chronic disease,"
and Shipton in his article in Sibley's Harvard Graduates, XII, 455–61, speaks
of his severe gout.

Sure it was well fixed, according to all his former Experience he took the potion went to bed, had a breathing Sweat all over, but his gouty foot Sweat very profusely, soon got to sleep, was well refreshed and got up in the Morning perfectly well. I believe you Know Middlecott Cook Esq;[7] the Clerk of Our Common Pleas. Last week or a week before, he was Seiz'd with a Violent fitt of the Gout, was ill three or four Days and could not bare to be stirr'd in his Bed, he took the Dose, (tho his root was steep'd in Spirit) I saw him the next day walking about his Chamber quite free of the gout, tho' as he told me he could not stir hand or foot the evening before. Mr. Cook has been for above 20 years past more afflicted with that disorder than ever I knew any one to have been. An other Gouty Gentleman of my Acquaintance has lately found the Same releif, by the Same Medicine. I know the plant, it grows wild in Many Low Lands, and in plenty. I have heard that one or two Gentlemen have wrote Home concerning this wonder working Plant, which has fairly baffled the Maxim of the Physician viz Nescit Medicina Podagram,[8] but I tho't my mentioning the same thing might be a benefit, to many excellent Men and to his Lordship particularly. And I am So confident of the Virtue of that plant, I would venture a Voyage to England upon the Credit of it. But I suppose Some of the Faculty will find it out, keep it a Secreet as they have done the Method of American Inoculation, and then run away with the Profit and Credit of it too.[9]

So much for Cauhouse.

Your Friends and relations in Boston are all well, and are exceedingly rejoyced, that you design for America next Spring. And before you come we wish you would put a Commission for the Government in your Pocket, but if you don't chuse to be at the Trouble; pray befriend your Native Town, and Province, so much as to procure it, for Some good man, who will deserve More Hon-

7. Middlecott Cooke (1705–1771), son and grandson of important political leaders in Mass., had large interests in Maine lands. *Sibley's Harvard Graduates*, VII, 160–3.

8. "Medicine is ignorant of the gout." *Nescit*, literally "does not know," may connote ignorance, and in a medical sense this expression could mean that medicine does not know what to do about treating the gout.

9. Probably a reference to Dr. George Muirson's method of inoculation through the use of mercury; above, XI, 356–7, esp. note 5.

our and Love than ever our present G--r[1] has had, or ever will have. This Province is a Large and I hope a Respectable Family but if we have a G--r disproportiond to the station of a Father, the Family in time may be ruined, by the bad hearts of those who grant Posts of Trust without a due reguard to Merit. It is well known that the best preaching, and the best Laws have not half the Tendency, to make a people Virtuous and wise, as One great and good Man has, at the Head of a Society. Virtue and Wisdom must be Inspired from our Betters, and they must be our Rulers too, or we shall never Attain it. Pray Sir If John Wilks Esqr. be the Author of that Most Divine Book, call'd Epistles Philosophical and Moral,[2] please to be so kind as to mention it in some one of your Letters, to some Friend of yours with whom I have the pleasure to be acquainted in Boston. That GOD, would bless you above even your wishes is the Sincere desire of your Friend   BENJA. KENT

Addressed: For The Honble. / Benjamin Franklin Esq; / Doctr of Laws / at the Pensylvania, or New England[3] / Coffee House / London / By Capt. Scott.

Endorsed: B Kent

Remarks on the Plan for Regulating the Indian Trade

Draft: Library of Congress

During June 1764 the Board of Trade had spent considerable time and effort preparing a "Plan for the Future Management of Indian Affairs," and on June 15 it ordered that copies be sent for comment to the superintendents of Indian affairs and the royal governors on the North American continent.[4] On July 10 drafts of the Board's explanatory letters to these officials were read and approved for signature. The Plan

1. Francis Bernard continued to serve as governor of Mass. until Aug. 1, 1769.
2. Kent was a great admirer of John Wilkes; see his letter of Oct. 5, 1768, *Proc. Mass. Hist. Soc.*, XLVII (1913–14), 194–6. The author of *Epistles, Philosophical and Moral* (London, 1759), was William Kenrick (1725–1779); *DNB*. This was a highly sceptical, philosophical poem, written in octosyllabics, that had appeared in an earlier form in 1756 with the title *Epistles to Lorenzo.*
3. This and the next line were struck out on the address page.
4. *Board of Trade Journal*, 1764–1767, pp. 65–71.

to which the letters referred has consequently been usually cited by this date: July 10, 1764.[5]

Sir William Johnson sent back an article-by-article commentary on this Plan with an accompanying letter dated October 8, and several governors also wrote their opinions.[6] The Board of Trade read these communications and from time to time considered doing something with the Plan, but never carried the discussions beyond the point of talk.[7] In the autumn of 1766, when Lord Shelburne had taken office as secretary of state for the Southern Department, he became definitely interested in placing the management of Indian affairs on a more systematic and effective footing. As one move toward this end he asked Franklin and Richard Jackson to examine the Plan of July 10, 1764, and submit to him their comments.

Just when Franklin prepared the draft "Remarks" printed below is not certain, but the date can be approximated. He wrote his son William on September 12 that he was to have a conference with Shelburne the following Tuesday, that is on the 16th; on October 11 he told Galloway that he had "occasionally had several Conferences lately" with the secretary of state.[8] On the second page of this draft (now transferred to near its start) he jotted down several memoranda of "Things to be mentioned to Lord Shelbourne," that had come to Franklin's attention in recent months. It seems highly probable, therefore, that this paper represents the draft of a document he planned to present to Shelburne during one of their "several Conferences" in September and October 1766. Jackson, who was out of town during the early autumn, dated his report in November 1766.[9]

The Plan on which Franklin was commenting consisted of forty-

5. *Ibid.*, p. 98. The Board's letter to Sir William Johnson is in *Documents Relative to the Colonial History of the State of New York*, VII (Albany, 1856), 634–6. The Plan is printed: *ibid.*, pp. 637–42; Adam Shortt and Arthur G. Doughty, eds., *Documents Relating to the Constitutional History of Canada*, I (Ottawa, 1907), 433–7; and Clarence W. Alvord and Clarence E. Carter, eds., *The Critical Period*, pp. 273–81.

6. *Board of Trade Journal*, 1764–1767, p. 149. The text of Johnson's comments is printed in *N.Y. Col. Docs.*, VII, 661–6; and Alvord and Carter, eds., *Critical Period*, pp. 327–42.

7. On Jan. 16, 1766, while the repeal of the Stamp Act was being considered, the Board of Trade agreed "that it would be advisable in the present state and situation of American affairs to postpone any representation" on the Plan. Previously the Board had considered the matter in February and March 1765. *Board of Trade Journal*, 1764–1767, pp. 149, 162, 244.

8. See above, p. 415, and below, p. 447.

9. See below, p. 486. Jackson's comments on this and other schemes are printed in Clarence W. Alvord and Clarence E. Carter, eds., *The New Régime*, pp. 422–30.

three numbered paragraphs or articles, and a final unnumbered one on financial matters to which Franklin referred in his comment as "44." He discussed less than a third of the articles, but these he examined with complete freedom. Characteristically, he seemed most interested in the workability and practical operation of the arrangements and regulations proposed. To make his remarks as intelligible as possible, each of his comments is preceded by a summary (or occasionally a direct quotation), set in brackets, of the corresponding article of the Board of Trade's Plan.

[September–October 1766]

REMARKS ON THE PLAN FOR REGULATING THE INDIAN TRADE
Written at the Request of Lord S.

The Regulations in this Plan seem to me to be in general very good; but some few appear to want Explanation, or farther Consideration.[1]

Things to be mentioned to Lord Shelbourne.

Map of proposed Colony[2]

Demand of Traders who suffered before the first War, and at breaking out of the second.[3]

Att[orne]y Generel of Virg[ini]a.[4]

Petitions relative to Gov[ernmen]t of Pennsylvania Paper Currency[5]

—— Islands in Delaware[6]

1. The first page of the draft begins with the heading as printed above and then proceeds directly to the comment on Article 3, which occupies the rest of the page. This obviously introductory sentence and the memoranda that follow here appear on the back of the first page, following a cancelled comment on Article 10. The remarks on Article 4 begin at the top of the third page. It seems clear that, although BF set down this sentence and the memoranda at a later time, he intended to place this opening sentence, at least, directly after the heading in his final copy. For convenience the memoranda are also placed before the comments on particular articles.

2. The proposed colony in the Illinois country in which Johnson, the Whartons, the Franklins, and others were interested.

3. The hopes of the "Suffering Traders" for compensation in land cessions by the Indians have been referred to in several letters from the Whartons in this and the previous volume.

4. For George Wythe's hope that BF would help him get appointed attorney general of Virginia, see above, p. 321.

5. On the Pa. Assembly's concern for paper currency, as well as BF's, see above, pp. 51 n, 204–7.

6. See above, XII, 219 n. Nothing seems to have been done about the possible grant of these islands during the past year.

———— Mr. Croghan's Demand[7]
Mr. Cox's Demand.[8]

[3. No trade to be allowed with Indians in Southern District except in towns belonging to tribes included in the district, and in the Northern District trade is to be fixed "at so many Posts and in such Situations" as thought necessary.]

3. Is it intended by this Clause to prevent the Trade that Indians living near the Frontiers may chuse to carry on with the Inhabitants by bringing their Skins into the Settlements? This Prevention is hardly practicable, as such Trade may be carried on in many Places out of the Observation of Government, the Frontier being of great Extent, and the Inhabitants thinly settled in the Woods remote from each other. The Indians too do not every where live in Towns sufficiently numerous to encourage Traders to reside among them, but in scattered Families here and there often shifting their Situation for the sake of better Hunting; and if they are near the English Settlements It would seem to them very hard to be obliged to carry their Skins for Sale to remote Towns or Posts, when they could dispose of them to their Neighbours with less Trouble and to greater Advantage, as the Goods they want for them are and must be dearer at such remote Posts.[9]

[4. "That all Laws now in Force in the Several Colonies for regulating Indian affairs or Commerce be repealed."]

4. Those Laws are the Result of long Experience, made by People on the Spot interested to make them good, and it seems they should be well considered before they are repealed to make way for new untried Schemes.

By whom are they to be repealed? By the Colony Assemblies? or by Parliament? Some Difficulty will arise here.[1]

7. For the uncertain nature of George Croghan's "Application" or "Demand," see above, p. 257 n.

8. It is uncertain whether this note refers to William, Daniel, or John Coxe, all of whom had some sort of claims to be pressed with the home government and would have been glad of BF's help.

9. Here as in several later instances Sir William Johnson, who favored tight control of the Indian trade, approved a proposal that BF criticized as too constricting.

1. Johnson declared that "Nothing can be more Necessary" than the repeal of these laws, thereby placing Indian affairs more directly under the Crown and the Crown-appointed superintendent—himself. Jackson, like BF, strongly

[13. No order to be issued by the governor or by an officer with military command of any fort in the Indian country for stopping the trade with any tribe in either district without the concurrence or consent of the agent or superintendent for Indian affairs in the district.]

13. The Districts seem too large for this. The Indians under the Care of the Northern Superintendant border on the Colonies of N Scotia, Quebec, New Hampshire Massachusets, Connecticut New York, New Jersey, Pensilvania, Maryland, Virginia. The Superintendents Residence remote from several of these may occasion great Inconvenience, if his Consent is always to be necessary in such Cases.[2]

[14. The agents or superintendents or their deputies are to visit all the posts or tribes in their districts once a year or oftener to take account of the behavior of their subordinates, to hear appeals or redress complaints of the Indians, to make proper presents, and transact all affairs relating to the Indians.]

14. This seems too much to be done, when the Vastness of the District is considered. If there were more Districts and smaller this might be more practicable.

[15. That the agents or superintendents and the commissaries at each post be empowered to act as justices of the peace with all usual powers and also authority to commit offenders in capital cases. In civil actions the commissaries may try "in a summary way" disputes between traders and Indians or between traders, up to £10 sterling, with liberty of appeal to the agent or superintendent or his deputy, whose judgment is final. 16. The evidence given by Indians is to be accepted under proper regulations in all criminal and civil cases as above, and admitted by courts of justice

---

opposed such a sweeping repeal. In his draft BF entered a comment on Article 10, which he later struck out. This article conferred almost complete power of conducting Indian affairs on the agent or superintendent, excluding the governors or military commanders, except "in case of great Exigency" or when the superintendent was too far away. BF wrote: "10. Will not this Clause interfere with the Charter to some of the Colonies, who are impowered to make Peace and War with the Natives, &c." His cancellation indicates that he had second thoughts about making this criticism.

2. Johnson highly approved this article, as might be expected. Jackson did not comment on it.

in the colonies in criminal cases under the normal rules concerning false evidence.]

15 and 16. Are these Agents or Commissaries to try Causes where Life is concerned? Would it not be better to send the Criminals into some civil Government for Trial, where good Juries can be had?[3]

[18. The Indians in each town of every tribe in the Southern District are to choose a "Beloved Man" to be approved by the agent or superintendent and to take care of the mutual interests of Indians and traders of the town. These "Beloved Men" of the tribe's towns are to elect "a Chief for the whole Tribe who shall Constantly reside with the Commissary in the country of each Tribe, or occasionally attend" on the agent or superintendent, as guardian of the Indians and protector of their rights. The chief is to be entitled to be present at all hearings or trials relating to the Indians before the agent, superintendent, or commissary, and give his opinion on all matters under consideration.]

18. *Chief for the whole Tribe who shall constantly reside with the Commissary,* &c. Provision must then be made for his Maintenance, as particular Indians have no Estates but live by Hunting, and their Public has no Funds. Being us'd to Rambling, it would perhaps not be easy to find one, who would be oblig'd to this constant Residence.

[22. The agent or superintendent and the commissaries are to take oath before a governor or chief judge of a colony in their district for the due execution of their trust. They and all subordinate officers are to be forbidden under proper penalties to carry on any trade, personally or in trust for others, or to accept any grants of land from the Indians.]

22. If the Agent and his Deputies and the Commissaries are not to trade, should it not be a Part of their Oath, that they will have no Concern in such Trade directly or indirectly? Private Agreements between them and the Traders for Share of Profits should

3. Johnson wanted greater judicial powers for the superintendent or his deputy and he wanted the court evidence of Indians restricted to those who by religion or experience really understood the nature of an oath. It is perhaps surprising that Jackson, the barrister, had no comments on these two articles.

be guarded against. And the same between them and Purchasers of Lands from Indians.[4]

[31. Persons trading with the Indians without a license and without previously giving security as required in an earlier section of the plan, "or trading at any other posts or places than those expressed in their licenses," are to forfeit the goods they are found trading with, pay a fine, and suffer imprisonment.]

31. *or trading at any other Post,* &c. This should be so express'd as to make the Master liable for the Offence of the Servant; otherwise it will have no Effect.[5]

[33. All trade with the Indians to be carried on by tariffs settled by the commissaries at the posts or truckhouses or in the countries of the tribes, in concert with the traders and Indians.]

33. I doubt the Settling such Tariffs will be a matter of Difficulty. There may be Differences of Fineness, Goodness and Value in the Goods of different Traders, and the like in the Peltry of different Indians, that cannot be properly allow'd for by general Tariffs: It seems contrary to the Nature of Commerce for Government to interfere in the Prices of Commodities. Trade is a voluntary Thing between Buyer and Seller, in every Article of which each exercises his own Judgment and is to please himself. Suppose either Trader or Indian is dissatisfied with the Tariff, and refuses to barter on those Terms: Are the Refusers to be compell'd? If not, Why should an Indian be forbidden to take more Goods for his Skins than your Tariff allows if the Trader is willing to give them; or a Trader more Skins for his Goods if the Indian is willing to give them? Where there are a number of different Traders, the separate Desire of each to get most Custom will operate in bringing their Goods down to a reasonable Price. It therefore seems to me, that Trade will best find and make its own Rates. And that Government cannot well interfere, unless it would take the whole Trade into its own Hands, as in some Colonies it does, and manage it by its own Servants at its own Risque.[6]

4. Johnson had no objection to this proposal but took occasion to declare that he had never been involved in acquiring any land from the Indians. Jackson commented cynically: "A Man must know very little of the Administration of publick affairs in any part of Europe to rely upon the Oaths of officers in any degree."

5. Neither Johnson nor Jackson spotted this loophole in the proposal.

6. Johnson strongly supported the idea of tariffs; Jackson, agreeing with

[38. "That no Trader shall sell or otherwise supply the Indians with Rum or other spirituous Liquors, Swan Shot or riffled Barrell'd Guns."]

38. I apprehend that if the Indians cannot get Rum of fair Traders, it will be a great Means of defeating all these Regulations that direct the Trade to be carried on at certain Posts. The Country and Forests are so very large it is impossible to guard every Part, so as to prevent unlicens'd Traders drawing the Indians and the Trade to themselves by Rum, and other Spirituous Liquors which all savage People are so fond of. I think they will generally trade where they can get Rum preferably to where it is refus'd them; and the propos'd Prohibition will therefore be a great Encouragement to unlicens'd Traders, and promote such Trade. If the Commissaries or Officers at the Posts can prevent the Selling of Rum during the Barter for other Goods, and until the Indians are about going away, it is perhaps all that is practicable or necessary. The Missionaries will doubtless among other things endeavour to prevail with them to live soberly and avoid Drunkenness.[7]

[39. In Indian trade no credit to be given for goods beyond the value of 50 shillings, and no debt for a larger amount shall be recoverable by law or equity.]

39. The Indian Trade so far as Credit is concerned has hitherto been carried on wholly upon Honour: They have among themselves no such Thing as Prisons or Confinement for Debt. This Article seems to imply that an Indian may be compelled by Law to pay a Debt of 50s. or under. Our legal Method of Compulsion is by Imprisonment. The Indians cannot and will not imprison one another, and if we attempt to imprison them, I apprehend it would be generally dislik'd by the Nations, and occasion Breaches. They have such high Ideas of Personal Liberty, and such slight ones of the Value of personal Property, that they would think the Disproportion monstrous between the Liberty of a Man and a Debt of a few Shillings and that it would be excessively inequitable and unjust to take away the one for a Default in Payment of the other. It seems to me therefore best to leave that Matter on its present

BF, called a trade carried on by such a method, when buyers and sellers were numerous, "little better than a Solecism."

7. Johnson opposed any sale of rifles to the Indians, but like BF he had strong doubts about the complete prohibition of the sale of rum.

Footing, the Debts under 50s. to be as irrecoverable by Law as this Article proposes for the Debts above 50s. Debts of Honour are generally as well paid as other Debts. Where no Compulsion can be used, it is more disgraceful to be dishonest. If the Trader thinks his Risque greater in trusting any particular Indian, he will either not do it, or proportion his Price to his Risque.[8]

[44 *(Actually unnumbered in the Plan)*. The estimated annual expense of supporting the proposed establishment, providing presents, and meeting other contingencies, is £20,000. It is proposed to defray this charge by a duty on the Indian trade: either as an export duty on skins or furs, or payable by the traders at the trading posts, whichever may be determined on further inquiry to be most practicable and least burdensome to trade.]

44. As the Goods for Indian Trade all go from England, and the Peltry is chiefly brought to England perhaps it will be best to lay the Duty here on the Exportation of the one, and the Importation of the other and avoid meddling with the Question of Right to lay Duties in America by Parliament here.[9]

If it is thought proper to carry this Plan into Execution, would it not be well to try it first in a few Posts to which the present Colony Laws of Indian Trade do not reach, that by Experience its Defects may be discovered and amended before it is made general and those Laws repealed to make way for it?

If the Indians find by Experience that they are better us'd in their Trade at the Posts under these Regulations, than at other Places may it not make them desirous of having the Regulations extended to other Places, and when extended better satisfy'd with them upon Reflection and Comparison.[1]

8. Johnson opposed the granting of credit beyond 50s. to Indians, but had nothing to say about how smaller debts were to be recovered from Indians. Jackson offered no useful comment here.

9. Johnson offered here an elaborate and lengthy scheme for raising the necessary money. Jackson declared flatly that if the duty was to be levied at the posts, it would "of itself, probably overthrow the Regulations for obvious Reasons." He thought very little of the plan as a whole and disliked giving the King's officers so much power. He then went on to prophesy the gradual elimination of the Indian problem in much the way it has come about over large parts of the United States.

1. This Plan was never put into operation even experimentally.

To Abbot Upcher[2] Draft: American Philosophical Society

Reverend Sir, Cr. Street London, Oct. 4. 1766[3]

Since my Return from abroad I have been inform'd of your good Purpose to purchase a land[ed?] Estate in America of the Value of One Thousand Pounds and to apply the Rents and Profits thereof to the Support of Schools for the Instruction of Negro Children. And I have been desired by the Associates to consider the Matter, and give my Opinion where, and in what Manner the Purchase may best be made. I do accordingly acquaint you, that I think the best Province to make the Purchase in is Pennsylvania, where Titles are generally clear, and that it would be well to impower three Persons in Philadelphia to purchase Ground Rents within that City and other safe and profitable Estate in or near the same, as Bargains may offer, in Trust for the Purposes you mention; drawing for the Money here from time to time as the Purchases are made; the Money remaining at Interest here till so drawn for. And the Rents as receiv'd by such Trustees to be applied as you direct. Any farther Advice or Assistance that I can give in the Choice of Trustees or otherwise,[4] shall not be wanting: being respectfully, Reverend Sir, Your most obedient humble Servant B F.

2. Abbot Upcher (1722–1770), B.A. Cambridge, 1741; ordained deacon, 1745; rector (or vicar) of St. Gregory's and St. Peter's, Sudbury, Suffolk; J.A. Venn, *Alumni Cantabrigienses*, Part 1, IV, 290; C.F.D. Sperling, *A Short History of the Borough of Sudbury* (Sudbury, 1896), p. 124. On June 28, 1766, Upcher wrote the secretary of the Associates of the late Dr. Bray (above, VII, 100 n) that he proposed to donate £1000 to buy real estate in America, the income to be used for Negro education. At the meeting of July 24 (BF being in Germany at the time) the Associates accepted the proposal and asked that BF acquaint Upcher "with the Circumstances of purchasing Lands in America." Richard I. Shelling, "Benjamin Franklin and the Dr. Bray Associates," *PMHB*, LXIII (1939), 289.

3. The first meeting of the Bray Associates that BF attended after his return to England from America was one on Oct. 2, 1766, two days before he wrote this letter. *PMHB*, LXXIII (1949), 39.

4. In the spring of 1767, when Upcher had paid in the second £100 of his gift, the Associates asked BF to buy improvable lands under the trusteeship of himself, Jacob Duché, Jr. (and in succession to him the future rectors of Christ Church), Francis Hopkinson, Edward Duffield, and David Hall. *Ibid.*, LXIII (1939), 289.

From Mary Owen: Bill and Receipt

ADS: American Philosophical Society

Before Franklin sailed from Pennsylvania in November 1764 his son William probably asked him to assume the immediate responsibility for the care and education of William Temple Franklin, the small son of an unidentified mother William had left in England two years before.[5] The two men seem to have agreed that Benjamin would charge to William's account all expenditures he made on behalf of the boy while in England.

During the first years of Franklin's second mission his financial records show several unexplained cash payments made to women and charged to William. Probably most of these simply represent purchases made from London shopkeepers for William or his wife, but one or two may indicate money given to a nurse or foster mother who was looking after the child.[6] Sometime in the spring of 1767 Franklin sent young Temple (as he came to be called) to a school in Kensington conducted by James Elphinston, brother-in-law of William Strahan. The boy remained there until February 1775, when his grandfather took him out of school to prepare for their voyage to Philadelphia together.

One document does survive to suggest something about the arrangements made for Temple before Elphinston took over. The bill printed

5. William Temple Franklin's tombstone in Père Lachaise Cemetery, Paris, states that he was born Feb. 22, 1762 (above, I, lxii), but twice BF indicated that the boy was about two years older than that date would make him. Writing to WF, Aug. 1, 1774 (British Museum), he said, "Methinks 'tis time to think of a Profession for Temple, (who is now upwards of 14)." Then, in a letter from Philadelphia to Jane Mecom, June 17, 1775 (Van Doren, *Franklin-Mecom*, p. 158), he told her, "I brought over a Grandson with me, a fine Lad of about 15." The bill printed here, in which Mary Owen is providing the boy with "Schooling" and one shilling pocket money a month, seems more appropriate to a boy somewhere between 6 and 7 years of age, as BF's statements would make him, than to a child of 4 years 8 months, as the tombstone date would indicate.

6. The entries in BF's Journal charged to WF that seem most likely to relate to Temple's maintenance are payments to Mrs. Margaret Nelson: Aug. 19, 1765, 5 guineas; Dec. 6, 1765, 6 guineas; Feb. 28, 1771, "Waterage &c. for Mrs. Nelson," 6s. Journal, 1764–1776, pp. 4, 6, 31. While the last of these entries comes long after Temple was in Elphinston's school, it appears in direct association with a charge against WF for £95 12s. 7d. "for Sundries disbursed for Master Temple." Perhaps BF had paid 6s. for Mrs. Nelson to go by boat on the Thames to visit her former charge in his school. The first entry in BF's Journal relating clearly to the boy is a payment to Alexander Small, Nov. 9, 1765, of 10 guineas "for inoculating Temple." Journal, 1764–1776, p. 5.

below shows that an otherwise unidentified woman, Mary Owen, had the boy in her care and under her "Schooling" for at least six months in 1766–1767.[7] The bill was presented to Mrs. Stevenson, who took a womanly interest in her tenant's grandson during all these years. She paid the bill for Franklin and, while there is no specific record in his Journal or Ledger of his repaying her, it was almost certainly included in the running account they kept with each other and on which he made lump-sum payments from time to time.

		£:	s:	d.
Oct. the 8th	Two pr. Shoes for Master Temple	0:	4:	0
1766	Cutting hair	0:	1:	0
	To A Quarters Board and Schooling due the 12 of Novbr. 1766	4:	10:	0
	To Pocket Money	0:	3:	3
	To plaisters	0:	0:	9
Janry the	To Cutting hair	0:	1:	0
2 1767	To A pr Stockings	0:	1:	9
	To mending Shoes	0:	0:	2
Janry 12.	To making 6 Shirts at 1s. each	0:	6:	0
	To Pocket Money	0:	3:	0
	To a Quarters Board and Schooling Due the 12th of Febry, 1767	4:	10:	0
		10:	0:	11

Febry, the 20th 1767 Recd of Mrs. Stevenson the Contents being in full of all Demands per me   MARY OWEN

Endorsed: No. 8 Mary Owens Bill for Mastr Temple Febry 20. 1767

To Deborah Franklin   ALS: American Philosophical Society

My dear Child   London, Oct. 11. 1766

I received your kind little Letter of August 26. per Packet.[8] Scarce any one else wrote to me by that Opportunity.[9] I suppose they imagin'd I should not be return'd from Germany.[1]

7. There seems to be no other mention of this Mary Owen in any of BF surviving papers or financial records.

8. Not found.

9. Joseph Galloway was one who did; see the second document below.

1. For BF and Sir John Pringle's trip to Germany in the summer of 1766, see above, pp. 314–5.

You mention writing to me by a Son of Mr. Potts's.[2] A Ship is come from Philadelphia, Capt. Golley. But I have only one Letter in her, and that is from Mr. Hall, to whom my Respects. I know not whether that is the Ship the young Gentleman was to come in.[3]

Pray did you ever get the Letters and Cambrick I sent you per Mr. Yates?[4] You told me he had lost them, but hop'd to find them again. You did not say in any of your subsequent Letters whether he found them; or whether our generous Adversaries have got them and keep them for their own Amusement, as you know they did some of my former.[5]

I wish you would always mention the Dates of the Letters you receive from me; for then, as I generally keep Copies, I should know what get to hand and what miscarry.

I grieve for the Loss of dear Miss Ross.[6] She was indeed an amiable Girl. It must be a great Affliction to her Parents and Friends.

In my last I desired you to get Mr. Rhoads to send me a little Sketch of the Lot and Wall; but I have since found one he sent me before; so it is not necessary; only tell me whether it takes in Part of the late controverted Lot,[7] and how high it comes on both sides, and whereabouts the Wall is. By the way you never have told me what the Award was. I wish I could see a Copy of it.

2. Jonathan Potts, son of John Potts, and Benjamin Rush sailed from Philadelphia at the end of August and arrived at Liverpool, Oct. 21, 1766. Several of BF's friends wrote him by these young men; if DF did, her letter has not been found.

3. *Pa. Gaz.*, Aug. 21, 1766, reported the clearance of the brig *Elizabeth*, Capt. Golley. For Hall's letter of Aug. 19, 1766, see above, pp. 380–1. Young Potts and Rush were aboard the *Friendship*, Capt. Pearce.

4. In his letter to DF of April 6, 1766 (above, pp. 233–5), BF mentioned sending "3 Ells of Cambrick" by a Mr. Yates. The fate of the letters carried by Yates is not known.

5. See above, IX, 15 n, 221–2 n.

6. For the death of Sally Franklin's close friend, Margaret Ross, Aug. 20, 1766, see above, p. 338 n.

7. This was a lot to the west of BF's property the title and exact bounds of which were in dispute between a group of Quakers and the heirs of one Fox. According to Charles Thomson, writing DF on Nov. 10, 1766, court-appointed arbitrators had reached a satisfactory decision on the matter sometime before that date. See above, XII, 166–7 n; this volume, p. 118 n; Thomson to DF, Nov. 10, 1766, Yale Univ. Lib.

Here are but two Franklins remaining in England descended from my Grandfather; to wit, my Uncle John's Grand Son Thomas Franklin, who is a Dyer at Lutterworth, in Leicester Shire, and has a Daughter about 13 Years of Age named Sally.[8] He brought her to town to see me in the Spring, and Mrs. Stevenson persuaded him to leave the Child under her Care for a little Schooling and Improvement, while I went abroad. When I return'd, I found her indeed much improv'd, and grown a fine Girl. She is sensible and of a sweet obliging Temper; but is now ill of a violent Fever, and I doubt we shall lose her; which particularly afflicts Mrs. Stevenson, not only as she has contracted a great Affection for the Child, but as it was she that persuaded her Father to leave her here.

Mrs. Stevenson presents her best Respects. Polly is gone home to her Aunt's at Kensington. My Love to our Children and all enquiring Friends I am, Your ever loving Husband B FRANKLIN

I must request you to procure of some Friend of ours, a Copy of our Fire Company Articles, and a Copy of the Insurance Articles,[9] and send them as soon as you can to Irenaeus Moe, Esqr. at Barbadoes, Bridgetown.[1]

To William Franklin

MS not found; reprinted from extract in [Jared Sparks, ed.,] *A Collection of the Familiar Letters and Miscellaneous Papers of Benjamin Franklin* (Boston, 1833), p. 279.

[October 11th, 1766]
I was again with Lord Shelburne a few days since, and said a good deal to him on the affair of the Ilinois settlement.[2] He was

---

8. Thomas Franklin (A.5.2.3.1.1), who coincidentally wrote BF on this day (see below, p. 454), was his first cousin once removed. Thomas' daughter Sarah (A.5.2.3.1.1.1) recovered from the illness mentioned later in this paragraph, married in 1773, and had four children before her death in 1781.

9. See above, II, 150–2; IV, 281–95.

1. Probably Irenaeus Moe, proposed as a member of the Barbados Council in 1766 and appointed by the King in 1768; *Board of Trade Journal*, 1764–67, pp. 330, 344; *Acts Privy Coun., Col.*, V, 653. Bridgetown had been almost destroyed by fire on May 14. *Pa. Gaz.*, June 12, 19, 26, July 3, 10, 1766, published letters describing the loss, and *London Chron.*, July 5–8, reprinted an account from the *Barbados Mercury*.

2. For an earlier interview with Shelburne on this subject, see above, p. 424.

pleased to say he really approved of it; but intimated that every new proposed expense for America would meet with great difficulty here, the treasury being alarmed and astonished at the growing charges there, and the heavy accounts and drafts continually brought in from thence. That Major Farmer,[3] for instance, had lately drawn for no less than thirty thousand pounds extraordinary charges, on his going to take possession of the Ilinois; and that the superintendents, particularly the southern one, began also to draw very largely.[4] He spoke, however, very handsomely of Sir William on many accounts.

To Joseph Galloway

ALS: William L. Clements Library

Dear Sir,   London, Oct. 11. 1766
    I received your Favour of Aug. 23.[5] almost the only one I had by that Packet. It gives me great Pleasure to learn that our Friends keep up their Spirits, and that you have little doubt of the next Election.[6] I have occasionally had several Conferences lately with

3. Major Robert Farmar (1735–1780) of the 34th Regiment was the commander of British forces at Mobile in 1763 and led the expedition which occupied Fort Chartres in the Illinois country, Dec. 2, 1765. In the summer of 1766 he was relieved and returned to Mobile. Governor Johnstone of West Florida criticized the expenses of his Illinois expedition, but Gen. Thomas Gage defended him. Clarence E. Carter, *The Correspondence of General Thomas Gage*, II (New Haven, 1933), 295, 344, 345, 508, 562–3.
    4. On Dec. 11, 1766, Shelburne wrote John Stuart, superintendent of the Southern District, that "the Expences of Your District run so much above all Expectation and Proportion that it is very necessary you should attend to this Point very minutely for the future." Clarence W. Alvord and Clarence E. Carter, eds., *The New Régime*, pp. 454.
    5. Not found.
    6. The anti-proprietary party scored a decisive victory in the provincial elections in October. Its victory in the city and county of Philadelphia was complete, all of its candidates being chosen in both polls. In Philadelphia County all of the incumbents were re-elected with the exception of former speaker Isaac Norris who had died July 13, 1766; his place was taken by BF's old friend, John Potts (above, XI, 484 n). In the city of Philadelphia the incumbent James Pemberton was re-elected, and John Ross defeated the proprietary party candidate, John Dickinson, for the other seat by a margin of 34 votes. The voting in 1766 was substantially lighter than in the preceding year; the leading vote-getter, Joseph Richardson, polled 3,019 ballots, 1313

447

our present Secretary of State, Lord Shelbourne,[7] and some on the Affair of the Petitions. He was pleas'd to assure me that he was of Opinion Mr. Penn ought to part with the Government voluntarily, and said he had often told him so; but however that might be, he said that the Relation between them could and should have no Influence with him, in the Disputes subsisting between the Proprietors and People, as possibly some might suppose, &c.[8] Mr. Jackson is not yet come to Town, nor is the Season of Business yet come on; but nothing in my Power shall be wanting to push the Matter vigorously to a Conclusion if possible this Winter; for besides my Concern for the Publick, I really want to be at home and at Rest.

You see by the late Papers that we have had several Changes in the Ministry this Summer.[9] I was in hopes now Mr. Pitt was in, that we should have had a Ministry more firm and durable; for really these frequent Changes are extreamly discouraging to all who have Business to transact with the Government: but they begin now to whisper that we are not yet fix'd, and that before the Meeting of Parliament, we shall see fresh Overturnings. This, however, I do not give much Credit to. There may be some Changes, but I hope not considerable ones.

You take notice, that in the London Merchants Letter there is mention made of a Plan for a general Currency in America, being under Consideration of the Ministry;[1] and you wish it may suit

---

fewer than Isaac Norris had received in 1765, when he led both tickets. For the 1765 election, see above, XII, 290–1 n. For the present year's election, see Philadelphia city and county election returns, [Oct. 1, 1766], APS, and Sally Franklin to WF, Oct. 3, 1766, Yale Univ. Lib.

7. See above, pp. 424, 446.

8. On Feb. 3, 1765, Shelburne married Lady Sophia Carteret, the niece of Thomas Penn's wife, Lady Juliana Fermor Penn. *Gent. Mag.*, XXXV (1765), 97. On Oct. 28, 1766, Galloway wrote BF that William Allen was "continually publishing" the fact of Shelburne's relationship to Penn, implying that it would help the proprietary cause. See below, p. 478.

9. For the more important of these changes, see above, p. 384 n. There were no "fresh Overturnings" before the meeting of Parliament, Nov. 11, 1766.

1. In a letter of June 13, 1766, from "the Merchants of London, trading to North-America, to the Committee of Merchants in this City [Philadelphia]," published in *Pa. Gaz.*, Aug. 21, 1766, it was stated that "The Regulation of Paper Currency is postponed, in order to communicate to the Colonies, and take their Opinion upon, a Scheme for a general Paper Currency through America which has been proposed to the Administration."

448

the Temper of the Americans. I will let you into the History of that Plan.[2] When we were opposing the Stamp Act, before it pass'd, Mr. Grenville often threw out to us, that the Colonies had had Notice of it, and knew it would be necessary for Government here to draw some Revenue from them, and they had propos'd nothing that might answer the End and be more agreable to themselves: And then he would say, Can you Gentlemen that are Agents name any Mode of Raising Money for Publick Service that the People would have less Objection to, if we should agree to drop this Bill? This encourag'd me to present him with a Plan for a General Loan Office in America, nearly like ours, but with some Improvements effectually to prevent Depreciation; to be established by Act of Parliament, appropriating the Interest to the American Service, &c. This I then thought would be a lighter and more bearable Tax than the Stamps, because those that pay it have an Equivalent in the Use of the Money; and that it would at the same time furnish us with a Currency which we much wanted, and could not obtain under the Restrictions lately laid on us. Mr. Grenville paid little Attention to it, being besotted with his Stamp Scheme, which he rather chose to carry through. But the Successors of that Ministry, when it fell into their Hands, took a fancy to it, and a good deal of Pains in considering it, had frequent Conferences with me upon it, and really strengthened one another and their Friends in the Resolution of Repealing the Stamp Act, on a Supposition that by this Plan of a Loan Office they could raise a greater Sum with more satisfaction to the People. However, when the Stamp Act was repeal'd, I did not press the other, but advis'd that when they had settled the Plan to their own Minds, they should send Copies to the several Governors and Assemblies in America, to the End they might receive all their Opinions, Objections and Improvements, that it might, whenever carried into Execution, be as perfect as possible, and, (if it might be) with general Consent, as it was a Matter of great Importance. In the meantime, I drew a Bill for our present Relief (at the Request of a Member) to take off the Restraint on our legal Tenders by the late Act.[3] I send you a Copy of it inclos'd. Nothing was done on it, the Session being nearly at an End. I wish for your Sentiments on it.

2. See above, XII, 47–61.
3. See above, pp. 204–7.

With this Bill among my Papers I find the inclos'd Draft of a Petition I gave Mr. Jackson to present against the Bill for extending to Scotland the Act for transporting Felons to America.[4] He did not think fit to present it, (and indeed it was not fit to be presented without some Alterations which I propos'd to make if it had been presented it being rather too ludicrous.) but he show'd it among the Members, and it occasion'd some Laughing; but it was said, the Way to get the Transportation of Felons abolish'd, would be for all the Colonies to remonstrate against it.

It is certainly high time, as you observe, that our publick Debts were discharged; but I hope no Consideration of your Agents will induce the House to any Compliances inconsistent with the Publick Good, in order to obtain an Act for discharging those Debts.

As soon as any thing of consequence occurs, I shall not fail writing to the Committee. Present my Respects to them, and believe me ever, Dear Friend, Affectionately yours,　　　B FRANKLIN

My kindest Respects to our Friends Mr. Hughes, and the Whartons, to whom I cannot now write.

Jos. Galloway Esqr

Endorsed: Benja. Franklin Esqr　Oct. 11. 1766

From Giambatista Beccaria

Translation from draft (in Italian and Latin):[5] American Philosophical Society

Most illustrious Sir　　　　　　　　　Turin, 11 October 1766

Twelve days after receiving your most gracious letter[6] I was overtaken by blind hemorrhoids, which have tormented me fiercely

4. See above, pp. 240–2.

5. The editors are grateful to Robert S. Lopez, Durfee Professor of History, Yale University, for making the translation printed here. Beccaria composed most of the letter in Italian; he composed the second paragraph (set in quotation marks) in Latin except for a few words, intending this paragraph as a postscript to his paper on electricity. This draft is the longer and more finished of two versions of the letter to BF among the Beccaria MSS at APS. Readers wishing to consult the original text will find it conveniently printed in Antonio Pace, *Benjamin Franklin and Italy* (Phila., 1958), pp. 374–6.

6. Above, pp. 286–9.

for three months and a half. Hence it is only now, as I begin to feel some relief from them, that I am able to thank both the Royal Society and you for the condescension you showed towards my endeavors whatever [they may be worth], and this I think I cannot do in a better manner than by continuing my experiments. In keeping with this goal, I am enclosing a few pages of experiments I had carried out before I fell sick. Among them you will find an improved and augmented table of my first experiments.[7] Should the Royal Society like to have the abovesaid pages as well, it seems to me that the first experiments could be printed, omitting the whole table, and starting again with the Theorem.[8] However, the number of the Transactions where the table is to be printed, such as I am sending it now, ought to be quoted. I do not know whether Mr. Maty has communicated to you a postscript I had added to those first experiments.[9] It should read as follows:

"I am adding an experiment, as it will be seen, which is elegant, easy, and not hard to explain: I wrap a band of velvety black silk cloth around a glass cylinder which is rubbed in an electric machine; I distend it, sew it, rub it against the hair of the skin of a wild animal (the very long hair of a wildcat does much better than that of a hare).[1] By such a not-so-strong friction there appears in the chain electricity [that is] more vehement than that appearing through the ordinary friction of glass, but is opposite to it. Moderate friction offers easiness in experimenting. The vehemence of the electricity both increases the easiness of experimenting and increases the effects of the experiments. The contrast in the vehemence of the electricity defines the question. Thus as a matter of fact, I see that those who denied the electricity of resin opposite

7. What appears to be this paper is among the Beccaria MSS in APS labeled "cartella No 11 (16)" and "14" and headed "Risultato d' sperienze."

8. Beccaria's paper, read at the Royal Society May 1, 1766, appears to have been printed in essentially its original form in *Phil. Trans.*, LVI (1766), 105–18.

9. Matthew Maty (1718–1776), foreign secretary of the Royal Society, 1763; secretary, 1765; principal librarian of the British Museum, 1772. *DNB*. With the change indicated in the next note, this postscript was appended in its original Latin to Beccaria's paper in *Phil. Trans.*, LVI.

1. The words within parentheses are in Italian in the MS. The Latin words immediately preceding the parenthetical remark are *qui extant ex pelle felis silvestris*, but when printed in *Phil. Trans.* (p. 118) they were converted into *qui extant ex pelle leporis*, thereby substituting the hare *(lepus)* for the wildcat *(feles silvestris)* that Beccaria preferred for the experiment.

to the electricity of glass were deceived by the weakness of its electricity."

Mr. Maty, in replying to my first letter, told me that you were very much occupied with American affairs. This is the only reason why, since I expected no reply from you, I addressed to Mr. Wilson[2] other additional pages of mine concerning the electricity of glasses. If I had hoped for the honor of correspondence from you, I would have addressed myself to you and would have explained more openly my theoretical impressions concerning those experiments, which I think detract nothing from your theory but only add something. As I gain strength I shall endeavor to support those impressions with additional facts and shall write you about them if you care for it. I am enclosing the printed copy (a)[3] of those pages of mine, sent to Mr. Wilson, which I beg you to look at and to write me something about them.[4] For the time being I shall only point out: first, that the more the glasses are heated by fire, the less they show the effects preceding the discharge, and the discharge itself also is less, but they show greater effects following the discharge; second, that when I want to see the colored areas, I apply glasses that overlap in their two naked, most polished surfaces, which have been exposed to fire; third, that whether the glasses are charged in the chain as usual, or are charged by laying them over some body and rubbing them, one must always distinguish the two electricities, for if immediately after rubbing the surface of one of two united glasses, I separate them, the one which was rubbed appears electric by excess, the other by defect. Only after some time do these electricities reverse themselves. I should like these three remarks to be added as footnotes to those

2. Benjamin Wilson; above, IV, 391 n. Here and later in the letter Beccaria spells the name "Vilson," there being no "W" in Italian.

3. In the lower part of an otherwise blank page of the draft, Beccaria placed an "(a)" and two sentences obviously intended to be inserted somehow at this point. They are translated as follows: "The circumstances in which I was, that I could not hope for a reply from you, and still more that I had to fear that all I was experimenting, even privately, might be spied upon by some people who very importantly are watching around me, has forced me to such printing. I hope that this will not cause the Royal Society to look at my works with a less benevolent eye."

4. The paper mentioned here was probably the one sent to the Royal Society, April 26, 1766, read there on June 4, 1767, and printed in *Phil. Trans.*, LVII (1757), 297–311.

experiments.[5] Here in Turin, Cigna, the physician, a student of mine a few years ago,[6] sent me on 23 February of this year a printed copy of a pamphlet of his, where, among other things, he deals with the rubbing of ribbons and with the electricity of glasses. I think you will have received such a pamphlet from Mr. La Grange,[7] a companion and great friend of the said Cigna. I was uncertain whether I ought to mention that pamphlet as I was dealing with glasses and ribbons. I decided not to do it, considering that such a quotation might look like a reproach, since my experiments concerning ribbons show the experiments of Cigna to be wrong in that part where they would coincide with mine; and you will see that the same is true in Cigna's experiments concerning glasses, because, among other things, he does not in any way distinguish the electricity before a discharge from that after the discharge. At any rate, Cigna could have made out a more ingenious pamphlet if he had less indulged his inclination to innovate and contradict.

Should you not have that pamphlet, I will send it to you. Likewise, I beg you to continue [sending] me the news of discoveries that happen there and I am awaiting with great eagerness the new and enlarged edition of your most original letters, of which the meteorological observations you have most courteously favored me with are a most worthy accompaniment. On the other hand, in regard to waterspouts I have two observations of my own, one of 12 September of last year, the other of the last day of Whitsuntide of this year, which I shall make bold to offer you, if it pleases you, so that you may decide by yourself whether the circumstances I observed prove that some of the phenomena included under the name of waterspouts are produced by electric fire, as I have suggested. Meanwhile with full gratitude, respect and esteem, I am[8]

5. The desired footnotes do not appear in the paper as printed in *Phil. Trans.*
6. See above, p. 423 n.
7. Probably Joseph-Louis Lagrange (1736–1813), distinguished mathematician of French ancestry, born in Turin, professor at the artillery school there, and a founder of the Academy of Turin.
8. The draft ends here, but immediately following is the draft of a Latin letter to Charles Morton, secretary of the Royal Society (above, x, 71 n), dated the same day as the letter to BF, asking him to give the accompanying experiments to BF if the latter should be in London; if not, then asking Morton to present them to the Society himself.

From Thomas Franklin[9]   ALS: American Philosophical Society

Sir   Lutterworth Octr 11 1766
   I have Received all the Letters You have been so good as to
Send and am not Able to Express my Self with humble thanks to
you for all these great favours I and My Daughter Receive from
you Likewise humbly thank Mrs. Stevenson for all her E[x]ter-
ordinary Goodness to my Daughter. It is joyfull news to me to
hear my Daughter is getting better I Bless God for it, I have made
bold to Send My Daughter a few Lines in Your Letter for I could
not tell which would be most proper to send a Letter to her or to
Write in Yours as I have I hope you and Mrs. Stevenson are Well
as I am att this time and Conclude With all humble thanks to you
and Mrs. Stevenson for all your great Goodness and am, Your
Obedient humble Servant: THOS: FRANKLIN

From James Parker   ALS: American Philosophical Society

Honoured Sir   New-York, October 11. 1766
   Notwithstanding you have not pleasured me with one Line now
three Packets, yet will I not refrain writing till forbid; though I
wish I could write more agreeable Matters than I generally do:
As your Friends from Philada. doubtless inform you of political
Matters, I have little to say to them: In my Letters of May and
June last I informed you of my coming to this City and the Situation of my Affairs with Regard to Holt, &c. I am yet in the very
same Case neither any Settlement or Account from him, nor
Money: I should have been glad of a little of your Opinion on
those Letters, as Affairs stand, about beginning any News-paper:
but finding Nothing to be done with him, I am thinking to begin
next Week; notwithstanding all the Depressions and Disadvantages I am under, which are numerous; for there are these.[1] Some

   9. For Thomas Franklin (A.5.2.3.1.1), BF's first cousin once removed, and
for Thomas' daughter Sarah (A.5.2.3.1.1.1), who had been visiting BF and
Mrs. Stevenson and had become ill while at Craven St., see above, I, li-lii;
and this volume, p. 446.
   1. Parker resumed publication of *The New-York Gazette: or, the Weekly
Post-Boy* with the issue of Oct. 16, 1766, assigning to it whole number 1241

Popularity he has acquired by the Writing about the Stamp-Act; all his Works new; the Books and Customers all in his own Hands; the Unpopularity of my Offices, especially in the Custom-House; all these are Disadvantages that I think would but whet and animate me the more and I should encounter them with Pleasure, as the greater the Difficulty, the more the Satisfaction in over-coming, but the Depressions that most discourage me, is the Hand of God upon me; the Sickness and Distress of my Family now full Sixteen Months since I have constantly had the Doctors to deal with, whose Bills are more than the Butchers. My Daughter [has] now been sick 32 Days, and not the best Prospect of soon recovering: my little Grand-Daughter, now about a Year old, has had the Fever-and-Ague excessive hard for four Weeks, and still racks her to pieces, she is too little to physick—her Mother has been poorly, but is a little on the Recovery. One of my Prentice now lies in the same Condition—one or other of us has been constantly down, ever since June was a year. Sometimes five of my Family at once: My poor Son I told you of before. He was advised to go off to Sea a little, I sent him to my Brother: I heard four Days after he went out, that he was poorer than when he sail'd, which was the second Day of September, and I have not heard a Word of him since: I have not had a Shillings Worth of Work since I came here but Stock-Work and of that have not sold as much as will pay the Paper only—I sell a few Things now in the Shop which gets me a little Market Money: Indeed the Times seem very bad here: but the Worst is we have had the wettest Summer ever remembered, and it has occasioned universal Sickness both in City and Country; so much in the Country as to disable the Farmers and Labourers from doing their usual Work, and many I am assured have not sowed their Grain yet which should generally be in the Ground the Beginning of September. Till within three Days past, we have not had two Days for four Weeks without Rain more or less, and some times Abundance: this has prevented

in direct sequence to Holt's issue of October 9. Holt brought out *The New-York Journal, or General Advertiser* with the issue of October 16, and gave it the same whole number, 1241, thereby emphasizing the continuation of his own paper though with a changed name. Clarence S. Brigham, *History and Bibliography of American Newspapers 1690–1820* (Worcester, Mass. 1947), pp. 636, 655.

both Wood-Cutters and Carters from bringing Wood to Market, and some Cool Weather now coming on, the Country all sick, Wood has surprizingly rose 5 and 6s. in a Cord in one Day only and is now as high as generally in the hardest Winter: this affects the Publick in general, and me as an Individual only: but it adds a little to the particular Distress of my Family. Amidst these Troubles I am thankful to God, that I myself enjoy such a tolerable Share of Health. Perhaps when all the Storms are over, a Calm may come; tho' I can safely say that since the first of May last my Expences have been more than all my Incomes, and I have not bought me one Rag of Cloaths, nor fitted any Thing for the Winter: and thus to begin a Paper I am afraid will look like Madness, when I have not Money to purchase Paper for to carry it on: but I am now like the Lepers at the Gate of Samaria:[2] If I continue thus, I shall be ruined, and I can but be ruined if I venture: but if I succeed I shall be saved: This seems to edge me on: The Lot is cast, but the Disposal thereof is in the Lord.[3] Amidst these Affairs, will it give offence, if I once more ask, if my Allowance in the Office could not be enlarged a little more according to Mr. Foxcroft's Opinion.[4] There being several more Offices now than there were three or four Years ago, and it adds considerably to the Business: Quebeck and Montreal Offices which we apprehended would scarce quit Cost, brings in a pretty considerable Sum, which helps the Revenue, as well as adds to my Business: If it could be advanced a little, it would greatly help me; in this very dear Place and if I fail in a News-paper, I have no other Dependance: However that God who has hitherto preserved me, will I am persuaded,

2. The reference is to II Kings 7: 3–8. The city of Samaria was in the throes of a severe famine because the Syrians were besieging it. Four lepers at the city gate concluded that if they went into the city they would die; if they stayed where they were they would die; but if they went to the Syrian camp there was a possible alternative: "If they save us alive, we shall live; and if they kill us, we shall but die." So they set forth. Meanwhile the Lord had frightened the Syrians, they had fled, and the lepers found the camp deserted. "They went into one tent, and did eat and drink, and carried thence silver, and gold, and raiment, and went and hid it." They repeated the process and then reported their discovery to the city, and the famine was ended.

3. Proverbs 16: 33: "The lot is cast into the lap; but the whole disposing thereof is of the Lord."

4. The allowance was enlarged by £20 a year, as Parker learned in December; below, pp. 525–6.

point out some Way for my Escape from Ruin: The New-Haven Affair is not ended:[5] I have had a Writ for Holt out these 5 Weeks, but tis said he has the Gout: However he is [not] to be seen: nor is he, I am afraid Worth much if taken and it grives me much to arrest any one. I told you before the New Haven Affairs, tho' I shall get but little of B. Mecom, as he does little, yet assoon as all Holt's Time is accounted for to me, I will account to Hunter for all I get of B. Mecom; but I fear Holt has spent all due to [me at] that Place: and I think since I can't come upon Holt for it, Col. Hunter should consider me, (but this I wrote of before).

You never sent the Bill of Lading for the Electrical Machine yet, so we cannot get it: There that rests yet.[6] Mr. Hughes keeps close yet: but keeps a School still: The Parcel of Stationary you sent over for him, which I took, and I told you would be willing to pay you Interest for from the Beginning of May, which is the Time I took them—very little else of it sells, except the Paper and Bound Books: and if you would (for I have not Money now to send) procure me —as much more Paper and Books only as there were in that, from two Quire to 6 Quire—bound, marbled Edges, except instead of two Ream of Small Post, to send two Ream of thick Post: and to add, one Ream of demi, and a Ream of Medium also a Roll of good Parchment: Also the same Quantity of Wafers in Boxes Sealing Wax and Ink-powder, as in that Invoice, but no other Stationary, as those are all the Articles I have sold any Thing of, and need supplying or all in any Likelihood of going: Paper you know never comes amiss to a Printer, only as that Cargo was all cut Paper it would suit better was most of it not cut. The chief Reason I ask this of you, is that I may owe you all I do owe; and I had as leive pay you Interest as another, and that you know the Interest is higher here than there: But if it be too inconvenient to you, I shall not be offended if you decline it[7]—If you send any, and the Box or Case should want something to fill up, either a Ream

5. Parker's difficulties with Holt and Mecom concerning their New Haven accounts, to which reference has often been made in previous letters.

6. On the machine BF sent over for Hugh Hughes of N.Y., see above, XII, 259–60 n, and repeated mentions in Parker's letters of this year.

7. On Jan. 29, 1767, BF paid Bloxam & Fourdrinier £50 2s. 9d., charging the payment to Parker, for "sundry Stationary sent him." Journal, 1764–1776, p. 10; Ledger, 1764–1776, pp. 10, 24. The marine insurance policy for the shipment to N.Y., Feb. 6, 1767, is in APS.

or two more of Paper or Six of Entick's Dictionaries,[8] a Doz. or so of small Testaments, or some Common Prayer Books: but none of Dilworth's Histories[9] sell here, as they are 8s. Sterl. per Doz. when Chapmen's Books are sold here by Merchants for 12s. 6d. per Doz. this Money, they say they cost them but 5s. 6d. Sterl. per Doz. and are as good as Dilworth's. Indeed few Books will sell here now, as Rivington, Noel and Gaine have all large Stores of them, But enough of this.

I have never ask'd, or ever heard, who was to pay me any Thing for the Office of Land Waiter: If its to be paid there, please to let me know. I shall order it all to you, if you are there when any of it comes due, tho' I know no more about it than the Mogul. If any Thing is to be done about the Post Office in Consequence of my coming to keep it here shall be glad of your Orders and Directions: I continue to go on as usual, in the best Manner I can tho' am often getting new Post-Masters, for now the Privilege of franking is taken away, it is a hard Matter to get a Person to take it: And as hard to get the Money from some of them after they have taken it. However we keep doing; tho' Money is really scarcer than ever I knew it here, and every Thing as dear as if we found Money in the Streets. The City is too great for the Country.

I have now almost exhausted my Budget, and indeed considering how little I can say to any Purpose, its a Wonder I have so much to say of any Kind. But so it is, the Sickness of my Family, the Difficulties that seem to surround me sometimes throws my Mind into gloomy Thoughts, at other Times, my Spirits revive in full Hopes and Confidence I shall not be left destitute; that I ought patiently and contentedly to submit to the Will of Heaven: knowing I am but a Creature of a feeble Make: Indeed, was the Strength of my Body equal to those Sallies of Spirit, I could do well: but I feel not the Ability I had to undergo Hardships, I once did. A little more Struggling thro' Life will probably carry me out of it, and Oh: if we do but go out with a cleer Conscience, a humble Mind,

8. John Entick (1703?–1773), schoolmaster and author, published among other works several popular school books, including a *Spelling Dictionary* in 1763. *DNB*. Apparently BF sent over none of the books Parker asked for.

9. Probably William H. Dilworth, listed in the British Museum Catalogue as the author of a series of histories and biographies first published between 1755 and 1760; not Thomas Dilworth, author of a famous spelling book.

and the Satisfaction of having done our Duty here: we have no more to fear, but a joyful Hope of a Rest from all our Labours.

I have now only to add: all my best Wishes for your safe Return: My Wife and Daughter from her Sick Bed send their humble Salutations: May my next be more agreeable both to you and to Your most obliged Servant   JAMES PARKER.

From Timothy Lane[1]   Copy:[2] The Royal Society

Sir   [Aldergate-Street,] October [15,] 1766[3]

Being employed in some Electrical Enquiries about the beginning of the year 1762 it occured to me, that many Experiments on this Subject might be made with a much greater degree of precision if we could determine with any tolerable accuracy the comparative quantity of Electric Fluid, with which for any given Experiment, the Coated Phial is impregnated.

An In[s]trument, which I have contrived for this Purpose, may not improperly be called an Electrometer. I have herewith sent you a drawing thereof,[4] with the Machine* to which it is fixed.

*This Portable Machine is the contrivance of Mr. Read Mathematical In[s]trument Maker at Knight[s]brid[g]e near London.

1. On Timothy Lane, member of the Apothecaries' Company and electrical experimenter, see above, p. 288 n. His inventive ability, demonstrated in this paper, appeared again in his creation of the Patent Graduated Measures, "which have proved very efficacious in preventing venders and purchasers from being deceived by such false measures as were detected by the Censors of the Royal College of Physicians in the years 1800 and 1801." *Gent. Mag.*, LXXVII (1807), 689.

2. This copy is in a set of relatively small pages stitched together, apparently in Lane's hand and apparently sent to the Royal Society to be used as printer's copy. The text appears on the right-hand pages, the left pages being reserved for additions to be inserted at points indicated by carets in the text. The letter was printed in *Phil. Trans.*, LVII (1767), 451–60. An occasional doubtful word has been supplied from the printed text. The paper was reprinted as a separate pamphlet in 1768. The cover page of the MS is marked "Received Aug. 1767" and "To Benjamin Franklin LLD. FRS," and carries in another hand a description of the contents.

3. The material in brackets does not appear in the MS but is supplied from the printed text.

4. Lane's original drawing does not survive. The illustration printed here is reproduced from Tab. XX, in *Phil. Trans.*, LVII, facing p. 451, the first page of the printed text.

Fig 1.

A   The Cylindrical Glass of the Machine used instead of a Globe. The Cylindrical part of the Glass is 6 inches in lenth and 16 in circumference.[5]

B   The Wheel at every turn of which the Cylindrical Glass revolves 4 times.

C   The Conductor

D   The Coated Phial

E   a Brass Wire Loop, passing through the wood work to a Tin Plate on which the Coated Phial stands

F   The Pillar of the Electrometer made of Wood bored cylindrically about ⅔ of its lenth and rendred Electrical[6] by being long baked in an oven and then boiled in Linseed Oil and again baked.

   At first the Pillar was made of Brass which tho it served very well to determine the Electric Stroke for Medical purposes, yet was defective in many Experiments, as the Table thereby became a ready Conductor.

G. Brass Work, having its lower part inclosed within the Bore of the Pillar

H. a Screw which passes through the Brass Work near the Bottom and fixes it in the Pillar

I   a Groove for the Screw H to move in when the Electrometer is moved higher or lower, as the different hights of different Condensing Phials may require.

K   a well polished haemispherical piece of Brass fixed to the Conductor

L   a Steel Screw passing through the Top of the Brass work, whose threads are distant nearly 1/24 of an Inch from each other.

M   a well polished spherical piece of Brass fixed to the Screw L and opposite to K. As the polish of K and M will often be destroyed by large Electrical explosions, the Polish should

---

5. Elements A, B, C, and D, as described here and shown on the plate, were merely one form of the familiar device by means of which frictional electricity was generated by revolving wheel B, and thereby cylindrical glass A, and was then transferred via conductor C to phial (or Leyden jar) D. The wire loop E was the only special feature of this assembly. The elements lettered from F through O constituted the electrometer proper.

6. That is, rendered non-conducting.

Fig.2.

Fig.3.

Fig.4.

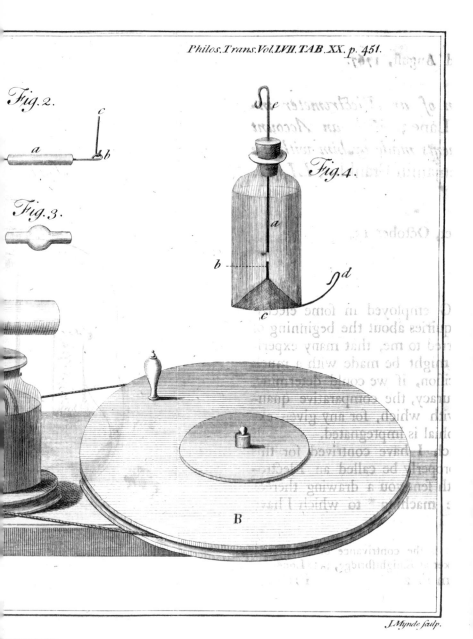

B

ectrometer

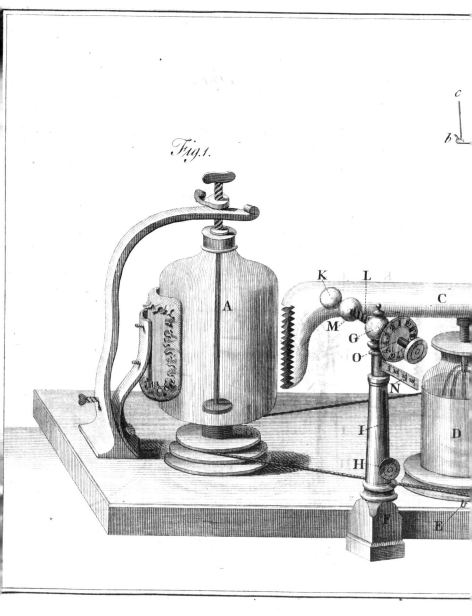

Fig.1.

Timothy Lane's E

again be restored, particularly where the Expe[riments] require accuracy.

N a Scale with divisions equal to each turn of the Screw.

O a Circular Plate fixed to and moving with the Screw, pointing at each turn to the Division upon the Scale. This Plate is also divided into 12 to denote the parts of each Turn.

The Principle on which the Electrometer acts, is very simple, being merely this. The Coated Phial is hereby rendred incapable of accumulating and retaining any more than a certain quantity of the Electric Fluid, for any intended Experiment when a Metallic or Non Electric communication is made from the Screw H to the wire loop E of the Machine. And that quantity will be proportionate to the distance of K and M from each other, and consequently the Explosion and stroke will thereby be regulated.

Thus if a Person holds a wire fastened to the Screw H in one hand, and another Wire fixed to the Loop E in the other, he will perceive no Stroke, if K and M are in contact notwithstanding the Cylindical Glass A acts strongly. But if by turning the Screw L. the Ball M is distant from K 1/100 part of an Inch a very small stroke will be perceived, with an Explosion from K to M, and if K and M are distant one inch from each other, the quantity of the Electric Fluid, at the time of the Explosion will be increased 100. times. For example it appears by Experiment that if the Explosion happens after 4 Turns of the Wheel B. when M is distant from K 1/24 of an Inch or 1 turn of the Screw, the same will happen at 8 turns of the Wheel when M and K are distant 2 turns of the Screw or 1/12 of an Inch. And if K and M are distant 3 turns of the Screw, the turns of the Wheel will be twelve at the time of the Explosion, the same proportion will continue so far as the distance K and M is equal to the condensing Power of the Coated Phial without wasting. By wasting I mean when the Phial is so fully charged that part of the Electric Fluid escapes from the mouth of the Bottle, or from the Conductor into the air or to some adjacent non Electric.

The Number of Turns of the wheel, when K and M are at any of the above distances, will be more or less in proportion to the state of the Air, the Cylindrical Glass, the Cushion against which the Glass is rubbed, or the Coated Phial which last will not give so great an explosion when the Air is damp as when dry.

The fewer the Number of Turns of the wheel at any given distance, the better the Machine worketh. Thus a Comparative difference between any two Machines may be determined.

A Wire in general is better than a Chain, unless the Chain is held very tight, particularly in very small Strokes the Electric fluid will be lost in passing from Link to Link of the Chain. By Experiment it also appears, that the quantity of Electric Fluid at every Explosion will be proportionate to the quantity of Coated Glass, either as to the size of the Coated Phial or to the Number of Phials added. For Example. If the Phial D has half of the Coating on each side of the Glass taken off the Explosion will happen after half the Number of Turns of the Wheel, at any of the above distances and if a Phial with twice the quantity of Coated Glass, is employ'd instead of D, the turns of the Wheel will be double the same will happen if two Coated Phials each equal to D are used, and if three Phials the Number of Turns will be triple &c.

The Phial D used in the following Experiments contains about 80 Square inches of Coating on the inside and also on the outside of the Glass, the mouth being stopped with wood prepared like the Pillar and the Coating not so near the mouth of the Phial as usual to prevent[7] the Electric Fluids wasting, and thereby the Phial may be more fully charged.

As K is part of the Conductor and M of the Electrometer, the distance between them is the distance of the Electrometer from the Conductor, whence it will be readily understood, when I relate the distance of the Electrometer in any Experiments for Example. The Electrometer at 20, that is M is 20 turns of the Screw distant from K or 20/24 of an Inch.

That Lightening and Electricty are of very near affinity, if not the same, evidently appears from the many discoveries you have made. And as the following Experiments tend to confirm the same as well as to illustrate the use of the Electrometer I hope they will not be unacceptable.

Experiment 1. A Peice of Moist Tobacco Pipe Clay rolled cylindrically, a. Fig 2. about an inch in lenth and about 2 or 3/10ths of an inch in diameter, having a Peice of Wire thrust into each end

7. *Phil. Trans.* reads here: "and the coating not too near the mouth of the phial, to prevent" etc.

bb, distant from each other about 1/10 of an Inch with the solid Clay between and the end of one of the Wires cc fixed to the Loop of the Machine E and the other fixed to the small Screw of the Electrometer H will with an Explosion at 20 of the Electrometer, be inflated as in Fig. 3, or if the Clay is too dry or the quantity of Electricity too great, it will burst in Peices leaving only the Clay concave near the ends of the Wires. And tho the Experiment will in appearance differ, yet it will always leave evident signs of an Explosive Power or sudden rarefaction, excepting when the wires in the Clay are at too great a distance from each other, then the Electric Fluid will only run over its moist surface. If instead of Clay a Mucilagenous vegetable paste is used, as wheat flower and Water &c. the Experiment will appear the same.

Experiment 2. A peice of common hard baked smoking Tobacco Pipe about an inch in lenth with the bore in the Middle filled with Clay and Wires put into each end as in Fig 2 and applied in the same manner to the Machine will burst into many peices, at 20 of the Electrometer, sometimes the peices will be driven near ten feet from the Machine.

Experiment 3. A small Square peice of Portland Stone with holes drilled at each end so as to admit the wires, was in like manner burst in peices, when a second Coated Phial was added to increase the Stroke.

The Iron cramps in stone Buildings are similar to the Wires, and when a Building is struck by Lightening produces a similar effect. I observed that when the Tobacco Pipe or stone was damp the Experiment succeeded better than when dry, and I frequently found that either of them after being first dipped in Water would be broken with a less explosion than before.

This observation, is different from the received opinion of many, not well acquainted with Electricity, that Lightening is less likely to do mischeif after a Shower of Rain than before. So far may be true that the Rain will bring down some of the Lightening, and also render Thatched Houses &c. less likely to take fire; but will not assist Buildings that have Metallic Ornaments near their Tops, as the Weather Cocks of Churches &c. As a metallic Conductor from the Tops of Buildings to the Earth will prevent the effects of Lightening on them, so will the smallest wire prevent the effects of Electricity on the Stone or Tobacco Pipe when in contact with the two wires cc. Fig 2.

If the Tobacco Pipe instead of Clay is filled as above with an Electric Substance as Wax, Powderd Glass or with any non Electric substance inferior to Metals as a Conductor, it will be burst in Peices, with nearly the same quantity of the Electric Fluid.

As the above Experiments succeeded better when the Stone or Clay were previously dipped in Water than before, I was induced to try Water only.

Experiment 4. Having made a hole without any cracks on the side thro the bottom of the Phial a Fig 4, which may easily be done if the Phial is conical at the bottom as in the Figure, by holding the Phial inverted in one hand and with the other strikeing a Pointed Steel Wire against the Apex of the Cone.

Through this hole I passed a Wire b. and filled the bottom c with melted Sealing Wax leaving the other end of the Wire out at d. When the Wax was cold, the Phial was about ¾ths filled with water, and stopped with a Cork thro which a Wire e. was passed downwards, till the Points of the two wires were distant from each other about 1/10 of an Inch as near as my Eye could determine: a Wire from the Electrometer was fixed to e and another from the Loop of the Machine was fixed at d. By an Explosion, at 20 of the Electrometer, the Phial burst in peices, the Top falling from the Bottom near the point of the lower Wire. Another Phial was fitted in the same manner and the Cork cut longitudinally that the air might freely pass at the time of the Explosion, but this made no sensible difference. Often times the Phial is so cracked as to resemble Radii from a Center.

If Oil is used instead of water, the Event will be the same.

The quantity of Electricity necessary to burst the Phial; appears to vary more in proportion to its thickness than its size. Many Phials of various sizes may be broken at 10 of the Electrometer while others nearly of the same size remain sound with a Stroke at 30 or even more.

I generally found Green Glass more difficult to break than white.

When the Phial is not broken by the Electric Stroke, the agitation of the Water may be sensibly observed at the instant of the Explosion, and the Electric Spark evidently seen to pass through the water from the point of one wire to the other.

464

This remarkable appearance of the Electric fluids passing through water may be observed, when the Electrometer is at a smaller distance from the Conductor, if the wires are nearer to each other.

I have broken many Phials by the Electric Strokes as above mentioned when the wires have been at the various distances, of above one inch to 1/20 of an inch from each other, as near as my Eye could determine. But the distance of about 1/10 of an Inch I usually prefer. The above experiments I have often repeated and may therefore be relied on: Want of leisure has prevented me from pursuing them more minutely. But I hope they will serve as hints to others of more abilities and leisure than Your respectfull Humble Servant [T LANE][8]

Pennsylvania Assembly Committee of Correspondence to Richard Jackson and Benjamin Franklin

Printed in *Votes and Proceedings of the House of Representatives of the Province of Pennsylvania, Met at Philadelphia* [October 14, 1766] (Philadelphia, 1767), pp. 8–9.

Gentlemen, [October 18, 1766]

You will perceive by the inclosed Resolves, that you are appointed joint Agents of this Province for the ensuing Year, to solicit and transact the Affairs thereof in Great-Britain, and that we are the Committee of Correspondence, to whom you will be pleased to communicate, from Time to Time, such Information as may be necessary to be laid before the House of Representatives.[9]

The present House concurring in Opinion with the three last preceding Assemblies, that it is necessary the present Government should be changed, from *Proprietary* to *Royal*,[1] and being earnestly desirous that this Measure may be accomplished with all convenient Speed, in case all their Charter and legal Rights and Privileges may be preserved and secured, it is therefore by their Order,

8. The signature, not on the MS, is supplied from *Phil. Trans.*

9. In the new Assembly, meeting on Oct. 14, 1766, Joseph Galloway was elected speaker, replacing Joseph Fox. On the 15th Jackson and BF were reappointed agents and the six men who, together with Speaker Galloway, signed this letter of instruction were named the Committee of Correspondence for the year. 8 *Pa. Arch.*, VII, 5938–40.

1. Above, XI, 193–200, 423–4; XII, 322; and this volume, pp. 51–2.

that we instruct you to prosecute the Petitions, for this Purpose, to an Issue, before His Majesty in Council; but at the same Time, they direct and enjoin, that you strictly observe the Instructions on this Head,[2] relative to the Preservation of all those civil and religious Privileges, which the People of this Province have a Right to enjoy, under the said Charter and Laws, which you have before received from the several preceding Assemblies, and to which we refer; and further, that in case the said Petitions should be finally rejected by His Majesty in Council, that you do not of yourselves, without first having the Approbation of Assembly, petition the Parliament on this Occasion.[3]

The House have taken into their Consideration the Act of Parliament passed at the last Session, for repealing certain Duties in the British Colonies and Plantations, &c. and although the last Assembly by their Committee fully instructed you, respecting the Mischiefs which will attend the Execution of this Statute,[4] yet they conceive it a Matter of so much Importance to the Welfare of the Colonies, that they have ordered us to renew those Instructions, and to press you to exert your utmost Industry and Abilities, at the next Meeting of Parliament, to obtain a Repeal of such Clauses of that Statute as tend to restrain the Trade between Ireland and the American Colonies.

It is difficult to describe the Distress which this Province, as well as other Colonies, labour under for Want of a Paper Currency, and it is no small Addition to the Concern of the Representatives of the People, on this Occasion, to find that this Distress is daily growing greater, and must continue to increase, until the present Restriction on striking Bills of Credit in the Colonies is taken off; it is therefore by Order of the House, that we earnestly desire that you will endeavour to make all the Interest in your

2. Above, XI, 219–20 n, 398 n, 403.

3. Technically, the Privy Council never "finally rejected" the petition for a change in government, though its action on Nov. 22, 1765, had virtually that effect. *Acts Privy Coun., Col.,* IV, 741, records that on that day consideration was "postponed for the present." Thomas Penn told Governor Penn, Nov. 30, 1765, that it was "postponed, sine die, that is (to use my Lord Presidents own expression) for ever and ever." Above, XII, 420–1 n.

4. On this act (which would have cut off colonial exports to Ireland) and the previous Assembly's special instructions relating to it, see above, pp. 419–21.

Power with the House of Commons, to obtain a Repeal of the Act of Parliament prohibiting the making Bills of Credit lawful Tender in the Colony Debts, agreeable to the Petition now before the House of Commons from the last Assembly;[5] and we cannot suffer ourselves to doubt but that you will be joined in this Measure by every Merchant in London trading to America; as without it their Exportation must be greatly diminished, and the People here compelled to go into Manufactures, which otherwise they might never attempt: We also hope you will not be inattentive to the Introduction of Fruit, Wine, and Oil directly from Spain, Portugal and Italy, into the Colonies, and the Exportation of Iron from thence to foreign Ports, as they are Regulations which our Merchants have much at Heart, and which are really necessary to the true Interest of Great-Britain and her Colonies.

We conclude that the Governor, agreeable to the Directions of the Royal Charter, has before this Time transmitted to His Majesty in Council, the several Laws passed by the last Assembly, and as some of them are of great Importance to the People, particularly the Act for regulating our Elections, that for erecting an House of Employment for the Poor, &c. and a Third for the Regulation of Pilots,[6] we doubt not you will do every Thing in your Power to obtain their Confirmation. We are, Your assured Friends,

JOSEPH GALLOWAY, JAMES PEMBERTON,

JOSEPH RICHARDSON, JOHN ROSS,

THOMAS LIVEZEY,   ISAAC PEARSON.

JOSEPH FOX,

P. S. We inclose a Copy of the Letter from the Committee of Correspondence of the last House, respecting the Trade with Ireland.

To RICHARD JACKSON, *and* BENJAMIN FRANKLIN, *Esqrs, Agents for the Province of* Pennsylvania, *in* London.

5. See above, p. 51 n.

6. The three acts named had all received Governor Penn's assent on Feb. 8, 1766, and were laid before the Privy Council for consideration on Feb. 11, 1767. All three were allowed to stand upon the passing of the six months' time limit prescribed by the charter. Their texts may be found in *Statutes at Large, Pa.*, VII, 32–40, 9–17, 19–27, respectively.

From Jonathan Potts[7]   ALS: American Philosophical Society

Worthy Sir   Liverpool October 22d: 1766
   You will receive by this post several Letters in my favour from
Gentlemen of your Acquaintance in Philadelphia[8] and by the first
Vessels from Pennsylvania you will receive Letters, in favour of
my Good friend and Relation Mr. Rush and myself from your Son
the Govenour of the Jerseys (who has honoured me with a Letter
to Sir Alex: Dick of Edinburgh) and also from my Father,[9] should
you think proper to write to any Gentlemen in Edinburgh in favour
of both Mr. Rush and Myself[1] it shall be acknowledged as a particular favour confered upon Sir your most Obedient and very
humble Servant   JONATHAN POTTS.

PS Please to enclose any Letters in our favour to me in Edinburgh.

To Benjamin Franklin Esqr.

Addressed: To / Benjamin Franklin Esqr. / Craven Street / London
/ per post / paid.

From Thomas Ronayne[2]   ALS: American Philosophical Society

[*Illegible*] Sir   Corke (in Ireland) October 22. 1766
   [*Illegible*] of last July I received your kind Letter bearing date
of April 20th.[3] together with your Book of Whirlwinds, Waterspouts, &c.[4] which I should have acknowledg'd before now but
that I was in daily Expectation of having opportunities for offering
these Remarks.

---

   7. For Jonathan Potts, who was traveling to Edinburgh with Benjamin
Rush, to pursue his medical studies, see above, pp. 387–8, 404 n; the two
young men arrived in Liverpool on October 21 (above, p. 445 n).
   8. See above, pp. 404–5.
   9. The letters from WF and Potts's father have not been found.
   1. See below, pp. 531–3, for BF's letters of recommendation to various
friends in Edinburgh.
   2. On Ronayne see above, IX, 350 n.
   3. Above, pp. 247–50.
   4. Presumably BF had sent an offprint of his "Physical and Meteorological
Observations, Conjectures, and Suppositions" that had been published in
Phil. Trans., LV (1765), 182–92.

As to what you observe how any large body electrified may cause smaller ones to be electrified the Reverse of what itself is, that might have often been the case when I had a Tin Tube which did not end in a sharp Point but the one I describ'd to you does, beside I made observations of several changes from Negative to positive and viceversa when I stood on a cake of Wax with a Pole in my hand round which a Wire* was twisted during the passing of what seem'd one Cloud and that not very extensive, so that if there was a succession of Clouds the Electricity of each must have been very great.

I have read your experiments in pursuance of those of Mr. Canton.[5] They together with your ingenious Conjectures in your letter shew how in some circumstances the Electricity may be changed in contrarium when the Lightning strikes to the Earth without supposing Electricity in the Earth to be the cause of Thunder as Beccaria Seems to think.[6]

I have since discoverd that the Reason why Electrical Experiments do not succeed in damp weather is owing to Silk imbibing Moisture from the Air; for bodies insulated by Sealing Wax or gum lac[7] retain Electricity very well at all times, and the Moistest Air conducts very slowly as I found by Electrifing it in a Room.

I also discover'd that Silk dryed and dipt in [*illegible*] melted, if kept in ones pocket is convenient to have [in rea]diness, but the best way of insulating bodies is thus, [*torn*] a Piece of Sealing Wax, or Gum lac at each end making a hole transversely through which you may put Silk, or even Twine. With two pieces in this manner a prime Conductor can be insulated.

I should have mentiond an Experiment favouring your principles, Viz. Let a pair of Cork balls suspended by dry silk be electrified by Glass, or wax, approach them with the Same and it will

---

*The Wire went beyond the Pole and was broken so it would not act in the Manner of Points.

5. Above, v, 516–19.

6. For this theory and BF's belief that it might, at least sometimes, be valid, see above, v, 396, 428.

7. *Gum lac* is one variety of a resinous incrustation (called *lac*) deposited on twigs of various trees in India and other parts of southern Asia by an insect known variously as *Tachardia lacca* or *Carteria lacca*. The *shellac* of commerce is a refined and processed form of *lac*.

never close them; so that the cause of the encrease or decrease of repulsion is not the Different density of internal and external Electricks Fluid, but what you said.

In a letter I wrote to you before I receivd your letter I conjecturd that Vapour, or a Cloud when electrified is more or less capable of exploding as 'tis more or less compress'd, this follows from your principles as it doth that Vapour can receive more Electricity than the same quantity converted into Water, therefore some Part of a Cloud may conduct much better than others at the same time; this perhaps may account for the changes during the Passing of what seems one Cloud or Nimbus, it may also serve to shew that when the Electricity upon a Flash appears and disappears the Equilibrium of any Cloud with the Earth may not be restor'd, and explain several Phenomena in Lightning, and variations in the Noise of Thunder; but I cannot to much recommend the Signals &c.

The foremost Clouds of a Shower &c. are generally Negative. In a Shower of Snow the Electricity tho on and of[f] at different times yet was always Negative, till after the Shower was just past there was a weak positive Electricity, discoverable only by Mr. Cantons Electrometer.[8] In haste I am Most excellent Sir Your most obedient humble Servant   THOS. RONAYNE

P.S. I attempted the Experiment I mentiond to you of the Wax to try whether hot Air at the Surface is what only makes Electricks per se seem conductors or not; the Experiment seem'd to favour the Affirmative tho not so small a Quantity of Wax would not keep in such perfect fusion as I could wish.

Addressed: To | Benjamin Franklin Esqr | Cravenstreet, Strand | London[9]

8. For this device, see above, IX, 351 n.

9. On the address page appears a series of financial calculations, apparently in BF's hand, involving sums in the hundreds of pounds. Their purpose or significance cannot be determined.

From Benjamin Rush[1]   ALS: American Philosophical Society

Sir   Liverpool Octobr: 22nd: 1766

As I have the Happiness of being born in the Province where you have resided many years, I was anxious to come under your Patronage, as I well knew your great Love and Partiality to the Province of Pennsylvania would readily induce You to favour any One of its Natives even though unknown to You. With this view I have procured a few Letters from some of your Friends,[2] of such Import I trust as will induce You to think any such Services will not be wasted or duly acknowledged by me.

As the Season is now so far advanced I cannot do myself the Honour of waiting upon you in person in London to intimate there my Desires to you: I must therefore beg of you to write to such of your Friends in Edinburgh in behalf of my good Friend Mr. Potts and myself as you think will be most usefull to us in the prosecution of our Studies.[3]

I hope Sir you will excuse the Fredom I have assumed in writing to you. During your late Stay in Philadelphia I was too Young, and my Confinement to Study too close to aspire after the Honour of an Acquaintance with you.[4] Although the high Esteem I was early taught to entertain of that Merit and learning which have procured you so much Reputation in the World would have prompted me to it.[5] I have the Honour to be with much Esteem your most Obedient Humble Servant   BENJAMIN RUSH

Addressed: To / Benjamin Franklin Esqr. / Deputy post master General / of / North America / in / London / per post paid

1. For Benjamin Rush, who was traveling to Edinburgh with Jonathan Potts to pursue his medical studies, see above, pp. 387 n, 468.
2. Only Charles Thomson's letter of Aug. 24, 1766, has been found; see above, pp. 387–8.
3. See below, pp. 531–3.
4. Born in 1746, Rush graduated from Princeton in 1760 and served as Dr. John Redman's apprentice until 1766. *DAB.*
5. Evidently Rush had changed his opinion about BF since Nov. 5, 1765, when he had exclaimed: "*O Franklin, Franklin,* thou curse to Pennsylvania and America, may the most accumulated vengeance burst speedily on thy guilty head!" See above, XII, 353 n.

From James Parker   ALS: American Philosophical Society

Honoured Sir   New York, Octob. 25. 1766.

Notwithstanding, I have not yet had the Pleasure of one Line from you this great while, and I have nothing worthy Notice to write, yet I must continue to scribble a little.

Whether you have received any of my Letters wrote since I have been in this City, I cannot say: but suppose you have them all, therefore to them must refer for many Things:[6] Finding no Prospect of getting Mr. Holt to a Settlement, notwithstanding all the Concessions I made to him, and that in the present Method of Life I was in, I must decline, and the Moment I should be removed from my Offices, I should be ruin'd, I have began a Paper, tho' under all the Disadvantages that could be conceived: A real Dulness of Times as well as News; Powerful Antagonists, Holt having acquired some Popularity by the Stamp-Act, and I in an unpopular Condition from perhaps too many concurring Circumstances, it must be next to a Miracle if I succeed: This is the second Paper I have printed;[7] and I have yet got but 20 single Subscribers in this City: and about as Many in the Country: yet I am not discouraged upon that Score, not doubting but Resolution, Perseverance and Diligence will work Wonders: But my greatest Discouragement is the Hand of God upon me, in the continual Distress and Sickness of my Family: having a Doctor continually in tow: My Daughter has been down sick now 7 Weeks, and is a little on the mending Hand; after taking two Vomits, sundry other Physick, and 30 Doses of the Bark: My Son poorly ever since last Winter,

6. This is the eighth surviving letter from Parker to BF in the less than six months since he moved to New York and took up his duties as landwaiter there at the beginning of May. The latter-day reader, like BF in 1766, is referred to those letters for the "many Things" Parker discusses here once more.

7. Parker had resumed publication of *The New-York Gazette; or, the Weekly Post-Boy,* with the issue of Oct. 16, 1766. By the date of this letter he would have brought out a second issue on the 23d, and this is probably what he meant here by "the second Paper I have printed." Or he may have thought of his earlier publication of the *Gazette,* alone or with partners, as his first New York paper, and the present venture as his second. In the present context he probably was not thinking of the *Connecticut Gazette* he had started in New Haven in 1755 as one of the two distinctly different newspapers with which he had been associated.

he was advised to go to Sea, eight Weeks ago he went to North-Carolina, and I have not heard a Word of him since, only 4 Days after he sail'd he was worse God only knows if he be alive: His Wife and Child have been sick above 5 Weeks past, and both my 'Prentices, have been sick: I bless God, I have had so little myself since I been here, only a very small Paroxysm of the Gout now above six Months: the Doctor's Bills are as large, and much worse than the Butcher's: We having had a very wet Summer, has made it generally very sickly: I heard from Burlington that your Son had a Spell of it also, but is getting better again:[8] This has thrown this City in my Imagination into a Distress they will be sensible of before Spring: Wood rose in 24 Hours near 10s. on a Cord: Oak-Wood, that used to be 16 and 18s. per Cord, is now 25s. and Hickory that was 28 to 30s. per Cord is now 40s.—And not plenty at that Rate; occasioned by the Country-People not able to cut and cart it, for the Fevers and wet Roads. In this very dear Place I find it hard to live; having not had 20s. worth of Employ from others since I have been here: only my Almanacks, and 4 other Printers here printing Almanacks also,[9] I shall be well off, to get above a Fifth of the Whole: I am a little in Hopes, that while I live in this City, as Comptroller to the Office, that you will consent to add the £20 Sterl. per An. to the Allowance for that Office; as Mr. Foxcroft thinks it will be but reasonable: It would please me, would the Allowance for the Land-Waiters Office, be made a little more adequate to the Trouble: for tho' £50 Sterl. was a very Considerable Allowance as that Office used to be attended a few year's ago, yet now as the Surveyor General of the Customs has given peremptory Orders for the continual reconnoitering the Harbour &c. it has rendered it the most laboroious Office in the Customs; however, I do not repine at it, it is perhaps more than the Benefits of the Office to the Crown; yet I should be glad if that could be a little enlarged; as it would help me to pay off my

8. Writing to Lord Shelburne, Dec. 16, 1766, WF excused his failure to answer letters received by the last packet on the score that "I was at that time greatly indisposed with a Fever." 1 *N.J. Arch.*, IX, 574.

9. Parker's almanacs were Roger More, pseud., *Poor Roger's American Country Almanack* and *Poor Roger's Universal Pocket Almanack.* Only three other New York printers are listed in Evans or Alexander J. Wall, *A List of New York Almanacs 1694–1850* (N.Y., 1921), p. 18, as publishing almanacs in this year: John Holt, Hugh Gaine, and William Weyman.

Doctor's Bills. I think I told you, that I know not who pays the Allowance I am to have, or where I am to look for it, having never asked any of the Custom-House Officers about the Pay; being desirous rather to hear from you about it: If it is to be paid there, and you will acquaint me of the Manner of it, I will order it into your Hands, if you are there at the Time of it: for you first to pay yourself, the Charges and Expences you have been at, and if any Thing further towards paying you, for the Stationary you have or may send to me; and if you please to order the Stationary as per annexed List[1] to be sent, such Payments shall be made as I may be able, or Interest paid to you for it; As I would gladly have all the Debts I owe, in one Hand only: Now, I do not know what to do with Holt on many Accounts, amongst which is that of Hamilton & Balfour of Edinburg; he having never settled Nothing about them, tho' he says he has many of the Books he had of them upon Hand—I have not been on speaking Terms with him for some Time, having issued a Writ 6 Weeks ago, but the Sheriff delays taking him, or he keeps close tho' tis said it is with the Gout: I know not how it is, but thus stands the Case: The New England Affair undetermined yet—nor can I get any Thing from thence. B. Mecom makes still but a poor Hand, and I am afraid, I shall never get much by him: But by a random Guess at the Business, during Holt's Partnership there there should be several Hundred Pounds coming to me, which Holt has spent: And I think Col. Hunter should be concerned either to see a Settlement made, or adequate Allowance: It seems Mr. Green accounted to Holt, tho' Holt never accounted to me, and Green in a Letter to me says the Business did not neat[2] to him, who was to have half of but little more than £100 per An. clear. On the Supposition, that it yielded no more the 3 or 4 Years Green had it, would have neated me near £200: and the three Years and a Half Holt had it; it should have neated me as much: 'Tis true as B. Mecom now carries it on, he can't pay a Rent of only 30 Dollars per An. altho B. Goddard[3]

1. No list of stationery Parker wanted has been found with this letter; it probably was much the same as that in his letter of October 11, above, p. 457.

2. In its rare use as a verb, "neat," here and later in the paragraph, means "to produce a neat return," that is, "to net a profit."

3. It was William Goddard, not "B. Goddard," to whom Thomas Green had sold his types.

paid Green for his Types, 100 Dollars. However when Holt's Share is accounted for to me, I will answer for one Half of the Rent B. Mecom is to pay me, whether ever I get it or not; which is all can be reasonably expected of me:

I am now in this City, agreeable to the Orders of the Post-Master General: I should be glad to know, if there be any Appendages to my Duty in the Post-Office other than what was usual at Woodbridge, or any other or different Duty, Behaviour or Carriage;[4] for [methinks?] I seem to be a very insigificant Animal here in it, and I could full as well do all the Duties at Burlington—or Woodbridge—as here: I should indeed have been glad to have spent the small Remains of Life I have at Burlington; and but for this Office should I believe have staid there: but it Matters little where I spend it, so I do it with Credit, and a good Conscience; If I could clear the World honourably, with a slender Prospect of a Competency for Life, I would not bustle so thro' it: but believe Providence knows best what is best for me, and I submit with Patence.

I this Day got home your Box, with the Electrical Machine from Capt. Berton, and paid him a Dollar and a half: Mr. Hughes does not chuse to take it till he can purchase and pay for it, so it lays in my Store Room, till further Orders from you: Hughes continues to keep close yet, and keeps a School, has a pretty large one; Indeed, Money seems very scarce, Trade very dull the City too full for the Country: The only Hopes seems to me is a very visible Retrenchment in many of the Luxury that too much abounds: Punch-Houses and Taverns not so full as usual, and every Thing very dear. Weyman, tis said keeps close: I am told, he owes but every Body, he has an Opportunity to owe.[5] Capt. Berton sails for London in about a Week after this Vessel perhaps I shall hear

4. This query and the passage that follows are in effect a repetition of a question in Parker's letter of June 11. One disagreeable feature of the move and of Parker's new duties was that Alexander Colden, at least nominally his subordinate in the Post Office, was now his superior in the Customs. Furthermore, Parker had discovered no added or changed responsibilities that might explain the requirement, imposed three thousand miles away, that the comptroller of the colonial Post Office must reside in New York.

5. On Weyman's financial difficulties and his running feud with Parker, see Beverly McAnear, "James Parker versus William Weyman," N.J. Hist. Soc. *Proc.*, LIX (1941), 1–23, esp. 20–1.

from you before that Time: Now let me conclude, with asking your Opinion, Shall I launch into Business; get Stock again buy and sell, push forwards, strive hard in my old Age, or be content with small Matters, and live as I do, without getting a-head; or, could I but have this or any equivalent Office in Burlington, I would chuse that: but am determined to sacrifice my Will, let it be what it may, to your Advice and Opinion, tho' with all the ill Presages that could be conceived: If I am to push, you will send me the annexed Stationary; if not, you will decline it.[6]

I forgot to tell you, that a Day or two ago Lewis Jones, the young Man whom I paid a Passage for, and took your Assignment,[7] left me, and got among the Soldiers, and I hear is listed for a Drummer: I don't know that the Loss of his Time would have given me any great Concern, but to descend so low: I don't know any Difference we have had and I was preparing to get him Cloaths, &c. only some Months ago, I two or three Times miss'd some small Matters, and I had Room to suspect him; therefore catechised him about, and remonstrated to him the Evil Consequences that would follow such a Conduct; but I did never strike him: It seems he told my other Lad, he never liked the Business, that he was forced in it, and he would not follow it: I had some Hopes even yesterday of getting him again, but to-day think it in Vain: He loves Drink rather too much, and he is now to be a Flogger and Drummer in the Army: so he is lost to Goodness and Virtue:[8] and I have lost the Money and Service due to me: This seems to be a small Help to the Discouragements I labour under.

If I should continue a News-paper, (which I really doubt from the very slender Encouragement I have a Prospect of) will you be so good as to send those I send you to some Coffe-House, or Person that would send me a Paper in Return; or would you speak

6. BF sent Parker stationery to the value of £50 2s. 9d. in January 1767, thereby giving him the desired push. Journal, 1764–1776, p. 10; Ledger, 1764–1776, pp. 10, 24.

7. On Lewis Jones, the ne'er-do-well youth whose father, a complete stranger, had sent him from London to BF to be trained as a printer, see above, x, 343–8, esp. n. 5.

8. The flogging of soldiers as a penalty for offenses in the British Army seems usually to have been done by the drummers. Edward E. Curtis, *The Organization of the British Army in the American Revolution* (New Haven, 1926), pp. 29–30.

476

to some Person to send me one of the best Weekly Papers &c.—
and I would try to pay them: but I shall write again either per
Capt. Berton or the next Packet, and shall know further. Mean
while we all send our humble Compliments, whilst I am your most
obliged Servant   JAMES PARKER.

Addressed: Dr B [*half the page torn away*] / per the Britannia / Capt.
Jeffries

From Sir Alexander Dick   ALS: American Philosophical Society

Dear Sir,   Prestonfield Octr. 28. 1766
    Your Letter of the 11th.[9] gave me and all my Family the greatest
pleasure it being so long since we heard from your self[1] of your
and your familys wellfare and particularly your Son the Governor.
    I return you and your Son my most hearty thanks for the very
great friendship you have shown to me and my friend Mr. Swinton
in taking so much effectual pains to be at the bottom of what he
wishd to know about his claim.[2] He was not come to Edinburgh
when your Letter arrivd else I had sooner made this return to you,
but so soon as he came and got the papers you enclosd than he
very joyfully said I thank God I have now got by your means a
real friend in America to put me at my witts end whither my
Family shall lose their Estate there or not. You may depend on
Mr. Swinton as being most gratefull excellent man and will long
to return this great favour. Lord Kaims has a great regard for him
and indeed he is his near neighbour in the Country.[3] A propos our
worthy friend Kaims is in the Country Still else I had shown him
your Letter: I know he puts the greatest value upon a Letter from
you of any of all his numerous correspondents. He is more active
if possible than ever and the great accession to his Estate by the

9. Not found.
    1. BF's last known letters to Dick are those of June 2 and July 5, 1765
(above, XII, 156–8, 197–8).
    2. Dick's friend, John Swinton (above, XII, 156–7 n), was a claimant to
certain lands in New Jersey and Pa. WF had obtained legal opinion from two
prominent New Jersey attorneys about the validity of his claims and had sent
them to BF, who had forwarded them to Scotland. See above, p. 322 n.
    3. Kames and Swinton both came from Berwickshire.

death of Lady Kaimss Brother Mr. Drummond of near 2 thousand pounds a year[4] has only given a keene edge to his Love for his Country and his friends.

I beg that my most hearty good wishes and all my familys may be made acceptable to you and yours and in a particular manner to your Son the Governor who I hear is the darling of the World. I ever remain Dear Sir your most obligd and obedient humble Servant ALEXANDER DICK

P.S. Enclosd is Mr. Swintons Letter[5] who desires you may draw on him for what ever has been laid out to serve him. Mr. Alex-[ande]r[6] will pay it. He is often here and begs his best Complimts to you all.

From Joseph Galloway

ALS: American Philosophical Society

Dear Sir   Philada. Octr. 28th. 1766.

It was with real Concern, we received the News of a Change of Ministry, as we conclude it will Retard, and, we fear will totally prevent the Change of Government, which we have made so noble a Struggle to obtain.[7] Our Proprietary Enemies hesitate at Nothing that tends to discourage every further Application for Relief. The C.J.[8] is continually publishing the great Interest of the Proprietaries with Lord Shelbourne, and his great Friendship for them—

4. Upon the death of her brother's infant son in May 1766 Kames's wife, the former Agatha Drummond, inherited the family estate of Blair-Drummond in Perthshire, which henceforth became the country residence of the Kames family. BF visited Lord Kames at Blair-Drummond in 1771. A.F. Tytler, *Memoirs of the Life and Writings of the Honourable Henry Home of Kames* (2d edit., Edinburgh, 1814), I, 148; II, 37–43. J. Bennett Nolan, *Benjamin Franklin in Scotland and Ireland 1759 and 1771* (Phila., 1938), pp. 182–7.

5. Not found.

6. Probably Robert Alexander (above, VIII, 444–5), who had previously carried letters between Dick and BF; see above, XII, 70–1, 156, 165.

7. Rumors of the impending change in the Ministry were reported in *Pa. Gaz.* and *Pa. Jour.*, Sept. 11, 1766, and the news became steadily more circumstantial and detailed in the later issues of that month.

8. William Allen, whose attacks on BF and support of the Penns in the Assembly have been mentioned several times in letters to BF.

His Intermarriage with a Neice of Lady Juliana &c. &ca., And a few Days ago in the Course of the Debates in the House,[9] he declared, that he had received a Letter from a Gentleman of undoubted Credit, (whose Name he took Care to conceal, tho called on to mention it) assuring him That you had applied to Secretary Conway for a Hearing on the Petitions at the last Season of Buisiness, "That the Secretary Rebuked you on the Occasion", and told you, "that the Petitions were laid aside by his Majesty in Council sine Die, with an Intent never to be resumed, desired that you woud not again attempt to obtain any further proceedings on them, For if you did, you might depend, you wou'd meet with such an Answer as woud be neither agreable to you or to the Assembly you represented." Altho the Chief Part of our Friends do not beleive this Declaration or any thing else that comes from the same Quarter without some Proof to Support it, Yet as it has some weight with the Weak and Credulous, I should be glad to have it in my Power to deny it. Be so good therefore, if it be not improper, to inform me in this Matter[1]—and further how the Petitions for a Change of Government is likely to be affected by the Change of Ministry—What is the Prospect of the Change? What Course it is likely to take, and where effected, if it shoud be effected? And particularly if any thing is wanting, which the Assembly can do, to Strengthen your Hands. Because from the present Temper of both Assembly and People, I think they will leave nothing undone, to get rid of the present Government, provided their priviledges remain safe. And if any other Mode shall be thought more likely to be crownd with Success, than the present I am confident, they

9. Probably during the debates on the instructions sent to Jackson and BF on October 18, for as soon as that matter was concluded the Assembly adjourned to Jan. 5, 1767. 8 *Pa. Arch.*, VII, 5943–8. If the conversation between BF and Conway took place approximately as reported in the passage that follows, it almost certainly happened sometime between Nov. 22, 1765, when the Privy Council postponed consideration of the petition "for the present," and May 24, 1766, when Conway exchanged his secretaryship for the Southern Department for that for the Northern Department and so gave up his responsibility for colonial affairs. It seems unlikely that Conway would have treated BF quite as brusquely as Allen reported, however discouraging he may have been.

1. Nothing has been found in BF's letters to Galloway or elsewhere in his papers either to confirm or to deny the accuracy of Allen's report.

will do all in their Power to effect their Purpose. Shoud you think it prudent to commit the Information I have mentioned to writing, you may be assured, whatever you communicate to me shall be confined to the Limits (whatever they be) prescribed by your Self and not one Iota further.[2] And yet, the Propriety of doing this, is entirely Submitted to you, who, being on the Spot where the thing is to be Transacted, must be the best Judge. Beleive me, my Dear Friend, with great Sincerity yours Affectionately

JOS. GALLOWAY

Benja. Franklin Esqr.

[*In the margin:*] I enclose with this a Letter to Mr. J.[3] open, which be pleased to Seal and deliver to him unless you think he may think I am forward in giving the Explanation of the Sense of the House. Then retain it.

November 5th.[4]

I received your Favor per Capt. Chancellor on Saturday last[5]—I was not uneasy about the Copies of my Letters, I was much so on Account of our poor Friend H —who of his own Hand, without consulting his Friends, I fear has wrote many indiscreet things to the Commissioners of the Stamps and the Treasury and they as indiscreetly have suffered them to become publick. He is now truly distressed—and much disliked by the People of both Parties. A few of his Friends are determined to support him, and I hope in a Short Time, he will recover his Spirits, tho not his Popularity. Humanum est errare—But it is the Nobility of Humanity to pass over with Tenderness the Mistakes of our Friends. You will have Seen before this comes to hand, what wicked Pains have been

2. Galloway may have remembered how a copy of a letter by BF to the former speaker, Isaac Norris, in 1758, calling Thomas Penn a "low Jockey," had fallen into Penn's hands and had caused much trouble; above, VII, 360–2; VIII, 312–13. Galloway was promising no similar leaks during his speakership.

3. Richard Jackson, BF's fellow agent. Galloway's letter to him has not been found.

4. This postscript appears on the same sheet as the earlier part of the letter.

5. Probably BF's letter of September 27, in which he reported that Hugh Williamson was reading letters from Galloway to BF, or vice versa, aloud in the coffee house; above, pp. 425–6. Galloway's comments below suggest a belief that Williamson was also responsible for making public John Hughes's indiscreet letters to British officials, recently printed in *Pa. Jour.*

taken to Slander him and my Self. Their Venom affected him, but has raised me still higher in the Favor and Opinion of my Country. I wish some Method coud be fallen on to raise him once More above the Malice of his unrelenting Enemies.

Our Friends never discovered greater Firmness or more Activity than in the last Election—The Wharton Family in particular Your Antient and my late, worthy friend Mr. Roberts, &c. &ca. &ca. And so Complete has our Victory been, that it is generally thought, the Proprietary Party another Year will not attempt an Opposition.[6] Dear Friend once more Adieu.   J G.

Our new Mode of Electing is acknowledged by Both Parties to be a very good one. It gives great dispatch, and prevents much Perjury and Fraud, so that we hope it will meet with the Royal Approbation.[7]

Our Worthy Friend Joseph Wharton the Elder just now comes in and desires to be kindly remembered to you, and that I would assure you of his best Prayers and wishes.

To Peter Templeman[8]   ALS: Royal Society of Arts

Sir   Cravenstreet, Oct. 29. 1766
    I received with the enclos'd Letter[9] an improv'd Compass for the Surveying of Land, sent me by Mr. Aaron Miller of New-

6. For the anti-proprietary party's clear victory in the election of October 1, 1766, see above, p. 447 n.

7. A new law enacted Feb. 8, 1766 (*Statutes at Large, Pa.*, VII, 32–40) introduced several reforms in the system. The voters in each township or district were to meet prior to the Assembly election and choose one inspector (two from each ward in the city) to join with other inspectors and officials in the county or city election in handling the voting in ways that would help to insure against fraud. Uniform polling hours were specifically set for the first time, and the voting in Philadelphia was transferred from the Court House in the middle of Market Street (declared by the act to be "inconvenient and improper" for the purpose) to the State House (Independence Hall). Sister Joan de Lourdes Leonard, "Elections in Colonial Pennsylvania," 3 *Wm. and Mary Quar.*, XI (1954), 385–401, esp. 394–8.

8. On Peter Templeman, secretary of the Society of Arts, see above, IX, 322 n.

9. The writer of the enclosure was William Alexander, called Lord Stirling, a large landholder in New Jersey; above, VI, 244 n; X, 151 n.

481

Jersey,[1] with a Request that I would lay it before the Society of Arts, which I will do whenever call'd upon for that purpose; I am, with great Respect for the Society, Sir, Your most obedient humble Servant   B FRANKLIN

[*Cut off*] Templeman

Endorsed: Octor. 29, 1766

[ENCLOSURE]

Sir,   New Jersey July 31st. 1765

Mr. Aaron Miller an Ingenous Man in the Province of New Jersey some time ago contrived a Method of fixing a kind of Index to the Circumferenter or Common Land Surveying Compass, which in the Manner of the Second hand to a Clock or Watch divides each Degree into 60 Equal parts or Minutes, he has lately very much improved on the first invention, and it's application to the Instrument is now so far Perfect, that it does not in the least incumber the use of it; but so far improves it that a Land Surveyor may now with Certainty divide each Degree into Minutes, whereas without this improvement, he was left to divide the Degrees on the Limb of the Circumferenter into 60 equal parts by his Eye only. The improvement of the Instrument will no doubt be of use to Surveyors of Land in General, more Especially in America where the Compass is constantly used in Surveying Lands; I have advised Mr. Miller to send one of his to Dr. Franklin who I make no doubt will be ready to Shew the use of it to the Society for the Encouragement of Arts Manufactures and Commerce whenever they will be pleased to give him an Opportunity, and I must beg the favour of you to lay this recommendation of it before them. I am, Sir, Your Most Humble Servant   STIRLING

To Peter Templeman Esqr. Principal Secretary to the Society for the Encouragement of Arts Manufactures and Commerce, London

1. Almost certainly Aaron Miller (d. 1778 or 1779) of Elizabeth, N.J., a maker of clocks, compasses, church bells, and surveyor's chains. N.J. Hist. Soc. *Coll.*, 1936, p. 154; 1 *N.J. Arch.*, XII, 418; XXXIV, 346.

To [Daniel Burton][2]   Draft: American Philosophical Society

Reverend Sir   [October 1766[3]]

At the Request of Mr. Spencer[4] I take the Liberty of mentioning to you, that if the venerable Society shall think fit to appoint him to Spotswood in New Jersey, a new Mission which he tells me is under Consideration, I will recommend him to the Countenance and Protection of the Governor of that Province.[5]

My Friend the Revd. Mr. Sturgeon of Philadelphia writes to me, that his Health has been so much on the Decline, as to oblige him to retire into the Country, and that he should think him self happy if the Society would appoint him to succeed Mr. Campbel at Burlington.[6] I suppose Trenton which is not far distant would equally suit him which if vacant, and I imagine he would be very agreable to the People there.[7] Will you be so good as to excuse my intermeddling in these Matters, and believe me to be with great Esteem and Respect, Revd Sir

2. The subject matter of this letter makes it virtually certain that it was intended for the Reverend Dr. Daniel Burton, secretary of the Society for the Propagation of the Gospel in Foreign Parts, usually referred to at this time as "the venerable Society," the term BF uses here. Spencer and Sturgeon, mentioned in the letter, both served under the Society's auspices.

3. In the second paragraph BF mentions Sturgeon's letter asking BF's help in getting him assigned to Burlington instead of Philadelphia. That letter (above, p. 406) was dated Sept. 1, 1766, and probably reached BF sometime in October. Hence this letter, in which BF complies with that request, is tentatively dated October 1766.

4. On George Spencer, see above, x, 104–5, and this volume pp. 385–6.

5. The Society did assign Spencer to Spotswood and also to East Brunswick, 1766–67; he transferred to Freehold, 1767, but was dismissed as "disreputable." He later went to North Carolina. Frederick Lewis Weis, "The Colonial Clergy of the Middle Colonies," *Proc.* Amer. Antiq. Soc., LXVI, part 2 (1956), 318.

6. William Sturgeon, who had resigned his positions at Christ Church and St. Peter's in Philadelphia, July 31, 1766, because of ill health, did not receive appointment to a New Jersey parish but died in Philadelphia, Nov. 3, 1770. *Ibid.*, p. 323.

7. BF revised and interlined this passage in his draft several times but did not quite succeed in maintaining grammatical construction.

From [Joseph] Johnson[8]   AL: American Philosophical Society

Paternoster row Nov 4. 1766.
J. Johnson's compliments to Dr. Francklin and sends those MSS for his inspection by order of Dr. Priestley who will esteem himself much oblig'd to the Dr. for looking over them as soon as possible.

Addressed: To Dr. Francklin

From François Willem de Monchy[9]

ALS:[1] American Philosophical Society

Honour'd sir   Rotterdam the 4 Nov. 1766.
With no small pleasure did I recive your kind letter of the 23 Oct.[2] where for I am much oblig'd to you.

I confess, that the care you have taken of my friends commission is very great,[3] and that I do'nt know any think to recompence it.

8. Joseph Johnson (1738–1809), bookseller and printer and in his later years deemed "the father of the book trade," was one of the publishers of Joseph Priestley's *The History and Present State of Electricity*, which had been put to press by Sept. 21, 1766 (see above, p. 421). Priestley continued to conduct experiments and incorporate their results in his book as it was being printed and the manuscripts which Johnson asks BF in this note to examine may be an account of one of Priestley's experiments. *DNB*.

9. François Willem de Monchy (1749–1796), medical student at Leyden, 1766–74, and later physician at Rotterdam, was elected, 1775, a member of the Batavian Society for Experimental Philosophy, of which his father, Solomon de Monchy (1716–1794) was an original member. P.C. Molhuysen and J.P. Blok, *Nieuw Nederlandsch Biografisch Woerdenboek*, I (Leyden, 1911), cols. 1342–3. BF and Pringle had certainly met both men in Rotterdam during the summer of 1766.

1. Following some of the questions and at the bottom of the page are numerous notations in BF's hand of data to be used in his reply. Most of these notations are so faint as to be indecipherable; others can be read only with difficulty and uncertainty. Whatever can be read with reasonable confidence is indicated below in footnotes.

2. Not found.

3. Neither the identity of the friend nor the precise nature of his commission is known. From the questions in this letter and from BF's endorsement it seems probable that BF had supplied some information about Matthew Boulton's experimental steam ("fire") engine; see above, pp. 166–8, 196–7.

Being come home last week from England, I have spoken with my friend and shew'd him your letter, who like wise return'd his thanks to you, at the same time he ask'd me to write you about the following questions.

1° How much the Iron Cylinder 30.9 Inch in Diam. 110. 0 Inch in Length and 00. 5⅜ Inch in Thickness Cost?[4]

2° How much the same Cylinder made of brass?

3° How much a Cylinder 30.9 Inch in diam. 80. 0 Inch. in Length and 00. 3⅜ Inch. in Thickness?[5]

4° How much the saem and made of brass?

5° How much the bottom and sucker[?] ?[6]

6° How much the whole machine without pumps, Iron, and wooden Pipes?

7° How much the same made of brass?

My father desir'd his Compliments to you. I am with great estime Honour'd Sir, Your most humble and Obedient servant

F: W. DE MONCHY

P.S. Pray give my compliments to Sir John Pringle, and tell him if you please that I will not fail to write him with the next post.[7]

Mr. B. Franklin

Addressed: To / Dr. B. Franklin at Mrs. Stevenson / Craven Street / in / London

Endorsed: De Monchy Queries concg. Fire Engin[e]

4. A note by BF begins: "24*s*. per Cwt." The rest of the note is illegible.

5. A note seems to read: "24*s*. per Cwt."

6. A note reads: "16*s*. per Cwt."

7. At the bottom of the page are two columns of notes. While a few words in the left-hand column can be read, too much is illegible to permit any useful reconstruction of the whole. The right-hand column is clearer and seems to consist of a tabulation of the costs of the parts of the steam engine and its house. It appears to read as follows, with the breaks between lines indicated here by slant lines: "Cylynder £35 / Beam 10 [*these two lines joined by a brace followed by* or £50] / Boiler of Iron 84 / Copper cheaper in the End / Regulator and other Pipes 40 / Leaden Cistern for Injection 10 / 184 / House 100."

To William Franklin

MS not found; reprinted from extract in [Jared Sparks, ed.,] *A Collection of the Familiar Letters and Miscellaneous Papers of Benjamin Franklin* (Boston, 1833), pp. 279–80.

[November 8th, 1766]

Mr. Jackson is now come to town. The ministry have asked his opinion and advice on your plan of a colony in the Ilinois,[8] and he has just sent me to peruse his answer in writing,[9] in which he warmly recommends it, and enforces it by strong reasons; which gives me great pleasure, as it corroborates what I have been saying on the same topic,[1] and from him appears less to be suspected of some American bias.

To Pennsylvania Assembly Committee of Correspondence

MS not found; abstract printed in *Votes and Proceedings of the House of Representatives of the Province of Pennsylvania, Met at Philadelphia* [October 14, 1766] (Philadelphia, 1767), p. 17.

[January 14, 1767]

Mr. Speaker laid before the House a Letter received from Benjamin Franklin, Esq; in London, dated November the 8th, 1766, acquainting the Committee of Correspondence, that the Chancellor of the Exchequer[2] had given him Assurances, that he had ordered a short Bill to be drawn for amending the Clause in the late Act of Parliament requiring Commodities intended for Ireland, to

---

8. See above, p. 330 n.

9. Jackson's report of November 1766 deals with several proposed plans for Indian trade and western settlement. It is printed in Alvord and Carter, *The New Régime 1765–1767*, pp. 422–30. In a brief passage on "The Plan of a Settlement on the Mississippi from Philadelphia, approved by Sir Wm. Johnson," Jackson commented that it was "certainly well framed, and that by Persons too well acquainted with the Country and with the Indians to be deceived by others, and too much interested in the Success of their Scheme, to attempt to deceive the King's Ministers in such a Case as the present, I have no doubt of its practicability or Utility, Improvements perhaps it may receive, but I dare not undertake to make any. . . ." *Ibid.*, pp. 425–6.

1. See above, pp. 424–5, 446–7.

2. Charles Townshend.

be first landed in Britain; and that he would himself present it to Parliament, as soon as they met, having no Doubt of its passing.[3] That with Respect to the Restraint laid by the late Act of Parliament on our making Paper Money a legal Tender, the Agents have Hopes of obtaining a Repeal of the said Act.[4]

To Joseph Galloway

ALS: William L. Clements Library

Dear Friend,   London, Nov. 8: 1766

I received your kind Letter of Sept. the 22d.[5] and from another Friend a Copy of that lying Essay in which I am represented as the Author of the Stamp Act, and you as concern'd in it.[6] The Answer you mention is not yet come to hand.[7] Your Consolation, my Friend, and mine, under these Abuses, must be, *that we do not deserve them.* But what can console the Writers and Promoters of such infamously false Accusations, if they should ever come themselves to a Sense of that Malice of their Hearts, and that Stupidity of their Heads, which by these Papers they have manifested and

3. On September 18 the Committee of Correspondence, on orders from the Assembly, had instructed Jackson and BF to ask for an amendment of an act of June 1766, 6 Geo. III, c. 52, in which faulty wording would have the effect of stopping most exports from the colonies to Ireland. For these instructions and their background, see above, pp. 419–20, and accompanying notes. As indicated there, the amending bill received the royal assent on Dec. 16, 1766.

4. In spite of repeated efforts by BF and other agents, the Currency Act of 1764 was never repealed prior to the Revolution, though it was somewhat modified in 1773. For a general account, see Jack M. Sosin, "Imperial Regulation of Colonial Paper Money, 1764–1773", *PMHB*, LXXXVIII (1964), 174–98.

5. Not found.

6. The Supplement to *Pa. Jour.*, Sept. 18, 1766, contained a long piece entitled "An Essay discovering the Authors and Promoters of The Memorable Stamp Act. In a Letter from a Gentleman in London, to his Friend in Philadelphia." The author, generally believed to be Hugh Williamson, undertook to "prove" that BF and his friends had been active abettors of the passage of the Stamp Act. He admitted that BF had declaimed against the act in his examination before the House of Commons, but argued that by that time BF could have done nothing else.

7. Galloway published a reply to the "Essay" and other attacks in both *Pa. Gaz.* and *Pa. Jour.*, Sept. 25, 1766.

exposed to all the World. Dunces often write Satyrs on themselves, when they think all the while that they are mocking their Neighbours. Let us, as we ever have done, uniformly endeavour the Service of our Country, according to the best of our Judgment and Abilities, and Time will do us Justice. Dirt thrown on a Mud-Wall may stick and incorporate; but it will not long adhere to polish'd Marble.[8] I can now only add that I am, with Sincerest Esteem and Affection, Yours,   B FRANKLIN

The Town begins to fill, and the Parliament sits down next week.

J. Galloway Esqr

From Jane Mecom

ALS: American Philosophical Society

Boston, Novr. 8 1766

You wonce tould me my Dear Brother that as our Numbers of Bretheres and Sisters Lessened the Affections of those of us that Remain Should Increes to Each other.[9] You and I only are now Left, my Affection for you has all ways been So grate I see no Room for Increec, and you have Manifested yours to mee in such Large measure that I have no Reason to suspect Itts strength, and therefore know it will be agreable to you to hear that my self and the childin I have the care of[1] are in no wors situation than when I last wrot you, and should Rejoyce to heare the same of you since I understand by sister you were in an Ill state of Helth and thought Proper to travel for the Recovery of it.[2] I hope in god you have Recovered it and will Live Long to make your Inemies ashamed, your Answrs to the Parlement are thought by the best Judges to

8. "Act uprightly, and despise Calumny; Dirt may stick to a Mud Wall, but not to polish'd Marble." *Poor Richard*, 1757; above, VII, 85.

9. Jane was paraphrasing a passage in BF's letter to her of Jan. 9, 1760; above, IX, 18. She was writing in this vein because of the death of Peter Franklin, July 1, 1766 (above, p. 332 n), of which DF probably informed her.

1. Jane's two grandchildren, Jane and Josiah Flagg, and her two grandnieces, Elizabeth and Sarah Ingersoll, appear to have been living with her at this time. See above, XII, 418 n.

2. DF had evidently written Jane after receiving BF's letter of June 13 (above, pp. 314–16), advising her of his ill health and of his intention to travel to Germany to attempt to recuperate.

Exeed all that has been wrot on the subject³ and being given in the maner they were are a Proof they Proceeded from Principle and suficent to stop the mouths of all gain-sayere—the vile Pretended Leter⁴ which no Doubt you have seen gave me some uneaseyness when I heard of it before I could git a sight of it, as considering when a grat Deal of Durt is flung some is got to stick but when I Read it I see it was filld with such bare faced falshoods as confute them selves, Thire [*their*] treetment of you among other things makes the world Apear a misereable world to me not withstanding your good opinyon of it,⁵ for would you think it our General Court has sett all most a Fortnight cheaffly on the subject of Indemnifieing the sufferers by the Late Mobs and cant yet git a Vote for it tho they sitt Late in the Evening and the friends to it strive hard to git it acomplishd.⁶ I have six good Honist old souls who come groneing Home Day by Day at the Stupidety of there Bretheren.⁷ I cant help Interesting my self in the case and feel in mere Panicke till they have Brought the matter to a conclution.

I writ this in hopes you will be in England when this gits there and that you will find time to writ me a few Lines by the barer Capt. freeman when he Returns.

And I have a small Request to ask tho it is two trifeling a thing for you to take care of. Mrs. Steevenson I Dont Doubt will be so good as to do it if you will give her the meterals it is to Procure me some fine old Lining or cambrick (as a very old shirt or cambrick hankercheifs) Dyed into bright colors such as red and green a Litle blew but cheafly Red for with all my own art and good old

3. BF's *Examination* before the House of Commons (above, pp. 124–62) was published in Philadelphia on Sept. 18, 1766, but Jane probably read a Boston edition of the work that the *Boston Evening-Post*, Sept. 29, 1766, announced would be published on October 2.

4. Probably the letter published in the Supplement to *Pa. Jour.*, Sept. 18, 1766, and mentioned by BF to Galloway in the letter immediately above.

5. On March 1, 1766, BF had written his sister: "Take one thing with another, and the World is a pretty good sort of a World." See above, p. 188.

6. On Dec. 9, 1766, Governor Bernard signed an act, compensating Thomas Hutchinson and other sufferers in the Boston Stamp Act riots. See above, XII, 340.

7. Jane may have meant that she had six boarders who were members of the Mass. General Court and who favored compensation.

unkle Benjamins[8] memorandoms I cant make them good colors and my Daughter Jeney[9] with a little of my asistance has taken to makeing Flowrs for the Ladyes Heads and Boosomes with Prity good acceptance, and If I can Procure them coulars I am In hopes we shall git somthing by it worth our Pains if we live till Spring. It is no mater how old the Lining is I am afraid you never have any bad a nouf.[1]

Present my Compliments to mrs. Steevenson and Excuse my Presuming to give her this troble.

I have had a Respectfull Leter from Gouvernor Franklin this sumer with a Present of Six Barrils of flower amounting to sixty odd Pounds old tenor which was a grat help to me and his notice of me a grat satisfaction, all our Relations and friends hear are well as useal my Daughters[2] Desire there Duty to you. I am Dear Brother your ever affectionat sister JANE MECOM

Addressed: To Doctor Benjamin Franklin / at Mrs. Stevensons in Cravin / Street att / London / per favour of Capt. Freeman

Endorsed: Sister Mecom Nov 8. 1766 answer'd per Capt Freeman and sent a Box of Millenery.

From James Parker

ALS: American Philosophical Society

Honoured Sir,   New-York, Nov. 11. 1766.

Yours of Sept. 1. by Way of Philadelphia,[3] I duly received, which is all I have been favoured with a great While: I congratulate you on your safe Return from Germany. I will do what is possible with B Mecom.

8. Benjamin Franklin the Elder (1650–1727; A.5.2.7), for whom BF was named, had been a silk-dyer in England. He had lived in his brother Josiah's home for four years after moving to Boston; above, I, 3–6.

9. Jane (Jeney) Mecom (C.17.9) was 21 years old at this time.

1. In a bill from Mrs. Stevenson to BF (above, XII, 324 n) there is an entry, Feb. 27, 1767, recording the expenditure of £5 3s. 6d. for "Sundries" from a London women's shop. Evidently this payment was for the "Box of Millenery" which BF notes having sent his sister in the endorsement to this letter and for which Jane wrote Mrs. Stevenson a letter of thanks, May 9, 1767. APS.

2. Jane's other daughter, Mary (Polly) Mecom (C.17.11) died the following year.

3. Not found.

With Respect to a new Supply of Types, I should either have been more explicit at first, or wrote again about them:[4] But amidst the Manifold Distresses, I had almost said Distractions, I am surrounded with, I know not what to say: I always imagined I had my full Share of the Troubles of Life, but all my former Life, till about 18 Months ago, has been but as Children's Play to that which for some Time afflicts me: I have and do endeavour to put the best Side outwards, and to behave like a Man under it: Knowing that though the Potsherds of the Earth may Strive with the Potsherds thereof, yet Man is not to Strive with his Maker.[5] Now the Hand of God is upon me, and has been so these 18 Months: Not one Thing is accompanied with even a common Blessing that I take in Hand, and the Sickness of my Family in that Time has never ceas'd: but all I get goes to the Doctor's or for the Relief of them: I have had five at a Time down, and always one or another, I have three now, and have been so this 6 Weeks and more: My Daughter Jane is slowly mending: but my Son's Wife and Daughter are both down. And my Son I believe to be no more: He had been taken last Winter, and continuing so poorly, was advised to go to Sea: Accordingly on the 2d of September last, he went in a small Schooner for North-Carolina, to see his Uncle, whom he had never seen: He was to return in 4 or 5 Weeks, we heard 4 Days after he went out, that he was worse, but we never heard one Syllable of either him or the Vessel afterwards, now 10 Weeks and more, and there has been much bad Weather. There is indeed a Possibility of his being alive, but very small Probability of it.[6] I desire to submit my Will to the Will of Heaven: While all my People lays so sick, my Mind is too much overwhelmed to determine what to say or do: I was in Hopes such a long Course of Sickness would stop some Time: but it has not yet: I have received

4. In several of his earlier letters Parker had mentioned the worn-out condition of his type, and in his letter of July 15 he had asked directly whether BF could help him get two or three fonts of Scots type.

5. Isaiah 45:9: "Woe unto him that striveth with his Maker! Let the potsherd strive with the potsherds of the earth. Shall the clay say to him that fashioneth it, What makest thou? or thy work, He hath no hands?"

6. Samuel Franklin Parker was indeed alive and returned to his father on December 12 of this year somewhat in the manner of the Prodigal Son of Scripture, but perhaps less repentant; below, p. 528.

Good at the Hand of the Lord, and shall I not receive Evil![7] Indeed, tho' I know I have too much of the fretful Temper you accuse me of, I have strove much to conquer it, and my constant Prayers are that Heaven would give me Wisdom to direct my Ways aright: However, I know it is easy for a Mind at Ease, to bear other's Troubles, but like the Gout, it is easier to preach Patience to the Sufferer, than to practise it one's self: Now amidst these Afflictions I do not desire to trouble you with my Sorrows tho' I can't help mentioning them: as they add Weight to the other common ill Run of Fortune or Luck, as it is called of which every Thing seems frowning and contrary: I have now been here above Six Months, in which Time have not had Five pounds worth of Work altogether, except an Almanack I did: which tho' 'tis really better done and was a more noted One than some of the others:[8] Nay, for years past Holt sold above 6000 of them, whilst the other Printers did as many as they do now, yet I have not sold one single Thousand yet whilst both Gaine and Weyman I am told are doing a second Impression of theirs, yet I have taken all proper Measures possible to publish mine, and there is more in them in Fact, than in theirs. I have not done one single Advertisement, tho' I should ask no more than others: nor any other Job: The News papers I have printed now 4 Weeks, I have got but 26 Customers in this City and about 40 or 50 in the Jerseys, and other Parts: I don't know that I behave worse than I use to do—nor do I take so much News from the others Papers, as they do from mine and I print them better than they do in general, and yet I can get none. Every Body will speak to me seemingly kindly enough, but if I ask any of my old Friends to take the Paper they either tell me, I had recommended them to Holt's Paper, and they can't leave him, or they are engaged to another Printer, and can't leave that &c. Thus if there be Such a Thing as good or bad Fortune, I am sure of the last. Tho' Holt and Weyman both keep close

7. Job 2: 10: "What? shall we receive good at the hand of God, and shall we not receive evil?"

8. Beginning with the issue for 1746, Parker had published his New York almanac in every year, with the exception of 1759, either alone or in partnership with Weyman, Samuel F. Parker, or Holt. The last one to bear his imprint was the one for 1770. Alexander J. Wall, *A List of New York Almanacs 1694–1850* (N.Y., 1921), pp. 10–20.

House[9] they live better than I in many Cases; they can each drink a Glass of Wine, or somewhat like it, every Day, whereas I seldom see or taste a Glass oftener than once a Week, if then:[1] This I do not regret: as it is all for the best perhaps at last: But amidst such a continued Run of the Displeasure of Heaven, is it a Wonder that I know not how to proceed. I have two 'Prentices and one Journeyman, but all the Money I get would not find them Victuals only, as every Necessary of Life is excessive dear in these Circumstances. I must necessarily go astern, which adds another Cross to all the rest. Now, if my Son be dead, as I think he is, and I am old and feeble I am at a Stand whether to get any New Letter or not, especially as I have no Prospect of Success. I have pretty good Letter at Woodbridge, but it is best to keep it there, to do such Jersey Work as may offer, which is generally more Profit in Proportion to the Work than any here.[2] However, I can't yet determine what to do: I have wrote you already in some of my former, something of my State here, and that tho' I sue Holt, I fear he will elude all I can do, for I am not a Master in Chicanry to equal him.

I wrote you, that Lewis Jones had left me: I never went after him; but after he had been gone a Day or two, he got foul of an Humble-Pie, and wrote me a Note that he would return, if I would forgive him, so I answered I would take No Notice of his Slip: and he thereupon returned to Work again and I have never had no Words with him about it: tho' indeed, I should not much have regretted his Loss: for the continual Misfortunes I have met with had quite absorb'd the Thoughts of any Loss by him. I could mention many other Losses of another Kind, but they are nothing to what I feel in general, and may be only called the common Afflictions of Life: And yet tho' I am so severely corrected by Heaven, my Hope is in God, who will still mix Mercy with his Judgments.

As to any other Matters, your Friends doubtless write you the

9. To avoid arrest for debt.

1. An eighteenth-century physician might have pointed out that this abstinence could explain Parker's relative freedom from gout during recent months.

2. Parker printed the New Jersey acts and Assembly proceedings in Woodbridge in 1767 and 1768, but Evans records nothing else he did there in the latter year.

needful. Only H. Hughes, who is the *Son of Liberty*, as he calls himself, is very much displeased both with his Brother and you:[3] He keeps close yet, and I visit him now-and-then; but we generally have some political Battles about you and his Brother, as I have in all I can defended you both: Hugh says your Examination is all a designed and premeditated Thing between you, and Mr. Grenville, &c. he being fully of the Mind you were a Friend to the Stamp &c.—Maugre all I can say to the contrary: But I observe, those who have little or nothing to lose, are the greatest Sons of Liberty: Holt, who is grown so elate and popular, by his Appearance against the Act, had Nothing to lose: for had he suffered for it, I should have Suffered the Loss of my Tools &c. whilst he got the Credit of it: He was really sorry, that the Act was repealed, because he was in Hopes it would have been attempted to be inforced, and he wanted to fish in troubled Waters, for he could not be worsted.

I told you, I think I cut a very insignificant or insipid Figure, in the Post-Office here; not knowing one Thing more easier to do here than at Woodbridge, unless it be spending the Wages I may get, and that can be done with vastly more Facility than there: If any Thing is needful or necessary for me to do in it here, other than there, shall wish to know it. About the other Office I wrote before, and if any Allowance according to what I before mentioned can be allowed, it would greatly help me to pay my Doctor's Charges.

The Quebeck Post-Offices yield a pretty considerable Sum to the Revenue—at least more by far than was expected, and I believe will in all Canada, equal either New-York or Philadelphia, in net Proceeds.

A Merchant Ship sailing soon for London, shall send my News papers with that: Mean while, yet refer you to my last per the Britannia Merchantman, Capt. Jefferies, who sailed about a Week ago,[4] for sundry Matters, and with all our Respects &c remain Your most obliged Servant   JAMES PARKER.

3. Hugh Hughes, the source of some of Parker's financial troubles, was a brother of John Hughes, stamp distributor for Pennsylvania; above, x, 290 n.

4. According to Parker's letter of November 15, which went by this unnamed "Merchant Ship," the present letter went on the *Harriot* packet. The letter by the *Britannia*, Capt. Jefferies, was his letter of October 25.

From Thomas Wharton

ALS: American Philosophical Society

My Dear Friend.   Philada. Nov 11 1766

My last was on the 24th. Ult. since which I received thy kind Favour of the 13th. Sep.[5] for which I thank thee. And rejoice to find the Tour thou took into Germany, proved servicable to thee; and restored the Health of One, whom many look upon, as the great Instrument in saving both our Mother-Country and this Continent from Ruin.

The kind sentiments, thou expresses relative to my little Babe, have closely affected its Parents.[6]

Immediately on receiving thy Letter, I communicated thy Sentiments to our Friend, G. Ashbridge, which afforded him real Pleasure.[7]

I return thee my thanks for thy kind Intentions of writing to Springet Penn:[8] I know, that, Edward Penington is his Agent; but he hath no power to sell.

It will give me particular Pleasure to receive from thee, the *Police* of Amsterdam:[9] And it must afford every true Lover of Mankind real satisfaction to find, that so large and populous a City, is govern'd, with such order, that it does not become necessary to make a Capital-Execution in 7 years![1] We are in great Hopes, that, the Work-House now erecting will greatly contribute to restore the Manners, and rectify the Lives of many dissolute Persons;[2] as

5. Neither Wharton's letter of October 24th nor BF's of September 13th has been found.

6. For the birth of a son whom Wharton named for BF, see above, p. 252, and for the baby's death, above, p. 338.

7. In May Wharton had reported the helpfulness of George Ashbridge of Goshen, assemblyman from Chester Co., in defending BF to the "Country Members"; above, p. 273.

8. Wharton was interested in acquiring some Philadelphia lots Springett Penn had inherited; above, p. 283. If BF wrote to Springett on this matter prior to the young man's death, the letter has not been found.

9. Probably a pamphlet or an official or unofficial report dealing with the administration of Amsterdam, including its protective services. BF could have acquired such a document, perhaps through his friends the Hopes, while passing through Holland on his way to or from Germany.

1. It should be remembered that in the eighteenth century most crimes regarded as major were punishable by death.

2. On the new almshouse or "Bettering House," see above, p. 262 n. In a

well as Implant in the Minds of the rising Youth, the Habit of Frugality and Industry. Our present Building is about 600 Feet in length by 44 in depth, and forms a hollow Square, with a Piaza all the way in Front, looking into the Yard.

It gives us great Pleasure, that, thou approves the Illinois Scheme; and altho' it was at that time thought it might be prudent to take in two Persons, such as thou should approve of, yet I conceive it will by no means be disagreable to our Company should thou enlarge the Number, if a proportionable number of Acres be granted.[3]

Our Governor, a few days past received a new Commission, which, I understand vests him with that power for three Years longer.[4]

The Bearer hereof, John Morton, being on a visit to his aged Parents, has requested the pleasure of delivering this Letter to thee, in order that he may see a Person, whom he much respects.[5] He is a Man of a fair Character, and one who has contributed to the Freedom of this City.

letter dated Sept. 12, 1766, Governor John Penn wrote his uncle, Thomas Penn, that the managers were applying for two lots in the city belonging to the Proprietors and had begun to erect "a very large building" on the site. Penn Papers, Hist. Soc. Pa.

3. The Articles of Agreement for the Illinois Co., had permitted the addition of two other members, but in his letter of Sept. 12, 1766, to WF, his father had expressed the wish that he had been allowed to name more than two British participants, thereby increasing "the weight of interest" in Great Britain; above, p. 415. He had probably expressed the same wish in the missing letter of September 13 to Wharton.

4. On Nov. 15, 1766, John Penn informed his Council that he had received from the Proprietors a new commission reappointing him lieutenant governor of the province of Pennsylvania and the Lower Counties for three years from Dec. 1, 1766, when his present commission would expire; and that he had also received two orders in council, both dated August 8, one formally approving his appointment and the other authorizing the governor of New York, "or any other of His Majesty's Governors in the neighbouring Provinces," to administer the oaths Penn was required by law to take. Penn informed the Council that he planned to get Governor Sharpe of Maryland to perform this service. *Pa. Col. Recs.*, IX, 345–7. His ignoring of the more conveniently located but politically hostile governor of New Jersey was obvious.

5. This John Morton has not been identified. He could hardly have been the John Morton of Chester Co., with whom BF had been associated in the Assembly and who would need no introduction. That man had just been appointed sheriff of Chester Co.

Our friend, Ross[6] is in the Country, shall not fail of informing him of thy kind Sentiments—as soon as I have the pleasure of seeing him.

Our Friend, Galloway sent thee by the Packet, (which sailed a few days past) the Resolves of our Assembly and their Instructions relative to the Change of Government;[7] and as he has informed thee of the additional Clause shall not trouble thee with my Sentiments.[8]

I find by a N'York-Paper of the 10th. Inst., that, its possitively asserted, that Governor Moore has received Instructions from London to assent to Bills, which may be offered by the Assembly for the Emission of Paper-Currency.[9]

We are informed that, Sir. Wm. Johnson has had a Treaty with Pondiac and a great number of Southern-Indians, at Oswego; and that he has settled Matters to their Satisfaction.[1]

I know of nothing particularly new among us at this time; Therefore conclude with informing thee, that my Father desires his sincere Respects may be paid thee, and be pleased to accept the same from Thy real Friend   THO WHARTON

To Benjamin Franklin Esqr

6. John Ross.

7. Above, pp. 465–7.

8. The "additional Clause" was probably the passage in the instructions directing that, if the petition for a change in government "should be finally rejected" by the Privy Council, the agents were not to petition Parliament without first getting the approval of the Assembly.

9. This report was printed in *Pa. Gaz.*, Nov. 13, 1766. Additional instructions, dated July 15, 1766, were sent to Gov. Henry Moore of New York, revoking his former instructions on paper money and permitting him to assent to a measure for issuing not more than £260,000 in bills of credit under certain conditions, including ample provision for their retirement within five years and the inclusion of a clause suspending the act until the King's pleasure should be known. Leonard W. Labaree, ed., *Royal Instructions to British Colonial Governors 1670–1776* (N.Y., 1935), I, 228–9.

1. For Johnson's treaty at Oswego, July 23–31, 1766, with Pontiac and the Southern (more accurately, Western) Indians, see *N.Y. Col. Docs.*, VII, 854–67. Johnson commented on this meeting to Baynton, Wharton, and Morgan, Sept. 16, 1766, saying it had been "much to my satisfaction and beyond my expectations." *Johnson Papers*, XII, 182.

From William Franklin

LS (incomplete):[2] American Philosophical Society

(Remainder of my letter dated November 13, [1766])[3]

Mr. Sherwood was not removed for any offence he had given, but by the Management of the East Jersey Proprietors in the Council, who have long wanted to have the Agent they employ appointed Provincial Agent.[4] They took Advantage of Sherwood's Letters about the Stamp Act, which were very short and trivial, and produced some of Mr. Wilmot's which were full and sensible. Then the Speaker,[5] who is in the Proprietary Interest, proposed him for Agent, which the House acquiesc'd in, without any Opposition, not knowing he was the Proprietary Agent. But since they have discovered who he is, they are, I am told, much displeasd, (as it is a Thing they have always been determin'd against) and are resolved to leave him out next year, in revenge for the Trick that has been play'd them. If so, perhaps they may appoint Sherwood again, who has behaved very complaisantly on his Dismission, tho' they are far from thinking him properly qualified. He is to be sure no ways equal to the other in Point of Abilities, tho' he is more equal to the Pimping Salary they allow. It is only £100 Currency, and £30 Sterling for Petty Expences. If you know of any Person of Credit that would accept of that Allowance, who is capable of doing the Duty, I believe I could manage to obtain the Office for him, if you acquaint me in Time. I am told that Mr. Wilmot's Reason for accepting of it is not only to serve the East Jersey Proprietors but as it will give him some Consideration with the Ministry.

It is now generally said to be Debert, and not Ray, who wrote that scandalous Aspersion of the Agents, printed in the New-York, and other Papers.[6]

2. The body of the letter is in the hand of WF's wife, Elizabeth. The first part of the letter has not been found.

3. The contents of the letter indicate the year.

4. For Joseph Sherwood, a Quaker lawyer who had served as N.J. agent since 1760, see above, X, 413 n. He was succeeded by Henry Wilmot, agent for Thomas Penn and for the East Jersey Council of Proprietors; see above, IX, 16 n. BF was appointed N.J. agent in 1769, apparently through the influence of his son.

5. Cortlandt Skinner; see above, p. 335 n.

6. Almost certainly a reference to an "Extract of a letter from an American

I really think it not at all unlikely that Mr. Allen is in some Degree out of his Senses. Upon finding that, Williamson's *Essay* publish'd in Bradford's Supplement[7] did not take with the People, he cried out against it in the House as much as any Body. And yet at the last Session, when the Assembly were about appointing their Agents, he made that very Piece the Foundation of a great deal of Abuse he threw out against you, and spoke from it as if it had been his Brief.

I have heard nothing further about Mr. Skinner, but perhaps I may now the Duke of Grafton is again in the Ministry.[8]

I Long to have your Copy of the Examination.[9]

Our Friends have been a considerable Time greatly disgusted with Mr. Hall, but his late Conduct to Mr. Galloway has determin'd them to throw him off entirely.[1] I have been above a Year fully convinced that he had a greater Attachment to Mr. Allen than to you; and as he treated me very insolently in a Letter he

---

Gentleman in London, to his Friend in New-Jersey. London, Feb. 25, 1766," which was reprinted in *Pa. Jour.*, May 17, 1766, from a printing in the *New York Gazette*, May 1, 1766. The letter writer bitterly attacked the colonial agents in London, averring that they had "SACRIFICED AND SOLD" the American people. It is not now possible to determine whether Dennys De Berdt (c.1694–1770), the Mass. agent since 1765, or Nicholas Ray (1716–1788?), a London merchant born in New York, wrote this calumny.

7. The supplement to *Pa. Jour.*, Sept. 18, 1766, published "An Essay Towards discovering the Authors and Promoters of the Memorable Stamp Act," supposed by BF's friends to have been written by an old literary adversary, Hugh Williamson, above, p. 425 n. The piece accused BF of being one of the principal promoters of the Stamp Act.

8. See above, p. 335, for WF's report of rumors that William Skinner, brother of the speaker of the N.J. Assembly, would be appointed to succeed him as governor of N.J., through the influence of the Duke of Grafton to whom he was distantly related by marriage.

9. The publication of BF's *Examination* before the House of Commons was announced in *Pa. Gaz.*, Sept. 18, 1766 (above, p. 126); WF evidently wanted a manuscript copy or one authenticated by British officials.

1. Although Hall in the Sept. 25, 1766, issue of *Pa. Gaz.* published Galloway's refutation of the charges made against him in the article in the *Pa. Jour.* Supplement, Sept. 18, 1766, in the same issue he published two comparisons of Galloway's sentiments in his *Americanus* pamphlet and in his letter to BF of Sept. 20, 1765 (above, XII, 269–70), with extracts from BF's *Examination* before the House of Commons, which were designed to show that Galloway favored the Stamp Act.

wrote to me on a Supposition that I was the Author of Jack Retort[2] I have eversince dropt all kind of Intercourse with him. I wrote you a Letter at the Time,[3] with a full Account of the whole Affair, but as I thought it would not be long before you return'd I did not send it, thinking it best not to trouble you till your Return when you would have an opportunity of hearing both Sides and enquiring into the Truth of the Accusations against him. I really had a Friendship for Mr. Hall and have frequently endeavor'd to remove the Prejudices our Friends had conceived against him; but I am now quite satisfied that he has no Friendship for you, and is as great an Enemy to your Side of the Question as ever Smith was. All the Difference is that Smith is so openly, and the other [cov]ertly —a meer Snake in the Grass. The Consequence is that your Friends (who would have set up a Press above a year ago, but that they did not know but you might chuse to be concern'd in the Printing Business on your Return) have at length engaged one Goddard,[4] who served his Apprenticeship with Mr. Parker, to set up a Printing Office in Philadelphia and publish a News Paper. Mr. Galloway, and Mr. Thos. Wharton for his Encouragement, have entered into Partnership with him and have agreed to advance what Money may be necessary.[5] But as their Motive for doing this is not merely for the Sake of Profit, but principally to have a Press henceforth as open and safe to them, as Hall's and Bradford's are to the other Party, they have put it into their Agreement as I understand, that when you return you shall have it in your Power to be concern'd, if you Chuse it, in the Place of one of them.[6] The young Man has brought several good Founts of Letter with him, but his Press he was obliged to leave with his Mother who carries on the Business

2. Jack Retort was the pseudonym which Isaac Hunt used for his 1765 anti-proprietary papers, *An Humble Attempt at Scurrility* and *Exercises at Scurrility Hall;* see above, XII, 44 n, 83 n.

3. This letter, probably written in the winter of 1765, has not been found.

4. For William Goddard, who began publishing the *Pennsylvania Chronicle* in January 1767, see above, XII, 287–8 n.

5. The articles of partnership are printed in Goddard's *The Partnership: or the History of the Rise and Progress of the Pennsylvania Chronicle &c.* (Phila., 1770), pp. 7–10.

6. Goddard, Galloway, and Wharton agreed that, if BF should return to Philadelphia and desire to join them in the printing of the *Chronicle*, he should have a two-ninths share of the enterprise.

at Providence. They therefore desired me to ask my Mother to lend them the old Press which Parker used here,[7] and they would either buy it of you, or pay you what you thought reasonable for the Hire. My Mother told me she had no Objection to my letting them have it, but she did not chuse to do it of herself lest Mr. Hall might be displeased with her for it. At the same Time she said that she should be glad that the Printer would take the old House in which it was, as it stood empty and has not brought in any Rent for a great while. I accordingly let them have the Press, and they have agreed with my Mother to take your old House in Market Street.[8] There is a new Mahogany Press there, which they seem desirous to purchase if you incline to part with it, but I suppose they will write to you on the Subject. What I have done is for the best, and I hope it will prove agreeable to you. There is, indeed, really a Necessity for their having a Press of their own, while their publick Affairs continue in their present critical Situation for it is with great Difficulty they can get Hall, or Bradford to consent to print any Thing for them, and when they do some of the Proprietary Party are sure to have it communicated to them before it is publish'd. Hugh Roberts, and many more of your old Friends, have determined to encourage the new Printer all in their Power, and to go about the several Wards to get Subscriptions to the News-paper. The Members of Assembly will do the same in their respective Counties, and let him have all the Publick Work. So that I am in hopes that by the Time you return they will lay the Foundation of a very valuable Business, worth your while to be concern'd in, if you should think it proper or convenient. But I am likewise in hopes that when you do return you will have something far better worth your Acceptance than that can possibly be made.[9]

7. That is, a press, formerly Benjamin Mecom's, which Parker had used at Burlington, N.J., and then had shipped to Philadelphia. See above, XII, 409; this volume, pp. 109, 110.

8. The *Chronicle* was issued at the "New Printing Office, in Market Street, near the Post Office." This was the house on the site of the present 326 Market St., just west of the Franklin property, where the family lived from 1761 until they moved into the new house in 1765. It belonged to Adam Eckert. See Hannah B. Roach, "Benjamin Franklin Slept Here," *PMHB,* LXXXIV (1960), 166–74.

9. WF appears to be expressing a wish that BF return to Pa. as royal governor, a position to which his enemies had accused him of aspiring.

However, as all Things in this Life are uncertain, it may not perhaps be amiss for you to have it in your Power to engage in this Affair. I am, Honoured Sir Your dutiful Son

WM: FRANKLIN

From Benjamin Gale[1]   ALS: American Philosophical Society

Dear Sir   Killingworth 15th N[ovember 1766][2]
  Had I been apprized of your Crossing [torn] a Second time in the Service of your Country [torn; Exp]erience of past favours, and the well known [torn] temper of your Mind, I should almost have been [torn] to have Asked the favour of you, to have recom-[mended] me to the notice of some Gentleman of Charecter eminent in the practice of Phisick in London, with whom You may have contracted an Acquaintance, Although I may not Flatter my self, that either the natural powers of my mind, or the advantages we enjoy in America, to obtain medical Knowledge, entitule me to the honour of such a corrispondence, yet I doubt not there are persons in Brittain as well as America, who take pleasure in rendring services to Mankind, and estimate the pleasure resulting from such kind and benevolent services, abundant satisfaction even where there is not the least prospect of returns.
  But I should not at this time have diverted You, either from the Interesting and important affairs in which you are engag'd for your Country, or even presum'd to disengage you one moment from your Freind, or the many amusements of the Town, had I not been greatly Concerned for a very Valuable patient, which I have long had under my care, labouring under a dropsey, which mended a [torn], when she first put herself under my Care [torn] to be a genuine Ascites, but since [I have] been convinc'd it is a dropsey of the ovaries, by [torn] prescriptions she Hath recovered a good Appetite, and [torn] great freedom from many Complaints incident to [such] disorders, but retains her Size, the waters not

  1. For Benjamin Gale, physician of Killingworth, Conn., son-in-law of Jared Eliot, see above, XI, 183 n.
  2. The upper corner of the leaf is torn off, causing the loss of some words on the first and second pages. The date is supplied from BF's endorsement.

being [drawn] off, either by Hydragogue Cathartics, or Diuret-
icks.[3]

Having lately seen in a Magazine an Account of the Effects of
the Meadow Saffron, or the *Colichicum Linnaei foliis planis lance-
olatis erectis* by Dr. Storke, Physian to the Empress Queen, and
that the same had been successfully usd in one of the Hospitals in
London,[4] And as I have heard You Say, if I do not misremember,
You had the pleasure of An Acquaintance with Dr. Pringle of
London, I should esteem it as a very great Favour if You would
be pleasd to request that Gentlemans Opinion of that Medicine,
and whether it has ever been us'd in either of the Hospitals in
London, and with what Success. From Long Acquaintance with
Dr. Elliots Practice in the Dropsey, as well as in my own, I have
never as Yet been Able to discover any one certain diuretic medicine, and should be glad to find, that even the most Deleterious
poyson should have so Salutary Effect, in so deplorable a Disease.
I must confess as Dr. Storke seems to lay great Stress on the most
deleterious poysons for the recovery of Health, I fear there is more
of Enthusiasm than reality in such prescriptions, however it must
with truth be confessd, that the most powerfull Medicines, if given
in undue quantities Act as poysons—if any Encouragement can be
given of its success, either in the Hospitals, or by Practitioners in
London, if it can be had in London and You would be pleas'd to

3. Mutilation of the MS and the use of technical phraseology complicate
this passage for the layman. Its purport is roughly as follows: When Gale's
patient first came under his care her condition improved somewhat and he
diagnosed her ailment as dropsy of the abdomen, that is, the collection of se-
rous fluid in the abdominal cavity, known as ascites. He has subsequently been
convinced that her ailment is what would today be called an ovarian cyst.
Her condition has in some ways improved, but her abdominal distention
remains and is unaffected by cathartic or diuretic medication designed to drain
off the excess fluid.

4. "Some Account of the Use and Effects of the Root of *Meadow Saffron;*
by Dr. Anthony Storck, Aulic Councellor and chief Physician to the Empress
Queen," *Gent. Mag.*, XXXIV (1764), 426–9. Meadow saffron, or autumn
crocus, now known as *Colchicum autumnale,* long regarded merely as a poison,
was introduced in the treatment of dropsy by Baron Anton Störck of Vienna
in 1763, but its value in cases of gout was well known to the Arabs much
earlier. Gale was in error in saying that the article in *Gent. Mag.* reported the
successful use of meadow saffron for dropsy in one of the London hospitals;
he apparently misunderstood a passage relating to a wholly different matter.

forward me a Quantity sufficient for a full tryal in this Case, to Mr. Colden, I should gratefully Acknowledge the Favour, and most gladly pay any Expence how greatsoever it may be.

December 26 1766

Since transmitting my Dissertation to Dr. Huxham on the Subject of Inoculation, with some Historical Memoirs, which You did me the Honour to read,[5] I have heard nothing from him, till Reading the Gentlemans Magazine for August Last, in the List of Books published in London, I found these Words, "It appears on the Authority of Dr. Huxham that Dr. Benjamin Gale of Connecticut in N England, since he has given Mercury and Antimony in preparing persons for Inoculation, has Lost only one patient out of 800 Inoculated whereas before he gave this Medicine, he usually lost one out of 100."[6] By this it Appears Dr. Huxham had published, or made mention, of those Accounts which I transmitted to him, which the remarker suppos'd was the result of my own practice, while I only deduced the General ratio of Mortality in Mercurial, and Unmercurial Inoculation, from the practices of others, particularly in the Town of Boston AD 1720, 1752, and 1764, but as it now Appears from the Magazines, it must set me in a Disadvantageous light, [*illegible*] in the Colony of Connecticut, where it is well known I did not Inoculate more than 70 or 80 persons, before the practice was Interdicted by the Legislature of the Colony, wherefore I have wrote Dr. Huxham on that Subject, and presum'd to Inclose it to You, for a more safe Conveyance which I hope You will the more easily pardon, as it is with me an Interesting point, as my veracity may thereby be Calld into Question, requesting him to Set that matter in its just and true light, in the Next Magazine, your Favour herein will be most gratefully

5. John Huxham (1692–1768), F.R.S., physician, winner of the Copley Medal in 1755, wrote chiefly on fevers and scurvy. *DNB*. On May 23, 1765, he read to the Royal Society Gale's paper, "Historical Memoirs, relating to the Practice of Inoculation for the Small Pox, in the British-American Provnces, particularly in New England: Addressed to John Huxham, M.D. F.R.S." It was published in *Phil. Trans.*, LV (1765), 193–204, but that volume did not appear until the summer of 1766.

6. *Gent. Mag.*, XXXVI (1766), 381–4, printed a review of a book on inoculation for smallpox by George Baker, M.D., F.R.S., in the course of which the reviewer cited Huxham and Gale in nearly, though not quite, the words in quotation marks here.

Acknowledged by Sir Your Most Oblidged Most Obedient Humble
Servant   BENJA GALE

P.S. I have Inclosd the Letter to Dr. Huxham Unseald which
please to read, if it Contains any thing that may offend, You will
please to Suppress it.[7] I hope You with Mr. Johnson will Concert
some measures, to Extricate me from the disadvantages I lye under
with regard to that Mistake which greatly troubles me which will
in some measure I hope plead my Excuse for the Trouble It gives
my freinds. Ut Sup.   B G

To Dr B. Franklin Esqr

Endorsed: Dr Gale Nov. 15. 66

From James Parker

ALS: American Philosophical Society

Honoured Sir.   New York Nov. 15. 1766
Four Days ago I wrote you per the Harriot Packet, in hopes
that will come safe to your Hands.[8] To that I refer for many Things,
as this serves only to inclose two or three of my News-papers, which
I did not think so proper to send then. I have now printed 5 Newspapers and have got 25 Subscribers in this City, and about 50 in all
in the Country: As many more about goes for Nothing, either to
Post-Masters or Printers to exchange: I print 200 and have a good
Parcel to spare: Is it worth the While for an Old feeble Fellow like
me, to strive with such small Force? Yes, I will try one Quarter:
Last Night I had the Pleasure of a Letter from my Son, who,
thank God, is yet in the Land of the Living:[9] He was returning

7. BF wrote Gale, Feb. 23, 1767, that the *Phil. Trans.* publication of Gale's
paper had stated Gale's claim accurately; that statements in the magazines
"are only abridg'd accounts or notes" of what is in the volume; that the
abridgers often make mistakes to which nobody pays any attention; and that
the full text of a paper in *Phil. Trans.* was understood to be "the only authentic publication." Therefore, BF had not given Huxham the trouble of Gale's
letter, but had suppressed it, as Gale had authorized him to do. Gale published this part of BF's letter in *Connecticut Courant,* June 26, 1769.

8. Above, pp. 490–4.

9. Samuel Franklin Parker had gone to North Carolina for his health in
early September, but had not communicated with his wife or parents since.
He returned to New York on December 12.

home the 18th of October, but by the violent Gales of Wind which we had, he was beat off, and quite back to South-Carolina, where he was the 4th of this Month: He had been very poorly ever since he went, till he arrived at Charles-Town, where he was got a little better: It was uncertain, whether he would come away this Winter: but as it is, I am thankful: May God in his Mercy compassionate my Afflicted Soul, and in due Time send Relief! His Will be done—Sickness yet predominates in my Family, but all in due Time, it will be removed, I hope.

By the next Packet, tho' not arrived here yet, I hope to send more pleasing Affairs, if any: We can only now send our Humble Salutations from Your obliged Servant   JAMES PARKER.

To Ann Penn

MS not found; reprinted from Albert H. Smyth, ed., *The Writings of Benjamin Franklin*, IV (New York, 1906), 466–7.[1]

Dear Madam,   London, Nov. 20, 1766.
I received yours of the eleventh Instant,[2] and condole with you most sincerely on the loss of your Son—my amiable young friend.[3]

It must have been a heavy loss to you; For he was truly a good Child; His last Will is only the last Instance of the affectionate dutiful Regard he always paid you, and of a peace with the rest.[4] I waive the common Topics of Consolation used on such Occasions. I knew that to a Person of your good Understanding they must all have occurred of them selves and I know besides by Experience, that the best Remedy for Grief is Time.[5]

I shall as you desire transmit the Account and Copy of the Will

1. Smyth noted that the MS was then in the possession of Miss Frances M.F. Donnel of Sunbury, Pa. In 1924 the ALS. was offered for sale in the Stan V. Henkels *Catalogue*, No. 1343 (Jan. 17, 1924), p. 31, as item 193. The present editors have been unable to trace the letter since then.

2. Not found.

3. Springett Penn died at Dublin early in November of tuberculosis; he had been seriously ill since at least September; see above, p. 417.

4. Springett devised all of his real and personal property to his mother. Howard M. Jenkins, "The Family of William Penn," *PMHB*, XXII (1898), 183.

5. For another expression of the same sentiments, see above, XII, 385.

to Mr. Pennington.[6] The Power of Attorney you send him must be acknowledged, or proved before the Lord Mayor of Dublin, and should be drawn with an express Clause enabling him to Sell Land;[7] in other respects the common form is sufficient. The Will should be a Certified Copy from the Office where wills are recorded. If in anything there or here I can do you acceptable service, it will be a Pleasure to Receive your Commands; being with great Esteem and Respect Dear Madam, Your most obedient Humble Servant   B. FRANKLIN

From Thomas Pownall   ALS: American Philosophical Society

Dear Sir   Westrop. Novr. 20. 66
I am scarce forgiven by Lady Fawkener[8] for not bringing you down with me to this place. She bids me say that she had flattered her with the hopes of seing you here. I have told her of your promise to come at Xmass and if you don't keep your word I shall be ruined.

You was so good to say that you would forward the enclosed for me. Pray be so good you will much oblige me. I have not a frank and all our neighbours who belong to the house are out of the Way so that I have not a frank.[9] I am ashamed to putt you to the Expence of a packet but do not know how to avoid it. I am Sir Your Obliged and Obedient Servant   T POWNALL

6. Edward Penington, a Quaker merchant and judge in Philadelphia, had looked after Springett's interests there. He was, in fact, a distant relative of the young man; see above, IX, 315 n. He replied to BF's notification on April 5, 1767.

7. Mrs. Penn changed her mind about selling her son's property in Pennsylvania after she married Alexander Durdin, a Dublin attorney, in February 1767. See Jenkins, "The Family of William Penn," pp. 183–4.

8. The widow of the former postmaster general, Sir Everard Fawkener (above, V, 334 n). She married Pownall in 1765, but continued to be called by the title and name derived from her first husband. Charles A. W. Pownall, *Thomas Pownall* (London, 1908), p. 185.

9. Had one of Pownall's neighbors who was a member of the House of Commons been available, he might have franked Pownall's packet; he himself did not become an M.P. until the next February.

To Daniel Burton   ALS: Society for the Propagation of the Gospel

Reverend Sir,   Craven Street, Nov. 21. 1766
Being informed that Mr. Jonathan Odell[1] purposes applying to the Venerable Society, for an Appointment to the Mission of Burlington in New Jersey, I beg leave to acquaint you that from the Character he bears I apprehend such Appointment may be very agreable to the Congregation there; and that if the Society think fit to favour his Request, I shall recommend him warmly to the Countenance and Friendship of the Governor of that Province. I am, with great Respect Reverend Sir, Your most obedient and most humble Servant   B FRANKLIN

Revd. Doctor Burton

Endorsed: Mr Odell's testimonium and recommendation Laid before the Board—Nov. 21. 1766.

From Margaret Stevenson[2]   ALS: American Philosophical Society

[*Torn*] Sir   Westbury Nov: 22 1766
I rived hear Thursday Night at Ten a Clock alramd [alarmed] all the wilage Mrs. Moriss gone to Bead but got up. I cant express

1. Jonathan Odell (1737–1818), Anglican clergyman, surgeon, vigorous satirist, active Tory, was born in Newark; graduated from the College of New Jersey, 1754; studied medicine; was ordained in London, January 1767. The S.P.G. appointed him to the mission in Burlington, where he served until after the beginning of the American Revolution. He was with the British Army in America, 1776–77, first as a surgeon, then as a chaplain. After the war he settled in the province of New Brunswick, where he was a councilor and secretary of the province, 1785 to his death. *DAB;* Frederick L. Weis, "The Colonial Clergy of the Middle Colonies," Amer. Antiq. Soc. *Proc.,* new series, LXVI (1957), 284–5.

2. From the phraseology of this letter it appears that BF's landlady was escorting his young relative Sarah (Sally) Franklin (A.5.2.3.1.1.1)—who had spent some months in the Craven Street house—back to her father's home in Lutterworth. They had stopped off in Westbury on the way to visit BF's cousins, Hannah Walker (A.5.2.3.3.1) and Eleanor Morris (A.5.2.8.1). Margaret Stevenson in England, like DF in Pennsylvania and Jane Mecom in Massachusetts, belonged to a generation in which female education had dealt rather lightly with spelling. Letters by their daughters among the Franklin Papers suggest a major change in this respect from one generation to the next

her Joy. I thought it wod have bin to much for her. It is a misrabl being for cold and hard Lod[g]ing. But Poor Mrs. Walker is every kind and car[e]full to keep me warm and gete me all the good [*torn*] she cane but how I am to geet to Luterworth I dont know they say it is near forty miles cross the Country. I beg you will wright to me by the return of the Post How you goe onn. I am goin to make Passtye and Bread for thay have one Overn and one Chimble. Saly is very well and Mrs. Moriss Mr. Walke &ct. He I think is Industrys at his work Boord and She too[3] but its a Poor Plass to geat Bread for them Selfe and three Childen and Provition dear[er] than in London expect Butter. I live as Chipe as Possable. No Tea for what thay have I cant Drink but I get milk. The Passon [Parson] has bin to visit me and offers his vine and Sent a Math [Mat] to lay under my feat, the Sqres [Squire's] Lady has sent for me so, my Dear Sir I am your verry humble Searvant

MARGT STEVENSON

Mrs. Morris and Walker &c. &c. Send thear Duty the talkeing of you fills up the time that I am rely hapey. Pray Dear Sir send a Carid [Card] that Ingravaed about the Colnies.[4]

Addressed: To / Docter Benn: Franklin / In Craven Street / London

Endorsed: Mrs Stevenson from Westbury Nov. 66

From the Earl of Morton[5]   AL: American Philosophical Society

Brook Street monday 24 November 1766
Lord Morton's Compliments to Dr. Franklin, Acquaints him that he has been elected one of the Auditors on the part of the Society, and desires the favor of his Company to Dinner on Saturday next

---

on both sides of the ocean. In any event, DF's and Jane's letters had given BF considerable practice before he had occasion to read many of Margaret Stevenson's.

3. It is not clear what trade Thomas Walker followed; his wife was a lacemaker.

4. One of BF's Stamp Act cards depicting "Magna Britania her Colonies Reduc'd." See above, pp. 66–72.

5. For James Douglas, 14th Earl of Morton, president of the Royal Society since 1764, see above, IX, 272 n.

the 29th, and that he would come about one o'Clock so as there may be time to Examine the Accounts before Dinner.

Addressed: To | Doctor Franklin

"Arator": On the Price of Corn, and Management of the Poor

Printed in *The London Chronicle,* November 27–29, 1766.

The first editor to identify Franklin in print as the author of this paper was Benjamin Vaughan, who included it in his 1779 edition of Franklin's writings.[6] Before that it had been twice reprinted. A periodical published by the French physiocrats, called *Ephémérides du citoyen,* printed a translation in February 1767, introducing it with a note beginning: "C'est à M. l'Abbé M. très connu dans la République des Lettres, que nous sommes redevables de la Lettre suivante, traduite sur le *London Chronicle* du mois de Novembre dernier."[7] The "Abbé M." was almost certainly André Morellet (1727–1819), who had not yet met Franklin but who later became one of his most congenial friends in France. Two years after this publication, an unidentified Englishman saw the French translation and sent the English text to a periodical entitled *De Re Rustica, or The Repository for Select Papers on Agriculture, Arts, and Manufactures,* with a letter signed "Columella" in which he described the author as "a gentleman well known to every man of letters in Europe, and perhaps there is none, in this age, to whom mankind in general are more indebted."[8] From this source, apparently, Vaughan

6. [Benjamin Vaughan, ed.,] *Political, Miscellaneous, and Philosophical Pieces; . . . Written by Benj. Franklin. LL.D. and F.R.S.* (London, 1779), pp. 57–63.

7. *Ephémérides du citoyen, ou bibliothèque raisonnée des sciences morales et politiques,* 1767. Tome Second, Première Partie. No. Premier, pp. 5–18. The note went on to caution readers not to be deceived by the paper's "apparence de badinage et de légereté"; there had been many disturbances in English cities caused by the dearness of grain, and the disputes between the farmers and the manufacturers, artisans, and merchants had divided England for a long time. The note concluded: "Les plaisanteries de l'"Ecrivain Anglois étoient propres à réussir auprès du Public pour lequel il écrivoit: elles prépareront nos Lecteurs à quelques remarques plus sérieuses sur le vrai *moyen politique* d'empêcher les *terreurs populaires,* les *murmures* et les *soulevements* de cette espece."

8. *De Re Rustica; or, The Repository for Select Papers on Agriculture, Arts, and Manufactures,* 1 (1769), 352–4 (Columbia Univ. Lib.). Credit for noticing

took the text, reprinting "Columella's" letter and giving the paper the title indicated above. Later editors have accepted Vaughan's identification of Franklin as the author, reprinted as he did the note by "Columella," and headed the paper with the title Vaughan gave to it.

The wheat crop of 1766 in most parts of Europe had been a failure, and in other areas, including Great Britain, it had been below normal.[9] In consequence, the price of wheat and flour had shot up on the Continent, and English producers, millers, and dealers were naturally tempted to ship much of their supplies to these profitable foreign markets. When the domestic price of wheat advanced as a result, the prices of other foodstuffs tended also to rise, and loud outcries began to be heard. On the advice of the Ministry the King issued a proclamation, September 10, to enforce long-standing acts against "Forestallers, Regraters, and Engrossers of Corn, &c.," but it proved ineffective.[1] The newspapers began to carry reports of demonstrations and mob violence in various parts of the country directed against the mills and other property of those suspected of engaging in the export trade.

An act already on the statute books had the effect of freely permitting the exportation of wheat after Aug. 26, 1766; the prompt repeal of that act and the imposition of a legislative embargo would have considerably relieved the situation. Most unwisely, however, the very day on which the futile proclamation was issued, the King, acting on the advice of his ministers, prorogued Parliament until November 11, making impossible the immediate passage of such legislation. The reports of mob actions soon convinced the Ministry that they faced an emergency. On September 26, therefore, the King and his ministers issued an order in council imposing an embargo on the exportation of wheat or wheat flour from any British port to foreign parts.[2] Although riotous demonstrations

---

the French translation and for sending the text to the English periodical has sometimes been assigned to Benjamin Vaughan, probably because he reprinted the "Columella" letter as part of a note in his edition of 1779, and because later editors, reprinting this note, have attached to it the initials "B.V." That Vaughan should have sent the piece to *De Re Rustica* in 1769 is most unlikely, however, for he attained only his eighteenth birthday in April of that year. *De Re Rustica* was sometimes cited as *The Repository*.

9. An account of this whole episode is found conveniently in Gipson, *British Empire*, XI, 83–7.

1. The text was printed in *London Chron.*, Sept. 13–16, 1766.

2. The embargo was to continue until November 14. A second proclamation of the same day prohibited "the making, extracting, or distilling, of any kind of low wines, or spirits, from any wheat, wheat meal, wheat flour, or wheat bran, or any mixture therewith," for the same period. The texts of both orders in council were printed in *London Chron.*, Sept. 27–29, 1766.

continued, local authorities began to take steps to regulate prices, and some public-spirited citizens undertook to make bread available to the poor. With the enforcement of the embargo these measures helped to avert the threat of a real famine. When Parliament reassembled on November 11 the Commons began action at once on a bill to forbid the export of wheat and flour or the extraction of low wines and spirits from these commodities. The bill became law on December 16.[3]

The order in council had been helpful in dealing with a crisis situation in the food supply and in the public peace, but it in turn created something of a constitutional crisis. The King, though acting on the advice of his ministers, had in fact exercised the same dispensing power for which James II had incurred great wrath before the Revolution of 1688; for George III had in effect dispensed with the act legalizing the exportation of wheat. Whether the seriousness of the emergency could justify such a violation of a constitutional principle became a subject of vigorous debate in Parliament and in the public press.[4] All through this autumn, in fact, the printers of newspapers and pamphlets were busy with writings on the subject of corn, as that commodity affected either the nation's economy, its foreign trade, its farmers, its deserving (or undeserving) poor, its public peace, or its constitution. To this discussion Benjamin Franklin—a city-dwelling colonial now temporarily living in the British metropolis—contributed this paper in stalwart defense of British farmers, among whom he probably was not personally well acquainted with a single one.

To Messieurs the PUBLIC and Co.   [November 29, 1766]

I Am one of that class of people that feeds you all, and at present is abus'd by you all; in short I am a *Farmer*.

By your News-papers we are told, that God had sent a very short harvest to some other countries of Europe. I thought this might be in favour to Old England; and that now we should get a good price for our grain, which would bring in millions among us, and make us flow in money, that to be sure is scarce enough.

But the wisdom of Government forbad the exportation.[5]

3. *Commons Journals*, XXXI, 46. The act is 7 Geo. III, c. 3.

4. On December 16 the King also assented to an act (7 Geo. III, c. 7) to indemnify all persons acting "for the Service of the Public" who had advised or carried out the order in council establishing the embargo. Recognition of the need for this act was close to an admission by the Ministry that the order in council had been a violation of the constitution.

5. In reprinting the paper in 1779 Benjamin Vaughan cautiously added a footnote at this point: "It is not necessary to repeat in what degree Dr.

Well, says I, then we must be content with the market price at home.

No, says my Lords the mob, you sha'n't have that. Bring your corn to market if you dare; we'll sell it for you, for less money, or take it for nothing.

Being thus attack'd by both ends *of the Constitution,* the head and the tail *of Government,* what am I to do?

Must I keep my corn in barn to feed and increase the breed of rats? be it so; they cannot be less thankful than those I have been used to feed.

Are we Farmers the only people to be grudged the profits of honest labour? And why? One of the late scribblers against us gives a bill of fare of the provisions at my daughter's wedding, and proclaims to all the world that we had the insolence to eat beef and pudding! Has he never read that precept in the good book, *Thou shalt not muzzle the mouth of the ox that treadeth out the corn;*[6] or does he think us less worthy of good living than our oxen?

O, but the Manufacturers! the Manufacturers! they are to be favour'd, and they must have bread at a cheap rate!

Hark-ye, Mr. Oaf; The Farmers live splendidly, you say. And pray, would you have them hoard the money they get? Their fine cloaths and furniture, do they make them themselves, or for one another, and so keep the money among them? Or do they employ these your darling Manufacturers, and so scatter it again all over the nation?

Franklin respected the ministers, to whom he alludes. The embargo upon corn was but a single measure: which, it is enough to say, an host of politicians thought well-advised, but ill-defended. Of the great and honourable services of the Earl of Chatham to his country, Dr. Franklin has borne the amplest testimony. E."

6. Given in this version in I Corinthians 9: 9, citing "the law of Moses," where it appears in Deuteronomy 25: 4 in a slightly different form. The newspaper account of the wedding of the farmer's daughter has not been located, but a very similar report of a farmer's christening party "within this fortnight" appeared in *London Chron.*, Nov. 15–18, 1766. The guests were numerous enough to have to be seated in two large rooms, and the table in each room was laden with: a buttock of beef, a filet of veal, a ham, three boiled fowls, a goose, a pigeon pie, a rice pudding, and an apple pie. The "Liquors" consisted of: red port and mountain wines, rum punch and brandy punch, three sorts of "made Wine," bottled beer, old October beer, and "Muld Ale."

My wool would produce me a better price if it were suffer'd to go to foreign markets. But that, Messieurs the Public, your laws will not permit. It must be kept all at home, that our *dear* Manufacturers may have it the cheaper. And then, having yourselves thus lessened our encouragement for raising sheep, you curse us for the scarcity of mutton!

I have heard my grandfather say, that the Farmers submitted to the prohibition on the exportation of wool, being made to expect and believe, that when the Manufacturer bought his wool cheaper, they should have their cloth cheaper. But the deuce a bit. It has been growing dearer and dearer from that day to this. How so? why truly the cloth is exported; and that keeps up the price.

Now if it be a good principle, that the exportation of a commodity is to be restrain'd, that so our own people at home may have it the cheaper, stick to that principle, and go thorough stitch[7] with it. Prohibit the exportation of your cloth, your leather and shoes, your iron ware, and your manufactures of all sorts, to make them all cheaper at home. And cheap enough they will be, I'll warrant you—till people leave off making them.

Some folks seem to think they ought never to be easy, till England becomes another *Lubberland,* where 'tis fancied the streets are paved with penny rolls, the houses tiled with pancakes, and chickens ready roasted cry, come eat me.

I say, when you are sure you have got a good principle, stick to it, and carry it thorough. I hear 'tis said, that though it was *necessary and right* for the M——y to advise a prohibition of the exportation of corn, yet it was *contrary to law;* and also, that though it was *contrary to law* for the mob to obstruct the waggons, yet it was *necessary and right.* Just the same thing, to a tittle. Now they tell me, an act of indemnity ought to pass in favour of the M——y, to secure them from the consequences of having acted illegally. If so, pass another in favour of the mob. Others say, some of the mob ought to be hanged, by way of example. If so, —— but I say no more than I have said before, *when you are sure that you have got a good principle, go thorough with it.*

You say, poor labourers cannot afford to buy bread at a high price, unless they had higher wages. Possibly. But how shall we Farmers be able to afford our labourers higher wages, if you will

7. "Thorough stitch": thoroughly, completely.

not allow us to get, when we might have it, a higher price for our corn?

By all I can learn, we should at least have had a guinea a quarter more if the exportation had been allowed. And this money England would have got from foreigners.

But, it seems, we Farmers must take so much less, that the poor may have it so much cheaper.

This operates then as a tax for the maintenance of the poor. A very good thing, you will say. But I ask, Why a partial tax? Why laid on us Farmers only? If it be a good thing, pray, Messrs. the Public, take your share of it, by indemnifying us a little out of your public treasury. In doing a good thing there is both honour and pleasure; you are welcome to your part of both.

For my own part, I am not so well satisfied of the goodness of this thing. I am for doing good to the poor, but I differ in opinion of the means. I think the best way of doing good to the poor, is not making them easy *in* poverty, but leading or driving them *out* of it. In my youth I travelled much, and I observed in different countries, that the more public provisions were made for the poor, the less they provided for themselves, and of course became poorer. And, on the contrary, the less was done for them, the more they did for themselves, and became richer. There is no country in the world where so many provisions are established for them; so many hospitals to receive them when they are sick or lame, founded and maintained by voluntary charities; so many alms-houses for the aged of both sexes, together with a solemn general law made by the rich to subject their estates to a heavy tax for the support of the poor. Under all these obligations, are our poor modest, humble, and thankful; and do they use their best endeavours to maintain themselves, and lighten our shoulders of this burthen? On the contrary, I affirm that there is no country in the world in which the poor are more idle, dissolute, drunken, and insolent. The day you passed that act, you took away from before their eyes the greatest of all inducements to industry, frugality, and sobriety, by giving them a dependance on somewhat else than a careful accumulation during youth and health, for support in age or sickness. In short, you offered a premium for the encouragement of idleness, and you should not now wonder that it has had its effect in the increase of poverty. Repeal that law, and you will soon see a change in their manners. St. Monday, and St. Tuesday, will cease to be holidays.[8] Six *days shalt thou labour,* though one of the old commandments long treated as out of date, will again be looked upon as a respectable precept; industry will increase, and with it plenty among the lower people; their circumstances will mend, and more will be done for their happiness by inuring them to provide for themselves, than could be done by dividing all your estates among them.

Excuse me, Messrs. the Public, if upon this *interesting* subject, I put you to the trouble of reading a little of *my* nonsense. I am sure I have lately read a great deal of *yours;* and therefore from you (at least from those of you who are writers) I deserve a little indulgence. I am, your's, &c.   ARATOR.

From the Associates of Dr. Bray[9]

Printed form with MS insertions in blanks: American Philosophical Society

Sir,   Associates Office,   17 *66*
    The Associates of Dr. Bray, for establishing Parochial Libraries, and instructing the Negroes in the British Plantations, meet on Thursday the *4* Day of *December* at Ten o'Clock, at their Office at the Angel and Bible, in Ave-Mary Lane.

Addressed: To | Dr. Franklin Near | The Strand

8. In describing his life as a young man among the London printers in 1724–26 in his Autobiography, BF used the expression "making a St. Monday" for a printer's absence from work on that day because of week-end dissipation. *Autobiog.* (APS-Yale), p. 101. Here he extends it to include Tuesday as well.

9. For the Associates of Dr. Bray, a philanthropic organization, one of whose principal concerns was the education of Negro children in North America, see above, VII, 100 n. BF was elected to membership in the organization during his first mission to England and in 1763, while in Philadelphia, reported to the Associates about the progress of their school there. See above, VII, 356 n, 377–9; IX, 12, 174; X, 395–6; and this volume, p. 442.

From [John] Blair[1]

AP: American Philosophical Society

Monday Decr 8th [1766][2]

Dr. Blair presents his Compliments to Dr. Franklin and has used the freedom of sending his Servant for a small parcell of the *Pine Tops*[3] which he was so obliging as to say he would give him.

From Jonathan Potts

AL: American Philosophical Society

Edinburgh December 10th: 1766

I wrote to you upon my arrival in Liverpool as did my Friend and Relation Mr. Benjamin Rush,[4] we also sent you some Letters from your Friends in Philadelphia in our favour,[5] the design of which Letters was that you would be so kind as to write to any

1. While the writer of this note might be Hugh Blair (1718–1800), a Scottish minister who was also Regius professor of Rhetoric and Belles Lettres at the University of Edinburgh and a friend of Hume, Robertson, and Adam Smith, the editors believe that the penman was more probably John Blair (d. 1782), a minister in the Church of England, who was elected to the Royal Society in 1755 on the strength of his *Chronology and History of the World, from the Creation to the Year of Christ 1753* (London, 1754). *DNB*. The editors prefer John Blair because the nature of this note suggests its author was a resident of London, as this man was. Another note in the same handwriting by a "Dr. Blair" is addressed from Princes Street, Leicester Fields.

2. December 8 fell on a Monday twice during BF's years in England: in 1760 and 1766. This note is placed in the latter year because of its reference to "Pine Tops," which were far more popular by 1766 than they had been six years earlier; see the next note.

3. Pine buds from America, brewed into a tea, came into vogue during the 1760s in England. In 1764 William Allen sent a box of them to William Pitt, explaining that, while the concoction would not cure the gout, it would render that disease less frequent. Lewis B. Walker, ed., *The Burd Papers. Extracts from Chief Justice William Allen's Letter Book* ([Pottsville, Pa.], 1897), pp. 58–61. By 1766 the use of pine buds had become popular in the British Isles. During that year an advertisement appeared often, though at irregular intervals, in *London Chron.*, announcing pine buds for sale at several outlets in the city and elsewhere, and recommending them highly for the treatment of colds, coughs, rheums, asthmas, scurvy, gout, and rheumatism.

4. Potts and Rush arrived in Liverpool, Oct. 21, 1766, and went immediately to Edinburgh to pursue their medical studies. For their letters see above, pp. 468, 471.

5. See above, pp. 387–8, 404, 404–5.

517

of your Friends in this place in our behalf, as I am somewhat apprehensive you have not received those Letters, I have taken the liberty to repeat my request, as I find since my arrival here that Letters from you in our favour would be of infinite service to us.[6] I am Sir with the utmost respect your most obedient and very humble Servant   JONATHAN POTTS

To Benjamin Franklin Esqr.

Addressed: To / Benjamin Franklin Esqr. / in Craven Street / London

From the Earl of Morton   AL: American Philosophical Society

Thursday 9 o'Clock [December 11, 1766?][7]
Lord Morton woud have spoke with Dr. Franklin but he was gone

6. For BF's letters of recommendation for Potts and Rush, all written on Dec. 20, 1766, see below, pp. 531–3. Mrs. Thomas Potts James, a genealogist of the Potts family, published a postscript to the present letter, which she noted as being "written on a separate slip of paper and enclosed," but which the present editors have not found, in which Potts observed that "Just after sealing this, news of the packet arrived this morning, I got yours of Nov. 11th. I shall answer it by the packet which I suppose will sail in a few days." The present editors have found no letter from BF to Potts of Nov. 11, 1766. Mrs. James published what purported to be such a letter but it is indubitably BF's letter to Potts and Rush of Dec. 20, 1766. There may have been a November 11 letter, but it appears more likely that the postscript which Mrs. James published belonged to another letter to another correspondent. The present editors find it highly unlikely that Potts would have sent a letter from Edinburgh to London by sea when an efficient overland postal service operated between the two places. See Mrs. Thomas Potts James, *Memorial of Thomas Potts, Junior* (Cambridge, 1874), pp. 172–3.

7. The phraseology of this note suggests that Lord Morton, president of the Royal Society from 1764 until his death, Oct. 12, 1768, scrawled it after one of the meetings of the Society's Council during the years 1765–68 when BF served on that body. Regular meetings were held on Thursdays, though special meetings might be held on other days. The minutes record one Thursday meeting in 1765 that BF attended, two in 1766, six in 1767, and nine in 1768 before Morton's death. It is probable that the meeting of Thursday, Dec. 11, 1766, is the earliest to which this note may have related, though it could have been almost any of the others. Among the Franklin Papers, APS, are ten printed notices of Council meetings during these years. Only five of them coincide with meetings at which he is recorded as being present: Dec. 11, 1766; July 15, Nov. 19, Dec. 10, and Dec. 14, 1767.

immediately after the Counsil; Should be oblig'd if the Dr. could breakfast with him to morrow about 10 and will send for an answer earlier.

Addressed: To | Dr Franklin | Craven Street

To Deborah Franklin   ALS: American Philosophical Society

My dear Child,   London, Dec. 13. 1766
   Since my last I have received your kind Letters of Sept. 28. and Oct. 4. I wonder you had not heard of my Return from Germany, as I wrote by the August Packet, and by a Ship from Holland just as I was coming over.[8]
   It is not amiss that the Reverend Doctor refused that Privilege.[9] We shall not want it. And it will be a good Reason for us to refuse him Conveniencies that incommode us. Only that his present Tenant is our good Friend Thomson, we might well object to their Back Gate opening thro' our Lot. Allison will in time want to cut off the Tail of his Lot to build on, and to have a Passage to the Street thro' ours: We may then remember his Civility. Now if he should change his mind and offer the Drain, I charge you not to accept of it.
   Let me ask you once more if you have paid off Mr. Siddons, and got the Deeds recorded? I have several times asked this Question, and received no Answer.[1]

8. None of the letters mentioned in this paragraph has been found.
   9. In the absence of DF's letters to which this is a reply, the matter to which BF refers here must remain somewhat conjectural. It would seem that the Reverend Francis Alison, D.D. (above, IV, 470 n), owned land abutting the Franklins, probably at the southern or Chestnut St. end of their property; that Alison had leased this property to Charles Thomson (whom BF has several times mentioned as a neighbor); and that Alison had refused DF permission to run a drain from the Franklin land through his. The political hostility between BF and Alison would explain some of BF's asperity here.
   1. The deed to the Syddon lot, Sept. 26, 1765, had certainly been recorded; see above, XII, 283–6. At the time the deed was signed Syddon gave his receipt for the whole £900 purchase price, but as DF told BF, Nov. 3, 1765, £400 of that payment was in the form of a bond on which John Hughes had been co-signer with DF; above, XII, 352. Whether she had paid off that obligation during the following year does not certainly appear from surviving records. She would presumably have answered this and the other questions BF asked below in some of her letters of February or March 1767, but no letters from her written in those months have been found.

I want also to know what Money you receiv'd of Brother Peter on Account of the Post Office.[2] Pray send me the Account directly, without delay. It is necessary for me to settle rightly here the Post Office Accounts.

I have fix'd in my Mind, God willing, to return homewards in [*torn*].[3] But yet as something may happen to [detain me?] somewhat longer, I would have you continue [wr]iting as if I were to continue here. Let me know how your Tenants pay, and what Rents you receive? Whether the Wall is equally carry'd up on both sides your Ground?[4] Whether you have insur'd the House?[5] Whether any Use is made of the House Mrs. Broughton liv'd in?[6] &c.

My Love to our Children and Relations, to Mr. Hughes and all Friends. I am, ever, Your affectionate Husband   B FRANKLIN

To Joseph Galloway
ALS: William L. Clements Library

Dear Friend,   London, Dec. 13. 1766

I congratulate you cordially on the News I see with much Pleasure in the Papers, that you are chosen Speaker of the Assem-

2. Presumably during Peter Franklin's tenure of the Philadelphia postmastership, 1764–66, he would be expected to pay over to DF his net receipts. She might use the money for household and personal expenses, but BF would be required to account for it to the postmasters general in England as part of his receipts. While some of the Philadelphia office's records during Peter's incumbency survive (above, XI, 398–402), these are not his actual financial accounts and would be of little help in establishing the net monetary liability of his estate to the Post Office authorities.

3. Unfortunately a hole in the MS here has caused the loss of words in this and the next two lines. Here the first letter appears to be "M" or "N" and the last letter to be "t." Between is enough space for six or eight letters. One may surmise that BF wrote "March next" or "May next," probably the latter.

4. Building of the wall on the west side of the property had been delayed by a dispute among other parties as to the title.

5. For the survey preliminary to the issuance of insurance, see above, pp. 379–80.

6. The lady has not been identified, though she was possibly the person who had made the "silly Complaint" of July 3, above, p. 329. The house probably stood on one of the Philadelphia lots BF owned (see map, above, II, facing p. 456), but it is impossible to say which one.

bly.[7] I foresee great Good to our Country from your being in that Station, as I know you will fill it ably and worthily.

It is long since I have heard from you; not a Line of later Date than Sept. 22.[8] not a Word since the Election, or the Sitting of the Assembly. I wrote to you per the last Packet,[9] and have little to add; for, ever since, there has been a Ferment at Court; every Day producing Changes or Resignations, or expected Changes; so that little else has been attended to, except the Corn Affair in Parliament, and the Act of Indemnity for those that advised the Embargo on Provisions, and acted under it.[1] We have however got the Act thorough [through] for amending the Act of last Year, relating to the Trade to Ireland, &c. which was complain'd of in a Letter from the Committee.[2] It is agreed to by the Lords, and will receive the Assent. Mr. Jackson intends to write if he has time, and will I suppose be more particular: But I expect to get a Copy of the Act on Monday, which I hope will not be too late for the Packet.

Lord Hillsborough is now gone from the Board of Trade to the Post-Office, and Mr. Nugent succeeds him at the Head of that Board.[3] I know not how he will prove, whether a Friend or other-

7. The new Assembly had chosen Galloway speaker on October 14 instead of Joseph Fox, who had held that office since the resignation of Isaac Norris, Oct. 24, 1764. Governor Penn had written his uncle, Thomas Penn, Sept. 12, 1766, that Fox was "lost to the party; he is convinced, that the *great Patriot* as Franklin is called, has been making fools of them all; he is an honest man I believe, and has great Interest in the Town. There is a design to turn him out of the house because he is too much with the Governor and Mr: Allen. This is what is propagated by the party, than which nothing can better shew their malice and rage, for I have not seen him to speak to him these six months that I know of, and he never was more than twice in my house in his life except upon publick business, but they never had any regard to truth." Penn Papers, Hist. Soc. Pa. Penn may have exaggerated Fox's feelings about BF; it seems clear, however, that Fox may have become too much of a moderate for the majority of the anti-proprietary party in the Assembly to accept him any longer as their leader.

8. No letter from Galloway of September 22 has been found.

9. BF's letter of November 8; above, pp. 487–8.

1. See above, pp. 510–16.

2. See above, pp. 419–21, 465–7. The amending act became law on December 16.

3. Lord Hillsborough became joint postmaster general with Sir Francis Dashwood, Lord Le Despenser. The news of their appointment and that

wise to America. He was indeed against us in the Affair of the Repeal: But here Men often alter. One Comfort is, that if he proves an Enemy, the Board has not the Power or Influence it had, being reduc'd to a meer Board of Reference, proposing or moving nothing of itself.[4] I call it a Comfort, because America has rarely, for many Years past, had a Friend among them. The Standing Secretary seems to have a strong Bias against us, and to infect them one after another as they come to it. But I hear he is about to quit.[5]

Mr. Jackson and myself, hoping since the late Changes, that the Ministry will now continue for a while, are using our best Endeavours to obtain a Repeal of the Act restraining the Emission of American Paper Money of legal Tender, which will come under Consideration after the Holidays;[6] and also our other main Point, making all the Impressions possible wherever we can be heard, preparatory to reviving the Petition: For tho' we have heard nothing from you or the Committee, we conclude from the Elections, and your being Speaker, that the Assembly tho' a new one, con-

---

of Nugent to the Board of Trade appeared in *London Chron.*, Dec. 4–6, 1766. Robert Nugent (1709–1788) was created Viscount Clare, Jan. 19, 1767, and Earl Nugent, July 21, 1776, both in the Irish peerage; M.P., 1741–84; a lord of the Treasury, 1754–59; vice treasurer of Ireland, 1760–65, 1768–82; president of the Board of Trade, December 1766–January 1768. He had opposed repeal of the Stamp Act and favored forcing the Assemblies to compensate sufferers from the riots. A former supporter of Newcastle and then of Grenville, he became an adherent of Administration and remained so until the resignation of Lord North in March 1782. *DNB;* Namier and Brooke, *House of Commons*, III, 218–22.

4. For some years the Board of Trade had functioned virtually as a ministerial executive office, with full authority in its own area, but by an order in council of Aug. 8, 1766, it became an office of reference only. Colonial governors were to communicate directly with the secretary of state for the Southern Department, sending to the Board merely copies of their letters to him.

5. John Pownall (1720–1795), brother of Gov. Thomas Pownall, had been on the clerical staff of the Board of Trade since 1741. He was joint secretary, 1753–58, and secretary, 1758–76; after the creation of a secretaryship of state for the Colonies in January 1768, he was also under-secretary of state until 1776, when he became a commissioner of the Excise. Namier and Brooke, *House of Commons*, III, 315–16. An able, knowledgeable, and tenacious civil servant, Pownall was far from quitting in 1766.

6. In spite of efforts, neither BF and Jackson nor the other colonial agents were able to win any general repeal, or even relaxation, of the Currency Act of 1764 during the next session of Parliament.

tinues of the same Mind with their Predecessors. With great and sincere Esteem, I am, Dear Friend, Yours affectionately

B Franklin

Joseph Galloway Esqr

From Deborah Franklin

ALS (incomplete):[7] American Philosophical Society

December the 13 1766

[*First part missing*] the Profile is Cume Safe and is the thing as everey one ses that has seen it I am verey much obliged to you for it everey bodey knows it that has seen it.[8] As to the Candil sticks and Corke Screw[9] thay will doe when you return in the Spring. Be So good as to give my love to Mrs. Stephenson and her Dafter tell me is Polley is a going to be marreyed. I think you sed sum such thing sum time a go. When Shee dus I hope it will be to one that will deserve her.[1] It Semes a dought with me wather Salley writes by this Ship as shee is setting for her Pickter for her Brother Shee is to be playing on the Armonekey.[2] The vesill is gon down so I muste seel this all thow I have not got aresete [a receipt] for the things. I am your a feckshonet wife   D Franklin

From Isaac Hunt   ALS (mutilated):[3] American Philosophical Society

Worthy Sir,   Philadelphia December 14th: 1766.
Your friendly and obliging Favour by Captain Falconer came

7. Only the last page of the letter survives. Fortunately DF placed the date at the end instead of at the beginning, as usual.

8. The "profile" was apparently a medallion made by Josiah Wedgwood, the model of which was a wax representation of BF by Isaac Gosset. See Charles C. Sellers, *Benjamin Franklin in Portraiture* (New Haven, 1962), pp. 69–73, 396.

9. On April 6, 1766 (above, p. 233) BF sent DF "a Gimcrack Corkscrew which you must get some Brother Gimcrack to show you the Use of."

1. BF's letter, mentioning Polly's plans to marry, has not been found. On June 22, 1767, he wrote DF that the prospective match was "quite broke off." APS.

2. This portrait of Sally, if it was ever finished, has not been found. Nor is the artist's name known.

3. The lower half of the sheet is torn away.

safe to Hand.[4] I think myself happy in so good a Friend, and shall always endeavour by an upright Conduct to deserve your Friendship.

The Judgment you have passed on my Essay does me great Honor, and [offers?] a Pleasure in reading that Part of your Letter which I want Words to express. I have not yet published it here, and if I do, shall pay due Attention to your Advice relative to the Dedication.

After great Opposition, I was admitted a few Weeks ago an Attorney of the Court of Common Pleas. The Justices struggled hard to oblige me to make Concessions to the Governor and themselves for my late political Conduct,[5] and for some Time made it the Terms of my Admission. They thought as my Bread depended I would readily comply, but it was a *Meaness* I could not stoop to commit, and bravely stood it out. When they found my Friends beginning to stir and me obstinate, they at length dropped the Proposal of Concessions. But even [so?] then no Favour was to be shewn me! They appointed two Gentlemen of their own Party Mr. Shippen and Mr. Dickinson[6] to examine me, which was accordingly done; and after Examination upon their reporting me qualified, I was sworn an Attorney of the Court, and am now getting my Bread in that Way. The [*half a line torn off*] be their Design what it may, as [*remainder of page missing*] villainous Lye of your being concerned in forming and supporting the Stamp Act.

I gratefully thank you for your good Advice and shall apply myself with great [zeal?] to my Studies, and endeavour to behave with that Diligence and Fidelity in the Prac[tice] which you so kindly recommend. I am also greatly obliged to you for recom-

4. BF's letter has not been found; it probably replied, in part at least, to Hunt's letter of May 21, 1766 (above, pp. 279–82), telling of the failure of his essay to win the Sargent Medal at the College of Philadelphia and of the refusal of the College Trustees to grant him the master's degree because of his political writings. In that letter Hunt had promised to write more fully "by the Packet," so in the missing letter BF was probably replying also to a second one from Hunt.

5. Hunt's *Exercises in Scurrility-Hall* attacking members of the proprietary party.

6. Edward Shippen, Jr. (1729–1806), judge of the Vice Admiralty Court and practicing lawyer, and John Dickinson (1732–1808), both of whom had taken active parts in the pamphlet war of 1764 on the proprietary side.

mending Capt. Falconer to Mr. Strahan. The Books are sent exactly agreeable to my Directions.[7]

I wish you a happy and successful new Year. May seventeen hundred and [sixty] seven be the glorious Æra on which the Change of Government might be effected. I am With Respect and Gratitude Your obliged Friend and humble Servant ISAAC HUNT

To Deborah Franklin

ALS: American Philosophical Society

My dear Child   London, Dec. 15: 1766

I omitted one thing in my Letter of Saturday,[8] which I intended to mention, viz. to desire you to send me three or four young Trees of the Newtown Pippin kind,[9] or else a few Cuttings for Grafts solder'd up in a Tin Tube to keep them from drying. Mr. Bartram or Mr. Roberts will be good enough to tell you which is best, and also the best time to send them. They are for a very good Friend here, whom I would fain oblige. I am, Your affectionate Husband

[Love] to Sally   B FRANKLIN

Addressed: To / Mrs Franklin / Philadelphia / Via New York / per Packet. / B Free FRANKLIN

From James Parker

ALS: American Philosophical Society

Honoured Sir   Nyork, Dec. 15. 1766

Not having received any more than one Letter from you since last May: and the Packet expected this Month not arrived, while this Opportunity offering by a Merchant-man, I take the Liberty to scribble again to you, especially as I this Post have News from Mr. Foxcroft that you consent to allow me £20, per Annum

7. The matters alluded to in this and the preceding sentence would probably be clarified if BF's letter and the one from Hunt "by the Packet" were available.

8. See above, pp. 519–20.

9. A type of apple. There are two varieties of Newtown pippins, the green and the yellow. Lewis Morris and Hugh Roberts sent BF bundles of Newtown pippin scions and of three other varieties of apples, sealed in a canister, the following February. L. Morris and H. Roberts, memorandum to BF, Feb. 21, 1767, Hist. Soc. Pa.

more,[1] for which I return you my Sincere and hearty Thanks assuring you I will always endeavour to have grateful Thoughts: and I hope the Honourable Board, who has Cognizance thereof will allow it, especially if the Additional Trouble and Benefit of the three Canada Offices only be taken into Consideration, which of themselves yield to the Revenue above £500 per An. clear of all Charges to the Revenue, and are a considerable Addition to my Trouble, not to mention 6 or 8 other new Offices more than were before. The Quebeck Post-Master has hitherto sent Bills on this City, generally to the Officers of the Army, the receiving of which gives me no small Trouble, as it will not do to quarrel with those Genttry, who are not the most punctual or honourable People in the World; at least I find them so: In getting the Pay of one £60, upon one of them, I spent as much Time and Shoe-Leather, as I might have earn'd 40s. at Journeyman's Wages only: I don't say this, as begrudging my Trouble, but as a Truth, that might induce the Board to think the additional Allowance not inadequate. However, between that and the Custom-House Office, I find pretty full Employ; as they oblige the Waiters now to a constant and continual Duty, and me in particular. But I have wrote you already about that.

You see I have began a News-paper, and continue it yet without the least appearance of Success, I have yet, but a bare exact 30 Subscribers in this City; and about 60 more in all in the various Parts of the Country, I believe in all that I may hope for Pay near 100; I endeavour after Success, but tis not in my Power to command it: I sent you some of my Papers and now send you a few more, with one of my small Almanacks for your Observation on the following Account.

My Letter, by this Almanack, tho' I did my best: you will see is quite gone: Mr. Holt's Hands abused it as much as used it: both Pica, Long-Primer and Brevier[2] are quite fit only for Old Letter: This Year I printed 3000 Almanacks only, and have the Luck not to sell one Half of them: tho' Holt for Years past, and when I

---

1. The addition to Parker's salary as comptroller and secretary of the American Post Office, for which he had repeatedly expressed a hope in his letters to BF. Most of the matters mentioned here will be familiar to readers of other letters from Parker in this volume.

2. These three type sizes correspond to 12-, 10-, and 8-point, respectively, in the modern American point system.

printed before, did 6000, and we never had many left on our Hands, yet I think mine is as good and as much in it as any of theirs. Now, when I was first set up I got as much Money always as enabled me to get new Letters when the Old were gone, but now tho' I have had new twice before of some Sorts, I am left unable to purchase new: The Money that I should have had of Weyman and Holt to purchase me new Letter with, they took to purchase themselves new with. As to Weyman, tho' he continues in this Goverments's Service, I am assured he owes but every Body that would trust him, and that he keeps close; that Writs are out for him. I have had Writs out for Holt, these 3 Months or more, but he keeps close, and can't be taken, yet he drives on Business somehow, and gets more News for his Paper, in his Chamber, than I can do by Scouring the Docks and trying every Vessel: So much is our Fortune's different, I get no other Work, and yet I do not think that I am worse looked on than I was formerly, or behave worse: Nay I really try to behave as much better as possibly I can. And I want Nothing of Holt, but a Settlement, and reasonable Security: but I can not get him to any Thing: not even the Affair of Hamilton & Bellfour,[3] which I suppose I shall be troubled about. I wrote you before something about Col. Hunter, who ought to see my first Affairs settled according to his Bond to me; tho' Holt has used him in my Opinion as base as he has me, only Col. Hunter is far more able to bear it than I am, and his is but a two Years Matter, whilst mine is a ten Year's Affair. If Holt could live with that Business, and I have starved upon it, whilst I had some other I leave any Man to judge what I must suffer by it, when I ought to have had Half.

As to Benny Mecom, he and I have had abundance of Altercations in Letters; he promises fair, but performs but little. I threaten to displace him and sue him: He says he will try to pay it, but if I sue him, he must go to Goal, and that will pay none: He pays one Rider pretty tollerably now and the Ballance over that is not much yearly, yet if left unpaid, it runs up: The Affair with Holt there not being yet determined, he has paid Holt no Rent, and I am told Holt threatens to distrain on him: How that will be, I don't know, but I am really at a Loss on all sides, If he does not pay this Winter, I believe we must try to put in another Post-Master at least,

3. The Edinburgh firm that said Parker owed them money.

527

tho' I was in Hopes Holt's Matter would have been terminated this Fall, and then I could have taken some Measures about it. Those Materials will be worn out, without my getting any Pay for them: for I will truly affirm, that I have never received one Quarter of the Money in the Whole from that Office, which I paid you for it, exclusive of all my Labour and Fatigue with it: But this is my Luck.

The Hand of God lays heavy on me, and he will remove it in his due Time: I imagine myself as one Strugling with Adversity: and I will not be cast down: but if I perish I will perish with Strugling thro' it.

I told you about my Son: He returned alive, and much recovered of his Sickness three Days ago: but has made a Flemish Voyage as we say: His Behaviour has not been as good abroad as it should have been: He had about £30 in Money and Effects with him; has been gone three Months and ten Days, spent all he had, and came home in Debt for his Passage: I thank God it is no worse, But this is my Luck still: I will still strive: for who knows, but the Tide may Turn one Time or other.

Inclosed is An Account of what Quantity of Letter I would be glad of, if you would answer it to Caslon; I will pay you Interest for it, from the Day you pay it, thankfully.⁴ I would send for Brevier, but I durst not venture it yet: I am really more behind-hand than ever I was, but I have yet Hopes, almost against Hope itself.

Thus have I told you all that occurs at present. You will excuse the bad writing, when I tell you, it is pretty cold, and I much to write various Ways oblige me to write as fast as I possibly can. Hope to write again by the Packet which is momentarily expected: Mean while, all our humble Salutations are sent from Your obliged Humble Old Servant   JAMES PARKER

Dec. 16. 1766

Just after Sealing this, News of the Packet arrived: This Morning, I got your of Octob. 11.⁵ I shall answer it by the Packet, who I suppose will sail in a very few Days.   J.P.

---

4. On March 10, 1767, BF charged Parker's account with a payment to Caslon of £49 5s. 3d. for type and a cash payment of £1 7s. 9d. for insurance. Journal, 1764–1776, p. 11; Ledger, 1764–1776, pp. 6, 7, 10.
5. Not found.

From Richard Price[6]

ALS: American Philosophical Society

Dear Sir   Newington-Green, Dec: 15th: 1766

I received the inclosed letter from Dr. Priestly last Saturday night.[7] I know nothing of the list of books on Electricity mentioned in it. I believe it was not in your letter to him, which pass'd thro my hands. He is in a hurry for it, and if you have it he will be much oblig'd to you for Sending it him, or conveying it to me that I may Send it to him. I am Sorry I [*torn*] the pleasure of meeting you at St. Paul's Coffee: house.[8] I was confined by the toothach and a Swell'd face. I hope nothing will deprive me of this pleasure next thursday night. I am, Dear Sir, with great regard, Your oblig'd humble Servant   RICHD: PRICE

Addressed: To / Dr Franklin / at Mrs Stephenson's / Craven-Street / Strand

Endorsed: Scroog

From [Samuel] Potts[9]

AL: American Philosophical Society

Genl. Post Office 19 Decr 1766

Mr. Potts presents his Compliments to Mr. Francklin and Dsires the favour of his Company to Dine on a Doe of the Postmaster Generals at the Kings Arms Tavern in Cornhill on Monday next at 3 OClock in Afternoon.

Addressed: To / Benjamin Francklin Esqr / Craven Street / Strand

6. On Price, see above, XI, 100 n.

7. Priestley's letter has not been found. The list of books mentioned in it and by Price here was almost certainly the bibliography on electricity Priestley had asked for in his letter to BF of September 21, above, p. 422.

8. At the gatherings of the Club of Honest Whigs, which met fortnightly on Thursday evenings at this coffeehouse; above, XI, 98 n.

9. For Samuel Potts, comptroller general of the General Post Office, see above, X, 149 n. This note has been attributed to Samuel Potts rather than to his uncle Henry, secretary to the General Post Office, on the basis of handwriting comparison.

To Benjamin Rush and Jonathan Potts[1]

ALS: Fordham University Library

Gentlemen,   London, Dec. 20. 1766.

With this I send you Letters for several of my Friends at Edinburgh.[2] It will be a Pleasure to me if they prove of Use to you. But you will be your own best Friends, if you apply diligently to your Studies, refraining from all idle useless Amusements that are apt to lessen or withdraw the Attention from your main Business. This from the Characters you bear in the Letters you brought me, I am persuaded you will do. Letters of Recommendation may serve a Stranger for a Day or two, but where he is to reside for Years, he must depend on his own Conduct, which will either increase or totally destroy the Effect of such Letters. I take the Freedom therefore of counselling you to be very circumspect and regular in your Behaviour at Edinburgh, (where the People are very shrewd and observing) that so you may bring from thence as good a Character as you carry thither, and in that respect not be inferior to any American that has been there before you. You have great Advantages in going to study at Edinburgh at this Time, where there happens to be collected a Set of as truly great Men Professors of the several Branches of Knowledge, as have ever appeared in any Age or Country. I recommend one thing particularly to you, that besides the Study of Medecine, you endeavour to obtain a thorough Knowledge of Natural Philosophy in general. You will from thence draw great Aids in judging well both of Diseases and Remedies; and avoid many Errors. I mention this, because I have observed that a number of Physicians, here as well as in America, are miserably deficient in it. I wish you all Happiness and Success in your Undertakings, And remain, Your Friend and humble Servant   B FRANKLIN

1. Because of its subject matter this letter is placed ahead of four others of the same date, three of which would normally take alphabetical precedence. This letter and the one below to Sir Alexander Dick are the ones of which Benjamin Rush sent copies to his mother, sending her into "Rapters," as DF put it, and winning for BF "much Credit" in Philadelphia. From DF, April [20–25], 29, 1767, APS.

2. For these letters, which Potts and Rush had requested on Oct. 22, 1766, and again on December 10, see the documents immediately below.

P.S. As the Packet would have been too large if all the Letters had been under one Cover, I have directed some of them under Cover to Mr. Potts.

Messrs. Rush and Potts

To William Cullen[3] Draft: American Philosophical Society

Sir,   [December 20, 1766][4]
I beg Leave to recommend to your favourable Notice two young Gentlemen the Bearers of this Letter, Messrs. Rush and Potts Sons of my Friends in Philadelphia. They are at Edinburgh to improve themselves in the Study of Physic, and from the Character they bear of Ingenuity, Industry and good Morals, I am persuaded they will improve greatly under your learned Lectures, and do Honour to your medical School. With the highest Esteem, I am Sir, Your most obedient humble Servant   B FRANKLIN
Dr. Cullen

To Sir Alexander Dick Draft: American Philosophical Society

Dear Sir,   [December 20, 1766]
I am heartily glad that the Information procur'd from my Son, affords any Satisfaction to your Friend Mr. Swinton.[5]
I beg Leave to recommend to your Countenance and Protection the Bearers of this Letter, Mr. Rush and Mr. Potts, Sons of my Friends in Philadelphia, who come to study in your Medical School. They are strongly recommended to me by many of my Acquaintance, as young Gentlemen of Ingenuity, Application, and excellent Morals; and I trust will do Honour to their Instructors. Your Advice as to the Manner of prosecuting their Studies, and sage Counsels as to their Conduct in other respects, must be of

3. For William Cullen, professor of physic at the University of Edinburgh and one of the most influential men in its medical school, see above, VII, 184 n.
4. The drafts of this and the three following letters appear together on a single sheet. The date for all is supplied from the ALS of the letter to Swinton, one of the four.
5. See above, p. 477 n.

great Service to them if you favour them therewith, and will highly oblige Dear Sir Your most obedient and most humble Servant

B F

Please to make My respectful Compliments acceptable to Lady Dick, and the rest of your amiable Family.

Sir Alexr Dick

To [William Robertson]⁶   Draft: American Philosophical Society

Reverend and dear Sir   [December 20, 1766]

The young Gentlemen who will have the Honour of presenting you this Letter are Mr. Potts and Mr. Rush, drawn to Edinburgh by the Fame your Medical School has so justly acquired; intending there to accomplishing them selves there in the Study of Physic. They are recommended to me in the fullest and strongest Manner, by a Number of my Acquaintance in Philadelphia; and are besides Sons of my particular Friends. I beg leave therefore to recommend them to your Countenance and Protection, and request that you would be so kind as to favour them with your good Advice, and wise Counsels, which must be of great Service to them, and will highly oblige, Dear Sir, Your most

To John Swinton

ALS: Josiah C. Trent Collection in the History of Medicine, Manuscript Division, Duke University Library; draft: American Philosophical Society

Sir,   London, Dec. 20. 1766

I am extreamly glad that the Intelligence procur'd from my Son, relating to your Lands in New Jersey, affords you any degree of Satisfaction.⁷ You may rely on his doing you any farther Service in his Power. He has not mention'd to me that he has been at any Expence.

6. So identified because the addressee was a Scottish clergyman who was also attached to the University of Edinburgh, and none of BF's friends fits this description as well as the historian William Robertson, principal of the University; above, IX, 220 n.

7. See above, p. 477 n.

The Bearers Mr. Rush and Mr. Potts, are Sons of two of my Friends in Pennsylvania. They are at Edinburgh to improve themselves in the Study of Physic, and bring with them to me most excellent Characters with respect both to their Ingenuity and Morals. May I take the Liberty of recommending them to your Friendly Offices, as they must, for some time, be Strangers in your City. Every Civility you are so good as to show them, I shall esteem and acknowledge as shown to me. I am, with great Regard, Sir, Your most obedient humble Servant   B FRANKLIN

Mr Swinton

Addressed: To / Mr John Swinton / Broun's Buildings / Edinburgh

Endorsed: B: Franklin Decr 20. 1766

From John Tunnicliff[8]   ALS: American Philosophical Society

Langley Lodge, Near Derby
Honoured Sir   Dec. the 21st. 1766.
I Received your kind Letters for which I return you my Best Thanks.[9] If I can get a good Plantation either in Pensylvania or the Jerseys provided the same, is in a good Neighbourhood and the House High and Ary Sittuation to render it Healthy and near the River Delaware or the River Schoolkill with sufficiant Meadow and Pasture of the White Honey-Suckle, Grass Sufficiant for Summering and Wintering Twenty Milking Cows if such a Plantation should come to your Knowledge Please to let me know of it but I Beg you will give yourself no trouble of making Enquiry as I shall not have it in my Power to render you any Amends, from your Friend and, Humble Servant,   JOHN TUNNICLIFF

I am sure you did not Receive the Woodcocks According to Expectation.[1]

8. Described by John Whitehurst of Derby in 1763 as "a farmer of good Credit, from this neighborhood," Tunnicliff had gone to Philadelphia in 1763 with a view to settling as a farmer in America, but had returned to England by 1765; above, X, 277, 296, 300; XII, 109.

9. No previous letters between BF and Tunnicliff have been found.

1. In October 1765 Tunnicliff had sent BF a hare "as a grateful acknowledgment of the favors confer'd upon him," according to Whitehurst. It was for-

I have Spoke to the Book keeper of the Coach who Saith he will make me Satisfaction if you do not Receive them in the Mean Time. I Beg your Exception of a Woodcock and Partridge.

Addressed: To / Benjamin Franklin Esqr. / at Mrs. Stephensons / Craven Street the Strand / London

From James Parker

ALS: American Philosophical Society

Honoured Sir   New York, Decem. 22. 1766

Yours of the 11th of October is now before me:[2] In Answering of which some various Passions intermix alternately in my Mind: In the first Place your kind Wishes for the Return of my Health, demands my grateful Acknowledgements—and, thank God, considering what Sicknesses have surrounded me, I have escaped wonderfully. The next Thing, you tell me Col. Hunter had given his half of the Printing-Materials to Holt, yet as he was bound for the Performance of the Agreement for the first two Years, and Nothing of it performed, I think he ought to see me have Justice done so far, because as Holt is not bound, nor is my Agreement with Holt, so I can not sue him upon that Account: Indeed I don't find I can upon any other: for he keeps close. In the third Place, you say my voluminous Complaints hurt you, which you suppose I designed they should do: This I think is a little unkind: for I never had any Design to give you any Pain about it: God knows my Heart, the utmost of my Intentions were, if there was Room for any Alteration or Amendment, I might be the Object: I never in my Life, acted any Thing with Design to pain you, but am fully convinced I have often done what has pained me to try if I could give you any Satisfaction: tho' my Endeavours perhaps have often been wrong, as they have failed of the Effect: I believe many

warded by the Derby stage to the coaching inn called The Swan with Two Necks, situated in Lad Lane, London; above, XII, 326–7. Probably the missing woodcocks and the gifts mentioned later in this postscript traveled by the same route. One may hope that the later remembrances reached their intended destination, but no note of thanks from BF to Tunnicliff has been found to settle the point.

2. Not found. It would appear from what follows here that in that letter BF had rebuked Parker more sharply than before for the "voluminous Complaints" with which his letters had been filled.

Times, my Actions have been construed hard by you in these Cases when I did not design it: I have seen it, and been grieved; and I think from an Affection our long Friendship[3] had implanted, I continued my Endeavours to serve you, more in Reality, than from any Fear of Poverty; for to me Distress has long been familiar, and one of the greatest Inducements for me to endeavour to be well in the World, was more from a Desire of not reflecting Dishonour to you, than for my own Sake, whilst you were pleased to favour me with your Friendship: knowing that an Old Friend was better than a new One whether you may think so or not: However the next part of your Letter of your Willingness to suffer me to return from this City,[4] would have given me great Pleasure if I had not began a News-paper again, which tho' I have not a good Prospect of Success in, yet I can't bear the Thoughts of being a Coward, after I have put my Hand to the Plough, to turn back in the Day of Battle. I had rather dye than fly; without the Retreat was laudable, which in the present Case I can't see: The Hand of God has been upon me now almost two Years: and tho' I will humble myself before him, yet will I not forego nor forsake my Integrity: If he slays me, yet will I trust in him: Perhaps the Tide may turn: and I can but fall at last: To come here and begin and make a Splutter, and then yield before I am beat out of the Field, is such a Mark of Cowerdice that I can not bear: However, if after a Year or two's Trial, when I have convinced my Antagonists, that I am not to be scared out of my Senses, if there be Room for a Retreat, I shall gladly embrace it: tho' had it not been for the Stamp-Act I believe I should last Year have fixed my Residence in Burlington; many Things seeming to invite me thither, but God in his Providence saw fit to order it otherwise: If any Thing I can say, can give You or that Gentleman[5] any Pleasure about the Office in the Customs I would do it; for altho' there is actually the Labour I have asserted in it, yet inasmuch as both yours and his Intentions

3. Parker had first begun to work for BF in or about 1733, and they had entered into a six-year partnership in 1742; above, II, 341–5.

4. This sounds as if BF had persuaded the postmasters general in England to relax their requirement that the American comptroller reside in New York, or at least that BF had said he would try to get such a relaxation. In neither case have the editors found any documentary evidence to support the supposition.

5. Presumably the unidentified individual in England through whose good offices BF had procured the post in the New York Customs House for Parker.

sprang from a Desire of befriending me, even tho' it were ten Times worse than it is, I should be an ungrateful Wretch not to return the most sincere Thanks to you both: Were there any Thing else in my Power that could shew my Gratitude I would do it; For tho' I cannot say in my Heart, it was the most acceptable Thing in the World in me, to come to this City; yet inasmuch as I would not pay that Disregard to your Kindness which a Refusal would do, I came the more Readier. And tho' I have the Misfortune not to meet with the Success I might flatter myself with, I know Diligence and Perseverance, will do much: Its true, I grow old, I cannot stand to my Work as formerly, my Legs and my Strength failing me, yet I will not despair. My Letters have been much abused in the latter End of Holt's Time; but perhaps I may get new soon; I will wait. And tho' this City is grown a very dear Place, yet inasmuch as you have been pleased to consent with Mr. Foxcroft to the advancing the Allowance in the Post-Office £20, more, I flatter myself I [shall] rub through, and if I can, will make you Amends for all your past Kindness: And if hereafter it shall please Heaven to smile on me any more, I will endeavour with a thankful Heart to behave as patiently as I can: I have met with a great many Crosses, and have deserved many more: I have met with many Favours and Blessings, and all these I have been undeserving of. I pray for Wisdom, Resignation and a thankful Heart, and whether I ever take your Advice or not, hope you will not refrain giving it, whenever it shall suit you so to do.

A few Days ago I wrote you per the Snow Amelia, Capt. St. Clair from this City;⁶ and sent for some new Types: If I have a Prospect of Success I may try for some more: with that I sent some News Papers, and beg you would please to speak to somebody to send me some, when Opportunities offer: which I must satisfy according to a reasonable Custom: I send the One printed since.

My Son I told you was just come home, pretty much recovered of [his] Sickness, but it had been a costly Voyage to me: Whether he will do better or not Time only will shew: The Appearance of Health begins to shew itself a little in my Family more than has been these two Years. I hope in God we shall once more have it: tho' my Gout often threatens me, yet have I had less of it this Fall, than I have these several Years.

6. Above, pp. 525–8.

Dec. 23. Nothing extraordinary this Day, but closing this Letter: And as I expect you will be preparing to return soon, I wish you a pleasant Voyage home. We all send our respectful Complements, whilst I remain Your most obliged Servant   JAMES PARKER.

Addressed: For | Dr Benjamin Franklin | London

Endorsed: Parker

From [Andrew] Cheap and from Mr. and Mrs. [Israel] Wilkes[7]   AL (two): American Philosophical Society

These two invitations are printed together because they are written on the same sheet of paper, though in different hands, and clearly relate to each other. They were certainly written on the same day. Though December 23 fell on a Thursday in 1760 as well as in 1766, this paper and its contents are assigned to the latter year because the people mentioned seem to have been friends of Franklin's second mission rather than his first.

Woodstock Street, near New Bond Street.
[December 23, 1766]
Mr. Cheap's Compliments to Dr. Franklin. He is afraid that he has been deprived of the Honour of his Company to Dinner by his not knowing the Situation of Woodstock Street.[8] He therefore presumes to desire he will be so good as [to] spend the Evening with Mr. and Mrs. Barrows[9] and some more of his Friends.

7. The Reverend Andrew Cheap (d. 1803), B.A., Oxford (Baliol), 1754; M.A., 1757; vicar of Sutton on the Forest, March 1768, in succession to Lawrence Sterne; prebendary of York, December 1776; *Gent. Mag.*, XXXVIII (1768), 146; XLVI (1776), 580; LXXIII (1803), pt. 2, 1260; Joseph Foster, *Alumni Oxonienses, 1715–1886* (London, 1887), I, 243. Israel Wilkes (d. 1805) was the elder brother of John Wilkes (1727–1797), the radical writer. Israel and his wife are often mentioned in later letters of the Stevensons and other friends of BF. A letter from Mrs. Emma Thompson to BF, Feb. 6, 1777, mentioned all the people whose names appear in these two notes. APS.

8. Woodstock Street is a short street running southeast from Oxford Street, parallel to and a little west of New Bond Street.

9. Probably Thomas Barrow, who served as a paymaster in the British Army under General Gage in 1772 (and possibly also under Bouquet in 1759). He and his wife were in New York City when the Revolution began; he took refuge on a warship in the harbor, while she remained in the city. BF called on her there in the spring of 1776 and, in answer to an inquiry from

Tuesday 23d Decr. [1766]
For fear Mr. and Mrs. Wilkes should not have the pleasure of seeing Dr. Franklin this Evening in Woodstock Street, they take this Opportunity of begging the favour of his Company on Thursday next at four in Red Lyon Square[1] to eat his Christmas dinner there with Mr. and Mrs. Barrow and Cheap.

From the Committee of America Merchants

AL: American Philosophical Society

Kings Arms Cornhill Monday 29th: [December 1766?][2]
The Committee of America Merchants meet this Evening 6 'Clock and desire Mr. Franklins attendance.

Addressed: For. / Mr: Franklin / Cravenstreet

From [William Franklin[3]]

AL (fragments):[4] American Philosophical Society

[December 1766][5]
[*Top part of first surviving sheet is missing.*] Side the Water. But, if

their mutual friend Emma Thompson, reported on this call in a letter of Feb. 8, 1777. Lib. Cong. Where their London residence was in 1766 is not known.

1. Red Lion Square lies to the east of Bloomsbury Square and Southampton Row and north of High Holborn.

2. While the 29th of a month fell on a Monday seven times during 1765–68, the editors are inclined to assign this note to Monday, Dec. 29, 1766, because during that winter the merchants and the American agents were meeting often to concert action in an attempt to obtain repeal of the Currency Act of 1764. BF played a leading role in these efforts, as several documents in the next volume will show.

3. Identified by handwriting comparison.

4. The lower parts of two half-sheets survive, each written on both sides. Almost half the lines at the top of each of the four pages are gone and, because the tears extend diagonally downward, parts of the first five or six surviving lines of each page are also lost. The remaining parts of these pages are printed here in what appears from the context to be the correct order, with the breaks and tears indicated within brackets.

5. Many of the matters mentioned in this letter show that it was written toward the end of December 1766, as the footnotes will demonstrate.

we [*torn*] late Publications in Virginia [*torn*] still remains a considerable Spirit [*torn*] and Opposition.[6] They have been told, and [*torn*] must know, that tho' the Parliament have solemnly [dec]lar'd their Right to tax America,[7] they do not mean to exercise it in future: Our pretended Patriots however are not satisfied that the Claim should lie dormant, but seem determin'd to oblige the Parliament to renounce it, or else to occasion fresh Disturbances. For this purpose, they are taking Pains to get the Assemblies to remonstrate against it, and to pass a Bill of Rights in Opposition to that of Parliament. Some are led to this Conduct in hopes of distinguishing themselves as the Friends of their Country, others with a View of promoting their Popularity and thereby securing their Elections, others out of a mere Propensity to Mischief, and others again in [*top part of verso page missing*] for a Dispute with [*torn*] among them, who have any [*torn*] fail to push him on Points [*torn*] cannot well avoid disputing, if [torn] with his Duty. I was therefore very sorry [*torn*] Letter from Mr. Deberdt to the Assembly of Massachusetts Bay [*torn*] in the Papers,[8] in which he mentions a Conversation with Lord S. nearly similar to that you had with him.

Many of our Friends were under a good deal of Apprehensions lest Lord S. should have a Partiality for the Proprietor on Account of the Family Connection. But I have made them very happy by acquainting them with the Sentiments his Lordship express'd to you on the Occasion.[9] Most certainly Mr. Penn had better part

6. Evidently a reference to an address of the Virginia House of Burgesses, Nov. 12, 1766, and a resolution of the House, Nov. 20, 1766, in both of which the King was thanked for repealing the Stamp Act, but in a manner that struck some as being not a little insolent. Gipson, *British Empire*, XI, 7–9.

7. In the Declaratory Act, March 18, 1766 (6 Geo. III, c. 12), Parliament affirmed its right "to make laws and statutes of sufficient force and validity to bind the colonies and people of America, subjects of the Crown of Great Britain, in all cases whatsoever."

8. *Pa. Gaz.*, Nov. 20, 1766, published a letter of Sept. 19, 1766, from Dennys De Berdt, the Massachusetts agent, to Thomas Cushing, speaker of the Mass. House, in which he described an interview with Shelburne on the preceding day. His Lordship was conciliatory toward the colonies, De Berdt wrote, but insisted that "the Dignity of Government must be maintained as well as a due Regard to the Administration here."

9. In an interview with Lord Shelburne in the fall of 1766, reported to Joseph Galloway in a letter of Oct. 11, 1766, BF said that Shelburne told him

with his Government if he inclines that either himself or his Posterity should be able to avoid having troublesome Contentions with the Inhabitants. Matters are now carried too far, and the [*end of first surviving sheet.*]

[*Top part of second surviving sheet is missing.*][1] Lordship's Dislike to you [*torn*] to the latter) has lately said that [*torn*] how it happens, but so it is, that [*torn*] the Ear of Lord S. and that you are full as [*torn*] respected[2] by him as ever you were by any of his [pr]edecessors in Office: For his Part, he don't know but a Change of Government may take place some Time or other, but that the Proprietor had lately assur'd him that if he did dispose of it to the Crown, he would take Care of all his Friends there, and make it a Condition that his Nephew John Penn should have the Government during his Life, so that none of those who push'd for the Change would probably be the better for it, if it should happen." This Alteration in Mr. Allen's Tone, added to what Lord S. said to you, makes our Friends incline to think that the Proprietor has serious Thoughts of parting with his Government and that it may be owing in some Measure to his Lordship's Advice [*top part of verso page missing*][3] be one there let who [*torn*] as Numbers of People un [*torn*] have an Idea of the Value of [*torn*] [con]tinually resorting there from all [*torn*] The Question therefore is, Whether it would [*torn*] eligible on all Accounts to have a well regu[lated?] Government established there at once, than to [wait?] till it is become the Residence of a numerous and lawless Banditti? Besides the Garrison which is now at Fort Chartres to keep Possession of that Country are

---

"that he was of the opinion Mr. Penn ought to part with the Government voluntarily, and said he had often told him so." Shelburne also assured BF that his marriage to Thomas Penn's wife's niece would not prejudice him against the Assembly. Above, p. 448.

1. What follows here is obviously part of an alleged quotation from Chief Justice William Allen. The renewed references to Lord Shelburne and to the possibility of Penn's surrendering his government suggest strongly that this passage is a continuation (with an unfortunate gap) of the discussion printed immediately above.

2. The last two tears are just about long enough to permit a guess that the missing words would make this passage read: ". . . that you have won the Ear of Lord S. and that you are full as much respected . . . ."

3. In the missing part of this page WF's topic has obviously changed to the prospective colony in the west.

oblig'd to depend on the French Inhabitants for their Provisions, who (as appears by a Journal which I have seen of an Officer just return'd from thence[4]) only supply them from Hand to Mouth, that they may have it in their Power when they see convenient to starve them. This has occasion'd the General to send them a Quantity, last Summer, all the Way from Fort Pitt. But [*end of second surviving sheet.*]

To [John Hughes] ALS (incomplete): American Philosophical Society

The addressee of the letter of which this is a fragment and the matter to which it refers are made clear by a letter Franklin wrote Galloway, June 18, 1767 (Princeton Univ. Lib.), and by entries in Franklin's accounts dated June 2, 1769. During Franklin's stay in America, 1762–64, one Mitchell (perhaps Abraham Mitchell, a Philadelphia hatter) asked him for a letter of credit to be used in England to buy some lands in partnership with John Hughes. Hughes engaged, Sept. 21, 1764, to guarantee Franklin against loss. On the strength of Franklin's letter of credit Mitchell borrowed £260 from the London banker, Henton Brown. Not being reimbursed by Mitchell, Brown began to press Franklin for payment, and Franklin now sought assurance that Hughes would meet his obligation promptly.

[1766][5]

[*First part missing*] satisfy Mr. Henton Brown as you desire, [*torn*] what you say that you shall be able to pay it [*torn*] four Months: My Expences here are very con[siderabl]e, and my Income much lessened of late by the [terminat]ion of my Partnership with Mr. Hall, so that I [shall?] be straitned in the Spring when about to

4. This journal is almost certainly that of Capt. Harry Gordon, Gen. Thomas Gage's chief engineer, who accompanied George Croghan on his mission to Fort Chartres in the summer of 1766. Charged with charting the courses of the Ohio and Mississippi Rivers, Gordon sailed down to New Orleans with Croghan at the conclusion of his negotiations and from there to New York, preceding Croghan (who arrived in New York harbor, Jan. 10, 1767) by a few weeks. Gordon's journal is printed in Alvord and Carter, eds., *The New Régime 1765–1767*, pp. 290–311. See also Nicholas B. Wainwright, *George Croghan Wilderness Diplomat* (Chapel Hill, [1959]), pp. 233–8.

5. Mention of the recent dissolution of the Franklin-Hall partnership and of BF's intention of returning home the following spring certainly dates this letter in the latter part of 1766.

return [if?] you disappoint me. I am and ever shall be with sincere Esteem Dear Friend, Yours very affectionately   B FRANKLIN[6]

Passages for Priestley's History of Electricity

Drafts: American Philosophical Society

As other documents in this volume show, Franklin was one of several friends who read sections of Joseph Priestley's *History of Electricity* while it was in preparation during 1766, offered information and suggestions, and on occasion submitted revised or expanded phraseology at various points. Among Franklin's surviving papers are two sheets containing passages in his hand which appear largely unchanged in Priestley's printed work. These papers contain cancellations and revisions themselves and are obviously drafts of suggested new or expanded phraseology that Franklin sent to Priestley and that the latter gratefully accepted, revised slightly, and then incorporated in the book.

The first passage appears in two parts in the *History of Electricity*. The first part of this passage, as far as the word "backwards," forms a short paragraph near the bottom of page 50. The second part becomes a paragraph near the top of page 51. The second and somewhat longer passage occupies almost the whole of page 424. Notes are appended here to indicate the changes Priestley made in each of Franklin's contributions.

[1766]

The Doctrine of two different Electricities produc'd by exciting different Substances and of their Effects on each other[7] seems to have been dropt after Monsr. Dufay[8]—and those Effects ascrib'd to other Causes; which is an Instance that Science sometimes goes backwards. Many Years after, Mr. Kinnersley,[9] a Friend of Dr. Franklin's, being at Boston in New England, made some Experi-

6. In the spring of 1769 Hughes paid the firm of Brown & Collinson £360 for Mitchell's loan and £81 12s. 10d. for accrued interest. Before the bills of exchange reached England £1 12s. 10d. more interest had accrued; BF paid it and charged it on his books to the account of his friend Hughes. Journal, 1764–1776, p. 19; Ledger, 1764–1776, pp. 14, 29.

7. In the place of the seven words following "Substances," Priestley wrote: "considerable as the discovery of it was."

8. See above, IV, 423.

9. Priestley: "It will be seen that, many years after, Mr. Kinnersley of Philadelphia," etc.

ments which again show'd that Difference of Electricities.[1] He communicated those Experiments to Dr. Franklin, who repeated and explain'd them. See Franklin's Letters.[2]

II

It ought to be so on Dr. F.'s Principles.[3] If one Side be rubbed by the Finger; it acquires from the Finger some of the Electric Fluid. This being spread on the Glass as far as the Rubbing extended, repels an equal Quantity of that contain'd in the other Side of the Glass, and drives it out on that Side, where it stands as an Atmosphere, and so[4] both sides are found *plus*. If the unrubb'd Side were in Contact with a Conductor communicating with the Earth, the Electric Fluid would be carried away, and then that Side would be left *apparently* in the natural State. If the electric Fluid found on the unrubb'd Side was really part of that which had been communicated by and from the Finger, and so had actually *perm-*[*eated*] the Glass, it might, when conducted away, be continually replac'd by fresh permeating Fluid communicated in the same Manner: But if the Effect is continually diminishing, while the suppos'd Cause repeated, continues the same, there seems reason to [doubt] the Relation[5] between that Cause and the Effect. It appears difficult to conceive how Electric Fluid having pass'd thro' a permeable Body, should make it more difficult for other Electric Fluid to follow, till at length none would pass thro' at all.[6]

1. Priestley: "of the two electricities."

2. Above, IV, 263–4, 275–6. These last words appear in Priestley as a footnote: "See his Letters." At a blank corner of this paper BF wrote in a different ink for some purpose unknown: "Devonshire Street Bishopgate street."

3. Priestley: "upon this I cannot help observing that it ought to be so on Dr. Franklin's principles."

4. Priestley: "so that."

5. Priestley: "the supposed relation."

6. Priestley revised the final sentence to read: "For it appears difficult to conceive how some electric fluid, having passed through a permeable body, should make it more difficult for other particles of the same electric fluid to follow, till, at length, none could pass at all."

From John Canton

AL: American Philosophical Society

[1766][7]

Mr. Canton presents his Compliments to Dr. Franklin and begs to be inform'd whether, or not, in Writing to Dr. Priestley, he has mention'd Mr. C's wanting Æpinus's *Tentamen Theoria Electricitatis et Magnetismi*[8] for Mr. Cavendish;[9] if not, Mr. C would beg the Favour of a Frank.

Addressed: To | Doctor Franklin

From Peter Collinson

AL: American Philosophical Society

[1766?–1768][1]

P Collinson very Respectfull Inquires after his Dear Friends Health hopes to See him next Thurday.

The Inclosed Letter Shows the purpose of the Ingenious Mr. Moors[2] waiting on You to Show his Curious Types.[3]

Addressed: To | Benn. Franklin Esqr | at Mrs Stephensons in | Craven Street

7. So dated by the reference to the book by Aepinus, which BF had sent Priestley in April, to assist in his preparation of his *History of Electricity;* see above, p. 246.

8. For this book, in which Aepinus tried to use BF's electrical theories to explain the phenomenon of magnetism, see above, X, 204.

9. Canton apparently means Henry Cavendish, not his father Charles; see above, X, 41 n. Henry developed Aepinus' theory at length in a paper, "An Attempt to explain some of the principal Phenomena of Electricity, by Means of an Elastic Fluid," published in *Phil. Trans.,* LXI (1771), 584–677.

1. This note cannot have been written later than Aug. 11, 1768, the date of Collinson's death.

2. This may have been Isaac Moor or Moore, a Bristol type founder, who established himself in London about 1766 in the firm of Pine & Moor, but it is more likely Edward Rowe Mores (1731–1778), antiquarian, student and collector of typographical materials, and author of a *Dissertation upon English Typographical Founders and Foundaries* (London, 1778). Mores and BF corresponded in 1773 and in his book Mores noted that Thomas James (d. 1736 or 1738), a famous type founder, had conducted his business in a building once occupied by Samuel Palmer, in whose house worked a journeyman (BF) "well known since in the philosophical world." For Mores, see *DNB*.

3. On an otherwise blank page of this letter are sketched some script types: an *h* alone, and the letters *h, i,* and *m,* and an em-quad set together.

From [John] Hunter[4]

AL: American Philosophical Society

Tuesday Noon [1766?]

Mr. Hunter intreats the favour of Docr. Franclin's Company to Tea this Evening as Mr. H. is going to Bath to Morrow, and Wishes to see Mr. Franclin very much first.

From George Maddison[5]

AL: American Philosophical Society

[1766?–1773]

G. Maddison called to acquaint Dr. Franklin that the Packets for America do not go from the Gen. Post Office till Saturday night.

From Thomas Osborne[6]

AL: American Philosophical Society

[c.1766][7]

Mr. Osborn's Compliments to Dr. Francklin and If he writes to

4. For John Hunter, a merchant of Hampton, Va., and a colonel in the Va. militia, who settled in England by the fall of 1765, see above, VI, 223 n; XII, 354. As a kinsman and bondsman of John Holt, Hunter may have wished to discuss with BF the involved business relations of Holt and James Parker, often mentioned in Parker's letters of this year.

5. George Maddison (1747–1783) had been brought into the Foreign Office of the Post Office by 1765 by his uncle, Anthony Todd, secretary of the Post Office. In 1773 Maddison entered the diplomatic service and was posted to the Hague, where he was secretary to the embassy until 1780. He was an under-secretary of state, 1782–3, and in 1783 he was secretary to the British embassy in Paris, where he was charged with negotiating the establishment of postal service with the independent United States, Kenneth Ellis, *The Post Office in the Eighteenth Century* (London, 1958), pp. 86, 94, 147; Todd to BF, June 25, Aug. 22, Sept. 19, 1783, APS.

6. For Thomas Osborne, the foremost London bookseller of his day, see above, VII, 176 n.

7. This curious note can not have been written later than 1767, the year of Osborne's death. Evidently it was written after BF returned to England in 1764, because if he had still been in Philadelphia, Osborne would doubtless have written him directly, as he had done before (above, XI, 478), rather than send a message to him by his former landlady, Mrs. Margaret Stevenson. The reference to the "Quakers bible," Anthony Purver's *A New and Literal*

Dr. Fothergill that He woud be so kind as to recomend me to the Dr. to publish or purchase the Quakers bible[8] and shoud be Oblidged If he woud Inform me what No. of Books might goe off in His part of the World. Mr. Bevan[9] is my friend and will serve me.

Endorsed:[1] Mr Osborne gave this to Mrs Stevenson when she was at Tunbridge and desired her to send the substance of it in better words to Dr Franklin. This way he is sure to have the substance.

From Joseph Priestley

ALS (incomplete): American Philosophical Society

[1766][2]

[*First part missing*] ly; and in a direct line, I some times inclosed them [in?] small glass tubes.

I make these experiments with great care, as my machine is constructed so as to electrify with equal strength by the rubber, or

---

Translation of the Old and New Testaments, could put the note in 1765, for the work was published late in 1764 and was selling throughout the British Isles and the colonies during the next year (*Pa. Ga₃.*, June 13, 1765, advertised it for sale). Of the 1766 dating the editors are not completely confident, however, and profess to be considerably perplexed by this note.

8. Fothergill had purchased the copyright to the Purver bible from the author for £1,000 and paid the cost of printing it from his own pocket. R. Hingston Fox, *Dr. John Fothergill and his Friends* (London, 1919), p. 27.

9. Probably Timothy Bevan, a wealthy London Quaker apothecary; see above, VIII, 437 n. His brother, Sylvanus, died in 1765.

1. The endorsement appears to be in the hand of Mrs. Stevenson's daughter, Polly.

2. This fragment is devoted to Priestley's electrical experiments and, since he was busy performing them in 1766 for his own edification and for the purpose of writing his *History of Electricity* with greater confidence, it is dated in this year. It is quite possible that the letter was written in the winter or the early spring of 1766 because Priestley mentions having sent John Canton an account of an experiment "which, proves that glass, when red hot, is pervious to electricity" and in letters to Canton of Feb. 14, 1766, and March 29, 1766, he describes two experiments he has made to prove this point. Robert E. Schofield, *A Scientific Autobiography of Joseph Priestley (1733–1804)* (Cambridge, 1966), pp. 15, 26–7.

by the conductor, and I can change the mode of operation in an [*instant?*].³

I am still in a course of experiments upon glass [*torn*] but have not yet brought any thing to a state worthy of presenting to you. Many things have occurred which surprize and puzzle me, but that gives me no concern.

I have desired Mr. Canton and Mr. Price to show you the letters I have written to them. I gave Mr. Canton an account of experiment which proves that glass, when red hot, is pervious to electricity.⁴ Dear Sir, the sense I have of the honour of your acquaintance, and the pleasure I have in communicating to you the result of my little experiments, give me an ardour in these pursuits, which I never felt before. I am with the greatest respect, and with compliments to Messr. Canton and Price, your &c. J Pries[tley]

Addressed: To / Dr Franklin / at Mrs Stephens' / in Craven street, in the Strand / London

From Sir John Pringle   AL: American Philosophical Society

Sat. Morning [1766–1775]⁵

Sir J Pringle's Compliments to Dr. Franklin and acquaints him that he now recollects that the gentleman from Geneva⁶ was not to call till 8 o'cl this evening and therefore begs that if Dr. F. is not engaged he would favour with his company, in order to gratify that learned gentleman.

Also, that Dr. F. would further oblige him by eating with him tomorrow his beef with a rice piloe [*pilau, pilaf*] after the Indian manner.

Addressed: Dr Franklin

3. Priestley described this machine in *History of Electricity,* pp. 530–4, and illustrated it in Plate VII.

4. Priestley described in *History of Electricity,* pp. 610–11, the experiment on this matter that he had reported to Canton on Feb. 14, 1766.

5. Pringle was made a baronet, June 3, 1766, and this note could have been written any time after that date until BF left England in 1775. Pursuant to editorial practice, it is placed here at the end of its earliest possible year.

6. Not identified.

From [Mary] Rich

AL: American Philosophical Society

Grosvenor Square fryday [1766–1769][7]
As Miss Rich finds her Servant deliverd the money and Reciept to a Little Girl, She is desirous to know that Dr. Franklin recievd it, therefore begs he will just write her a line by the penny Post. She will also be obligd to him for the Direction to the man that made the Spindle &ca in Case She Should at any time want his Assistance. She finds so much difficulty in keeping the Glasses turning the right way, that She has some thoughts of having a handle made by which it may be turnd by another person while She plays.[8]

Addressed: To / Doctor Franklin / in Craven Street / near the / Strand.

7. If the writer of this note is indeed Mary Rich, the daughter and sister of distinguished soldiers (both named Sir Robert Rich), a friend of Horace Walpole, and, as this note reveals, a player of the armonica, then it can not have been written later than July 18, 1769, the date of her death. *London Chron.,* July 20–22, 1769. One reason for placing this note here is the reference to the "Little Girl" at Craven Street, to whom Miss Rich's servant delivered money; this was probably Sally Franklin, BF's second cousin once removed (A.5.2.3.1.1.1), who came to stay with Mrs. Stevenson in the spring of 1766. See above, p. 446.

8. Some armonicas were indeed made to be turned by a handle in this manner instead of by a foot treadle. One such, privately owned, is illustrated in R.T.H. Halsey *et al,* compilers, *Benjamin Franklin and His Circle A Catalogue of an Exhibition* (N.Y., Metropolitan Museum of Art, May 11–Sept. 13, 1936), p. 133.

548

Index

Compiled by Mary L. Hart

INDEX

Hughes, 107, 265; visits DF, 117; prints BF's Examination, 126; receives BF's books, 203; and BF electrical machine, 203, 265, 307, 342, 394, 410, 457, 475; business affairs with Weyman, 264–5, 527; printing of *N.Y. Gazette*, 264 n, 306 n, 454, 472 n, 492, 505; on weather, 266, 392, 455–6, 473; delivers customs certificate and bond, 300, 325; on New Haven post-office affairs, 301, 341 (*see also* Holt, John; Mecom, Benjamin); prints *Connecticut Gazette*, 301 n; prints broadside against Holt, 306 n; illness in family, 312, 455, 472–3, 491; wants instructions on N.Y. post office, 475; customs salary of, 326 n, 343, 394, 458, 473–4; post-office salary, 328, 394, 456, 473, 525–6; business affairs with J. Chew, 328; on slow business in N.Y., 341; comment on BF-Hall accounts, 341–2; appointed New Haven postmaster, 341 n; type for, 343–4, 491 n, 528; prints N.J. *Laws* and *Votes*, 345, 393 n, 493 n; prints almanac, 393 n, 410, 473 n, 492; books and stationery for, 457–8, 474, 476 n; account of, charged, 457 n; N.Y. post-office duties, 458; questions need for N.Y. move, 475, 494; relationship to Colden in N.Y. offices, 475 n; asks BF's advice, 476; apprentice leaves, 476; but returns, 493; wants to exchange newspapers, 476–7; trouble with son, 491, 505–6; sends almanacs and newspapers to BF, 505, 526; on friendship with BF, 534–5; letters from, 10–18, 104–10, 202–4, 262–6, 300–12, 325–8, 340–5, 392–5, 409–13, 454–9, 472–7, 490–4, 505–6, 525–8, 534–7; mentioned, 193, 379 n, 500 n, 545 n
Parker, Jane: marriage, 379 n; illness, 455, 472, 491; greetings from, 459
Parker, Mary Ballareau, greetings from, 459
Parker, Samuel (nephew of James): debt to J. Parker, 10 n; in Parker-Holt dispute, 301–3; absconds to West Indies, 302 n
Parker, Samuel Franklin: illness, 11, 12, 14, 32, 117 n, 203, 312, 345, 392, 455, 472–3; voyage to N.C., 392–3, 392 n, 412, 455, 473, 491, 505 n; death rumored, 412–13, 491; Parker gets letter, 505–6; returns to N.Y., 491 n, 505 n, 528, 536; mentioned, 11 n
Parliament: relationship of colonies, assemblies to, 22, 211; addresses to king, printed, 39; compensates colonies, 76; colonial attitude to, after Stamp Act, 136; colonial views on right to regulate trade, commerce, 142, 161; authority of,

disputed, 308; and establishment of Georgia, Nova Scotia, 361; in session, 448 n; in domestic crisis over wheat shortage, 511–12. *See also* Commons, House of; Lords, House of; Representation, parliamentary; Taxation, parliamentary.
Patent Graduated Measures, creation of, 459 n
Paving, of Chancery Lane, 9
Paxton Boys, attack Indians, 181 n
Pearce, Capt., commands *Friendship*, 445 n
Pemberton, Israel, mentioned, 260 n
Pemberton, James: biog. note, 260 n; advises BF on reporting to Committee of Correspondence, 260; defends BF, 295; in 1766 election, 447 n; letter from, 260–2; mentioned, 177 n, 262 n, 314
Pendergrass, in N.Y. riots, 334
Penington, Edward: identified, 507 n; to advise S. Penn on Pennsbury Manor, 177; forwards letter to S. Penn, 177; sends account of N.J. land, 333; S. Penn's will to be sent to, 506–7; replies to BF, 507 n; letter to, 177; mentioned, 495
Penn, Ann: identified, 417 n; greetings from, 124, 417; condolences to, 506; BF advises, 507; marriage, 507 n; changes mind on Pa. land sale, 507 n; letter from, 417; letter to, 506–7; mentioned, 124 n
Penn, John: quoted, 292–3 n, 396 n, 521 n; and Pa. stamp demonstrations, 283 n; 294–5 n; issues proclamation on squatters, 398 n; assents to Assembly acts, 467 n; reports building of Bettering House, 495–6; reappointed governor, 496; protection for, in change of government, 540; mentioned, 466 n
Penn, Lady Juliana Fermor, mentioned, 448 n
Penn, Springett: identified, 123 n, 283 n; receives Penington letter, 123; BF encourages proprietorship claim, 123 n; wants loan for lottery ticket, 124; BF's letter forwarded to, 177; may sell Pennsbury Manor, 177, 333; stays in Ireland, 177; illness, death, 283 n, 417, 417 n, 506 n; T. Wharton asks about Pa. property, 283–4; T. Penn feared taking advantage of, 333 n; BF on death of, 506; will to go to Penington, 506–7; terms of will, 506 n; BF advises on estate of, 507; letter from, 123–4; mentioned, 495
Penn, Thomas: extract of letter sent to BF, 179, 190; quoted, 179–80 n, 466 n; is assured against change of Pa. government, 190; claim to part of Pennsbury Manor, 190; account of N.J. land sent to, 333; feared taking advantage of S. Penn, 333 n; and quitrent, land sales in Pa.,

570

Printing office, valuation of Franklin & Hall's, 60–3, 105
Printing press, Mecom's: sent to Phila., 109, 110; Goddard uses, 500–1
Privy Council: BF's application for land grant, 123; and Pa. petition for royal government, 180 n, 466 n; action on Pa. acts, 267 n, 467 n; in domestic crisis over corn shortage, 512
Proprietary government, Pa.: Galloway on abuses under, 180–1; constitution of colonies under, 358; quitrents, land purchase under, 358; and appointment of judges, in Pa., 361
Proprietary party: strengthened by rumored rejection of Pa. petition, 190; and proposed change to royal government, 318–19, 324; doubts authenticity of BF's Examination, 396–7; attacks on BF, 268 n, 273, 285, 313; opposes Pa. resolve on King's requisitions, 293–4; and Pa. stamp demonstrations, 294; Shelburne expected to be partial to, 448 n, 539; electoral defeat, 481
Proprietors of the Pennsylvania Land Company in London. See London Land Company.
Protests against Stamp Act repeal: BF's marginalia in, 207–32; printed, 207–8; imprint of, 208 n; BF sends to Pa., 240
Providence Gazette, Goddard prints, 306 n
Public Advertiser, BF pieces in, 4, 54, 382
Purdy (Purdie), Alexander, prints Va. Gaz., 108 n
Purver, Anthony, translates Bible, 545 n
Pyrlaeus, John Christopher, and Mohawk grammar, 407 n

Quakers: support sought for colonial independence, 37; in Pa., 132; in dispute over Syddons lot, 445 n
Quebec, post office in, 412, 456, 494
Quitrents: in Pa., 358, 359–60; in colonies, 374; in Va., 374

Ramsey, William, in BF-Hall account, 92, 113
Ramsey, William (d. 1785): identified, 92–3 n; possible debt to BF, 92–3 n
Randolph, John, appointed Va. attorney general, 321 n
Randolph, Peyton, elected Va. speaker, 321 n
Raspe, Rudolph Erich: biog. note, 345 n; handles correction, payment of BF's bill, 345, 407; sends piece for Monthly Re-

view, 406; review of book displeases, 406–7 n; letter, goods sent to, 407, 408; publishes book on fossils, 407 n; advised on proposed move to America, 408; Exper. and Obser. to be sent, 408; authorship of Baron Munchausen's Travels, 408–9 n; letters to, 345, 406–9
Rattlesnakes, proposed transportation to England, 240
Ray, Nicholas, mentioned, 499 n
Read, Mr. (instrument maker), builds electrometer, 459
Read, Charles: identified, 198 n; advises of goods sent to Sally, 198–9
Read, George: biog. note, 32 n; advises DF on Dunlap's land, 32; seeks job as port collector, 246–7, 257; marriage, 246 n; BF seeks job for, 313, 405; letters from, 246–7, 405; letter to, 313; mentioned, 379 n
Read, John (brother of DF): identified, 319 n; seeks commissary post, 319; letter from, 319–21
Read, Mary, marriage, 379 n
Read, Mary Howell, greetings to, from, 313, 405
Red Lion Square, mentioned, 538 n
Redman, Dr. John: identified, 387 n; Bettering House manager, 284; recommends Rush, 387; Rush apprenticed to, 471 n
Redstone Creek: identified, 398 n; settlers on, 398–9
Reed, Joseph, mentioned, 430 n
Religion: in Scotland and America, 47; toleration in England, America, 48; in colonies, 362–3, 362 n
Remarks on the Plan for Regulating Indian Trade, 433–41
Remarks concerning the Savages of North-America, Indian legend in, 349 n
Repository, The. See De Re Rustica.
Representation, parliamentary: for colonies, not favored in America, 3, 65–6, 84; original basis for, 42–3; inequities in, 42–3; of Scotland, satire on, 46; BF's views on, for colonies, 65 n, 268–9
Requisitions, royal: as means of colonial financial support, 25; colonial willingness to answer, 143–4
"Retort, Jack," WF accused of writing, 500
Rhine river, BF travels on, 315, 384 n
Rhoads, Hannah: identified, 117 n; visits DF, 117
Rhoads, Samuel: builds BF's house, 31 n; DF gives money to, 117; advises DF on vaults, 176 n; mentioned, 445
Rhoads, Samuel, Jr., marriage, 117 n

St. Thomas (island), free port in, 370
Salt: production of, 369; in colonial shipping trade, 370
Samp, in American diet, 7
Sardine (ship), stamped paper put aboard, 30 n, 294 n
Sardoine (ship). See *Sardine* (ship).
Sargent Aufrere. See Sargent, Chambers and Co.
Sargent, Chambers and Co., defends BF, 295 n
Sargent, John: identified, 415 n; share in Illinois Co. to be offered to, 415; mentioned, 280
Saur, Christopher, Jr., prints German newspaper, 191 n
Savile, Sir George: identified, 145 n; in BF's Examination, 145 n, 157 n; constituency, 170 n
Saybrook, Conn., postrider hired, 301
Scalping, Indian method, 350–1
Scotland: and New England compared, 45; BF's satire on parliamentary representation, taxation of, 46; English relation to, 48; BF's attitude toward, 48 n; bill for transporting felons to America, 240; BF's petition against, 240–2, 450; annual value of trade, 371
Scots, in the advancing of frontier settlement, 353–4
Scott, Rev. James, identified, 304 n
Seamen, impressment of: bill for preventing in colonies, 238–9; BF opposes, 239
Sears, Mr., mentioned, 253
Seneca Indians. See Six Nations.
Senegal, mentioned, 369
Sermon on Education: in BF-Hall accounts, 96
Servants, classes of, in colonies, 355–6
Sevells, Mr., mentioned, 402
Sharpe, Horatio, to administer oath to Penn, 496 n
Shawanese Indians: to surrender lands to compensate traders, 172; Croghan makes treaty with, 397
Shelburne, Lord: submits Pa. address to king, 384; in Pitt ministry, 384 n, 414 n; and responsibility for colonial affairs, 385 n; BF's interview with, 415, 446, 447–8; and scheme for Illinois colony, 424–5; and plan for regulating Indian trade, 434; quoted, 447 n, 539 n; T. Penn's kinship to, 448, 448 n, 478–9, 539; marriage, 448 n; views on change in Pa. government, 539–40 n; mentioned, 385
Sherwood, Joseph: identified, 498 n; replaced as N.J. agent, 498

Shewell, Miss, mentioned, 337
Shewell, Mrs., mentioned, 337
Shewell, Robert, mentioned, 337 n
Shewell, Stephen, mentioned, 337 n
Ship money, defined, 215 n
Shippen, Edward, Jr.: identified, 524 n; examines Hunt for admission to bar, 524
Shippen, Joseph: identified, 337 n; son dies, 337
Shippen, Joseph (son of Joseph), death, 337 n
Ships, shipping: building in colonies, 365; restrictions on colonial, 369–70; importance of colonial, 370
Shirley, William: sends Board of Trade plan to BF, 120; BF's letters to, printed, 278 n
"Short Sketch of the Arguments for and against the American Stamp Act," printed, 52 n
Shorter Catechism of the Reverend Assembly of Divines, in BF-Hall account, 96
Silk, culture, in colonies, 363
Simitière, Pierre Eugene du, marginalia on "Magna Britannia," 69 n
Singel Gracht, mentioned, 386 n
Six Nations: to surrender land to compensate traders, 172; formation, tribes in, 351, 351 n; relationship to Britain, 351; Croghan makes treaties with, 397; and Croghan's journey to Illinois, 400–1; Mohawk grammar, 407 n
Skinner, Cortlandt: biog. note, 335 n; mentioned, 498; rumored successor to WF, 335, 499 n; mentioned, 499
Slaves, in America: corn in diet, 46; value of, 46
Small, Alexander: incloses bill, 312; inoculates Temple Franklin, 323, 443 n; letter from, 312
Small, Maj. John, identified, 118 n
Small, William: identified, 197 n; greetings to, 197; mentioned, 312 n
Smallpox, Indian reaction to, 351
Smith, Mary ("Goody"): identified, 198 n; illness of, 33, 117, 234; death, 33 n, 117 n, 198, 234 n
Smith, Richard, death, 254 n
Smith, Samuel, authorship of N.J. history, 12 n
Smith, Susannah, BF pays, 322 n
Smith, William: in Dunlap affair, 86 n; and controversy on American bishops, 320; mentioned, 34, 51 n, 254 n
Smitham (smeddum), duties on, 403 n
Smuggling: in Britain and colonies, 22, 370; BF's letter on, printed, 73 n; an-

to Lutterworth, 508 n; wants Stamp Act card, 509; carries Osborne message, 546; letter from, 508–9
Stevenson, Mary (Polly): invites BF to dinner, 196; in Kensington, 196 n, 446; greetings to, 199, 523; prospective marriage, 336–7, 336 n, 523, 523 n; letter from, 196; mentioned, 546 n
Stiles, Ezra: wants lists of holders of doctorates, 174; receives Edinburgh degree, 174 n; wants correspondence with Watson, 175; wants title for BF, 175; Stevens carries letter, 175; wants to publish BF letters, biography, 175, 175 n; sights comet, 235–6; letters from, 174–5, 195–6, 235–6
Stirling, Lord, BF forwards letter, 481–2
Stirling, Capt. Thomas, mentioned, 171 n
Störck, Dr. Anthony, introduces, writes on medicinal use of meadow saffron, 503 n
Story, Enoch, Bettering House manager, 284
Stove: BF advises on, 197; BF's development of smoke-consuming, 197 n
Strahan, Margaret Penelope, illness, 427
Strahan, William: Parker's debt to, 13, 13 n; report to, on Pitt's Stamp Act speech, 39–44; on difficulty of obtaining reports of Stamp Act debates, 40–1; in BF-Hall accounts, 91, 112; BF seeks view on copyright, 101; prints Post's journals, 113 n; and Stiles's request for list of Scottish doctorates, 174; prints extracts of BF-Thomson letters, 179 n; recommends B. Towne, 289; use of BF's franking privilege, 331, 331 n; greetings to, 332; returns to London, 427; mentioned, 120 n, 385, 390, 443
Stratford, Conn., post office in, 16 n
Stretch, Mr., mentioned, 108
Strettell, Amos: identified, 274 n; demands interest money from DF, 31; and Dunlap land transaction, 31 n; election as hospital manager, 274
Strettell, Mrs. Amos, mentioned, 165 n
Stuart, John: draws funds for Southern District, 447; Shelburne writes, 447 n
Sturgeon, William: identified, 406 n; wants Burlington, N.J. mission, 406; resigns, 406 n, 483 n; BF recommends, 483; death, 483 n; letter from, 406
Succotash, in American diet, 7
Sugar: possible reduction of duty on muscovado, 237; in colonial trade, 237, 370; West Indies receives concessions on, 237 n; storage in American ports, 308 n; maple, in colonies, 365; treatise published on, 365 n

Sugar Islands. See West Indies; and individual islands.
"Summary of the Arguments against repealing the Stamp-Act," printed, 208
Susannah (DF's maid), mentioned, 337
Swan with Two Necks (inn), mentioned, 534 n
Swedish Academy of Sciences, Transactions, cited, 364–5
Swift, Jonathan, mentioned, 64, 382 n
Swift, Samuel: identified, 235 n; mentioned, 235
Swinton, John: and title to N.J., Pa. lands, 322 n; legal opinion forwarded to, 477 n; to pay BF, 478; letter forwarded to BF, 478; Rush, Potts recommended to, 532–3; letter to, 532–3; mentioned, 531
Syddon, Anthony: DF and down payment on lot, 90 n; dispute over lot, 445 n; deed for lot, 519 n
Syng, Philip: receives books from BF, 189; Bettering House manager, 284; letter from, 189–90

Tacitus, quoted, 321 n
Taxation, local colonial: compared to Britain, 121; amount, 374; assemblies' right to assess, 375. See also Taxation, Pa.; Poll tax, Pa.
Taxation, parliamentary: views on right of, 25, 40, 41–2, 137–8, 143–4, 159, 214–15, 375, 539 n; satire on, 46; of Ireland, 54; BF opposes, 119, 278 n; proposed plan of, for N.Y., 138; external vs. internal, 139, 160, 156–7; of colonies, necessity for, 217–18. See also Stamp Act.
Taxation, Pa.: base for, 130; as burden to British trade, 134, 135; amount, 134, 135, 161; of Negroes, 355. See also Poll Tax.
Temperature, general level in colonies, 348
Templeman, Peter: letter forwarded to, 481; letter to, 481–2
Thames River: BF on obstructions in, 382–3; geography of, 382 n
Thomlinson & Hanbury, mentioned, 378 n
Thompson, Mrs. Emma, mentioned, 537 n, 538 n
Thomson, Charles: Enquiry printed, 113 n; letters printed, 178 n, 277 n, 428 n; praises BF, 278; on colonial loyalty to Britain, 278–9; introduces Rush, Potts, 387, 404 n; letters from, 277–9, 387–8; letters to, 178–9, 428; mentioned, 519
Thomson, Ruth Mather: identified, 33 n; greetings from, 33; greetings to, 179, 428
Three Lower Counties on Delaware. See Delaware Counties.

Walker, Hannah Farrow: sends condolences to BF, 418; gifts to BF, Mrs. Stevenson, 418–19; Mrs. Stevenson visits, 508–9; greetings from, 509; occupation, 509 n; letter from, 417–19
Walker, Thomas, mentioned, 509
Waller, Benjamin: identified, 289 n; B. Towne recommended to, 390 n; letter to, 289–90
Walnut, tea from leaves of, 8
Walpole, Horace, mentioned, 168 n
Walpole, Robert, mentioned, 66
Ward, Samuel, mentioned, 59
Warder, Jeremiah, Bettering House treasurer, 284
Warren, Miss, mentioned, 336
Waterspouts: Beccaria observes, 453; BF's paper on, sent to Ronayne, 468
Watson, William: identified, 175 n; Stiles wants correspondence with, 175; Priestley meets, 185 n; sends Cigna tract to Priestley, 422–3; advises Priestley on book, 421 n
Watts, Isaac, catechism in BF-Hall accounts, 96
Wayne, Anthony: identified, 32 n; DF pays, 32
Wedgwood, Josiah, as designer of BF medallion, 523 n
Wesley, John, translation of address, printed, 346 n
West Indies (British): and export duty on sugar, 145; rights of colonists in, 161; gets concessions on sugar export, 237 n; no impressment of seamen in, 239 n; settlement of, 351–2; colonial government in, 358; standard of living in, 366; annual value of trade with, 371
West Indies (French and Spanish), prohibition of colonial trade, 369
Weyman, William: identified, 303 n; prints *N.Y. Gazette*, 265 n; Parker's business affairs with, 264–5, 527; prints almanac, 473 n, 492; financial difficulties of, 475; mentioned, 302 n, 303, 344, 492
Weyman's New-York Gazette. See New-York Gazette.
Whales, whaling, in colonies, 364
Wharton, Franklin: birth, 252; death, 252 n, 337 n
Wharton, James, mentioned, 235 n
Wharton, Joseph, Senior: and formation of Illinois Co., 257 n; Bettering House manager, 284; greetings from, 284, 481, 497
Wharton, Joseph (son of Thomas), death, 252 n, 337 n
Wharton, Joseph II: seeks financial aid

from BF, 234–5; gives BF bill of exchange, 235 n
Wharton, Samuel: quoted, 247 n; and formation of Illinois Co., 257 n; at Pittsburgh, 324 n; returns from Fort Pitt, 397; sends Sally's letter to BF, 404; introduces Potts, Rush, 404; letters from, 324–5, 404
Wharton, Thomas: urges BF write Committee of Correspondence, 191, 268 n; visits WF, 192; favors colonial bishop, 251 n; names son after BF, 252; and formation of Illinois Co., 257 n; interested in S. Penn's lands, 283–4; quoted, 285 n; death of sons, 337–8; and funeral of Mary Franklin, 339; BF to send Amsterdam pamphlet to, 495; agrees to enlarged membership in Illinois Co., 496; and partnership with Goddard, 500; letters from, 190–2, 250–2, 272–5, 282–4, 313–14, 495–7; mentioned, 181 n, 500 n
Wharton family: greetings to, 450; success in elections, 481
Wheat: BF on the price of, 510–16; domestic crisis over, in England, 511–12
Whirlwinds, BF's paper on, sent to Ronayne, 468
Whitefield, George: identified, 176 n; visits BF, 176; praises BF's Examination, 176 n; quoted, 255 n; prosecution, in ecclesiastical court, 362 n; mentioned, 254, 416 n
Whitehurst, John, quoted, 533 n
Wichmann, Johann Ernst: identified, 409 n; greetings to, 409
Wilcke, Johan Carl: Priestley wants remainder of treatise, 422; sends book to BF, 422 n; mentioned, 246
Wilkes, Mr. and Mrs. Israel: identified, 537 n; asks BF to Christmas dinner, 538; letter from, 538
Wilkes, John, mentioned, 433, 537 n
William III, mentioned, 359
William, Fort (Scotland), described, 217 n
William and Mary College, fund for support of, 145
Williams, Grace, expects baby, 253 n
Williams, John: identified, 187 n; carries letters, 187, 252; appointed to customs post, 252 n
Williams, Capt. John: WF buys china from, 322; advertises personal goods for sale, 322 n
Williams, Jonathan, Senior: greetings to, 188; letter to, 252–3; mentioned, 187 n
Williams, Josiah, BF to get armonica for, 253
Williams, Sally, death, 253 n
Williamsburg, Va., mentioned, 368